Enhancing Democracy With Coalition Governments and Politics

Ndwakhulu Stephen Tshishonga
University of KwaZulu-Natal, South Africa

A volume in the Advances in Public Policy and
Administration (APPA) Book Series

Published in the United States of America by
    IGI Global
    Information Science Reference (an imprint of IGI Global)
    701 E. Chocolate Avenue
    Hershey PA, USA 17033
    Tel: 717-533-8845
    Fax: 717-533-8661
    E-mail: cust@igi-global.com
    Web site: http://www.igi-global.com

Library of Congress Cataloging-in-Publication Data

Names: Tshishonga, Ndwakhulu, 1964- editor.
Title: Enhancing democracy with coalition governments and politics / edited
  by Ndwakhulu Tshishonga.
Description: Hershey, PA : Business Science Reference, 2024. | Includes
  bibliographical references and index. | Summary: "This book considers
  critical discourses on the notion of coalition politics or coalition
  governments, its formation and management in the context of Africa's
  quest for sound electoral democracy and democratic governance"--
  Provided by publisher.
Identifiers: LCCN 2024009400 (print) | LCCN 2024009401 (ebook) | ISBN
  9798369316542 (hardcover) | ISBN 9798369316559 (ebook)
Subjects: LCSH: Coalition governments. | Coalition governments--Case
  studies. | Democracy. | Democracy--Case studies.
Classification: LCC JF331 .E65 2024 (print) | LCC JF331 (ebook) | DDC
  324--dc23/eng/20240316
LC record available at https://lccn.loc.gov/2024009400
LC ebook record available at https://lccn.loc.gov/2024009401

This book is published in the IGI Global book series Advances in Public Policy and Administration (APPA) (ISSN: 2475-6644; eISSN: 2475-6652)

British Cataloguing in Publication Data
A Cataloguing in Publication record for this book is available from the British Library.

All work contributed to this book is new, previously-unpublished material. The views expressed in this book are those of the authors, but not necessarily of the publisher.

For electronic access to this publication, please contact: eresources@igi-global.com.

Advances in Public Policy and Administration (APPA) Book Series

ISSN:2475-6644
EISSN:2475-6652

MISSION

Proper management of the public sphere is necessary in order to maintain order in modern society. Research developments in the field of public policy and administration can assist in uncovering the latest tools, practices, and methodologies for governing societies around the world.

The **Advances in Public Policy and Administration (APPA) Book Series** aims to publish scholarly publications focused on topics pertaining to the governance of the public domain. APPA's focus on timely topics relating to government, public funding, politics, public safety, policy, and law enforcement is particularly relevant to academicians, government officials, and upper-level students seeking the most up-to-date research in their field.

COVERAGE

- Government
- Law Enforcement
- Political Economy
- Politics
- Public Administration
- Public Funding
- Public Policy
- Resource allocation
- Urban Planning

IGI Global is currently accepting manuscripts for publication within this series. To submit a proposal for a volume in this series, please contact our Acquisition Editors at Acquisitions@igi-global.com or visit: http://www.igi-global.com/publish/.

The Advances in Public Policy and Administration (APPA) Book Series (ISSN 2475-6644) is published by IGI Global, 701 E. Chocolate Avenue, Hershey, PA 17033-1240, USA, www.igi-global.com. This series is composed of titles available for purchase individually; each title is edited to be contextually exclusive from any other title within the series. For pricing and ordering information please visit http://www.igi-global.com/book-series/advances-public-policy-administration/97862. Postmaster: Send all address changes to above address. Copyright © 2024 IGI Global. All rights, including translation in other languages reserved by the publisher. No part of this series may be reproduced or used in any form or by any means – graphics, electronic, or mechanical, including photocopying, recording, taping, or information and retrieval systems – without written permission from the publisher, except for non commercial, educational use, including classroom teaching purposes. The views expressed in this series are those of the authors, but not necessarily of IGI Global.

Titles in this Series

For a list of additional titles in this series, please visit: http://www.igi-global.com/book-series/advances-public-policy-administration/97862

Global Trends in Governance and Policy Paradigms
Mahani Hamdan (Universiti Brunei Darussalam, Brunei) Muhammad Anshari (Universiti Brunei Darussalam, Brunei) Norainie Ahmad (Universiti Brunei Darussalam, Brunei) and Emil Ali (Universiti Brunei Darussalam, Brunei)
Information Science Publishing • © 2024 • 453pp • H/C (ISBN: 9798369317426) • US $240.00

Soft Power and Diplomatic Strategies in Asia and the Middle East
Mohamad Zreik (School of International Studies, Sun Yat-sen University, China)
Information Science Reference • © 2024 • 386pp • H/C (ISBN: 9798369324448) • US $265.00

Economic and Societal Impact of Organized Crime Policy and Law Enforcement Interventions
Alicia Danielsson (University of Bolton, UK & Hume Institute for Postgraduate Studies, Switzerland)
Information Science Reference • © 2024 • 350pp • H/C (ISBN: 9798369303276) • US $240.00

The Convergence of Traditionalism and Populism in American Politics From Bannon to Trump
Adrian David Cheok (Nanjing University of Information Science and Technology, China)
Information Science Reference • © 2024 • 288pp • H/C (ISBN: 9781668492901) • US $235.00

Regulating Fair Competition Toward Sustainable Development Goals
Siti Faziiah Abdul Shukor (University of Tunku Abdul Rahman, Malaysia) Farahdilah Ghazali (University of Malaysia Terengganu, Malaysia) Nur Yuhanis Ismon (University of Tun Hussien Onn, Malaysia) and Aerni Isa (Taylor's University, Malaysia)
Information Science Reference • © 2024 • 285pp • H/C (ISBN: 9798369303900) • US $275.00

Analyzing Energy Crises and the Impact of Country Policies on the World
Merve Suna Özel Özcan (Kirikkale University, Turkey)
Engineering Science Reference • © 2024 • 283pp • H/C (ISBN: 9798369304402) • US $240.00

Using Crises and Disasters as Opportunities for Innovation and Improvement
Saeed Siyal (School of Economics and Management, Beijing University of Chemical Technology, China)
Information Science Reference • © 2024 • 323pp • H/C (ISBN: 9781668495223) • US $240.00

701 East Chocolate Avenue, Hershey, PA 17033, USA
Tel: 717-533-8845 x100 • Fax: 717-533-8661
E-Mail: cust@igi-global.com • www.igi-global.com

Table of Contents

Preface..xvii

Chapter 1
Factors and Conditions Triggering the Formation of Political Coalitions...1
  Fako Johnson Likoti, Lesotho Public Service Commission, Lesotho

Chapter 2
Nature of Conditions and Characteristics to the Politics of Party Alliances and Coalitions in
Formation of Governments in Africa...17
  Sushant Shankar Bharti, Indira Gandhi National Open University, India
  Mukesh Shankar Bharti, Jawaharlal Nehru University, India

Chapter 3
A Comparative Study of Coalition Governments in Post-Conflict Societies.....................................33
  Mbuyiseni Simon Mathonsi, University of KwaZulu-Natal, South Africa
  Ndwakhulu Stephen Tshishonga, University of KwaZulu-Natal, South Africa

Chapter 4
It Takes Two to Tango: 2010 British Con-Dem Coalition...50
  Sureyya Yigit, New Vision University, Georgia

Chapter 5
Governments of National Unity (GNU) as the Democratic Governance Model in Selected Africa
Countries...74
  Ndwakhulu Stephen Tshishonga, University of KwaZulu-Natal, South Africa

Chapter 6
Mozambique's Singular Path in Southern Africa's Coalition Governance Landscape 92
  Maximino G. S. Costumado, University of KwaZulu-Natal, South Africa
  Delma C. Da Silva, University of the Witwatersrand, South Africa
  A. D. Chemane, University of KwaZulu-Natal, South Africa

Chapter 7
Local Experiences of Local Government's Coalition Politics in South Africa 112
  Kgothatso Shai, University of Limpopo, South Africa

Chapter 8
Israel's Coalition in Power and Its Implications on Israel-Palestinian Relations and Conflict........... 124
Ndwakhulu Stephen Tshishonga, University of KwaZulu-Natal, South Africa

Chapter 9
Critical Reflections on Coalition Politics: Prospects and Challenges From an African Perspective.. 144
Bhekie Mngomezulu, Nelson Mandela University, South Africa

Chapter 10
Challenges of Coalition Formations and Government: The Case of Some African Countries 157
Levy Ndou, Tshwane University of Technology, South Africa

Chapter 11
Strides and Struggles of Coalition Governments in Southern Africa: The Case for Zimbabwe 172
Menard Musendekwa, Reformed Church University, Zimbabwe

Chapter 12
Coalition Government and Democratic Instability: An Analysis of the City of Johannesburg's
2021 Coalition Government... 188
Bonolo Debra Makgale, University of Pretoria, South Africa

Chapter 13
The Confluence of Soft Power Diplomacy and Coalition Politics: A Comparative Analysis of
China's Strategies in Africa and the Middle East 201
Mohamad Zreik, Sun Yat-sen University, China

Chapter 14
Navigating Coalition Dynamics in the City of Johannesburg: A Lefortian Perspective on Political
Power... 223
Mpho Tladi, University of the Witwatersrand, South Africa

Chapter 15
The Role of Coalition Governments as Sustainable Democracy Enhancing in South Africa 246
Mukesh Shankar Bharti, Jawaharlal Nehru University, India

Chapter 16
Coalitions in South African Local Government and the Implications for Public Service Delivery... 263
Thokozani Ian Nzimakwe, University of KwaZulu-Natal, South Africa
Sakhile Zondi, University of KwaZulu-Natal, South Africa

Chapter 17
Examining the Impact of Coalition Governments on Service Delivery: The Case of ANC-Led All. 277
Mbuyiseni Simon Mathonsi, University of KwaZulu-Natal, South Africa
Ndwakhulu Stephen Tshishonga, University of KwaZulu-Natal, South Africa

Chapter 18
Investigating the Dynamics of Coalition Governance in South African Local Government............. 300
    Mohale Ernest Selelo, University of Limpopo, South Africa
    Khutso Piet Lebotsa, University of Limpopo, South Africa

Chapter 19
Critical Reflections on Coalition Governments in the 30th Year of South African Democracy........ 316
    Daniel N. Mlambo, Tshwane University Technology, South Africa
    Thamsanqa Buys, Tshwane University of Technology, South Africa
    Thabo Francis Saul, Tshwane University of Technology, South Africa

Compilation of References 337

About the Contributors 384

Index 388

Detailed Table of Contents

Preface.. xvii

Chapter 1
Factors and Conditions Triggering the Formation of Political Coalitions... 1
Fako Johnson Likoti, Lesotho Public Service Commission, Lesotho

Party coalitions have become very important in contemporary African politics in parliamentary and presidential systems. The dawn of democracy in the third world, and Africa in particular, witnessed significant democratic developments. African political parties have increasingly seen the value of cooperation and have built coalitions and alliances to achieve similar goals. Key amongst these developments have been the formation of political coalitions. Several factors and conditions have triggered the formation of political coalitions and alliances in most African countries. A coalition is a grouping of rival political parties that, in most cases, are motivated by the perception of a common threat or recognition that their goals cannot be attained by not coalescing. The management of a coalition is also critical in order to attain stability. The rationale is that stability becomes important to parties when they enter their coalition pact.

Chapter 2
Nature of Conditions and Characteristics to the Politics of Party Alliances and Coalitions in
Formation of Governments in Africa... 17
Sushant Shankar Bharti, Indira Gandhi National Open University, India
Mukesh Shankar Bharti, Jawaharlal Nehru University, India

The purpose of this study is to discuss the politics of party alliances and conditions in the formation of the government in the countries of Africa. Since the 1990s, many African countries have adopted either parliamentary or presidential forms of democratic rule to strengthen the rule of law, respect human rights and the rights of minorities, children, and women. After the end of colonial rule, the South African countries started the development process and good governance for the establishment of the welfare of the people. The democratic and democratization process has been strengthening the government institutions of countries' public and private entities for better governance. This chapter used a theoretical approach of debate to discuss Samuel P. Huntington's third wave of democratization and coalition theory to understand the democratization process which has been led by democratic government through general elections. In this electoral process, only one party was unable to form the government because it did not obtain a majority in parliament. This is why many emerging coalition governments have been established in many African countries. Moreover, this research uses the qualitative approach to describe and answer many research questions about the success and failure of the coalition governments in Africa. The case study also imposed and scanned to study of the various coalition governments in the countries of Africa. As a result, the formation of coalition governments is unusual in African countries because parties are not getting the popular vote to form a single-party government.

Chapter 3

A Comparative Study of Coalition Governments in Post-Conflict Societies.. 33
Mbuyiseni Simon Mathonsi, University of KwaZulu-Natal, South Africa
Ndwakhulu Stephen Tshishonga, University of KwaZulu-Natal, South Africa

The establishment of coalition governments as transitional arrangements on nations bedeviled by conflicts has become an automatic solution in many countries of the world. Multiparty electoral processes or processes that include as many contesting parties and interests as possible have for years been dubbed as important building blocks for peace and smooth transition, especially in countries devastated by civil wars or violence. This chapter argues that that single party governments make governing straightforward and keep the executive/legislatures fully accountable to voters as the incumbent governing party has nobody else, but itself to blame for mediocre performance. While multi-party governments involve bargaining informed by compromises on the interests of voters and coalition bargaining are fashioned more on the interests of the leaders and actors in the bargaining table. In the Third World countries, especially those experiencing violence or civil wars, exogenous superpowers mainly from the West are quick to broker coalition governance with externally imposed rules as panacea for progress. The chapter further argues that externally imposed coalition formations and rules more often than not benefit the interests of the outside superpowers than the domestic interests of citizens. While endogenously crafted, formulated, and implemented coalition processes are more likely to benefit domestic interest of the people than outside powers. The chapter seeks to contribute to the current literature on the formation of coalition governments as transitional arrangements and peace brokers for parties or groups in conflict. The chapter used desktop research to solicit information from peer reviewed journals and scientific research papers.

Chapter 4

It Takes Two to Tango: 2010 British Con-Dem Coalition.. 50
Sureyya Yigit, New Vision University, Georgia

British politics has traditionally been identified as a two-party political system throughout the post-war period. Single parties have formed governments in the United Kingdom, with the two major parties squeezing out any third-party challenger. The year 2010 was an anomaly. The result of the general election proved inconclusive, ending in a hung parliament. For the first time in over 60 years, coalition negotiations took place between the three main parties, and the Con-Dem coalition was agreed to. This coalition pushed forward constitutional changes relating to the timing of elections and proposed reforming the electoral system. The coalition endured for its full five-year term, although its effects were short-term. The subsequent conservative government reneged on its previous support for constitutional changes. This chapter focuses on the challenges of coalition politics in a British context.

Chapter 5

Governments of National Unity (GNU) as the Democratic Governance Model in Selected Africa Countries.. 74

Ndwakhulu Stephen Tshishonga, University of KwaZulu-Natal, South Africa

This chapter interrogates the notion of government of national unity (GNU) as an emerging model for democratic and coalition governance in Africa. Considering Africa's dismal record of governance, coupled with socio-economic developmental challenges, coalition governance is imperative. African countries such as Kenya, Lesotho, Malawi, South Africa, and Zimbabwe were selected as case studies to demonstrate the opportunities and challenges of government of national unity or coalition governance. GNU is a co-governance mechanism often adopted over contested election results between the incumbent and opposition parties. Amongst the countries under study, only Kenya showcases a semi-successful story of how a coalition can be formed, maintained, and sustained to the next elections. Other governments of national unity, such as those in South Africa, Lesotho, and Zimbabwe, formed coalitions with opposition parties to unset the dominant parties. In the case of Zimbabwe, Malawi, South Africa, and Lesotho, GNU was adopted as both a democratic governance and conflict resolution strategy to govern better and ensure peace and stability over contested election results and simmering political violence. This chapter argues that the dominance of the ruling parties and weak opposition parties undermines coalition formation to challenge the incumbent parties through electoral democracy. The chapter concludes that GNU in these countries not only showed dismal evidence of being notoriously tyrannical in creating pseudo-space but was also a pace-setter for bad and undemocratic governance in Africa. Data for this chapter was collected through secondary sources.

Chapter 6

Mozambique's Singular Path in Southern Africa's Coalition Governance Landscape 92

Maximino G. S. Costumado, University of KwaZulu-Natal, South Africa
Delma C. Da Silva, University of the Witwatersrand, South Africa
A. D. Chemane, University of KwaZulu-Natal, South Africa

This in-depth comparative study explores the complexities of coalition governance in Southern Africa, specifically focusing on Mozambique's remarkable absence of coalition governments. It sets it apart from neighboring countries where coalition experiences and party alliances are firmly established. The tumultuous contestation of the October 2023 municipal election results, marked by allegations of fraud and favoritism, sheds light on critical challenges within Mozambique's electoral system. This contentious episode highlights the need for comprehensive changes in the country's electoral regulatory framework, which is crucial for alignment with regional contexts and cultivating a political environment conducive to joint governance, particularly at the local level. In addition, it requires a re-evaluation, leading to improvements that increase transparency, fairness, and public confidence in the nation's electoral processes, and could bring the country closer to standards of electoral integrity.

Chapter 7

Local Experiences of Local Government's Coalition Politics in South Africa 112
    Kgothatso Shai, University of Limpopo, South Africa

Coalition politics has become a key feature of many countries' political landscapes in the 21st century. Among others, countries such as South Africa, Zimbabwe, Mauritius, and Germany have experimented with the system of political coalitions at different levels and with varying degrees of success. However, scholars and practitioners have not uniformly understood coalition politics, regardless of the attempt to locate the thinking in this regard within the Westernised perspective. Against this backdrop, this chapter uses 2021 as an ending point for research to examine the historical emergence of local government coalition politics in South Africa. While this chapter's primary focus is on South Africa, the line of thought is located within a global context to generate a broader understanding. It is also unavoidable to make sense of local government's coalition politics without linking it to national politics. This is because there is no level of politics or governance that exists in a vacuum, and this is even more expressive within the cooperative governance model of South Africa. Given the explanatory and analytical power of theories, this chapter first discusses the theories and types of municipal coalitions and politics and then intentionally proposes Afrocentricity as an alternative contextual and theoretical lens to make a better sense of this phenomena (local government's coalition politics) in Africa and South Africa, in particular. At the core of the research analysis for this chapter is the interface between municipal governments and coalition politics with specific reference to Tshwane and Johannesburg metropolitan municipalities.

Chapter 8

Israel's Coalition in Power and Its Implications on Israel-Palestinian Relations and Conflict........... 124
    Ndwakhulu Stephen Tshishonga, University of KwaZulu-Natal, South Africa

This chapter discusses Israel's recent coalition government and its implications for internal governance, its conflictual agenda to destabilize the Middle East region, and particularly, its relations to the raging war between Israel and Palestine in the Occupied Gaza and West Jerusalem respectively. Considering how the state of Israel was formed, the chapter argues that the far-right coalition formed in 2022 post-general elections led by Netanyahu is bound to entrench Palestinian oppression and Apartheid as well as sour relations in the region. The inclusion of ultra-nationalists and ultra-Orthodox parties in Israel's formed coalition has far-reaching implications for Israel's democracy and its ability to manage peace and stability in the Middle East and with Palestinians. Evidence from the raging Israel-Hamas war leads one to conclude that the coalition is being used and abused to undermine the international organisations and laws that prohibit Israel's illegal occupation of Palestinian land. Secondary data was used to comprehend the complex dynamics of the coalition formed under the Netanyahu leadership, focusing on Israel's internal democracy and conflictual relations with Palestine and the region.

Chapter 9

Critical Reflections on Coalition Politics: Prospects and Challenges From an African Perspective.. 144
    Bhekie Mngomezulu, Nelson Mandela University, South Africa

Political coalitions have a deep history which transcends geographical boundaries. The rationale for establishing them varies. In the absence of a guiding framework, coalitions become unsustainable. The aim of this chapter is threefold. Firstly, it traces the history of coalition politics. Secondly, it discusses prospects for successful coalitions. Thirdly, it considers challenges involved in coalition politics. While conceding that coalitions are a global phenomenon, the chapter focuses on Africa. It argues that since the dawn of democracy in Africa, different forms of coalitions have been used with different results. As the number of political parties increase in each election, coalitions have become a reality.

Chapter 10
Challenges of Coalition Formations and Government: The Case of Some African Countries 157
Levy Ndou, Tshwane University of Technology, South Africa

The establishment and existence of coalition governments, its theory, and practice have their roots and dominance mainly in the experiences of central, eastern, and western European countries. Coalition governments have become a norm in Europe. Between 1945 and 2014, 88% of the governments in Europe are regarded as coalition governments. Coalitions are mostly formed at any given time without establishing guidelines or a framework to work on. Coalition partners spend a lot of time managing coalitions rather than focusing on providing services to the people. This chapter is of the view that coalitions should be established to benefit the citizens and enhance governance and stability. Coalitions appear not to be working in most African states that are discussed in this chapter. Though there are many municipalities that are run through coalitions in South Africa, coalitions are blamed for instability and poor governance in the South African metros. The same can be said in the selected countries that are of specific focus in this chapter. This chapter will specifically look at the coalition governments in countries such as Mozambique, Lesotho, Kenya, Zimbabwe, and South Africa. The challenges associated with coalitions will be discussed and possible solutions will be provided.

Chapter 11
Strides and Struggles of Coalition Governments in Southern Africa: The Case for Zimbabwe 172
Menard Musendekwa, Reformed Church University, Zimbabwe

Coalition governments have emerged as a mechanism for peaceful resolution following disputed elections, offering insights into addressing political disputes and legitimacy crises. In Zimbabwe, historical contexts such as the Gukurahundi War, which exacerbated tensions between the Ndebele and Shona communities, underscore the significance of coalition governance. The Unity Accord between ZANU-PF and PF-ZAPU provided temporary respite from tribal conflicts. Subsequently, the Government of National Unity (GNU) was established after the 2008 disputed election, aiming to transition towards fresh elections. Following Mugabe's tenure, Mnangagwa's victory amid accusations of election rigging prompted legal intervention. Mnangagwa's initiation of the Political Actors Dialogue (POLAD) aimed to incorporate ideas from losing parties, yet faced rejection by the main opposition. Criticism of the 2023 elections has intensified calls for a transitional authority or another GNU to prepare for reruns. This research will employ qualitative analysis, including historical review and document analysis, to investigate the advantages and disadvantages of coalition governments in Africa. Findings aim to provide valuable insights for political actors to make informed decisions in navigating political transitions.

Chapter 12
Coalition Government and Democratic Instability: An Analysis of the City of Johannesburg's
2021 Coalition Government 188
    Bonolo Debra Makgale, University of Pretoria, South Africa

Since the first local government elections in 2000, South Africa has habitually produced 'hung councils', where no political party wins more than 50% of the municipal seats. This chapter examines the 2021 coalition government in the City of Johannesburg and its democratic instability. The chapter argues that one of the factors contributing to this trend of instability in local government is the lack of a conducive environment in which coalition governments can thrive. It also examines coalition governments, taking into account existing theories of democratic principles and theories of coalition formation. The chapter outlines the findings that political ideological struggles and the lack of a conducive democratic environment underpinned the instability of the coalition government in the City of Johannesburg. The chapter also recommends mature coalition political leadership, collaborative governance and a legal framework to strengthen democratic principles in coalition governments.

Chapter 13
The Confluence of Soft Power Diplomacy and Coalition Politics: A Comparative Analysis of
China's Strategies in Africa and the Middle East 201
    Mohamad Zreik, Sun Yat-sen University, China

China's growing influence through soft power diplomacy is a parallel storyline to Africa's current experience with coalition politics and electoral democracy, especially in the Middle East and East Asia. This chapter examines how China employs coalition politics to enhance its larger diplomatic efforts in Africa with the goal of connecting these two crucial storylines. This chapter uses examples from the Middle East and East Asia to explore the complexities of coalition governments in Africa and how they might help or hurt China's soft power ambitions. This study, which takes an interdisciplinary approach, will shed new light on the complex dynamics at play when coalitions of politicians, democratic governments, and foreign governments interact. The chapter finishes with concrete suggestions for policymakers, stressing the importance of a comprehensive knowledge of these overlapping domains for the development of effective and democratic approaches to government in Africa. Policymakers, academics, and practitioners in the fields of politics, international relations, development studies, and sociology are among the many who will find value in this chapter.

Chapter 14
Navigating Coalition Dynamics in the City of Johannesburg: A Lefortian Perspective on Political
Power 223
    Mpho Tladi, University of the Witwatersrand, South Africa

This chapter offers a theoretical analysis of coalition politics in South Africa, with a focus on the City of Johannesburg's Metropolitan Municipality. It uses Claude Lefort's political theories to examine the fluctuating dynamics of political power in the nation's coalition governments, particularly at the local government level. The chapter traces the emergence and instability of coalitions, highlighted by the African National Congress' (ANC) loss of majority and the subsequent power shifts in Johannesburg. These changes, including the formation of different coalition arrangements and the 2021 Local Government Elections' outcomes, reflect the unstable nature of coalitions in South Africa. The chapter aims to discuss the impacts of these coalitions on governance quality and service delivery, addressing the broader socio-political and economic challenges of the country. Two case studies, focusing on fiscal management and trust in Johannesburg's coalition government, will provide deeper insights into the practical implications of such political arrangements.

Chapter 15
The Role of Coalition Governments as Sustainable Democracy Enhancing in South Africa 246
Mukesh Shankar Bharti, Jawaharlal Nehru University, India

The aim of this study is to discuss the nature of coalition government and its role in strengthening the norms of democracy in South Africa. Over the past two decades, South Africa has continued to focus on the progressive development of the country's political institutions under the ethos of the democratic principle of coalition government. This chapter also discusses the various South African governments' roles in the establishment of democratization in the country. The research method used in this study is the qualitative approach to search for actual research output. The empirical method would also involve discussing research gaps on the nature and characteristics of coalition government for better governance. Moreover, this study will answer the following research questions: How is the coalition government in South Africa paving the way for the healthiest democracy? There is the second question: Why are the people of South Africa electing a coalition government in the country? This study also uses the third wave of democratization theory of Samuel P. Huntington, which contributed to the democratic transition and the establishment of democratic governments in the late 1980s in developing countries, namely in Africa, Latin America, and Central and Eastern Europe. Apart from Samuel P. Huntington's idea on democratization, this study also utilises other modern democratic theories to discuss South Africa's democratization process under the coalition government. Finally, the chapter outlines how political alliances are conceptualized and operationalized for the democratization of South Africa.

Chapter 16
Coalitions in South African Local Government and the Implications for Public Service Delivery ... 263
Thokozani Ian Nzimakwe, University of KwaZulu-Natal, South Africa
Sakhile Zondi, University of KwaZulu-Natal, South Africa

The decision to establish coalition governments in South Africa is one that lies firmly on political parties. Ultimately the electorate does not have a say in its formation. It is assumed that representative democracy finds expression in the formation of coalitions. The stability of the government will formally depend on the urges of the elected representatives of political parties in a legislative body. It is more likely to depend on political party leaders who, for various reasons, retain considerable control over the conduct of their elected representatives. Coalitions seem to be the solution when political parties in democracies do not win by outright margins and majority governments have to be constituted. Yet, the way in which political parties and politicians practice coalitions in South Africa means coalitions are, at best, a tense alternative. The South African Constitution of 1996 vests legislative and executive authority in the municipal council. As the highest decision-making body, the council must steer the municipality, determine its strategic direction, and take crucial decisions. In coalitions, this requires close cooperation between coalition partners to ensure that the responsibilities of the council are carried out effectively. This chapter argues that, however, in practice, coalition governments have often been unstable and terminated before the end of the council term. Instability in a local coalition can have a severe impact as it may compromise the municipality's ability to adopt policies and by-laws, make senior management appointments, or even adopt a budget. Ultimately, local communities will continue to bear the brunt of unstable coalition politics. The conclusion is that more stable coalitions will therefore contribute to improved service delivery.

Chapter 17
Examining the Impact of Coalition Governments on Service Delivery: The Case of ANC-Led All. 277
Mbuyiseni Simon Mathonsi, University of KwaZulu-Natal, South Africa
Ndwakhulu Stephen Tshishonga, University of KwaZulu-Natal, South Africa

Formation of coalition governments and politics before and after elections is the manifestation of the absence of overwhelming winner in national, provincial, or local government elections. This chapter aims to contribute to the nascent literature on coalition government and politics within the context of South Africa by examining the historic coalition of the ANC, SACP, COSATU, and SANCO. The chapter is conceptual in approach and it uses a desktop method. The research acknowledges that the tripartite coalition/alliance is without precedent on the African continent and with few parallels throughout the world. Coalition governing is now a phenomenon defining South African body politics, and it is likely to be the future system of government in this country. In terms of the South African system of government, national, provincial, and local governments are critical platforms for service delivery and the overall development of the country that is currently riddled by the triple challenges of unemployment, poverty, and inequality.

Chapter 18
Investigating the Dynamics of Coalition Governance in South African Local Government.............. 300
Mohale Ernest Selelo, University of Limpopo, South Africa
Khutso Piet Lebotsa, University of Limpopo, South Africa

The dynamics of coalitions in South Africa's democratic landscape can be attributed to the ANC government's shortcomings or failure in providing services to communities and its pervasive issues of corruption. The chapter argues that enhancing governance, service delivery, and fostering unity in South Africa requires a political centre, consistent policy agenda, and capable politicians. This is essential to fulfil the service delivery mandate, and it also suggests the need for a legislative framework to regulate coalition governments, considering their inevitability in the current political climate of South Africa. The current South African political climate of coalitions is clouded by political immaturity which is a receipt for poor service delivery. An analysis of several motions of confidence passed in coalition governance in many municipalities across the country shows that coalition governance in the contemporary South African political climate is characterized by instability, political egos, no commonality of interest, and political patronage which are ingredients of poor service delivery, particularly as the next 2024 national and provincial elections draw near. Coalition governments typically include parties with varied ideological orientations and policy preferences. The task of reconciling these differences to establish a unified policy agenda can pose significant conundrums and delays in service delivery. What ordinary people need on the ground is very simple, which is just the provision of basic services not political ideologies. However, different policy agendas from political parties haunt the delivery of basic services to the constituencies. This chapter sees it as imperative to demonstrate contextual and institutional effects that supplement emergent discoveries in the literature of coalition governance. Thus, it adopts a literature-based approach, which is conceptual, to assess the dynamics of coalition governance in South African local government, looking at policy implementation, political stability, and service delivery inter alia.

Chapter 19

Critical Reflections on Coalition Governments in the 30th Year of South African Democracy 316

Daniel N. Mlambo, Tshwane University Technology, South Africa
Thamsanqa Buys, Tshwane University of Technology, South Africa
Thabo Francis Saul, Tshwane University of Technology, South Africa

This chapter comprehensively explores the detailed evaluations of coalition governments in the 30th year of South African democracy. Despite being a relatively recent concept in our political discussions, implementing coalition arrangements is frequently mishandled, posing a hurdle to efficient administration in local municipalities. The main contention of this chapter is that if coalition agreements in South Africa were motivated by a sincere aspiration for effective governance and the provision of services, they would have had positive outcomes for the general public.

Compilation of References 337

About the Contributors 384

Index 388

Preface

Coalition politics has played a pivotal role in power dynamics globally, be it through electoral alliances, legislative coalitions, or governance coalitions (Basson & Hunter, 2023; Jolobe, 2018; Masina, 2021, Schreiber, 2028). However, in post-colonial Africa, the rise of coalition governments holds particular significance, reshaping electoral landscapes and challenging established political orders. African nations such as Congo Kinshasa, Zimbabwe, Nigeria, Mauritius, South Africa, and Lesotho exemplify the diverse and complex nature of coalition formations to address ethnic and racial tensions while promoting democratic stability. In Europe, especially in countries such as Denmark, and Germany, coalition governance was formed for the benefit and betterment of the voters (Bassin & Hutter, 2023). A coalition is a governance model that several rival parties or groups form to achieve shared aims or objectives (see Heywood, 2019).

Albala, Borges, and Couto (2023) contend that coalitions are frequently formed when no party has the majority to govern unilaterally. Oppermann, Brummer & Van Willigen (2017) state that all parties decide under a coalition governance style instead of only one organization. Müller and Meyer (2014) add that coalition members must negotiate and make concessions to establish an agreement on policies and actions because they may have diverse interests. Since coalitions need collaboration and coordination from various stakeholders, they are usually more flexible than one-party regimes. One of the advantages of Coalition Governance is representation. Bowler, Freebourn, Teten, Donovan and Vowles (2023) posit that compared to one-party regimes, coalitions frequently reflect a wider range of interests and points of view. Islam, Ahmed, and Sakachep (2023) add that coalitions improve stabilization by bringing together different groups and encouraging collaboration and consensus-building. Coalition governance fosters inclusiveness by including a range of viewpoints and views in the decision-making process. Klüver and Spoon (2020) also note the advantage of coalition governance: the coalition members divide the power according to their abilities and negotiating positions.

ROLE AND IMPORTANCE OF COALITION INTERNATIONALLY

Coalitions may emerge around any subject and at every level of society, from local concerns to worldwide conflicts. Coalitions play an important role in international relations and politics, allowing players to coordinate their actions to accomplish similar goals. This is supported by Daphi, Anderl, and Deitelhoff (2022), who assert that coalitions play an important role in international relations because they bring together numerous nations or people to overcome similar difficulties or attain shared goals.

Coalitions allow governments to combine diplomatic resources and use collective influence to achieve shared objectives in international forums (Earsom, 2023). Such as the United Nations, G7, and G20. Security and defense are two of a coalition's roles. Military coalitions are established to battle terrorism, maintain peace, deal with security concerns, and handle humanitarian emergencies. The Global Coalition to Defeat ISIS and NATO (North Atlantic Treaty Organisation) are two examples. Economic alliances support trade agreements, advance economic growth, and fortify regional integration including the European Union (EU), the Association of Southeast Asian Nations (ASEAN), and Mercosur (Malamud, 2020). Collective action against climate change, promotion of sustainable development, and environmental protection are the goals of coalitions like the Climate Vulnerable Forum and the signatories to the Paris Agreement (Unger and Thielges, 2021).

Coalitions encourage a sense of shared responsibility and unity in confronting shared issues by dividing up the workload of addressing global crises among several parties. Coalitions can attain economies of scale and optimise the effectiveness of interventions in domains like scientific research, peacekeeping operations, and development aid by pooling their financial, human, and technical resources (Sandler, 2017). .Coalitions may be very helpful in settling disputes, encouraging communication between parties involved, and assisting in developing peaceful solutions through initiatives for peacebuilding or diplomacy (Dworack, Lüttmann, von Messling, and Vimalarajah, 2021). Coalitions for shared ideals, tenets, and guidelines that direct conduct in domains like environmental preservation, human rights, and disarmament help to shape international norms, standards, and laws.

Coalitions encourage shared responsibility and unity in confronting shared issues by dividing the workload of addressing global crises among several parties. Coalitions can attain economies of scale and optimise the effectiveness of interventions in domains like scientific research, peacekeeping operations, and development aid by pooling their financial, human, and technical resources (Sandler, 2017). Coalitions may be very helpful in settling disputes, encouraging communication between parties involved, and assisting in developing peaceful solutions through initiatives for peacebuilding or diplomacy (Dworack, Lüttmann, von Messling, and Vimalarajah, 2021). Coalitions for shared ideals, tenets, and guidelines that direct conduct in domains like environmental preservation, human rights, and disarmament help to shape international norms, standards, and laws.

Coalition governance plays a pivotal role in post-conflict situations. Coalition governance can be essential to fostering peace, harmony, and the establishment of democracy in post-conflict countries. After a battle, nations are sometimes severely split along racial, religious, or political lines, which makes it difficult to set up an effective government that serves the interests of all citizens. Coalition agreements have several benefits in such delicate situations. Paudel, Winterford, and Selim, (2023) posit that coalition governments can ensure that various groups or communities are involved in the decision-making process in post-conflict countries. By addressing complaints, fostering trust, and preventing marginalised groups from feeling alienated or excluded from the democratic system, this representation helps to resolve issues.

Gumede (2023) believes that in post-conflict countries, coalition governments are less prone to abrupt shifts or disruptions brought on by internal dissension or power struggles than single-party bureaucracies. Abdulhalim (2022) contends that rebuilding institutions, resuming public services, and luring investment necessary for post-conflict recovery depends on this stability. Coalition governance provides a practical method for handling difficult transitions in post-conflict countries by encouraging stability in representation policies.

CHALLENGES OF COALITION GOVERNANCE IN POST-CONFLICT NATIONS

However, coalitions are not without challenges of their own. Challenges of Coalition Governance include conflict management; handling disagreements among coalition members who have different goals can be difficult and could impede efficient government. According to Unger, Mar & Gürtler (2020), because of the coalition members' differing objectives and interests, ensuring the successful execution of policies agreed upon can be difficult, and maintaining the coalition accountable for its activities and decisions can be challenging because several parties share accountability. Thus, coalition as a governance model entails acknowledging its collaborative character, shared decision-making procedures, and the challenges and opportunities it brings in accomplishing common goals through collaboration among various stakeholders.

Although coalition arrangements offer clear benefits in post-conflict environments, they also confront major obstacles that may limit their efficacy and long-term viability. Forming a coalition government after a battle is a significant difficulty since many parties and groups must agree to cooperate and reach a settlement, even though they frequently have conflicting interests and a strong mistrust of one another after fighting (McGarry and O'Leary, 2009). A coalition agreement can require extensive and challenging negotiations since the parties must agree on several issues, including power-sharing arrangements, policy goals, and the distribution of cabinet posts. (Mukherjee, 2006).

In post-conflict settings, coalition governments are frequently precarious and vulnerable to impasse, disintegration, and rekindled hostilities (Cameron & Taflaga, 2017). Divides of many kinds, including ideological, racial, and religious ones, might jeopardise unity. Parties in the coalition government may frequently undercut one another or pursue competing agendas without a shared vision or mutual trust, resulting in policy gridlock and incoherence (Papagianni, 2008). According to McCulloch (2013), accommodating various parties in the cabinet through power-sharing quotas may lead to dissatisfaction if, for example, extreme groups obtain excessive influence given their size and popularity. Group involvement in agreements on power-sharing might exacerbate rather than lessen social divides (Sriram, 2008).

COALITION IN POST-COLONIAL AFRICA

However, in post-colonial Africa, coalition governments' emergence witnessed former liberation parties' electoral base being consolidated or threatened. Thus, the coalition governments in Africa have been renewed and given a political impetus by forming political parties contesting power against the dominance of liberation movements (Ndou, 2022; Patel, 2021; Oyugi, 2006). In the 21st century, various African countries are experimenting with coalition governments juxtaposing the dominance of the former liberation movements in power (Matlosa, 2021). Some countries that have been in coalition arrangements include Malawi, Kenya, Congo, Kinshasa, Zimbabwe, Nigeria, Mauritius, South Africa, and the Kingdom of Lesotho (Jones & Brown, 2018; Khadiagala, 2021; Likoti, 2021). At the center of these coalitions' formation were mainly geared towards dealing with deepening socio-economic challenges and disparities, corruption, and mismanagement by the seating government and regional and ethnic-racial divisions.

Sadly, in countries where the opposition parties contested elections through a coalition formation, internal conflicts and scrambling for positions become the major weakness, cascading to democratic instability and deficit in all spheres of government (Basson & Hunter, 2023). In essence, coalitions riddled with internal conflicts and based on narrow-capitalist and self-interest agendas and interests cannot be used for conflict resolution and democratic governance models (Murali, 2017). Without corporations and compromise, coalitions can undermine African electoral democracy (Schreiber, 2018). Within coalition arrangements, where coalitions are driven by ethnic and regional power-grabbing, the voters have not gained in terms of service delivery. Typical examples are South Africa and Zimbabwe, where coalitions are short-lived and destabilize the state's operational function (Matsika, 2019; Shai & Vunza, 2021). Within the multiparty systems, coalitions were formed either before or post-elections, most times comprising political parties that did not share a common ideology but entered into such an alliance only to contest political power and authority.

Political coalitions have become an alternative governance vehicle in countries where dominant party systems are entrenched, and opposition parties cannot assume power. Pre- and post-elections became optional in Africa, where the former liberation overstayed in power without much transformational change. Thus, the collation through coalition governments; small parties came together mainly to challenge the political hegemony of the liberation movement, which has ascended into power since the dawn of political liberation. Since independence, most liberation movements have enjoyed political euphoria, being tagged as the liberators. Hence, they became complacent in radically addressing their electorates' socio-economic challenges. A radical agenda is needed to ward off rampant corruption, maladministration, and abuse of political power for amassing personal wealth. Most citizens in the developing world are languishing in abject poverty and material deprivations, hence resentment, despondency, and democratic deficit.

CHAPTER OVERVIEW

Chapter 1: This chapter explores the significance of party coalitions in contemporary African politics, focusing on their formation, triggers, and management, particularly in parliamentary and presidential systems. It delves into the motivations behind coalition building, the common threats or goals that drive rival parties to coalesce, and the critical role of stability in coalition management.

Chapter 2: This chapter discusses the politics of party alliances and the conditions influencing government formation in African countries. It examines the transition towards democratic rule in the post-colonial era, highlighting the role of parliamentary and presidential systems in strengthening governance, rule of law, and human rights.

Chapter 3: This chapter addresses the establishment of coalition governments as transitional solutions in conflict-affected nations worldwide. It focuses on multiparty electoral processes, coalition bargaining dynamics, and the impact of externally imposed coalition rules on domestic interests and international dynamics.

Chapter 4: This chapter analyzes the challenges of coalition politics within the context of British governance, with a focus on the unique dynamics of coalition negotiations, constitutional changes, and the short-term effects of coalition governments on policy and electoral systems.

Chapter 5: This chapter investigates the Government of National Unity (GNU) model as a mechanism for coalition governance in Africa, using case studies to illustrate the opportunities, challenges, and implications of coalition governance in contested election contexts.

Chapter 6: This chapter provides a comparative study of coalition governance in Southern Africa, emphasizing Mozambique's absence of coalition governments and the challenges within its electoral system. It advocates for electoral reforms and transparency to align with regional standards.

Chapter 7: This chapter explores the historical emergence and dynamics of local government coalition politics in South Africa, contextualizing it within a global perspective to enhance understanding of municipal governance and political alliances.

Chapter 8: This chapter discusses Israel's recent coalition government and its implications for internal governance, regional conflict dynamics, and international relations, focusing on the Netanyahu-led coalition's policies and challenges.

Chapter 9: This chapter traces the history of coalition politics globally, focusing on Africa's experiences, discussing the prospects, challenges, and impacts of coalition governments on governance and political landscapes.

Chapter 10: This chapter examines challenges facing coalition formations and governments in African countries, discussing the dominance of coalition governments in Europe and proposing solutions to enhance coalition stability and service delivery.

Chapter 11: This chapter explores coalition governance as a mechanism for resolving political disputes following disputed elections, using Zimbabwe's historical context and experiences with coalition governments as case studies.

Chapter 12: This chapter analyzes democratic principles and challenges within coalition governments in South Africa, focusing on local government instability, ideological struggles, and recommendations for effective coalition governance.

Chapter 13: This chapter investigates China's use of coalition politics in Africa to enhance its soft power diplomacy, examining the interactions between coalition governments, democratic processes, and foreign influences.

Chapter 14: This chapter offers a theoretical analysis of coalition politics in South Africa, using political theories to understand power dynamics, governance quality, and service delivery challenges within coalition governments, particularly at the local level.

Chapter 15: This chapter discusses the role of coalition government in strengthening democracy in South Africa, focusing on its historical development, party dynamics, and governance structures to promote national interests and welfare.

Chapter 16: This chapter examines the practical challenges and instabilities within coalition governments in South Africa, highlighting their impact on municipal governance, policy implementation, and service delivery.

Chapter 17: This chapter contributes to the understanding of coalition government and politics in South Africa, examining the impact of coalition governance on service delivery and development, particularly in the context of the ANC-led coalition.

Chapter 18: This chapter evaluates the dynamics of coalition governance in South African local government, emphasizing the challenges of governance, service delivery, and political stability within coalition arrangements.

Chapter 19: This chapter provides a comprehensive evaluation of coalition governments in South Africa's democratic landscape, discussing their impact on governance efficiency, service provision, and public welfare over the past 30 years.

CONCLUSION

As the editor of this book, I am thrilled to introduce a comprehensive exploration of coalition politics and governance, focusing on Africa's journey towards robust electoral democracy and democratic governance. The emergence and evolution of coalition governments have become central to global political dynamics, offering alternatives to entrenched dominant party systems and fostering inclusive governance.

This book aims to delve deeply into the conceptual underpinnings of coalitions and coalition governments, tracing their historical trajectories, examining the triggers behind coalition formations, and evaluating their impact on African electoral democracy. We seek to understand the intricacies of coalition politics at both local and national levels, exploring how coalitions shape electoral processes and influence the quality of governance.

Our audience includes policymakers, practitioners from government, private sectors, and civil society, as well as scholars and researchers in Politics, Sociology, Public Administration, Development Studies, and related fields. We invited contributions illuminating various facets of coalition politics and governance, including theoretical discussions, factors driving coalition formations, models of coalition governments, challenges faced by coalition governments, and the democratic opportunities and governance outcomes they bring.

The chapters in this book offer theoretical insights and empirical analyses into the formation, management, and sustainability of political coalitions, providing valuable frameworks for governments, political parties, and oppositions to navigate coalition dynamics effectively. We aim to foster a deeper understanding of how coalitions can enhance democratic governance, promote inclusivity, and address governance challenges in diverse political contexts.

The thematic areas covered in this book include:

- Theoretical discourses underpinning coalition politics and governments.
- Factors and conditions triggering the formation of political coalitions.
- Approaches and models of coalition politics and governments.
- Challenges facing coalition formations and governments.
- Democratic opportunities and governance outcomes of coalition governments.
- Regulatory frameworks for coalition governance.

We hope this book will significantly contribute to the ongoing discourse on coalition politics and governance, offering valuable insights for policymakers, practitioners, scholars, and researchers engaged in shaping democratic processes and governance frameworks.

Ndwakhulu Stephen Tshishonga
University of KwaZulu-Natal, South Africa

REFERENCES

Abdulhalim, N. (2022). *Investment Opportunities in Post-Conflict Countries How Can Post-Conflict Countries Attract Foreign Direct Investment: The Case of Syria* (Doctoral dissertation, Marmara Universitesi, Turkey).

Albala, A., Borges, A., & Couto, L. (2023). Pre-electoral coalitions and cabinet stability in presidential systems. *British Journal of Politics and International Relations, 25*(1), 64–82. doi:10.1177/13691481211056852

Basson, A., & Hunter, Q. (2023). *Who will Rule South Africa? The Demise of the ANC and the Rise of a New Democracy.* Flyleaf Publishing & Distribution.

Bowler, S., Freebourn, J., Klüver, H., & Spoon, J. J. (2020). Teten, P., Donovan, T. and Vowles, J., (2023). Preferences for single-party versus multi-party governments. *Party Politics, 29*(4), 755–765. doi:10.1177/13540688221081783

Cameron, A., & Taflaga, M. (2017). Coalition government: The Australian experience. In A. Cameron & M. Taflaga (Eds.), *Coalition governance in post-conflict countries* (pp. 177–192). Springer.

Daphi, P., Anderl, F., & Deitelhoff, N. (2022). Bridges or divides? Conflicts and synergies of coalition building across countries and sectors in the Global Justice Movement. *Social Movement Studies, 21*(1-2), 8–24. doi:10.1080/14742837.2019.1676223

Dworack, S., Lüttmann, C., von Messling, B., & Vimalarajah, L. (2021). Basics of Mediation: Concepts and Definitions. In *Peace Mediation in Germany's Foreign Policy* (pp. 97–110). Nomos Verlagsgesellschaft MbH & Co. KG. doi:10.5771/9783748926160-97

Earsom, J. (2023). It's not as simple as copy/paste: The EU's Remobilisation of the High Ambition Coalition in international climate governance. *International Environmental Agreement: Politics, Law and Economics, 23*(1), 27–42. doi:10.1007/s10784-023-09592-z

Gumede, W. (2023). *Policy Brief 46: Improving Coalition Governance. Democracy Works Foundation.* Retrieved February 14, 2024, from https://www.democracyworks.org.za/policy-brief-improving-coalition-governance/

Heywood, A. (2019). Politics (5th ed.). MacMillan International & Red Globe Press.

Islam, N., Ahmed, M., & Sakachep, M. (2023). Governance in collaboration: Evaluating the advantages and challenges of coalition politics. *The Journal of Research Administration, 5*(2), 2142–2149.

Jobela, Z. (2018). The politics of dominance and Survival: Coalition Politics in South Africa 1994-2018. In S, Ngubane (Ed.), Africa Dialogue: Complexities of Coalition Politics in South Africa (pp. 73-106). Durban: The African Centre for the Constructive Resolution of Disputes (ACCORD).

Jones, M., & Brown, A. (2018). The Evolution of Coalition Politics in Southern Africa: A Historical Perspective. *American Journal of Political Science, 25*(1), 78–95.

Khadiagala, G. (2021). Coalition Political in Kenya Superficial assemblages and momentary vehicles to attain power. In S. Booysen (Ed.), Marriages of Inconvenience: The Politics of Coalitions in South Africa (pp. 157-180). Johannesburg: Mapungubwe Institute for Strategic Reflection (MISTRA).

Klüver, H., & Spoon, J. J. (2020). Helping or hurting? How governing as a junior coalition partner influences electoral outcomes. *The Journal of Politics, 82*(4), 1231–1242. doi:10.1086/708239

Likoti, F. (2021). The impact of coalition politics on political parties 'ideologies in Lesotho, 2012-2020. *Coalition politics in Lesotho: a multi-disciplinary study of coalitions and their implications for governance, 1*, 157.

Malamud, A. (2020). Mercosur and the European Union: comparative regionalism and interregionalism. Oxford Research Encyclopedia of Politics. doi:10.1093/acrefore/9780190228637.013.1085

Masina, M. (2021). *Future Realities of Coalitions in South Africa: Reflections on Colation Government in the Metros: 2016-2021.* SAAPAM.

Matlosa, K. (2021). Electoral systems, party systems and coalitions: Lessons from Southern Africa. In S. Booysen (Ed.), Marriages of Inconvenience: The Politics of Coalitions in South Africa (pp.97-124). Johannesburg: Mapungubwe Institute for Strategic Reflection (MISTRA).

Matsika, T. (2019). *The politics of sustainability: discourse and power in post-2000 Zimbabwean political texts* (Doctoral dissertation, University of the Free State).

McCulloch, A. (2013). Does moderation pay? Centripetalism in deeply divided societies. *Ethnopolitics, 12*(2), 111–132. doi:10.1080/17449057.2012.658002

McGarry, J., & O'Leary, B. (2009). Power shared after the deaths of thousands. In R. Taylor (Ed.), *Consociational theory: McGarry & O'Leary and the Northern Ireland conflict* (pp. 15–84). Routledge.

Mukherjee, B. (2006). Why political power-sharing agreements lead to enduring peaceful resolution of some civil wars, but not others? *International Studies Quarterly, 50*(2), 479–504. doi:10.1111/j.1468-2478.2006.00410.x

Müller, W. C., & Meyer, T. M. (2014). Meeting the challenges of representation and accountability in multi-party governments. In *Accountability and European Governance* (pp. 137–164). Routledge.

Murali, K. (2017). Economic Liberation, electrola Coliations and Invsetment Policies in India. In States in the Developing World (pp. 248-290). Cambridge University Press.

Ndou, L. L. (2022). *An analysis of a coalition government: a new path in administration and governance at local government level in South Africa* (Doctoral dissertation, North-West University, South Africa).

Oppermann, K., Brummer, K., & Van Willigen, N. (2017). Coalition governance and foreign policy decision-making. *European Political Science, 16*(4), 489–501. doi:10.1057/s41304-016-0082-7

Oyugi, W. O. (2006). Colaition Politics and Colaition Governments in Africa. *Journal of Contemporary African Studies, 24*(1), 53–79. doi:10.1080/02589000500513739

Papagianni, K. (2008). Participation and State Legitimation. In T. Charles (Ed.), *Building States to Build Peace.* Lynne Rienner. doi:10.1515/9781685856670-005

Patel, L. N. (2021). Political parties, alliance politics and the crisis of governance in Malawi. In S. Booysen (Ed.), Marriages of Inconvenience: The politics of coalitions in South Africa (pp. 207-231). Johannesburg: Mapungubwe Institute for Strategic Reflection (MISTRA). doi:10.2307/j.ctv2z6qdx6.15

Paudel, P., Winterford, K., & Selim, Y. (2023). Exploring the Need for an Integrated Conflict Sensitivity Framework in Development Assistance that Contributes to Peaceful and Sustainable Post-conflict Societies. In *Integrated Approaches to Peace and Sustainability* (pp. 11–31). Springer Nature Singapore. doi:10.1007/978-981-19-7295-9_2

Sandler, T. (2017). International peacekeeping operations: Burden sharing and effectiveness. *The Journal of Conflict Resolution*, *61*(9), 1875–1897. doi:10.1177/0022002717708601 PMID:28989181

Schreiber, L. (2018). *Coalition Cuntry" South Africa after the ANC*. Tafelberg.

Shai, K. B., & Vunza, M. (2021). Gender Mainstreaming in Peacebuilding and Localised Human Security in the Context of the Darfur Genocide: An Africentric Rhetorical Analysis. *Journal of Literary Studies*, *37*(2), 69–84. doi:10.1080/02564718.2021.1923715

Sriram, C. L. (2008). Justice as peace? Liberal peacebuilding and strategies of transitional justice. *Global Society*, *21*(4), 579–591. doi:10.1080/13600820701562843

Unger, C., Mar, K. A., & Gürtler, K. (2020). A club's contribution to global climate governance: The Case of the Climate and Clean Air Coalition. *Palgrave Communications*, *6*(1), 99. doi:10.1057/s41599-020-0474-8

Chapter 1
Factors and Conditions Triggering the Formation of Political Coalitions

Fako Johnson Likoti

ⓘD https://orcid.org/0000-0002-8922-6887

Lesotho Public Service Commission, Lesotho

ABSTRACT

Party coalitions have become very important in contemporary African politics in parliamentary and presidential systems. The dawn of democracy in the third world, and Africa in particular, witnessed significant democratic developments. African political parties have increasingly seen the value of cooperation and have built coalitions and alliances to achieve similar goals. Key amongst these developments have been the formation of political coalitions. Several factors and conditions have triggered the formation of political coalitions and alliances in most African countries. A coalition is a grouping of rival political parties that, in most cases, are motivated by the perception of a common threat or recognition that their goals cannot be attained by not coalescing. The management of a coalition is also critical in order to attain stability. The rationale is that stability becomes important to parties when they enter their coalition pact.

INTRODUCTION

A Coalition government is a democratic mechanism through which willing parties come together to power to lead the Nation. Their agreement is usually based on a shared policy agreement they want to pursue in government. The critical aspect of Coalitions is that they enhance democracy. When political players work together, the net results benefit the broader electorate. The rationale for forming Coalitions was to strengthen democracy. It can also be argued that democracy is unthinkable without democratic parties, and we cannot have political parties without democracy. Additionally, "political parties created modern democracy, and modern democracy is unthinkable save in terms of the parties." (Schattschneider,1942, pp. 1-2). Therefore, political parties and democracy are mutually inclusive. You cannot have one without the other.

Diamond (1995 and 1999) defines democracy as the best form of government, better than any imagined option. He views it as the only business in town. In any democracy, political parties are critical for entrenching democratic culture and practice. Democracy has given political parties a high premium of cooperating and strengthening democracy by forming Coalitions. For instance, some parties at the "local government level, Coalition or multiparty governments were formed to ensure that the business of government was carried out" (Kadima, 2006, p.15).

Since independence, most African countries, such as Mauritius, have been governed through Coalition governments. In other countries like Kenya," the National Rainbow Coalition (NARC) won the 2002 elections, giving meaning, for the first time in nearly 40 years, to democratic alternation" (Kadima, 2006, p. vii). In South Africa, alliances were formed amongst opposition parties and Coalitions during the first democratic elections to strengthen democracy in governing the country and, thus, contribute to nation-building and reconciliation. These alliances and Coalitions formed by different political parties within the Southern African Development Community (SADC) region and throughout Africa were instrumental in triggering democratic consolidation. It must be stated that "some party Coalitions were formed for either strengthening the governing party or creating a viable and stronger opposition" (Kadima, 2006, p.15). Therefore, democracy is strengthened more by the establishment of Coalition governments.

In most African countries in the 1960s, multiparty politics were banned, and immediately after independence, they were replaced by one-party dominant systems. In Lesotho from 1970 to 1986, political parties were banned by the then ruling Basotho National Party (BNP) (Khaketla, p.1971). During military rule, these parties were banned from 1986 to 1993 (Matlosa and Sello, 2005). Political parties in Lesotho were only allowed to function after the 1993 Constitutional reforms, which allowed a free democratic process. Conversely, this period ushered one dominant political party, the Basotho Congress Party (BCP), until 1998, when electoral reforms were introduced, and a new electoral Model of Mixed Member Proportional Representation (MMP) was introduced (Likoti, 2009).

This chapter is divided into five sections, including this introduction. The following section defines a Coalition government. This section forms a framework for understanding Coalition governments. Section three discusses the various reasons for forming Coalitions. It presents an overview of the constellations of factors that provide a rationale for forming Coalition governments. The fourth section discusses the management of Coalitions to ensure their stability and efficiency. The sections emphasise stability as one of the prerequisites for managing this cooperation, amongst other factors. The section put forward some essential factors which must be considered in managing a successful Coalition government that will strengthen democracy. The conclusion forms the last section of this chapter.

BACKGROUND

Towards Definition of Coalitions Governments

The advent of Coalition governments has become a global phenomenon. The composition, nature and life expectancy of Coalition government varies from country to country, depending on specific political circumstances. The emergence of pluralistic politics in the early 1990s motivated the emergence of Coalition governments to secure sufficient seats in Parliament to form stable governments. These power-sharing governments were so popular in most developing countries, especially in Southern Africa, where "others have been accused of being unprincipled because their members were ideologically remote and therefore perceived as political opportunists interested in short-term gains rather than long-term policy goals" (Kadima,2006,p.1).

While Coalitions have been defined differently by various authors, what is important to note is that Coalition governments are always composed of two or more parties that come together to form a stable and efficient government. A Coalition government is, therefore, a form of government representing political parties with diverse interests. Coalition governments aggregate diverse interests and manage them to stabilise their government. These political parties are "broad governing Coalitions that had the job of aggregating interests and a whole package of policies into programmes" (Dearlove and Saunders, 1991, p.131). These types of government consist of two or more political parties that must compromise on principles and shared mandates to govern the country (Finley, 1984).

Coalition parties, therefore, work on mutual trust and agreed procedures that encourage collective decision-making and responsibility while respecting each party's identity (Finn, Mike., Seldom, Anthony., Finn, Michael, 2015). Furthermore, Coalition partners, individually and collectively, must display strong unity to forestall any latent fragmentation. That notwithstanding, Cabinet parties must still adhere to the concept of collective responsibility. Cabinet decisions remain binding to all Coalition partners, and consultation forms the hallmark of this vital agreement to maintain the stability of the government. This type of government usually comprises different parties, sometimes different ideologies. A Coalition government, therefore, leads to consensus-based politics and reflects the popular opinion of the electorate within a country.

A Coalition government, on the other hand, takes time to form a government. Parties must subject themselves to a laborious and lengthy negotiation process to plead with other partners to downgrade their demands and expectations. Israel has gained notoriety for taking months to negotiate to form Coalitions. After the April 9, 2019, elections, it took five months for Israel to form a Coalition government on September 17, 2019 (Levush, 2019). Despite these limitations, Coalition governments play a pivotal role in democracy.

Factors and Conditions Triggering the Formation of Political Coalitions

The world has witnessed several Coalitions since the Second World War. Nigeria has since 1954 seen most governments based on one form of Coalition or the other (Nnoli, 1986). While factors and conditions triggering the formation of Coalitions vary globally, Coalition precipitants remain the same. Some of these precipitants motivating Coalition formation, the first and the most apparent cause, are related to political discontent (Yellappa, 2020). Coalitions are a result rather than a cause of political unrest. The dissatisfaction with the single majority rule and its failure to respond to the changing public needs forces the electorate to resort to other alternatives. In Lesotho, for instance, the formation of the Coalition, which was led by the All-Basotho Convention (ABC) in 2012, was motivated mainly by anti-Mosisili (Then Prime Minister and leader of Democratic Congress (DC) sentiments (Motsamai, 2015). These parties feared congress dominance under Pakalitha Mosisili, especially his welfare policies of free education and old-age pension policy that appeared to be attracting more followers. Ironically, all Lesotho Coalitions and political parties adopted these policies. Their fears were not grounded in ideology but motivated by an office-seeking mentality. This also proved that their ideological outlook (ABC, LCD and BNP) was similar to that of the DC Leader (Motsamai, 2015).

In Lesotho, for instance, it can be argued that the emergence of Coalition governments was a direct reflection of "the failure of Lesotho's political elites to cooperate for the greater good, itself a manifestation of the historical legacy of elite fragmentation and mistrust produced what was described as the assurance or coordination dilemma"(Monyake,2020,p.3). This manifested a lack of trust amongst political elites without coordination and reciprocity. The absence of compromise and collaboration between rival political elites has made the emergency of consensus-building difficult. It was for this reason that, the Coalitions in Lesotho became so unstable (The Post newspaper, 2015).

Political parties form Coalitions for various reasons. In Germany, as elsewhere in Europe, political parties chose to be in power rather than in opposition. The 2010 Coalition government in the UK was motivated by a similar argument of being inside rather than outside (Martin and Vanberg, 2011). Political parties form Coalitions because they are interested in supporting an existing cabinet or party or fear that other opposition parties will form an alternative government.

Parties in Coalition tend to search for a common ground rather than conviction and politics of principle (Heywood, 1997). For any successful formation of a Coalition government, the politics of principles had to be conveniently abandoned to achieve this project. While this realism can be regarded as "implicitly corrupt, in that parties are encouraged to abandon policies and principles in their quest for power" (Heywood, 1997, p.246), this does not mean parties will conduct themselves politically incorrectly.

Rational for Coalition Formation

Political parties are rational and goal-oriented. They all seek to be elected to office. Coalition stability and partners' cooperation incentivise office-seeking parties to maintain the Coalition to avoid the loss of executive posts. Therefore, these parties have strong incentives to avoid activities that might risk the government's break-up. This office-seeking behaviour drives their interests and, if not well managed, can easily risk the Coalition's stability and cause the government to collapse. Riker (1962) saw this office-seeking mentality as instrumental in winning elections to control the Executive offices. This forms the primary motivation for being in politics in the first instance.

Similarly, Anthony Downs (1957), in his celebrated work, 'An Economic Theory of Democracy', argues that parties are political firms selling policy packages to maximise votes to win and enjoy the fruits of government office (Likoti, 2008). These two imperatives of winning votes and policy prioritisation have made it difficult for Coalition parties to ensure their government's stability. To ensure stability, Coalition partners must coordinate their efforts.

The 1960s and 1970s saw the emergence of Coalition theories based on size and ideology (Kadima, 2006). Most of these theories drew their experience from Western Europe. These theories mainly aimed to explain Coalition government formation in European parliamentary democracies. While these theories are critical, they could have been more comprehensive in explaining Coalition government formation in most African countries. That being the case, "they centre on the effects of a potential Coalition size and ideology on its chances of formation and may be subdivided into office-seeking and policy-seeking theories" (Kadima, 2014, p.4). Therefore, office-seeking theory assumes that political parties' primary goal is to assume power. This is derived from the belief that government formation is vital, especially with ample seats.

The theory assumes that it is more desirable for a few political parties to form a Coalition government. The number of members of Parliament must be sufficient to guard against any contemplated vote of no confidence, which must be won. The 2022 Coalition government of four political parties in Lesotho and the 2017 Coalition of four parties were formed on this basis. The view here is that the fewer the parties that form a Coalition government, the better the payoffs (Gamson 1961, Riker 1962). The propounders of this view argue that it is better to exclude more passengers. For them., it is easier for a few political parties to reach a consensus than many parties.

Government formation is critical to any political party, and Cabinet positions are the ultimate payoffs. Government formation is a matter of a win-and-lose scenario. Since cabinet portfolios are essential to political parties, a majority Coalition in Parliament would not allow the existence of a minority government. Instead, it would take the spoils of office itself. For this reason, office-driven theories are known as office-seeking or office-oriented (Kadima, 2006).

When political parties enter a Coalition government, they gain power, and more political benefits are guaranteed with power. The most central benefit is enacting policies and controlling the entire state apparatus (Lynch and Fairclough, 2010). However, unlike political parties in single-party governments, which can independently decide legislation, political parties in Coalition governments are constrained by their Coalition partnership.

The central dilemma of Coalition parties has been the governance of the Coalition government itself. Once in a Coalition, political parties must demonstrate unity to govern together. They cannot independently select and prioritise their issues, unlike when they are outside the Coalition partnership at will. In a Coalition, they are constrained in their selective issue emphasis once they enter a Coalition government. They should align their issue priorities with those of other Coalition partners (s). They cannot make unilateral decisions, unlike in a single-party government, where political parties can make decisions of their own free will.

Most major parties tend to dislike Coalitions because the grouping tends to overstate the strength of minor parties. For instance, the 2015 Coalition government in Lesotho was a composition of seven political parties. Four parties won one proportional seat each, while the fifth got three seats. Each of the four political parties had to be given a Ministerial position, and the fifth party was given two Ministers: a cabinet Minister and a Deputy Minister. Additionally, the leading parties had to treat these minor parties as if they had won more seats. It was clear that the strength of these minor parties had been overrated.

Homogeneous Ideology

The end of the Cold War in Europe witnessed ideological shifts in most developing countries. Most countries in Africa went through ideological changes that were influenced by socioeconomic changes,

Even in those few countries with relatively more delineated ideologies (e.g., Mauritius and South Africa), high poverty levels have forced party leaders to grant the state a comparatively large role in the market economy to fast-track national socioeconomic development. This convergence of the main priorities creates a degree of connection among the majority of mainstream political parties, thus justifying why most parties can compatibly share power. Divisions tend to be, in essence, personality-driven rather than ideologically based. (Kadima, 2014, p.5)

It has been asserted that African political parties have "no significant ideological differences" (Svasand, 2014, p.87). Surveys showed that voters could identify the parties as offering alternative policy issues. This has been the case with Lesotho's major political parties, which have similar ideologies and policies. One major political party, "the BCP, for example, has split five times, with no major ideological differences between the resulting parties" (Kabemba, 2003, p.28). This demonstrates that it has been easy for these parties to form Coalition governments. Kabemba (2003) notes that:

... 19 parties that cover Lesotho's political space show minimal variation in ideological orientation, policy position, organisational structure or geographical dispersion, and they hardly present any alternative sets of policies for addressing the socioeconomic challenges facing the country and for taking the country forward. (Kabemba, 2003.p.27)

Therefore, Lesotho's political parties have remained consistent in their ideological orientations. Several political parties dominate the current Lesotho political landscape. Lesotho has over 54 political parties with similar ideologies originating from the first political party in Lesotho, the Basotho Congress Party (BCP), which was established in 1956. These "parties only differ in names and colours ... party manifestos are the same ... the difference is only in the language used in writing the manifesto and leadership" (Kabemba, 2003, p.27). Arguably, their ideological similarity has made it easier for these parties to coalesce. Additionally, Coalition formation in Lesotho, Mauritius and Kenya presents one similar feature of insuring elite circulation and cooperation in Coalition governments. Political parties in these countries are governed by people from one major political party in each of these polities.

To a large degree, these parties embraced the now reigning hegemonic world's neo-liberal ideology (Kapa, 2013). This neo-liberal ideology refers to pluralistic politics and free- market-oriented reform policies of deregulation of capital markets, eliminating price controls and lowering trade barriers. This neo-liberal ideology is sometimes called "pluralism" since it focuses on the plurality of actors who play a significant role within global markets (Tansey, 2008). These actors advocate for "free trade together with the minimisation of state intervention" (Garner, Ferdinand and Lawson, 2009, p.344).

Neo-liberals see the plethora of actors' roles as interdependent, hence the term "complex interdependence" within a given market environment. Since political parties are also interdependent within a country regarding some policy outlook and ideological similarities, they coalesce with each other, where the dominant goal is not security but the welfare of their citizens (Garner et al., 2009).

While Lesotho political parties have convergent ideological proximity, this (ideology) does not mean that the trigger for their Coalition formation derives from this ideology. Kadima (2006) maintained that in countries like Kenya, South Africa, Mozambique, Malawi and Mauritius, their ideological orientation did not determine Coalition formation. Their neo-liberal orientation only moved them to the center, a factor like that of Lesotho Coalition parties. Therefore, "the ideological realignment of the main parties ... towards the center has reduced the importance of ideology as a differentiating factor for Coalition building, collapse and revival" (Kadima, 2006, p.229). This ideological realignment of political parties has also been a significant factor in Coalition formation, which the existing electoral system has reinforced, among other factors.

The Electoral System

There is a major interplay between the electoral system and Coalition formation. One of the most interesting political developments in Lesotho has been the issue of electoral system. This aspect was brought to bear as a result of major political conflict in 1998 in Lesotho, where the First Past the Post Electoral System (FPTP) that the country used since independence kept on producing one dominant political party. This conflict precipitated the review of this electoral system from majoritarian to a mixed member electoral system (MMP). It was this electoral system (MMP) that facilitated the emergence of Coalition governments and political alliances in Lesotho. This model was more appreciated that the previous winner-take-all model since it was a transformational model away from the previous FPTP into the current Mixed member proportion representation that cater for both party Alliances and Coalition governments.

Lesotho adopted a Mixed Member Proportional (MMP) Representation Electoral system or what is known as the Compensatory Model (Likoti, 2009). The MMP environment encourages political parties to form Coalitions, just like the PR system used in Germany. However, this does not mean that the Fist-Past-the-Post (FPTP) or Majoritarian system used in the United Kingdom of Great Britain and Northern Ireland (UK/ Britain) cannot countenance Coalition formation. The MMP electoral system in force in Lesotho is founded on the principle that governments are formed by an agreement of willing parties. These parties' main interest is influencing government policies and programmes in the direction favoured by their political philosophies. These perspectives are crucial when comparing Coalition stability in Lesotho, Germany, and the United Kingdom.

Coalition governments require coordination and compromise among Coalition parties. Jones and Baumgartner (2005) have referred to this coordination requirement as institutional friction caused by PR electoral systems such as the one practised in Germany and the MMP Electoral System used in Lesotho.

Coalition formation has been a successful concept in countries like Germany and Britain. In Germany, Coalition formations have become a custom. This can be seen by the Proportional Representation (PR) Electoral system that Germany has adopted. The European countries have a long and vibrant history of Coalition governments. For instance, "all Belgian cabinets since 1954 have been Coalitions of two or more parties with more than merely a bare majority of Legislative seats" (Lijphart,1984,p.24). The 2010 British Coalition government between the Conservative and Liberal Democrats is a case in point of a successful Coalition formed on trust, respect, consultation, and shared political mandate. Negotiations and reconciliation typically characterise Coalition politics.

Nnoli (1986) argued that three distinct features characterise Coalition government or multiparty system; firstly, the legal framework between three or more parties. Secondly, the high degree of the fragmentary electoral basis of each of these three or more political parties; finally, the political parties" inability or any single one of them to form a government on its own, thus giving rise to the emergence of Coalitions of several parties to form government"(Nnoli, 1986,p.143).

In most multiparty systems where PR and MMP systems are used, none of the political parties can win a majority of legislative seats, as has been the case in point with recent Lesotho and Germany elections. In these cases, Coalition governments of at least two or more different political parties must consult their Coalition partner (s) before deciding not to risk the government's instability and premature collapse (Warwick, 1994; Lupia and Strom, 1995). The PR electoral system and MMP in South Africa and Lesotho respectively, can be construed as triggers for Coalition formation in these countries.

Hung Parliament

In most cases, election results tend to produce a hung Parliament where significant parties failed to gain most seats. Lesotho has had five successive Coalition governments since 2012 as a result of hung parliament. In all these elections no party was able to gain the minimum requirement of 50 plus one seats to form government on its own. The formation of these governments, were based on coalition agreements. However, a comprehensive analysis of these agreements reveals in adequate preparation or vague understanding as to how the said agreement had to be drafted. There was lack of understanding as to how these agreements which forms the basis of these Coalitions resulting from hung parliament had to include or not include. It was for this reason that the split was bound to emerge between the partners sooner than later.

This hung Parliament has often been utilised as a trigger for Coalition formation and as a factor to prevent some political parties from forming a Coalition of their own with the pretext that they threaten democracy. The 2005 German Federal elections produced Parliament, where traditional Coalition partners needed more seats to form a government. While another Coalition led by SPD, Greens, and the Party of Democratic Socialism (PDS), the successor party to East Germany and a former partner of the then East German ruling Socialist Unity Party, could be formed, this was strategically and politically prevented by the leaders of the SPD and the CDU/CSU. These leaders conveniently agreed to form a Grand Coalition with CDU leader Angela Merkel as chancellor with an equal number of cabinet seats for each party. This was another testimony that parties with similar ideological outlooks could work together and exclude a party that does not share their ideological outlook, such as PDS above. Merkel was elected Chancellor on November 22-2005 (Gallagher et al., 1992).

The next regular election in September 2009 led to another change in the composition of the German government as the CDU/CSU coalesced with the liberal FDP (Koalitionen, 2021). The 2009 Federal elections saw the end of the Second Grand Coalition in German history and the formation of another Coalition of CDU/CSU and the FDP under the leadership of Merkel as Chancellor for the second term. The 2013 elections saw another successful effort that prevented the formation of a centre-left (successor party to the PDS) Coalition government with the SPD and the Greens. The Grand Coalition was strategically formed once again.

These left parties have been left out of government by all these major Coalition partners. Grand Coalitions of 1st, 3rd and 4th Merkel cabinets (2005–2009, 2013–2018, 2018) strategically prevented these left parties from forming a Coalition government or participating in these Grand Coalitions. The Coalition was composed of many political parties with diverse interests. What brought all these political parties together was said to safeguard democracy that was threatened by radical political parties such as the KPD and NSDAP.

Britain had a Coalition government in 2010 after the elections that brought about a hung parliament, which was the first in Britain in 36 years (United We Stand, 2021, p.1). In their Coalition agreement of 2010, David Cameron, Leader of the Conservative Party and Nick Clegg, Leader of the Liberal Democrats, argued that "we share a conviction that the days of big government are over; that centralisation and top-down control have proved a failure" (The Coalition,2010,p.7). The two parties committed themselves to liberal values that they shared. They listed 31 policy areas to govern and guide their Coalition government (The Coalition, 2010). They vowed not to establish a big government or grand Coalition like their predecessors during the war period but a consensual Coalition government that would open opportunities for both the rich and the poor to practice their talents and improve their capabilities (The Coalition, 2010). The rationale for forming this Coalition was to have many seats in parliament and break, the Labour party 13-year control over the British Parliament, and dislodge it (Labour) from power. Conversely, national crisis in Britain has been able to bring these parties (Conservative and Labour parties) together and force them to form a Coalition government.

National Crisis (War)

National crisis, primarily (war) has arguably been one of the triggers of Coalition formation. From 1954 onwards, Coalitions were formed after elections and during political crises, predominantly during significant conflicts such as war. During this crisis (war), Coalitions are considered to be favourable option to keep the nation united against a foreign enemy (Finley,2012).

Unlike the Federal Republic of Germany, the United Kingdom has no long tradition with Coalition governments. While Germany often entered Coalition governments, Britain, on the other hand, was not persuaded to follow this route (Kuttner, 2021). Grand Coalitions were, however, formed only occasionally during the national crisis. The reason was that British political parties come from different ideological traditions. The two main parties which dominated the political landscape since the Second World War did not trust each other because of their different political outlook. The Labour Party was more socialist in orientation, while the conservative party adopted a Liberal ideological outlook. Coalition governments in the UK are commonly known as National Governments. These Coalitions were formed during the First and Second World Wars.

The most prominent Coalition in British political history was the National Government of 1931 to 1940. This was regarded as the most successful wartime Coalition in British political history. It was forged during wartime by Winston Churchill and Labour Leader Clement Attlee as Deputy Prime Minister. Churchill was the Prime Minister, and several Labour and conservative personalities occupied critical positions in this wartime government. Churchill's Grand Coalition government saved Britain from Hitler (Kuttner, 2021). Unfortunately, in 1945, voters punished him at the polls, and the Labour Party won the elections massively (Kuttner, 2021). Labour and Conservatives have always been arch-enemies pursuing different ideologies. Therefore, it was easier for their marriage to collapse once the war ended. This was because they were brought together by this crisis (war), not policies or ideological outlooks. Despite the British having an antipathy towards the National government (Coalition), on average, they formed them when it was expedient to do so and, most importantly, when it was in the national interest. This was another trigger of Coalition formation. However, for these Coalitions to be sustainable, good leadership and management skills are required from the political leadership of the Coalition government itself.

Management of Coalition Government

Those who led successful Coalitions agree that the most significant contribution to a successful Coalition is stability, trust, respect among leaders and good relationships amongst political parties in the Coalition marriage. This is why Coalition stability is so crucial in consolidating democracy. Efficiency and stability are the essential characteristics of a Coalition government management strategy. For the Coalition to be stable, it must have more robust parliamentary support. Coalition control of many seats in Parliament is linked to consensus decision-making.

Kostova (2004) argued that the presence of a Coalition agreement, where available, serves as a mechanism to overcome the mutual mistrust amongst parties and to create a definite certainty. In a Coalition government formation, the issues that divide the partners are the ones to be discussed rather than the ones that unite them. While parties concern themselves with giving and taking, this does not eliminate tensions that may crop up between the parties. One way to ensure Coalition stability is the partners' ability to manage many of the challenges of Coalition governments through adherence to Coalition agreements. Coalition agreements are agreements on policies and procedures entered into by cabinet parties. These agreements foster Coalition stability since all partners will know from the onset what can reinforce the Stability of their Coalition (Kostova, 2004). From an agenda-setting perspective, Coalition agreements set the government's policy agenda, determining which issues it should try to promote (and avoid) during its governing period.

A Coalition agreement is a contract constraining the behaviour of individual party supporters, cabinet parties, and Ministers' behaviour, preventing the Coalition enterprise's destabilisation. The contract also constitutes a vertical constraint. It constrains all party levels, from Ministers to Members of Parliament and ordinary rank-and-file members. Hence, one crucial aspect of Coalition agreements is that they promote stability and regulate relations between and within parties. In this sense, Coalition agreements are pre-commitments, by which the parties bind themselves to the mast so that when they go through unpleasant situations, the Coalition government does not meet a premature death (Kostova, 2004).

It (Coalition agreement) is a viable document that provides Coalition leadership with the mechanism by which they can resist temptation and pressure from their respective parties to renege on their agreements. This agreement serves as radar that guides the ship through troubled waters (instability). The nonexistence of this Covenant can bring about unpalatable consequences. The stability of the Coalition government depends on a Coalition agreement. This agreement must meet the partners' expectations. Expectations on Ministerial positions and government seats commensurate to the number of resources brought into the Coalition by each partner must be spelt out.

Coalition governments are interested in prioritising their unity rather than managing their diversity. Coalition governance is a mixed-motive game in which Coalition parties must reconcile the tension between policy compromise to maintain government stability and policy differentiation to ensure electoral success (Thies, 2001, Martin and Vanberg, 2011, Falco-Gimeno, 2014).

For Kostova, (2004,a), the formation and management of a successful Coalition depend on maintaining strong party discipline and loyalty. He observed that when party discipline is weak, rebellions and party divisions will likely cause the Coalition to collapse. He stressed that the Coalition will weaken if party loyalty and divisions are not managed and controlled by the party leadership. This was a case in point in Lesotho when the seven-party 2015 and four parties 2017 Coalition governments collapsed, respectively. In 2015, the leading Coalition party, the Democratic Congress (DC), fragmented, and in late 2016, the rebellion within DC necessitated a vote of no confidence that precipitated the collapse of that Coalition government in February 2017. In 2017, the leading Coalition party suffered the similar fate like Democratic congress. During the elections of its National Executive Elections (NEC), All Basotho Convention (ABC) also engaged in factional conflicts that collapsed their Coalition government in May 2020.

Even though Coalition parties often have diverging preferences, they must portray and demonstrate unity to remain stable. To achieve stability, research on Coalition governance has demonstrated that Coalition parties use control mechanisms such as Coalition agreements, conflict management committees within their members, especially those outside government and portfolio committees to keep their Coalition partners on track (Thies, 2001, Muller and Strom, 2008a, Muller and Meyer, 2010, Martin and Vanberg, 2011, Falco-Gimeno, 2014).

Stability is a vital ingredient for the durability of Coalition governments in parliamentary democracies. The Coalition leadership must ensure that the Coalition marriage is stable. Without stability, Coalition government termination is almost inevitable. The key to Coalition governments' sustainability has always been their stability and efficiency in government. Coalition governments are usually volatile and collapse easily. There are various reasons for this instability. In most cases, parties that coalesce with each other tend to disagree on many policy areas. Therefore, the Coalition government tends to be fractious and prone to disharmony since some partners may hold differing views. Some of them may not have a history of working together, as it has been stated with political parties in Lesotho that formed Coalitions.

While these parties may find themselves compelled to work together due to election outcomes or circumstances beyond their control, establishing trust and unity may necessitates a lot of work. The Coalition collapses quickly because some partners may not agree to sacrifice for a policy they think will cost them at the next elections. In most cases, some of these parties developed hostility towards each other before forming the Coalition government itself.

Under the Westminster parliamentary system that Lesotho and Britain have adopted, governments are invariably formed by a party that controls most seats (Read, 1993). When the Coalition enjoys the most seats in Parliament, its legislative programme usually needs not be met with challenges. Similarly, consensus decision-making in the Cabinet is also closely linked to the majority of parliamentarians they have. Greater consensus can also stabilise the Coalition during political and economic instability. For this consensus to endure during these crises, strong social support is also needed to stabilise the government (Kostova, 2004). Each party needs the support of partners, and without it, a Coalition could break down since parties have diverse interests.

Cooperation in this regard pays dividends. Therefore, the value of cooperating in government is much greater than differences, as government stability ensures control over state resources. Partners outside the Coalition government usually manage conflictual issues. Parties' primary priority has been to minimise the ferocity of conflict from not spilling into cabinets. This ensures that, these conflicts are managed and resolved elsewhere, not within the Cabinet (Lynch and Fairclough, 2010). Parties look for compromise on potential issues and ensure that the Stability of the Coalition is sustained. This is how the Coalition builds consensus policies amongst themselves. Coalition parties, therefore, place more premiums on dealing with global Coalition issues that gain support from all partners rather than focus on their narrow partisanship priorities (Muller, 2008b, Muller and Meyer 2010). Therefore, partners' demonstration of unity has become a prerequisite for government stability.

The Coalition government needs strong leadership of the cooperative type of the President, who can fully use his office's powers to secure the Coalition (King, 1993). The President's political and individual sources of authority are crucial in reinforcing his or her leadership style. Constantly seeking support from other Ministers can significantly benefit him or her and the Coalition's Stability (Blondel, 2001). The other strategy the President can adopt to stabilise the Coalition is the persistent usage of his or her position of controlling information. The President controls the communication and policy of the government. He or she has the authority to control many policy areas. The President can use critical roles and information networks to stabilise the Coalition Kostova (2004).

The critical role of the President, amongst others, is to preserve harmony between partners and manage Coalition conflicts successfully. Coalition stability depends on the leadership's ability to manage differences that may emerge from time to time. Management of Coalition priorities requires hierarchy. The President must use his or her primary sources of authority extensively. These sources include his or her right and duty to chair the Cabinet and use his or her influence to stabilise the Coalition. Since this type of government was formed through negotiations, the President is well placed to utilise this skill to stabilise the Coalition (Blondel, 2001). Cabinet stability is vital for the Coalition to succeed and govern effectively. Coordination of cabinet efforts must be maintained at all times.

King (1993) argued that, for the Coalition government to be stable and efficient, it must overcome barriers that can hurt it. First, it must overcome weak leadership. The leader must be strong and be a skilled negotiator. Secondly, it must guard against the substantial interference of political parties in government business. When these are present, the government may be stable but needs to be more compelling. Cabinet conflicts are typical in Coalitions. If the leadership is weak, these conflicts can spiral out of control and collapse the Coalition. Thirdly, the Coalition must eliminate politicised programmes because they threaten the Coalition itself (King, 1993).

Coalition unity forms "an important precondition for the functioning and the survival of a Coalition government" (Martin and Vanberg, 2008, Martin and Vanberg, 2011). Unity is achieved by prioritising policy issues supported by all Coalition members while avoiding issues on which they disagree. Despite parties having different policies, they must compromise to achieve stability by collectively adopting joint policy initiatives. Since the benefits of cooperation outweigh its costs, Coalition parties must focus on common issues of mutual interests. It can be argued that once a Coalition government has been formed, the partners' priority is strengthening government stability and cohesion to effectively pursue their legislative agenda (Lynch and Fairclough, 2010). The legislative programme must accommodate the views and demands of other partners. This is done notwithstanding the parties' divergent policy goals. By demonstrating unity, the stability of the government is assured. Coalition partners must also maintain their independence by signifying their profile. They must reconcile the tension of building their profile and ensuring that they do not temper with government stability and thus break the government.

The strength of political parties is also vital in determining the stability of the Coalition government (King, 1993). Most European political parties, especially in Germany and Britain, have a long history and tradition of forming sustainable Coalition governments, unlike Coalition governments in Lesotho. The strength of the Coalition depends on internal parties' cohesion, which Lesotho political parties need to improve, unlike their European counterparts. Because of their unity, trust among themselves and vast experience in Coalition formation, European parties can negotiate quickly with aspirant Coalition partners. Their ability to negotiate and balance the interests of the Coalition during formation is critical. Prasad (2013) argued that forming Coalitions in Lesotho does not allow thorough negotiations to flourish. He observed that the two-week Constitutional requirement of forming a government after "election day resulted in a rushed Coalition formation" (Prasad, 2013, p.28), where even trust, respect and unity cannot be developed between parties.

Additionally, the Stability of the Coalition, according to Kostova (2004), depends on creating a collegial environment. A collegial environment built integrity, teamwork, and decision-making style amongst Coalition partners. The principle of collegiality means that

The 'best', the most authoritative, decision in the British government must be collective decisions of the whole Cabinet, not just of one member of it or of any group of members...; if the best decision were to be collective decisions, then the collective's members had the right to be consulted about the most important of them and to participate in the taking of them.., collective decisions having been taken, all the members of the Cabinet and the government had the duty to defend them publicly. Political strength lies in unity. (King, 1993, p.53)

For Coalition government to be stable, cabinet decisions must be made collectively. The success of any Coalition depends on all partners participating in the decision-making process. This decision must be taken in the Cabinet. If the President has strong negotiation skills, the Coalition will be more effective, and conflicts between partners will be well-managed and less explosive. Therefore, the less conflictual the Coalition, the more effective and stable it will be (Blondel, 2001).

Like elsewhere, Coalition governments in the above three countries have significant internal and external challenges. The reason is simple: Coalitions can make government more fractious and unstable. Conversely, as has been argued in Coalition literature, "it would nevertheless be a mistake to suggest that Coalitions are always associated with instability, as the record of the stable and effective Coalition government in Germany and Sweden demonstrates" (Heywood, 1997, p.246).

CONCLUSION

In conclusion therefore, it can be argued that, Coalitions are crucial in strengthening democracy. Through Coalitions, political parties coalesce together to enrich democracy to be sustainable. Coalitions are like marriages; parties must work at them to keep them stable. All parties come together in good faith. Coalitions always require compromise and negotiations to steer successful pathways that meet the aspirations of the electorate, which did not give any party the mandate to govern on its own. The importance of Coalition stability in a democracy cannot be overemphasised.

There are several conditions which form primary triggers for Coalition formations. These are not limited to policies, ideological homogeneity, and factors such as national crises or even conflicts among political parties, which, in the end, produce a hung Parliament. Electoral systems such as proportional representation, mixed member proportion, or events first past the post-electoral system could trigger Coalition formations. In most cases, these factors can be crucial in enhancing and consolidating democracy. It should also be noted that some of these factors can weaken democracy in some cases, predominantly where a Coalition government is composed of many parties with fewer seats who may demand more than their share of their electoral outcome (fewer seats), as in the case of 2015 Lesotho seven-party Coalition demonstrated.

Since the gestation period of Coalitions, as discussed above, can be very short, this calls for proper management of Coalitions themselves. This means that Coalition arrangements must be well thought-out. With proper management of Coalition government, democracy is strengthened and becomes sustainable. Political parties can only play this game (democracy) if they manage Coalition arrangements, as discussed above. As a result of proper management, Coalition stability can create sustainable conditions that enhance democratic sustainability.

REFERENCES

Blondel J., & Muller, R. (Eds.). (2001). *Cabinets in Eastern Europe*. Palgrave.

Dearlove, J., & Saunders, P. (1991). *Introduction to British Politics* (2nd ed.). Polity Press.

Dearlove, J., & Saunders, P. R. (2000). *Introduction to British politics*. No Title.

Diamond, L. (1995). *Developing Democracy: Toward Consolidation*. Johns Hopkins University Press.

Diamond, L. (1999). *Developing democracy: Toward consolidation*. JHU press. doi:10.56021/9780801860140

Downs, A. (1957). *An economic theory of democracy*. Harper.

Falco-Gimeno, A. (2014). 'The use of control mechanisms in Coalition governments: The role of preference tangentiality and repeated interactions'. *Party Politics*, *20*(3), 341–356. doi:10.1177/1354068811436052

Finley, M. (2012). *Coalition Agreement for Stability and Reform*. Cabinet Office.

Finn, M., Seldom, A., & Finn, M. (2015). *The Coalition Effect, 2010-2015*. Cambridge University Press.

Gallagher, M., Laver, M., & Mair, P. (1992). *Representative Government in Western Europe*. McGraw-Hill, Inc.

Gamson, W. (1961, June). 'A Theory of Coalition Formation'. *American Sociological Review*, *26*(3), 373. doi:10.2307/2090664

Heywood, A. (1997). *Politics*. Macmillan Foundations. doi:10.1007/978-1-349-25543-6

Jones, B. D., & Frank, R. B. (2005). *The Politics of Attention: How government prioritises problems*. University of Chicago Press.

Kadima, D. (Ed.). (2006). *The politics of party Coalitions in Africa*. EISA.

Kadima, D. (2014). An introduction to the politics of party alliances and coalitions in socially-divided Africa. *Journal of African Elections*, *13*(1), 1–24. doi:10.20940/JAE/2014/v13i1a1

Khaketla, B. M. (1971). *Lesotho 1970: An African Coup Under the Microscope*. Morija Printing Works.

King, A. (1993). Cabinet Coordination or Prime Ministerial Dominance? A Conflict of Three Principles of Cabinet Government. In The developing British Political System: 1990s. Longman.

Koalitionen. (2021). https://www.bundestagswahl-2021.de/koalitionen

Kostova, D. (2004a). *Coalition Governments and the Decision Making Process in CEE*. Paper prepared for the ECPR Joint Session of Workshops, University of Uppsala, Sweden.

Kuttner, R. (2021). *Britain's Unlikely Grand Coalition (Don't Mention the War)*. https://robertkuttner.com

Levush, R. (2019). *Here We Go Again: Forming a Coalition Government Israeli Style*. https://blogs.loc.gov/law/2019/09/here-we-go-again-forming-a-Coalition-government-israeli-style/

Lijphart, A. (1984). *Democracies: Patterns of Majoritarian and Consensus Government in Twenty-One Countries*. Yale University Press. doi:10.2307/j.ctt1ww3w2t

Likoti, F. J. (2009). The 2007 General Elections in Lesotho. The Application and Challenges of the Electoral System. *African Studies Quarterly,* *10*(4). africa.ufl.edu/asq/v10/v10i4a3.htm

Lupia, A., & Kaare, S. (1995). Coalition termination and the strategic timing of legislative elections. *The American Political Science Review*, *89*(3), 648–665. doi:10.2307/2082980

Lynch, P., & Fairclough, P. (2010). UK Government and Politics. Hachette.

Martin, L. W., & Georg, V. (2011). *Parliaments and Coalitions: The Role of Legislative Institutions in Multiparty Governance*. Oxford University Press. doi:10.1093/acprof:oso/9780199607884.001.0001

Matlosa, K. (1999). Conflict and Conflict Management: Lesotho's Political Crisis after the 1998 Election. *Lesotho Social Science Review*, 5(1), 163–196.

Matlosa, K. (2017). Understanding Political Crisis of Lesotho's Post-2015 Elections. In M. Thabane (Ed.), *Towards an Anatomy of Political Instability in Lesotho 1966–2016* (pp. 131–161). National University of Lesotho.

Matlosa, K., & Sello, C. (2005). *Political parties and democratisation in Lesotho*. Academic Press.

Monyake, M. (2020). A. ssurance dilemmas of the endangered institutional reforms process in Lesotho. *Canadian Journal of African Studies / Revue canadienne des études africaines*. https://www.tandfonline.com/loi/rcas20

Motsamai, D. (2015). Elections in time of Instability: Challenges for Lesotho beyond 2015 Poll. *Institute for Security Studies, 3*, 1-16.

Muller & Strom. (2008b). Coalition agreements and cabinet governance. In *Cabinets and Coalition Bargaining*. Oxford University Press.

Muller, W., & Kaare, S. (2008a). *Cabinets and Coalition bargaining: The democratic life cycle in Western Europe*. Oxford University Press.

Muller, W., & Thomas, M. M. (2010). Meeting the Challenges of Representation and Accountability in Multiparty Governments. *West European Politics, 33*(5), 1065–1092. doi:10.1080/01402382.2010.486135

Nnol, O. I. (1986). *Introduction to Politics*. Longman.

Peter, C. (1991). World Politics Since 1945. Longman.

Read, M. (1993). The Place of Parliament. In The developing British Political System: 1990s. Longman.

Riker, W. H. (1962). *The Theory of Political Coalitions*. Yale University Press.

Roy, J. (2001). *Churchill*. Macmillian.

Sangeeta, Y. (2020). Coalition Governments in India. *Political Perspective Third Concept*, 21–31.

The Coalition. (2010). *Our Programme for Government*. London Her Majestry's Government.

The Coalition Agreement for Stability and Reform. (2015). *Lesotho's Second Coalition Government Agreement*. Author.

The Constitution of Lesotho. (1993). *The Constitution of Lesotho*. Government Printer.

The Post Newspaper. (2015, Apr. 16). *The Collapse of Lesotho First Coalition Government*. Author.

Thies, F. F. (2001). Keeping Tabs on Partners: The Logic of Delegation in Coalition Governments. *American Journal of Political Science, 45*(3), 580–598. doi:10.2307/2669240

United We Stand. (2021). *Coalition Government in the UK*. https://www.Instituteforgovernment.org.uk/publication/united-we-stand

KEY TERMS AND DEFINITIONS

Coalition Government: Where more than one political party after winning seats in Parliament come together to form government.

Hung Parliament: Where election results did not give any competing political party an outright majority to govern alone.

Ideology: A set of beliefs that binds people together. It, therefore, provides a set of values that political supporters adhere to. It shapes how people identify themselves.

National Crisis: A situation whereby a sovereign state is facing external aggression from another state.

Political Alliance: A situation where political parties outside Parliament group together to fight government policies.

Rational Choice: It is a theory which states that individual have the right to choose who rule them and why in a democratic system.

Stability: A situation whereby government governs without intra or inters governance challenges, from any political party or individuals within itself or outside it.

Chapter 2
Nature of Conditions and Characteristics to the Politics of Party Alliances and Coalitions in Formation of Governments in Africa

Sushant Shankar Bharti
https://orcid.org/0000-0002-2998-7713
Indira Gandhi National Open University, India

Mukesh Shankar Bharti
https://orcid.org/0000-0002-3693-7247
Jawaharlal Nehru University, India

ABSTRACT

The purpose of this study is to discuss the politics of party alliances and conditions in the formation of the government in the countries of Africa. Since the 1990s, many African countries have adopted either parliamentary or presidential forms of democratic rule to strengthen the rule of law, respect human rights and the rights of minorities, children, and women. After the end of colonial rule, the South African countries started the development process and good governance for the establishment of the welfare of the people. The democratic and democratization process has been strengthening the government institutions of countries' public and private entities for better governance. This chapter used a theoretical approach of debate to discuss Samuel P. Huntington's third wave of democratization and coalition theory to understand the democratization process which has been led by democratic government through general elections. In this electoral process, only one party was unable to form the government because it did not obtain a majority in parliament. This is why many emerging coalition governments have been established in many African countries. Moreover, this research uses the qualitative approach to describe and answer many research questions about the success and failure of the coalition governments in Africa. The case study also imposed and scanned to study of the various coalition governments in the countries of Africa. As a result, the formation of coalition governments is unusual in African countries because parties are not getting the popular vote to form a single-party government.

DOI: 10.4018/979-8-3693-1654-2.ch002

INTRODUCTION

Since 1990, in several countries in Africa, pre-electoral alliances and post-election coalitions have gained prominence in the analysis of African politics. This phenomenon has become a crucial aspect of understanding the continent's election dynamics and government formation. Several factors contribute to the growing significance of alliances and coalitions in African politics (Arriola, 2013; Kadima, 2023; Kapa, 2008; Karume, 2003; Resnick, 2013). In African political landscapes, pre-electoral alliances can be significant due to various factors, including diverse ethnic and cultural considerations, historical contexts, and the nature of political competition. Recognizing the prevalence of pre-electoral alliances in Africa implies that coalition theories should be adapted and expanded to better capture the nuanced dynamics of political collaboration and power-sharing in this context. Africa is known for its diverse political systems, and many countries on the continent have experienced variations in their governance structures. Many African countries experienced shifts between democratic governance and authoritarian rule. While some countries made progress in democratic consolidation, others faced challenges with electoral integrity, human rights abuses, and consolidation of power by incumbents. The emergence of the multi-party-political systems in the countries of Africa is realties since 1990. Many African countries operate within a multi-party system, and elections often feature multiple political parties competing for power. Some African countries have experienced coalition governments formed after elections, where parties join forces to secure a parliamentary majority. This is often a response to the challenges posed by fragmented political landscapes.

The term "alliance" is defined as the coming together of at least two political parties before an election with the primary objective of maximizing their votes. This type of alliance is formed as a strategic move before the election, where parties collaborate to enhance their electoral prospects. The cooperation is temporary and aims to pool resources and support for mutual benefit in the upcoming electoral contest. Unlike alliances, coalitions extend beyond the electoral phase and involve parties collaborating in the governance and legislative processes. The collaboration is based on the results of the election, and these parties may have different levels of influence or representation within the government or legislative bodies. By adopting Kadima's definitions, the analysis can provide a more precise examination of the evolving dynamics of political parties in South Africa, particularly in the context of elections and subsequent governance (Booysen, 2014; Kadima, 2006). It allows for a nuanced understanding of the different phases of political cooperation within the African political landscape. An alliance formation indicates that political parties often align themselves with others based on shared racial or cultural profiles. This suggests that these alliances may be rooted in common identities or interests related to ethnicity and culture.

Moreover, Smaller political parties are described as having relatively exclusive racial-cultural profiles. This implies that smaller parties may appeal to specific demographic groups based on shared racial or cultural affiliations. The exclusivity of these profiles may reflect a targeted approach to garnering support. The larger political parties face challenges in overcoming barriers imposed by race, ethnicity, and culture. This could indicate that larger parties, with more diverse constituencies, may encounter difficulties in appealing to voters across different racial and cultural backgrounds. This study discusses the potential trends or changes in the nature of political parties in Africa and their implications for democratic governance. Further, this chapter broadly provide a comprehensive understanding of the dynamics surrounding political parties in Africa and their contributions to democratic governance. The end of the Cold War was a significant factor that contributed to the democratization process in Africa.

The changing global geopolitical landscape created an environment that influenced domestic political developments on the continent.

Theoretical Approach of Coalition Government

The applicability of theories of party alliances and coalitions developed in other settings, particularly continental Western Europe, to African contexts is a complex and nuanced issue. While some principles of coalition politics may be universally relevant, it's crucial to recognize the unique historical, cultural, and political dynamics that characterize African nations. Many African countries are characterized by diverse ethnic and cultural landscapes. This diversity can influence political alliances and coalition formations in ways that may not be fully captured by theories developed in less ethnically diverse contexts. The colonial history of African nations has had a profound impact on their political structures and party systems. The legacy of colonial borders, the imposition of governance systems, and the manipulation of ethnic divisions can shape the nature of political alliances in ways that differ from European experiences. Socioeconomic factors, such as poverty, inequality, and development issues, can play a significant role in shaping political alliances in African countries. The priorities and concerns of the electorate may differ from those in more economically developed regions. The strength and effectiveness of political institutions can vary widely across African countries. The institutional context, including electoral systems and the legal framework for coalition building, can impact the formation and stability of alliances. The process of post-colonial state-building and nation-building is ongoing in many African countries. This dynamic can influence party systems and the strategies employed by political actors in forming alliances. The theories of party alliances and coalitions can be necessary when applied to African contexts (Axelrod, 1969; Dodd, 2015; Gamson, 1961; Luebbert, 1983; Marradi, 1975; Riker, 1962).

The role of the European Community (EC) in promoting and consolidating democracy in southern European countries during the third wave of democratization. This historical context is significant for understanding the dynamics between democratization processes and European integration. Soviet leader Mikhail Gorbachev introduced a series of political and economic reforms in the mid-1980s, known as perestroika and glasnost. These reforms aimed to revitalize the Soviet economy and open up political discourse. However, they inadvertently contributed to a loosening of control over the Eastern Bloc countries, fostering an atmosphere conducive to political change. The withdrawal of Soviet power and the subsequent end of the Cold War marked a historic shift in the political landscape of Eastern Europe, paving the way for the establishment of democratic governments and the eventual integration of several countries into Western political and economic structures. The third wave of democratization that began in the late 1980s in Eastern Europe continued in 1990 (Huntington, 1991, 1993, 1997). Countries such as Bulgaria and Romania experienced significant political changes. In Bulgaria, the Bulgarian Communist Party relinquished its monopoly on power, and multi-party elections were held in June 1990. In Romania, the overthrow of Nicolae Ceauşescu's regime in December 1989 marked the end of communist rule. In the aftermath, Romania transitioned toward a more democratic system (Bharti, 2022d, 2022b, 2022a; Huntington, 1997).

The events in Eastern European Countries (CEE) had a ripple effect on some Arab countries. The "upheaval in Eastern Europe" influenced political dynamics, prompting leaders in Egypt, Jordan, Tunisia, and Algeria to respond to popular demands by opening up more political space. The interconnectedness of these movements and the inspiration drawn from one region to another characterized the geopolitical landscape of the early 1990s, reflecting a broader global shift toward democracy and political change.

The term "snowballing" aptly captures the idea that democratic movements in one area could catalyze similar movements in neighboring regions, creating a chain reaction of political transformation in the countries of Africa. The "third wave" of democratization refers to a global surge in the establishment of democratic governments that occurred from the mid-1970s to the early 1990s. This wave was characterized by the transition from authoritarian rule to democratic governance in various regions of the world. Latin America and Tropical Africa were significant arenas for democratization during this period (Huntington, 1993; Randall, 1993).

The end of apartheid in South Africa in the early 1990s marked a historic moment in the democratization process. Nelson Mandela's release from prison and subsequent negotiations led to the dismantling of apartheid and the establishment of democratic elections in 1994. The third wave of democratization represented a significant shift in global politics, with a multitude of countries embracing democratic principles and institutions. The factors driving democratization were diverse and included popular movements, economic challenges, and changes in the global political climate. This wave contributed to the spread of democratic ideals across different continents, leaving a lasting impact on the political landscapes of Latin America and Tropical Africa (Kamrava, 2005; Randall, 1993; Sakwa, 2022). To the scanning of party-politics in African context can be understood through the applying saliency theory to party competition in Africa involves examining how political parties strategically respond to and prioritize issues that are most relevant and significant to the electorate. It provides a framework for understanding the dynamics of political competition in terms of issue salience, which, in turn, shapes party strategies, electoral outcomes, and the broader political landscape (Budge, 1993; Budge & Farlie, 1983; Klüver & Sagarzazu, 2017). According to saliency theory, political parties can gain advantages by strategically emphasizing specific issues, irrespective of their actual policy positions. These strategic priming influences voter perceptions, shapes the political agenda, and can contribute to a party's electoral success.

Saliency theory posits that political parties can strategically gain advantages by emphasizing certain issues, regardless of their actual policy positions on those issues. This approach involves "priming" voters, which means influencing their perceptions of issue importance and making specific issues more salient in their decision-making process. Saliency theory suggests that parties can strategically choose to highlight specific issues during election campaigns, focusing on those where they perceive themselves to have an advantage. This is done to shape the political agenda and influence voter perceptions. Saliency theory underscores the idea that voters, influenced by the selective highlighting of issues, may prioritize these issues in their decision-making process. This can create a situation where voters place more importance on specific issues, potentially overlooking other aspects of a party's platform.

In-group favoritism refers to a preference for and positive treatment of individuals belonging to one's own group or community. This bias may manifest in various forms, such as preferential treatment, shared benefits, or positive attitudes toward in-group members. The realistic conflict theory, suggesting that competition over real or perceived resources can contribute to intergroup conflict. In the political context, this theory may be applied to understand how power struggles and resource allocation influence group dynamics. realistic conflict theory underscores the potential impact of resource competition on intergroup. Group dynamics are complex, and the statement recognizes that the relationship between in-group and out-group sentiments is not one-dimensional. It depends on various factors, including political strategies, identity mobilization, and power competition. Political competition for power is highlighted as a factor influencing the reciprocal relationship between in-group and out-group sentiments. As parties vie for influence and control, they may leverage group identities to rally support and distinguish themselves from rival factions (Brewer, 1999; Hahm et al., 2023; Muzafer & Sherif, 1953).

Conceptual Background and Literature Issues

The social and political justice, as integral components of democracy, are multidimensional. This implies that justice in a democratic context goes beyond a single aspect and encompasses various dimensions that contribute to a fair and equitable society. T.H. Marshall's classification is referenced as a framework for understanding rights in the context of citizenship. Marshall's work is foundational in the study of citizenship and social rights. Civil rights are categorized as a component of citizenship and encompass property rights, legal guarantees, and various freedoms. These rights are fundamental to ensuring individual liberties and protections within a democratic society. Political rights, as outlined by Marshall, include the right to vote and be voted for, rights to associate, constitutional participation, and other elements that empower individuals to actively participate in the political processes of a democracy. Social rights constitute another dimension of citizenship according to Marshall's classification. These rights are related to broader social and economic issues, aiming to ensure that individuals have access to basic necessities and a decent standard of living. The interplay between social and political justice within the context of democracy, drawing on T.H. Marshall's classification of rights based on citizenship. This framework provides a theoretical foundation for analyzing the multidimensional nature of justice in democratic societies (Kura, 2008).

Miller's work explores the means necessary for a good life and underscores the importance of these entitlements within the framework of social justice. However, the statement also notes that, despite the recognition of the multi-dimensionality of social justice, some scholars argue for differences in importance among these classifications. Miller's focus on basic entitlements like education, health, social care, income, and housing suggests that these are fundamental elements necessary for individuals to lead a good life. These elements are often considered essential components of social justice. Miller's concept of "deserts" as entitlements in the context of social justice, emphasizing the importance of basic elements for a good life. However, the acknowledgment of debates on the differences in importance among these classifications highlights the complexity and subjectivity involved in discussions about social justice. Through the political transformation in Africa people will get their social rights (Dean & Melrose, 1999; Lister, 2003).

Plant (2000) suggests a perspective that social justice can be pursued through a government-market system collaboration, even though this may appear at odds with the normative principles of a neo-liberal agenda. The complexities of balancing state intervention with market forces in the pursuit of social justice reflect ongoing debates in political and economic thought. The term "normative exigencies" implies the normative demands or imperatives associated with a neo-liberal agenda. These demands may include a preference for limited government, free markets, and an emphasis on individual freedom and choice. Doyal & Gough (1991:230) emphasizes a balanced approach to social justice, opposing extreme free-market views while recognizing the importance of economic success. It further contends that ruling political parties are the super-force in the process of providing comprehensive social justice, highlighting their pivotal roles in governance, leadership, and policy shaping. Ruling political parties are identified as central forces in various aspects, including the formation of government, social mobilization, political education, leadership recruitment, and public and social policy making and implementation. The indispensable role of ruling political parties in the formation of government implies that the composition of the government, including key decision-makers, is significantly influenced by the political party in power. Ruling political parties are attributed with roles in social mobilization and political education.

This suggests that parties are not only instrumental during elections but also in shaping public opinion, awareness, and understanding of political issues (Salih, 2003; Strøm & Müller, 1999; Tordoff, 1988).

The character of democracy and the nature of ruling parties are positioned as crucial indicators for assessing the commitment to social justice. This implies that the way democracy is practiced and the values upheld by ruling parties significantly impact social justice outcomes. the character of democracy and ruling parties as a yardstick for measuring the commitment to social justice within a political community. It notes a potential gap or neglect in studies on social justice, where the linkage between the provision of social justice and the nature and character of party government is either neglected or undermined in the several African countries. The democratization waves had a profound impact on re-shaping political landscapes across Africa. They marked a significant departure from authoritarian rule and contributed to the establishment of multi-party democracies (Shiner, 2004). The late 1980s and early 1990s witnessed the spread of the third wave of democratization across Africa. This period marked a departure from authoritarian rule and saw the emergence of democratic governance in various countries.

Methods and Data

Thematic content analysis is a qualitative research method used to identify, analyze, and report patterns (themes) within textual data. The analysis is described as inductive, indicating that the themes and patterns were derived from the data itself rather than being predefined or driven by preconceived categories. Inductive approaches allow themes to emerge organically during the analysis process. The qualitative analysis involved establishing categories, patterns, and themes. Categories are groups of content that share common characteristics, patterns represent recurring sequences or regularities, and themes are overarching concepts that capture the essence of the data to discusses political landscape of Africa (Marshall & Rossman, 2011). Qualitative research is an approach that seeks to understand phenomena in their natural settings, often exploring the depth and complexity of human experiences for the development of democratic institutions in Africa. It involves a flexible and iterative process of data collection and analysis. The paper aims to contribute to the existing body of knowledge on coalition governance formation since 1990 in Africa (Creswell & Miller, 2000; Makole et al., 2022). By doing so, it suggests an intention to build on, extend, or enrich the current theoretical framework or understanding in the field. Theory-building involves innovating and contributing new insights to a particular area of study. The paper's focus on the African phenomenon of coalition governance formation implies a desire to contribute novel perspectives, concepts, or explanations to the existing literature.

The study relies on qualitative data, indicating a focus on rich, non-numeric information to explore the challenges and opportunities inherent in coalition governance in the context of countries of Africa. The emphasis on primary and secondary data implies the use of existing records, documents, or literature to make sense of the research problem. The study relies on a diverse range of secondary data sources, including extant literature, secondary documents, archives materials, government gazettes, government legislation, newspapers, and journal articles. This approach is beneficial for obtaining a comprehensive understanding of the subject matter from various perspectives.

Why Do Parties Form Alliances and Coalitions in Africa?

The ruling party may engage in coalition formation as a strategic move to co-opt and demoralize smaller political parties, particularly those that could pose a potential threat in the long term. The powerfully dominant ruling party in South Africa that faces no significant electoral threats. This dominance provides the ruling party with the flexibility to consider coalition formation from a position of strength. The ruling party may form coalitions with smaller parties to effectively co-opt them. By bringing smaller parties into a coalition, the ruling party may be seeking to integrate them into the political system, thereby neutralizing any potential challenges or threats they could pose. Coalition dynamics can be complex, and the statement suggests that the ruling party may use coalitions strategically to demoralize junior partners. This demoralization could result from a power imbalance within the coalition, with the ruling party maintaining a dominant position. A dominant ruling party in South Africa may be driven by a desire to co-opt and neutralize smaller parties, preempting potential challenges and threats to its long-term political dominance. Analyzing the motivations behind coalition strategies provides insights into the dynamics of political power and competition in the South African context (Lodge, 2014).

In South Africa, the ruling party may engage in coalition formation as a strategic move to neutralize or weaken junior partners to stop gaining majority in the parliamentary elections, particularly smaller parties that could potentially pose a threat to its dominance. The term "co-opt" implies the process of bringing smaller parties into the ruling coalition, possibly by offering them incentives or benefits. This could range from ministerial positions to policy influence, effectively integrating them into the ruling structure. The demoralization of junior partners is presented as a strategic outcome. By being part of a coalition dominated by the ruling party, smaller parties may feel marginalized or disempowered, potentially reducing their capacity to emerge as significant competitors in the future. Coalition formation, in this context, is portrayed as a means to maintain political stability and control. By consolidating power through coalitions, the ruling party can secure its dominant position and minimize potential disruptions from smaller parties.

It is unusual for opposition coalitions to win elections indicates that single-party dominance has been a prevalent feature in many African political landscapes. This dominance might be attributed to factors such as historical legacies, party strength, or electoral systems. There is a shifting trend over time, with the possibility that coalition formation is gradually making alternation of parties in government more frequent. This could indicate a growing acceptance and effectiveness of coalition politics in challenging established political forces. The effects of coalitions on the functioning of the party system suggests that coalition dynamics have implications beyond individual elections. Coalitions can influence party structures, electoral strategies, and the overall configuration of political forces. An assessment of the impact of coalitions on the functioning of the government more generally. This includes considerations of governance effectiveness, policy stability, and the ability to address national challenges in a coalition government setting. The potential increase in alternation of parties in government, facilitated by coalition dynamics, may be indicative of evolving democratic norms in certain African countries. It suggests a departure from the historical trend of single-party dominance.

The dynamics of coalition politics can vary significantly based on country-specific factors, such as political culture, institutional structures, and historical contexts. Therefore, the assessments of coalitions may be contingent on the unique circumstances of each country. The coalition politics in Africa continues to evolve in response to changing political contexts, societal dynamics, and external influences. While challenges persist, coalition governments have the potential to foster inclusive governance, consensus-building, and political stability in diverse African contexts., with a suggestion that opposition coalitions may be gradually influencing the alternation of parties in government. The divided assessments at the symposium indicate that the impact of coalitions on the party system and government functioning is a nuanced and complex issue that may vary across different African countries. Motlamelle Kapa and Victor

Shale (2013) showed that coalitions seriously undermine party cohesion in this country. They can also weaken the opposition in general. In fact, they could eliminate the opposition altogether, as happened in Mauritius in 1982 and 1995, when the main parties formed coalitions that won all the seats. the impact of coalitions in Mauritius, particularly addressing concerns related to the under-representation of women, the inclusion of individuals perceived as mediocre in government, and the potential constraints on meritocratic considerations in the appointment of Cabinet members. It also mentions how coalitions might block democratic advances, using the example of Indian state parties preventing the delimitation of constituencies.

The impact of coalitions in Mauritius, particularly in relation to gender representation, the quality of government officials, and potential challenges to democratic processes. These issues underscore the complexities and trade-offs involved in coalition politics. McMillan indicates that there is academic inquiry and scholarship exploring the impact of coalitions on democratic processes and outcomes. Understanding the specific findings and methodology of such research can provide additional insights. The under-representation of women is a recognized issue in Africa, and it notes that this concern can be addressed through quota requirements. Quotas are often implemented to ensure a more equitable representation of women in political positions. The political practitioners provide insights into the practical implications of pre-election coalitions in the specific context of Zimbabwe. Despite disagreements on other issues, there appears to be a consensus among the Zimbabwean politicians on the positive impact of pre-election coalitions in terms of conflict mitigation. This suggests that the observed positive effect is a point of agreement among diverse political perspectives. Understanding the specific context of Zimbabwe is crucial for a nuanced interpretation of the statement. Zimbabwe has experienced periods of political turbulence, and the positive testimony about pre-election coalitions implies a potential role in easing political tensions.

Pre-election coalitions are often formed with the goal of achieving shared objectives. The collaborative nature of coalition-building can foster a sense of cooperation among different political parties, potentially contributing to a more harmonious political climate. Zimbabwe provides real-world context to this observation, demonstrating that, at least in certain situations, coalitions can play a constructive role in promoting political cooperation and reducing confrontations (Mangwana et al., 2013). The power-sharing government in Zimbabwe indicates a specific period in the country's political history when political parties, including former opposition parties, collaborated in a shared governance structure. Power-sharing arrangements can be challenging, especially when there are significant power imbalances or historical animosities between the parties involved. A power-sharing government is often expected to promote inclusivity and protect democratic values, and any shortcomings in this regard may have implications for the overall health of the democratic system.

During the power-sharing government in Zimbabwe, which occurred between 2009 and 2013, former opposition parties faced several significant challenges. This government was formed following a disputed presidential election in 2008 and aimed to address the country's political and economic crises. The two main opposition parties involved were the Movement for Democratic Change (MDC), led by Morgan Tsvangirai, and the smaller MDC faction led by Arthur Mutambara. It underscores the complexities and limitations associated with such arrangements, particularly when it comes to restraining authoritarian tendencies within ruling parties (LeBas, 2011).

One-Dominant-Party System in African Countries

Egypt, Senegal, and Botswana are cited as examples of African countries with a one-dominant-party system. Despite the formal existence of multiple parties, the ruling parties in these countries have been successful in maintaining entrenched power, limiting the realistic chances of opposition parties to win elections. The existence of a one-dominant-party system raises questions about the health of democratic practices in these countries. While they may formally have multiparty structures, the dominance of one party challenges the core principles of competitive and pluralistic democracy. The concept of a one-dominant-party system reflects a scenario where, despite the existence of multiple parties, one party significantly controls the political landscape and restricts the ability of other parties to compete effectively for power. The examples provided from Egypt, Senegal, and Botswana illustrate the practical challenges faced by opposition parties in such systems. The ruling parties in certain African countries have manipulated elections to maintain themselves in power. This manipulation often involves harassment of the opposition, reducing them to a symbolic role. The emerging trend described involves ruling parties manipulating elections. This manipulation could take various forms, including changes in electoral laws, gerrymandering, electoral fraud, or other tactics aimed at securing an advantage for the ruling party.

The primary objective of the manipulation is noted to be the perpetuation of power by ruling parties. This implies a strategic use of political power to extend the duration of the ruling party's stay in office, potentially circumventing the democratic principle of regular alternation of power. The opposition parties, according to the statement, face harassment as part of the manipulative strategies employed by ruling parties. Harassment can take various forms, including legal challenges, restrictions on political activities, or even physical intimidation. The impact of the manipulation is described as reducing the opposition to a symbolic role. This implies that the opposition, despite its formal existence, may face significant challenges in effectively challenging the ruling party's hold on power. The use of the term "emerging trend" suggests that this phenomenon has been observed over an extended period since the early 90s. The manipulation of elections and harassment of the opposition raise concerns about democratic backsliding. These practices may undermine the core principles of democratic governance, including free and fair elections, political pluralism, and respect for opposition rights. It's important to recognize that the observed trend may vary across different African countries. The nature and extent of electoral manipulation and opposition harassment can be influenced by specific political, historical, and social contexts. the ongoing struggle for democratic governance in certain African countries, where ruling parties seek to entrench their power through electoral manipulation and suppression of opposition voices. Addressing these challenges requires concerted efforts to strengthen democratic institutions, uphold the rule of law, and protect fundamental freedoms. This raises significant concerns about the state of democracy in those contexts (Bharti, 2022c; Joseph, 2011).

The impregnable autocracies falling in North Africa suggests a broader trend of political transformation and change across the African continent. This may include instances such as the Arab Spring movements that led to regime changes. The characterization of most countries in sub-Saharan Africa as nominally democratic indicates that, on the surface, they have embraced democratic features such as regular elections and opposition party participation. However, the use of "nominally" implies a distinction between formal structures and the effective practice of democracy. The fact that regular elections are held, and opposition parties compete for elective offices signals adherence to democratic processes. This is a positive aspect of democratic governance, providing mechanisms for political competition and power alternation. The reference to the Freedom House survey from 2010 provides a specific timeframe for the assessment. The mention that the survey suggests a deterioration in political rights and civil liberties implies challenges in the effective practice of democracy in the subsequent years. Political dynamics are fluid, and the situation can change over time. Continuous assessments, beyond the 2010 survey, are essential to capture evolving political landscapes and dynamics in sub-Saharan Africa. The political evolution in sub-Saharan Africa, highlighting the move towards nominal democracy but expressing concerns about the deterioration of political rights and civil liberties, in line with a global trend. Ongoing scrutiny and analysis are essential to understand the complexities of political developments in the region.

The reintroduction of the multiparty system in Africa has brought both opportunities and challenges for democratic governance, political stability, and socio-economic development. The evolving nature of multiparty politics continues to shape the continent's trajectory and prospects for democratic consolidation, one emerging trend has been the increasing role and influence of technology and social media in shaping political dynamics across the continent. This trend has significant implications for political participation, electoral processes, and governance. The ruling parties in certain African countries have manipulated elections to maintain themselves in power. This manipulation often involves harassment of the opposition, reducing them to a symbolic role. The re-introduction of the multiparty system established in Africa in the early 90s. This period marked a significant shift away from single-party dominance or authoritarian rule toward a more pluralistic political landscape. Ethiopia's geopolitical significance and strategic importance may play a role in the international community's decisions regarding aid. Geostrategic considerations could outweigh concerns related to political freedom, leading to continued support. The juxtaposition of Ethiopia's political demotion and its status as a significant aid recipient raises broader questions about the effectiveness of foreign aid in promoting political and democratic reforms in recipient countries. the reconfiguration of Marxist-Leninist ideologies in Ethiopia, the downgrade in Freedom House's 2010 survey, and the suggestion that this demotion may not substantially impact the country due to its significant receipt of overseas development aid. The complex interplay between political assessments, foreign aid, and geopolitical considerations in international relations is underscored by this observation. China is an international actor has been playing an important role in Ethiopia under the Belt and Road Initiative (BRI) in the country (Bharti, 2023; Joseph, 2011).

The regime in Ethiopia is described as prioritizing its capacity to project force, suggesting that military strength and security considerations play a central role in its approach to governance. The term "regional gendarme" implies that Ethiopia is perceived as a regional enforcer or stabilizer. The country may be playing a role in maintaining regional security and stability, possibly at the behest of external powers. Ethiopia is described as a very diverse country with a population of 90 million. The diversity, both in terms of ethnicity and cultural differences, adds complexity to the governance challenges faced by the regime. The regime's approach appears to prioritize stability, security, and socioeconomic development over a strict adherence to democratic principles.

The historical perspective on South Africa's democratic journey, highlighting the significance of the 1994 elections in ushering in a new era and the dominance of the African National Congress (ANC) in subsequent elections. The outcome of the 2024 general election will shape South Africa's political landscape and governance priorities for the coming years, also suggesting that it could be one of the most important in the country's history, potentially paving the way for a coalition government at the national level. The ANC, led by figures like Nelson Mandela, played a central role in the post-apartheid political landscape. The mention of the democratic journey suggests the ongoing evolution of South Africa's political system and the maturation of democratic processes over the years. The anticipation that the 2024 general election could be one of the most important indicates a sense of critical juncture or change. The outcome of this election may have far-reaching implications for the country's political direction. The statement introduces the possibility of a coalition government at the national level. While South Africa has experienced coalition governments at local and provincial levels, a national coalition government would represent a significant departure from the historical dominance of a single party. A coalition government is formed at the national level following the 2024 election, it would be an unprecedented development in South African politics. This reflects a potential shift in the political landscape and power dynamics. The coalition government at the national level implies the potential for political realignment, with parties forging alliances and cooperation to navigate the complexities of governance. The 2024 general election in South Africa that could lead to the formation of a coalition government at the national level, a departure from historical electoral patterns in the country (Cassimjee, 2023).

CONCLUSION

The coalition governments do exist in certain African countries, particularly in contexts where no single party secures an outright majority in elections or where power-sharing arrangements are necessary to promote political stability and inclusivity. Examples include Kenya, South Africa, and Zimbabwe, where coalition governments or alliances have been formed in response to fragmented party systems, disputed election outcomes, or post-conflict reconciliation efforts. In recent years, there has been a gradual shift towards multiparty democracy and coalition politics in some African countries, driven by demands for greater political pluralism, accountability, and inclusivity. However, the prevalence of coalition governments in Africa remains contingent on various political, institutional, and socio-economic factors specific to each country's context.

This study highlights that South Africa is grappling with economic difficulties. Collaborative initiatives in key sectors can be instrumental in finding solutions to economic challenges. South Africa faces significant challenges, and addressing these challenges requires a comprehensive and collaborative approach involving both the public and private sectors. The political groups of the country have been prioritizing the economic challenges in South Africa, with an emphasis on the critical role of the full professionalization of public services for effective government delivery. The focus on long-term governance effectiveness and the recognition of the importance of skilled public service personnel underscore a commitment to overcoming challenges irrespective of political changes. South Africa and other African countries have been facing significant socio-economic challenges because of political instability on this continent. These challenges may include issues related to unemployment, poverty, inequality, access to education and healthcare, and broader economic development concerns.

The importance of considering the character of democracy and ruling parties in discussions on social justice, challenges the simplistic link between authoritarianism and social justice, and directs attention to the nuances within African democracies and their experiences with authoritarian tendencies. In this context, this study elucidates that democracy promotion is in fragile position in African countries and party system is also not working systematically across the continent. Further, the historical overview of political governance in post-colonial Africa underscores the complex interplay between authoritarianism and democratization, highlighting both progress and persistent challenges in the quest for democratic governance and respect for human rights on the continent. The role of Western donor countries and international organizations in influencing African leaders to embrace democratic reforms and proper electoral process in several countries of Africa. Financial support for re-democratization projects came with conditions tied to democratic governance. In spite of the EU and UN supports, there is need to more work for establishment of democratic culture in the Central Africa and other region as well. The pressure for political openness led to the introduction of multiparty elections for better political opportunity for downtrodden people in across the Africa. The move towards multi-party systems allowed for increased political competition and participation.

The ultimate goal of the suggested reforms is to prevent the development of authoritarian dominant ruling parties. By addressing both the general and specific environments, the framework aims to create conditions conducive to democratic pluralism and social justice. The research also suggest that reforms aim to create a conducive environment for democratic development and prevent the consolidation of power within ruling parties. The complexities of simultaneous reforms, the difficulty in defining boundaries, and the shared involvement of political elites are acknowledged challenges. The success of the framework depends on the political will and collaboration of relevant stakeholders, underscoring the importance of a cooperative and committed approach to reform efforts. By and large, the geopolitical and geoeconomics agenda of global economies in the Global South is creating new political transformation in the countries of Africa. The democratic system is still in fragile conditions in many African countries. This research has reached at the top agenda of African political system is negotiation to rule the country through the pre-poll and post-poll alliances. It is reality of the African countries and the European Union has been providing all support for democratic development in the region because the EU's key agenda is that democracy establishment in the world.

REFERENCES

Arriola, L. R. (2013). *Multi-ethnic coalitions in Africa: Business financing of opposition election campaigns*. Cambridge University Press.

Axelrod, R. M. (1969). *Conflict of Interest: A Theory of Divergent Goals with Applications to Politics*. Yale University.

Bharti, M. S. (2022a). Democratisation and Institutional Development in Romania after 1989. *Journal of Scientific Papers. Social Development and Security*, *12*(1), 104–117. doi:10.33445/sds.2022.12.1.11

Bharti, M. S. (2022b). Political Institution Building in Post-Communist Romania. *Central European Political Studies*, *1*(1), 73–97. doi:10.14746/ssp.2022.1.4

Bharti, M. S. (2022c). The Development of China's Economic Cooperation in the Horn of Africa: Special Reference to the Belt and Road Initiative. *African Journal of Economics. Politics and Social Studies*, *1*(1), 17–30. doi:10.15804/ajepss.2022.1.12

Bharti, M. S. (2022d). The Economic Integration of the Central and Eastern European Countries into the European Union: Special Reference to Regional Development. *Copernicus Political and Legal Studies*, *1*(2), 11–23. https://doi.org/doi.org/10.15804/CPLS.20222.01

Bharti, M. S. (2023). The Sustainable Development and Economic Impact of China's Belt and Road Initiative in Ethiopia. *East Asia (Piscataway, N.J.)*, *40*(2), 175–194. doi:10.1007/s12140-023-09402-y PMID:37065271

Booysen, S. (2014). Causes and impact of party alliances and coalitions on the party system and national cohesion in South Africa. *Journal of African Elections*, *13*(1), 66–92. doi:10.20940/JAE/2014/v13i1a4

Brewer, M. B. (1999). The Psychology of Prejudice: Ingroup Love and Outgroup Hate? *The Journal of Social Issues*, *55*(3), 429–444. doi:10.1111/0022-4537.00126

Budge, I. (1993). 'Issues, Dimensions, and Agenda Change in Postwar Democracies: Long-Term Trends in Party Election Programs and Newspaper Reports in Twenty-Three Democracies. In W. H. Riker (Ed.), *Agenda Formation* (pp. 41–80). University of Michigan Press.

Budge, I., & Farlie, D. (1983). *Explaining and predicting elections: issue effects and party strategies in twenty-three democracies*. Allen & Unwin.

Cassimjee, M. (2023, December 1). South Africa weighs a new election outcome: coalitions. Chatham House. Retrieved from https://www.chathamhouse.org/publications/the-world-today/2023-12/south-africa-weighs-new-election-outcome-coalitions

Creswell, J. W., & Miller, D. L. (2000). Determining Validity in Qualitative Inquiry. *Theory into Practice*, *39*(3), 124–130. doi:10.1207/s15430421tip3903_2

Dean, H., & Melrose, M. (1999). *Poverty, Riches and Social Citizenship*. Routledge. doi:10.1057/9780230377950

Dodd, L. (2015). *Coalitions in parliamentary government* (Vol. 1247). Princeton University Press. doi:10.1515/9781400868070

Doyal, L., & Gough, I. (1991). *A Theory of Human Need*. Macmillan. doi:10.1007/978-1-349-21500-3

Gamson, W. A. (1961). A theory of coalition formation. *American Sociological Review*, *26*(3), 373–382. doi:10.2307/2090664

Hahm, H., Hilpert, D., & Konig, T. (2023). Divided We Unite: The Nature of Partyism and the Role of Coalition Partnership in Europe. *The American Political Science Review*, 1–19. doi:10.1017/S0003055423000266

Huntington, S. P. (1991). How countries democratize. *Political Science Quarterly*, *106*(4), 579–616. doi:10.2307/2151795

Huntington, S. P. (1993). he third wave: Democratization in the late twentieth century (Vol. 4). University of Oklahoma Press.

Huntington, S. P. (1997). After twenty years: The future of the third wave. *Journal of Democracy*, *8*(4), 3–12. doi:10.1353/jod.1997.0059

Joseph, R. (2011, November 9). *Democracy and Reconfigured Power in Africa*. Brookings. Retrieved from https://www.brookings.edu/articles/democracy-and-reconfigured-power-in-africa/

Kadima, D. (2006). The study of party coalitions in Africa: Importance, scope, theory and research methodology. In *The politics of party coalitions in Africa*. Konrad Adenauer Stiftung and EISA.

Kadima, D. (2023, May). *An Introduction to The Politics of Party Alliances and Coalitions in Socially-Divided Africa*. Electoral Institute for Sustainable Democracy in Africa (EISA). Retrieved from https://www.eisa.org/storage/2023/05/2014-journal-of-african-elections-v13n1-introduction-politics-party-alliances-coalitions-socially-divided-africa-eisa.pdf

Kamrava, M. (2005). Democracy and Democratisation. In J. Haynes (Ed.), *Palgrave Advances in Development Studies* (pp. 67–88). doi:10.1057/9780230502864_4

Kapa, M. A. (2008). The Politics of Coalition Formation and Democracy in Lesotho. *Politikon: South African Journal of Political Studies*, *35*(3), 339–356. doi:10.1080/02589340903017999

Karume, S. (2003). Conceptual Understanding of Political Coalitions in South Africa: an Integration of Concepts and Practices. *Political Party Coalitions: Strengthening Democracy through Party Coalition Building*.

Klüver, H., & Sagarzazu, I. (2017). Coalition Governments and Party Competition: Political Communication Strategies of Coalition Parties. *Political Science Research and Methods*, *5*(2), 333–349. doi:10.1017/psrm.2015.56

Kura, S. (2008). *African Ruling Political Parties and the Making of 'Authoritarian' Democracies*. ACCORD. Retrieved from https://www.accord.org.za/ajcr-issues/african-ruling-political-parties-and-the-making-of-authoritarian-democracies/

LeBas, A. (2011). *From Protest to Parties: Party Building and Democratisation in Africa*. Oxford University Press. doi:10.1093/acprof:oso/9780199546862.001.0001

Lister, R. (2003). *Citizenship: Feminist Perspectives*. Palgrave. doi:10.1007/978-0-230-80253-7

Lodge, T. (2014). Some preliminary conclusions on the causes and consequences of political party alliances and coalitions in Africa. *Journal of African Elections*, *13*(1), 233–242. doi:10.20940/2014/v13i1a10

Luebbert, G. M., Dodd, L., & Swaan, A. D. (1983). Coalition theory and government formation in multiparty democracies. *Comparative Politics*, *15*(2), 235–249. doi:10.2307/421678

Makole, K. R., Ntshangase, B. A., & Adewumi, S. A. (2022). Coalition Governance: Unchartered Waters in South African Political Landscape. *Business Ethics and Leadership*, *6*(4), 23–37. doi:10.21272/bel.6(4).23-37.2022

Mangwana, P., Dube, N., & Moyo, L. (2013, September). *Panel presentations to the EISA 8th Annua Symposium*. Academic Press.

Marradi, A. (1975). Abram de Swaan, Coalition Theories and Cabinet Formations, Amsterdam, Elsevier, 1973. Italian Political Science Review/Rivista Italiana Di Scienza Politica, 5(3), 592–594.

Marshall, C., & Rossman, G. B. (2011). *Designing Qualitative Research* (5th ed.). Sage Publications.

Muzafer, S., & Sherif, C. W. (1953). *Groups in Harmony and Tension; An Integration of Studies of Intergroup Relations*. Harper & Brothers.

Plant, R. (2000). Social Justice. In R. Walker (Ed.), *Ending Child Poverty*. Policy Press.

Randall, V. (1993). The media and democratisation in the Third World. *Third World Quarterly, 14*(3), 625–646. doi:10.1080/01436599308420346

Resnick, D. (2013). Do electoral coalitions facilitate democratic consolidation in Africa? *Party Politics, 19*(5), 735–757. doi:10.1177/1354068811410369

Riker, W. (1962). *The Theory of Political Coalitions*. Yale University Press.

Sakwa, R. (2022). Democratisation. In *Routledge Handbook of Russian Politics and Society* (pp. 33–45). Routledge. doi:10.4324/9781003218234-5

Salih, M. M. A. (2003). Introduction: The Evolution of African Political Parties. In M. M. A. Salih (Ed.), *African Political Parties: Evolution*. Institutionalisation and Governance.

Shiner, C. (2004, October 28). *Challenges remain to consolidating democracy in several African countries*. Voanews. Retrieved from https://www.voanews.com/english/archive/2004-10/2004-10-28-voa38.cfm?CFID=117984128&CFTOKEN=79037326

Strøm, K., & Müller, W. C. (1999). Political Parties and Hard Choices. In *Policy, Office, or Votes? How Political Parties in Western Europe Make Hard Decisions*. Cambridge University Press. doi:10.1017/CBO9780511625695.001

Tordoff, W. (1988). Parties in Zambia. In V. Randall (Ed.), *Political Parties in the Third World*. Sage Publications.

ADDITIONAL READING

Basedau, M., Erdmann, G., Lay, J., & Stroh, A. (2011). Ethnicity and party preference in sub-Saharan Africa. *Democratization, 18*(2), 462–489. doi:10.1080/13510347.2011.553366

Bekker, M., Runciman, C., & Roberts, B. (2022). Beyond the binary: Examining dynamic youth voter behaviour in South Africa. *Politikon: South African Journal of Political Studies, 49*(4), 297–317. doi:10.1080/02589346.2022.2151687

Bratton, M., Bhavnani, R., & Chen, T.-H. (2012). Voting intentions in Africa: Ethnic, economic or partisan? *Commonwealth and Comparative Politics, 50*(1), 27–52. doi:10.1080/14662043.2012.642121

Dlakavu, A. (2022). South African electoral trends: Prospects for coalition governance at national and provincial spheres in 2024. *Politikon: South African Journal of Political Studies, 49*(4), 476–490. doi:10.1080/02589346.2022.2151682

Grinin, L., & Korotayev, A. (2011). The Coming Epoch of New Coalitions: Possible Scenarios of the Near Future. *World Futures, 67*(8), 531–563. doi:10.1080/02604027.2011.625749

Ishiyama, J. (2012). Explaining ethnic bloc voting in Africa. *Democratization, 19*(4), 761–788. doi:10.1080/13510347.2011.623354

Karreth, A. K. (2018). Schools of democracy: How trade union membership impacts political participation in Africa's emerging democracies. *Democratization, 25*(1), 158–177. doi:10.1080/13510347.2017.1339273

Khambule, I. (2022). Governing Through Turbulent Coalitions: Will ActionSA Bring Stability to Gauteng Metropolitan Municipalities? *Politikon: South African Journal of Political Studies, 49*(4), 411–427. doi:10.1080/02589346.2022.2151686

Mitlin, D. (2023). The contribution of reform coalitions to inclusion and equity: Lessons from urban social movements. *Area Development and Policy, 8*(1), 1–26. doi:10.1080/23792949.2022.2148548

Ndjio, B. (2023). Rhizomic authoritarianism: Power, biopolitics and transnational authoritarian practices in Cameroon. *Globalizations*, 1–18. doi:10.1080/14747731.2023.2207272

Oyugi, W. O. (2006). Coalition politics and coalition governments in Africa. *Journal of Contemporary African Studies, 24*(1), 53–79. doi:10.1080/02589000500513739

Poupko, E. S. (2017). An exploratory study of constitutional design in three island states: Seychelles, Comoros, and Mauritius. *Journal of Contemporary African Studies, 35*(3), 324–348. doi:10.1080/02589001.2017.1341624

Sanches, E. R. (2020). Transitions to democracy, institutional choices and party system stability: Lessons from small African islands. *Journal of Contemporary African Studies, 38*(2), 186–204. doi:10.1080/02589001.2020.1774048

Szmolka, I. (2015). Inter- and intra-party relations in the formation of the Benkirane coalition governments in Morocco. *Journal of North African Studies, 20*(4), 654–674. doi:10.1080/13629387.2015.1057816

KEY TERMS AND DEFINITION

Coalitions Politics: Coalition politics in Africa, much like in other parts of the world, often emerge in situations where no single political party can secure an outright majority in elections. This necessitates parties to form coalitions or alliances with other parties to gain the necessary parliamentary seats to govern. The dynamics and reasons behind coalition formations in Africa can vary widely based on historical, social, and political contexts within each country. Many African countries are characterized by diverse ethnic and regional populations. Political parties often represent specific ethnic or regional interests, leading to fragmented party systems. Coalition-building may involve parties aligning along ethnic or regional lines to secure broader support bases. The electoral system used in a country can significantly influence coalition politics. Proportional representation systems, for example, tend to produce more fragmented parliaments and encourage coalition formation. In contrast, first-past-the-post systems may lead to more dominant single-party governments.

Party Alliance: Parties may form alliances before elections to maximize their chances of winning seats. This could involve agreements to avoid competing against each other in certain constituencies or forming joint candidate lists to pool their support bases.

Chapter 3
A Comparative Study of Coalition Governments in Post-Conflict Societies

Mbuyiseni Simon Mathonsi
University of KwaZulu-Natal, South Africa

Ndwakhulu Stephen Tshishonga
University of KwaZulu-Natal, South Africa

ABSTRACT

The establishment of coalition governments as transitional arrangements on nations bedeviled by conflicts has become an automatic solution in many countries of the world. Multiparty electoral processes or processes that include as many contesting parties and interests as possible have for years been dubbed as important building blocks for peace and smooth transition, especially in countries devastated by civil wars or violence. This chapter argues that that single party governments make governing straightforward and keep the executive/legislatures fully accountable to voters as the incumbent governing party has nobody else, but itself to blame for mediocre performance. While multi-party governments involve bargaining informed by compromises on the interests of voters and coalition bargaining are fashioned more on the interests of the leaders and actors in the bargaining table. In the Third World countries, especially those experiencing violence or civil wars, exogenous superpowers mainly from the West are quick to broker coalition governance with externally imposed rules as panacea for progress. The chapter further argues that externally imposed coalition formations and rules more often than not benefit the interests of the outside superpowers than the domestic interests of citizens. While endogenously crafted, formulated, and implemented coalition processes are more likely to benefit domestic interest of the people than outside powers. The chapter seeks to contribute to the current literature on the formation of coalition governments as transitional arrangements and peace brokers for parties or groups in conflict. The chapter used desktop research to solicit information from peer reviewed journals and scientific research papers.

DOI: 10.4018/979-8-3693-1654-2.ch003

INTRODUCTION AND BACKGROUND

The phenomenon of coalition governments has become a dominant form of governing, especially areas where the parliament or municipalities are hung. It happens when no one party can form a government due to constitutional imperatives. In this case parties come together and form multi-party governments; hence, Resnick (2013) defines coalition government as a cabinet of a parliamentary government in which several parties come together using economies of scale to pull together resources (both human and financial) into a more substantial collection and conduct a larger campaign to form a unity government. However, coalition governments have also been employed as conflict resolution strategies that serves as transitional arrangements that create conditions for a matured democracies (Hamid and Daniel, 2022). This phenomenon is mostly adopted by countries undergoing civil wars or violent conflicts that are mostly on based on ethnic, religion and rationalistic based conflicts. In this instance, coalition governments are adopted to assist the country transit to democracy.

Coalition agreements have become a key aspect of governance throughout the world. Conti and Marangoni (2014) point out that a coalition agreement is an agreement negotiated between the parties that form a coalition government and it collates the most important shared goals and objectives of the cabinet. Conti and Marangoni (2014) add that a coalition government is one in which <u>political parties</u> enter into a power-sharing arrangement of the <u>executive</u> and that such governments usually occur when no single party has achieved an absolute <u>majority</u> after an <u>election</u> process based on <u>proportional representation</u>. Resnick (2013) defines coalition government as a cabinet of a parliamentary government in which several parties come together using economies of scale to pull together resources (both human and financial) into a more substantial collection and conduct a larger campaign to form a unity government. Coalition is the association of two or more parties who agree to work together to form government based on election outcomes (Mokgosi, Shai, Ogunnubi, 2017). Kadima (2014) argues that coalitions are objectives driven and are processes of organising coalition parties towards a common goal which is explicit agenda to control the executive. Negotiating such government arrangements does not only take time and resources but it also involves compromises.

While coalitions are not a choice, but a necessity, Conti and Marangoni (2014) argue that coalition governments are a potential high risk since they are based on serious compromise of the voters' mandate and their decision-making processes are tedious as parties must keep accommodating deviant parties for the purposes of maintaining the coalition. The ability of citizens to hold governments to account for their past actions is one of the pivotal functions of elections. However, Mokgosi, Shai and Ogunnubi (2017) contend that the complex political context of coalition governments is a hindrance to accountability. Single-party governments are homogenous and make governing a straightforward process that ensures more accountability to both the constitution and voters as the governing parties has no liberty to blame other parties for errant approaches taken by the government. In this case, opposition party strengthen accountability of the single governing party when they play their role as opposition parties more than they do when they are part of government (Mokgosi, Shai, Ogunnubi, 2017). However, Pottie, (2014) posits that coalitions represent a maturity of democracy and are important arrangements not only to prevent instability but to also ensure that small parties and all interests and all citizens feel accommodated, while improving the legitimacy of the government.

This is a comparative study of coalition governments in post-conflict societies of Sudan, Somali, Columbia, Brazil and Iraqi. The chapter is split into sections: (a) Introduction Background, (b) Conceptualising Coalition and coalition governance, (c) International perspective on Coalition governance; (d)

Coalition as a Conflict resolution strategy; (e) Theories of democratic governance, (f) Profile of selected case studies (Sudan, Somalia, Iraq and Colombia) (g) Findings and analysis (h) Future directions and (i) Conclusion and recommendations. The profile of each selected country analysis the history of violent conflicts, mandate of the transitional government (coalition government), the preferred government structure and electoral system, the extent to which the mandate was conducted if it were and reasons for non-accomplishment. Coalition governments are also reflect each country's political institutions; political actors; political culture; and societal, geographic, and ideological rifts. It has been established that in many of the countries, changes in the constellation of parties in government are emblematic of important political, social, and economic changes.

CONCEPTUALIZING COALITION AND COALITION GOVERNANCE

These forms of transitional governance (coalition arrangements) are normally exogenously imposed by the United Nations (UN) as a strategy to achieve domestic peace. The United Nations (UN) is the world institute tasked with maintaining international peace and security. Overtime the UN developed complex and interconnected systems of subsidiary organs to prevent the escalation of violence, manage and resolve violent disputes, and prevent the recurrence of war. There are many United Nations Peace Initiatives (UNPI) which are directed at conflict prevention and crisis management, mediation, peacekeeping, and peace-building and by 2015 there were already more than 450 such initiatives since 1946 (Clayton, Dorussen and Bohmelt, 2021). In his first statement to the United Nations (UN) Security Council in January 2017, the new Secretary-General, António Guterres, emphasised that the UN must do more to prevent war and sustain peace. Prevention is on the top of the agenda because the human and economic costs of managing conflict have reached levels that are over-whelming the international system (De Coning, 2018. Sustaining Peace: Can an innovative approach change the UN? The urgent need for sustaining peace concept gained even more momentum during the adoption of Agenda 2030 for sustainable development in 2015. Agenda 2030 is underpinned by 17 Sustainable Development Goals (SDGs). In his sustaining peace report, the Secretary-General contended that there can be no sustainable development without peace and no peace without sustainable development. SDG16 is the main goal for "fostering peaceful, just and inclusive societies which are free from fear and violence".

A bourgeoning literature explores the different Models adopted by the UN, International, and Regional and National organs as interventions to create peace and instability in countries devastated by civil wars and or violence. This chapter examines government coalitions as models of peace initiatives adopted with the view to achieve peace and stabilise as critical building blocks on which to build sustainable democracy. The chapter also discusses coalition government approaches preferred in 3 countries in 2 continents: Somali and Sudan (Africa), and Iraqi (Asia) under the topic "Examining the effects of government coalitions in countries which suffered violence/civil wars; Sudan, Somalia, and Iraqi". Hamid and Daniel (2022) argue that states in the post-conflict phase often engage in democratic state building involving institutional-design choices in which the political class must decide on the suitable electoral system for the context at hand. For countries recovering from a civil war sparked by competition for power and resources, this is crucial as the system provides peaceful ways of achieving power (Hamid and Daniel, 2022). Sekatle and Sebola (2020) point out that government coalitions as state administrations formed either before or after elections in presidential or parliamentary or mixed systems and are usually a manifestation of failure of the competing political parties to garner majority of votes required to control parliaments or legislative assemblies. Sekatle and Sebola (2020) further note that this form of governance is usually adopted as a short-term intervention and as a platform to foster the mood of national unity within a country and not as a permanent measure.

INTERNATIONAL PERSPECTIVE ON COALITION GOVERNANCE

The history of Government Coalitions are more traceable in Western Europe, a continent which is historically referred to as the heartland of parliamentarism. Most European countries have gained experience on formation and stabilising coalition governments. However, Kadima (2014) points out that most Western Europe coalitions are post–electoral in nature in the sense they are arrangements entered into based on there not being a party that appropriates the majority of legislative seats hence unable to govern without other parties. This is opposite to pre –electoral coalitions, which means the conjoining of two or more political parties by developing their agenda before and conduct elections under one banner to capture presidential or legislative elections. Hence, understanding theories that guide coalitions can help researchers understand why parties and individuals behave the way they do when they enter coalitions government or when they enter government (Fisher and Hobolt, 2010). According to Neumann (1953) and Morgen (1962) it is through theoretical reasoning that parties are likely to hamstrung coalition government if their mission of entering government were purely office-seeking whose only motivation is to seek power and prestige bestowed in the office for the purposes of addressing their individual or narrow interest. Axelrods (1970) argues that minimal connected winning theory posits that coalitions last if they are formed by parties with similar ideological dimension or where ideological interests are not too much at variant with one another. However, Schofield (1998) points out that that institutions largely determine the nature and character of the coalition government likely to be formed. If institutions are based on the constitution, they have more chances to stay longer than those that rely solely on the agreed upon coalition chatter.

Coalition governments are not only a European phenomenon but have now become increasingly common in many countries with multi-party-political systems. Coalition government experiences from countries in Asia, Europe, and Africa show that invariably some areas of public policy formulation and implementation is adversely affected at various degrees, as a result of coalition politics (Ravi, 2013). Corruption is one such area. It is dominant and there is ample evidence that shows its levels in many developing and some developed countries. Hence, more countries opt for coalition governments which have in some instances resulted in poor governance. Coalition governments tend to shy away from serious efforts to fight or eliminate corruption, as this can threaten the stability or the very existence of these governments. To an extent in his study "Innovation with information technology: coalition governments and emerging economies – fighting corruption with electronic governance", Ravi (2012) suggests that electronic governance (e-governance) may be adopted as part of the mechanisms to fight corruption. Ravi (2012) defines electronic governance as vital in the provision of simple, moral, accountable, responsive and transparent (SMART) governance using information and communications technologies (ICTs).

There are many factors that motivate countries of the world, and Africa in particular, to consider coalition or alliance-based governments. Kadima (2014) enumerates the reasons as follows: a) The presence of the legal framework governing alliances and coalitions: even to date political parties and their alliances and coalitions are generally affected either by the absence or the inadequacies of legislation. In Malawi, the legal framework does not explicitly recognise party coalitions. As a result, alliances and coalitions have no status beyond that of unwritten agreements. b) The electoral system factor: Distinct kinds of electoral systems give rise to several types of instrumental calculations among political parties. The nature and character of the electoral system also predetermines the natural inclination of parties to opt for coalitions or alliances. c) The political regime factor: The type of political regime has an impact on the formation of electoral alliances and coalition governments. In a parliamentary regime (Mauritius, South Africa and Lesotho), the government's survival depends on the confidence of Parliament. As a result, coalition partners work hard to maintain the cohesion of the governing party or coalition. d) The ideology factor: this is the least considered factor in alliance or coalition formation. Since the end of the Cold War, most African political parties have realigned themselves ideologically by moving to the centre. Because Africa faces huge challenges; extremely prevalent poverty levels, unemployment, poor education and health delivery etc. parties align themselves based on the urgent need to alleviate these challenges rather than being concerned with socialist or liberal ideologies.

The next section discusses the critical factors that motivate most African countries to consider coalition governance favourably.

Theories of Coalitions

Analyses of government formations are also characterized by their motivational assumptions about politicians. The theories of party coalitions are essentially based on the experiences of continental Western Europe and are focused on predicting and explaining models of government formation and termination in parliamentary democracies (Martin and Vanberg (2014). The basis of this theoretical section starts from the presumption that the influence of parties in any coalition corresponds to their relative weight in the coalition and this is reflective of the recent findings by Martin and Vanberg (2014). It can be argued that overall coalition policies and deployment of portfolios reproduce the nature of a compromise between government parties. There are a few theories that the researcher seeks to highlight and are, as much as possible, relevant to the study under review and each of the country's coalition processes will be examined in accordance with these theories.

Such theories are based on size and ideology. These theories emerged during 1960s and 1970s and are divided into two areas, which are office-seeking and policy-seeking theories Bäck, Müller and Nyblade, 2017). Office-seeking theories presuppose that the main goal of political parties during coalition formation is the access of power and cabinet portfolios are regarded as the quintessential payoff for office-seeking politicians (Resnick, 2013). According to Resnick (2013), government creation is a win-lose scenario where Cabinet portfolios are the settlements criteria and in achieving these cabinet portfolios, a majority coalition cannot accept minority parties, instead would rather share the spoils of office for itself (the majority government). The minimal winning theory to government formation was developed by William Gamson (1961) and later polished by William Riker (1962). The theory assumes that government coalitions should encompass as few political parties as possible – just enough to win the legislature's vote of confidence. William Riker (1962) posits that the minimum winning theory emphasises on the minimisation of the number of political parties in the coalition because that maximises office benefits make consensus easy to reach. Minimum winning governments "carry no passengers." The core arguments of office-seeking theories are relevant in African contexts because the main motive for the formation of alliances and coalitions in Africa, just like elsewhere, is to hold public office. However, the argument that minimal winning governments carry no passengers become sterile in the African context, especially where pre-electoral alliances are deliberately formed as large as possible to ensure electoral victory a more desired outcome than that of maximising the benefits. Similarly, Abram De Swaan (1973) notes that political parties form the minimal winning coalition with the smallest ideological range, which positions the hypothesis of 'ideologically compact winning coalitions. Warwick (1994) concurs with Axelrod's and De Swaan's views by arguing that ideologically diverse governments tend not to survive because of the greater policy compromises coalition members have to make.

According to Neumann (1953) and Morgen (1962) theoretical reasoning, parties are likely to hamstrung coalition government if their mission of entering government were purely office-seeking whose only motivation is to seek power and prestige bestowed in the office for the purposes of addressing their individual or narrow interest. Axelrods (1970) states that minimal connected winning theory posits that coalitions last if they are formed of parties with similar ideological dimension or where ideological interests are not too much at variant with one another. However, Schofield's (1998) theory posits that institutions largely determine the nature and character of the coalition government likely to be formed. If institutions are based on the constitution, those have more chances to stay longer than those relying solely on the agreed upon coalition chatter.

PROFILES OF SELECTED COUNTRIES

Somalia Coalition Government 2004-2012 and Transitional Challenges up to 2024

The coalition government was adopted in 2004-2012 to create conditions that could revive Somalia from its failed state condition, looking back 12 years down the line, seem to have failed dismally in that mandate (Kahiye, 2021). The Charter that gave mandate to the coalition government dubbed the Transitional Federal Government (TFG) expected 5 key areas to be accomplished before the end of the transitional authority (Mohamoud (2015). These include a) create conditions for peace and unity, free and sovereign nation; b) re-establish peace, democracy, rule of law, social justice, the dignity and integrity of all Somalian; c) establish and nurture Transitional Government for Somalia Republic and d) foster Conciliation, national Unity and good governments.

The new constitution was adopted on 1 August 2012 and elections successfully held on 20 August 2012. The president and Prime Minister were elected in 2013. However, the government administration that followed in 2016 – 2021 and 2021-2026 were/are, in essence, illegitimate because they were not products of state level or direct elections but were indirect, short cut elections. The inability of the 2004-2012 Transitional Federal Government to meet the mandates in the charter has made the situation in Somalia fragile that as the African Union transition mission in Somalia (ATMIS) is currently (in 2024) winding up its activities in the country. There are no convincing signs for peace, an in fact there is all evidence that the country is unstable and that civil war is still raging. For example, there are reports that from 9 September to 13 October 2023, Somalia registered 279 political violence events and 1,752 fatalities, while on 9 December – 19 January 2024, 300 political violence events were reported and 726 people killed (Hybe, 2024). Other than the conflict between Federal Government of Somalia and the government of Somaliland which is assisted by the Ethiopian government, the Federal Government of Somalia has since 2007 faced the insurgence by the Islamic militia group and to date (20 February 2024) the Somalian government is still asking the UN to lift the arms embargo that have been in place since 1991 (Hybe, 2024).

The people of Somalia have had no peace since 1991 when Said Barre who had ruled Somalia since 1961 was assassinated in 1991. From 1991 to 2011 Somalia has been suffering serious tragedies in the form of civil war that had claimed thousands of lives and famine that bedevilled the country for years (Devecioğlu, 2022). Since the fall of the Said's regime, there has been intense military rivalry among various factions all vying for power to rule Somalia. These factions include mainly the faith based organizations called Islamic Courts Union, Al-shabaab and other impermanent groups that are causing Somalia to become an environment with accumulated incompatible interests, and power struggle that has ascended to be the cornerstone objectives almost without giving due attention to choices of the citizens (Devecioğlu, 2022). Somalia consists of many ethnic groups; hence, its civil wars and conflicts are also shaped by contradictory interests of these ethnic groups (Bryden, 2013).

A variety of attempts to peace and stability by the 2004 -2012 coalition government, was key in implementing the Charter as well as the role of external actors like the UN and AU. The Transitional Federal Government was made up of the Presidents and Prime Ministers who had the authority to pass a veto law and ran government with Somalia majority of four clans that occupied 61 seats and the alliance of minority clans with 31 seats (Sekatle and Sebola 2020). According to Pottie (2014), the TFG faced challenges that made it take more than 5 years to deliver democratic elections.

Furthermore, Bryden, 2013) posits that the presence and dictatorship of the international actors denied the Somali people their right to decide, as a nation, the kind of political system that could work in Somalia, decide on what type of state suitable in Somalia given their unique social and political environment. Given a chance, the Somali people could have turned down the establishment of the Federal System in favour of a unitary state given the complex nature of Somalia either socially, politically or territorially (Bryden, 2013). For example, power sharing and political jealousy between the President and the Prime Minister in Somalia has often been a domestic political phenomenon which Somalia had never suffered from since the post- colonial history in 1960.

On this basis it could clear that the exogenous strategies adopted including the imposed electoral system and form of government adopted by Somalia are the main reasons Somalia is far from fulfilling the required criteria for federalism (Danida, 2014). even the Somalia Constitution which was approved in late 2012 has not defined and clearly outlined the concept of federalism. Moreover, countries that practice workable federal systems have qualified either through separate colonial systems of the federating parts or ethnic variations. Somalia has not attained these features due to the fact that it had only one colonial experience (that of Italy), and since British Somaliland has dissolved the union or reclaimed its independent and self- determination in 1991(Danida, 2014).

Bryden (2013) and Danida (2014) argue that the denial of Somalia people by international actors (US, UN and AU) to determine their future has resulted in the government's post 2012 dispensation suffer from the following a) there is no specific territorial map that SFG is able to administer, b) no effective government institutions that can carry on the obligatory mandate of the SFG; c) Despite, the huge external support to this nascent state of Somalia, the political and security crisis is yet rampant, and this socio-political and economic vulnerability became the arsenal of terrorism, foreign exploitation, piracy, international drug trafficking, human trafficking and unacceptable political behaviours that disrupted the stability in region.

Given the influence of external actors interfering in the running of transitional government, Lane and Preker (2018) posit that the political parties as main actors both in government formation are critical in the distribution of executive power, their corresponding seats and its exercise. Political parties are formed with one aim; the attainment of highest political office in the country and the exercise of its power. Hence, Weber (2012) retorts that political parties are not the end in themselves, but they are instruments with which to capture state power, hence they are only means to an end. Jessop (2012) advances the view that "state" power is interconnected with class relations in economics, politics and ideology and that in capitalist social formations, the state becomes an instrument considered secure the conditions for economic class domination.

SUDAN TRANSITIONAL GOVERNMENT: 2019 - 2023

Subsequent to the enormous popular uprising in December 2018 against the long-reigning kleptocratic "Ingaz" regime of General Omer al-Bashir, the Sudanese armed forces (SAF) and Rapid Support Force) RSF leaders conspired to collapse the administration in April 2019 and introduced a ruling "Transitional Military Council (TMC) (Elbadawi, Amin, Elobaid, Alhelo, Osman, and Suliman, 2023). Sudan had been under the leadership of the authoritarian regime of Omar Al- Bashir for 30 years (1989- 2019). The woes of Sudan started during the 1990s when the Western financial and commercial markets imposed sanctions against Sudan forcing the country to explore non-Western means of financing and went East Asia and the Arabian Gulf (Hamid and Daniel, 2022.). Currently and because of the overlap in the two streams of financing adopted by Sudan, it has been difficult to accurately calculate its debt hence creating an opportunity for different elites to coalesce and declare Sudan over-indebted in order to impose a program of fiscal austerity and economic liberalization. Hamid and Daniel (2022) point out that it is this neoliberal program that had hamstrung the ruling alliance and made change difficult by country's already delicate political transition.

The cause of transition from an authoritarian regime to an alternative democratic transition was made possible by what Sudanese refer to as "2019 revolution" (Cross, 2023). Cross (2023) posits that from around 19 December 2018 to 11 April 2019 there was a four-month long civil disobedience and violent protests in many Sudanese towns and cities that compelled President Omar al-Bashir to resign as state president. The protest movement was initially motivated by the shortage of bread and fuel as well as the scarcity of local currency (Elbadawi at al., 2023). When this protest crisis reached its boiling point, the Supreme Security Council forced al-Bashir regime to concede defeat and allow for transfer of power (Hamid and Daniel, 2022). Since then, the country had entered a transition route through a transition government. However, conflicts and civil wars continue to plague the country. Due to many years of the notorious al-Bashir regime characterised by civil wars and conflicts; Sudan is currently facing a plethora of challenges that the transitional government should attend to. For an example, according to ACLED (2024) in the population of 45 Million people, 5.9 million are internally displaced, 1.4 million had fled as refugees, 25 Million people are in need of humanitarian help, and there is a looming food crisis and hence the possibility of famine records report that just between 25 November 2023 and 5 January 2024, there has been over 640 Political violence incidents and 720 reported fatalities and most of these events are more dominant in Khartoum. There is a raging war between Sudanese Armed Forces (SAF) and paramilitary Rapid Support Forces (RSF).

The Sudanese coalition government (Civilian-Military Alliance) was formed by Sudanese Transitional Military Council (TMC) an organisation of armed military forces (formed of the armed forces, the police, the security and intelligence agencies, and the Rapid Support Forces (RSF)) and groups of civil society organisations led by the Sudanese Professionals Association (SPA) joined by various organisations to form an organising platform known as the Forces of Freedom and Change (FFC) (Cross, 2023.).

Judging from the easier and the smooth way by which this coalition government was formed, it can be concluded that talks, negotiations, and compromises took place between members of the SSC (renamed the Transitional Military Council (TMC), and opposition Sudanese groups which led to the partnership between the military and the FFC long before the December 2019 (Cross, 2023.) and indeed it appeared that the TMC had long established communication networks with some opposition parties long before the revolution of December 2019 meaning that the army had secretly and gradually distanced itself from the regime and got biased towards change (Elbadawi at al. 2023). This section looks at the strategies employed by the Transitional Sudanese Coalition government to bring about transition from authoritarian system to a democratic system.

The prominent role in delivering this transitional government was played by three left-wing minority parties (the Sudanese Communist Party (SCP), the Sudanese Baath Party, and the Unionist Democratic Nasserist Party), the Sudanese Congress Party, and some professional and civil society organisations (Elbadawi at al., 2023). These are the organisations that had challenged the regime beneath the banner of the Declaration of Freedom and Change, and they were the political incubator for the 'revolutionary government.' It was they who drafted the Constitutional Charter, defined the governmental structures and hierarchy, and shared power with the TMC (Hamid and Daniel, 2022).

What made the coalition easily accepted was the Constitutional Charter that showed that both alliance partners had a common ideological stand that rejected regional or outside interventions in Sudanese affairs. This common approach on outside interventions within the FFC, first and between FFC and TMC confirmed that internal differences were not about tactics and therefore resolvable within the framework of the greater aim. The importance of adopting a common coalition government program, in this case the constitutional Charter, is further reinforced by de Haan et al. (2013) who argues that the coalition policy agreement is a critical control mechanism that limits policy discretion of individual parties and ministries in their delineated portfolios and jurisdictions. This argument is further emphasised by "fiscal institutionalists" who suggest the policy agreement ensures that that spending targets by individuals deployed to cabinet executives are negotiated and should lead to smaller deficits (Martin and Vanberg, 2013). The partners in the Sudanese coalition government, given commonality of thinking, agreed to share executive power on the basis of the Constitutional Charter that they signed with FFC obtaining a number of seats in the Sovereignty Council and all the ministerial portfolios in the cabinet except for Defence and Interior. This supports the argument by Resnick (2013) that portfolio distribution is the critical function in any coalition government because political parties are office-seeking actors. After these distribution of portfolios and responsibility the TMC's presidency ended (Hamid and Daniel, 2022.) and the term of the transitional coalition government began 2019 where Abdalla Hamdok became prime minister (2019-2022), and Lieutenant General Burhan became chairman of the Sovereignty Council in the framework of a grand pact backed by around seven political parties. However, Hamdok resigned on 2 January 2022 because of violent protests and Osma Hussein acted as Prime Minister since 19 January 2022.

The Sudanese transitional government is different from the Somali Transitional Government of 2004-2012 which was a product of external forces (US and UN in particular). The Sudanese transitional coalition arrangement was internally crafted and directed with UN and UN only pledging their support. The Supreme Security Council had created the Military Council to be responsible for the country's security during the transitional period of not more than two years. According to Cross, 2023 the Salient features of the constitution Charter were as follows:

- To help the country transition from "Salvation" regime (Omar al-Bashir's) to new and alternative political system founded on the new Constitutional Charter.
- Destroy Salvation Regime institutions of oppression
- Hold constitutional Convention towards the end of the coalition government term (3 years) to prepare for permanent Sudanese constitution that would define the form of government as well as decide on the electoral system.
- The ruling coalition had to be done with creating conditions for permanent government within 3 years and be ready to conduct democratic general elections by July 2023

However, the fact that by now in February 2024 the Sudan democratic government is still illusive, bears testimony to the fact that the transitional coalition government could not fulfil the constitutional charter instructions. The opposite is true that now in 2024 and there is no sign of peace in Sudan and instead from the April 2023 civil war between the generals has now escalated to a conflict in which rebel groups,, ethnic militias, and international actors are now participating. It is reported that about 13 000 people have died thus far and about 7 million people displaced amid claims of ethnic cleansing, deteriorating humanitarian conditions, human rights violations etc. it is predicted that the war in Sudan is unlikely to end soon and the transitional government reigns more than the time stipulated, and democratic government remain elusive. The researcher sketches out a few reasons for this failure.

Amongst the challenges was economic instability. Following the sanctions by Western Financial institutions on Sudan during the 1990s and the country's turning to Asia countries for fiancé assistance the international elites declared the country over indebted and forced the transitional authority to apply neoliberal policies of austerity and that lowered the coalition government's capacity to deliver on key areas of the Charter like refashioning institutions of the previous oppressive regime and in their place build democratic organs (Elbadawi at al., 2023).

The coup that took place on 25 October 2021 disoriented the transitional government and created retrogression in many areas already covered. The coup was led by General Abdel Fattah al-Burhan while he was chair of the Sovereignty Council, but he dissolved the government and arrested many of its members including Prime Minister Hamdok. This severely hampered the functioning of the coalition government and created massive civil disobedience and protests. Although the transitional authority was reinstated on 21 November 2021, worse with most civilian members replaced by military appointees, but a lot of damage had been incurred. In 2023 Sudan descended into civil war, once again. Characterising the self-centred behaviour of al-Burhan Lane and Preker (2018) posit that political parties are formed with one aim and one aim only, the attainment of highest political office in the country and the exercise of its power. Jessop (2012) argue that individuals and political parties are primarily ideological platforms and that they enter into coalition governments with an intention to accomplish the realisation of substantive political ideals. Coalition governments can be governments' instruments that either alter or reconfigure power relations in line with a particular mode for class domination. April 2023 war between Sudanese armed forces (SAF) (led by General Abdel Fattah al- Burham and Rapid Support Forces (RSF), (an elite force), led by Mohamed Hamdan Degalo further elucidate the above theoretical construction. These generals were chair and deputy chairperson of the transitional Sovereign Council respectively that served the transitional coalition government since nobody could fathom that they would work against the transitional government efforts 2019. hence Jessop (2012) advances the view that "state" power is interconnected with class relations in economics, politics and ideology and that in capitalist social formations like Sudan at the time, the state becomes an instrument critical to secure the conditions for economic class domination that is why Lane and Preker (2018) advances the view that Parties reside in the sphere of power. Jessop (2012) concludes that problems in coalitions are exacerbated by sheer lack of understanding deeper foundations in the social structure and he advises that any study of government formations should focus more on the causal interconnectedness of the exercise of (state) power and either the reproduction and/or transformation and class domination. According to Lane and Preker, (2018) the mere act of sabotaging the transitional route to democracy is reflective unrestrained unitary actors with insatiable determination to exploit well-defined coalition possessions like office positions for proximity to scarce resources.

However, Bawn and Rosenbluth (2006, p. 251) blame the Sudanese Model of government coalition for failure to implement the Charter. Their theoretical construal argue that coalitions of fragmented parties are usually associated with reaching less proficiency because a multiplicity of political interests needs representation in cabinets and parliament which also has a bearing on government spending. Meyer (2010) agrees and contends that coalition arrangements retard government performance because of their portfolio allocation model that deploys coalition party ministers or party officials to particular portfolios which are considered the ultimate jurisdiction of those deployed ministers often without any mechanism for oversight.

TRANSITIONAL GOVERNMENT USED TO AVOID DEMOCRACY

According to Hamid and Daniel (2022) Sudanese political parties were not ready for democracy and hence they opportunistically used ideological reasons to avoid extend the transitional period and avoid general elections. This is easy to detect because the ideological orientations of some of the constituent organisations (like Bath Party and military) are inconsistent with democratic principles. Also, the Sudanese Communist Party (SCP) baulks at the notion of re-democratisation for ideological reasons, having questioned the value of democracy since the mid-1960s. (Devecioğlu, 2022.). The SCP argued at times that Sudanese social foundations were too weak to support a Western-style parliamentary system due to the disproportionate weight of the country's conventional feudal forces, hence other times it had pronounced a new democracy that would limit the activities of counterrevolutionary forces. This, according to SCP a 'democracy of the society' is a dispensation where the people would have a practical and tangible role in policy design and decision-making and to achieve that, they believed, Sudan needed more than Western bourgeoisie elections and democratic methodology. But what seems the main practical reason why even left-wing organisations in the coalition avoided democratic elections was that the electoral process would open space to political forces undesirable to be in government because they had been dominant parties in the old Omar al-Bashir regime, like the Umma Party, the Democratic Unionist Party, together with some traditional social organisations. Most of the small parties that dominated Sudanese political space during transition like the Sudanese Baath, the Nasserist Democratic Unionist Party, and the Sudanese Communist Party feared losing their influence if free elections were to be held (Devecioğlu, 2022.).

The key features of electoral management, as part of the democratic transition process in deeply divided societies such as Sudan, usually vary from case to case. In sensitive, pluralist, and arguably sectarian societies that have experienced conflict and violence on identity-concentrated issues may call for complex power-sharing. This may sometimes involve forms of territorial self-governance under a federal system. Under federal governance, power is redistributed across 'multiple layers of government' (Norris, 2012:

157. As such, each respective regional government, as it is in the case of Iraq, has a relative independent say in regional matters. This also means that governments under such a model are typically split up into regional jurisdictions, as emphasised by constitutional arrangements that enforce this 'split.' This makes it harder to break the federal structure by embedding regional jurisdictions into the constitution, as well as clearly defining territorial jurisdiction, a process known as 'legislative entrenchment' (King, 1993: 94). Territorial power in federal constitutions, then, is distributed between the central government and the regional administrative units (Ibid: 96). As a result, the federal government still has a say in decisions affecting politics at a national level (Lijphart, 1979: 502).

IRAQI Coalition Arrangement

Since the United States (US)-led invasion in 2003, Iraqi suffered a long period of instability, with armed groups like the self-proclaimed Islamic State taking advantage of the power vacuum left by the disbandment of the military and the ban on Saddam Hussein's Baath party. Islamic state (IS) was a dominant organisation that took advantage of this vacuum and by 2014 it had captured a reasonably large territories from Iraqi especially the Anbar province, Mosul and the Northern part of Iraqi. In 2014, the Islamic State advanced into Iraq from Syria and took over parts of Anbar province, eventually expanding into the northern part of the country and capturing Mosul in June 2014. However, in 2017 the Trump government retook all IS conquered areas and brought IS insurgents to an end.

Iraqi is the nation of many sad episodes. It has become a laboratory where concepts (including security and democracy) had been evaluated and applied often in an intolerant mode against local dynamics and with little consideration for local needs in the planning (Costantini and O'Driscoll, (2023). According to Costantini and O'Driscoll, (2023) the only beneficiaries of insecure Iraqi had been the United State, European Countries and North Atlantic Treaty Organization – NATO, or the European Union – EU) who have also contributed to an insecure environment in Iraqi. The change by the US foreign policy from containment strategy installed on Iraq following the Persian Gulf War in 1991 into the strategy for US-led invasion and occupation which led the civil war period (2003– 2008) is what led to the sever destruction of lives and livelihoods in Iraqi and opened condition that led to a coalition government adopted as the solution to rebuilding the country. Under this policy of containment, the United States and its international coalition imposed economic sanctions, weapons inspections, no-fly-zones, and occasional military strikes on Iraq in order that Iraq can be militarily weak such that it is prevented from being a threat to neighbouring countries (Ulrazzaq, 2022.). Ulrazzaq (2022) argues that the implementation of US's new security strategy of invasion and occupation in 2002 joined by the EU in 2003 marked a rupture with the Cold War's prevalent understanding of security which sought to secure small, weak states fragile the threat of foreign attacks and usher in a new strategy that views weak, fragile and failed states as a threat to international security. This change in strategy sought to primarily create conditions for Saddam Hussain's removal from Presidency and put a puppet government under the guise of looking for weapons of mass destruction (Costantini and O'Driscoll, 2023).

Iraqi as a predominantly etho-secterian country, like all deeply divided societies has experienced growing intercommunal violence and mass killing throughout. Such types of conflict, Ulrazzaq (2022), are often protracted and painstakingly embedded in the identity of the groups involved. For years, Iraq has been dealing with a multidimensional conflict originating from the escalation of Saddam Hussein's Ba'ath Party in 1989, the Gulf Wars of the 1990s, the US invasion, the drafting of a new constitution in

2005, and the increased threats of the infighting that was dominantly among <u>Sunni Islamic</u>, <u>Shia Islamic</u>, <u>Kurdish</u> and other religious or ethnic groups (Gunter, 2015: 102).

<u>Iraq</u> is a <u>federal</u> <u>parliamentary</u> <u>representative democratic</u> <u>republic</u>. It is a <u>multi-party system</u> in which the <u>executive power</u> is exercised by the <u>Prime Minister</u> of the <u>Council of Ministers</u> as the <u>head of government</u>, the <u>President of Iraq</u> as the <u>head of state</u>, and <u>legislative power</u> is vested in the <u>Council of Representatives</u>. The <u>federal</u> <u>government</u> of <u>Iraq</u> is defined by a <u>constitution</u> which is <u>Islamic</u>, <u>democratic</u>, <u>federal</u> <u>parliamentary</u> <u>republic</u>. The federal government is composed of the <u>executive</u>, <u>legislative</u>, and <u>judicial</u> branches, as well as numerous independent commissions (centre for Preventive Action, February 13, 2024).

This section discusses the extent to which the power-sharing arrangements in a divided society like Iraq has contributed to heal the rift and help the country transition to fully fledged democracy. In this case the chapter focuses on the role of the coalition government of parties led by the Shiite cleric Muqtada al-Sadr from May 2018 to 2021. This coalition government won the Iraq's May 2018 parliamentary election. In Iraqi, the coalition government for the period under review was based on consensus (Petrikkos, 2019). Consensus-based coalition government, according to Petrikkos (2019) represents a general contract through which all participating political parties run the country's affairs on consensual bases notwithstanding the size of their parliamentary representation (large parties and small parties). This system had been resilient in Iraq is because the constitution which was the product of the 2005 referendum by the people, and enforced a broad-based consensus in the selection of a president, requiring a two-thirds parliamentary majority (if this fails, as it frequently does, a run-off election takes place) (Norris, 2012). The intent of this instrument was to avoid a return to tyranny and canvass the buy-in by most of Iraq's ethno-sectarian constituents in forming a government. This system has endured over the years because Iraq does not have a culture of parliamentary opposition. The traditional political parties always <u>refuse to take opposition benches</u>, irrespective of how many seats they have won because to them it means missing out on influence, positions, and access to state resources (Norris, 2012))

The consensus system can be traced back to policies and governing methods of many European governments formed after World War 2, especially in Britain. The consensus principle or methodology is an antithesis of competitive democracy or representative democracy and was designed specifically to as it resolves racial, ethnic and societal divisions as well as frequent waves of violence between societal components. The system had also been employed in situations where there was failure of the democratic system based on the majority where the rule of the majority did not meet all the aspirations and desires of the people (Petrikkos, 2019) The consensus mechanism was both relevant and necessary for post-2003 Iraq, especially because it followed a phase when there was a monopoly of power and the deprivation of the majority of the people from participating in government and public affairs (Norris (2012)). One of the requirements for consensus is the existence of real and balanced political institutions and an open political system for the societal and political organizations that the parties represent primarily. According to Norris (2012) this calls for building a value system, i.e., activating the values of democracy and political transition and making them effective and capable of distributing power in society to achieve real democracy, not formal or institutional, and this means acknowledgment of pluralism within an effective value system (Abd Ulrazzaq, 2022.) The main advantage of a democratic system based on consensus is the existence of a broad coalition to rule a country which can either be in the form of a large presidential coalition, a government coalition or through a committee with broad powers. The consensus systems require a written constitution that plainly comprises the mechanism of governance, clarify how power is transferred and how elections are organized (Abd Ulrazzaq, 2022).

The Iraq coalition government has had some successes and is considered to have established some internal equilibrium in Iraqi (Petrikkos, 2019).

Findings and Analysis

The chapter deliberated on the effects of government coalitions in countries which suffered violence/ civil wars; Sudan, Somalia, and Iraqi. The chapter concludes that while the three countries under review from two continents (Africa, Somali, Sudan and Asia, Iraqi) are distant from each other, but there are remarkable similarities about their history of internal strife, conflicts or civil wars. For example, all of them suffered internal conflicts based on regionalism, ethnicity and religion-based differences and at the centre of such conflicts is Islamic insurgency. In all these countries there is a questionable role played by international actors, especially UN and US. In Iraqi and Somalia, in particular, both US and UN withdrew security measures while internal strife or civil war and Islamic insurgency was still raging and thereby making states vulnerable to being taken over by Islamic States. It is also noted that for Somali and Iraqi their transitional methodology was imposed by external players, and they do not reflect the countries socio-cultural and traditional values. For example, in Somalia they imposed federalism while most Somalians preferred a unitary state as a result to date and long after the Transitional Federal Government, Somalia and also Iraq with its imposed government are still far away from people centred and people driven democracies. While Sudan resorted to internally driven transition, however, embargos and austerity strategies imposed by external institutions like International Monetary Fund (IMF) ensured that Sudan find it hard to transition to democracy. What has also come out clear is that coalition governments are far from being considered as capable of bringing about democracy. The situation of Somali and Sudan are living examples and also Iraq management of a consensus government is always done for pacifying only the coalition government players at the expense of the will of the people and their varying interests.

The failure of coalition governments is also indicative of the failure or crisis that liberal democracy has and is going through. The so-called Global democracy recession the world is currently going through supports the view that democracy and voting not solution to people's problems observed from objective poverty, endemic corruption and poor governance. The solution, as the philosophy of the ancient African democracy suggests, is about equitable distribution of the objects and instruments of production.

DIRECTIONS FOR FUTURE RESEARCH

The research study is desktop research, the investigation of secondary material, further research study that collects data from primary sources may shed more light on this subject. Also, the research study was based on only two continents and covering only 3 countries. Further research examining the effects of government coalitions in more than 3 countries which suffered violence/civil wars.

CONCLUSION AND RECOMMENDATIONS

Indeed, coalition governments have been capable of helping countries transit to democracy, especially in Western Europe, the heartland of liberal democracy, but that in non-European settings, especially where there are conflicts and civil wars, coalition governments are more often unable to resolve the impasse and help countries transition to democracy. Hence any attempt at transition may need to take the history and context of the country into consideration. The study proves that Africa has, since the 1884 Berlin Conference, been the product of a Eurocentric ideology of one size fits all. This Berlin Conference initiated ideology has ignored the significance of the ancient history of Africa where democracy was clan based and exercised through designated African organs composed of the Family (with family, the basic unit of society with own values kinked upwardly to those of whole community), the clan (a close-knit group of interrelated families of all families and the Ethnic Group (grouping of people who identify with one another on the basis of perceived shared attributes that set them apart from other groups) with the King as the overall Head or President. The King was not above the law but could be deposed upon transgression. Hence, most of the transitional arrangements are unable, mainly in Africa to lead to a genuine democratic dispensation.

The chapter recommends that coalition government created as conflict resolution measures, while they should operate under external guidance, from UN in particular, it is important that decisions like the nature and composition of coalition government or transitional authority must be decided by citizens themselves or internal political actors based on their socio-cultural traditions and inclinations than by outside actors. Coalition governments should not be considered as the only panacea for resolving the crisis of nations engulfed by internal conflicts, violence or civil wars, consideration of the socio-cultural background ethnic and regional composition of the nation in crisis should be strictly analysed and considered to bring about corresponding and palpable interventions than to always opt for a one size fits all strategy of coalition governance.

REFERENCES

Ammar, S. (2022). *National Reconciliation in Libya: Challenges and Perspectives*. Academic Press.

Arriola, L. R. (2013). *Multiethnic Coalitions in Africa: Business Financing of Opposition Election Campaigns*. Cambridge University Press.

Campbell, K. L. (2020). Democracy in Western Europe. Democracy in Crisis around the World.

Clayton, G., Dorussen, H., & Böhmelt, T. (2021). United Nations peace initiatives 1946-2015: Introducing a new dataset. *International Interactions*, *47*(1), 161–180. doi:10.1080/03050629.2020.1772254

Conti, N., & Marangoni, F. (Eds.). (2014). *The challenge of coalition government: the Italian case*. Routledge. doi:10.4324/9781315746937

Costantini, I., & O'Driscoll, D. (2023). Twenty years of externally promoted security assistance in Iraq: Changing approaches and their limits. *International Peacekeeping*, *30*(5), 562–584. doi:10.1080/1353 3312.2022.2149501

Davis, M. (1977). Inheritance, Magoc and Political Power on South East Papua. *Journal of Pacific Studies*, *3*, 69–88.

Dodd, L. (2015). *Coalitions in parliamentary government* (Vol. 1247). Princeton University Press. doi:10.1515/9781400868070

Fisher, S. D., & Hobolt, S. B. (2010). Coalition government and electoral accountability. *Electoral Studies*, *29*(3), 358–369. doi:10.1016/j.electstud.2010.03.003

Foa, R. S., Klassen, A., Slade, M., Rand, A., & Collins, R. (2020). *The global satisfaction with democracy report 2020*. Academic Press.

Freeman, W. (2023). Colombia Tries a Transformative Left Turn. *Current History (New York, N.Y.)*, *122*(841), 69–74. doi:10.1525/curh.2023.122.841.69

Glassman, R. (2017). *The Origins of Democracy in Tribes, City-States, and NationStates*. Springer. doi:10.1007/978-3-319-51695-0

Hassan, Q., Algburi, S., Sameen, A. Z., Salman, H. M., & Jaszczur, M. (2023). Implications of strategic photovoltaic deployment on regional electricity self-sufficiency by 2050: A case study in Iraq. *Renewable Energy Focus*, *46*, 338–355. doi:10.1016/j.ref.2023.07.007

Haybe, A. (2024). Somalia: making the most of EU-Somalia Joint Roadmap. *Watch List*, p. 1.

Hristov, J., & Arias, J. C. (2023). Beyond the politics of love: The challenges of paramilitary violence and the land question for Colombia's President Gustavo Petro. *Studies in Political Economy*, *104*(1), 55–68. doi:10.1080/07078552.2023.2186022

Hübscher, E. (2019). The impact of coalition parties on policy output–evidence from Germany. *Journal of Legislative Studies*, *25*(1), 88–118. doi:10.1080/13572334.2019.1570599

Isakhan, B., & Stockwell, S. (Eds.). (2011). *The secret history of democracy*. Palgrave Macmillan. doi:10.1057/9780230299467

Jalata, A. (2018). The Contested and Expanding Meaning of Democracy. *JIS, 2*(2).

Jalata, A. (2018). The Contested and Expanding Meaning of Democracy. Journal of Interdisciplinary Studies, 2(2), 1-29.

Kadima, D. (2014). An introduction to the politics of party alliances and coalitions in socially-divided Africa. *Journal of African Elections*, *13*(1), 1–24. doi:10.20940/JAE/2014/v13i1a1

Klä, H., Bäck, H., & Krauss, S. (2023). Coalition Agreements as Control Devices: Coalition Governance in Western and Eastern Europe. Oxford University Press.

Lu, J., & Chu, Y. H. (2021). *Understandings of democracy: Origins and consequences beyond western democracies*. Oxford University Press.

Oesterdiekhoff, G. W. (2015). Evolution of democracy. Psychological stages and political developments in world history. *Cultura (Iasi, Romania)*, *12*(2), 81–102. doi:10.5840/cultura201512223

Rosenau, J. N. (2021). Governance in the Twenty-first Century. In *Understanding Global Cooperation* (pp. 16–47). Brill. doi:10.1163/9789004462601_003

Stieb, J. (2019). *The Regime Change Consensus: Iraq in American Politics, 1990-2003*. The University of North Carolina at Chapel Hill.

ADDITIONAL READING

Figueiredo, A. C. (2023). Government coalitions in Brazilian democracy. *Brazilian Political Science Review*, *1*(2), 182–216. doi:10.1590/1981-3834200700020006

Ravi, S. P. (2013). Innovation with information technology: Coalition governments and emerging economies–fighting corruption with electronic governance. *International Journal of Business and Emerging Markets*, *5*(1), 46–66. doi:10.1504/IJBEM.2013.050741

Reiter, B. (2021). The African origins of democracy. *Academia Letters, 2.*

Shay, S. (2019). *The escalation of the war in Libya*. Research Institute for European and American Studies. Available at http://rieas. gr/images/editorial/shaulshaydec19. pdf

KEY TERMS AND DEFINITIONS

Coalition: When two or more parties combine their votes for government.

Democracy: Is government ruled by the people.

European Union: A supranational political and economic union of 27 member states located primarily in Europe.

NATO (North Atlantic Treaty Organisation): Intergovernmental military alliance of 31 member states, 29 Europe and two North America.

Sudanese Communist Party: The Marxist Party of Somalia.

Sustainable Development Goals: These are UN goals aimed at transforming the world.

Transitional Federal Government: Somalian transitional authority that was in charge of governance and administration.

Transitional Military Council: Somali armed forces headed by president as commander in Chief.

UN (United Nations): An intergovernmental organisation whose stated purpose is to maintain international peace and security.

Chapter 4
It Takes Two to Tango:
2010 British Con-Dem Coalition

Sureyya Yigit

https://orcid.org/0000-0002-8025-5147

New Vision University, Georgia

ABSTRACT

British politics has traditionally been identified as a two-party political system throughout the post-war period. Single parties have formed governments in the United Kingdom, with the two major parties squeezing out any third-party challenger. The year 2010 was an anomaly. The result of the general election proved inconclusive, ending in a hung parliament. For the first time in over 60 years, coalition negotiations took place between the three main parties, and the Con-Dem coalition was agreed to. This coalition pushed forward constitutional changes relating to the timing of elections and proposed reforming the electoral system. The coalition endured for its full five-year term, although its effects were short-term. The subsequent conservative government reneged on its previous support for constitutional changes. This chapter focuses on the challenges of coalition politics in a British context.

INTRODUCTION

"If you're not a liberal at twenty you have no heart, if you're not a conservative at forty, you have no brain." ~ Winston Churchill

Man is a social animal, according to Aristotle. As humans have increased over time, they have come to settle in communities, small at first limited to blood relatives, after which in greater numbers in cities such as Alexandria, Babylon, Athens and Samarkand, to name just four. In ancient times, the political system attributed to Athens was quite unusual regarding participation. Their decision-making and lifestyle choices first interested Greek philosophers and, later, the medieval Christian thinkers, culminating with the Enlightenment and contemporary political science.

Ancient Athens is identified as the birth of democracy. Not as we know it today, of course. The modern definition of democracy does not exclude voters based on gender, let alone accept a category

DOI: 10.4018/979-8-3693-1654-2.ch004

of enslaved people. Nevertheless, the basic understanding of greater participation in deciding policy remained. Regarding the modern democratic state, decision-making or governance has pursued multiple paths. Some states, such as the United States, have chosen a presidential form of government. Others have opted for parliamentary democracy. The United Kingdom of Great Britain and Northern Ireland is classified as a Parliamentary-democratic hereditary monarchy. Interestingly and quite uniquely, it has no written constitution. The constitutional order is based on unwritten law and individual statutes, including the Magna Carta of 1215 and the Habeas Corpus Act of 1679 (Wert, 2010). This chapter endeavours to highlight the challenges faced by the Conservative-Liberal Democrat Coalition of 2010, which was a unique development in terms of British post-war politics as there had never been a formal coalition government since 1945.

METHODOLOGY

When addressing the first elements of the research process, one may define it as the way of accessing knowledge concerning the question, that is, the method. To locate the importance of the method in science, it will suffice for us to recall that any discipline which aims to be autonomous must necessarily define an object - what is the specific object that is studied, and a method - how one proceeds to study this object. The first systematic method stemmed from the work of Descartes, who advocated doubt (Cartesian doubt), which has remained the major concern of all self-respecting positivist researchers.

This is the procedural logic of science, that is, the set of particular practices that are put to logic of science, that is, the set of particular practices that she puts to work so that the progress of its demonstrations and theorisations are either clear, obvious or irrefutable. The method consists of a set of rules which, within the framework of a given science that are relatively independent of particular contents and facts studied as such. It translates, on the ground, into concrete procedures for preparing, organising, and conducting a search.

The approach is considered an intellectual approach that does not involve steps, a systematic path, or particular rigour. A general provision locates the philosophical background or the researcher's metatheory or research. In such a meaning, one refers to Marxist, functionalist, culturalist, structuralist, or systemic approaches.

It is a precise means of achieving a partial result at a specific level and moment of the research. This direct achievement of results concerns the concrete, the observed fact, the practical, and the limited stage. The techniques in this meaning refer to covering the stages of limited operations - while the method is concerned about the overall design coordinating several techniques. These are tools that are momentary, circumstantial, and limited in the research process, such as a survey, interview, sociogram, role-play, and tests.

The methodology can be defined as the study of the proper use of methods and techniques. It is not enough to know them; one still needs to know how to use them properly, that is, how to adapt them as rigorously as possible to the precise object of the research or of the study envisaged and to the objectives pursued. Otherwise, the methods and techniques retained in a given research must be the most capable of considering the subject studied and leading the researcher towards the goals fixed in the work outcome. It is unnecessary to specify that this must be the subject of justifications and arguments on the researcher's part. The researcher must define, formulate, and develop his/her problem, which is referred to as the "problem" in research, to the utmost detail. An inter-conditioning is necessary between the problem, the way of posing it, the method adopted, and the techniques are retained.

In conclusion, it is important to emphasise that scientific work is only possible with method and methodology. It is what distinguishes, for example, the journalist or the researcher. The second is characterised by explicit, absolute, and systematic rigour in the quest and processing of information collected. There, s/he must demonstrate the method, which is how that s/he relates to the community as a scientist.

Of the established six main types of methods, which are:

i.   The deductive method.
ii.   The inductive method.
iii. The analytic method.
iv.   The clinical method.
v.   The experimental method.
vi.   The statistical method.

Three are relevant to this particular research. The deductive method consists of analysing the particular from the general, reading a specific concrete situation using a general pre-established theoretical grid—for example, applying the government coalition model to study the political system of a unitary constitutional parliamentary democracy.

The inductive method is more common than the first; it consists, on the contrary, of attempting generalisations from cases of individuals. We observe specific characteristics of one or several individuals or political parties and demonstrate the possibility of generalising these characteristics to political relations. It is the succession of observation - analysis - interpretation - generalisation. It is very often used in social sciences and relies heavily on inference techniques and statistics (tests which make it possible to measure the risk of error and the extent of the possibilities of generalisations -extrapolations). The opinion poll and the market study both fall under this method.

The analytical method decomposes the object study, ranging from the most complex to the simplest. As chemistry breaks down molecules into simple, indecomposable elements, one decomposes all the elementary parts to reconstruct the overall diagram. This method, which seeks the smallest possible component, the basic unit of phenomena, is favoured in laboratory conditions for studying inert objects or phenomena that are not susceptible to rapid transformation. It is also used in historical research involving archives and documents.

There are several different kinds of problems that one can use for research. One can identify several types of problems, constituting many research genres distinguished by objectives, including theoretical, verification, confirmation, and experimentation dimensions. A fundamental issue is a problem that concerns so-called fundamental research, that is, research that attacks the foundations of any aspect of a given field. It relates to a theoretical problem within the framework of theoretical research. As its name suggests, an applied issue is an application of theoretical notions or, more directly, a study focusing on a specific aspect of reality. A case study is a problem that requires a detailed and in-depth study of several limited objects, individuals, and events. This research into that category.

LITERATURE REVIEW

Quinn, Bara, and Bartle compare the coalition agreement with the manifestos of the coalition partners to determine the extent of their alignment (Quinn, Bara & Bartle, 2013). To achieve this, the article uses the Comparative Manifestos Project to analyse the agreement's content, particularly in regard to the parties' left-right position. The CMP is a comprehensive database of political party manifestos from over 50 countries worldwide. The article highlights the importance of manifestos as crucial policy documents in countries like the UK. They are the main tool used by political parties to communicate their policy platforms to voters before an election. Therefore, a coalition agreement that is inconsistent with the parties' manifestos could be seen as a breach of trust with voters. Additionally, the article examines the feasible coalitional options and the preferences of the major parties after the election. By analysing the possible outcomes of different coalition scenarios, the article provides insights into how the political landscape may change post-election. Finally, the article concludes by considering the allocation of cabinet portfolios. This is a crucial aspect of coalition formation, as the allocation of portfolios determines which party will be responsible for which policy areas. The article examines the potential implications of different portfolio allocations and how they may impact the success of the coalition.

Daddow conducts an in-depth analysis of the coalition government's foreign policy from 2010 to 2015 (Daddow, 2015). The study employs qualitative discourse analysis to unpack the ideological underpinnings that influenced the government's foreign policy practices. The research identifies the foreign policy principles that informed the British identity that liberal Conservatives constructed and the values and interests that the government aimed to express through its foreign policy. The article argues that the liberal Conservative foreign policy was an attempt to address the challenges that impinged on Britain's international agency, including the legacy of the New Labour years, reduced economic resources in the 'age of austerity,' and the increasingly limited capacity for Britain to exercise ideational entrepreneurship in the international community. The analysis highlights how liberal Conservatism adapted, without fundamentally restructuring, the established British foreign policy tradition of merging values and interests in complex ways. The article substantiates the extant literature claim that the liberal Conservative foreign policy was an attempt to come to terms with the limits on Britain's international agency. The study concludes by emphasizing that the coalition government's foreign policy had significant implications for the country's role in the international community and its relations with other nations.

Matthews and Flinders consider the UK as the archetype of Westminster democracy, a system that is seen as the opposite of the power-sharing coalitions that exist in Western Europe (Matthews and Flinders, 2017). Relying on recent scholarship which has delved deeper into the institutional dynamics that shape the UK's democratic system, revealing a more nuanced picture they seek to contribute to this body of work by situating the recent chapter of coalition government within the broader context of the UK's democratic evolution. To achieve this, they draw on a refined framework that enables systematic comparison over time, utilizing a two-dimensional typology of democracies. In doing so, it shows that between 2010-15, the UK underwent another period of majoritarian modification. This was driven by various factors, including the long-term influence of constitutional forces that had been set in motion under the previous Labour government and the short-term impact of coalition management. The article makes several noteworthy contributions. Firstly, it offers a critical response to debates regarding the relationship between institutional design and democratic performance. Secondly, it demonstrates that the tools of large-scale comparison can be effectively scaled down to facilitate case analysis. Finally, it provides a series of conclusions regarding the tenability of the UK, offering insights that are relevant not just within the UK but also beyond. Overall, this article offers a detailed examination of the UK's democratic system, exploring the ways in which it has evolved over time, and highlighting the factors that have driven this evolution. By doing so, it provides a more nuanced understanding of the UK's political landscape, which will be of interest to scholars, policymakers, and other stakeholders.

Dunleavy closely scrutinizes the 2010 British election results, examining the shape of the basic outcome and delving into how voting behaviour changed in response to the evolving strategies of competing political parties (Dunleavy, 2012). He also takes a deep dive into the intricacies of the British electoral system, exploring the ramifications of the election for the long-term trends towards multi-partyism in British politics. Furthermore, Dunleavy delves into the transition to a coalition government formed between the two parties, led by Cameron and Clegg. He analyses the parliamentary arithmetic and electoral situation the new government faced and considers how it navigated this new political landscape. Lastly, Dunleavy looks beyond the election's immediate aftermath to consider the longer-term potential for change in British politics. He explores the opportunities for constitutional reform that have emerged from the election and its aftermath and considers the possibilities for another wave of political change in British society.

Johnson, Chandler, Seldon and Finn focus on the UK government's progress in reducing the deficit which they find has been disappointing due to slower economic growth (Johnson, Chandler, Seldon, & Finn, 2010). The government pushed austerity measures for a decade, and the shape of the state in 2020 would be quite different from pre-recession. Health, pensions, and debt interest are predicted to make up a larger share of public spending. The Bank of England played a central role in keeping interest rates at record lows, implementing a large quantitative easing programme, and using unconventional monetary tools. The Chancellor had implemented aggressive cuts to corporation tax, and the tax-free personal allowance has become the focal point of policy.

Lees argues the formation of the UK coalition by utilizing insights from theoretical and empirical studies of coalition behaviour in multi-party politics (Lees, 2011). The author argues that the formation of the coalition is not a rare occurrence in historical terms or in the context of contemporary European politics. Moreover, the article provides a comparative analysis of the impact of Britain's electoral system, such as the First-Past-The-Post (FPTP) and Alternative Vote (AV) systems, on party competition. The article argues that if the UK retains the FPTP electoral system, it is highly likely to return to single-party government in 2015. However, if the AV system is introduced, the article suggests that it is not inevitable that it would significantly advantage the Liberal Democrats. In addition, the article highlights the performance of the AV system, which allows voters to rank candidates in order of preference. The author examines how the AV system could influence the formation of coalitions and argues that it would help to reduce the number of wasted votes. Lees provides essential insights into the functioning of the UK's political system and its impact on party competition. It also highlights the importance of studying the coalition behaviour in multi-party politics to understand the formation and functioning of coalitions.

Martin and Whitaker focus on the ability of a legislature to keep a check on the activities of the executive branch, which is crucial for ensuring transparency in governance (Martin & Whitaker, 2019). This oversight is primarily achieved through the committee system of the legislature. The committee system is a mechanism through which legislative body members can scrutinise government policies, programs, and activities. The committee system is considered necessary for the legislature to help regulate policy compromises between parties in a multiparty government. However, other mechanisms can perform this role effectively. One such mechanism is parliamentary questions. Parliamentary questions force ministers to reveal information about their legislative and extra-legislative activities. These questions are an essential tool for coalition members to monitor their partners. By asking parliamentary questions, coalition members can gain insights into their partners' behaviour, which can help them make informed decisions. A new dataset of parliamentary questions in the House of Commons covering the 2010-15 coalition was built and analysed to test this argument. Government MPs asked more questions as the divisiveness of a policy area increased. Parliamentary questions are separate from the committee system. The committee system remains the most effective mechanism for overseeing the executive branch. However, parliamentary questions can be an essential supplement to the committee system, especially in cases where the committee system is weak. Legislatures conventionally considered weak due to the lack of strong committees may play an important role in oversight through other parliamentary devices, including helping to police the implementation of coalition agreements.

BACKGROUND

State structure and regional structure in Great Britain is governed and administered centrally. However, in devolution, powers are limited to the regions - Scotland, Wales and Northern Ireland - and the capital, London. On July 1, 1999, the regional parliaments in Edinburgh and Cardiff were elected, and on May 4, 2000, the direct election of a mayor for Greater London took place for the first time (Larsen, 2002). There has been increasing discussion about whether England should also create its own parliament as part of devolution and elect assemblies for the eight English regions - in addition to London. These already have the first approaches to regional administration with the regional development agencies financed from the central budget. Regarding the right to vote, there is an active right to vote from 18 years of age for citizens of the United Kingdom, a Commonwealth country or the Republic of Ireland - residing in one of the constituencies.

The head of state is the monarch, the head of the commonwealth of nations. From 1952 until 2022, this had been Queen Elizabeth II, under whom fifteen prime ministers had already been in power. When she died on 8 September 2022 King Charles III ascended the throne (Murphy, 2022). Formally, the king rules in Parliament: he appoints the government and opens the parliamentary session with the throne speech in the Upper House. However, this speech can be equated with the government declaration because the head of government writes it. The head of state also has supreme command over the armed forces.

Britain has a Bicameral Parliament: Lower House with 650 directly elected members and Upper House with approximately 800 members, a majority of whom are life peers appointed for life, the 26 Anglican bishops and only 92 holders of hereditary titles of nobility. In the United Kingdom, parliamentary sovereignty applies, meaning that Parliament's legislation also binds the Crown. When one talks about the "British Parliament", what is usually meant is the British House of Commons. Political power lies in the lower House, as the government majority lies in the lower House. The Members of Parliament (MPs) elect the head of government, are responsible for legislation and control the government. However, almost all legislative initiatives come from the government itself. Until the Coalition government, there was no fixed cycle for elections to the House of Commons. The legislative period could last a maximum of 5 years, but the exact time for new elections was not set by law. The government usually sets the date, with the Prime Minister proposing to the monarch to dissolve Parliament or call new elections.

Elections are based on universal, equal and direct suffrage. Members of the royal family are also eligible to vote. Each voter has one vote for a candidate in their constituency. The system of simple majority voting in constituencies of one - 650 in total - applies. The politician who wins the majority of votes in his constituency enters Parliament. All remaining votes are forfeited. A candidate can run in multiple constituencies; in case s/he wins in several constituencies, s/he has to decide within a week which constituency s/he wants to represent.

The British electoral system has the advantage of creating clear majorities, and there are usually no minority or coalition governments. However, a party's number of parliamentary seats varies from its actual vote share. To illustrate this point, this phenomenon was also evident in the Labour Party's election victory 1997: with only 43.3% of the vote, it received 63.6% of the seats in the House of Commons. The number of seats won by the Liberal Democrats appeared even more paradoxical, as they could double their seats with a lower share of voters. Occasionally, there are even grotesque distortions of the voters' will: in 1983, for example, the Liberal Alliance received only 23 seats (3.5%) with 25.4% of the vote, while Labour received 209 seats (32%) with 27.6% of the vote. Even a reversal of the majority is possible: In 1951, the Conservatives won an absolute majority of seats, even though Labour had received more votes. In the 1974 election, although the Conservatives won the majority of votes, Labour achieved an absolute majority of seats.

Great Britain is the prime example of relative majority voting. However, critical voices have been increasing. The final report of the Roy Jenkins Commission of 1998 on the reform of British electoral law stated that a new electoral system should create extensive proportionality and expand voters' options (McLean, 1999). At the same time, however, the existing government stability must be secured, and the personal connection between the MPs and their constituencies must be maintained.

The result of such a reform would be a mixed system in which, on the one hand, voting in single-member constituencies would be retained. However, on the other hand, additional large constituencies would be created that enable - a certain - proportional balance. 85% of all seats in the House of Commons should, therefore, continue to be determined by majority voting, and the rest should be distributed among the parties according to the proportional system. The regional electoral systems are also slowly weakening the traditional British majority electoral system. Proportional representation systems were used for the first time in the Welsh Assembly and Scottish Parliament elections in 1999.

As part of the Blair government's reform of the House of Lords, over five-sixths of the hereditary lords were abolished (Bogdanor, 2007). The House of Lords still has over 800 members - apart from 92 hereditary nobles who are no longer allowed to pass on their seats after the latest reform, especially so-called life peers, distinguished former politicians, artists, and scientists nominated to be appointed by the government for life. The upper House has a one-year suspensive veto over certain bills; 12 members (Law Lords) form the Supreme Court. The Speaker of the House of Lords (Lord Chancellor) also assumes the role of Minister of Justice (excluding criminal law, which is the responsibility of the Minister of the Interior). He is also one of the Law Lords and, therefore, simultaneously belongs to the executive, legislative and judicial branches.

DEVOLUTION AND REGIONAL PARLIAMENTS

The Scotland Act, passed in 1998, provides for establishing a Scottish Parliament and an Executive (Mitchell, 2000). The law followed a referendum in 1997 on the Blair government's proposals to transfer parts of central government power to Scotland. 1,775,045 Scots (74.3%) voted in favour of the government's autonomy plans, with 614,400 (25.7%) against.

In the first elections to the Scottish Parliament and the Welsh Assembly on June 6, 1999, the Scottish National Party (SNP) and the Welsh National Party Plaid Cymru came second after the Labour Party. In the elections in May 2007, the SNP, which advocates Scotland's separation from the United Kingdom, won a majority in the regional Parliament for the first time with 47 seats (Labour 46). In 2021, the SNP increased its seats to 64 (Labour 22).

The areas of responsibility delegated to the Scottish Parliament include health, education and training, local government, housing, economic development, home affairs, civil and criminal law, transport, the environment, agriculture, fisheries and forestry, sport and Art. The Scottish Parliament can amend, repeal or make new laws in these areas. A mixed procedure has been in place in regional elections in Scotland and Wales since 1999, which is similar to that used in German federal elections and is called the additional member system in Great Britain (Schakel & Jeffery, 2013). Voters have two votes. With the first, voters elect the representative from their constituency based on a simple majority (as in the lower house elections). With the second, they elect a list in a larger constituency. Considering the direct mandates won by the parties with the first votes, the list mandates are distributed proportionally among the parties campaigning based on the second votes. This allows parties that achieve a high vote percentage but have only received a few direct mandates to make up some ground.

The Scottish Parliament is made up of 129 members elected for 4-year terms. Seventy-three of them are directly elected in single-member constituencies. The remaining fifty-six seats are distributed based on the list of votes using proportional representation. The regional government of Scotland (Scottish Executive), based in Edinburgh, is headed by a First Minister. It is responsible for all authorities and public institutions whose functions and services have been transferred from London to Edinburgh and is accountable to the Scottish Parliament. The "First Minister" (Prime Minister) is the SNP politician Humza Yousaf.

The Welsh National Assembly The government's proposals for Welsh autonomy received the support of 559,419 Welsh people (50.3%) in a referendum in 1997; 552,698 (49.7%) were against it. The Welsh Assembly consists of 60 MPs, 40 elected by majority vote in single-member constituencies and the remaining 20 by regional lists using proportional representation. On July 1, 1999, the Welsh Assembly took over virtually all the functions previously held by the Minister for Wales. However, the National Assembly for Wales, based in Cardiff, has no primary legislative power; it is responsible for economic development, agriculture, education, housing, industry, and local government. Responsibility for foreign affairs, defence, taxation, economic policy, and social welfare, as well as radio and television, continues to lie with the central government in London. A President chairs the Executive Committee, whose members may not bear the title of Minister.

The multi-party talks in Belfast ended in April 1998 with the agreement that became known as the "Good Friday Agreement" (Tannam, 2001). A law was then passed in London allowing a referendum and elections for a Northern Irish Assembly. In May 1998, A referendum was held in both parts of Ireland in which the agreement received clear support. Northern Ireland voted 71.1% in favour and 28.8% against; the result in the Irish Republic was 94.3% in favour and 5.6% against. A Northern Ireland Assembly was elected in June 1998 and met for the first time the following month. In July 1998, bills for Northern Ireland's autonomy and the official administration handover were introduced in the British House of Commons, which came into force by royal assent in November of the same year.

After the Northern Ireland Assembly had been suspended for several years due to a lack of progress in completely disarming the Irish Republican Army (IRA), it came to an end after the general election of March 7, 2007, in which the Protestant Unionist Party (DUP) was the strongest with 36 of 108 seats, the Catholic Sinn Fein emerged as the second strongest force with 28 seats, a historic compromise. The leader of the DUP, Ian Paisley, became the new head of government, and the former fighter of the IRA, Martin McGuinness, his deputy. In 2011, the DUP and Sinn Fein each gained slightly at the expense of the smaller parties. The Northern Ireland Assembly is made up of 108 members. Its Executive Committee comprises a First Minister, his deputy and ten other ministers. The single transferable vote system applies in Northern Ireland - as in the Republic of Ireland. This was intended to create a fairer and more representative electoral system that considers both denominational groups equally and does not severely disadvantage the numerically smaller Catholic population group as in the majority electoral system.

Unlike Scotland, Wales and Northern Ireland, England does not have a regional parliament or a ministry responsible for its central administration (Pearce, Mawson & Ayres, 2008). The affairs of England fall under the responsibility of the central government departments in London. The British central government wants to give the regions of England higher accountability regional administrations where this is needed. The first step is to establish nine Regional Development Agencies: East, East Midlands, London, North East, North West and Merseyside, South East, South West, West Midlands, Yorkshire and the Humber. The government appoints them, and regional chambers supervise their activities. They are monitored, and local authorities appoint their members.

In most of England, local government consists of two separate administrative levels: the counties with the county councils form the upper administrative level, and the districts with the district councils form the lower administrative level (Martin, 2002). There is only one administrative level in some areas - metropolitan or metropolitan counties. The members of the 34 county councils and the 238 district councils are elected by relative majority voting. Since 2000, the mayor responsible for Greater London, including the City of London, and the 25-member assembly of the Greater London Authority have also been elected in direct general elections. The City Parliament is responsible for issues affecting the whole of London, such as transport, economic development, environmental protection, strategic planning, policing and fire services. The metropolitan county of Greater London consists of 32 boroughs - the London Boroughs – as well as the City of London, the city's historic core and centre of its financial economy. Each borough has an elected council responsible for its district's local administration.

WESTMINSTER

Regarding political systems, Westminster has been categorised as a model of parliamentary democracy. It is regarded as the oldest functioning Parliament in the past millennium. Possessing such a long history, it is no surprise that the political factions or parties have changed throughout the centuries. Two major parties characterise the post-war British political system. Perhaps the most well-known are the Conservatives due to their longevity. A major rival emerged with the Labour Party at the beginning of the 20th century. After the Second World War, the political system became identified as a two-party system as the aforementioned parties became dominant on the political scene. Electoral victories meant an alternation of governance between Labour and Conservative. No third party came close to forming an administration on its own. During the 1970s, however, due to almost parity in popular support for the two major parties, a third party, the liberal party, came into prominence, possessing the opportunity to affect the balance of power. While they did not take place in government, they did support Labour in parliamentary votes to keep them in power throughout the mid-to-late 1970s. After the electoral success and domination of Thatcher's Conservative Party for 18 years, Labour returned to power with Blair and held office until the general election of 2010. At the time, the opinion polls predicted that whilst Labour as the party of government had lost support, the opposition Conservatives were not popular enough to form a government on their own. This was the political scene as the general elections in the spring of 2010 in the United Kingdom allowed the advent of a government coalition which had not been seen since the Second World War.

Despite the uncertainties weighing on its future, agreement was reached between the two political parties concerning major reforms which should be implemented as soon as possible, especially concerning constitutional matters. Therefore, the initial effort to transform institutions started by New Labour in 1997 was intended to continue. In particular, the Conservatives and Liberal Democrats wanted to improve the functioning and organisation of Parliament, making it more efficient and democratic.

Participation in the election had reached 65.1%, almost two-thirds of registered voters, which laid the foundations for a possible notable political renewal (Lewis, 2011). The extremely serious economic situation that the country had been experiencing since the end of 2008 first required the parties to propose realistic programs for the nation's efforts. This sincerity undoubtedly returned to the political actors some of the credibility they had collectively lost during the expense report scandal. Whilst it did indeed create a major institutional crisis, the election had the merit of removing the most unscrupulous personalities from Parliament and the government. In addition, due to a notable television performance by the Liberal Democrat leader, Nick Clegg, the most critical voters preferred to vote for the centre rather than taking refuge in abstaining from the two major political parties (Drake & Higgins, 2012).

For the first time during an electoral campaign, whereas a sluggish campaign was predicted, the emergence of a third candidate for the post of prime Minister and the high probability that no majority would emerge made the 2010 election one of the most exciting of the post-war period. A Parliament without a majority resulting from the polls led to suspense lasting several days to determine whether the conservatives would manage to agree with the Liberal Democrats to form a government. The sequence finally concluded with a mutual agreement.

It is important to focus on the constitutional consequences of the Coalition in order to understand the contemporary changes in British parliamentary democracy. The government's first measures were not surprisingly certainly related to the economy, but three essential factors led to significant constitutional developments:

- The participation of liberal democrats in government since the Second World War;
- The very strict anti-terrorism legislation adopted during the Labour era, which the ruling parties had strongly contested;
- The expense report scandal, which seriously called into question the authority and sincerity of the parliamentary as an institution

The coalition government's program took these three elements into account by committing to specific political reforms mentioned in point 24 of the agreement, which stated that there was a desire to strengthen the control of the people and Parliament, to seek a solution to the West Lothian question alongside changing the manner in which petitions would be organised and the reform of the civil service (Matthews & Flinders, 2017).

Adopting a new Bill of Rights would be a means for conservatives to repatriate the protection of fundamental rights into the national fold. The Human Rights Act of 1998 clearly showed its limits according to them. Despite the novelty of certain provisions, these were less significant developments than those announced by the Labour government, which took office in 1997. A new Constitution as such would be very different from that faced by the Coalition to that of Tony Blair, who had directly launched the basis of major constitutional reforms: devolution and the transposition into national law of the Convention for the Protection of Human Rights and fundamental freedoms, as well as the reform of the House of Lords.

The Coalition faced economic difficulties and attempted to provide generally cyclical responses to recurring criticism of certain aspects of British political life. Furthermore, the latent opposition between the constitutional ideas of the conservatives and the liberal democrats could undermine any desire for major reform, as was later evidenced by the failure of the referendum of May 5, 2011, on the evolution of the voting method (Curtice, 2013). Without prejudging the results that the government would obtain on constitutional grounds, the analysis of the common program and the mode of operation of the Coalition nevertheless allowed observers to glimpse a real desire to continue with institutional adaptations. Three themes were essential on this subject: reviewing the functioning of the chambers, modifying the method of designating parliamentarians, and reconsidering relations with the territories benefiting from devolution. On this last point, the government was content to give guidelines in favour of a referendum on its deepening in Wales and Scotland by applying the Calman report (McLean, 2010). It provided, in particular, for increasing powers and establishing a commission to deal with the West Lothian question. This question referred to the argument made in 1977 by Tam Dalyell. These subjects were of certain importance, nevertheless, these modifications continued to evolve without a desire to break with the direction that had been followed since the end of the 1990s.

On the other hand, the recent crisis experienced by the House of Commons and the growing questioning about the place of the lower houses in rationalised parliamentary regimes marked by the "elective dictatorship" of the government was an important issue. This was an expression used by Lord Hailsham in 1976. It developed a study of future developments in the House of Commons concerning two essential aspects: its relations with the government and the method of appointing its members. On the first point, the scope of the envisaged reforms remained relative. As for the second, it failed following the failure of the aforementioned referendum on May 5, 2011, as the alternative vote was rejected by 67.90% of the voters. It retained a historical value since it was planned to end the First-Past-The-Post (FPTP) system.

The coalition program highlighted two reforms relating to the relationship between the House of Commons and the Executive. The most important concerns were questioning the royal prerogative of dissolving the lower House. The date of the next renewal of the members of the House of Commons could only occur after the end of five years of the legislature. Adopting the Fixed-term Parliaments Act 2011 appeared to be a real constitutional revolution even when compared to what prevailed for other parliamentary systems, whose constitutions already regulated this question. The Coalition also proposed following the Wright Commission's recommendations to strengthen the House of Commons functions vis-à-vis the Executive (Russell, 2011). Again, this approach revealed a real desire to increase the influence of parliamentarians. However, it only continued by deepening what Labour had previously achieved with the Constitutional Reform and Governance Act of 2010.

Adoption of the Fixed-Term Parliaments Act 2011

Considered by some politicians as being unconstitutional or even undemocratic, establishing a fixed date for the next election of members of Parliament was unprecedented in the history of the United Kingdom. Fixed-term Parliaments Bills were regarded as proof of the goodwill of the two parties in power to govern together for the long term in a country that doubted the Coalition's solidity. Disraeli's words, according to which "England does not like coalitions", were repeated often (Lees, 2011). This view is only partially accurate when one pays closer attention to history. Before the 1830s – marked by the expansion of the right to vote, the establishment of the first political groups in the modern sense of the term, and the formalisation of the function of Prime Minister – the idea of a partisan majority dominating the House of Commons was unknown. The designations of Tories and Whigs did not prejudge the positions of each of the Members of Parliament regarding any particular political project. One must recall that such a tradition was maintained from 1885 to 1945, whereby minority or coalition governments ruled the country for half a century.

In reality, the distrust towards the Coalition resulting from the elections of May 2010 could be explained by inconclusive experiences at the beginning of the 20th century and the non-existence of the phenomenon after the Second World War. The last coalition governments took place after the 1910 elections – on February 10 and December 10 – due to a crisis between the Cabinet and the House of Lords, which refused to approve Lloyd George's progressive budget. The beginning of the 20th century was also marked by the rise of Irish autonomist demands, whose representatives at Westminster became essential to constitute a majority. In 1924, the Liberal-backed Labour minority government lasted only a few months.

In explaining the content of the Fixed-term Parliaments Bill, it was tabled on July 22, 2010, by Deputy Prime Minister Nick Clegg and obtained the Royal Assent on September 15, 2011 (Norton, 2020). The reform was far from unanimous, particularly from a legal point of view. Under the text, the next election of members of Parliament was to take place on May 7, 2015. The following ballots would be held every first Thursday of May, five years after the previous election. There were exceptions to this. In the first case, the House of Commons could adopt a motion in favour of holding an early election; the motion adopted by an official vote and by parliamentarians greater than or equal to two-thirds of the seats in the House, including vacant seats, would lead to an early election. As a second option, the House of Commons could adopt a motion of no confidence in the government on a specific day and for 14 days after the above-mentioned day; if the House of Commons did not pass a motion expressing confidence in any government, then a general election would be necessary. The power of dissolution could not be used outside of these two specified circumstances.

Seemingly simple, the system had its critics. When reading the coalition government's program, an initial controversy led to the review of the project. Initially, it was planned that a qualified majority of 55% of MPs would be necessary for a dissolution to be pronounced. There were concerns regarding the unsatisfactory nature of the measure given the composition of the Chamber resulting from the elections. Although the Coalition had 57% of the seats, the Conservatives, who largely dominated the Cabinet, could easily be put in the minority since they only benefitted from 48% of the seats. Moreover, the defection of forty-two Liberal Democrats would be enough to bring down the coalition government through the adoption of a motion of censure.

On the other hand, the possibility of dissolving the Chamber would be much more difficult given the qualified majority required. To achieve this, the almost unanimous consent of both parties in power would be required. Consequently, if the censure motion was easily possible, the same was not true for dissolution. This mechanism did not benefit the opposition or the government due to a 55% majority that was almost impossible to achieve for one and easily lost. It would also have thwarted a classic principle of the parliamentary system: the adoption of a motion of censure must be followed by an unconditional dissolution to resolve the conflict between the legislative and executive powers.

The solution finally presented to parliamentarians was more measured. Firstly, dissolution may result from the inability to form a new government within 14 days of the adoption of a motion of censure. The link between Parliament's lack of confidence in any government and the power of dissolution was thus partially re-established. Secondly, the qualified majority necessary for adopting a motion in favour of early elections was raised to ensure that the choice to dissolve the Chamber is independent of the majority's will in place. With a two-thirds threshold, the majority and opposition were equal. Despite these adjustments, the law had at least three limitations.

The first concerned the principle of parliamentary sovereignty. A key rule of the British Constitution is one whereby one Parliament of a legislature cannot bind the next, which can revise texts that have been previously adopted. The second criticism related to the Prime Minister requesting a motion of censure in order to achieve a dissolution, according to the conditions provided for in the law. If the latter makes exercising the right of dissolution more difficult, it in no way protects the House of Commons from practices similar to those found, for example, in Germany. The Prime Minister can ensure that the majority supporting him adopts a motion of no confidence at his request and refuses to support a new government. Misuse of the procedure is not excluded. This aspect led Parliament to reject the initial idea of having the dissolution decision validated by a certificate from the Lord Speaker.

Ultimately, after listing the criticisms relating to legislation governing the use of the power of dissolution, the reluctance resulted more from attachment to constitutional conventions than insurmountable legal obstacles. Several laudable objectives were being pursued. The first of these was to prevent the sovereign from dissolving the Commons according to the goodwill of the Prime Minister. This prerogative was undoubtedly an advantage for the party in power. S/he can choose the most opportune – or least unfavourable – moment to enter the campaign, thus reaping the benefits of a surging popularity rating or considering the beginnings of an electoral debacle. Although this strategic process has not always been successful, it has often benefited the Prime Minister in place, attenuating the chances of victory for an opposition taken by surprise. Establishing a fixed term in the legislature restored a balance between the ruling party and the opposition. Another decisive argument was put forward. The Fixed-term Parliaments Act 2011 ended a possible blockage of the monarch. It aligned the dissolution regime with most parliamentary democracies—finally, the new law clarified the definition and procedures of distrust in the government. The control mission of the House of Commons would then be enhanced, which seemed essential in a broader context of strengthening its functions.

Strengthening House of Commons Functions

Since 2009, Parliament had been the subject of two major scandals leading to resignations that had not been seen since the 17th century. Both houses were affected, one of which concerned the House of Lords (the Cash for Amendments scandal) and the other the Commons (the Expenses scandal); it was undeniable that they encouraged and confirmed the suspicion of the British about their Parliament upholding common values and shared ethics (Hine & Peele, 2016).

The Wright report led to a change in the functioning of the committees and an overhaul of working methods (Russell, 2011). On the first point, the composition of the commissions became more transparent and legitimate. The Chamber had a right of review over the choice of presidencies, which was largely controlled by the government previously. A new process for appointing committee members was also introduced, calling into question an essential prerogative of party leaders and the whips. To this end, a secret ballot vote within the parliamentary groups was planned according to a public procedure verified by the House administration. To these measures must be added the reduction in the number and size of committees to a maximum of eleven parliamentarians, the representation of the smallest parties within them being ensured. The second point is that the intervention of the reform of the House of Commons Select Committee made it possible to grant the Commons greater control over parliamentary debates. In contrast, the government-controlled the agenda without any real sharing.

These various developments gave rise to mixed feelings. The possibility offered to citizens to participate more actively in parliamentary debates – while the right to petition was not new in the United Kingdom – was quite demagogic. In reality, it must be admitted that reforms aimed at extending the influence of parliamentarians in the legislative process were, in part, in vain since the model in question remained rationalised parliamentarism linked to the idea of a majority. However, this observation did not conceal the evolution towards enhancing Parliament's control mission. Four elements can be identified in this regard.

Already, the institutionalisation of the opposition benefited, as such, from status and advantages, which is considered a government in waiting and is favourable to the control function. More recently, the notion of opposition has been intended to integrate, in certain circumstances, minority parties, even those that do not belong to the official opposition. The opening of and access to committees for minority political groups illustrated this.

Secondly, strengthening Parliament's oversight role increasingly involved a system of impartial and effective committees. Inspired by the American example, these parliamentary bodies, embryonic at the beginning of the 20th century, have been essential since the end of the 1970s despite governments objecting to the constant increase in their powers. In recent years, emphasis has been placed on the evaluation function accompanied by a substantial information duty on the part of the government. Every bill is subject to a regulatory impact assessment, which draws up its adoption's advantages, disadvantages and possible risks and at the same time, each commission dedicated to an area of action of the Executive - Departmental select committee - evaluates the implementation of the text three to five years after it enters into force (Jacobs, 2005).

Thirdly, beyond the sole case of the House of Commons, the function of monitoring the legislative work of the government by Parliament has also been better assumed by the House of Lords in recent years. With legitimate expertise, it has, on several occasions, defeated government projects, particularly on human rights issues. The high quality of the debates there analyses the Upper House, which is essential to upgrading the Westminster Parliament. On this subject, the ruling Coalition had to ensure, despite the renewed desire for a partial or total election of its members, to maintain the impartiality and tranquillity of the discussions. Finally, the Fixed-term Parliaments Act 2011 was expected to re-establish a balance between the House of Commons and the government regarding the general election date.

Given these elements, the United Kingdom undoubtedly made progress in putting Parliament back at the heart of the conduct of national affairs. This approach was part of the larger project of a better balance between powers. In addition to upgrading the chambers' role, the externalised control of legislation, whose main initiator is the Executive, was strengthened by applying the HRA. On this issue, the United Kingdom asserted itself as a relevant example of the new model of constitutionalism specific to the main Commonwealth States. This model was located between political regimes characterised either by the sovereignty of Parliament or by constitutional supremacy guaranteed by one or more judicial organs.

Reforming MP's Method of Election

One of the sine qua non conditions set by the Liberal Democrats for their participation in the coalition government with the Conservatives was to obtain the latter's promise to hold a referendum relating to the method of election of MPs. The Tories' agreement was far from certain, and it is possible to argue that in its absence, the Monarch would have had to dissolve Parliament to provoke new elections. Indeed, the conservatives had always excluded the possibility of modifying a voting method – first-past-the-post – which had proven itself in simplicity and governmental stability. Conversely, the Liberal Democrats supported electoral reform, allowing them to be better represented in the House of Commons. For its part, Labour had rallied around this idea during the 1990s.

Despite the clashes and contradictions between the parties, the government program adjusted the voting method applicable to MPs at the heart of modernising political life, assigning the Deputy Prime Minister the responsibility of carrying it out. The majority of the British people initially supported it according to opinion polls as a year earlier, 69% of the population favoured such a move. The desire for reform was based on relevant reasons, justifying the disappearance of a unique electoral tradition in Europe. However, the May 5, 2011 referendum failed for many reasons, including the strong mobilisation of Conservative MPs supported by David Cameron.

Although belonging to the same Coalition, the growing unpopularity of Nick Clegg was a negative factor (Seawright, 2013). The other, more technical factor related to the chosen voting method – the alternative vote, Alternative Vote or AV – was quite complex. The failure of the popular consultation revealed a real curse attached to the Alternative Vote. The method of election of members of the lower House of Parliament at Westminster remains a characteristic feature of the political system of the United Kingdom. An essential example for any lecturer of constitutional law who wishes to explain as educationally as possible the contrast in results between majority and proportional voting systems, first-past-the-post (FPTP) is also the one most rooted in the tradition of a European state. For a large part of the British political class, this historical value almost alone justifies the relevance of its maintenance. The conservative approach considers that, as long as a system works, there is no reason to question it. The crisis of legitimacy that the House of Commons was going through undermined this position. Reconciliation between citizens and their elected representatives and better election participation requires greater electoral justice, which the first-past-the-post voting system does not allow.

The current circumstances could not obscure three aspects which attenuated the British attachment to the FPTP and justified the evolution towards a fairer voting method. Firstly, the UK had only sometimes seen widespread application of FPTP. It should be remembered that first-past-the-post voting did not become a majority until 1884 (Dunbabin, 1988). Next, controversies surrounding the FPTP were recurrent. If the first-past-the-post voting system has established itself through its simplicity and the centuries-old polarisation of political life around the Whigs and the Tories, a part of the political class had always questioned it.

The first was the expression of a minority, strong and constant opposition to the system. In the 1910s, Unionists in the south of Ireland declared themselves in favour of a more proportional voting system which would prevent the creation of a massively Catholic Northern Irish Parliament. The British also saw it as a means of reconciling the various parties in the Irish independence conflict. The Home Rule Bill of 1912, adopted but not applied, provided for this. In the same spirit of defence of particular interests, certain free-trade conservatives wished to preserve their seats against the protectionists. The working class, while growing, was growing very late in obtaining satisfactory representation in the Chamber.

Several laws gradually emerged after the Great Reform Act of 1832, often dependent on electoral agreements with the Liberals. Some Labour workers saw the need for a fairer voting system. These multiple demands justified that in 1909-1910, a Royal Commission considered the possibility of implementing the alternative vote in the United Kingdom. The Representation of the People Bill of 1917-1918 also expressly provided for using this voting method for the first time in a bill. It was reintroduced in the Representation of the People Bill, discussed in 1931.

The second movement favouring greater proportionality developed after the Second World War among Labour, then the Liberals who became Liberal Democrats in 1988. Both parties' feelings of electoral injustice justified less categorical opposition to the FPTP. From 1951, more and more voices were heard in the ranks of Labour to ensure that the perverse effects of first-past-the-post voting were limited. Although benefiting from the most votes in the October 23, 1951 election, Labour obtained fewer seats than the Conservatives, with 48.8% of the votes cast for Labour. However, it was not until the 1970s and 1980s that the protest found greater resonance. Two factors contribute to this: on the one hand, electoral injustice coupled with political uncertainty resulting from the elections of 1974; on the other hand, the questioning of the hegemony of the two parties in power. If political stability returned in 1979 with the large victory of the conservatives, the elections of February 1974 allowed the liberals to acquire a real place in the political game by mobilising more than two million voters in their favour. This electoral breakthrough made them essential for the two larger parties. This position grew through electoral alliances and the merger in 1988 with the Social Democratic Party despite their status as the third political force in the country (Jones & Jones, 2011).

Since 1983, with the electoral alliance and then the partisan merger, the Liberal Democrats have remained in the minority in Parliament and were the main victims of the FPTP. Their electoral manifestos continued to support proportional representation. They were partially joined by Labour, who sought to destabilise the conservative majority in the Commons. In the 1987 elections, the Conservatives had 376 seats. Once returned to power in 1997, Labour kept everything about the voting system the same, despite electoral promises and the Jenkins report it had requested. This should undoubtedly be seen as a new rallying to the FPTP, which made it possible to lead the country with a solid majority in the House of Commons despite the low real representation of Labour.

Since 1997, due to ever-increasing participation and the number of votes it gained, it justified the Lib Dem contestation of the FPTP. It was due to the success of mixed and proportional ballots in the United Kingdom. Despite the reform projects favouring alternative voting, which has punctuated British political history, this voting method has remained the same in a major election. The incomprehension also resulted from the complex modalities of the alternative vote. These criticisms are justified, but it is appropriate to put them into perspective in three respects. There is no perfect voting method that would guarantee the constitution of clear parliamentary majorities, a guarantee of political stability, and would ensure the representation of all currents of opinion in the electorate. In addition, certain criticisms levelled against the AV may constitute advantages. The possibility that a candidate who did not obtain the greatest number of preferential votes in the first count could be elected through vote carryover is not necessarily shocking. This result favours the consensus candidate, allowing for a more peaceful and less polarised political life.

There is, moreover, a contradiction in accusing the alternative vote of leading to difficulties for the constitution of a majority and of being even more unfair than the FPTP. It is important to remember that AV is a majority voting method whose effects are attenuated by preferential voting. It is not fundamentally different from the FPTP, which is also not a guarantee against parliaments without a majority. Finally,

AV retains significant advantages. The main argument lies in the resulting stronger bond between voters and candidates, promoting participation. Rather than being a default or tactical method of designation to which the FPTP often leads, the AV requires contenders to adopt positive behaviour to benefit from first place on the ballot. Candidates can only be elected if they have been the subject of an explicit choice by the voter in his favour, which comes from the classification. This important aspect explains why the AV limits the possibility of extremist parties obtaining seats. If the AV appeared to be a good compromise, the failure of the May 5, 2011, referendum can be explained by the complexity and a context unfavourable to its supporters. The Liberal Democrats had bet a lot on this deadline, even if it meant renouncing electoral commitments in terms of university fees.

Comparative European Coalitions

Coalition governments function differently in Europe compared to the UK. The life cycle of a coalition typically starts with elections, but it can also end as a consequence. This is where the first regional differences become noticeable. In Central and Eastern Europe, the end of a coalition does not imply the end of the government. While new elections often follow a coalition break in Western Europe, Eastern European government members delay elections. This is one outcome of the endeavour.

Voters in Eastern Europe tend to penalize governments more frequently than in Western Europe, so they avoid new elections and try to stay in power for as long as possible, if necessary, with a swap of coalition partners or through a minority government. In these countries, it is common for a new government to be established or a party to leave within the same legislative period. The unstable party system and the high percentage of swing voters frequently bring new parties into Parliament, but they quickly vanish again. This instability of the party system leads to more diverse coalitions but also results in an uneven distribution of power, often favouring those in power.

Romania

Romania is a country where the President holds significant powers according to the country's constitution (Gherghina, Tap & Farcas, 2023). When the President expresses support for a political cabinet, Romanian MPs frequently switch or give up their party membership to back the government. This means that the cabinet is not empowered by the voters but by the wishes of the current ruler. Post communist states must go through a long learning phase. They first must come to terms with their political past and then establish new structures enabling coalitions. Concluding coalition agreements is an initial step, but these contracts must be monitored and executed. Eastern European states developed structures for coalition formation and controlled relatively quickly, and they were faster than their Western neighbours after World War II. Eastern European states had the advantage of learning through implementation and also had the West as a role model, which had to invent these mechanisms first. However, these mechanisms still need to be more efficient. Despite coalition compromise being the dominant pattern of governance in Western Europe, Eastern Europe is different in two ways: on the one hand, there is a greater tendency towards fragmented governance, where each party has a free hand for "its" ministries, and on the other hand, there is too strong leadership by the Prime Minister. So far, research on coalitions has mainly focused on the beginning and end of coalitions rather than the entire life cycle – the beginning, the end, and everything in between.

Germany

In Germany, forming a coalition between deputies from two or three parties is almost always necessary to achieve a majority to elect a government and the Chancellor. The party that comes first, or another party having a significant score and capable of uniting a majority around it, can begin several preliminary discussions to evaluate the possibilities of an alliance with the other parties before engaging in more detailed discussions with one or two of these parties to form the coalition. This process can last several weeks or even months. The parties define their red lines, points of disagreement, and the common projects they intend to carry out. Traditionally, this results in a "coalition contract," which becomes the basis of government action (Gross & Krauss, 2021).

The logic of coalition, based on the construction of a stable majority with a clear mandate and a roadmap constructed by the coalition partners, gives real political weight to the two or three coalition parties – provided, of course, especially for small parties, that the negotiation was well conducted. The life of the coalition is organized by the regular holding of an informal commission called the "coalition commission", composed of representatives of the member parties of the coalition, the Chancellor, and the vice-chancellor, which decides, in particular, on the laws under discussion and on possible political disagreements.

France

The French Fifth Republic is particularly flexible and in no way prohibits a coalition agreement during the presidential mandate between several parties to have a majority with a clear and written contract on the reforms to be made, and this, without dissolution or even a change of power. The prime minister or government reshuffles necessarily, a potentially unique situation in Europe. A situation permitted by the semi-presidential or mixed parliamentary regime multiplies the options. Establishing a coalition leads to a form of "chosen cohabitation", which allows reforms to be pursued (Paxton, & Peace, 2021). The use of coalitions works very well among different European neighbours.

Germany is a federal state and a parliamentary democracy organized under the principle of the separation of powers. Thus, the government is responsible to Parliament. On the other hand, the latter can only overthrow the government by replacing it through a constructive motion of censure. Each new Chancellor poses a question of confidence by calling new legislative elections. Note that early legislative elections can only be caused by a lost vote of confidence. Finally, the Federal President appoints the list responsible for proposing a coalition, which must agree on a "coalition contract" resulting from negotiations between the parties who want to form it. When the government proposes a text, it goes through three readings in the Bundestag. Both houses can amend the bill. It goes through a conciliation committee of the two chambers. The final reading takes place in the Bundestag. In the end, the text must be signed by the Federal President, who very rarely uses his veto.

Italy

Italy is a decentralized parliamentary democracy with a bicameral Parliament (a Chamber of Deputies and a Senate) where parliamentarians elect the President in a joint session and for a mandate of 7 years. In consultation with the political parties, the latter appoints the President of the Council of Ministers, who takes the head of the government. If the "incarito" (person responsible for forming the government) fails to form a government, s/he must return his mandate to the President of the Republic (Conti, Pedrazzani & Russo, 2022). If s/he has her/his government, the President of the Council must obtain a vote of confidence in Parliament, as well as the approval of the President of the Republic. The latter also can veto laws as a last resort if he deems them unconstitutional. In Italy, political parties are accustomed to announcing the coalition of their choice before the election. Voters, therefore, have the possibility of "choosing" the coalition. This government emanates from the composition of the majority within the Chamber of Deputies, which currently has 238 deputies. However, the Italian ballot is particular: one third majority voting, two-thirds proportional.

Historically, Italy was known for a relatively unstable parliamentarism, reminiscent of the Fourth Republic in France. This instability resulted from perfect bicameralism between the Senate and the Chamber of Deputies and too many parliamentarians. In 2015, a law was passed to guarantee 55% of seats to the leading party. Then, a 2020 referendum introduced the current system, favouring the search for majorities (Chessa & Fragnelli, 2022). The Italian system is affected by two trends: the splitting of votes - bipartisanship has disappeared for a very long time - and the search for stability in recent years, which can lead to the formation of improbable coalitions or the polarization of life.

Poland

The Polish political system is similar to France's. In fact, the President of the Republic enjoys a more important role than in many European countries and is elected by direct universal suffrage for five years. At the same time, the Prime Minister leads the country's policy and represents Poland abroad. In the lower house (the Diet), the multi-member proportional vote determines the composition, as in Italy, which has prefabricated coalitions that present themselves before the elections. Like Parliament and the government, the President of the Republic has the legislative initiative (Markowski, 2020). He can veto a bill, which can be cancelled if three quarters of the parliamentarians censure it. The President of the Republic can also request an opinion from the Constitutional Court on a bill. However, this Supreme Court has been very dependent on the executive for several years.

The President also has the power of the head of the armies and can decide on general mobilization in times of war. In Spain, Italy, and Germany, the head of state (King or President) has the role of guarantor of the institutions; in Poland, he has a role similar to that of a Gaullist president. Therefore, Poland is a parliamentary regime that tends to become presidentialized under the leadership of the Law and Justice Party, which almost succeeds in governing alone by obtaining almost half of the votes. There is certainly a coalition system, but in reality, it is a coalition with a central party and small parties that join together.

Sweden

Sweden is a parliamentary monarchy, one of the oldest in the world, alongside the United Kingdom. The Swedish Parliament is made up of only one chamber, the Riksdag. Deputies are elected by single-member proportional representation. Only parties having gathered at least 4% of the votes cast across the entire territory are eligible for the distribution of seats. Failing this, a party which would have obtained at least 12% of the votes in a constituency may have elected representatives but cannot benefit from compensatory mandates. MPs can propose a motion of censure, which requires an absolute majority. A single minister or the government as a whole may be affected by this motion. The vote on a motion of censure has no effect if the censored government organizes early elections within one week. In the event of the government's fall, the President of the Royal Diet (i.e. the President of Parliament) must propose a new Prime Minister after consultation with the groups' presidents. This proposal is then put to a vote in the Riksdag: it is adopted if less than half of the deputies vote against it. In Sweden, too, the government is responsible to Parliament. The King has only an honorary role. His political role is limited to maintaining a privileged relationship with the head of government and meeting ministers four times a year. Unlike other monarchies, the King cannot, even constitutionally, veto a law (Persson & Persson, 2020). When the Riksdag adopts a law, two ministers must sign it.

The European examples above demonstrate that using government coalitions is common among Britain's European neighbours, who all have (whether federal or unitary states) strict parliamentary regimes or even with a presidential tendency for Poland. Strict parliamentary logic, therefore, requires that the government be responsible to Parliament and necessarily implies the organization of legislative elections before any coalition pact. France, from this point of view, is situated in another logic since its semi-presidential regime and its practice of rationalized parliamentarism places the government and its head, the Prime Minister, under the double dependence of the President of the Republic (who appoints the second and dismisses him upon presentation of the resignation of his government) and of Parliament before which he engages his responsibility. In this sense, the establishment of a coalition and a government pact may not have to give rise to a resignation of the current government but to a simple reshuffle, or even no reshuffle, if one takes the Swedish example where the Sweden Democrats support government action without taking part in it (Johansson & Vigsø, 2021). The French constitution is, therefore, particularly flexible in this regard, depending on the legislative balance of power. Until now, presidential readings of the regime or cohabitation readings until the establishment of the five-year term have emerged, depending on the congruence or mismatch between the presidential and legislative majority, but viewing it as parliamentarian is just as legitimate in the event of a breakdown of political forces. This culture has been long lost since the end of the Fourth Republic 65 years ago, and France needs to reappropriate it. As can be seen from the continental European examples of coalition forming and governance the British experience is quite different.

CONCLUSION

During the election campaign, all three parties offered their perspectives and proposals to counter the nation's challenges making extensive use of political rhetoric (Yigit, 2022). Equally, they harshly criticised their opponents' views and suggestions. Facing a hung parliament, compromises had to be made with the Liberal Democrats holding the balance of power. They negotiated with the major parties and opted into government with the Conservatives had, hoping to achieve their primary, most cherished goals. By the time the five-year coalition had run its course, and a new general election was called for, the conservatives had been able to outmanoeuvre and manipulate their coalition partners. The Labour Party had changed its leadership and campaigned vehemently against the coalition (Yiğit, 2015). The Coalition had acquiesced to five-year fixed parliaments but ensured the FPTP electoral system remained to ensure their partners would remain perennially embedded as the third party without hope of forming a single-party administration. If the Lib Dems had allied with the social-democratic Labour Party, they would have had a greater chance of implementing their core aims, given the closeness of their political values and ideologies. The Coalition was a hard lesson for the Liberal Democrats but an even harder endurance for the electorate. They suffered from socially insensitive and exclusionary policies and economic mismanagement, with the national debt increasing. Despite supporting the Lib Dem aim of establishing five-year fixed parliaments, the Conservatives made a sharp U-turn after winning the 2019 election, reverting to giving the Prime Minister the right to call an election whenever s/he wanted. This demonstrated their fair-weather relationship with the Lib Dems based purely on party interest to allow them to gain power. There had been no genuine commitment to political or constitutional change, paying only lip service to enter government as the coalition's senior partner and immediately reneging on the constitutional change they had supported in Parliament.

Since the 2010 election, there have been three elections in 2015, 2017 and 2019, all of which have been won by the Conservatives; hence, there was no need for a coalition. The Con-Dem Coalition helped the senior partner and destroyed the credibility of the junior partner. That is a lesson the Liberal Democrats may not quickly forget: entering a coalition with a right-wing party does not ensure concrete permanent constitutional reforms nor increase popularity and electability. It has led to them becoming an obscure and less than influential third voice in British national politics. The political system entering into 2024 remains as it always was since the Second World War - apart from the blip in 2010 – a two-party race between Labour and the Conservatives.

REFERENCES

Bogdanor, V. (2007). The Historic Legacy of Tony Blair. *Current History (New York, N.Y.)*, *106*(698), 99–105. doi:10.1525/curh.2007.106.698.99

Chessa, M., & Fragnelli, V. (2022). The Italian referendum: What can we get from game theory? *Annals of Operations Research*, *318*(2), 849–869. doi:10.1007/s10479-022-04927-6

Conti, N., Pedrazzani, A., & Russo, F. (2022). Policy polarisation in Italy: the short and conflictual life of the 'Government of Change'(2018–2019). In *The Politics of Polarisation* (pp. 64–97). Routledge. doi:10.4324/9781003317012-5

Curtice, J. (2013). Politicians, voters and democracy: The 2011 UK referendum on the Alternative Vote. *Electoral Studies*, *32*(2), 215–223. doi:10.1016/j.electstud.2012.10.010

Daddow, O. (2015). Constructing a 'great'role for Britain in an age of austerity: Interpreting coalition foreign policy, 2010–2015. *International Relations*, *29*(3), 303–318. doi:10.1177/0047117815600931

Drake, P., & Higgins, M. (2012). Lights, camera, election: Celebrity, performance and the 2010 UK general election leadership debates. *British Journal of Politics and International Relations*, *14*(3), 375–391. doi:10.1111/j.1467-856X.2011.00504.x

Dunbabin, J. P. D. (1988). Electoral reforms and their outcome in the United Kingdom, 1865–1900. *Later Victorian Britain, 1867–1900*, 93-125.

Dunleavy, P. (2012). *The British general election of 2010 and the advent of coalition government*. Academic Press.

Gherghina, S., Tap, P., & Farcas, R. (2023). Informal Power and Short-Term Consequences: Country Presidents and Political Parties in Romania. *Political Studies Review*. doi:10.1177/14789299231187220

Gross, M., & Krauss, S. (2021). Topic coverage of coalition agreements in multi-level settings: The case of Germany. *German Politics*, *30*(2), 227–248. doi:10.1080/09644008.2019.1658077

Hine, D., & Peele, G. (2016). The expenses crisis: Statutory regulation and its difficulties. In *The regulation of standards in British public life* (pp. 104–124). Manchester University Press. doi:10.7228/manchester/9780719097133.003.0005

Jacobs, C. (2005). *Improving the quality of regulatory impact assessments in the UK* (No. 1649-2016-135960). Academic Press.

Johansson, B., & Vigsø, O. (2021). Sweden: Lone hero or stubborn outlier? In Political Communication and COVID-19 (pp. 155-164). Routledge.

Johnson, P., Chandler, D., Seldon, A., & Finn, M. (2010). The coalition and the economy. *The coalition effect*, 159-193.

Jones, T., & Jones, T. (2011). Liberals, Owen and the Social Market Economy: 1983–1988. *The Revival of British Liberalism: From Grimond to Clegg*, 118-142.

Larsen, H. O. (2002). Directly elected mayors—democratic renewal or constitutional confusion? In *Local Government at the Millenium* (pp. 111–133). VS Verlag für Sozialwissenschaften. doi:10.1007/978-3-663-10679-1_6

Lees, C. (2011). How unusual is the United Kingdom Coalition (and what are the chances of it happening again)? *The Political Quarterly*, *82*(2), 279–292. doi:10.1111/j.1467-923X.2011.02192.x

Lewis, M. (2011). An Analysis of the Relationship Between Political Blog Reading, Online Political Activity, and Voting During the 2008 Presidential Campaign. *The International Journal of Interdisciplinary Social Sciences: Annual Review*, *6*(3), 11–28. doi:10.18848/1833-1882/CGP/v06i03/52046

Markowski, R. (2020). Plurality support for democratic decay: The 2019 Polish parliamentary election. *West European Politics*, *43*(7), 1513–1525. doi:10.1080/01402382.2020.1720171

Martin, S. (2002). The modernization of UK local Government: Markets, managers, monitors and mixed fortunes. *Public Management Review*, *4*(3), 291–307. doi:10.1080/14616670210151595

Martin, S., & Whitaker, R. (2019). Beyond committees: Parliamentary oversight of coalition government in Britain. *West European Politics*, *42*(7), 1464–1486. doi:10.1080/01402382.2019.1593595

Matthews, F., & Flinders, M. (2017). Patterns of democracy: Coalition governance and majoritarian modification in the United Kingdom, 2010–2015. *British Politics*, *12*(2), 157–182. doi:10.1057/s41293-016-0041-5

McLean, I. (1999). The Jenkins Commission and the implications of electoral reform for the UK constitution. *Government and Opposition*, *34*(2), 143–160. doi:10.1111/j.1477-7053.1999.tb00475.x

McLean, I. (2010). Calman and Holtham: the public finance of devolution. In PSA: Territorial Politics Conference, Oxford, UK.

Mitchell, J. (2000). New parliament, new politics in Scotland. *Parliamentary Affairs*, *53*(3), 605–621. doi:10.1093/pa/53.3.605

Murphy, P. (2022). Queen Elizabeth II and the Commonwealth: Time to Open the Archives. *The Journal of Imperial and Commonwealth History*, *50*(5), 821–828. doi:10.1080/03086534.2022.2136299

Norton, P. (2020). Fixed-term Parliaments: Fixed or not so fixed? In Governing Britain (pp. 115-127). Manchester University Press.

Paxton, F., & Peace, T. (2021). Window dressing? The mainstreaming strategy of the rassemblement national in power in French local government. *Government and Opposition*, *56*(3), 545–562. doi:10.1017/gov.2020.11

Pearce, G., Mawson, J., & Ayres, S. (2008). Regional governance in England: A changing role for the Government's regional offices? *Public Administration*, *86*(2), 443–463. doi:10.1111/j.1467-9299.2007.00699.x

Quinn, T., Bara, J., & Bartle, J. (2013). The UK coalition agreement of 2010: Who won? In *The UK General Election of 2010* (pp. 175–192). Routledge.

Russell, M. (2011). 'Never Allow a Crisis to Go to Waste': The Wright Committee Reforms to Strengthen the House of Commons. *Parliamentary Affairs*, *64*(4), 612–633. doi:10.1093/pa/gsr026

Schakel, A. H., & Jeffery, C. (2013). Are regional elections really 'second-order' elections? *Regional Studies*, *47*(3), 323–341. doi:10.1080/00343404.2012.690069

Seawright, D. (2013). 'Yes, the census': The 2011 UK Referendum campaign on the Alternative Vote. *British Politics*, *8*(4), 457–475. doi:10.1057/bp.2013.23

Tannam, E. (2001). Explaining the Good Friday agreement: A learning process. *Government and Opposition*, *36*(4), 493–518. doi:10.1111/1477-7053.00078

Wert, J. J. (2010). With a little help from a friend: Habeas Corpus and the Magna Carta after Runnymede. *PS, Political Science & Politics*, *43*(3), 475–478. doi:10.1017/S1049096510000600

Yiğit, S. (2015). 2010 Labour Party Leadership Election. Alternatives. *Turkish Journal of International Relations*, *14*(3), 26–35. doi:10.21599/atjir.20754

Yigit, S. (2022). Cicero and the Art of Rhetoric. In *Media Literacy Forum, Social Sciences in the Age of Digital Transformation Proceedings Book*. Iksad Publications.

ADDITIONAL READING

Garnett, M., Dorey, P., & Lynch, P. (2020). *Exploring British Politics*. Routledge. doi:10.4324/9780429030864

Hayton, R. (2014). Conservative Party statecraft and the politics of coalition. *Parliamentary Affairs*, *67*(1), 6–24. doi:10.1093/pa/gst019

Lee, S. (2011). 'We are all in this together': the coalition agenda for British modernization. In *The Cameron—Clegg Government: Coalition Politics in an Age of Austerity* (pp. 3–23). Palgrave Macmillan UK. doi:10.1057/9780230305014_1

Lee, S., & Beech, M. (Eds.). (2011). *The Cameron-Clegg Government: Coalition Politics in an Age of Austerity*. Springer. doi:10.1057/9780230305014

Whitaker, R., & Martin, S. (2022). Divide to conquer? Strategic parliamentary opposition and coalition government. *Party Politics*, *28*(6), 999–1011. doi:10.1177/13540688211042859

Wright, T. (2020). *British politics: a very short introduction*. Oxford University Press. doi:10.1093/actrade/9780198827320.001.0001

KEY TERMS AND DEFINITIONS

Cabinet: A small group of the most important people in government, who advise the prime minister and make important decisions.

Campaign: To try to achieve the election of someone to a political office, by taking part in a number of planned activities.

Coalition: The joining together of different political parties or groups for a particular purpose, usually for a limited time, or a government that is formed in this way.

Compromise: A situation in which the people or groups involved in an argument reduce their demands in order to reach an agreement.

General Election: An election usually held at regular intervals in which candidates are elected in all or most constituencies of a nation or state.

Government: A small group of persons holding simultaneously the principal political executive offices of a nation or other political unit and being responsible for the direction and supervision of public affairs.

Leadership: Guiding and influencing others toward a common vision or goal which entails inspiring and motivating one's team, encouraging collaboration, and making sound decisions.

Parliament: In the UK, the highest legislature, consisting of the Sovereign, the House of Lords, and the House of Commons; the members of this legislature sit for a particular period, especially between one dissolution and the next.

Politics: The art of the exercise of power; the combination of individuals or parties or groups making decisions that affect others and institutions (i.e., government, legal system, military, police) that governs based on those decisions.

Chapter 5
Governments of National Unity (GNU) as the Democratic Governance Model in Selected Africa Countries

Ndwakhulu Stephen Tshishonga
University of KwaZulu-Natal, South Africa

ABSTRACT

This chapter interrogates the notion of government of national unity (GNU) as an emerging model for democratic and coalition governance in Africa. Considering Africa's dismal record of governance, coupled with socio-economic developmental challenges, coalition governance is imperative. African countries such as Kenya, Lesotho, Malawi, South Africa, and Zimbabwe were selected as case studies to demonstrate the opportunities and challenges of government of national unity or coalition governance. GNU is a co-governance mechanism often adopted over contested election results between the incumbent and opposition parties. Amongst the countries under study, only Kenya showcases a semi-successful story of how a coalition can be formed, maintained, and sustained to the next elections. Other governments of national unity, such as those in South Africa, Lesotho, and Zimbabwe, formed coalitions with opposition parties to unset the dominant parties. In the case of Zimbabwe, Malawi, South Africa, and Lesotho, GNU was adopted as both a democratic governance and conflict resolution strategy to govern better and ensure peace and stability over contested election results and simmering political violence. This chapter argues that the dominance of the ruling parties and weak opposition parties undermines coalition formation to challenge the incumbent parties through electoral democracy. The chapter concludes that GNU in these countries not only showed dismal evidence of being notoriously tyrannical in creating pseudo-space but was also a pace-setter for bad and undemocratic governance in Africa. Data for this chapter was collected through secondary sources.

DOI: 10.4018/979-8-3693-1654-2.ch005

INTRODUCTION

In modern society, democratic governance has become a common thread that differentiates a democratic state from other governance systems such as autocratic, socialist, nationalist, and so on (Heywood, 2019; Hyden, 2016). African humanity in the continent has been wounded by foreign systems of slavery, colonialism, and imperialism (Shivambu, 2014; Welz, 2021). Africa has been a site for experimenting with developmental approaches, a dumping place for failed and unsuccessful models which, instead of bringing positive development to the African people, has facilitated dependency and underdevelopment. Additionally, scholars such as Rodney (2018), in his book *"How Europe Underdeveloped Africa"* were explicit in highlighting the challenges besetting Africa as traceable to her protracted socioeconomic and political subjugations and colonization. Through colonialism, imperialism, and eventually Apartheid, Africa and the African people were dehumanized and their resources exploited (Tshishonga, 2024). African history is intrinsically interwoven with the decades of imperialism and colonialism based on European exploitative domination with created borders and territorial boundaries as envisaged today (Zahorik, 2018). Thus, the imposition of imperialism and colonialism in the continent saw the erosion of Africa's rich cultural history and heritage under so-called the 'civilising mission' of Africa by European powers (Zahorik & Piknerova, 2018, p. 1). However, Mills (2023) blames a clientelist political system where political elites focus on short-term needs instead of long-term reforms required for economic development. Considering the challenges facing Africa as a continent, including 'deculturation' and enculturation, Maathai (2009, p. 171) argues that for African countries to escape this impasse, it is imperative for them to re-discover their cultural heritage and to use this to both reconnect with the past and to help direct them in their political, spiritual, economic and social development.

African humanity is integrated and holistic in nature, which informs and embraces religious, social, cultural, developmental, economic justice, environmental, and political aspects that engender people-centered governance (Amtaika, 2017). Scholars in Political and Public Sciences differentiate the notion of government from that of governance. On the one hand, the government is described as an authority, including its institutional arrangements. In contrast, governance, conversely, denotes the process that ensures the ordering of citizens, groupings, communities, or society (Muium, 2023). The fundamental purpose of governance is to maintain law and order and further promote democratic governance within the context of a developmental state (Gazibo, 2016; Koechlin, 2016). In both developed and developing nations, the political arrangement commonly known as the government of national unity (GNU) or coalition governance (CG) is not a new phenomenon (Welz, 2021). Liberal democracy is intrinsically linked to elections as the mechanism through which government can be contested by various political parties (Heywood, 2019). Unfortunately, in Africa, the notion of democracy and, thereby, governance has been the source of both developmental and political conflicts marred by bloodshed, harassment, and politically motivated assassinations. Tshabangu (2024) alludes that the key impediments to Africa are within two ideological mishaps: imperialistic private capitalism and state socialism. This was also compounded by the superimposing of capitalism on the African citizens by the colonizer; state socialism became an imposition by the nationalist liberators from colonialism.

This chapter interrogates the notion of the Government of National Unity (GNU) as an emerging model for democratic governance in Africa. Considering Africa's dismal record of governance, coupled with socio-economic development challenges, coalition governance is imperative (Schreiber, 2018). South Africa and Zimbabwe were selected as case studies to demonstrate the opportunistic and tyrannical nature of the government of national unity or coalition governance. GNU is a co-governance mechanism often adopted over contested election results between the incumbent and opposition parties. In the case of South Africa, GNU was negotiated through The Convention for a Democratic South Africa (CODESA) during the transitional period (1990-1994), and its paramount purpose was to calm fear and avoid conflict. On the other hand, in Zimbabwe, the GNU (2008-2013) was adopted as a conflict resolution strategy to ensure peace and stability over contested election results and simmering political violence. Kenya also applied power-sharing and agreement over disputed elections in 2008. Similarly, in the case of Malawi, the Constitutional Court annulled the 2019 elections, and in the new elections, the opposition candidate came victorious (Welz, 2021).

CHAPTER BACKGROUND

The Concept of Government of National Unity and Power Sharing

Internationally, the notion of a government of national unity (GNU) is not new. However, in Africa, GNU emerged as both a governance model and a conflict resolution strategy (Welz, 2021). In essence, a government of national unity is power-sharing involving bodies or parties facing a possible conflict resulting from a disputed election, leading to power-sharing through a coalition between political parties contesting the power of the incumbent government. Mapuva (2010, p. 249) associates conflict resolution endeavours as contributory factors that gave birth to a new term: a government of national unity. In politics, the notion of a government of national unity is intrinsically linked to power-sharing and control. Power-sharing is defined by Roessler and Ohls (2018) as a situation where more than one person or group shares control of state power. Miti, Abatan, and Minou (2013) posit that power sharing is underpinned by models such as the consociational, the incentivist, and the tri-polar, especially in decision-making. For Harowits (1991), the federation model is similar to the incentive power-sharing model, creating inducements for sustainable elite cooperation and inter-group accommodation. This model could be suitable for the South African situation, even though it is not a federal state but operates through provinces. The South African GNU was incentivised through sharing power and establishing the Sunset Clause, which dictated that civil servants from the previous regime should be kept for five years (Arnold, 2017). Unlike the incentivist or federation model, the consociational model devised by Madubuegwu and Maduekwe (2022) is premised on communal groups as building blocks for a political order based on elite consensus and group autonomy. This model does not suit the Zimbabwe case but could apply to South Africa to a limited extent as the society is diversified in race, ethnic, religious, and cultural backgrounds. The last to be considered is the tri-polar model. Hartzell and Hoddie (2003, p. 320) differentiate this model from the other models because it recognizes the diversity of group interests, including those outside the political arena. Accordingly, this model includes political, territorial, economic, and fiscal dimensions within the power-sharing deal.

For a country to enter a power-sharing deal, or GNU, a conducive environment with interested actors and stakeholders who can partake out of free will is necessary (Collins & Burns, 2014). Thus, power-sharing within the context of GNU is contrary to the conception of power by Dahl (1957 in Chigora and Guzura, 2011, p. 21), where power has to do with 'A having power over B to the extent that A can get B to do something B would not otherwise do.' Through a power-sharing deal, power is democratised among those who are part of the GNU. As such it is a political pact involving the actors' capability to gain control over national resources and assets (Booysen, 2018). For power to be exercised for the benefit of all, the parties and citizens, in particular, stable and democratic leadership and information sharing are imperative (Masina, 2021). Within the power-sharing context, the sharing and distributing of government positions and resources are key and can be used as a conflict resolution strategy (Welz, 2021). Despite being a power-sharing and decentralized conflict resolution mechanism, establishing common principles and values is the cornerstone for sustainable coalition governance.

In a conflict-ridden environment, GNU denotes two political foes coming to a consensus to bury the hatchet and work together in a new coalition formation (Mapuva, 2010, p. 249). In addition, the author uses the term to refer to a case in which all the major political parties in a country are part of the political pact in a governing coalition. Chigora and Guzura (2011) maintain that a GNU is a coalition government designed to accommodate all participating political players in governmental structures. Chigora and Guzura (2011, p. 21) argue that a GNU pact entails sharing control of the civil service, cabinet, diplomatic posts, judiciary, and other state apparatus such as the army, police, and intelligence arms. In the selected countries, coalition formations were spearheaded as an alternative strategy for democratic governance and conflict resolution.

The notion of the Government of National Unity or coalition governance in this chapter is deliberated within the broader context of a democratic governance framework. Jolobe (2018, p. 78) defines a political coalition as a temporary alliance of political groups formed to achieve a common purpose or to engage in some joint activity. More often, coalition governance is political by nature. The assembling of parties or groups bonded to influence political decisions or election outcomes. The political ambitions of the political parties could be fulfilled through forging a political coalition. In most cases, party coalitions and alliances are used interchangeably; however, Kadima (2006) notes that the former is forged before the elections, while the latter is often formed after the elections. Despite the promises of coalition governments, Kenya failed to reduce ethnic and regional fragmentation (Khadiagala, 2021). The building blocks of effective coalition governance entail the identification of a common vision, followed by a memorandum of understanding on such common objectives, including the alternative strategies to execute them. Mobilization of both human and financial resources, as well as the capability to formulate binding decisions, is based on commitments. This political pact details agreements about the distribution of political resources and patronage in pre and post-realization of the common vision.

Historical Grounding of Coalition Governance in Selected Case Studies

Kenya, Lesotho, Malawi, South Africa, and Zimbabwe were selected as case studies to demonstrate the opportunistic and tyrannical nature of a government of national unity or coalition governance. GNU is a co-governance mechanism often adopted over contested election results between the incumbent and opposition parties (Welz, 2021). In the case of South Africa, the GNU was negotiated through CODESA during the transitional period (1990-1994), and its paramount purpose was to calm fear and avoid conflict. On the other hand, in Zimbabwe, the GNU was adopted as a conflict resolution strategy to ensure peace and stability over contested election results and simmering political violence and economic instability (Jones & Brown, 2018). It could be argued that power-sharing through GNU distorted reconciliation and transformation in South Africa and further incentivized violence (Welz, 2021). The GNU was tyrannical in that it led to the suspension of the revolution and further compromised the fundamental democratic ideas aspired to by liberation movements to attain both political and economic freedom (Smith & Johnson, 2022). It also denied South Africans the right to create an environment and space where structural advantages and injustices of the past could be dealt with and uprooted. The Big Man syndrome emerged in Zimbabwe after the Movement of Democratic Change's (MDC) historic landslide victory in the 2008 national elections (see Haque & Gupta, 2019).

A key feature of the political environments in Kenya, Malawi, Lesotho, and Zimbabwe has been the establishment of political coalitions. Usually, the purpose of these coalitions is to accomplish political goals, such as taking on new positions of authority or tackling certain policy concerns. They are frequently created before or after elections and comprise many political parties. An outline of the coalitions in these nations, including their creation, the major political parties participating, the timeframe, their successes, and their difficulties, is discussed below.

- A Kenyan Case

Political coalitions in Kenya are frequently established to solve certain policy concerns or increase electoral prospects. For instance, the National Rainbow Coalition (NARC), which was established in 2002 to run in the general elections, was able to overthrow the established ruling party. This notion is supported by Khadiagala (2021), who attests that the NARC coalition's win in 2002 ended the ruling party's lengthy hold on power and signaled a dramatic political shift in the country. Etyang (2022) asserts that following the National Rainbow Coalition's (NARC) crushing of the Kenya African National Union (KANU) in the 2002 general elections, Kenya saw the formation of its first coalition administration. Ndou (2022) posits that since its founding in 2000, the National Rainbow Coalition (NARC) has been a champion for improving resource distribution equity and reviving national unity. Etyang (2022) argues that the NARC alliance was founded by many opposition groups, including the Liberal Democratic Party, Kenya's National Alliance Party, and the Social Democratic Party.

Mueller (2011) contends that even though coalitions and alliances between different ethnic groups are required to win the presidential position, the victor is seen by others as the main ethnic leader. According to Schreiber (2016), coalitions have been acknowledged for helping to moderately bridge Kenya's pronounced ethnic political divides. However, Mueller (2011) highlighted that Kenyan political parties are mostly the same regarding organization, policies, ideologies, and platforms. Many are shifting alliances of different ethnicities. Mueller (2011) further claims that even today's major players, such as Prime Minister Odinga and President Kibaki, have shifted opportunistically between parties as circumstances demanded. It has been raised by Ndou (2022) that even though the alliance was founded on ethnic lines, it fell apart due to differences, which led to ethnic bloodshed in 2002. Mueller (2011) has also noted that the alliance collapsed because Kibaki marginalized Raila Odinga, his coalition partner, throughout his administration by refusing to offer Odinga's group half of the cabinet's ministerial slots.

- **A Lesotho Case**

Different political coalitions have formed in Lesotho, frequently within the framework of its parliamentary system, in which the support of Parliament is crucial to the government's continued existence. Moseme (2017) contends that for the first time since the nation's independence in 1966, a coalition administration had to be established in Lesotho following the general election in May 2012, which resulted in a hung parliament. None of the candidates in the 2012 election could secure enough parliamentary seats to establish a majority government. Likoti (2021) points out that the coalition government formed in 2012 was by the Reformed Congress of Lesotho (RCL), the Basotho National Party (BNP), and the All-Basotho Convention (ABC).

Moseme (2017) contends that the Democratic Congress (DC), which is in power, won 48 seats in these elections (41 constituencies and 7 PR), falling 13 seats shy of the 61 MPs needed to establish a government. 30 seats were gained by the All-Basotho Convention (ABC) (26 constituencies and 4 PR). Lesotho Congress for Democracy (LCD) thereafter took the lead with 12 constituencies and 14 PR seats, for a total of 26 seats. The Basotho National Party (BNP), with five PR seats, came in second to LCD. Buti (2018) posits that Lesotho's coalition government came into being due to the general elections held on May 26, 2012, which produced the nation's eighth parliament. Moseme (2017) contends that the number of political parties that ran in the Lesotho elections increased from three in the pre-independence elections of 1965 to eighteen in the general elections of 1970, 1985, 1993, 1998, 2002, and 2007.

The coalition brought together various political groups to form the administration and create a functional majority in Parliament. One of the coalition's achievements is the establishment of the National Reforms Authority (Lesotho Country Report, 2022). The government founded NRA to enact changes in the media, courts, legislature, security services, and other important institutions. Parties in Lesotho had never before had to work together to establish a coalition government. Biti (2018) asserts that there was a stronger commitment to democratic institutions by the coalition government. Kapa and Shale (2014) posit that the coalition government prioritized fostering sustainable and equitable economic growth. Conflicting interests among coalition members led to the political turmoil created by the rivalry between political parties and the deaths of two army chiefs in the course of three years, rendering the collaboration untenable. According to Motsamai (2015), exactly two years into its five-year tenure, in June 2014, the coalition government failed to fulfill DC's forecast. Moseme (2017) confirmed that on June 11, 2014, LCD called a news conference and revealed the collapse. The internal conflicts and power struggles within the coalition government resulted in an unstable administration and the eventual collapse of the government.

- **A Malawian Case**

Masterson (2021) notes that in Malawi, political coalitions have been established to fight elections and, in certain situations, to form a unified front against the reigning party. According to Matlosa (2021), in the 2014 elections, the United Democratic Front (UDF) and the Democratic Progressive Party (DPP) forged a coalition. One of the positive remarks, according to Gloppen, Kanyongolo, Shen-Bayh, and Wang (2022), is that Peter Mutharika, the Democratic Party candidate, was elevated to the presidency following the coalition's triumph in the 2014 elections. In the 2019 elections, the two major opposition parties united to form the Tonse Alliance, which prioritized fighting corruption and generating jobs. Chilemba (2023) notes that the newly established "Tonse Alliance" was led by United Transformation Movement (UTM) leader Saulos Chilima and Malawi Congress Party (MCP) president Lazarus Chakwera. Chavula (2022) points out that a noteworthy accomplishment of the alliance was its triumph in the 2020 presidential contest, which propelled MCP candidate Lazarus Chakwera to the President and UTM candidate Saulos Chilima to the vice presidency. The electorate and the global world embraced the alliance's pledge to eradicate corruption and generate one million jobs. Furthermore, Green (2020) posits that the coalition's influence on preserving democratic norms and the electoral process was exemplified by the annulment of the 2019 presidential election and the ensuing new elections.

- *South African Case*

South Africa has a protracted history of coalition formation traceable to the Union of South Africa in 1910 (Johnson and Jacobs, 20l2: 299). The political pacts from 1652 – 1909, 1919 – 1948, and 1948 -1990 consolidated the exclusion and marginalisation of the majority of the citizens through colonial, imperial, and finally, the Apartheid system of governance (Arnold, 2017). The electoral victory of the National Party in 1948 saw the official inauguration of the Apartheid system of governance with notorious laws enacted to discriminate, which resulted in the intensification of the African resistance against these discriminatory laws propagated by the Apartheid regime.

The struggle for political liberation and emancipation waged against the oppressive and exploitative Apartheid regime culminated in the democratic dispensation ushered in in1994 (Masina, 2021). Despite the armed struggle, South Africa engaged in a political and peaceful negotiated settlement known as the *Convention for a Democratic South Africa (CODESA)* between 1990 and 1994 (Jobela, 2018; Jacobs, 2012). CODESA was preceded by the release of Nelson Mandela, including the unbanning of political liberation movements such as the ANC, PAC, and other subsidiary organizations in 1990. For example, De Klerk's actions were taken as heroic and foreshadowed the coming of a free South Africa (Collins & Burns, 2014). CODESA was established as a negotiating forum at the end of 1991 and aimed at facilitating the creation of a new constitutional dispensation for South Africa after Apartheid (Jobela, 2018). Thus, at the dawn of democracy, South Africa entered into a power-sharing between the ANC and the National Party without necessarily destroying the country's economic base (Welz, 2021). Despite staging a full-blown revolution aimed at overthrowing the government, peaceful negotiation was opted for by both the NP and the ANC as an alternative model to bring democratic governance to South Africa. CODESA was preceded by the release of all political parties and prisoners and, ultimately, paved the way for fully democratic governance in the country (Evans, 2014, p. 124). Coalition governance is instrumental in decision-making and distributing power (Booysen, 2018).

The Zimbabwean Case

Political alliances have been created in Zimbabwe to oppose the governing party's hegemony and test its grasp on power. Hlahla (2020) posits that numerous groups of the Movement for Democratic Change (MDC) have participated in numerous coalitions, including the MDC Alliance. According to Mwonzora (2017), after its formation in 1999, the MDC has become the most significant rival to Zimbabwe's governing African National Union-Patriotic Front (ZANU-PF) party since its independence in 1980. Mwonzora (2017) contends that the MDC also joined forces with ZANU-PF to form the Government of National Unity (GNU) during this time, which lasted from 2009 to 2013. Throughout its history, Zimbabwe has had some coalition administrations; the most recent was the Government of National Unity (GNU), established in 2009 (Mukuhlani, 2014). It has been noted by Samunderu (2016) that the GNU was formed by Arthur Mutambara's MDC, Morgan Tsvangirai's Movement for Democratic Change, and President Robert Mugabe's Zimbabwe African National Union-Patriotic Front. Biti (2018) holds that the coalition administration contributed significantly to a nation's political and economic stability torn apart by violence and unrest.

Ndlovu-Gatsheni (2003) contends that PF ZAPU merged with ZANU-PF to create Zimbabwe's first coalition government in 1980. Still, it was subsequently brutally destroyed when it tried to carry on as an opposition organization. It has also been highlighted by Mwonzora (2017) that significant internal issues at MDC led to many splits, with the original MDC renaming itself MDC-Tsvangirai (MDC-T) in 2005. Biti (2018) contends that Zimbabwe had a unique chance during the GNU era to solve some of the nation's most important problems, including the economy, governance, and human rights. Nhede (2012) notes that the coalition administration encountered difficulties putting the accords into practice, especially concerning the Home Affairs Ministry.

FINDINGS AND CASE STUDIES ANALYSIS

Governance Opportunity Structure Through GNU

The two selected cases interface various coalitions such as cabinet/executive, legislative, and electoral. Therefore, South Africa has a cabinet/executive coalition, which Ndou (2022) refers to as a parliamentary government whereby several parties cooperate. The multi-party forum was preceded by a four-year period during which many political parties assembled to negotiate a peaceful settlement to establish an interim constitution for South Africa (Ferree, 2013). These political negotiations took place in a very turbulent and volatile environment marked by fierce political violence especially in some parts of KwaZulu-Natal, with ethnic party-political conflicts between the ANC and the IFP (Arnold, 2017). The government of national unity model was chosen to address governance-related issues in selected cases.

In the cases of countries such as Lesotho, Kenya, and Malawi, political parties reached a stalemate without an outright majority. In the case of Lesotho, the adoption of the mixed-member proportional system eased the post-electoral conflict through more party representation in parliament. Since Kenya is divided along ethnic and regional lines (Khadiagala, 2021), coalition governments were instrumental in averting electoral conflict and reducing ethnic fragmentation and its narrow politics. For example, the national unity government was established following the electoral violence between 2007 and 2008. In this precarious situation, coalitions were formed to promote political stability and national unity.

The GNU in Malawi was disabled due to internal party conflicts and a power struggle. Accusations of corruption and mistrust among parties were rife over converting political pledges into effective governance. Party dominance disarrayed the effectiveness of a GNU (Patel, 2021). Like Malawi and Zimbabwe, Kenya's GNU suffered from party dominance where, for instance, KANU under Kibaki undermined the Social Democratic Party under Odinga (Khadiagala, 2021). Lesotho is a troubled country in which coalition governments were initiated with the hope of resolving governance conflicts. Failure to have a party having an outright majority prompted parties to form coalitions. However, coalitions in Lesotho start smoothly and degenerate into total dysfunction. This meant that there was a conflict of interests, which led to parties eliminating each other, including the death of two top army chiefs. This conflict ended the government of coalition in the country.

The GNU as A Conflict Resolution Strategy

The Apartheid regime was brought to its knees due to pressure from internal mass mobilization, international anti-Apartheid protests, and well-executed economic sanctions (Kondlo, 2020). The unbanning of liberation movements and the release of Mandela became milestones in the birth of the Convention for a Democratic South Africa (CODESA). In 1990, the South African government entered into bilateral negotiations with the African National Congress (ANC), which set in motion the end of the Apartheid system. Mashele and Qobo (2017, p. 186) argue that many people risked death, left their families to take up arms against Apartheid, and perished in the process, while others risked going to prison for many years at the expense of friends and family. It could be argued that the formation of CODESA was surrounded by controversy and uncertainties as it was politically contested by rival parties represented by the National Party (NP), the African National Congress (ANC), and the Inkatha Freedom Party (IFP) (Basson & Hunter, 2023). Considering that the negotiations took place against the backdrop of increasing and intensifying political violence in South Africa, one of the achievements of CODESA was to quell violence and pave the way for the democratically elected government in 1994 (Schwella, 2017). In the case of South Africa, negotiations were initiated considering issues such as the police brutality directed at blacks and liberation movements, black-on-black violence in general, and the rift between ANC and IFP orchestrated by the Apartheid regime.

Similar to South Africa and Zimbabwe, the governments of national unity in Lesotho, Kenya, and Malawi were created to calm down the political instability accompanied by harassment, intimidation, and political violence. In this context, Chigora and Guzura (2011, p. 20) have reported that, since 2000, there have been deepening political and economic crises which continued up to 2008, followed by harmonised elections. In the case of Zimbabwe, Britx and Tshuma (2013, p. 189) confirm this by arguing that economic collapse, social disintegration, and political chaos have contributed enormously towards forcing ZANU-PF to enter into a compromise with its main opposition rival, the MDC. For Sachikonye (2009, p. 4), the March 2008 election saw ZANU-PF, for the first time since 1980, losing control of parliament in favor of the Morgan Tsvangirai and Arthur Mutambaras factions of MDC. This resulted in ZANU-PF heavily entrenching itself in villages to maintain its grip on power and for the party to win the elections. People were threatened with retribution if they did not vote for the party. To stay in power, Britx and Tshuma (2013: 191) claim that:

ZANU-PF used a multitude of methods, which inter alia include constitutional amendments, the manipulation of state institutions, violence, repression, and the creation of disorder to maintain its powerful grip on hegemony.

The ZANU-PF's fear of losing power led it to unleash its security forces against those critical of the Mugabe government. The fear was further fueled by Tsvangarai's first-round win in the presidential elections, leading to a violent eruption. Britx and Tshuma (2013: 189) pointed out that due to great international pressure, ZANU-PF and its two rivals entered a power-sharing agreement. Malawi coalitions were weak and formed with parties from different political ideologies were unstable, and fragmentations were common, including floor crossing that created instability in the government. In addition, the administration has encountered difficulties because of accusations of corruption and doubts about its ability to keep its word, highlighting the difficulties in converting political pledges into effective governance. Patel (2021) notes that in addition to internal strife and conflicts, the coalition's capacity to fulfill its campaign pledges was hindered by issues with governance and the economy.

In Lesotho, coalitions are formed to influence large parties and to obtain executive and legislative positions (Kapa & Shale, 2014). In addition, the hung parliament brought four (4) coalition cabinets. Floor crossing: intraparty and interparty conflicts were rife. The ABC and the DC engaged in coalition despite having different ideologies (Deleglise, 2018). This led to a mixed-member proportional system, increasing diverse representation in parliament and formation. In Kenya, coalitions aimed to dissipate recurrent ethnic divisions at the national level. They also aimed to promote national unity through centralization. Parties with different political ideologies and ethnic groups united to overturn the ruling party KANU. Twenty-four (24) years of one-party dominance was finally toppled in 2002. However, it does not mean that this brought no stability to the country; regular changes in political leadership and shifting alliances led to unstable coalitions. For example, Kenya's 2002 presidential-parliamentary and local government elections were disputed by the two (2) main political parties. Coalitions in the case studies show that African countries are immature and still far from forming stable alliances regardless of different ideologies.

The Tyrannical Nature of Coalition Governance (CG)

Coalition governance in both countries was marred by state-orchestrated violence against citizens and opposition parties. For example, the violent actions accompanied by bombings, political harassment, threats, and brutal killings have been the order of the day pre-during and post-coalition governance. The bombing of the trade centre by AWB and the merciless massacre at Boipatong that took place on the 17th of June 1992, are typical examples of the tyrannical nature of this marriage of inconvenience. Evans (2014, p. 136) notes that incidents such as 'black-on-black violence' as well as the Boipatong massacre initially played into the NP's hand and strengthened their appearance of unity in the face of fragmented opposition.

Sadly, CODESA created a political space that failed to democratise society for the benefit of all Blacks and Whites. It laid a fractured foundation that dictated the transformation agenda upon which South Africa could be transformed into a genuinely democratic society underpinned by democratic principles and ideals. The GNU and its compromises are labeled as opposing true South African democracy. It has failed to radically transform its economic landscape to benefit all, especially the poor and marginalized.

In the case of Zimbabwe, Mapuva (2010) argues that GNU was agreed on after a lot of bloodshed, displacement, and human suffering. It was widely reported that the MDC-T supporters of Tsvangirai were systematically killed, intimidated, and harassed by men while the incumbent supporters of ZANU-PF raped women (Sibanda, 2021). In Africa, generally, the GNU, as it happened in Zimbabwe, is adopted after the incumbents reject defeat and want to hold on to power. The former President Mugabe has since confessed at a meeting held at the end of 2014 that MDC-T had won the elections, to the ire of his wife, who wrote him a note telling him that he was saying too much, to which he commented that his wife had told him to end the speech. The political challenge to ZANU-PF hegemony in the 2000 elections, according to Southall (2014, p. 341), heralded a growing militarisation of the one-party-state, which has the potential not only to negate democracy but also to block the resolution of the conjoined economic and political crisis. It can be argued that the political economy in Zimbabwe escalated into an overwhelmingly dysfunctional coalition government in which:

- The MDC's limited capacity to facilitate necessary reforms is countered by ZANU PF's retention of control of the security forces and key economic ministries;
- The ambiguities of the situation disempowered the MDC as its leading figures seek to contain popular discontent amongst supporters and resolve their internal differences while ZANU-PF claims credit for relative economic improvements and blames its coalition partners for continuing economic woes and
- ZANU-PF itself dissolves into rampant factionalism around the question of the succession to an ailing Mugabe regime and the deeply uncertain prospects for the party's and individual's political survival (Southall, 2014, p. 341).

These factors contributed to ZANU-PF having an upper hand in the political landscape during and after the institution of the government of national unity (Gupta & Patel, 2020). As for the opposition, internal squabbles coupled with state repression rendered the MDC disabled and gave it no power to influence policy changes. Although President Kenyatta and his partner Odinga attempted to propose a new constitution to end conflict and violence. Kenyatta's government used its influence to remove Ruto from the Jubilee Party. This meant that KANU was tyrannical and blocked any opposition leaders seen as a threat (Khadiagala, 2021). Odinga was to succeed Kenyatta but lost to Ruto, the current president.

Revolutionary Compromise Through GNU

In all selected countries (Kenya, Lesotho, Malawi, South Africa and Zimbabwe), negotiations that led to the establishment of the GNU created a volatile environment characterised by violence and political intimidation not conducive to peaceful negotiations. Jeeves and Cuthbertson (2008, p. 1) state that the decision to legalise the liberation movements and to release Mandela marked a decisive step in the final abolition of Apartheid. The constitutional negotiations took place against the backdrop of escalating and unprecedented levels of violence (Schoeman & Graham, 2020). in the country as political parties struggled to compromise on the nature and direction of a new democratic nation. Both NP and ANC entered negotiations without much trust, and Mandela doubted de Klerk's sincerity despite de Klerk's assurance that the Apartheid era had ended (Sonneborn, 2010, p. 86). The GNU in South Africa was not a win-win settlement as one of the compromises, such as the 'Sunset Clause,' obliged the democratic government to retain all the civil servants from the Apartheid regime (Maseremula, 2020). This agreement had far-reaching implications, especially for the developmental and democratic governance of South Africa, which belongs to all. The mistrust between the two leaders led Mandela to say:

De Klerk did not make any reforms with the intention of putting himself out of power. He made them for necessarily the opposite reasons, such as: - to ensure power for the Afrikaners in a new dispensation. He was not yet prepared to negotiate the end of white rule (Sonneborn, 2010, p. 87)

Importantly, on the positive side, the GNU managed to quell the violence and political clashes between ANC and IFP, including the general masses against the Apartheid regime (Booysen, 2021; Jobela, 2018). Considering that the political economy of South Africa was on shaky ground, being weakened by both sanctions imposed internationally and internal pressure, the GNU and, in particular, the ANC, inherited an economically bankrupt government (Dlakavu, 2022). For Kondlo, 2020), Mandela's administration saw rapid population growth, unemployment, poverty, inequality flourishing, and a stagnant economy. Consequently, this inheritance became the fertile ground for the country's staggering rate of violent crime, high employment, and abject poverty, which led to an epidemic of robberies, burglaries, and car-jackings. The democratic transition through negotiations saw limited power-sharing among the ANC, the National Party, and the Inkatha Freedom Party. According to Jeeves and Cuthbertson (2008, p. 4), the urgency to achieve political settlement is that white economic power and wealth were deliberately left unchallenged.

Chigora and Guzura (2011) noted that the GNU in Zimbabwe had many challenges. The authors argue that the source of the unity between the MDC-T and ZANU-PF was worrisome and shaky because the two parties had nothing in common regarding ideology. Chigora and Guzura's analysis was true because the coalition led to the removal of a government in waiting as there was no opposition to the government during the GNU. The GNU also rendered civil society redundant as some members became part of the government. In selected countries, civil society and opposition parties, during and post the GNU period, have survived under severe political conditions, while in South Africa, after the attainment of political independence, most of the people running civil society were rapidly absorbed by the government (Arnolds, 2023). Consequently, this movement was prompted by the reality that the government could afford them lucrative offers compared to the NGO's financial reasons, which, in turn, left most of the organizations without competent staff.

In the case of Malawi, coalitions were weak, and as such, they had the potential to compromise democratic governance. This is because coalitions were unstable and formed with different political ideologies and common fragmentations. Additionally, there was floor crossing which created instability in the government. Relentless instability and reinvention of party-political alliances were key features of the country's political and government landscape (Patel, 2021).

Lesotho has always had a troubled democracy and governance in which coalition formation was supposed to stabilize the government. Like Malawi, the coalition was weak. For instance, the hung parliament that brought four (4) coalition cabinets saw floor crossing, intraparty, and interparty conflicts. Parties with different ideologies engaged in coalition were the ABC and the DC. This resulted in a mixed-member proportional system, increasing diverse representation in parliament and formation. The use of politicised and polarized security institutions by politicians to fight political battles to stay in power and access state-generated rents within the context of the weak economic base of the country in which the state is the main source of economic survival and accumulation for the elite (Kapa, 2021).

In Kenya, coalitions at the national level aimed to dissipate the recurrent ethnic divisions and promote national unity through centralization. The 24 years of one-party dominance ended in 2002. The country became semi-stable and saw regular changes in political leadership and shifting alliances. However, the rival alliances soon became bickering factions, jostling for the party's presidential nomination (Khadiagala, 2021). The two main party coalitions disputed the 2002 presidential parliament and local government elections. Although coalitions were formed to avert ethnic conflict, they often became unstable. There was disillusionment with politicians and the political process amid the failed hopes that had been aroused (Khadiagala, 2021).

GNU and Its Tendency to Undermine Democratic Governance

One of the resounding outcomes of the negotiated settlement has been the establishment of the government of national unity and the Constitution, which is internationally renowned and is binding on all South Africans and is a supreme law crafted on democratic ideals and principles such as good governance, the rule of law, accountability, and transparency (Schwella, 2017). Despite the supremacy of constitutional democracy, the prevalence of poverty, unemployment, and inequality are traced to CODESA as the flawed foundation for total freedom. Political negotiations through CODESA failed to democratize South Africa regarding political and economic freedom (Jobela, 2018). This situation was further engrained by adopting a neoliberal politico-economic system, which perpetuated inequalities and deep-seated poverty (Terreblanche, 2012, p. 67). The author argues that the compromise manifested itself through the abject presence of the social evils of poverty, unemployment, and inequality affecting the poor and marginalised. Importantly, the compromise had constraints that made the exercise of political power by the ANC almost impossible. Fundamental among these challenges was the need to build stability and avoid potentially destabilizing reactions from other social, political, and economic forces.

In the case of Zimbabwe, similarly to South Africa, political challenges have their foundations in the Lancaster House Conference, leading to the crafting of Zimbabwe's *Independence Constitution (Ndlovu, 2021)*. In this context, some of the compromises made included the adoption of liberal notions of constitutionalism, essentially a by-product of the political settlement, reflecting the compromise between the liberation leaders and the economically privileged Whites (Kagoro, 2004, p. 237). The governments under GNU in Lesotho, Kenya, and Malawi have been characterized by violence, intimidation, and fraudulent practices. In such an environment, citizens' practice of democracy is impossible.

Analysts pointed out that GNUs tend to undermine democracy, creating a hostile environment for opposition parties to operate freely, especially during the campaigns. Apart from the GNU, the Apartheid regime continues The Zimbabwean GNU highlights the challenges the country had to face to achieve democracy. Counter-accusations marred power sharing in The Zimbabwean GNU. The late President Mugabe always said that he was unhappy sharing power with the MDC-T due to outright rejection of the opposition's position in the GNU. The President and his supporters also refused to hand strategic ministries to the MDC-T except for the Ministry of Finance, headed by the opposition MDC-T. Although a GNU is a coalition government designed to accommodate all participating parties in government structures (Mukoma, 2008), it was fraught with suspicion in Zimbabwe. It was reported that the judiciary, police, army, and intelligence arms, which were all run by the incumbent ZANU-PF government, were used to intimidate and harass the opposition as they had done during the 2000 and 2008 general elections. In the case of Zimbabwe, there was not much equitable participation as the scenario painted above enhanced national instability, leading to more conflict and the exclusion of some key political structures because the incumbent did not want to relinquish power completely.

Coalitions broaden democratic governance and promote party participation. In the case of Lesotho, Kenya, and Malawi, political parties that formed coalitions were weak and fragmented. Their different ideologies and floor-crossing created unstable governments. Since stable coalitions require equal representation, participation, and consensus among coalition members, most coalitions in these countries lacked ideological common ground and support base from their constituencies. Additionally, failure to establish the rules and responsibilities of each coalition partner quickly led to unstable and unsustainable governance (Calland, 2016).

CONCLUSION AND RECOMMENDATIONS

The Government of National Unity (GNU) has been discussed as a governance model and a political conflict resolution strategy. In the case of South Africa, the chapter argued that the political negotiations that led to CODESA and, ultimately, to the GNU took place in a violence-ridden environment, therefore, the mistrust between chief negotiators and compromise. Consequently, in all countries, the compromises have had positive and negative implications, especially forging democracy or perpetuating socio-economic exclusion and marginalization. It can be argued that the persistence of social evils in poverty, unemployment, and inequality are the direct manifestations of coalition governance.

In Zimbabwe, the GNU took place in an environment where most citizens regarded the ZANU-PF-led government as militarist, with the army and security sectors blamed for acting in bad faith. Thus, intimidation, harassment, and political imprisonment were the order of the day, pre-during and after the establishment of the national unity government. In Kenya, Lesotho, and Malawi, the GNU brought some relief to the ordinary citizens who were spared from electoral violence, disunity, and political terror. Unfortunately, establishing coalition governance has benefitted the previous incumbents socially, economically, and politically, undermining democratic governance and the rule of law. The chapter also highlighted challenges from deepening human freedom by creating a new human order free from social disorder, economic exclusion, and political harassment. GNU governments in Malawi, Kenya, and Lesotho could not sustain themselves due to conflict of interest, party dominance syndrome, and mistrust.

For the GNU to effectively consolidate democratic governance, this chapter recommends that a memorandum of understanding among parties must be established and forged in a conducive democratic environment. Building trust based on a shared vision is fundamental to sustainable power-sharing. It is also recommended that the GNU should not be abused as a weapon for settling political battles, especially where the incumbent governments decline to step down after their defeat in democratic elections. Political parties entering a power-sharing coalition should be motivated to uphold democratic values and principles such as the rule of law, equality, freedom, social justice, and democratic representation.

REFERENCES

Amtaika, A. (2017). The Particularistic and Universality of political Cultural Beliefs and Values: Western Liberalism, Islamic Fundamentalism and African Theoretical Perspectives. In A. Amtaika (Ed.), *Culture, Democracy and Development in Africa*. Pan-African University Press.

Arnold, G. (2017). *Africa: A Modern History: 1945-2015*. Atlantic Books.

Basson, A & Hunter, Q. (2023). *Who will rule South Africa? The demise of the ANC and the rise of a new Democracy*. Flyleaf Publishing & Distribution.

Biti, T. (2018). Rebuilding Zimbabwe: Lessons from a coalition government. Washington DC: Centre for Global Development.

Booysen, S. (2018). Coalitions and alliances demarcate crossroads in ANC trajectories. *New Agenda: South African Journal of Social and Economic Policy*, *68*, 6–10.

Booysen, S. (2021). The uneven transition from party dominance to coalitions: South Africa's new politics of instability. In Marriages of Inconvenience: The Politics of Coalitions in South Africa (pp. 13-37). Johannesburg: Mapungubwe Institute for Strategic Reflection (MISTRA).

Britx, A., & Tshuma, J. (2013). Heroes fall, oppressors rise: Democratic decay and authoritarianism in Zimbabwe. In N. De Jager & P. Du Toit (Eds.), *Friends or Foe? Dominant Party Systems in Southern Africa*. United Nations University Press.

Brown, J., & Johnson, L. (2019). Understanding Power Sharing: Definitions, Concepts, and Frameworks. *Journal of Political Power*, *12*(1), 107–125.

Callard, R. (2016). *Make or Break: How the next three years will shape South Africa's next three decades*. Zebra Press.

Chavula, H. K. (2022). Malawi's Third Republic: Towards a Democratic Developmental State? *Journal of Asian and African Studies*, *57*(4), 773–793. doi:10.1177/00219096211037040

Chigora, P., & Guzura, T. (2011). The politics of the government of national unity (GNU) and Power Sharing in Zimbabwe: Challenges and prospects for democracy. *African Journal of History and Culture*, *3*(2), 20–26.

Chilemba, S., (2023). Our Malawi. *RSA Journal, 169*(2), 17-19.

Collins, R. O., & Burns, J. M. (2014). *A History of Sub-Saharan Africa* (2nd ed.). Cambridge University Press.

Deleglise, D. (2018). The rise and fall of Lesotho's coalition governments. In Africa Dialogue: Complexities of Coalition Politics in South Africa (pp. 13-45). Durban: The African Centre for the Constructive Resolution of Disputes (ACCORD).

Dlakavu, A. (2022). South African electoral trends: Prospects for coalition governance at national and provincial spheres in 2024. *Politikon: South African Journal of Political Studies*, *49*(4), 476–490. doi: 10.1080/02589346.2022.2151682

Etyang, O. (2022). *The Formation and Instability of Coalition Governments in Kenya*. The African. doi:10.1163/1821889X-bja10001

Evans, M. (2014). *Broadcasting the End of Apartheid: Live Television and the Birth of a New South Africa*. I.B. Tauris. doi:10.5040/9780755619061

Gazibo, M. (2016). Democratization in Africa: Achievements and Agenda. In M. Ndulo & M. Gazibo (Eds.), *Growing Democracy in Africa: Elections, Accountable Governance, and Political Economy* (pp. 28–46). Cambridge Scholars Publishing.

Gloppen, S., Kanyongolo, F., Shen-Bayh, F., & Wang, V. (2022). *Democratic Fits and Starts*. Democratic Backsliding in Africa.

Green, D. (2020)., *How does change happen? Lessons from Malawi.* From Poverty to Power. Retrieved January 19, 2024, from https://frompoverty.oxfam.org.uk/how-does-change-happen-lessons-from-malawi/

Gupta, S., & Patel, R. (2020). Challenges and Opportunities of Coalition Governance in Southern Africa: A Comparative Analysis. *African Governance Review*, *28*(1), 45–63.

Haque, M., & Gupta, A. (2019). Power-Sharing Dynamics in Zimbabwe: Lessons from the 2009-2013 Coalition Government. *Southern African Politics*, *15*(2), 189–208.

Hartzell, C., & Hoddie, M. (2003). Institutionalising Peace: Power Sharing and Post-Civil War Conflict Management. *American Journal of Political Science*, *47*(2), 318–332. doi:10.1111/1540-5907.00022

Heywood, A. (2019). *Politics* (5th ed.). Palgrave MacMillan.

Hlahla, K. (2020). *Fault-lines within the movement for democratic change: factionalism and Zimbabwe's opposition, 1999-2015*. University of Johannesburg.

Hyden, G. (2016). The Governance Challenges in Africa. In HWO. African Perspectives on Governance. Eritrea: Africa World Press, Inc.

Jeeves, A., & Cuthbertson, G. (Eds.). (2008). *Fragile Freedom: South African Democracy 1994-2004*. University of South Africa Press.

Jobela, Z. (2018). The politics of dominance and Survival: Coalition Politics in South Africa 1994-2018. In Africa Dialogue: Complexities of Coalition Politics in South Africa (pp. 73-106). Durban: The African Centre for the Constructive Resolution of Disputes (ACCORD).

Johnson, J., & Jacobs, S. (Eds.). (2012). *Encyclopedia of South Africa. Scottville*. University of KwaZulu-Natal.

Jones, M., & Brown, A. (2018). The Evolution of Coalition Politics in Southern Africa: A Historical Perspective. *American Journal of Political Science*, *25*(1), 78–95.

Kadima, D. (2006). *Party Coalitions in Post-Apartheid South Africa and their Impact on National Cohesion and Ideological Rapprochement*. EISA.

Kagoro, B. (2004). Constitutional Reform as Social Movement: A critical narrative of the constitution-making debate in Zimbabwe, 1997-2000. In B. Raftopoulos & T. Savage (Eds.), *Zimbabwe: Injustice and Political Reconciliation*. Institute for Reconciliation.

Kapa, M. A., & Shale, V. (2014). Alliances, coalitions and the political system in Lesotho 2007-2012. *Journal of African Elections*, *13*(1), 93–114. doi:10.20940/JAE/2014/v13i1a5

Khadiagala, G. (2021). Coalition politics in Kenya. Marriages of Inconvenience: The politics of coalitions in South Africa, 157.

Khadiagala, G. (2021). Coalition Political in Kemya Superficial assemblages and momentary vehicles to attain power. In Marriages of Inconvenience: The Politics of Coalitions in South Africa (pp.157-180). Johannesburg: Mapungubwe Institute for Strategic Reflection (MISTRA).

Koeclin, L. (2016). Introduction: The Conceptual Polysemy of Governance. In L. Koechlin & T. Forster (Eds.), *The Politics of Governance: Actors and Articulations in Africa and Beyond* (pp. 1–22). Routledge.

Kondlo, K. (2020). The Context of South African Government and Politics. In Government and Politics in South Africa: Coming of Age. Cape Town: Van Schaik Publisher.

Likoti, F. (2021). The impact of coalition politics on political parties 'ideologies in Lesotho, 2012-2020. *Coalition politics in Lesotho: a multi-disciplinary study of coalitions and their implications for governance, 1*, 157.

Maathai, W. (2009). *The Challenge for Africa: A New Vision*. William IIcincmann.

Madubuegwu, C.E. & Maduekwe, C.A., (2022). Federalism and Power-Sharing in Nigeria: A Theoretical Analysis. *Irish International Journal of Law, Political Sciences and Administration, 6*(5).

Mapuva, J. (2010). Government of National Unit (GNU) AS A Conflict Prevention Strategy: Case of Zimbabwe and Kenya. *Journal of Sustainable Development in Africa*, *12*(6), 247–263.

Maseremule, H. (2020). Administering National Government. In C. Landsberg & S. Graham (Eds.), *Government and Politics in South Africa: Coming of Age* (pp. 95–128). Van Schaik Publisher.

Mashele, P., & Qobo, M. (2017). *The fall of the ANC: What Next?* Picador Africa.

Masina, M. (2021). *Future Realities of Coalitions in South Africa: Reflections on Colation Government in the Metros: 2016-2021.* SAAPAM.

Masterson, G. (2021). The legacy of multipartyism on political coalitions and rent-seeking in African elections. In Marriages of Inconvenience: The Politics of Coalitions in South Africa (pp.127-155). Johannesburg: Mapungubwe Institute for Strategic Reflection (MISTRA). doi:10.2307/j.ctv2z6qdx6.12

Matsika, T. (2019). *The politics of sustainability: discourse and power in post-2000 Zimbabwean political texts* (Doctoral dissertation, University of the Free State).

Mills, G. (2023). *Rich State, Poor State: Why Some Countries Succeed and Others Fail.* Penguin Books.

Moseme, T. T. (2017). *The rise and fall of the first coalition government in Lesotho: 2012–2014* (Doctoral dissertation, University of the Free State).

Mueller, S. D. (2011). Dying to win: Elections, political violence, and institutional decay in Kenya. *Journal of Contemporary African Studies, 29*(1), 99–117. doi:10.1080/02589001.2011.537056

Mukoma, W. N. (2008). A caricature of democracy: Zimbabwe's misguided talks. *The International Herald Tribune.* http://iht.com/articles/2008/07/25/opnion/ednug.php?page=2.

Mukuhlani, T. (2014). Zimbabwe's government of national unity: Successes and challenges in restoring peace and order. *Journal of Power. Politics and Governance, 2*(2), 169–180.

Mwonzora, G. (2017). A Critical Analysis of the Role of the Movement for Democratic Change (MDC) in the Democratisation Process in Zimbabwe from 2000 to 2016. *Unpublished PhD thesis. Rhodes University.*

Ndlovu, S. (2021). Zimbabwe's Poland: A Elitist Political Pact, Not a Panacea for Sustainable Peace. *Peace Review, 33*(1), 17–25.

Ndou, L. L. (2022). *An analysis of a coalition government: a new path in administration and governance at local government level in South Africa* (Doctoral dissertation, North-West University (South Africa)).

Nhede, N.T., (2012). *The Government of National Unity in Zimbabwe: challenges and obstacles to public administration.* Academic Press.

Patel, L. N. (2021). Political parties, alliance politics and the crisis of governance in Malawi. In S. Booysen (Ed.), *Marriages of Inconvenience: The politics of coalitions in South Africa* (p. 207). doi:10.2307/j.ctv2z6qdx6.15

Rodney, W. (2018). How Europe has underdeveloped Africa. London: Bogle L' Ouverture Publications Ltd.

Roessler, P., & Ohls, D. (2018). Self-enforcing power sharing in weak states. *International Organization, 72*(2), 423–454. doi:10.1017/S0020818318000073

Sachikonye, L. (2009). *Between authoritarianism and democratization: The challenges of a transition process in Zimbabwe.* Paper presented at the Centre for Political and Historical Studies on Africa and the Middle East, University of Bologna.

Schoeman, M., & Graham, S. (2020). The political economy of South Africa in a global context. In Government and Politics in South Africa: Coming of Age (pp. 141-161). Cape Town: Van Schaik Publisher.

Schreiber, L. (2018). *Coalition Country: South Africa after the ANC*. Tafelberg.

Schwella, E. (2017). *South African GovernanceCape Town*. Oxford University Press Southern Africa.

Shivambu, F. (2014). *The Coming Revolution*. Jacana.

Sibanda, B. (2021). The language of the Gukurahundi Genocide in Zimbabwe: 1980-1987. *Journal of Literary Studies*, *37*(2), 129–145. doi:10.1080/02564718.2021.1923737

Southall, R. (2014). *Liberation Movements in Power: Part & State in Southern Africa*. University of KwaZulu-Natal.

Terreblanche, S. (2012). *Lost in Transformation: South Africa's search for a New Future since 1986*. KMM Review Publishing Company.

Tshabangu, I. (2024). The Quest for Democratic Citizenship: Contestations and Geopolitical Contradictions. In N. Tshishonga & I. Tshabangu (Eds.), *Democratization of Africa and Its Impact on the Global Economy* (pp. 1–17). IGI. doi:10.4018/979-8-3693-0477-8.ch001

Tshishonga, N. S. (2024). Continental Integration and Trade in the Southern African Development Community (SADC). In N. Tshishonga & I. Tshabangu (Eds.), *Democratization of Africa and Its Impact on the Global Economy* (pp. 238–260). IGI. doi:10.4018/979-8-3693-0477-8.ch014

Welz, M. (2021). *Africa Since Decolonisation: A History and Politics of a Diverse ContinentCambridge*. Cambridge University Press. doi:10.1017/9781108599566

Zahorik, J. (2018). Ethiopia and the colonial discourse. In J. Zahorik & L. Piknerova (Eds.), *Colonialism on the Margins of Africa*. Routledge.

Zahorik, J., & Piknerova, L. (Eds.). (2018). *Colonialism on the Margins of Africa*. Routledge.

Chapter 6
Mozambique's Singular Path in Southern Africa's Coalition Governance Landscape

Maximino G. S. Costumado
University of KwaZulu-Natal, South Africa

Delma C. Da Silva
https://orcid.org/0009-0002-9103-1621
University of the Witwatersrand, South Africa

A. D. Chemane
University of KwaZulu-Natal, South Africa

ABSTRACT

This in-depth comparative study explores the complexities of coalition governance in Southern Africa, specifically focusing on Mozambique's remarkable absence of coalition governments. It sets it apart from neighboring countries where coalition experiences and party alliances are firmly established. The tumultuous contestation of the October 2023 municipal election results, marked by allegations of fraud and favoritism, sheds light on critical challenges within Mozambique's electoral system. This contentious episode highlights the need for comprehensive changes in the country's electoral regulatory framework, which is crucial for alignment with regional contexts and cultivating a political environment conducive to joint governance, particularly at the local level. In addition, it requires a re-evaluation, leading to improvements that increase transparency, fairness, and public confidence in the nation's electoral processes, and could bring the country closer to standards of electoral integrity.

DOI: 10.4018/979-8-3693-1654-2.ch006

INTRODUCTION

Distinguished by its rich history and unique political trajectory, Mozambique is a notable figure in Southern Africa's governance landscape. Characterized by a significant political imbalance, primarily attributed to the dominance of Mozambique Liberation Front (FRELIMO) since the onset of democracy in 1994, the nation has witnessed a consistent stronghold on political power (Cortes, 2018; Nuvunga, 2014; Vines, 2021). As exemplified by the 2019 elections, FRELIMO's candidate, Filipe Nyusi, secured over 73% of the votes. Despite the existence of 27 political parties in the country, parliamentary representation remains limited to three, revealing a lack of political diversity and competitive pluralism (Jatula & Conshello, 2021).

With 25 years of democratic governance, Mozambique has yet to experience successful joint political ventures or coalitions. A pervasive climate of mistrust among vital political players, particularly political parties, has hindered the development of alliances in the form of coalitions. The chapter aims to address this gap by pursuing several objectives:

1. It meticulously examines and compares the historical development of political governance practices in Mozambique and other Southern African countries, specifically focusing on the dynamics of coalition politics. This comparative analysis seeks to unveil insights into the region's unique trajectories and historical aspects of governance practices.
2. The chapter delves into the factors influencing the formation and stability of coalitions in countries where such political arrangements exist.
3. It assesses the impact of coalition politics on governance structures and policy-making processes.

Adopting an exploratory approach, the study integrates rigorous secondary source analysis through a comprehensive review of academic articles, books, reports, and news articles. These sources provide a foundational understanding of coalition politics and party alliances in selected Southern African countries and the noticeable absence of such dynamics in Mozambique. The chapter identifies Southern African countries with established coalition governments for a meaningful comparison. Information was also obtained from social media focused on posts from Mozambican political parties and respected individuals on platforms like Facebook and Twitter, renowned for political discourse. Thematic analysis categorizes social media posts based on key themes, including public sentiment, political discourse, and coalition-related discussions. The subsequent comparative study aims to distinguish commonalities, differences, and pertinent patterns, contributing valuable insights into Mozambique's governance and political stability implications.

This chapter embarks on a comprehensive exploration of Mozambique's experience with coalition governance, aiming to unravel the complexities and peculiarities that define its political evolution. The introduction provides a concise overview, emphasizing the distinctive nature of Mozambique's political journey within the Southern African region. As a guide to the reader, the chapter objectives are clearly outlined, setting the stage for an in-depth examination of Mozambique's intricate path in coalition governance or party alliances.

BACKGROUND

During the tumultuous period spanning the 1970s to the 1990s, national liberation movements, including the one in Mozambique, emerged as dominant political forces in southern African countries (Funada-Classen, 2013; Manning & Malbrough, 2009). The proliferation of multiparty elections in sub-Saharan Africa during the 1990s is attributable to the continent's broader democratic transition (Adejumobi, 2000; Lindberg, 2007). In these transformative times, extensive political and constitutional engineering processes accompanied elections to establish democratic institutions and structures (Adejumobi, 2000).

Mozambique's political evolution reflects a subtle interplay of political agreements and periods characterized by the prominent absence of such alliances. A detailed exploration of historical engagement with coalition politics unveils instances where political forces converged and diverged. In the pre-independence era, Mozambique witnessed the formation of political alliances with the founding of FRELIMO, the liberation party, in Dar es Salaam, Tanzania, in 1962. This coalition brought together three regional nationalist movements: the Mozambican African National Union (MANU), the National Democratic Union of Mozambique (UDENAMO), and the National African Union of Independent Mozambique (UNAMI). The political joint aimed to liberate the land and its people, as outlined in FRELIMO's 1980 documentation (Nuvunga, 2014).

Driven by Marxist ideology, FRELIMO asserted its one-party dominance during pre- and post-independence eras (Levitsky & Way, 2012). In the post-independence period from 1975 to 1990, FRELIMO established a constitutional framework for a one-party socialist state, prohibiting the formation of additional political parties, ostensibly to exclude groups seeking participation in the independence process (Nuvunga, 2014). The end of the Cold War and support from the Soviet army regime posed a threat to FRELIMO's dominance, leading to a devastating civil war from 1977 to 1992. The Rome General Peace Accords, signed between conflicting parties—FRELIMO and the former rebel movement turned opposition party, RENAMO (Green & Otto, 2014)—opened the door for coalition governance, as highlighted by Harrison (1996).

Under substantial international pressure, FRELIMO adopted a multiparty constitution, negotiating peace with RENAMO and collaborating with various political factions. Despite the optimism surrounding the democratic transition, analyzing multiparty democracy and regular elections in Mozambique requires exploration from diverse perspectives to enrich reflections on the quality of relations between political parties and illuminate critical elements surrounding the current multiparty system and its contribution to good governance. According to Nuvunga (2005), RENAMO alleged that FRELIMO formed new political parties to secure its political influence within Mozambican society and on the international stage.

Political collaboration thrived during the early 1990s as Mozambique transitioned to a multiparty system. However, conflicts, often rooted in ideological differences, shaped periods of solitary governance, prompting the formation of coalitions among opposition parties. In 1992, Daviz and Lutero Simango founded the National Convention Party (NCP) (Lundin, 1995, cited in Nuvunga & Adalima, 2011). In 1999, the NCP and nine other opposition parties formed a coalition with Renamo called the RENAMO-Electoral Union. This coalition led to Simango becoming the official RENAMO candidate, triumphing over FRELIMO's candidate and assuming the role of Beira's mayor in local government elections (Nuvunga & Adalima, 2011:9).

Since establishing the multiparty system in 1994, Mozambique has consistently held regular elections. With six general elections (the last in 2019) and six municipal elections (the latest in 2023) over 25 years of multiparty politics, Mozambique's legal framework provides a foundation for democratic elections.

It encompasses constitutional provisions, national laws, and procedures concerning electoral processes (Da Silva, 2022; Nuvunga & Adalima, 2011). In analyzing Mozambique's trajectory toward democracy, Hanlon (2020) contends that the desire to end the civil war and establish a multiparty system overcame challenges in peace negotiations and enacting electoral legislation at the process's outset.

Nevertheless, challenges have tainted subsequent elections, with deteriorating electoral integrity observed in each occurrence. Contested elections have become widely used to consolidate fragile peace in emerging democracies like Mozambique (Kumar, 1998; Mazula,1995; Reilly, 2003; Vine, 2017;2021). In such contexts, elections play a critical role in choosing governments, making them a vital element of democratization (Reilly, 2003:9). The relevance of considering regional alignment and electoral frameworks is key in democratic nations. Mozambique, as a member of the Southern African Development Community (SADC), leverages various regional platforms and treaties to shape its governance principles. Therefore, the influence of regional bodies like SADC-PF, the Electoral Commissions Forum of SADC Countries, and civil society organizations is vital.

Exploring the Interplay of Electoral Systems, Processes, and Government Coalitions in Southern Africa

This section explores the conceptual framework guiding the examination of electoral systems, processes, and government coalitions in Southern Africa. It emphasizes the connection between electoral structures and the formation and functioning of government coalitions, elucidating how electoral processes influence political party representation and coalition dynamics.

The connection between "Examining Electoral Systems and Processes" and "Government Coalitions" lies in exploring how electoral systems and processes influence the formation and functioning of government coalitions. The link will likely explain the impact of electoral structures on political party representation, the dynamics of forming coalitions, and how these factors contribute to the governance landscape in a specific setting.

As Clark (n.d) suggested, citizens, also known as voters, the electorate, or the governed, exercise their civic right to choose representatives periodically, a frequency that differs from country to country. The conceptual functions of elections include providing routine processes for recruiting individuals who will occupy seats, allowing for the review of governments' records, assessing their mandate according to elected governments both domestic and international legitimacy, moral title to rule, and promoting conducive environments for political socialization and political integration, ultimately projecting national unity (Norris, Frank, & Coma, 2014).

Electoral processes are generally articulated through an electoral regulatory framework that states draft based on segments of a country's legal framework concerning electoral processes. This framework, as asserted by Clark (n.d) and Obiagu et al. (2021), preserves the independence and integrity of the electoral process. Given the complexity of electoral processes and actions, this framework should be legally well-defined with clear, comprehensive, simple, and understandable terms for all involved parties (ibid).

In the Southern Africa region, the adoption of democratic governance practices and the culture of establishing electoral systems gained prominence around the 1990s, marking a post-war and conflict transformation when most member states transitioned from mono-party, particularly military rule, to multi-party and democratic governance (Matlosa, 2002;2003). Most of Southern Africa's member states acquired the experience and capacity to hold multi-party democratic elections, initially under the United Nations (UN) (Pottie, 2001). Historically, regional states inherited colonial electoral systems, mainly the

British system, except for South Africa and Lesotho, which have adopted their unique systems (Pottie, 2001; Kadima, 2003; Southall, 2019).

The first-past-the-post electoral (FPTP) system, also known as the single-member plurality system (SMP), rooted in the global north, is expressed in countries like Botswana, the DRC, Lesotho, Malawi, Tanzania, Swaziland, Zambia, and Zimbabwe (Gunathilake, 2018; Kadima, 2003; Matlosa, 2002). While this system is perceived as favouring dominant parties, Kadima (2003) credits it with holding Members of Parliament accountable to their constituencies. Furthermore, other southern African states embrace more complex electoral systems, such as the Proportional Representation (PR) system rooted in social democracies. It entails contestants contending through the party list strategy, as seen in countries like Mozambique, Namibia, and South Africa (Matlosa, 2002; Kadima, 2003). As shown by electoral processes in Mozambique and South Africa, besides encouraging inclusivity and fairness in governance, this system is credited for favouring coalition governments and politics of consensus and compromise (Matlosa, 2002).

Evolution of Electoral Systems and Democratic Governance in Southern Africa: A Historical Perspective and Regional Dynamics

The electoral system encompasses rules governing how votes are cast and assigned seats (Blais & Massicotte, 2002). This involves administrative, procedural, and institutional mechanisms guiding the electoral process. The rules and procedures for casting votes and assigning seats vary significantly from country to country (Blais & Massicotte, 2002; Reilly, 2003). Electoral systems are often classified based on how they function proportionally to translate votes into seats for political parties. Generally, Governments worldwide employ three electoral systems: plurality, semi-proportional, and proportional representation (Reilly, 2003; 2015). Mozambique, falls into the last category, having conducted elections under proportional representation rules.

At the onset, the political landscape of most post-independence African states, including those in Southern Africa, was marked by either civilian or military authoritarian regimes, particularly around the 1960s, 1970s, and 1980s (Matlosa, 2002). This trend was broken in the 1990s as a wave of regime change and political transformations swept the region, accompanying the democratic governance practices and the holding of elections (ibid). This shift was driven by the global recognition of the centrality of democratic governance in development (UNDP, 2002). African governments, including those in Southern Africa, began taking measures through continental and regional institutions to express their commitment to democratization (Fomunyoh, 2020; Matlosa, 2002).

The transition to multi-party structures and democratic governance in Southern Africa was not only a response to internal challenges but also part of a broader regional strategy aimed at overcoming the historical exploitation by Western forces through their colonial systems (Saunders, 2020). In many instances, these countries formed regional alliances or cooperated to confront a common adversary, namely the Western forces that exploited them through their colonial systems (Yohannes, 2002). An illustrative example is the support extended by Mozambique and other regional nations to the South African ANC party and its anti-apartheid activists. This collective effort aimed to dismantle the segregationist system perpetuated by Western colonial powers.

The region witnessed significant democratic transitions, such as establishing civilian rule through elections in Lesotho in 1993. However, challenges persisted, as exemplified by failed elections in Angola, contributing to post-1992 instability (Makoa, 2004). Despite these burdens, the introduction of elections in Southern Africa represented a crucial step toward conflict resolution, peacebuilding, reconciliation, and overall regional stability. Positive political trajectory is evident in the successful shifts to democracy in countries like Namibia (1989), Mozambique (1994), and South Africa (1994). These countries political transitions resulting from intra, and external collaboration reflect a broader historical context wherein nations sought solidarity to overcome the challenges imposed by external domination and colonial legacies. In Mozambique, the Constitution and electoral laws delineate procedures, rules, and regulations governing elections. Article 73 of the Constitution establishes a multi-party democratic system based on universal, direct, equal, secret, and periodic elections. The Constitution recognizes political rights, including freedom of assembly, expression, the press, and political association for Mozambicans (Governo de Moçambique, 2004).

External influences, including international affiliations, significantly impact the deep values of countries' governance. Mozambique, a member of the SADC, approved platforms like the 1992 SADC Treaty, the Regional Indicative Strategic Development Plan (RISDP), the SADC Gender and Development Protocol, the Protocol on Politics, Defense, and Security Cooperation, the Strategic Indicative Plan of the Organ (SIPO), and the SADC Principles and Guidelines Governing Democratic Elections (Matlosa & Lotshwao, 2010). Regional bodies like the SADC-PF and the Electoral Commissions Forum of SADC Countries, along with civil society agencies like the SADC-CNGO and the Electoral Institute for the Sustainability of Democracy in Africa (EISA), support these regional institutions (Matlosa & Lotshwao, 2010).

Studies identified key principles of democratic governance. These include ensuring elected officials are accountable to the electorate and expected to consider the will and concerns of the people in decision-making (Hue & Tung-Wen Sun, 2022; Malik, 2023; Oluwasuji & Okajare, 2021). Effective governance in countries is marked by regular, free, and fair elections, allowing citizens to choose their leaders through democratic voting (John & Aderemi, 2023; Krishnarajan, 2023). The nation upholds the rule of law, ensuring that laws are applied impartially to all citizens, and it maintains an independent judiciary to guarantee justice (Moosa, 2023). The branches of government—judiciary, executive, and legislative—are distinct and autonomous (Dube, 2020; Waldron, 2020). The country actively safeguards and advances human rights to show its commitment to democratic values by guaranteeing access to essential services, individual freedoms, equality, and protection against discrimination (Malik et al., 2021; Nampewo et al., 2022; Yermek et al., 2020).

The analysis of emerging democracies emphasizes the need to distinguish between countries progressively developing liberal democratic practices and the majority that are not moving in that direction. Examining the conventional theoretical correlation between elections and democratization, scholars like Kumar (1998), Reynolds (2005), and Kühne (2010) propose that the holding of elections does not straightforwardly contribute to the democratic legitimacy of competitive elections. Kumar and Kühne argue that while elections are a crucial step toward democratization, they are insufficient conditions in themselves. Many emerging democracies are essentially electoral, demonstrating a commitment to multi-party systems through regular elections (Rosário, 2020). The inclusion of government coalitions implies an exploration of the role and impact of political alliances or coalitions in the context of elections and governance. This could involve understanding how different political parties come together to form coalitions and govern.

FINDINGS

Political Parties, Alliances, and Evolution in Mozambique's Democratic Landscape

A retrospective analysis of historical alliances, fractures, and shifting commitments provides crucial insights into the fluid relationships characterizing Mozambique's political scenario. Notable political structures such as the long-standing ruling party, FRELIMO, historically driven by Marxist ideology, and opposition parties like RENAMO, contribute distinct perspectives to Mozambique's political discourse, providing valuable insights into their contributions to the complex democratic political fabric of the nation.

For instance, FRELIMO's historical dominance as the liberation party and its subsequent recognition as the leading party promoting multiparty governance in the early 1990s that translated into the adoption of democracy exemplify the adaptive strategies employed by the Mozambican Government. Other examples from African countries that transitioned from the era of dominant-party systems to a multiparty system include Mali, Senegal, and Zambia (Doorenspleet and Nijzink, 2013). However, despite establishing the multiparty system in Mozambique, the country still experienced a dominant-party system, with FRELIMO winning all five presidential and legislative elections of 1999, 2004, 2009, 2014, and 2019 (Cortes, 2018; Nuvunga, 2014). Many countries in the SSA region observed this trend, with Lindberg (2007) identifying 21 electoral democracies, 11 of which could be characterized as stable, and eight having a dominant-party system. Additionally, Schrire (2010: 139) highlighted instances of former liberation parties evolving into dominant parties, such as the cases of South Africa's African National Congress (ANC) and Namibia's South West African People's Party (SWAPO).

Like Mozambique, the political landscape in Southern Africa is characterized by a diverse array of political parties and alliances, each contributing to the region's dynamic political scene. Countries such as South Africa and Zimbabwe feature prominent political entities, each with distinct ideologies, historical backgrounds, and policy priorities. For instance, in South Africa, the ruling party, the ANC, played a central role in leading the liberation efforts from the segregationist apartheid system that benefitted the white minority in the country for several decades (Mosala, 2022).

Historical incidents, including the 1992 peace agreement in Mozambique, significantly influenced the formation and dissolution of coalitions. Concurrently, opposition parties in Mozambique, such as RENAMO, and emerging ones, like the National Convention Party (NCP), bring alternative visions and policy proposals, enriching the diversity of the political discourse. For instance, RENAMO, the party that took part in the signature on 4 October 1992 of a General Peace Agreement with FRELIMO, was the main opposition party in the first democratic elections in the country held in October 1994 (Nuvunga, 2014). In the period of transitioning from a one-party political system to the establishment of a multiparty system, RENAMO was perceived as the insurgent faction. At the same time, the remaining opposition parties were commonly referred to as the non-armed opposition parties (Nuvunga, 2005). These other opposition parties often resulted from breakaways from the country's leading political party, RENAMO.

According to Simutanyi (2009:6), a breakaway faction or party emerges when significant disagreements between a party's leaders and certain officials or members lead the latter to resign and establish a new group or party. Such divisions often arise from perceived threats to party leadership, resulting in purges that prompt individuals to form their parties, usually to address unresolved issues. One example is the Mozambique Democratic Movement (MDM) emerged in March 2009 as a fragmented party originating from the former rebel movement, RENAMO. This breakaway occurred following an internal power dispute, primarily disrupting the bipolarization that had defined Mozambican politics since the inception of democratic elections in 1994 (Nuvunga & Adalima, 2011).

Another party that resulted from the breakaway of the main opposition party, RENAMO, is the Party for Peace and Development (PDD) of Raúl Domingos (Nuvunga & Adalima, 2011). Following the inaugural national democratic elections in Mozambique in 1994, several political parties emerged through breakaway movements. The Social Liberal and Democratic Party (SOL), is separated from the Liberal and Democratic Party (PALMO). Additionally, the Party National Democratic Congress (PACODE) originated from the National Convention Party (PCN). At the same time, the Labour Party (PT), emerged from the People's Progress Party of Mozambique (PPPM). Post the 1994 general elections, the formation of the Communist Party of Mozambique (PACOM) and the National Unity Party (PUN) also took place (Lundin, 1995).

Mirroring occurrences in neighboring countries, the first local government elections in South Africa witnessed a partnership between the Democratic Party, the New National Party (NNP), and the FA party (Boysen, 2014:78). In Zimbabwe, the Zimbabwe African National Union-Patriotic Front (ZANU-PF) has been a dominant political force to free its people from the subjugation of English dominance (Gwekwerere et al., 2019).

The emergence of political parties through breakaways is a recurring trend in various African countries. In Zambia, the United National Independence Party (UNIP) originated as a breakaway from the African National Congress (ANC), leading to the establishment of new political entities like the United Party for National Development (UPND), Forum for Democracy and Development (FDD), Heritage Party, and Patriotic Front (PF) (Simutanyi, 2009). Malawi witnessed the formation of several parties as breakaways from the United Democratic Front (UDF), including the Democratic Progressive Party (DPP). In Zimbabwe, the ruling ZANU-PF resulted from a breakaway from ZAPU. Namibia experienced the creation of the Rally for Democracy and Progress (RDP) as a breakaway from the ruling SWAPO party. South Africa saw the establishment of the Congress of the People (COPE) in December 2008 as a breakaway from the ruling African National Congress (ANC) (Simutanyi, 2009). Additionally, the Economic Freedom Fighters (EFF) party in South Africa, founded by Julius Malema in July 2013, emerged as a breakaway from the ANC due to political and ideological differences, particularly regarding economic policies, land reform, and social justice (Mbete, 2015).

In summary, the installation of multipartyism in Mozambique has allowed the proliferation of political parties and groups that have mostly emerged from breakaways from the larger parties. The same has happened in other countries in the Southern African region. However, this did not translate into greater strength in the power struggle, much less in the exercise of more democratic governance, since these parties did not have much political expression and muscle and were often gobbled up by the larger parties. This overview not only narrates events but interprets the underlying dynamics, providing a unique understanding of Mozambique's political evolution and its implications for the broader Southern African context.

Leadership Dynamics in Post-Independence Mozambique

The post-independence multiparty system in Mozambique introduced diverse political actors, with figures like Samora Machel, the first President of Mozambique, gaining notable recognition for his pivotal role in the country's struggle for independence from Portuguese colonial rule. Machel died in 1986 and is remembered for his contributions to the liberation movement and his efforts to establish a socialist state post-independence (Jopela, 2017; Sumich, 2020). From earlier 90s Mozambique embarked on a transition from a centrally planned economic system to economic liberalism and the adoption of multiparty politics. In 1994, Frelimo nominated Joaquim Chissano as their candidate in the inaugural presidential elections, and he held the presidency for two consecutive terms before stepping down in 2004 (Cortes, 2018). However, within Frelimo, particularly among war veterans, Chissano was perceived as weak due to alleged concessions to RENAMO during the negotiations leading to the signing of the peace agreement in 1992 (Weimer & Carilho, 2017).

Armando Emilio Guebuza, another prominent political figure, succeeded Chissano. Nuvunga (2014:11) noted a shift in leadership style from Chissano's reformist approach to Guebuza's more party-centric and authoritative style. Guebuza revitalized and reorganized the party, strengthening its presence within the state, in contrast to Chissano's separation of the party from the state (Nuvunga, 2014:11). Under Guebuza's leadership, Frelimo's influence over the state intensified, marked by the reactivation of party cells within the state apparatus and the utilization of state resources, such as the District Development Fund ('7 Millhões'), to stimulate economic development in the country's districts (Orre & Forquilha, 2012). This period witnessed increased Frelimo hegemony and exacerbated political intolerance (Chichava, 2010; Kleibl & Munck, 2017). Subsequently, Filipe Jacinto Nyusi, another FRELIMO candidate, assumed the presidency, becoming the third individual to hold the office through the electoral process (Cortes, 2018). President Nyusi's tenure has been marred by controversy and significant criticism regarding the nation's state. In an article titled "The State of the Nation is painful, pathetic, poignant, putrefying, and pariah. Not recommended!" published in 2023, Mosse expressed his dissatisfaction with Nyusi's governance, describing it as marked by an autocratic leadership style. Mosse argues that this leadership style has led the country into despair, manifested through a weakened democracy characterized by fraudulent elections. He further contends that a compromised National electoral system and the entanglement of the state judiciary and military bodies support these elections.

In addition to the FRELIMO leaders, Afonso Dhlakama, the deceased leader of the main opposition party, RENAMO, played a crucial role in establishing the democratic path and promoting peace in the country. Recognized for his successful guerrilla campaign during the civil war (1977-1992), Dhlakama was the RENAMO presidential candidate in four successive elections. The ceasefire agreement signed in Rome on October 4, 1992, involving President Joaquim Chissano and RENAMO leader Afonso Dhlakama, marked a significant moment in Mozambique's history (Vine, 2017:125). He was always known for being vocal and critical of the ruling party's governance intervention. In some circles, Dhlakama was viewed as lacking strong public speaking skills, exhibiting insecurity, indecisiveness, and a tendency to change positions (Vines,2017:122). Nevertheless, the author highlighted a significant improvement in his speeches and rallies during the 2014 election campaign, potentially contributing to RENAMO's enhanced electoral performance (Vines, 2017:122).

After the passing of Dhlakama, RENAMO's leadership fell to Ussufo Momade, a party veteran who had held various roles, including party general, Member of Parliament, and party general secretary (VOA Portugues, 2019). Momade faced challenges gathering support from youth voters and certain senior party members (Saraiva, 2023). This difficulty resulted in the emergence of a Military Junta comprising around 200 armed individuals, causing armed disruptions in the central region of Mozambique in 2019 (Vines, 2021). Notably, Momade's leadership has been criticized for its inadequacy in managing the demilitarization, demobilization, and social reintegration of RENAMO guerrillas in line with agreements made with the Government (Saraiva, 2023; VOA Portugues, 2019).

Social media pages affiliated with opposition parties such as RENAMO, academic Adriano Nuvunga, investigative journalist Marcelo Mosse, and private media outlets such as *Canal de Moçambique*, *SA-VANA,* and *Justiça Nacional* reveal an exciting trend. Despite a perceived decline in the popularity of RENAMO's current president, Momade, two party Members of Parliament, Venancio Mondlane and Antonio Muchanga, who contested as party candidates in the October 2023 local government elections in Matola and Maputo city, respectively, are widely seen by many in the country as potential counterbalances to the dominance of the ruling party.

A Glance at the Formation of Alliances in Mozambique and Other Southern African Countries From the Perspective of Democratic Coalition Government: Lost Opportunities?

Party alliances played a crucial role in defining Mozambique's political landscape, contributing to establishing the democratic process and socio-economic development. A notable instance occurred in 1999 with the formation of the RENAMO-Electoral Union, a coalition comprising ten unarmed parties alongside RENAMO, the main opposition party, also known as the rebel party. This Alliance resulted in the election of two of its prominent members, one to parliament and the other as a candidate and winner of the local elections in the city of Beira in 2003. This played a pivotal role in the founding of MDM in 2009, later becoming the third-largest party in the country (Nuvunga & Adalima, 2011).

The critical role of these alliances in influencing the nation's political trajectory reflected at the time a commitment to democratic principles and addressing the needs of the people. Scholars studying Mozambique's governance, public administration, and politics have documented legal measures implemented by the government to incorporate democratic principles into its programmatic activities. The nation operates under a system of a "superficial" representative democracy, where elected officials represent the interests and will of the people (Cortes, 2018; Da Silva, 2022; Jatula & Conshello, 2021; Nuvunga & Adalima, 2011; Nuvunga, 2014). In this system, Mozambican nationals do not directly decide on laws and policies; instead, they elect representatives to make decisions on their behalf.

Mozambique has been struggling to adopt adequately the key democratic principles in the country's governance and still grapples with challenges related to ensuring political stability originating from historical conflicts. This arises due to a fragmented governmental system and institutions needing help to uphold the rule of law, exacerbated by ineffective opposition parties that fail to pressure these institutions to serve the population. According to Jatula and Conshello (2021), despite its abundant natural resources, Mozambique faces challenges including political instability, corruption allegations, and economic difficulties. Additionally, the ruling party FRELIMO has maintained its dominance in Mozambique's political landscape since the onset of multiparty elections, exerting considerable control over the country's economic trajectory, administrative functions, and the judicial and legal system (Cortes, 2018; Jatula & Conshello, 2021; Vines, 2017; 2021). Furthermore, ineffective party alliances among opposition parties, marked by internal disagreements and conflicting interests, aggravate the situation, contributing to the country's precarious political and economic State.

Mozambique scores poorly on most democracy indicators. Since 1994, Mozambique has been classified as "partly free" in terms of political rights and civil liberties by Freedom House (Pitcher, 2020). According to the latest electoral democracy index from the Varieties of Democracy project, which measures critical aspects of democracy such as clean elections, the extent of suffrage, freedom of expression, and independent media, the score for Mozambique is halfway between non-democratic and fully democratic

(Varieties of Democracy, 2020). Over the period 2009 to 2019, Mozambique's score declined from 0.49 to 0.41, signaling the deterioration of its fragile democratic institutions and rising autocracy. The country was classified as a "hybrid regime", between authoritarianism and a flawed democracy (Pitcher, 2020).

One of the negative impacts of the absence of established party alliances through coalition governments is the erosion of democratic values within the political system. Simutanyi (2011) pointed out certain drawbacks within the African political system, such as underdeveloped bureaucratic and organizational structures, a deficiency in internal democracy characterized by a reluctance to accommodate dissent, a scarcity of internal debate, and a lack of competition for elective positions.

For instance, between 1999 and 2013, Dhlakama perceived Raul Domingos, a key political figure who served as a former guerrilla soldier, chief negotiator during the 1992 Civil War's Rome peace, and lately as the head of the parliament in RENAMO, as a threat to his leadership, and expelled him (Slattery 2003: 129). The expulsion of Domingos weakened the party leadership's authority and eroded public and internal support (Vine, 2017). Further internal conflicts within the party arose from concerns Dhlakama and other members expressed regarding the rising support for David Simango, resulting in Simango's expulsion from the coalition party (Nuvunga & Adalima, 2011). This expulsion prompted Simango's independent candidacy in the 2008 local elections, where he secured a decisive victory with 62%, surpassing candidates from both FRELIMO and RENAMO (Hanlon, 2010). In response to disputes with RENAMO's leadership, Simango took the initiative to establish the MDM, playing a pivotal role in breaking the parliamentary bi-polarization dominated by FRELIMO and RENAMO in Mozambique (Nuvunga & Adalima, 2014).

MDM party rose as the third biggest party in the country, has been advocating for transparency and accountability, a fundamental democratic principle while aiming to reduce the President's powers substantially and position itself as a viable alternative to the long-standing rivals, FRELIMO and RENAMO (VOA Portugues, 2019).

Other examples of the disintegration of democratic values due to unstable party alliances occurred in African countries such as Kenya, Malawi, South Africa, and Zambia that feature parties with different political ideologies, leading to fragmentation of the already established coalitions (Arriola et al., 2021; Lembani, 2014; Mistra, 2021). South Africa, for instance, with the ruling party, African National Congress (ANC), dominating the political scene, as in Mozambique, has also seen several coalitions governments formed due to the willingness of a minority party to unseat a ruling party by joining forces and winning elections or because parliament lacks a political party with the majority vote (Makole et al.,2022; Netswera & Khumalo, 2022). Instability in leadership within coalition governments in South Africa affected the execution of municipality responsibilities and the oversight of the party group's governance practices (Mamokhere, 2022; Mistra, 2021).

Malawi also has seen at least five party coalitions formed starting in 1994 to 2019 between opposition parties and some other small parties (Kadima, 2014; Mistra, 2021). Unfortunately, these political alliances in Malawi proved to be unstable. This instability of coalition parties in the country was the result of the awareness of party leaders or local councilors about the power of voters to push out specific politicians due to their discontentment about their inability to solve people's problems (Lembani, 2014; Muriaas, 2013). When alliances lack cohesion or are formed based on narrow interests rather than a shared commitment to democratic principles, the result can be a weakening of democratic institutions. This erosion may manifest through compromised electoral processes, reduced political transparency, and challenges to the rule of law (Kadima, 2014; Lembani, 2014; Mistra, 2021).

Another consequence of compromised party alliances or their absence is the obstruction to policy implementation. As highlighted by Cortes (2018), although the 1990 constitution mandates a separation between the State and the party, this separation is only nominal, leading to the common practice of using State resources for party purposes, particularly by party members. Consequently, the economic benefits of the country's apparent progress are enjoyed by only a minority of Mozambicans affiliated with the ruling party (Cortes, 2018; Jatula & Conshello, 2021). Indeed, as stated by Jatula and Conshello (2021), despite the apparent political stability throughout the post-independence period, continuous international donor support to almost half of the yearly national budget, and a rising Gross Domestic Product (GDP), the living standards of most Mozambicans remain poor.

Party alliances are instrumental in the formation of government and policy implementation. In Mozambique, a dominant ruling party with complete control of the executive and legislative governance structures may lead to ineffective service provision to its people and ultimately cause political instability, impeding the ability to enact and sustain effective policies. As such, from 2016 onward, extensive economic mismanagement and significant trade imbalances have exacerbated vast multidimensional poverty, even with the debt forgiveness and restructuring efforts of the International Monetary Fund (WBG 2020).

Divergent views against the ruling party FRELIMO or poorly aligned alliances may result in legislative gridlock, preventing the implementation of crucial socio-economic initiatives. This, in turn, has adverse effects on the country's development agenda (Cortes, 2018). Indeed, a significant number of respondents in a study conducted in 2021 concurred that the judicial system under Frelimo's control exacerbated corruption in the country. This situation is further exacerbated by the lack of accountability, transparency, and efficiency within Mozambique's Government (Jatula & Conshello, 2021).

The section concludes by highlighting the negative impacts of compromised party alliances, such as hindering policy implementation and perpetuating economic disparities among Mozambicans. It draws parallels with other African countries, like South Africa and Malawi, to emphasize the broader consequences of unstable party alliances on democratic institutions and governance.

DIRECTIONS FOR RESEARCH

Exploring Mozambique's political landscape and the state of party alliances and coalition governments in the country has illuminated critical aspects of democracy, governance, and electoral systems. Several avenues for future research can deepen our understanding and contribute to the ongoing discourse.

A more in-depth analysis of the historical and contemporary dynamics of party alliances and coalitions in Mozambique is needed, offering valuable insights into the country's political trajectory. Understanding how these alliances evolve, their internal functioning, and the implications for democratic governance could provide essential perspectives, especially considering the limited recent studies on this subject.

The recurring issue of party fragmentation and instability in Mozambique and its evident negative impact on governance structures necessitates investigating the consequences of party fragmentation. This research should explore how the absence of cohesive party alliances affects the effectiveness of government projects, resource distribution, and overall public service delivery. Such an inquiry would contribute significantly to comprehending Mozambique's intricate relationship between party dynamics and governance outcomes.

Examining the influence of international and regional bodies, such as SADC and the African Union, on Mozambique's governance and electoral processes emerges as a promising avenue. Understanding how these external factors shape domestic policies and contribute to or hinder democratic practices can provide a broader context for Mozambique's political scenario. In the present situation characterized by fragile governance structures, external pressure from regional bodies could catalyze reforms. Mosse (2023) proposes that, given the recent fraudulent elections and the evident fragility in governance structures, the Nyusi Government should actively endorse reforms in the country's constitution to enhance democracy.

Another crucial area requiring further research involves investigating public perceptions of the democratic process and the factors influencing political participation. While various social media pages, academics, and non-governmental organizations (NGOs) have highlighted negative public perceptions, more in-depth and scientific studies are necessary to understand how Mozambican citizens perceive electoral systems, political parties, and governance structures in the current political context. This knowledge is critical for informing strategies to enhance civic engagement and strengthen democratic practices.

Empirical comparative studies with other African nations facing similar governance and party politics challenges are imperative. Drawing similarities and contrasts with countries that have experienced successful democratic transitions or faced similar obstacles can provide a broader perspective on Mozambique's unique circumstances. South Africa and other regional countries such as Botswana, Lesotho, and Malawi have vast experience in forming and disestablishing coalition Governments. These can be helpful case studies as a comparative approach to enable a unique understanding of effective party alliances or the establishment of coalition governments.

As criticism of the current government in Mozambique grows, investigating the role of technological innovations in electoral processes becomes crucial. Future studies analyzing possibilities for integrating technological innovations could offer strategies to improve transparency, efficiency, and public trust in Mozambique's electoral system as highlighted by Monday & Aluko (2023) in their study to assess the role of ICT technology in elections management in Nigeria. Thus, the chapter contends that a study Assessing the benefits and challenges of adopting new technologies in elections is essential for modernizing democratic practices and addressing concerns about electoral integrity.

Lastly, there is a need to analyze the long-term impacts of coalition governments on political stability, economic development, and governance in Mozambique. Policymakers must understand the sustainability of such alliances and their influential role in the nation's future. Scholars engaging in these research directions can contribute to a deeper understanding of Mozambique's political scenario, offer evidence-based policy recommendations, and enrich the global discourse on democracy and governance in the African context.

CONCLUSION AND RECOMMENDATIONS

In conclusion, this chapter highlights the unique trajectory of Mozambique within Southern Africa's coalition governance landscape and emphasizes the need for ongoing research to comprehend the evolving dynamics of coalition politics in the country. Despite historical challenges, such as the Civil War, Mozambique has demonstrated adaptability in its political landscape, marked by the ruling party's dominance. The impacts of ineffective party alliances extend beyond immediate political consequences, affecting democracy and socio-economic development.

The chapter underlines the essential role of party alliances in promoting democratic principles and addressing the people's needs. While Mozambique is committed to democratic values, persistent challenges include political instability, corruption, and economic difficulties. The absence of established party alliances contributes to the erosion of democratic values, evidenced by internal conflicts within parties and the dominance of FRELIMO.

One significant consequence of the lack of effective party alliances is the impaired socio-economic development in Mozambique. The correlation between effective governance and socio-economic development is well-established, and ineffective party alliances can lead to governance challenges, hindering progress in key areas such as poverty reduction, education, and healthcare.

Furthermore, a lack of established coalition governance can foster Political Fragmentation. This means that ineffectual party alliances may promote political fragmentation, resulting in a fractured political landscape. The resulting fragmentation can diminish the effectiveness of opposition parties, reducing their capacity to act as checks and balances on the ruling coalition. A fragmented political environment can lead to a lack of accountability, inhibiting the overall health of Mozambique's democracy.

The chapter supports Jatula's (2021) proposed measures, emphasizing the importance of initially passing the Freedom of Information Bill. This legislative action is a crucial step to unlock the country's political space, promote transparency, and alleviate tensions between FRELIMO and RENAMO. Additionally, the chapter aligns with Jatula's recommendation to advocate for state support directed towards local firms and entrepreneurs. The goal is to facilitate their transition into more diversified and productive industries, ultimately enhancing competitiveness on a continental scale. This dual-pronged approach, involving legislative reforms and economic support, is essential for addressing existing challenges and promoting positive transformations in Mozambique's political and economic landscape. The volatile political landscape highlights opposition parties' need to forge strong coalitions, actively engaging in governance processes. This strategic approach aims to balance power and reduce the ruling party's dominance, ultimately serving the voters' best interests.

In terms of reforms, while some progress has been made in electoral governance reforms in southern African countries, there is a need for studies exploring empirical processes of electoral systems reforms in many African states. The suggestion is that adopting blended electoral systems, aligned with each member state's political culture and national vision, could enhance the region's cultivation and consolidation of democratic governance. Mozambique's political scenario shifted from bipartisan to coalitions in 1999, resulting in the ruling party, FRELIMO, losing some constituencies. Understanding electoral systems' interconnectedness is crucial for comprehending government coalition formation, stability, and functioning in Southern Africa.

Moreover, it is imperative to differentiate between pseudo-democracies and electoral democracies that fall short of thoroughly liberal democratic practices. Addressing national discontent requires strong party leadership to restore public confidence and address economic challenges. The complexity of Mozambique's political scenario necessitates continuous research to inform evidence-based policy recommendations and contribute to the global discourse on democracy and governance in the African context.

REFERENCES

Adejumobi, S. (2000). Elections in Africa: A fading show of democracy? *International Political Science Review, 21*(1), 59-73.

Arriola, L. R., Devaro, J., & Meng, A. (2021). Democratic subversion: Elite cooptation and opposition fragmentation. *The American Political Science Review, 115*(4), 1358–1372. doi:10.1017/S0003055421000629

Blais, A., & Massicotte, L. (2002). Electoral systems. In L. LeDuc, R. G. Niemi, & P. Norris (Eds.), *Comparing democracies* (2nd ed., pp. 40–69). Sage.

Booysen, S. (2014). Causes and impact of party alliances and coalitions on the party system and national cohesion in South Africa. *Journal of African Elections.*, *13*(1), 66–92. doi:10.20940/JAE/2014/v13i1a4

Clark, J. G. (n.d.). *The Legal Framework: The Context for an Electoral Management Body (EMB)'s Role and Powers*. Academic Press.

Cortês, E. R. D. O. (2018). *Velhos amigos, novos adversários: as disputas, alianças e reconfigurações empresariais na elite política Moçambicana*. PhD Thesis.

Da Silva, D. C. (2022). *Electoral Integrity in Mozambique–Institutions, Structures and International Players*. Master thesis.

Doorenspleet, R., & Nijzink, L. (2013). One-Party Dominance in African Democracies: A Framework for Analysis. In R. Doorenspleet & L. Nijzink (Eds.), *One-Party Dominance in African Democracies* (pp. 1–25). Lynne Rienner Publishers. doi:10.1515/9781626372658-002

Dube, F. (2020). Separation of powers and the institutional supremacy of the Constitutional Court over Parliament and the executive. *South African Journal on Human Rights*, *36*(4), 293–318. doi:10.1080/0 2587203.2021.1925954

Funada-Classen, S. (2013). *The origins of war in Mozambique: A history of unity and division*. African Minds. doi:10.47622/978-1-920489-97-7

Governo de Moçambique. (2004). *Constituição da República* [Constitution of the Republic]. Boletim da República.

Green, C., & Otto, L. (2014). *Resource abundance in Mozambique: Avoiding conflict, ensuring prosperity*. Academic Press.

Gunathilake, L. D. (2018). *Electoral Reform in Former British Colonies: A Comparative Case Study of Sri Lanka and South Africa*. Villanova University.

Gwekwerere, T., Mutasa, D. E., Mpondi, D., & Mubonderi, B. (2019). Patriotic narratives on national leadership in Zimbabwe: Zimbabwe African National Union-Patriotic Front (ZANU-PF) and Movement for Democratic Change (MDC) song texts, ca 2000–2017. *South African Journal of African Languages*, *39*(1), 56–66. doi:10.1080/02572117.2019.1572323

Hanlon, J. (2010). FRELIMO landslide in tainted election in Mozambique. *Review of African Political Economy*, *37*(123), 92–95. doi:10.1080/03056241003638019

Hanlon, J. (2020). Integridade eleitoral em Moçambique: Uma perspectiva política e histórica (Ser. Democracia Multipartidária em Moçambique, pp. 151–169). Maputo: EISA Mozambique.

Hue, T. H. H., & Tung-Wen Sun, M. (2022). Democratic governance: Examining the Influence of citizen participation on local government performance in Vietnam. *International Journal of Public Administration*, *45*(1), 4–22. doi:10.1080/01900692.2021.1939713

Jatula, V., & Conshello, S. (2021). Democratic Deficits and Underdevelopment in Mozambique. *Journal of the Humanities and Social Sciences*, *13*(2).

John, T. A., & Aderemi, A. K. (2023). The challenges of promoting centripetal forces in Nigeria's sustainable development. *ACU Journal of Social Sciences, 1*(1).

Jopela, A. (2017). *The Heritagization of the Liberation Struggle in Postcolonial Mozambique*. Academic Press.

Kadima, D. (2014). An introduction to the politics of party alliances and coalitions in socially-divided Africa. *Journal of African Elections*, *13*(1), 1–24. doi:10.20940/JAE/2014/v13i1a1

Kadima, D. K. (2003). Choosing an electoral system: alternatives for the post-war Democratic Republic of Congo. *Journal of African Elections, 2*(1), 33-48.

Krishnarajan, S. (2023). Rationalizing democracy: The perceptual bias and (un) democratic behavior. *The American Political Science Review*, *117*(2), 474–496. doi:10.1017/S0003055422000806

Kumar, K. (Ed.). (1998). Post-conflict elections, democratization, and international assistance. Boulder: Lynne Rienner Publishers.

Lembani, S. (2014). Alliances, coalitions and the weakening of the party system in Malawi. *Journal of African Elections*, *13*(1), 115–149. doi:10.20940/JAE/2014/v13i1a6

Levitsky, S. R., & Way, L. A. (2012). Beyond patronage: Violent struggle, ruling party cohesion, and authoritarian durability. *Perspectives on Politics*, *10*(4), 869–889. doi:10.1017/S1537592712002861

Lindberg, S. (2007). Institutionalization of Party Systems? Stability and Fluidity among Legislative Parties in Africa's Democracies. *Government and Opposition*, *42*(2), 215–241. doi:10.1111/j.1477-7053.2007.00219.x

Makoa, F. K. (2004). Electoral reform and political stability in Lesotho. *African. The Journal of Conflict Resolution*, *4*(2), 79–85.

Makole, K. R., Ntshangase, B. A., & Adewumi, S. A. (2022). Coalition Governance: Unchartered Waters in South African Political Landscape. *Business Ethics and Leadership*, *6*(4), 23–37. doi:10.21272/bel.6(4).23-37.2022

Malik, A. A. (2023). Parliamentary Democracy: Mechanisms, Challenges, and the Quest for Effective Governance. *Revista Review Index Journal of Multidisciplinary, 3*(4), 1-9.

Malik, F., Abduladjid, S., Mangku, D. G. S., Yuliartini, N. P. R., Wirawan, I. G. M. A. S., & Mahendra, P. R. A. (2021). Legal Protection for People with Disabilities in the Perspective of Human Rights in Indonesia. *International Journal (Toronto, Ont.)*, *10*, 539.

Mamokhere, J. (2022). Understanding the Complex Interplay of Governance, Systematic, and Structural Factors Affecting Service Delivery in South African Municipalities. *Commonwealth Youth & Development, 20*(2).

Manning, C., & Malbrough, M. (2009). Learning the Right Lessons from Mozambique's Transition to Peace. *Taiwan Journal of Democracy*, *5*(1), 77–91.

Matlosa, K. (2002). Review of electoral systems and democratization in Southern Africa. *International Roundtable on the South African Electoral System, Cape Town.*

Matlosa, K. (2003). Political culture and democratic governance in Southern Africa. *American Journal of Political Science, 8*(1), 85–112.

Matlosa, K., & Lotshwao, K. (2010). *Political integration and democratisation in Southern Africa: Progress, problems and prospects.* Academic Press.

Mazula, B. (1995). *Moçambique: eleições, democracia e desenvolvimento.* Inter-Africa Group.

Mbete, S. (2015). The Economic Freedom Fighters-South Africa's turn towards populism? *Journal of African Elections, 14*(1), 35-59.

MISTRA. (2021). Marriages of Inconvenience: The politics of coalitions in South Africa. Johannesburg: Mapungubwe Institute for Strategic Reflection.

Moosa, I. A. (2023). Western Exceptionalism: The Rule of Law, Judicial Independence and Transparency. In *The West Versus the Rest and The Myth of Western Exceptionalism* (pp. 91–130). Springer International Publishing. doi:10.1007/978-3-031-26560-0_4

Mosala, S. (2022). From a Liberation Movement to a Governing Party: An Interrogation of the African National Congress (ANC). *Journal of Nation-Building and Policy Studies, 6*(3), 67–89. doi:10.31920/2516-3132/2022/v6n3a4

Mosse, M. (2023). *O Estado da Nação é penoso, patetico, pungente,putrefacto e pária. Não se recomenda! Carta de Moçambique.* Available from https://www.cartamz.com/index.php/blog-do-marcelo-mosse/item/15607-o-estado-da-nacao-e-penoso-patetico-pungente-putrefacto-e-paria-nao-se-recomenda

Muriaas, R. L. (2013). Party affiliation in new democracies: Local reactions to the split of the ruling party in Malawi. *African Journal of Political Science and International Relations, 7*(4), 190–199. doi:10.5897/AJPSIR10.096

Nampewo, Z., Mike, J. H., & Wolff, J. (2022). Respecting, protecting and fulfilling the human right to health. *International Journal for Equity in Health, 21*(1), 1–13. doi:10.1186/s12939-022-01634-3 PMID:35292027

Netswera, M. M., & Khumalo, P. (2022). The Coalition-building Process in South Africa: Reflection on the 2021 Local Government Elections. *African Journal of Democracy and Governance, 9*(34), 103–125.

Norris, P., Frank, R. W., & Coma, F. M. (Eds.). (2014). *Advancing electoral integrity.* Oxford University Press.

Nuvunga, A. (2005). *Multiparty Democracy in Mozambique: Strengths, Weaknesses and Challenges.* EISA Report Number 14.

Nuvunga, A. (2014). *From the two-party to the dominant party system in Mozambique, 1994- 2012. Framing Frelimo party dominance in context.* PhD thesis. Erasmus University of Rotterdam.

Nuvunga, A., & Adalima, J. (2011). *Mozambique Democratic Movement (MDM): an analysis of a new opposition party in Mozambique.* Academic Press.

Obiagu, U. C., Abada, I. M., & Mbah, P. O. (2021). Autocratization verity: Insights from democratic setbacks in Africa. *African Review (Dar Es Salaam, Tanzania)*, *48*(2), 301–332. doi:10.1163/1821889X-12340051

Oluwasuji, O. C., & Okajare, O. E. (2021). Participatory Democracy, Local Government Elections and the Politics of the States' Ruling Parties in Nigeria. *International Journal of Research and Innovation in Social Science*, *1*, 370–378.

Pitcher, M. A. (2020). Mozambique elections 2019: Pernicious polarisation, democratic decline, and rising authoritarianism. *African Affairs*, *119*(476), 468–486. doi:10.1093/afraf/adaa012

Portugues, V. O. A. (2019). *Moçambique Eleições: Perfil de Ossufo Momade*. https://www.voaportugues.com/a/mo%C3%A7ambique-elei%C3%A7%C3%B5es-perfil-de-ossufo-momade/5120507.html

Pottie, D. (2001). Electoral management and democratic governance in Southern Africa. *Politikon: South African Journal of Political Studies*, *28*(2), 133–155. doi:10.1080/02589340120091628

Reilly, B. (2003). *International Electoral Assistance: A review of donor's activities and lessons learned* (Ser. Working Paper 17). The Hague: Clingendael Institute.

Reilly, B. (2015). Electoral systems. Routledge handbook of Southeast Asian democratization, 225-236.

Rosário, D. (2020). *Órgãos de administração eleitoral em Moçambique: Entre a (im)parcialidade, (in) dependência e a procura de transparência nas eleições competitivas em tempos de regimes híbridos: 1994-2019. Democracia Multipartidária em Moçambique*. EISA Mozambique.

Saraiva, R. (2023). Adaptive Peacebuilding in Mozambique: Examples of Localized International Non-Governmental Organizations (L-INGOs) in a Complex and Uncertain Environment. In *Adaptive Peacebuilding: A New Approach to Sustaining Peace in the 21st Century* (pp. 121–150). Springer International Publishing. doi:10.1007/978-3-031-18219-8_5

Saunders, C. (2020). Visions of Unity: Southern Africa and Liberation. *Visions of African Unity: New Perspectives on the History of Pan-Africanism and African Unification Projects*, 133-155.

Schrire, R. (2010). The realities of opposition in South Africa: Legitimacy, strategies and consequences. *Democratization*, *8*(1), 135–148. doi:10.1080/714000189

Southall, R. (2019). Electoral systems and democratization in Africa. In *Voting for Democracy* (pp. 19–36). Routledge. doi:10.4324/9780429428036-2

Sumich, J. (2020). 'Just another African country': Socialism, capitalism and temporality in Mozambique. *Third World Quarterly*, *42*(3), 582–598. doi:10.1080/01436597.2020.1788933

Varieties of Democracy. (2020). *Clean Elections Index*. Varieties of Democracy V-Dem.

Vines, A. (2017). Afonso Dhlakama and RENAMO's return to armed conflict since 2013: the politics of reintegration in Mozambique. *A. Themnér, Warlord democrats in Africa Ex-military leaders and electoral politics*, 121-152

Vines, A. (2021). Violence, Peacebuilding, and Elite Bargains in Mozambique Since Independence. In T. McNamee & M. Muyangwa (Eds.), *The State of Peacebuilding in Africa: Lessons Learned for Policymakers and Practitioners* (pp. 321–342). Springer International Publishing. doi:10.1007/978-3-030-46636-7_18

Waldron, J. (2020). Separation of powers in thought and practice? *Revista de Direito Administrativo, 279*(3), 17–53. doi:10.12660/rda.v279.2020.82914

Weimer, B., & Carrilho, J. (2017). *Political economy of decentralisation in Mozambique— Dynamics, Outcomes, Challenges*. IESE.

World Bank Group. (2020). *Global Economic Prospect: Slow Growth, Policy Challenges*. Retrieved May 20 2021 from: file:///C:/Users/UTAH/Desktop/ Global%20economic%20prospects%202020.pdf

Yermek, B., Zhanna, K., Dinara, B., Gulzhazira, M., Gulim, K., & Lidiya, B. (2020). Human dignity-the basis of human rights to social protection. *Wisdom*, (3 (16)), 143–155.

Yohannes, O. (2002). The United States and Sub-Saharan Africa After the Cold War: Empty Promises and Retreat. *The Black Scholar, 32*(1), 23–44. doi:10.1080/00064246.2002.11431168

ADDITIONAL READING

Aslanidis, P., & Rovira Kaltwasser, C. (2016). Dealing with populists in government: The SYRIZA-ANEL coalition in Greece. *Democratization, 23*(6), 1077–1091. doi:10.1080/13510347.2016.1154842

Brito, L. (1993). Estado e Democracia Multipartidária em Moçambique. In L. Brito & B. Weimer (Eds.), *Multipartidarismo e Perspectivas Pós-Guerra*. UEM/ Friedrich Ebert Foundation.

Haass, F. (2021). The democracy dilemma. Aid, power-sharing governments, and post-conflict democratization. *Conflict Management and Peace Science, 38*(2), 200–223. doi:10.1177/0738894219830960

Manning, W. (2010). *The role of elections in emerging democracies and post-conflict countries: Key issues, lessons learned and dilemmas*. Friedrich Ebert Stiftung - International Policy Analysis. https://library.fes.de/pdf-files/iez/07416.pdf

Resnick, D. (2014). Compromise and contestation: Understanding the drivers and implications of coalition behavior in Africa. *Journal of African Elections, 13*(1), 43–65. doi:10.20940/JAE/2014/v13i1a3

Rosário, D. (2020). *Órgãos de administração eleitoral em Moçambique: Entre a (im)parcialidade, (in)dependência e a procura de transparência nas eleições competitivas em tempos de regimes híbridos: 1994-2019. Democracia Multipartidária em Moçambique*. EISA Mozambique.

Somolekae, G. (2002). Democracy, Civil Society and Good Governance in Botswana. In A. Bujra & S. Adejumobi (Eds.), *Breaking Barriers, Creating New Hopes: Democracy, Civil Society and Good Governance in Africa*. Africa World Press.

Teshome, B. W. (2008). Democracy and elections in Africa: Critical analysis. [Online]. *International Journal of Human Sciences, 5*, 2. http://www.insanbilimleri.com

KEY TERMS AND DEFINITIONS

Coalition: Is an alliance between political parties created to achieve a purpose which is common and beneficial to all parties involved or to engage themselves in joint political ventures or activities.

Coalition Governance: Is a political arrangement in which multiple parties form a government. In many cases, this collaboration implicates sharing power, decision-making responsibilities, and representation to achieve a majority in a legislative body. Political parties typically form coalition governments when no party secures a clear majority in an election.

Corruption: Involves institution representatives abusing power, position, or authority for personal gain or violating ethical standards for dishonest or unfair benefits. It is translated as bribery, embezzlement, nepotism, fraud, or other unethical practices undermining the integrity and fairness of institutions, organizations, or individuals in both the public and private sectors.

Democracy: Is a system of government in which power is granted to the people, either directly or through elected spokespeople. It adopts principles such as political equality, participation, and the principle of popular freedom, ensuring that people have the right to participate in decision-making processes to protect their fundamental rights and freedoms.

Democratic Values: Are the principles and beliefs that direct a democratic system of government and aim to ensure fair and inclusive governance where the rights and interests of all individuals are respected and protected. These values include, but are not limited to, political equality, individual freedoms, protection of human rights, rule of law, transparency, accountability, and the participation of people in decision-making processes.

Electoral Systems: Define how votes are cast, counted, and transformed into seats or representation in a political structure, including the legislature or executive component.

Governance Structures: Are the organizational frameworks, systems, arrangements, and instruments that guide institutions' management, control, and decision-making process, including the Government. Those mechanisms are essential to ensure accountability, transparency, and the efficient functioning of institutions.

Party Alliances: Are the collaborative engagements and agreements between political parties to cooperate and work to achieve common goals or objectives. These partnerships are likely to be adopted to strengthen the political influence of the engaged parties, increase election victory, or solve people's needs.

Chapter 7
Local Experiences of Local Government's Coalition Politics in South Africa

Kgothatso Shai
University of Limpopo, South Africa

ABSTRACT

Coalition politics has become a key feature of many countries' political landscapes in the 21st century. Among others, countries such as South Africa, Zimbabwe, Mauritius, and Germany have experimented with the system of political coalitions at different levels and with varying degrees of success. However, scholars and practitioners have not uniformly understood coalition politics, regardless of the attempt to locate the thinking in this regard within the Westernised perspective. Against this backdrop, this chapter uses 2021 as an ending point for research to examine the historical emergence of local government coalition politics in South Africa. While this chapter's primary focus is on South Africa, the line of thought is located within a global context to generate a broader understanding. It is also unavoidable to make sense of local government's coalition politics without linking it to national politics. This is because there is no level of politics or governance that exists in a vacuum, and this is even more expressive within the cooperative governance model of South Africa. Given the explanatory and analytical power of theories, this chapter first discusses the theories and types of municipal coalitions and politics and then intentionally proposes Afrocentricity as an alternative contextual and theoretical lens to make a better sense of this phenomena (local government's coalition politics) in Africa and South Africa, in particular. At the core of the research analysis for this chapter is the interface between municipal governments and coalition politics with specific reference to Tshwane and Johannesburg metropolitan municipalities.

DOI: 10.4018/979-8-3693-1654-2.ch007

INTRODUCTION AND BACKGROUND

Globally, there is no consensus among scholars and practitioners on the definition of a coalition. The definition of a coalition within the scholarly and political circles remains an unsettled polemic and practical question. The latter is not limited to this term (coalition); it is commonplace in Social Sciences (Shai & Vunza, 2021). This chapter does not seek to provide a definite definition of a coalition. However, for the purposes of this chapter, the coalition is generally taken to mean an association of two or more political parties which is normally informed by an electoral outcome, and it is meant to foster cooperation in administration or government at a particular level (Booysen, 2014). While coalitions in most countries are negotiated after elections, Mauritius is an exceptional case. Because the country has always been governed through coalitions since independence in the year 1968, coalitions in this country are negotiated pre-polls. Even then, there is room for negotiations to be taken to another level by bargaining informed by the realities of shared electoral spoils (Sithanen, 2003).

According to Maserumule (2020), compromise adds to cooperation as the fundamental principle of a coalition. A coalition can be negotiated in a manner that results in a written and signed agreement among all the parties involved. Alternatively, a coalition can be based on a principle of reciprocity. This means policy convergence and ideological alignment form critical aspects of a principle of reciprocity. Thus, the coalition between the defunct Democratic Party (DP) and Independent Democrats (ID) in the City of Cape Town Metropolitan Municipality in South Africa was largely based on the shared ideology of economic liberalism (Shai, 2017). The contestation about the conception of a coalition was evident in South Africa following the 2016 local government elections. In certain metropolitan municipalities such as the City of Johannesburg Metropolitan Municipality and the City of Tshwane Metropolitan Municipality, the 2016 local government elections did not produce any outright winner and thus, resulting in hung municipalities. In these two cases, the Democratic Alliance (DA) was under the impression that it is in a coalition with the Economic Freedom Fighters (EFF) and other small political parties. Contrary to this position, the EFF's political and populist rhetoric suggested that the party was not in a coalition with the DA in those municipalities. But it was having a voting arrangement on an issue-to-issue basis (Maserumule, 2020). This opportunistic stance by the EFF allowed the party to unduly influence decision making in municipalities that are led by the DA while leaving a room to distance itself from any municipal failures. For example, the coalition with the DA had allowed the EFF to swindle decisions in the municipality regarding strategic appointments such as City Manager. While still in a coalition, the EFF was able to distance itself from allegations of corruption facing the DA led City of Tshwane Metropolitan Municipality. Central to these scandals was the irregular appointment of GladAfrica in a R12 billion deal for infrastructural management within the city (Maserumule, 2020).

While coalition politics in South Africa's local government sector gained traction in the year 2016, the reality is that political coalitions are not new to South Africa and Africa at large (Mare, 2000). The experience from other African countries shows that coalitions do not have a rich historical prominence. This is because most of the African states, particularly in Southern Africa are led by liberation movements cum dominant political parties (Shai & Zondi, 2020). Due to the dominant party system espoused in South Africa and other parts of Africa, the notion of a coalition was largely deemed by politicians as irrelevant (Masina 2021). As such, the trend in terms of the decline of the electoral fortunes of the dominant political parties in Africa is alive to the reality of coalitions. Thus the 2016 local government elections in South Africa represented the massive decline of African National Congress's (ANC) electoral support in the Gauteng province, a development that resulted in the DA coalescing with the EFF and other small parties for the purpose of wrestling power from the ANC in the City of Johannesburg and the City of Pretoria Metropolitan Municipal councils. For example, in the year 2016 the ANC only obtained 41.2% of the votes cast in City of Tshwane. In contrast, the DA amassed 43.15% of the votes. On the other hand, less than 2% of the votes were split between the Freedom Front Plus (FF+), African Christian Democratic Party (ACDP) and the Congress of the People (COPE) (Maserumule, 2020). Following the 2016 local government elections, the electoral decline of the ANC in the City of Tshwane may not be delinked from rampant corruption in the public sector - a punishable sin in the eyes of the middle class and youth who do not have any emotional attachment to the party (Shai & Zondi 2020).

Before the year 2016 elections, South African local government had experienced 97 municipal coalitions since the year 2000 (Ndletyana, 2018, p. 139). A case in point is that in the year 2006 the DA led coalition snatched the City of Cape Town Metropolitan Municipality from the ANC. Besides South Africa, coalitions also feature in politics across the globe. For instance, in Zimbabwe a coalition took the form of the 2009 Government of National Unity (GNU) between the Zimbabwe African National Union-Patriotic Front (ZANU-PF) and Movement for Democratic Change (MDC). The coalition in Zimbabwe was necessitated by the massive decline in the electoral support of the ZANU-PF in a highly contested March 2008 general election and violence ridden re-run. The latter resulted in MDC's Morgan Tsvangirai withdrawal from the race, an eventuality that left ZANU-PF's Robert Mugabe as a sole contestant. This produced a government which faced serious questions of illegitimacy across all angles and subsequently, pressured to cobble into a coalition as a means of gaining legitimacy especially in the eyes of the international community (Raphala & Shai, 2016). At the helm of economic instability in the year 1950, Indian National Congress (INC) and the State of Travancore-Chochi entered into a coalition in India (Masina, 2021). In December 2011 close to two thirds of the countries affiliated to the European Union (EU) were experimenting with coalitions (Mokgosi, Shai, & Ogunnubi, 2017). Among others, these countries include Canada, France, Australia and Italy. The foregoing narrative is a clear demonstration that coalitions are a feature of electoral politics in Africa, Asia, Europe and elsewhere. Regardless of all of this, what emerges from the literature on coalition is that the experience in Africa is not adequately researched. Because political parties do not settle for coalition as an alternative but due to political pressures of the moment, this phenomenon has not attracted adequate attention of the scholars. As such, this chapter adds to the prevailing discourses about coalitions in Africa. While it is necessary to locate the research and writing of the subject of this chapter within the historical and broader context, it is worth noting that one size fits all model does not apply in this context. Hence, we have success and failure stories in terms of coalition governments. It is also important for a study of this subject in Africa to be based in an Afrocentric lens; as opposed to previous studies that were largely located within the Euro-American world view (Breakfast, 2020).

THEORISING MUNICIPAL COALITIONS AND POLITICS

Much of the limited body of knowledge on coalition politics in South Africa reflects an inclination towards a positivist approach in research. The positivist approach seeks to achieve the knowledge of reality from a neutral and measurable standpoint. This situation cannot be delinked from a strong tide in South Africa to wrongly locate Public Administration in Management Sciences instead of Social Sciences (Vermeulen, 2019). The inclination towards the positivist approach is not aligned with the international trends in the discipline, which are more in favour of inter-disciplinarity (Shai, 2021). Because of the forced marriage between Public Administration as a discipline and Management Sciences, the discipline in South Africa finds itself in a state of theoretical despair. The latter should be understood within the context that generally, research in Management Sciences is theoretically and philosophically weak. This epistemic dilemma cannot be delinked from the reality that Public Management is less concerned about human behaviour in its totality but much more concerned about the managerial dimension of this behaviour. Against this setback, this chapter pauses to look at the theoretical perspectives to the study of coalition politics. This is worth looking at because, like models, theories have an explanatory value in our quest to understand human behaviour (that is, coalition) as they attempt to provide a simplified representation of the real world.

Theories of Coalitions

Maserumule's (2020) study of coalition politics is based on causal theory (also read as theory of causality. The central principle of the theory of causality is the relationship of events (Goodman, Ullman & Tenenbaum 2021). On the other hand, Breakfast's (2020) study of coalition politics is based on integrative theory. According to Wofford (1982, p. 27) integrative theory "…emphasises the role of the leader in assessing the deficiencies in the follower's abilities, motivation, role perception or environmental conditions and in taking action to alleviate deficiencies which inhibit follower performance. Determinants of leader behaviour and environmental influence are also central to the theory". This theory has been overly used in Conflict Management and Leadership Studies. Meanwhile, Mokgosi, Shai, and Ogunnubi (2017) underpin their work on coalition politics in the Gauteng Province of South Africa on the elitist theory. They consider coalitions as a product of the values and preferences of the governing elite. Other scholars base their studies of coalition politics on the theory of realism, whose value of rationality also finds expression in the theory of causality.

The common feature of all the works consulted in the preparation of this chapter is that they are all located within the Euro-American worldview. This does not come as a surprise because most scholars who ventured into this subject emanate from Political Science and its offshoot, Public Administration. Traditionally, the ancestral roots of Political Science and Public Administration as academic disciplines are traced from the Euro-American world. Besides this, coalition politics is dominant in Europe (Mokgosi, Shai, & Ogunnubi, 2017; Masina, 2021). While the value of the aforementioned theories in the study of coalition politics at municipalities and beyond cannot be disputed, this chapter presents Afrocentricity as an alternative theory to study this subject. This decision is informed by the general desire to decolonise Political Science and Public Administration disciplines while making a case for an indigenous epistemology (Maserumule, 2014; Mathebula, 2018).

This chapter is foregrounded by Afrocentric theory (also read as Afrocentricity) as propagated by Asante (2003). It also draws from the works of other Afrocentric scholars such as Modupe (2003) and Legodi (2019), inter alia. Modupe (2003) identified grounding, orientation and perspective as the tenets of Afrocentricity; which are in turn operationalised as the analytical categories of this chapter. Afrocentricity asserts that when Africans view themselves as central in their own history, politics and administration, they see themselves as agents, actors, and participants rather than as marginal and on the periphery of political, administrative and socio-economic experiences. The choice of Afrocentricity as the contextual and theoretical lens of this chapter was informed by its underlying desire to unmute genuine African voices on discourses about public affairs in Africa and South Africa in particular (Maleka & Shai, 2016). While the utility of North[ern] angled theories alluded to above in the study of municipal coalition and politics cannot be disputed, it is argued that a study based on Afrocentricity could potentially paint an alternative and qualitatively rich picture of the phenomena being studied. Asante (2003) lends credence to the foregoing by asserting that there is absolutely nothing that our Afrocentricity cannot explain. For him (Asante, 2020), Afrocentricity can stand on its own and it does not need the help or support of alien theories to capture the essence of African reality. The choice and use of South Africa as a test case for this chapter was informed by the propensity of case study designs to generate a crispy understanding of a phenomenon being studied in a context of limited participants (Shai, 2016). To add, the Afrocentric epistemic location of this chapter is dismissive of the binary standing of knowledge as either empirical/ non-empirical, good/evil and qualitative/quantitative (Maserumule, 2011; Shai & Nyawasha, 2016). In this spirit, the empty perceptual space between the researcher (also read as author) and the researched is non-existent. Such space is rejected as a cheap and false façade of Western scholarship.

Emerging from the above, it goes without saying that this chapter touches on critical issues that are currently of interest for those working in the field of municipal governance and coalition politics in Africa as well as bringing attention to a relatively new case study – the Afrocentric as against the Eurocentric perspective in knowledge production. Although of current interest, coalition politics in South Africa appear to be borne out of selfish interests of the governing elite and less about the interests of the people. The selfishness tendencies of the governing political elite laid bare in this chapter are a by-product of Eurocentric value system (Shai, Nyawasha & Ndaguba, 2018). Hence, they potentially possess a dangerous recipe for municipal instability and sabotage. To this end, Ubuntu/ botho/ humanness is a pillar of the Afrocentric value system which is equally critical to understanding the prevalence of strained relations between coalition partners in Africa and South Africa in particular. Far from the Eurocentric value system's embodiments of individualism, selfishness and competition; this chapter openly embraces oneness, cooperation, interdependence and collaboration as the anchors of the Afrocentric value system which ought to define the municipal governance architecture of South Africa and Africa as a whole. The latter is a non-negotiable pre-condition for the sustainability of municipal coalitions. This submission may be debatable because of the fluid nature of African politics, which is also a subject of Arabic and Euro-American cultural influences. Despite this, I argue that as Africans we have points of convergence in terms of what is good or bad. For example, all religions in Africa (and elsewhere) condemns violence.

TYPOLOGY OF MUNICIPAL COALITIONS

There is no globally accepted typology of coalitions. This is because coalitions are at times loosely and/ or interchangeably used with party alliances. Before one can present and discuss the common types of coalition, it is important to highlight the key distinctions. That is party alliances are normally forged before elections to project unity and strength to win elections. A classic example of an alliance is South Africa's Tripartite Alliance between the ANC, Congress of South African Trade Unions (COSATU), and the South African Communist Party (SACP). Recently, these three have been joined by the South African National Civic Organisation (SANCO). But the ANC led-alliance also has features of a coalition, and the post-election period also sees them engaging one another in ministerial deployments. While examples of a coalition have been presented in the introductory section of this chapter, it is necessary to acknowledge that this chapter borrows from Booysen's (2014) typology of coalitions. According to her, there are three main types of coalitions, namely:

Governing Coalitions

In the case of South Africa, governing coalitions are normally considered at local and provincial spheres especially in the absence of a party with outright majority (Booysen, 2014). A case in point of governing coalitions can be observed in a range of municipalities in Kwazulu Natal (KZN) Province of South Africa which were co-governed by the ANC and National Freedom Party (NFP) since the year 2011 local government elections. Following the fall out between Zanele kaMagwaza-Msibi and her former political home, Inkatha Freedom Party (IFP); she went on to establish her own political party (NFP). As such, the ANC then capitalised on her political mileage and that of her new party to forge a coalition for the purpose of snatching the governance of certain municipalities from the IFP. Such a coalition then led local municipalities such as Abaqulusi, Nkandla, Imbabazane and Indaka and Umvoti (Mkhize 2013). Despite their ability to wrestle power from the IFP, the ANC-NFP coalition has proven to be unsustainable as almost all municipalities where they co-governed plunged from one crisis to the other. Perhaps, we should acknowledge that the NFP and ANC have fundamentally different policy and ideological positions. For example, NFP is rooted in the IFP tradition of Zulu chauvinism which the ANC openly espouses nationalism (Ngqulunga, 2017). Their members also have a rich history of hostility linked to violence that characterised the ANC and IFP in the early 1990s (Shai, 2009; Ngqulunga, 2020). Equally, this coalition was negotiated and agreed upon at a higher level with little input from the local structures. A combination of all of these factors has laid a fertile ground for the collapse of the coalition between the ANC and NFP.

Sub-Party Coalitions

For Booysen (2014) sub-party coalitions eye for power and are mostly used to generate and maintain political hegemony. For example, the apartheid era saw the coalition between the ANC, Congress of Democrats, South African Indian Congress, Coloured People's Congress, and the South African Congress of Trade Unions (collectively known as the Congress Alliance). These organisations collectively formulated and adopted the Freedom Charter (1956) as a blueprint for the transformation of South Africa from NP led white minority rule to freedom and democracy (Boddy-Evans, 2019). This coalition later metamorphed into a tripartite alliance between ANC, SACP and COSATU. With the ANC as the leader of this coalition, the relationship is largely based on the desire to retain/ maintain the hegemony of ANC in government. Some observers regard the relationship between the ANC, SACP, COSATU and SANCO as a false coalition. They argue that there is an ideological collision cause between them (Kotze, 2017). They further argue that ANC only agreed to partner with SACP for tactical and strategic reasons. Hence, the ANC previously needed SACP for the purpose of attracting support and solidarity from Eastern Europe during the heydays of apartheid (Clark & Worger, 2011). In fact, there is also a sense that in exile, for one to become an ANC leader s/he needed to come through the SACP. It is on this basis that upon return to South Africa, some ANC leaders such as Thabo Mbeki and Jacob Zuma terminated their membership to the SACP. Essentially, the basis of the relationship between the ANC and SACP was never about class question but race. Hence, non-racialism was a dominating value for their engagement.

Returning to the question of the ANC leadership in exile, of the members of the party's National Executive Committee (NEC) between 1962-1969 only Oliver Tambo, Johny Makathini and perhaps, Joe Modise were not members of the SACP. This is because the SACP largely controlled the ANC in exile and this fact was strongly articulated in 1960 by Yusuf Dadoo, then Indian leader of the SACP. This rendered the issue of the ANC-SACP alliance, practically speaking, a myth. This backfired upon the legal operations of the ANC and SACP in the country after the unbanning (Shai 2009). The issue of becoming leaders, particularly members of the ANC through the SACP, ended. Individuals like Thabo Mbeki settled accounts with those like Joe Slovo calling the shots in exile.

Co-Option Coalitions

Booysen (2014) contends that co-option coalitions are largely about a limited engagement of certain individuals from small or opposition parties in government to enhance the credibility of the seating government. Co-option politics have always been an integral part of the politics of post-apartheid South Africa. They can also be observed in the post-colonial Zimbabwe (Rogers, 2019). Some observers regard co-option coalitions as the manifestation of the politics of accommodation. As a result of the coalition between the ANC and NFP, former President Jacob Zuma previously appointed Zanele kaMagwaza-Msibi as Deputy Minister of Science and Technology. Before this, former President Thabo Mbeki appointed Azanian People's Organisation's (AZAPO) Mosibudi Mangena as the Minister of Science and Technology. Following the 1st non-racial general elections in 1994 in South Africa, then President Nelson Mandela also appointed the defunct National Party's (NP) Frederick W. De Klerk as his deputy alongside Thabo Mbeki (Mandela & Langa, 2017). To add, Marthinus Van Schalkwyk was also a cabinet minister for some time because of the coalition of NNP and ANC. Of course other members of the NNP went to join the DA in protest. While the co-option coalitions have material benefits for the co-opted individual, the reality is that they are largely not good for their political parties. Hence, the co-opted individuals are then kept busy with government work in such a way that result in them neglecting their political parties or being dis-connected to their support base due to their belonging to the ruling elite. Being part of the executive authority could paralyse their effectiveness in terms of playing opposition politics. As a result of the co-option coalitions; NP, AZAPO and NFP were either swallowed by the ANC and other political parties and/or simply shrunk in terms of electoral support.

Similarly, the ANC Mayor of Maruleng Local Municipality (2016-2021) in Limpopo province of South Africa is accused in certain circles for running the municipality through the opposition parties, the EFF and Civic Warriors of Maruleng (a local political party that won three seats during 2016 elections) in particular. Whether that is true or not is beyond the scope of this chapter. However, the basis of the allegation of running a municipality through opposition is alive of the reality of the Mayor's association with some of the councillors from the EFF and Maruleng Warriors. This view is strongly propagated by some of the ANC councillors who feel that the Mayor gives much attention to members of the opposition than her fellow ANC councillors during decision making. These feelings may not be far-fetched especially when one considers the active involvement of individual members of Maruleng Warriors in meetings where the Mayor has a dire interest and they are often presented as bouncers/ officers for ensuring the security of the Mayor and her close political allies in terms of the ANC's factional template.

Beyond South Africa, the co-option of the late Morgan Tsvangirai (MDC) as the Prime Minister of Zimbabwe following the inauguration of the GNU in 2009 has compromised his party's politics of opposition (Rodgers, 2019). Consequently, this co-option coalition legitimised a lot of wrongdoing on the part of the ZANU-PF; or essentially rendered MDC irrelevant as the alternative to ZANU-PF. The danger of co-option coalition is even worse in political parties that are built around the personality of a particular individual. Because the co-option of such an influential leader could serve as a recipe for dis-organisation and/or instability for his/her political party. The act of agreeing for co-option by one's political enemy may also cause a leader to lose confidence of the members of his/her party.

Despite the usefulness of the above typology, Labuschagne (2018) presents an alternative to it. He argues that coalitions can be categorised into two: majority and minority coalitions. The former would fit the closer relationship between the ANC and IFP following the 1999 general elections which resulted in their coalition co-governing KZN province. This was critical for the maintenance of peace and stability in a province that was previously torn apart by Black-on-Black violence between the members of the two political parties (Mare, 2000). Majority coalitions are common across the globe. However, Labuschagne (2018, p. 102) submits that "A minority coalition, or an alliance, is also possible and occurs where the parties collectively still lack a parliamentary majority. In Denmark, a minority coalition is a regular phenomenon. This was also the case in Italy before the transformation of its party system". In the case of Italy, March 2018 votes produced a hung parliament. This should be understood within the context that the dominant Five Star Movement's (M5S) was too weak to constitute a parliament alone. Equally important, neither the Right wing alliance (including League, Forza Italia, and Fratelli d'Italia) nor Left wing alliance (including Partito Democratico (PD) obtained votes that are enough for a parliamentary majority (Kappeli, 2018).

Interface Between Coalition Politics and Municipal Governance

There is a causal relationship between the mode of coalition politics and municipal governance (Ndle-tyana, 2020). That is, the nature of a coalition directly affects municipal governance, democracy and the future of any coalition partner. This partly explains why certain municipal coalitions succeed while others fail. The DA leaders often claim that where the DA or a DA-led coalition leads, service delivery is good (Maserumule, 2020). It then follows that the City of Cape Town Metropolitan Municipality is used as an example of DA led coalition's success story in governance. While the pace of service delivery and financial accountability in the City of Cape Town Metropolitan Council is generally deemed better as compared to other metropolitan municipalities that the ANC leads, it does not necessarily mean that all is well. The City of Cape Town Metropolitan Municipality is still battling with gangs violence, and this has been the case for some time now. While there is a case for this, the DA draws from Schedules 4 and 5 of the 1996 Constitution to argue that this is a competency of the South African Police Service (SAPS) (Republic of South Africa, 1996). This means the City cannot take responsibility for this nature. Despite these purported imperfections, the DA-led coalition in the City is generally considered as a success story. This success can be attributed to the ideological convergence between the DA and its coalition partners, which serves as a pre-condition for municipal stability.

When one looks at then DA led coalition within the City of Johannesburg Metropolitan Municipality, it represents a flop. Hence, its only basis was the desire to take ANC out of power. One will also note that the relationship was not really between the two parties, but it was largely between the EFF and Herman Mashaba (the DA Mayor) (Maserumule, 2020). Shortly after the 2016 local government elections, the ideological and policy discord between the EFF and DA was apparent. This was reflected in the National Assembly when the DA opposed the EFF sponsored motion for the expropriation of land without compensation. Due to this policy disagreement, EFF's Commander in Chief (CIC), Julius Malema then pronounced that all DA Mayors should be removed in municipalities where the two parties have a voting arrangement. This spirit was further fuelled by the persecution of Black leaders such as Mmusi Maimane and Herman Mashaba within the DA; an act that was broadly considered as an affirmation of DA as a racist political party. It is for this reason that the political upheavals became the order of the day in DA led coalitions in the City of Johannesburg and City of Tshwane Metropolitan councils. At the end, DA led coalitions in the two municipalities collapsed. While the ANC took over in the City of Johannesburg Metropolitan Municipality, the situation in the City of Tshwane Metropolitan Municipality was still legal conundrum during the writing of this chapter (for 2016-2021 municipal council). Hence, EFF and ANC councillors in City of Tshwane simply sabotaged the DA through walkouts from council meetings, which resulted in such gatherings not reaching quorum for the purpose of executing the municipal business. As Integrated Development Programme (IDP) budget could not be approved due to the failure to meet council quorum, the delivery of socio-economic services especially in the townships was impaired.

CONCLUSION AND RECOMMENDATIONS

Based on global and local experiences, this chapter has sought to trace the emergence of coalition politics in South Africa and elsewhere within a historical context. It also briefly described theories that are useful in explaining municipal coalitions and politics. This also necessitated that the common types of municipal coalitions be identified and discussed. What emerged here is that there is an overlap in terms of the conception and articulation of a coalition, whether at a municipal, provincial and/or national levels. The narrative of this chapter was then zoomed to a focused analysis of the interface between municipal governance and coalition politics, with specific reference to the City of Johannesburg and City of Tshwane Metropolitan Councils. Municipal coalitions are crucial for the health of electoral democracy, which is at times stifled by the dominant party system as witnessed in countries such as South Africa and Zimbabwe. However, municipal coalitions are also having a rich potential to un-do the wishes and aspirations of the electorate. This should be understood within the context that when the electorate is canvassed for votes, political parties and candidates present manifestoes which are often used to win the hearts and minds of the voters. But the political elites do not involve ordinary voters in decision making about swindling of votes to form a governing coalition. In the same breath, councillors are elected to represent the interests of those who elected them to the municipal council. But decisions like non-participation in council meetings (also read as sabotage) as previously witnessed in the City of Tshwane Metropolitan Municipality constitute the betrayal of the electoral mandate and it shows the extent of the selfish nature of the governing political elite; even at the altar of the basic needs and services of the people.

REFERENCES

Asante, M. K. (2003). *Afrocentricity: The Theory of Social Change*. African American Images.

Boddy-Evans, A. (2019). *The Freedom Charter in South Africa*. Retrieved March 1, 2019, https://www.thoughtco.com/text-of-the-freedom-charter-43417

Booysen, S. (2014). Causes and Impact of Party Alliances and Coalitions on the Party System and National Cohesion in South Africa. *Journal of African Elections*, *13*(1), 66–92. doi:10.20940/JAE/2014/v13i1a4

Breakfast, N. B. (2020). The Nexus between Conflict Management and Coalition Politics in Three Selected Metropolitan Municipalities in South Africa. *African Journal of Peace and Conflict Studies*, *9*(3), 65–80. doi:10.31920/2634-3665/2020/v9n3a4

Clark, N. L., & Worger, W. H. (2011). South Africa: The Rise and Fall of Apartheid. Longman.

Goodman, N. D., Ullman, T. D., & Tenenbaum, J. B. (2021). *Learning a Theory of Causality*. Retrieved July 1, 2021, https://web.stanford.edu/~ngoodman/papers/LTBC_psychreview_final.pdf

Kappeli, A. (2018). *Italy's Vote for Change: Potential Coalitions and their Implications for Development*. Retrieved March 16, 2018, https://www.cgdev.org/blog/italys-vote-change-potential-coalitions-and-their-implications-development

Kotze, D. (2017). South Africa's communist party strips the ANC of its multi-class ruling party status. *The Conversation*. Retrieved December 7, 2017, https://theconversation.com/south-africas-communist-party-strips-the-anc-of-its-multi-class-ruling-party-status-88647

Labuschagne, P. (2018). South Africa, Coalition and Form of Government: Semi-Presidentialism A Tertium Genus? *Journal of Contemporary History*, *43*(2), 96–116.

Legodi, L. T. (2019). *An exploration of China's foreign policy towards Sudan from 2006 to 2016: An Afrocentric Perspective*. Unpublished Master of Arts (International Politics) dissertation, University of Limpopo.

Maleka, M. S., & Shai, K. B. (2016). South Africa's Post-Apartheid Foreign Policy Towards Swaziland. *Journal of Public Administration*, *51*(2), 194–204.

Mandela, N., & Langa, M. (2017). *Dare Not Linger: The Presidential Years*. Macmillan.

Mare, G. (2000). Versions of Resistance History in South Africa: The ANC Strand in Inkatha in the 1970s and 1980s. *Review of African Political Economy*, *83*(83), 63–79. doi:10.1080/03056240008704433

Maserumule, M. H. (2011). *Good Governance in the New Partnership for Africa's Development (NEPAD: A Public Administration Perspective*. Unpublished PhD Thesis. Pretoria: University of South Africa.

Maserumule, M. H. (2014). In search of African epistemology- a reflection of an editor. *Journal of Public Administration*, *49*(2), 439–441.

Maserumule, M. H. (2020). Democratic Alliance-Led Coalition in the City of Tshwane: Strange Bedfellows Coming Apart at the Seams. *Journal of Public Administration*, *55*(3), 310–341.

Masina, M. (2021). *Future Realities of Coalition Governments in South Africa*. South African Association of Public Administration and Management (SAAPAM).

Mathebula, N. E. (2018). Pondering over the Public Administration discipline: A move towards African epistemology. *Bangladesh e-Journal of Sociology*, *15*(2), 17–25.

Mkhize, N. 2013. Municipality in turmoil as ANC-NFP pact collapses. *BusinessDay*. Retrieved July 15, 2013, https://www.businesslive.co.za/bd/politics/2013-07-15-municipality-in-turmoil-as-anc-nfp-pact-collapses/

Modupe, D. S. (2003). The Afrocentric Philosophical Perspective: Narrative Outline. In A. Mazama (Ed.), *The Afrocentric Paradigm*. Africa World Press.

Mokgosi, K., Shai, K., & Ogunnubi, O. (2017). Local Government Coalition in Gauteng Province of South Africa: Challenges and opportunities. *Ubuntu: Journal of Conflict and Social Transformation*, *6*(1), 37–57. doi:10.31920/2050-4950/2017/v6n1a2

Ndletyana, M. (2018). A Note from the Policy Editor: Coalition Councils: Origin, Composition and Impact on Local Governance. Journal of Public Administration, 53(2), 139-141.

Ndletyana, M. (2020). *Anatomy of the ANC in Power: Insights from Port Elizabeth, 1990-2019*. Human Sciences Research Council (HSRC) Press.

Ngqulunga, B. (2017). *The Man Who Founded the ANC: A Biography of Pixley ka Isaka Seme*. Penguin Books.

Ngqulunga, B. (2020). The Changing Face of Zulu Nationalism: The Transformation of Mangosuthu Buthelezi's Politics and Public Image. *Politikon: South African Journal of Political Studies*, *47*(3), 287–304. doi:10.1080/02589346.2020.1795992

Raphala, M. G., & Shai, K. B. (2016). *Re-evaluating the EU's external human rights and democritisation policy: a critical analysis on Zimbabwe*. Governance in the 21st Century Organisations, the Proceedings of the 1st International Annual Conference on Public Administration and Development Alternatives (IPADA), The Park (Mokopane), South Africa.

Republic of South Africa. (1996). *The Constitution of the Republic of South Africa*. Government Printers.

Rogers, D. (2019). *Two Weeks in November: The Astonishing Untold Story of the Operation that Toppled Mugabe*. Jonathan Ball Publishers.

Shai, K.B. (2009). *Rethinking United States-South Africa Relations*. Hoedspruit: Royal B. Foundation.

Shai, K. B. (2016). *An Afrocentric Critique of the United States of America's foreign policy towards Africa: The case studies of Ghana and Tanzania, 1990-2014*. Unpublished PhD Thesis. University of Limpopo.

Shai, K. B. (2017). South African State Capture: A Symbiotic Affair between Business and State Going Bad. *Insight on Africa*, *9*(1), 62–75. doi:10.1177/0975087816674584

Shai, K. B. (2021). From the Guest Editor: About Lies, of Truths in Public Administration Scholarship. Journal of Public Administration, 56(1), 1-2.

Shai, K. B., & Nyawasha, T. S. (2016). A critical appraisal of the post-Cold War United States of America's foreign policy towards Kenya: An Afrocentric perspective. *Commonwealth Youth and Development*, *14*(2), 151–169. doi:10.25159/1727-7140/1925

Shai, K. B., Nyawasha, T. S., & Ndaguba, E. A. (2018). [De] constructing South Africa's Jacob Zuma led ANC: An Afrocentric perspective. *Journal of Public Affairs*, *18*(4), e1842. Advance online publication. doi:10.1002/pa.1842

Shai, K. B., & Vunza, M. (2021). Gender Mainstreaming in Peacebuilding and Localised Human Security in the Context of the Darfur Genocide: An Africentric Rhetorical Analysis. *Journal of Literary Studies*, *37*(2), 69–84. doi:10.1080/02564718.2021.1923715

Shai, K. B., & Zondi, S. (Eds.). (2020). *Dynamising Liberation Movements in Southern Africa: Quo Vadis?* Ziable Publisher and IPAD.

Sithanen, R. (2003). *Coalition politics under the tropics: office seekers, power makers, nation building A case study of Mauritius*. A paper presented at an Electoral Institute of Southern Africa (EISA) Roundtable: Political party coalitions - Strengthening Democracy through Party Coalition, Building Vineyard Hotel, Claremont, Cape Town, 19 June 2003. Retrieved July 1, 2021, https://aceproject.org/ero-en/topics/parties-and-candidates/mauritius.pdf

Vermeulen, L. (2019). A domum naturalia for public administration in a university structure. *Journal of Public Administration*, *54*(2).

Wofford, J. C. (1982). An Integrative Theory of Leadership. *Journal of Management*, *8*(1), 27–47. doi:10.1177/014920638200800102

Chapter 8
Israel's Coalition in Power and Its Implications on Israel–Palestinian Relations and Conflict

Ndwakhulu Stephen Tshishonga
University of KwaZulu-Natal, South Africa

ABSTRACT

This chapter discusses Israel's recent coalition government and its implications for internal governance, its conflictual agenda to destabilize the Middle East region, and particularly, its relations to the raging war between Israel and Palestine in the Occupied Gaza and West Jerusalem respectively. Considering how the state of Israel was formed, the chapter argues that the far-right coalition formed in 2022 post-general elections led by Netanyahu is bound to entrench Palestinian oppression and Apartheid as well as sour relations in the region. The inclusion of ultra-nationalists and ultra-Orthodox parties in Israel's formed coalition has far-reaching implications for Israel's democracy and its ability to manage peace and stability in the Middle East and with Palestinians. Evidence from the raging Israel-Hamas war leads one to conclude that the coalition is being used and abused to undermine the international organisations and laws that prohibit Israel's illegal occupation of Palestinian land. Secondary data was used to comprehend the complex dynamics of the coalition formed under the Netanyahu leadership, focusing on Israel's internal democracy and conflictual relations with Palestine and the region.

DOI: 10.4018/979-8-3693-1654-2.ch008

INTRODUCTION

Internationally, coalitions and their different categories have a protracted history of existence, formation and operations. Indeed, political coalitions are attached to party political systems and often use of political parties as the link between the state and electorates in the modern politics (Heywood, 2015). In essence, political coalitions are forged not only out of a common ideological standpoint but also through facing a common threat or enemy (Heywood, 2019). Scholarly political scientists have graduated beyond the what, who, and why to embrace the ontological and epistemological questions on how coalition governments impact governance and development. Within the multiparty democratic systems, coalitions are preferred to defuse the emergence of a dominant-party system. In conflict-saturated regions, democratic coalitions could be instrumental in accommodating cultures, ideologies of ethnic groups, traditions, and religions in order to promote access to opportunity and resources for inclusive governance and sustainable development (Gumede, 2023). Mithani and O'Brien (2021) view a coalition as a short-term alliance or collaboration of two or more political parties or groups that come together to work toward a shared objective, usually forming a government or gaining a majority in a legislative body. Conceptually, a coalition is a government made up of ministers or council members from various political parties, regardless of whether the parties have run against one another in elections (Dalmases, 2021). According to Beukes and De Visser (2021), a coalition government is the result of a convenient union of two or more political parties. Ndou (2022) highlights that coalitions are often established between parties to maximize their chances of achieving a specific goal or, more generally, to boost their electoral support.

Politics of coalitions is associated with electoral democracy (Bassin & Hunter, 2013). Thus, electoral democracy affords the electorates are afforded the electorates the golden democratic right to choose their representatives. An electoral democracy is "a democratic government based on a system that allows all citizens to choose one candidate for elected positions from a list of candidates" (Chauke, 2020, p. 38). In a democratic system of government, elections are tied to democracy, and democracy comes in different forms such as representative and direct democracy and others inclusive of authoritarian democracy (Held, 2006; Doorenspleet & Pellikaan, 2013). Representative democracy is a form of government in which the law is enacted by elected representatives (Heywood, 2019). This is different from direct democracy where larger numbers exert their dominance for compulsory compliance to smaller groups for their benefit (Held, 2006). Representative democracy is common in modern industrial and post-industrial societies (Ife, 2016, p. 141). Heywood (2019) holds that a representative democracy is limited to an indirect form of democracy. It is limited in that popular participation in government is infrequent and brief, being restricted to the periodic act of voting. On the other hand, there is a direct form of democracy where people engage directly in the country's governing procedure, and decisions are made directly by the public. If a new law or regulation is to be enacted, citizens have to vote against or in favour of it, and only then will it be approved or rejected (Germann & Serdult, 2017). It is also known as 'pure democracy' because there is no direct involvement of any intermediaries who make decisions on behalf of the citizens (Milic, Feller & Kubler, 2019). Direct democracy is a representation of common sovereignty and the right of citizens to make fundamental decisions directly with no intervention of their representatives (Colombo, 2018). No other model of democracy assures a greater degree of transparency and openness among the people and authorities. Public discussions and debates on major issues are held through participation (Mueller, Vatter & Schmid, 2016).

The democratic electoral principles aim to represent the core principle of making leaders responsive to citizens, which is accomplished through electoral competition for electorate approval under conditions in which voting is widespread. According to Coppedge, et al. (2016), p. 586) "political and civil society organizations can operate freely; elections are free of fraud or systematic irregularities." Therefore, inclusion, plurality, retrospectivity, transparency, and reactivity should be built into the electoral democratic system. There are numerous electoral democratic systems in use around the world, and there is little agreement on which fosters transparency and political stability. Cheeseman (2018) postulates that it is preferable for each country to select a model that best suits its specific circumstances, past, and political setting while also contributing to the advancement of democratic governance. Coalitions are, therefore, mechanisms for democratic governance by political parties, especially where there is no outright majority winner (Norries, 2012). Few states have made a concerted effort to rethink their electoral and democratic model in ways that address immediate difficulties to democratic essentials such as transparency, participation, and political stability (Emerson & Emerson, 2020).

This chapter wrestles with the dynamics of coalition governments in Israel and their implications in forging internal democracy and relations with Palestine in the Middle East. Thus, in both developed and developing nations, the dynamics of coalition formation and building have direct implications for the (in) stability of governance of such countries. Due to the fragmented governance system, Israel has adopted a coalition government framework under the leadership of Prime Minister Netanyahu and the extremist parties to consolidate its supremacy and Apartheid governance system within the region and dislodging Palestine. Israel recent coalition governments have devastating implications for internal governance and relations in Palestine and the Region. Over four decades, Netanyahu's grip to power is alleged to have had a conflictual agenda to destabilise the Middle-East region and particularly is escalating the raging war between Israel and Palestine in the Occupied Gaza and West Jerusalem respectively.

BACKGROUND INFOMATION

Politics of Coalitions Broadly

Coalitions are created when two or more individuals or organizations temporarily cooperate to accomplish a shared objective. Dalmases, (2021) states that a coalition government is made up of two or more political parties that have representatives in the national assembly or parliament. Empirical evidence from throughout the globe point out that acquiring political power is the main motivation behind coalition building (Law and Calland, 2018). Thus, global coalition politics has a history demonstrating the volatility with inclusionary and exclusionary binary. Debus and Gross (2016) assert that coalition politics describes the establishment and operation of a government composed of many political parties. To get enough seats parties band together to create a coalition to obtain a majority in parliament and successfully run the nation. Mwangi (2021) argues that the policy aspirations of all parties may not be completely realized at the same time under a coalition administration. For Labuschagne (2018), this implies that to come to an agreement on policy and successfully rule, parties must compromise and make compromises.

For Law and Calland (2018), global coalition politics have a history that demonstrate the volatility. Law and Calland (2018) posit that coalition research makes it abundantly evident that party cooperation has the capacity to strengthen national cohesion. Kenya, Mauritius, Denmark, Germany and India are all excellent examples of functional coalitions. In these nations, groups with disparate racial, cultural, and religious backgrounds united to bring peace during turbulent times. Gumede (2023) asserts that in modern African history, it has been the most effective system of governance since colonialism ended in the aftermath of World War II. With the exception of Botswana, Mauritius and Cape Verde, three of the 54 African nations most successful in terms of harmony, prosperity, and inclusivity, have been led by coalitions for the past century. Similarly, coalition governance is common in Europe, with countries such as Denmark and Germany being the typical examples. Coalition governance arrangements have both positive and negative elements. Positively, coalition-based governance could help opposition parties to defuse power and further challenge one party dominance and coalition politics can be a decisive feature of the national political development mostly in war-torn countries (Basson & Hunter, 2023).

A Brief History of Israel

Geographically, Israeli is in the Middle East and was established in 1948. Economically, Israel is without oil and other natural resources and has only 20 percent of arable land upon which its agriculture is derived (Mills, 2023). However, through innovations and the use of technology especially the drop-and direct-feed computerized irrigation systems, Israeli's agricultural outputs did not only increased, but also it produces half of the fresh produce inclusive of flowers, vegetables and exotic fruits (Mills, 2023).

Despite its progress economically, Israel is characterized by images dominated by conflicts, wars, and military confrontations with its neighbours, with Palestine being a contested territory. Since its existence, Israel has been embroiled in wars and confrontational encounters with its Arab neighbours such as Lebanon, the United Arab Emirates, Jordan, Syria, and the embryonic Palestinian state (Mills, 2023).

Figure 1. Israel jumbo country map
Source: Https://www.google.com/search?q=map+of+israel&rlz=1C1CHBD_enZA822ZA825&oq=map

Within the Arab land and North Africa, Israel is despised for being an intruder and its illegal occupation of Palestine (Arnold, 2017). Israel has a history of terrorism in foreign lands and the fact that it does not have a constitution, leaving the Supreme Court and the cabinet as the governance structure. Thus, the electoral system in Israel is anchored on proportional representation whereby power-seeking by political parties is often based on coalition arrangements (Renwick, 2011). On a governance perspective, Israel has been governed through crisis based on atrocities inflicted on its people and particularly the Jews-Palestinians residing in Israel which constitute 20 percent of the Israel population. With the renewed Israeli-Gaza war since 7th October 2023, it became clear that Israel is governed by the warring-far-right coalition government which is hungry to create a Jewish State at whatever cost. Through coalitions, Netanyahu has become the longest-serving prime minister in Israel. Vengeance through bombardment and genocidal mass killing against Palestinians in illegal Gaza and West Bank describe the prevailing governance in Israel (Madonsela, 2023).

Contextual Background of Coalition in Israel

Israel has had coalition governance arrangements from its inception. It became historical and apparent that since its establishment in 1948, Israel (Heywood, 2015 & 2019) has been ruled and marred with governance instability and conflicts with the Middle East. For example, in the 2009 legislative election, the Likud won 27 seats, Kadima 28, and Yisrael Beiteinu came third with 15 seats. Netanyahu was called upon to form the government with the right-wing camp having the majority of seats (Kingsley, 2022). It was in May 2012 that Prime Minister Benjamin Netanyahu reached an agreement with the Head of Opposition, Shaul Mofaz, for Kadima to join the government, which led to the cancelling of the September early planned elections. meant to be held in September (Wootliff, 2020). Unfortunately, due to a dispute concerning military conscription for ultra-Orthodox Jews in Israel, the Kadima party left Netanyahu's government in July. It was also in the 2023 elections that Benjamin Netanyahu got elected as the Prime Minister after the Likud Yisrael Beiteinu alliance won most seats (31) and a coalition government was formed with secular centrist Yesh Atid party (19), rightist, The Jewish Home (12) and Livni's Hatnuah (6), excluding Haredi parties (Lintl, 2023). The political picture of Israel is a mess as parties continuously hop from one partnership to the other while at the same time partnerships are short-lived.

The 2019–2022 political crisis featured political instability in Israel leading to five elections to the Knesset over a 4 year time period. The April 2019 and September 2019 elections saw no party able to form a coalition leading to the March 2020 election (Holmes, 2019). Without the leading part to govern, Netanyahu, and Blue and White leader, Benny Gantz, managed to establish a unity government based on a planned rotating prime ministership. In such a pact, Netanyahu was earmarked to serve first and later be replaced by Gantz (BBC, 2020). This coalition was short-lived due to a dispute over the budget, and new elections were called for March 2021, which saw the signing of a coalition agreement with Yair Lapid and different parties opposed to Netanyahu on the right, center, and left. The agreement was that Bennett would serve as Prime Minister until September 2023 and then Lapid would assume the role until November 2025 (BBC, 2021). An Israeli Arab party, Ra'am, was included in the government coalition for the first time in decades (Jerusalem Post, 2021). In June 2022, following several legislative defeats for the governing coalition, Bennett announced the introduction of a bill to dissolve the Knesset and call for new elections to be held in November 2022 (Gumede, 2022). Yair Lapid became the new interim Prime Minister (Jerusalem Post, 2022). After the 2022 elections, Netanyahu was able to return as Prime Minister under a coalition that included Likud, Shas, United Torah Judaism, Religious Zionist Party, Otzma Yehudit and Noam, in what was described as the most right-wing government in the country's history (France 24, 2022). The political picture of Israel is a mess as parties continuously hop from one partnership to the other while at the same time partnerships are short-lived. The government has overseen an uptick in violence in the Israeli–Palestinian conflict, driven by military actions such as the July 2023 Jenin incursion as well as Palestinian political violence, producing a death toll in 2023 that is the highest in the conflict since 2005 (UN News, 2023). In October 2023, the 2023 Israel–Hamas war started under the watchful eye of the coalition government. People, mainly the Palestinians, are the main victims of this war, with children and women being the main casualties. Thus, the coalition formed under Israel's Primister Natanyau continues to consolidate itself through the bombardment of Gaza and the West Bank. With the potential to spill into the Region.

Figure 2. 2022 Israel elections and outcomes
Source: Lintl, 2023, p. 2.

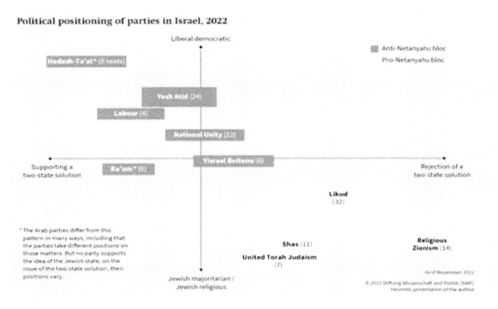

Israel's proportional representation electoral system, which frequently produces a fractured political landscape, is the primary cause of the country's need for coalitions. Hermann (2020) highlights that in Israel, a single party has hardly ever won an absolute majority in the Knesset since the country's founding in 1948. Based on the percentage of votes each party wins, the electoral system allots seats in the Knesset. Dodd (2015) posits that several parties therefore enter the parliament, making it difficult for one party to obtain the majority required to establish a government. This has resulted in coalition governments occurring more frequently. Perry (2023) contends that notable coalitions in history include the Likud coalition and the Alignment, which was the Labour Party's forerunner. Arjakas (2019) refers to the current Israeli government coalition as "the most right-wing government" in Israel's history. It was created following the 2015 election. Lintl (2018) claims that although the government is not a monolith, all of the coalition's parties—Kulanu, Shas, Torah Judaism, Jewish Home, and Yisrael Beitenu can be seen as being to the right of the center. Yisrael Beitenu entered the cabinet just a few months after Shas. In Israel, coalitions represent convergence of political and economic power elites with political and economic transformation (Murali, 2017).

Theoretical Frameworks of Coalitions

According to Zahariadis and Exadaktylos (2016) Riker is frequently credited with developing the idea of the minimal winning coalition in 1962. Damiani (2022) highlights that the theory known as the Minimum Winning Coalition (MWC) has its origins in cooperative game theory, specifically in the field of political science and coalition building. According to Bergman, Angelova, Bäck, and Müller (2024), it denotes to the smallest coalition of players that can prevail in a vote or secure a majority. Thus, the notion of minimal winning coalition theory in political science relates to the lowest coalition of parties that may create a majority in a legislative body. Lenine (2020) asserts that the theory is founded on the premise that politicians seek to establish winning, minimal-size coalitions. Debus and Gross (2016) posit that the minimal winning coalition is the least coalition that can win a vote, whereas the least minimal winning coalition is the smallest coalition that can achieve a vote but cannot be reduced any more.

FINDINGS AND ANALYSIS

Re-emerging Coalitions in Israel (2019-2023): When, Why, How, and for What Purpose

Mahler (2022) posits that the Israeli government has always been founded on political coalitions, which are transitory alliances of different political parties, and these coalitions have influenced how the government acts and what it achieves. Israel's election system of proportional representation has resulted in a history of coalition governments. Such systems typically result in coalitions since no single party can obtain a majority (Evans, 2019). In these coalitions, various parties collaborate to establish a government. Nyadera, and Kisaka, (2022) are of the view that the Israeli political system is parliamentary, which entails that the government is established by parties with a majority in the Knesset (parliament). According to Jönsson (2020) prominent instances comprise the Benjamin Netanyahu-led administration of 2013–2015, which comprised the Likud, Yesh Atid, and Hatnuah parties. After the Knesset election, the current cabinet of Israel, known as the Thirty-seventh government, was constituted.

According to Lintl (2023), Likud, United Torah Judaism, Shas, Religious Zionist Party, Otzma Yehudit, Noam, and National Unity 1 are the seven parties that make up the coalition government. It is headed by Benjamin Netanyahu. Matusiak (2023) notes that Netanyahu became Israel's sixth prime minister after taking office. Mahler (2016) asserts that Israel has always had coalition administrations since its establishment in 1948. However, Rahat, Hazan and Ben-Nun Bloom (2016) notes that in Israeli history, no coalition has ever been formed by less than three coalition partners, and no election has resulted in the formation of the government by a single party. That image amply illustrates the divisions throughout Israeli society, which calls for a more socio-political approach to Israel's coalition politics. Mahler (2022) posits that Israel's legislative politics are based mostly on coalitional patterns, which seem to represent the divisions within Israeli society. Schiff, (2018) contends that Israeli politics are shaped by divisions within Israeli society between Ashkenazi and Mizrahi Jews, as well as between the religious and secular sectors. Mahler (2022) adds that the Israeli coalition government is facing a struggle during a political upheaval, and the deck is being rearranged in a way that might drastically alter the Israeli government's appearance.

Shamir and Rahat (2022) posit that Israel has seen many elections and government changes since 2019. According to Reiter and Feher, (2023) following the Israeli parliamentary election of 2021, the most recent coalition, the Bennett-Lapid government, was established on June 13, 2021. Gerner (2018) points out that the goal of the coalition parties has always been to strengthen Jewish supremacy and Palestinian oppression. Majoritarian democracy is the goal of the current Israeli government, which views these limitations. The triumphant hard-right alliance is committed to upholding Israel's right to continue enslaving the Palestinian people. According to Averbukh and Lintl, (2022) Israel remains politically immobilized from the spring of 2019 to the summer of 2021 as no stable government could be established. Shamir and Rahat (2022) on June 13, 2021, a new government was sworn in after four elections. Zanotti (2021) argues that Benjamin Netanyahu was not simply removed from office as prime minister after a 12-year tenure. A coalition was established that encompasses nearly the whole political spectrum.

Role of Coalition Governments in Israel's Democratic Governance

In Israel, coalition governments play a crucial role in the country's democratic governance. Jafari (2016) states that Israel's political change started in 2015 when a right-wing majority solidified its hold on the Knesset and the conservative mainstream grew radicalized, has resulted in the establishment of coalition administrations. Nyadera, and Kisaka, (2022) posit that coalition governments are formed when political parties with differing ideologies join forces to form a majority in the Knesset, Israel's unicameral legislature. Kugler, (2018) states that this arrangement allows for the formation of a stable government capable of enacting legislation and implementing policies. Kraitzman and Ostrom (2023) contends that coalition governments are essential to the formulation of public policy and the mechanisms by which decisions are made in Israel's democratic government. There is paradox brought by mis-governance by extremist coalition has a devastating effects for both Israelis and Palestinians alike. On one hand, coalition-led government under the premiership of Netanyahu, promised not only safety and security of the Israelis, but also ensure socio-economic prosperity under Jewish state. On the other hand, for 67 years of occupation, Palestinians have witnessed brutality, harassment, mass killings and since 7th October 2023 the endless bombardment and destruction of infrastructure and denial of humanitarian aid.

The coalition government in Israel is the convergence of conflict and collaboration between various groups inside a political party are referred to as intra-party politics (Giannetti and Laver, 2008). This involves jostling for leadership posts, the creation and implementation of party programs, and the building of coalitions and factions. According to Cross (2013) Intra-party politics pertains to the internal allocation of power inside a political party. Caillaud and Tirole (2002), note that politicians are kept on their toes by intra- and interparty rivalry however it may tempt them to undermine sound policies and pursue competitiveness along socially undesirable lines. Intra party dynamics can lead to a variety of various outcomes. It can cause strife and division within the group. It could also result in modifications to the party's platform and guidelines. Intra-party politics can occasionally result in the creation of new political parties.

Political Power Dynamics

Coalitions by their nature are the outcome of power contestation and power is defined as persuasion (Kaswan, 2015). According to Andrushko (2021), political power is seen more as a spoken, intellectual term than as a component of the state's institutional framework. In this regard, democratic power is contested through what Heywood (2015, p. 49) called 'coalition of the willing' where civic order is maintained through state-and nation-building. Oprea (2014) is of the view that political power is the universal social responsibility that allows individuals to make broad choices in line with the interests of people who govern the power system. In the case of Israel, parties with a common agenda of reinstating the Jewish state and building Israel as a capable nation state in the Middle East. The fact that Israel has undergone the Holocaust and went through genocide, and the current oppressive behaviours and Gaza's bombardment are reflective of the long memories of the Jews (Polovin, 2024). In this context, Andrushko (2021) claims that political power is critical in managing social processes and political dominance in the Middle East. In essence, political power dynamics are the connections between various political actors and the tactics they use to exert influence over one another. Harris (1957) maintains that political power usually implies the use of physical force, either in the present or in the future. Nester and Nester (1993) argue that access to political power may be obtained through the use of financial resources, which can then be utilized to further the buyer's interests by promoting policies in their favour.

Naamna, (2018) contends that to obtain a majority in the Knesset, Israel's legislative body, these coalitions are established by several political parties coming together with common objectives and aims. Different viewpoints and interests are reflected through the establishment of coalition governments, re-sulting in a more inclusive and representative decision-making process. Furthermore, Akgül-Açıkmeşe, Kausch, Özel, Lecha (2023) highlight that in Israel, coalition governments encourage reaching agreements and making concessions to other political groups.

Role and Impact (Social and Political) of Coalitions on Israeli Democracy

Since Israel has a parliamentary form of government, coalitions are important to Israeli democracy. According to Kenig (2013), since 1948, the governments in Israel have been established through coalition agreements between many parties considering that no one party has ever achieved an absolute majority in the Knesset (the Israeli parliament). This qualifies Israel to be a coalition country with its complex relationship with the Arab nations in the Middle East. Israel is a parliamentary democracy, consisting of legislative, executive and judicial branches. Its institutions are the Presidency, the Knesset (parliament), the Government (cabinet), the Judiciary and the State Comptroller. However, due to the discrimination of the Palestinian Israelis and the military occupation of Palestine by their state, some scholars such as Beck (2019) concluded that Israel is not a democracy. While other scholars argue that the achievements of Israel and its leaders since its establishment in 1948 attest to the fact that Israel is the only genuine democracy in the Middle East (Dieckhoff, 2016).

Coalitions on Israeli democracy have a role in government formation (Stapleton, Biygautane, Bhasin and Hallward, 2023) as the establishment of a stable government depends on coalitions. To gain a majority in the 120-member Knesset, the ruling party or coalition engages in negotiations with other parties. This frequently entails giving in and compromising to consider different political interests. It has been high-lighted that the coalition's makeup influences policy decisions. Fortunato, Lin, Stevenson and Tromborg (2021) posit that voters find it difficult to properly assign blame for results when coalition government distributes the power to make policy among several parties. The Israel's society is embodied in politics in religion where religious fundamentalism has become the rallying point for Zionism based on militant and religio-political movement (Heywood, 2015). In this context, Heywood (2015, p. 198) added that:

In Israel, a collection of small ultra-orthodox Jewish parties and groups have become more prominent in transforming Zionism into a defence of the greater Land of Israel… and this has been expressed in a campaign to build Jewish settlement in territory occupied in the six-Day war of 1967 and then formally incorporated into Israel.

Despite the divergent coalition formations throughout the history of Israel, the central vision has been to build a strong and militant Israeli society in the Middle East capable of protecting itself from its enemies. Through Netanyahu led-coalition, the Israel government has been accused of being intoxicated with power to impose apartheid and displace Palestinians from their land. Under the pretence of fighting Hamas since 7th October 2023, Israel through its War Cabinet has orchestrated atrocities which are categorised as genocide by the international organisations, civil society organisations and governments alike.

Coalitions on Israeli democracy have a role in representation. Haklai, and Norwich (2016) maintain that parties representing many facets of Israeli society form coalitions. Coalitions encourage cooperation and compromise amongst disparate political interests by requiring members to cooperate and find common ground on a range of subjects. Rosner (2022) supports this as it promotes harmony and accommodation between the divergent political agendas. Socially, the situation is further aggravated by the Minister of Defence and War cabinet being at the forefront of arming the Israelis in occupied Gaza and West Bank as well as East Jerusalem. Globally, there is intensified demand for ceasefire, humanitarian aids, two-state solution by pro-Palestine and anti-USA funding Israel bombardment and mass killing in Gaza, West Bank and East Jerusalem by protests and demonstrators. Within Israel, protests organised by coalition of Human Rights and those opposing occupation are growing and Netanyahu's leadership and policies in the Middle East especially in relations to Gaza is brought under scrutiny. To restore peace and stability in Israel and the region, protestors are demanding Netanyahu to resign and the coalition government dissolved.

Impact (Social and Political) of Israeli Coalition on Israeli-Palestinian's Relations

The Israeli coalition has a profound and intricate effect on Israeli-Palestinian relations. The goals of the new coalition administration could have a significant impact on Palestinian rights and peace chances if it was crafted with inclusive developmental agenda. Amia (2023) posits that the coalition's intentions to deepen settlements and boost their legal validity may make it harder to create a Palestinian state since they would further solidify Israeli rule in the West Bank. According to Kurtzer-Ellenbogen (2023), concerns have been voiced regarding the coalition government's potential effects on regional relations and the Israeli-Palestinian conflict due to its creation, which includes far right political parties. Kurtzer Ellenbogen (2023) posits that Israeli allies in the UcddAE and Jordan have expressed concerns about the coalition government, with UAE foreign minister warning Ben Gvir's inclusion and Jordan's King Abdullah advising against crossing Jerusalem's red lines. It is apparent that the extremists' coalition, people in Gaza and West Bank would realise human rights and social justice as Israel continue to violate international laws such as Geneva Conventions and other UN-humanitarian organisations (Madonsela, 2023). The Palestinian-Israeli conflict was triggered by Hamas invading Israel and murdering Israeli civilians. Consequently, Israel retaliated by declaring war on Hamas by carpet-bombing Gaza with almost 24 000 fatalities which are still on the rise.

Bishara (2023) notes that as tensions between Prime Minister Benjamin Netanyahu and top generals Benny Gantz and Yoav Gallant grow, the coalition government is split on tactics and goals in the continuing war with Hamas. According to Chotiner (2023), some claim that the Israeli protest movement against judicial reforms has not given enough attention to Palestinian rights. The coalition administration is charged with intensifying its harsh oppression of Palestinians, including committing crimes against humanity like as apartheid and persecution. Chotiner (2023) posits the economic landscape in Israel and the West Bank may be impacted by the policies and actions of the coalition government, potentially having long-term effects on both Israelis and Palestinians. Socially and politically, the world is polarised with different schools of thought (Madonsela, 2023, p. 13). The first school of thought justified that Hamas' invasion of Israel on 7th October 2023 form the basis for the Palestinians' s denial of self-determination in their homeland by Israel illegal occupation. The second school condemned Hamas as a terrorist group and the collateral damaged suffered by Palestinians is acceptable. The third school claims that both Hamas and Israel are on the wrong to harm civilians by international law and as such obligated to protect children, hospitals and journalist (Madonsela, 2023. p. 13).

Shift of Power Dynamics Through Coalitions

Coalition is a potent instrument for enacting social change in Israel. The shift in power dynamics brought on by the establishment of coalitions among diverse political players is referred to as the distribution of political influence and authority to make decisions. According to Ryan (2014) it's necessary to form strong coalitions with a variety of players and accept conflict as a necessary component of social change. Bawn, Cohen, Karol, Masket, Noel and Zaller (2012) assert that as they enable parties to combine their resources and authority, coalitions may be a potent weapon for shifting power dynamics. There are a several of ways in which coalitions can shift power dynamics. Ideas (2018) points out that one strategy is to make a minority group more visible. This means that coalitions can shift power dynamics through uniting disparate groupings of individuals and organizations to work towards a single objective. Thus, shifting political power through coalition is key in promoting cooperative governance and building consensus for a stronger and stable democracy (Mashatile, 2023).

Political governance is the activity of authority and power in managing of a nation's concerns (Fagbadebo and Ile, 2022). The idea of political governance is intricate and varied, including many facets of political life, such as the division of power, the function of institutions, and the interaction between the state and society. A coalition government is created when two or more political parties pool their votes in order to elect a government and support the actions it performs (Bochel and Powell, 2016). For Netswera and Khumalo (2022), coalition governments are established when no one political party has won a complete majority after an election. In Israel, coalitions are frequent and fragmented as democratic governance mechanisms. Weak opposition parties and the dominance of Likud Party makes governance dynamic and complex. The current forged coalition pact comprising of extremist parties does not only undermine democratic governance in Israel, but also used to weaken smaller parties and further arm the military to depopulate Palestinians in their own homeland. On making the 100 days of Israel bombardment on Gaza, anti-Netanyahu protestors are demanding Netanyahu to resign. Thus, accusing him of prolonging the war in order to stay in power.

Having undergone their best efforts to advance the ideals of inclusive governance, coalitions present a number of key difficulties for member parties as they try to uphold their party identities while also fulfilling their obligations to coalition partners (NDI, 2015). Coalition governments continue to be uncontrolled and turbulent despite being a significant aspect of the Israeli-based coalition politics. Socially, coalition government including the recent one has been a disaster with dismal failure to hold the society together especially in the eve of Hamas attached on the 7th October 2023. Under Netanyahu's administration, Israel is at the verge of collapsing socially and economically with protracted war on Gaza costing more than 217 billion shekels ($59.3 billion), thus, costing Israeli around $272 million every day. Thus, the political economy of Israel coalition politics is based on patronage with long histories of civil conflict since the formation of Israel in 1948 (Ferree, 2013). This means that financially Israel will always be financially stable through patronage. Money will always flow into the country to help with socio-economic and political development.

Impact of Israeli Coalition on Israel-Palestinian Ongoing Conflict

The nature of the Israeli-Palestinian conflict can be greatly influenced by the Israeli government and its actions (Zanotti, 2021). Under Netanyahu's administration, relations between Israel and the Palestinians have soared with perceived pretence for peace negotiation. It is neither conceivable nor meaningful for peace negotiations to appear feasible given the low degree of confidence (Zanotti, 2021). Policies pertaining to the war are significantly shaped by the makeup of the Israeli coalition, which is made up of many political parties joining forces. Greene (2019) claims that there may be differences in opinion among the coalition's political parties over the Israeli-Palestinian issue. Paudel (2021) contends that while some parties might be in favour of a two-state solution, others might be in favour of taking a more proactive stance when addressing security issues. Internationally, organised mass protests for Israel to stop the war in Gaza and West Bank is gaining momentum daily. Simultaneously, anti-Israel war to Palestinians protestors are demanding ceasefire and urge USA administration to stop financing and supplying weapons to Israel (Rabkin, 2024).

Parallel mass demonstrations were organised in Tel Viv demanding Netanyahu's administration to bring back the remaining hostages. Through these protests and demonstrations, are raging with criticism towards a coalition government's failure to handle the war. By South Africa lodging a genocide case to the International Court of Justice (ICJ) on December 2023, accusing Israel of committing genocide against Palestinians in Gaza and West Bank adds salt on the open wound. As a counter to SA submission, Israel together with USA and UK as well as other Western nations dismissed the claim as 'meritless, counterproductive and completely without any basis' (in Khoza, 2024, p. 7). South Africa invoked Genocide Convention and accused Israel for contravening it. South Africa is joined by coalition inclusive of Progressive International, the International Association of democratic Lawyers, the Samidoun Palestinian Prisoner Solidarity Network, the Black Alliance for Peace, democracy for Arab World Now; the Palestinian Assembly for Liberation, Popular Resistance, CodePink and the National Lawyers Guild in strengthening the case for the ICJ to impose provisional measures to stop Israel genocide against Palestinians in Gaza and west Bank (Smith, 2024). In pursuit of Article 74(4) of the Rule of Court, South Africa is requesting and demanding the ICJ's President to stop genocide committed by Israel in Gaza (Swana, 2024).

Lehrs (2016) posits that critical to the peace process and negotiations with the Palestinians is the coalition's position. The chances of a two-state solution may be impacted by the coalition's stance on Israeli settlements in the West Bank and East Jerusalem. McInnis (2013) highlights that the coalition's strategy for enforcing border controls and conducting military operations can have an impact on the region's general security environment and degree of tension. Grossman, Manekin and Margalit (2018) note that decisions made by the Israeli government concerning the war may also be influenced by public opinion in the country. When formulating its policies, the coalition may consider the inclinations and opinions of the Israeli people. Baraka (2021) contends that the international community has failed to come up with a long-term solution to the Palestine issue since the 1967 War between Israel and a coalition of Arab governments. Rather, there have been repeated incidents of violence between Israel and Palestine, with the Palestinian people usually bearing the brunt of the conflict's disproportionate effects as seen in the current war.

Advantages and Disadvantages of Israeli's Coalitions in the Region: Middle East

Israel's coalition governments unite many political groups and viewpoints, perhaps resulting in more varied policymaking and representation. According to Rosner (2022), political parties join hands to present a unified face on several subjects, such as the war. Lintl (2023) contends that strong rightward shifts characterize the current Israeli coalition administration, which prioritizes settling major issues that have shaped Israeli society, such as the conflict with the Palestinians. This strategy has effects on the peace process and the area. Rosner (2022) asserts that coalitions force parties to cooperate, negotiate, and come to an agreement on policies, even those that touch on the contentious issues, which can result in more stable governance.

Lintl (2023) posits that the policy orientation of the current coalition administration may favour maintaining authority over some areas and making decisions unilaterally, which could impede attempts to find a settlement and end the dispute. Rosner (2022) posits that parties in coalitions frequently hold divergent beliefs, which can create internal conflicts and make it difficult to pursue a cohesive strategy for resolving disputes and promoting peace. Brown and Hamzawy (2023) state that there could be difficulties in interacting with important regional and international parties as a result of the Israeli coalition government's rightward turn, which could affect regional dynamics and peace chances. Miller (2021) claims that the current coalition administration in Israel undermine democratic institutions, particularly the Palestinian people's standing, the Supreme Court's authority, and the system of checks and balances.

Lessons to Be Drawn From Future Israeli Coalitions

For the nation to have efficient government and political stability, Israeli coalitions must be formed and maintained. Lintl (2023) posits that this entails managing the difficulties presented by the electoral process, accommodating outside influences, and striking a balance between political views. Gaining insight into these factors can help one comprehend the intricacies of Israeli coalition politics and the significance of establishing common ground between disparate political players. In Israel, forming and sustaining a coalition necessitates striking a careful balance between various political interests. Rosner (2022) argues that parties must work within the larger coalition structure while navigating their respective ideologies and policy preferences. Cox and Kernell (2019) note that the formation of a unified government requires cooperation and common ground among coalition members on several areas. Rosner (2022) contends that this procedure promotes harmony and accommodation between the divergent political agendas. According to Müller, Bergman and Ilonszki (2019), in Israel, the creation of surplus majority coalitions permits the prime minister to preserve political independence while guaranteeing the survival of the government.

FUTURE RESEARCH DIRECTIONS

This chapter deliberated on the dynamic imperative of the formation and maintenance of coalitions in the context of Israel. The efficacy of Coalition politics and coalition governments is camouflaged by nation building and imposition of Apartheid state in Palestine as well as the re-emergence of sectarian and racial politics. Despite its economic performance, Israel's coalitions and coalition governments have been the driven by sectarian and racial politics as opposed to building national unity. Evidently, under Netanyahu's administrative premiership, coalition politics and formations thrived on instability and frequent breaks-ups due to differences among coalition members. Given this scenario, there is a need for a comprehensive evidence-based research on how Israel uses ideology as one of the ingredients for

CONCLUSION AND RECOMMENDATIONS

This chapter has wrestled with dynamics of political power through coalition politics as an integral part of power-sharing focusing on Israel in the Middle East. Historical evidence showed that Israel is famous for coalition formation and building dynamics are a difficult and dynamic field. Despite the extremism nature of the coalition formed between Netanyahu and other seven political parties, Israel managed to galvanise support apart from parties having opposed ideologies, policies and principles. Positively, the Israel political legitimacy has been based on basic law of ministerial rotation among coalition partners with some budget reforms, reduction of unemployment and dealing with budget deficit as well as effectively managing the COVID pandemic. Coalitions in this context have proven to be a viable strategy to change the balance of power and through coalitions, ideologically varied parties band together and work collectively towards arching Israel developmental agenda and the advancement of illegal occupation of Gaza and West Bank. However, coalition politics as depicted by this chapter should move away from elitism to embrace even dissent voices from the smaller parties and civil society as well as ordinary citizens.

The chapter recommends that inclusivity and accountable coalitions should be advanced as a potent strategy for amplifying voices and help in bringing about developmental change in Israel. Through the promotion of active participation in electoral democracy and governance, transparent and accountable coalitions could change the power relations in Israel and in the Middle east at large. This entails making sure that every person has an equal chance to take part in the democratic process. It also entails informing people of their rights and obligations.

REFERENCES

Akgül-Açıkmeşe, S., Kausch, K., Özel, S., & Lecha, E. S. (2023). *Stalled by Division: EU Internal Contestation over the Israeli-Palestinian Conflict*. Academic Press.

Amiar, J. (2023). *Israeli-Palestinian relations are deeply affected*. Mitvim. Retrieved December 27, 2023, from https://mitvim.org.il/en/publication/israeli-palestinian-relations-are-deeply-affected/

Andrushko, V.I. (2021). Політична влада: аналіз інноваційних підходів. *Вісник НЮУ імені Ярослава Мудрого. Серія: Філософія, філософія права, політологія, соціологія, 49*(2), 153-168.

Arjakas. (2019). *On the Reciprocal Relation between Israeli foreign and Domestic policy in regard to the Israeli-Palestinian Conflict, 2009-2019.* Academic Press.

Arnold, G. (2017). *Africa A Modern History: 1945-2015.* Atlantic Books.

Averbukh, L., & Lintl, P. (2022). *Israel: Half a year under the Bennett government* (No. 4/2022). SWP Comment.

Baraka, A. (2021). Intractable Conflicts: How Israeli occupation and manifestation of Apartheid policy contribute to social and economic impacts on Palestinians. *Turan-sam*, *13*(51), 147–157.

Basson, A & Hunter, Q. (2023). *Who will rule South Africa? The demise of the ANC and the rise of a new democracy.* Flyleaf Publishing & Distribution.

Bawn, K., Cohen, M., Karol, D., Masket, S., Noel, H., & Zaller, J. (2012). A theory of political parties: Groups, policy demands and nominations in American politics. *Perspectives on Politics*, *10*(3), 571–597. doi:10.1017/S1537592712001624

BBC, (2020). *Israel's Netanyahu and Gantz sign unity government deal.* BBC.

BBC. (2021). *Netanyahu out as new Israeli government approved.* BBC.

Beck, M. (2019). *Israel: A Democratic State?* https://www.e-ir.info/2019/08/25/israel-a-democratic-state/

Bergman, M., Angelova, M., Bäck, H., & Müller, W. C. (2024). Coalition agreements and governments' policy-making productivity. *West European Politics*, *47*(1), 31–60. doi:10.1080/01402382.2022.2161794

Beukes, J., & De Visser, J. (2021). *A framework for coalitions in local government.* Academic Press.

Bishara, M. (2023). Fanatics vs generals: The strange Israeli rift over Gaza. *Al Jazeera.* https://www.aljazeera.com/opinions/2023/10/27/fanatics-vs-generals-the-strange-israeli-rift-over-gaza

Bochel, H., & Powell, M. (2016). *Coalition Government and Social Policy.* Policy Press.

Brown, N. J., & Hamzawy, A. (2023). *Arab Peace Initiative II: How Arab Leadership Could Design a Peace Plan in Israel and Palestine.* Academic Press.

Caillaud, D., & Tirole, J. (2002). Parties as political intermediaries. *The Quarterly Journal of Economics*, *117*(4), 1453–1489. doi:10.1162/003355302320935070

Chotiner, I. (2023). *How Israel's Democratic Crisis Affects Palestinians.* Retrieved December 27, 2023, from https://www.newyorker.com/news/q-and-a/how-israels-democratic-crisis-affects-palestinian

Cox, G., & Kernell, S. (2019). *The politics of divided government.* Routledge. doi:10.4324/9780429313844

Dalmases, J. M. (2021). *Guide to forming a coalition government.* Edicions Universitat Barcelona.

Damiani, G. (2022). *Looking for a" genuine science of politics": William H. Riker and the game theoretical turn in political science.* Center for the History of Political Economy at Duke University.

Debus, M., & Gross, M. (2016). Coalition formation at the local level: Institutional constraints, party policy conflict, and office-seeking political parties. *Party Politics*, *22*(6), 835–846. doi:10.1177/1354068815576292

Dieckhoff, A. (2016). What Kind of Democracy Is Israel? De Gruyter Oldenbourg. doi:10.1515/9783110351637-050

Dodd, L. (2015). *Coalitions in parliamentary government* (Vol. 1247). Princeton University Press. doi:10.1515/9781400868070

Evans, M. (2019). Coalitions through a comparative politics lens. *Coalition Government as a Reflection of a Nation's Politics and Society: A Comparative Study of Parliamentary Parties and Cabinets in 12 Countries.*

Ferree, K. E. (2013). *Framing the Race in South Africa: The Political Origins of Race-Census Elections.* Cambridge University Press.

Fortunato, D., Lin, N. C., Stevenson, R. T., & Tromborg, M. W. (2021). Attributing policy influence under coalition governance. *The American Political Science Review*, *115*(1), 252–268. doi:10.1017/S0003055420000763

France. (2022). *Israel's Netanyahu back with extreme-right government.* Academic Press.

Geenah, N. (2022, Nov. 6). Netanyahu's pact with extremists 'a threat to justice peace'. Sunday World, p. 3.

Gerner, D. J. (2018). *One land, two peoples: The conflict over Palestine.* Routledge. doi:10.4324/9780429494918

Giannetti, D., & Laver, M. (2008). Party cohesion, party discipline, and party factions in Italy. In *Intra-party politics and coalition governments* (pp. 146–168). Routledge. doi:10.4324/9780203889220

Greene, T. (2019). Foreign policy anarchy in multiparty coalitions: When junior parties take rogue decisions. *European Journal of International Relations*, *25*(3), 800–825. doi:10.1177/1354066119828196

Grossman, G., Manekin, D., & Margalit, Y. (2018). How sanctions affect public opinion in target countries: Experimental evidence from Israel. *Comparative Political Studies*, *51*(14), 1823–1857. doi:10.1177/0010414018774370

Gumede, W. (2023). *Policy Brief 46: Improving Coalition Governance.* Retrieved December 29, 2023, from https://www.democracyworks.org.za/policy-brief-improving-coalition-governance/

Gumede, W. (2023). Coalitions can work well with strange bedfellows. *Sunday Tmes*, *13*(August), 14.

Haklai, O., & Norwich, L. (2016). Bound by tradition: The exclusion of minority ethnonational parties from coalition governments—a comparison of Israel and Canada. *Ethnopolitics*, *15*(3), 265–284. doi:10.1080/17449057.2015.1052612

Haklai, O., & Rass, R. A. (2022). The fourth phase of Palestinian Arab politics in Israel: The centripetal turn. *Israel Studies*, *27*(1), 35–60. doi:10.2979/israelstudies.27.1.02

Hermann, T. (2020). Public Opinion in Israel. In *The Oxford Handbook of Israeli Politics and Society* (p. 247). Oxford University Press.

Heywood, A. (2015). *Global Politics* (2nd ed.). Palgrave MacMillan.

Heywood, A. (2019). *Politics* (5th ed.). Palgrave MacMillan.

Holmes, O. 2019). Benjamin Netanyahu tells Israeli president he cannot form government. *The Guardian*. www.theguardian.com

Ideas, M. (2018). *Understanding power dynamics in Cross-Class coalitions*. Mobilizing Ideas. Retrieved October 18, 2023, from https://mobilizingideas.wordpress.com/2018/03/30/class-and-movement-building-how-does-class-shape-participation-in-movements/

Jafari, S. (2016). *Constraints on Diplomacy: The Rise of Right-Wing Political Cultures in Israel*. University of California.

Jerusalema Post. (2022a). Yair Lapid officially becomes Prime Minister of Israel. *The Jerusalem Post*.

Jerusalema Post. (2022b). Israeli government to be sworn in on Sunday, coalition complete. *Jerusalem Post*.

Jönsson, A., (2020). *Populism in Israel: A study of the manifestation of populist rhetoric among Israeli right-wing political actors between 2015 and 2020*. Academic Press.

Kaswan, M. J. (2015). *Politics as the Dynamics of Power*. In Western Political Science Association Annual Conference. Las Vegas, NV.

Kenig, O. (2013). *Israeli Government - Coalition building in Israel: A guide for the perplexed*. The Israel Democracy Institute. Retrieved December 23, 2023, from https://en.idi.org.il/articles/10248

Khoza, A. (2024, January 14th). Assurance comes as SA prepares for backlash from West. *Sunday Times*, ●●●, 7.

Kingsley, P. (2022). Israel's Government Collapses, Setting Up 5th Election in 3 Years. *The New York Times*.

Kraitzman, A. P., & Ostrom, C. W. Jr. (2023). The Impact of Governmental Characteristics on Prime Ministers' Popularity Ratings: Evidence from Israel. *Political Behavior*, *45*(3), 1143–1168. doi:10.1007/s11109-021-09752-4

Kugler, J. (2018). *Political capacity and economic behavior*. Routledge.

Labuschagne, P. (2018). South Africa, coalition and form of government: Semi-presidentialism a tertium genus? *Journal of Contemporary History*, *43*(2), 96–116. doi:10.18820/24150509/JCH43.v2.6

Law, M., & Calland, R. (2018). *South Africa is learning the ropes of coalition politics – and its inherent instability*. The Conversation. Retrieved December 29, 2023, from https://theconversation.com/south-africa-is-learning-the-ropes-of-coalition-politics-and-its-inherent-instability-96483

Lehrs, L. (2016). Jerusalem on the negotiating table: Analyzing the Israeli-Palestinian peace talks on Jerusalem (1993–2015). *Israel Studies*, *21*(3), 179–205. doi:10.2979/israelstudies.21.3.09

Lenine, E. (2020). Modelling coalitions: From concept formation to tailoring empirical explanations. *Games*, *11*(4), 55. doi:10.3390/g11040055

Lintl, P. (2018). Israel on Its Way to a Majoritarian System? The Current Government's Fight against Principles of Liberal Democracy, the› Constitutional Revolution‹ and the Supreme Court. *Israeli European Policy Network Papers 2018*.

Lintl, P. (2023). *Israel's anti-liberal coalition: the new government is seeking fundamental changes in the political system and in the Israeli-Palestinian conflict* (SWP Comment, 5/2023). Berlin: Stiftung Wissenschaft und Politik -SWPDeutsches Institut für International.

Madonsela, T. (2023). *Will Human Rights and social Justice Prevail in Gaza?* City Press.

Mahler, G. (2022). Coalition Politics and Government in Contemporary Israel. In *The Palgrave International Handbook of Israel* (pp. 1–20). Springer Singapore.

Mahler, G. S. (2016). *Politics and government in Israel: the maturation of a modern state.* Rowman & Littlefield.

Mashatile, P. (2023). *Time to build framework for coalitions.* Mail & Guardian.

Matusiak, M. (2023). *Netanyahu for the sixth time: The new Israeli government.* Academic Press.

McInnis, K. J. (2013). Lessons in coalition warfare: Past, present and implications for the future. *International Politics Reviews, 1*(2), 78–90. doi:10.1057/ipr.2013.8

Miller, A. D. (2021). *Israel's new coalition government is more stable than it looks.* Foreign Policy. Retrieved December 28, 2023, from https://foreignpolicy.com/2021/06/14/israel-bennett-coalition-government-stable/

Mills, G. (2023). *Rich State, Poor State: Why Some Countries Succeed and Others Fail?* Penguin Books.

Mithani, M. A., & O'Brien, J. P. (2021). So what exactly is a "coalition" within an organization? A review and organizing framework. *Journal of Management, 47*(1), 171–206. doi:10.1177/0149206320950433

Müller, W. C., Bergman, T., & Ilonszki, G. (2019). Extending the Coalition Life-cycle Approach to Central Eastern. *Coalition Governance in Central Eastern Europe, 1.*

Murali, K. (2017). Economic Liberalisation, Electoral Coalitions, and Investments Policies in India. In States in Developing World (pp. 248-279). Cambridge University Press.

Mwangi, O. G. (2021). Conceptual and theoretical approaches to coalitions in parliamentary democracies. *Coalition Politics in Lesotho: A Multi-Disciplinary Study of Coalitions and Their Implications for Governance*, 13-27. https://doi.org/ doi:10.52779/9781991201690/02

Naamna, M. (2018). Political-electoral transformations in Israel in the contemporary period: Historical and political approach. *Moldoscopie, 83*(4), 91–99.

Ndou, L. L. (2022). *An analysis of a coalition government: a new path in administration and governance at local government level in South Africa* (Doctoral dissertation, North-West University, South Africa).

Nester, W. R., & Nester, W. R. (1993). *The Shifting Balance of Political Power: Hearts, Minds and Policies.* American Power, the New World Order and the Japanese Challenge.

Netswera, M. M., & Khumalo, P. (2022). The Coalition-building Process in South Africa: Reflection on the 2021 Local Government Elections. *African Journal of Democracy and Governance, 9*(34), 103–125.

Norris, P. (2004). *Electoral Engineering: Voting Rules and Political Behaviour.* Cambridge University Press. doi:10.1017/CBO9780511790980

Nyadera, I. N., & Kisaka, M. O. (2022). The State of Israel. In *The Palgrave Handbook of Comparative Public Administration: Concepts and Cases* (pp. 567–592). Springer Nature Singapore. doi:10.1007/978-981-19-1208-5_20

Oprea, V. B. (2014). The specific of the power relationship. *International Letters of Social and Humanistic Sciences*, (23), 45–52.

Paudel, B. (2021). *Two-state Solution Between Israel And Palestine: Viable or Obsolete Idea* (Doctoral dissertation, Department Of International Relation & Diplomacy).

Perry, G. E. (2023). Israel and Palestine. In *Government and Politics of the Contemporary Middle East* (pp. 255–344). Routledge. doi:10.4324/9781003198093-10

Polovin, R. (2024). We cannot an will not forget tose who were killed on October 7. *Sunday Times*, *14*(January), 13.

Rabkin, F. (2024). The Case that Woke up the World. *Sunday Times.*, *11*(January), 11.

Rahat, G., Hazan, R. Y., & Ben-Nun Bloom, P. (2016). Stable blocs and multiple identities: The 2015 elections in Israel. *Representation (McDougall Trust)*, *52*(1), 99–117. doi:10.1080/00344893.2016.1190592

Reiter, Y. & Feher, V. (2023). The Politics of Arab Israelis. *Polarization and Consensus-Building in Israel: The Center Cannot Hold.*

Renwick, A. (2011). *The Politics of Electoral Reform: Changing the Rules of Democracy.* Cambridge University Press.

Rosner, S. (2022). *Israel's Coalition Didn't Fail. It Set a New Bar.* Retrieved December 27, from 2023, https://www.nytimes.com/2022/07/05/opinion/israel-coalition-government-collapse.html

Ryan, M. J. (2014). Power Dynamics in Collective Impact. *Stanford Social Innovation Review*, *12*(4), A10–A11. doi:10.48558/N8Y6-E936

Schiff, G. S. (2018). *Tradition and politics: The religious parties of Israel.* Wayne State University Press.

Shamir, M., & Rahat, G. (Eds.). (2022). *The Elections in Israel, 2019–2021.* Taylor & Francis. doi:10.4324/9781003267911

Smith, S. (2024). Back SA's Israel Genocide case. Mail & Guardian.

Stapleton, S., Biygautane, T., Bhasin, T., & Hallward, M. C. (2023). Democracy Under Occupation: Coalition Government Formation and Survival in Iraq and Palestine. *Middle East Law and Governance*, *15*(3), 398–422. doi:10.1163/18763375-20231397

Swana, S. (2024). SA takes Israel to the International Court of Justice for Genocide. Sunday World.

UN Envoy. (2023). *Israeli-Palestinian death toll highest since 2005: UN envoy.* UN.

Wootliff, R. (2020). Israel calls 4th election in 2 years as Netanyahu-Gantz coalition collapses. *Times of Israel.*

Zahariadis, N., & Exadaktylos, T. (2016). Policies that succeed and programs that fail: Ambiguity, conflict, and crisis in Greek higher education. *Policy Studies Journal: the Journal of the Policy Studies Organization*, *44*(1), 59–82. doi:10.1111/psj.12129

Zahorik, J. (2018). Ethiopia and the colonial discourse. In Colonialism on the Margins of Africa. Routledge.

Zanotti, J. (2021). Israel: Background and US relations in brief (Vol. 16). Congressional Research Service.

KEY TERMS AND DEFINITIONS

Coalition: Is a collaborative efforts between political parties especially where there is no outright or absolute majority in electoral democracy.

Dominant-Party System: A dominant-party system, or one-party dominant system, is a political occurrence in which a single political party continuously dominates election results.

Electoral Democracy: Is the type of democracy in which political parties are afforded an opportunity to compete for political office through free and fair elections.

Government of National Unity: This is the type of government in which various political parties especially the major ones are included in the democratic governance pact.

Israel: Is a state which came into existence in 1948 and situated in the Middle East.

One-Party System: Is a form of government where the country is ruled by a single political party, and only one political party exists and the forming of other political parties is forbidden.

Power-Sharing: Implies a situation where power is shared among political parties such as government posts.

Proportional Representative Electoral System: Is an electoral system in which the electorates vote for political parties instead of individuals to represent them in government structures (Parliament and councils, etc.).

Chapter 9
Critical Reflections on Coalition Politics:
Prospects and Challenges From an African Perspective

Bhekie Mngomezulu
Nelson Mandela University, South Africa

ABSTRACT

Political coalitions have a deep history which transcends geographical boundaries. The rationale for establishing them varies. In the absence of a guiding framework, coalitions become unsustainable. The aim of this chapter is threefold. Firstly, it traces the history of coalition politics. Secondly, it discusses prospects for successful coalitions. Thirdly, it considers challenges involved in coalition politics. While conceding that coalitions are a global phenomenon, the chapter focuses on Africa. It argues that since the dawn of democracy in Africa, different forms of coalitions have been used with different results. As the number of political parties increase in each election, coalitions have become a reality.

INTRODUCTION

Coalition politics have become a general norm across the globe due to a variety of reasons. While some coalitions are planned, others are necessitated by the outcome of an election. It should not come as a surprise, therefore, that some coalitions have survived while others have had a short lifespan. Geys et al. (2006, p. 957), aver that, "coalition formation is often an important part of the political process." Implicit in this statement is the view that coalitions are a necessity. As mentioned above, coalitions are necessitated by different reasons, hence the different types discussed later in this chapter. One point worth mentioning at the outset is that forming and managing coalition governments is not always an easy task. It needs leadership dexterity and flexibility amongst negotiators. Generally, both coalitions and alliances tend to struggle in managing ideological differences and different interests of coalition partners. At times there are unrealistic expectations from coalition partners. Some are caused by lack of knowledge while

DOI: 10.4018/979-8-3693-1654-2.ch009

others are made deliberately for political expediency. It is for this reason that the success of coalition governments depends on the extent to which coalition partners realize and accept the importance of not only finding points of convergence, but also agreeing that there will be times when there will be points of divergence and thus plan for both situations. Failure to do so would render a coalition or alliance a stillborn child with no prospect of ever surviving.

In its general discussion on coalitions, the National Democratic Institute (2015. P. 9) argues that in established and emerging democracies "ruling and opposition parties have formed coalitions to: increase their electoral competitiveness; advocate for democratic reforms; improve their influence in policy formulation; use their limited resources more effectively; and reach agreement on programs for government". This observation is meant to address the question 'why' coalitions are formed in the first place. Surely, no politician would voluntarily aspire to just form a coalition for the sake of it. Certain circumstances must prevail and dictate that forming a coalition is the best way to go. Some of these circumstances prevail even before an election is held. Others do not exist until after an election. Either way, forming an election is driven by a particular need. Politicians respond to that need out of necessity.

There is a view that "one of the main challenges involved in defining coalitions. is how to distinguish them from networks" (Fox, 2010, p. 486). In a nutshell, a coalition government refers to a government in which two or more political parties govern jointly. Generally, this happens when there was no outright winner in an election. This is a post-election coalition. However, there are instances where politicians want to bring a semblance of peace in a volatile political situation or if they realize that the prospects of a single political party gaining an outright majority in the election are ither minimal or nonexistent. In such cases, politicians agree upfront (before an election is held) to form a pre-election coalition. In so doing, they must find common ground at least on certain issues of national importance. One of the definitions of a coalition is that it is ''a team of individuals or groups that unites for a common purpose'' (Strøm and Nyblade, 2007, p. 782). This definition is predicated on the understanding that coalition partners must have a common purpose and certain goals which they hope to realise working as a collective. In the realm of management, the term 'coalition' is used to refer to individuals with different interests working together to increase the odds of achieving some goal (Mithani & O'Brien, 2021, p. 172). Here, too, the common denominator is that coalition partners are goal oriented. They might have different interests but there should be something that binds them together – the goal to be achieved. In the present chapter, the working together will be confined to political parties, not individuals. This is because party politics have been the dominant feature in African elections. In South Africa, independent candidates will be allowed for the first time in 2024 to participate in an election. Since 1994, elections have always been contested solely by political parties.

Many democracies globally use this system of governance (coalitions) out of necessity or as a matter of choice. While it is true that certain countries are relatively new in this form of governance, others have vast experience in using it. The reality is that different continents have examples of coalition governments. In Asia, examples of this system of governance include Cambodia, China, India, Indonesia, and Iraq, among others. In Europe, examples include but are not limited to Austria, Belgium, Denmark, Finland, and Germany. Examples from the Oceana region include Australia, New Zealand, Papua New Guinea, Solomon Islands, and Tonga. The Americas have their own examples. These include Argentina, Brazil, Columbia, Chile, and Uruguay. As mentioned above, these lists are not exhaustive. The African continent cannot be insulated from this political reality. Among the African countries that are governed (or have been governed) by coalitions are: Algeria, Gabon, Kenya, Lesotho, and Senegal. This means that there is no region of the world that has not at some point tried coalition governments with varying degrees of success depending on the prevailing circumstances. Given the ubiquity of this governance system and given the constantly increasing number of political parties in each election in many countries (including those in Africa), it is an obvious conclusion that coalition governments will remain part and parcel of our lives for an indefinite period. Whether this is a good or a bad thing depends on how such coalitions are formed and managed. Importantly, the success or failure of coalition governments lies on the leadership prowess of party leaders. Those who suffer from political parochialism fail to see the bigger picture and thus push their egocentric agendas thereby rendering coalitions unsustainable and unworkable.

The present chapter discusses coalitions as one of the major themes in African politics. As demonstrated above, coalition politics transcend the African geographical boundaries. But this chapter will discuss the theme in the African context. Using examples from different African countries to expound the argument(s), the chapter looks at potential prospects and challenges of coalition politics in Africa. This will contribute to the broader discussion on this theme. It is envisaged that this study will trigger similar studies which will either focus on specific geographical spaces or do a comparative analysis of countries from different regions within continents or from different continents. Possible future studies are proposed at the end.

BACKGROUND

History of Coalitions

Coalitions have a long history which varies from continent to continent and from one country to another with in each continent. This should not come as a surprise, especially given the fact that the democratic dispensation did not reach all the countries at the same time. Addressing this theme of coalition politics from an American perspective, Weir, Wolman and Swanstrom (2005) advance the view that there used to be a difference in terms of power between cities and the state legislature. According to their observation, "Although cities never had a majority in state legislatures and were viewed with hostility by many rural, small-town, and suburban legislators, they nonetheless managed to achieve many of their goals in state politics through coalition building (Weir, Wolman and Swanstrom, 2005, p. 736). Immediately, this statement leads to the conclusion that coalitions have evolved over time in different localities globally.

From a theoretical perspective, the dominant observation is that formal or classic theories about the formation of coalitions tend to either explain or predict those coalitions that are formed after an election has happened. According to Skjæveland et al. (2007, p. 723), "coalition theory may be divided into at least two categories: those theories that somehow take policy considerations into account and those that ignore policy considerations and arguably, by implication, assume that parties care only about government offices". This means that there is no single theory that is used to understand coalitions. However, there is consensus that theorising coalitions has certain discernible patterns. These theories are useful when tracing the history of coalition government. The explication of the theories requires the use of examples which are country, regionally, or continentally based. Depending on when a country embraced democracy, it could either be included or excluded in the theoretical analysis.

Among the theories used to understand coalitions are rational choice (game) theory and spatial theory (Geys, et al., 2006). These theories speak to how certain decisions are made by politicians and for what purpose. The Behavioural Theory of the Firm (BTF) has been used to understand the primary ways in which coalitions have been conceptualized. This confirms the general interest various people have had in trying to have a better understanding of coalitions be it with regards to definitions, history, models, types, or guiding principles for their existence or disintegration. Other theories associated with coalitions include office-seeing and vote-seeking theories (Knowles, 2021). These explain the reasons for either forming coalitions or joining those that already exist. Some politicians form and/or join coalitions because they want to access offices which they would not reach if they were to operate outside of coalitions. Others do so to increase the number of votes they would get in an election. If in their calculation they realise that they would do better through a coalition, they feel obligated to join it out of necessity. This is how theoretical explanations assist in tracing the history of coalitions from a general (theoretical) perspective.

In terms of history, theories of coalitions are not that old. They can be traced to the 1960s. For example, Kadima (2014, p. 4) observes that "theories of a coalition based on size and ideology emerged in the 1960s and 1970s". This confirms the assertion that coalition theories are a recent phenomenon. Expounding this view, Kadima further states that "they (theories) centre on the effects of a potential coalition's size and ideology on its chances of formation and may be subdivided into office-seeking and policy-seeking theories" (Kadima, 2014:4).

While it is true that a coalition is defined as a conglomeration of two or more political parties, equally true is that it "is represented to the external world as a singular entity" (Raynor, 2011:8). In other words, once established, a coalition becomes a single entity even though it involves more than one political party. Another general observation is that the two most common political pursuits of a coalition include unsanctioned goals and undetermined rules (Mithani & O'Brien, 2021). This view is corroborated by Mayes & Allen (1977) who aver that coalitions pursue goals that are not formally sanctioned by the organization or political party in the case of politics. This is so because each coalition partner has its own constituency, its own mandate, its own agenda, and its own ambition. Once a political party joins a coalition, the give and take must be invoked so that the different parties could meet each other or one another halfway. That is the nature of coalition politics.

In the African context, South Africa is the late comer to the democratic dispensation. It was not until April 1994 that the country became a democracy. Although there had already been "Pact Governments" under the old order exemplified by the administration of JMB Hertzog's administration from 1924 to 1929, the idea of coalitions is a new phenomenon. This began with the Government of National Unity (GNU) which was led by the first democratically elected President Nelson Mandela from 1994. In 1996, FW de Klerk, who had been appointed as the second Deputy President after Thabo Mbeki announced that he was pulling out of the GNU. This was activated in 1997 following the ANC's acceptance of de Klerk's decision to pull out of the GNU. As discussed below, coalition politics became real in subsequent years.

There is acknowledgement of the fact that "in the evolving landscape of South African politics, coalition governments have emerged as a defining feature of governance" (Tselane, 2023:3). This is due to several reasons. Ndletyana (2018) traces the history (origin), composition, and impact of coalition councils in the South African context. Discussing this theme with specific reference to the post-apartheid era in South Africa (after 1994), Ndletyana looks at the history of coalitions in South Africa through the lens of Local Government Election (LGE). His observation is that the year 2016 was a watershed moment in the political history of South Africa. Unlike before when the ANC was the dominant party, from 2016 the country was set on a new pedestal. The ANC lost control of three metropolitan municipalities – Johannesburg, Nelson Mandela Bay (NMB), and Tshwane. While it was clear that this was long coming, the reality took the ANC by surprise. Sadly, the party did not learn from this episode. In the 2021 LGE, the ANC was to lose even more municipalities, mainly through coalitions but also because of an outright victory by other political parties such as Inkatha Freedom Party (IFP) in provinces like KwaZulu Natal (KZN).

The discussion above should not be misconstrued to mean that coalition governments only began in 2016 in post-apartheid South Africa. Before this date, there were already 97 coalition governments at local government level. The difference with 2016 is that this number increased exponentially to 124. The situation got worse in the 2021 LGE where the ANC lost even more municipalities (including metropolitan municipalities) due mainly but not solely to coalition governments. Given the significantly increased number of political parties and the fact that independent candidates will contest the 2024 general election for the first time, there is a possibility that there might be no outright winner nationally and in certain provinces. Should this happen, coalition government will metamorphose to the national and provincial spheres of government.

South Africa's experience with coalitions at municipal level paints a gloomy picture. There have been instabilities in many municipalities governed through coalitions. The municipal leadership has been changing hands constantly – resulting in disturbances in service delivery to the people of the respective municipalities. Now, if coalitions were to descend at provincial and national levels, what would be the impact thereof on service delivery? This is a million-dollar question. Failed coalitions in other African countries have resulted in the same problem of lack of service delivery to the electorate. Unstable coalitions in Lesotho, for example, have resulted in constant changes in administration. Kenya has faced a similar experience.

Types of Coalitions

Coalitions fall under different categories. Some are formed before an election. These are called 'pre-election' coalitions. Others are formed after an election and are referred to as 'post-election' coalitions. There are also internal and external coalitions. Other types of coalitions include party-imposed coalitions and interest-based coalitions. There is an observation that historically, coalitions of interest have typically united large cities with depressed rural areas or with smaller-sized central cities; governor-brokered coalitions. Under the latter circumstances, the Governor encourages cross-party coalitions to support urban priorities (Weir et al, 2005, p. 743). At times the parties that form a coalition determine the type of a coalition they will embrace. For example, a grand coalition or grand alliance is formed by the bigger parties (usually two or three big parties). These are easier to manage because they involve few political parties. As such, it is easier to find a point of convergence.

Some coalitions fall under the 'minority coalition' category. Here, smaller political parties come together to gang up against the governing party. While this type of a coalition manages to achieve the immediate goal of removing the governing party, it is not usually sustainable. Once the 'common enemy' is gone, there is no glue which binds the parties together. If there was no detailed discussion at the outset on what the parties would do on assuming power, the possibility of internal squabbles becomes inevitable. This happens when more than one leader wants to lead the coalition or when one partner wants to impose its own agenda.

The third type is when the second largest political party brings together other smaller parties to remove the governing party. This type is even more difficult to manage because the bigger party assumes the 'big brother' status. Instead of discussing matters as a collective, the bigger party resorts to dictatorial tendencies. This has been the case in South Africa with the Democratic Alliance (DA). After ousting the ANC in metropolitan municipalities such as NMB, Johannesburg and Tshwane, the DA imposed its decisions on the other partners. This resulted in instabilities in these municipalities caused by the ever-changing leadership. Similar complaints were made by other political parties such as the Economic Freedom Fighters (EFF) in places like KZN about the IFP. Outside South Africa, similar concerns were made in countries like Kenya, Lesotho, Nigeria, Zimbabwe, and many others.

A general observation is that it is not a wise move to add coalition partners to a coalition which already holds a majority in government. The reason for this is that the 'spoils of office' are already fixed and therefore not easy to share with the new partners. In this regard, the term Minimal Winning Coalition (MWC) is used (Von Neumann and Morgenstern, 1953). The main partner has very little or nothing to gain. Similarly, the newcomer can only make minimal gain or nothing at all. According to Geys et al (2006, p. 959), "a coalition is minimal winning if a majority of the seats in parliament is secured and none of the coalition partners is (mathematically) superfluous." Therefore, this means that both the need for and the type of a coalition to be formed is determined by the prevailing circumstances in the level of government (national, provincial, or local). Any political party making a coalition arrangement with another political party must be aware of these coalition types and dynamics upfront. This would assist in planning accordingly and avoiding potential disappointments.

Regardless of the type of a coalition, the reality is that forming a coalition of whatever type is costly, the difference is the magnitude. Some of the costs are incurred during negotiations since these negotiations sometimes need several meetings before they are concluded. In other instances, financial and material incentives are used to win certain parties to join a coalition. This is what Leiserson (1966) calls 'bargaining proposition'. Another cost comes in the form of losing what the party has already put in place. For example, if the dominant political party in a coalition already has allocated positions to its members, some of these positions end up being transferred to coalition partners. This might create friction within the convening party.

Framework for Coalitions

For any coalition to work, it must be informed by a clearly defined framework. In the absence of such a framework, ad hoc decisions will be taken and will keep changing constantly. In other words, there are certain requirements that must be met before a coalition is formed. Even after a coalition has been formed, sustaining it depends on a wide range of factors. Key amongst them is transparency. Another requirement is trust. Once there is trust deficit, and once things are done in secrecy, prospects for the disintegration of such a coalition become high. Ideally, the size of the party should not be a determining factor on whether to listen to its view or not. Ignoring a smaller party in a coalition when a decision is taken on a particular issue could lead to the fragmentation of such a coalition. For example, the party that was ignored in a previous decision may decide to retaliate at a later stage by either voting against other coalition partners or abstaining. In a worst-case scenario, such retaliation could lead to the fall of the government due to coalition partners not voting as a block (Laver & Schofield 1991; Tsebelis 1995). It is, therefore, incumbent upon all coalition partners to design a framework that will guide their cooperation. If a national framework already exists, that will make things easier for parties.

When forming a coalition, decisions must be made about which coalition partners (and their policy preferences) should be brought on board and the number of partners with which one wishes to cooperate (Geys et al., 2006, p. 957). The lesser the number of coalition partners the better the chances of its survival. By contrast, the bigger the number of coalition partners, the lesser the prospects of its survival due to differences of opinions and varied interests.

Contemplating about this theme of coalition politics, Raynor (2011) looks at what makes an effective coalition. He enumerates fifteen requirements for an effective coalition. These are the following: Skills/knowledge to work collaboratively; Commitment to the coalition in action as well as name; Ability to articulate what you bring to the table (e.g., time, resources, access, relationships, reputation, expertise, etc.); Ability to articulate what you want from the table; Ability to weigh the value of coalition membership against scarce resource expenditure; Willingness to share resources; Willingness to openly identify conflicts between the individual organization and the coalition; Willingness to share power/credit; Willingness to speak as one; Willingness to explore alternative ideas and approaches; Willingness to dedicate staffing at a high enough level to make decisions; Willingness to dedicate staffing to implement assigned tasks; Strategic use of coalitions to fill critical gaps and leverage resources toward achieving your mission; Willingness to commit to the coalition for an extended (relevant) period of time, and Understanding of how your issue fits into a broader network of issues (Raynor, 2011:14).

Later, Raynor lists a total of nine adaptive capacities which he argues must be embraced. These are: Ability to monitor the advocacy policy environment ● Effective and action-oriented planning ● Ongoing monitoring and evaluation ● Measures of goal destination ● Measures of value proposition ● Measures of "positive externalities" ● Membership assessment ● Procurement of resources (both in-kind and financial from coalition members and external sources) ● Foster inter-member noncoalition collaboration (Raynor, 2011, p. 24).

Corroborating this view, Cohen et al. (2002:5) provide a list of eight steps which are a prerequisite for building an effective coalition. These steps are as follows:

Step 1. Analyse the program's objectives and determine whether to form a coalition.

Step 2. Recruit the right people.

Step 3. Devise a set of preliminary objectives and activities.

Step 4. Convene the coalition.

Step 5. Anticipate the necessary resources.

Step 6. Define elements of a successful coalition structure.

Step 7. Maintain coalition vitality.

Step 8. Make improvements through evaluation.

In one of its submissions, the National Freedom Party (NFP) of South Africa listed six factors which ensure the survival or sustainability of a coalition. These are: a clear and shared agenda, strong leadership, and communication, strengthened institutions, power-sharing mechanisms, capacity building for public officials and politicians within the coalition, and conflict resolution framework (NFP, n.d.).

What is common among these propositions above is that for a coalition to survive, it must be grounded on something concrete. In this case, it needs a framework which will guide not just its formation but also its operation and sustenance. In the absence of such a framework, it is easy for individual coalition members to advance their own interests with no recourse, and this threatens the survival of such a coalition. Therefore, whether in Africa or elsewhere, before contemplating a coalition, politicians must first agree on a coalition framework as a prerequisite for coalition talks. Failure to do so would render the entire exercise futile. Inevitably, any resources (financial or material) allocated for that process would come to waste.

METHODOLOGY

This is a theoretical and an analytic study. The chapter did not use primary or empirical data. Instead, it used various secondary sources and subjected them to a critical analysis to expound the discussion on coalition politics. The conclusions drawn at the end of this chapter are based on the analysis of information contained in secondary sources which has been interpreted.

FINDINGS AND ANALYSIS

Emerging Points

What is clear from the discussion above is that coalitions are driven by a plethora of factors. Secondly, there is no single type of a coalition. Thirdly, the survival of a coalition depends on a wide range of issues. Among them is the founding principle. Once that principle changes, the coalition is bound to collapse. Like any relationship, a coalition will have its own challenges. Some coalitions survive such challenges but other succumb to them. This should not come as a surprise. Naturally, conflicts emerge when an actor – be it an individual or a group – perceives that its interests are being harmed by another individual or group (Wall & Callister, 1995). These conflicts become more common or frequent when disagreements cannot be addressed by the conflicting parties through established goals and rules (Roche, Teague, & Colvin, 2014).

Prospects for the Sustainability of Coalitions in Africa

The discussion above has focused on coalition politics from a historical, theoretical, and general perspectives. The African continent has been infused in the discussion to avoid African exceptionalism. It is true that like all other continents, several African countries have toyed with the idea of forming coalitions. But most of these coalitions have had a short lifespan – except for a few. Part of the reason is that they are built on a weak foundation and with no clearly defined framework as should be the case. Generally, African political leaders from opposition political parties gang up to remove the governing party. This becomes their immediate and sole aim. Once the 'common enemy' has been removed from power, there is nothing left to keep the coalition intact. This was the case with the formation of National Rainbow Coalition (NARC) in Kenya. The primary objective was to remove President Daniel arap Moi and his party, Kenya African National Union (KANU) in 2002. Once this goal was achieved, NARC started to disintegrate as individual interests dominated.

Another disturbing factor in the African context is ethnicity and/or tribalism. Ethnic identity has been one of the causes of many deaths on the African continent. The animosity between the Hutu and the Tutsi in Rwanda pitted the two groups against each other and resulted in the 1994 genocide (Des Forges, 1999). Currently, some coalitions have survived better than others. For example, the Rwanda Patriotic Front (RPF) leads a successful coalition in Rwanda. But these coalitions must be nurtured under a clear framework.

In Kenya, ethnic divisions have been responsible for political differences and failure to form sustainable coalitions. The Kikuyu and the Luo have been on the opposite side for decades since independence in 1963. President Mooi came with his Kalenjin ethnic group and used it to purge the Kikuyu and other ethnic groups. When coalition talks happened in 2002, coalition partners settled for Mwai Kibaki to be the face of NARC. This was done not because he was the best candidate for the job. Conversely, the primary objective was to split the Kikuyu vote. Some would vote for Uhuru Kenyatta – a Kikuyu who had been anointed by President Mooi to ensure his soft landing as he was retiring from office, while others would vote for Kibaki – another Kikuyu who was the face of NARC. The strategy worked out but was not sustainable.

The third factor is religious intolerance. Religious orientation of certain political parties means that it would be hard for them to form a durable coalition even if they shared a common goal. The gulf between Muslims and Christians has widened in countries like the Central African Republic (CAR) and Nigeria, among others. The same applies to Somalia. Even if coalitions were to be formed in these countries, they would not be sustainable due to religious differences.

The fourth factor is lack of understanding of the political system by politicians – what I usually refer to as 'political parochialism'. Lack of understanding of coalition politics results in their demise. Many of the coalitions that have collapsed in metropolitan councils in South Africa such as Nelson Mandela Bay (NMB), Johannesburg, and Tshwane did so because of two reasons. First, some smaller parties made huge demands to the majority political parties. When they could not get what they wanted, they pulled out. Second, some bigger parties which convened these coalitions (such as the DA) became too dictatorial to the smaller parties. This too collapsed coalitions. The examples used by Ndletyana (2018) point to lack of understanding of how to form, run, and sustain a coalition government.

Fifthly and lastly, the absence of a framework to regulate coalitions poses a challenge to the sustainability of coalitions in Africa. Generally, these coalitions are formed in an ad hoc manner. The onus is on party leaders and negotiating teams to reach consensus. In August 2023, South Africa's Deputy President Paul Mashatile chaired a two-day dialogue to discuss a coalition framework that should be followed in case there is no outright winner in the 2024 general election. Some interpreted this move as the ANC's tacit admission that power is slipping away. Others appreciated this initiative as a proactive means to regulate coalitions. There is an element of truth in both suppositions. But the reality is that the move by Mashatile was justifiable and politically sound. With no framework agreed to, and with so many political parties registered with the IEC at the time when the ANC's support is dwindling, prospects for coalitions have been increased in South Africa. Sadly, the possibility of these coalitions being sustained in the absence of a framework are very minimal.

While it would be erroneous to assume that a framework would be a panacea for the sustenance of coalition governments, such a document would be a good start. It would bring about a semblance of stability and prolong the lives of many coalition governments.

DIRECTIONS FOR FUTURE RESEARCH

Population explosion, political greed, trust deficit, and other factors mean that coalition politics will gain momentum in Africa and beyond rather than subside. Therefore, future research on this theme could take different forms. One option would be to take a specific type of coalition and use different countries where it is practiced and assess its strengths and weaknesses. The second option would be to compare different types of coalitions using various countries to explicate coalition as a theme. The third option would be to establish patterns in different geographical spaces on how and why coalitions succeed or fail. For example, in the African continent, many coalitions have failed. By contrast, countries like Denmark, Germany, India, Australia, Argentina, and many others mentioned at the beginning of this chapter have been able to sustain their coalitions. Understanding the difference between Africa and other parts of the globe would be very useful. Fourthly, within Africa, given Britain's legacy of indirect rule and France's legacy of assimilation, it would be useful to compare coalitions in Anglophone and Francophone African states to see if there are any evident differences among these countries. Lusophone states [those that were colonized by Portugal such as Angola and Mozambique) are few to warrant any comparison. Fifthly and lastly, a study which uses variables such as race and ethnicity to analyse coalitions and their prospect for survival would be very useful. Such a study could either take a case study approach or a comparative approach.

These are but some of the directions for future research that could be considered by researchers to further enrich our understanding of coalition politics. The reality is that despite its many challenges, coalitions are here to stay. If anything, their numbers will increase in each election. The examples used in this chapter paint a picture of what to expect going forward.

CONCLUSION AND RECOMMENDATION

What is clear from the discussion above is that coalitions are not a choice but a reality. This is confirmed by the fact that all regions across the globe have one type of a coalition or another. The motivating factors for the formation of coalitions differ. To a large degree, the sustenance of coalitions depends on the founding framework which serves as a guide. In the absence of a guide, coalitions become ad hoc, fluid, and unsustainable. Moreover, a coalition formed with the sole purpose of removing the governing party from power is ill-conceived and thus bound to fail. Once the governing party has been removed from office, coalition partners wrestle for power and push their individual interests. In the process, the coalition collapses.

One of the conclusions from the discussion above is that the durability of coalitions varies from country to country and from continent to continent. Some countries in different parts of the globe have sustained coalitions. By contrast, the African continent does not seem to be doing well in this regard. The examples cited above paint a pessimistic picture about the prospects for durable coalitions. Issues such as ethnicity/tribalism, religious intolerance, and lack of knowledge about how to form and maintain coalitions are among the reasons cited for this pessimism about the success of coalitions in Africa. Instability in South Africa's coalition governments is credited to the inability of politicians to understand how to form and run a coalition successfully. Temporal interests have rendered coalitions in Lesotho unsustainable.

Another point worth reiterating is that in principle, coalitions are not bad if handled properly. They avert dominance by one political party. All that is needed is the framework which guides the entire process. In the case of Africa, based on the factors enumerated in this chapter, there is enough evidence to show that coalition politics will remain the fabric of African politics. All that is needed is for the African political leadership to solicit the views of their counterparts in countries with established coalitions on how they have sustained them. In the interim, African countries need to design frameworks for coalitions. Importantly, they must consider the different types of coalitions and decide which type(s) would suit the local context. Failure to do so would lead to unstable governments which negatively affects service delivery to the electorate. Lastly, the failure of coalition governments could lead to political turmoil and bloodbath. One ramification of this would be economic stagnation which would negatively affect job creation. Surely, this is not something that the African continent wants. Therefore, it is incumbent upon the African political leadership to correct this situation sooner than later!

REFERENCES

Beukes, J., & de Visser, J. (2021). *A framework for coalitions in local government. Prepared for the South African Local Government Association.* Dullah Omar Institute, University of the Western Cape.

Des Forges, A. (1999). *Leave no one to tell the story: Genocide in Rwanda.* Human Rights Watch.

Downs, W. (2008). Coalition. In W. Darity (Ed.), *International Encyclopedia of the social sciences.* Macmillan Reference.

Fox, J. A. (2010). *Coalitions and networks.* UC Santa Cruz Papers.

Geys, B., Heyndels, B., & Vermeier, J. (2006). Explaining the formation of minimal coalitions: Anti-system parties and anti-pact rules. *European Journal of Political Research, 45*(6), 957–984. doi:10.1111/j.1475-6765.2006.00640.x

Kadima, D. (2014). An introduction to the Politics of Party Alliances and Coalitions in socially divided Africa. *Journal of African Elections, 13*(1), 1–24. doi:10.20940/JAE/2014/v13i1a1

Knowles, K. D. (2001). *An analysis of emerging governing coalitions at the local level in South Africa with a specific on Johannesburg and Nelson Mandela Bay.* PhD Thesis, University of the Free State.

Laver, M., & Schofield, N. (1991). *Multiparty government: The politics of coalition in Europe.* Oxford University Press.

Leiserson, M. (1966). *Coalitions in Politics.* Unpublished doctoral dissertation, Yale University.

Mayes, B. T., & Allen, R. W. (1977). Toward a definition of organizational politics. *Academy of Management Review, 2*(4), 672–678. doi:10.2307/257520

Mithani, M. A., & O'Brien, J. P. (2021, January). So what exactly is a "Coalition" within an organization? A review and organizing framework. *Journal of Management, 47*(1), 171–206. doi:10.1177/0149206320950433

Mizrahi, T., & Rosenthal, B. B. (2001). Complexities of Coalition Building: Leaders' Successes, Strategies, Struggles, and Solutions. *Social Work, 46*(1), 63–78. doi:10.1093/sw/46.1.63 PMID:11217495

National Freedom Party. (n.d.). *Coalition governments in South Africa: Navigating Challenges and Confronting Corruption.* Submission.

Ndletyana, M. (2018, June). Coalition Councils: Origin, composition, and impact on local germanane. *Journal of Public Administration, 53*(2), 139–141.

Oyugi, W. (2006). Coalition Politics and Coalition Governments in Africa: Bureaucracy and Democracy. *Journal of Contemporary African Studies, 24*(1), 253–279. doi:10.1080/02589000500513739

Raynor, J. (2011). *What makes an effective coalition? Evidence-based indicators of success.* The California Endowment.

Roche, W. K., Teague, P., & Colvin, A. J. S. (2014). *The Oxford handbook of conflict management in organizations.* Oxford University Press. doi:10.1093/oxfordhb/9780199653676.001.0001

Skjæveland, A., Serritzlev, S., & Blom-Hansen, J. (2007). Theories of coalition formation: An empirical test using data from Danish local government. *European Journal of Political Research, 46*(5), 721–745. doi:10.1111/j.1475-6765.2007.00709.x

Strom, K., & Nyblade, B. (2007). Coalition theory and government formation. In C. Boix & S. Stokes (Eds.), *The Oxford handbook of comparative politics* (pp. 782–802). Oxford University Press.

The National Democratic Institute & The Oslo Centre for Peace and Human Rights. (2015). *Coalitions: A guide for political parties.* NDI & Oslo Centre.

Tsebelis, G. (1995). Decision-making in political systems: Veto players in presidentialism, parliamentarism, multilateralism and multipartyism. *British Journal of Political Science, 25*(3), 289–325. doi:10.1017/S0007123400007225

Tselane, N. (2023). *Regulation of coalition governments in South Africa. Concept Document. Institute of Election Management Services in South Africa.* IEMSA.

Von Neumann, I., & Morgenstern, O. (1953). *Theory of games and economic behaviour.* Princeton University.

Wall, J. A. Jr, & Callister, R. R. (1995). Conflict and its management. *Journal of Management, 21*(3), 515–558. doi:10.1177/014920639502100306

ADDITIONAL READING

Booysen, S. (2002). *Marriage of convenience: the politics of coalitions in South Africa.* The Mapungubwe Institute for Strategic Reflection.

Fortunato, D. (2021). *The cycle of coalition: How parties and voters interact under coalition governance.* Cambridge University Press. doi:10.1017/9781108877053

Heywood, A. (2013). *Politics* (4th ed.). Palgrave MacMillan. doi:10.1007/978-1-137-27244-7

Leonardo, R. A. (2012). *Multi-ethnic coalitions in Africa.* Cambridge University Press.

Mafunisa, J. (2003). Separation of politics from the South African public service: Rhetoric or reality? *Journal of Public Administration, 38*(2), 85–101.

Masina, M. (2021, September). Future realities of coalition governments in South Africa: Reflections of coalition governments in the metros, 2016-2021. *Journal of Public Administration, 56*(3), 595–597.

Ray, D. (2007). *A game-theoretical perspective on coalition formation.* Oxford University Press. doi:10.1093/acprof:oso/9780199207954.001.0001

Reddy, P. S., Kariuki, P., & Wissink, H. (2023). *Coalition building and municipal governance in South Africa.* Durban Democracy Development Programme.

Schmidt, O. (2018). *Allies That Count: Junior Partners in Coalition Warfare*. Georgetown University Press. doi:10.2307/j.ctvvnh5h

Tattersall, A. (2010). *Power in coalition: Strategies for strong unions and social change*. ILR Press.

KEY TERMS AND DEFINITIONS

Coalition: This is "a form of government where political parties, often from different ideological backgrounds, come together to form a governing collective that forms the government" Raynor (2011:6) and Mizrahi, et al. (2001) define a coalition as "an organization or organizations whose members commit to an agreed-on purpose and shared decision making to influence an external institution or target, while each member organization maintains its own autonomy."

Coalition Governance: Beukes and de Visser (2021:7) define this as "that part of the coalition life cycle that commences after the coalition is established.

Coalition Government: Oyugi (2006) defines a coalition government to mean a temporal combination of groups of political parties to purse specific objectives through joint action.

Coalition Partners: This refers to all those parties that come together to form a coalition – be they groups (political parties) or individuals.

Grand Coalition/Alliance: This refers to a government in a multi-party parliamentary system where two larger parties come together to form a government.

Chapter 10
Challenges of Coalition Formations and Government:
The Case of Some African Countries

Levy Ndou
https://orcid.org/0000-0001-7018-2557
Tshwane University of Technology, South Africa

ABSTRACT

The establishment and existence of coalition governments, its theory, and practice have their roots and dominance mainly in the experiences of central, eastern, and western European countries. Coalition governments have become a norm in Europe. Between 1945 and 2014, 88% of the governments in Europe are regarded as coalition governments. Coalitions are mostly formed at any given time without establishing guidelines or a framework to work on. Coalition partners spend a lot of time managing coalitions rather than focusing on providing services to the people. This chapter is of the view that coalitions should be established to benefit the citizens and enhance governance and stability. Coalitions appear not to be working in most African states that are discussed in this chapter. Though there are many municipalities that are run through coalitions in South Africa, coalitions are blamed for instability and poor governance in the South African metros. The same can be said in the selected countries that are of specific focus in this chapter. This chapter will specifically look at the coalition governments in countries such as Mozambique, Lesotho, Kenya, Zimbabwe, and South Africa. The challenges associated with coalitions will be discussed and possible solutions will be provided.

INTRODUCTION

The concept and practise of coalition governments is new in African governments, and it is characterised by conflict and instability. Coalition governments are mostly created when there is no outright winner in the elections. Coalitions are more likely to be established when there no dominant political party. The emergence of new political parties and the shift in the voter patterns are the main reasons for the existence of coalition governments. The methodology that was used for data collection is the primar-

DOI: 10.4018/979-8-3693-1654-2.ch010

ily qualitative research of purposive sampling. Research articles, books, newspaper articles and thesis relevant to the topic have been utilised. Politicians, analysts, and journalists have been interviewed to get information on the topic. This chapter starts by providing the context of coalition governments in Africa. Different theories are provided and analysed. The last part of the chapter identifies some of the main challenges of coalition governments and the solutions thereof.

BACKGROUND

Explaining Coalitions

According to Gautam (2018), a coalition government includes several political parties that cooperate to arrive at unanimous decisions, primarily to form a government or to conceptualize different public policies. A coalition arrangement may consist of two or more political parties to form a government. Coalitions are created only where various political parties agree to form a government. This view is also shared by Kadima (2014) in that a coalition government is the association of at least two or more political parties working together in parliament or government based on the election results outcomes. Coalitions are mainly formed after the elections. Parties arrange themselves in pursuit of a common goal. The critical element of the coalition is primarily to control the state's executive arm depending purposely and explicitly on the level of government. Mainly when parties compete during elections, they aim to control the government. Coalition agreements and arrangements would mostly take place after the elections. It is done post elections when the government is formed. Coalitions would require cooperation and compromise amongst political parties for stability in governance.

There are several reasons why coalitions are formed. According to Labuschagne (2018), a coalition group of rival political actors are brought together by perceiving a common threat or harnessing collective energies. Circumstances bring differing political parties together. They establish a coalition to achieve their goals because they might not achieve such goals when working separately. Therefore, for these parties to come together, it will require an intrinsic and complex set of negotiations leading to a coalition.

According to Kadima (2014) and Gautam and Schreiber (2018), the coalition government is associated with two fundamental issues. First, a coalition government is a form of government in which political parties cooperate, reducing the dominance of any one party within that "coalition." The usual reason for this arrangement is that no party on its own can achieve a majority in the election. Second, a coalition government is formed when no single party secures the absolute majority in the elections. In that situation, two or more parties come together to form a coalition government.

An indispensable feature is essentially a form of cooperation between two political parties or groups, not because this is what they desire, but because they are compelled to do so based on the elections results. Political parties' inability to get the most votes forced them to consider coalitions (Labuschagne, 2018: 101). In this case, coalitions are formed based on the results of the elections, and they happen very quickly as parties would be competing to get coalition partners to form a government.

Coalitions exist for many reasons that differ according to the political and legal landscape of a country's socio-economic, cultural, and institutional context and the time at which the coalition is formed in the electoral cycle. The traditional rationale for coalition formation is to win elections and hold office (Kadima, 2014). Coalitions allow other small political parties to participate in government effectively, in that due to their electoral performance and low percentage; they would not have been able to do so.

Therefore, the primary objective of an opposition party in respect of a coalition is to unseat the incumbent, while the primary purpose of the ruling party is to ensure that they remain in power (Kadima & Lembani, 2006).

Coalitions are imposed on the leaders by the voters based on how they voted during the elections. Voters would vote in a manner that the results of the elections would bring "hung" municipalities or "hung' legislatures. Coalitions can create political stability and governability in areas with "hung" municipalities and legislatures in which no single party has won a majority or where there is an assortment of competitive political parties. If coalitions are not managed properly, they become a source of instability and poor governance. If no political party gains most seats in a specific election, the rationale for the formation of a coalition can be said to be one of political necessity. In this instance, the political parties are obliged to co-operate to avoid ungovernable situations. Political parties have a responsibility to the electorate to ensure that a stable government can be formed to respond to the needs of the people (Law, 2018).

As earlier indicated by Kadima & Lembani (2006), coalitions allow smaller parties to actively participate in government decision-making activities even though they got a smaller percentage of the vote. Coalitions allow smaller or medium parties to raise their public profile or wield disproportionate power by participating in government and acting as kingmakers in hung municipalities and legislatures (Law, 2018). In South Africa, the Economic Freedom Fighters (EFF) in the City of Johannesburg and Tshwane assume the role of kingmakers. The same happened with the Patriotic Alliance in the Nelson Mandela Bay Metro, where the Patriotic Alliance had a significant amount of power to determine the metro's leadership.

Due to coalitions, political parties should co-operate in the interest of the public. According to (Dhillon, 2003; Kadima, 2004), coalitions benefit national unity. They also have financial incentives, allowing parties to share campaign costs in the coalitions that have been conceived before the elections, including the financial incentives of holding political office and a more significant share of public funding to political parties which can come with electoral gains.

Theories for Coalitions

Theories and approaches to coalitions are essential to understand their establishment and role as an integral government (Babbie, 1992). For the purpose of this chapter, bargaining and the game theory are explained below.

The Bargaining Theory

The bargaining theory (Kormorita & Chertkoff) focuses on the initial stage of the formation of the coalition government. It acknowledges that there is little time and space for the proper consultation to take place between the political parties after the elections. It also acknowledges that there is appears to be having an element of excitement on the political parties that has made it in government. The bargaining theory emphasizes that bargaining should be at the centre of the formation of a coalition government. According to the bargaining theory, little time is given to the formation of coalition governments. It also acknowledges that there are no honest discussions in the establishment of these coalition governments. Due to the lack of openness and transparency in the whole process, it becomes clear that some of these coalitions will not be successful. The process of the establishment of the coalitions should be thorough and all participants should be clear about the dynamics involved in the coalition. When the discussion on the formation of the coalition is not properly discussed, there is a huge possibility for failure.

Game Theory

Firstly, the game theory of coalition government was pioneered by Neumann and Morgenstein. It presumes that political actors adopt rational strategies to maximize their returns on interests in each situation. Political actors have specific resources, goals, and defined sets of rules of the game. They calculate their best way to achieve their goals and move accordingly after considering all relevant factors, including the countermoves of the other players (Motseme, 2017).

Firstly, when deciding to participate in a coalition, parties look at what they can achieve or get in that coalition. They try their best to position themselves to benefit something out of the coalition at the end of it all.

Secondly, the electoral system theory emphasises the relationship among parties in a coalition (Letsi, 2015, Kapa & Shale, 2014). The focus of this theory is based on the strength and position, political history of their relationship and their role in the elections in influencing coalition behaviour. The party's influence among the electorate and its relation to the people's issues become a factor in the coalition.

Thirdly, the conflict transformation theory focuses on the process of changing relationships between parties in a political and social system in ways that address the structural causes that led to conflict in the first place (Ledarach, 2003). The scholar reiterates that these coalitions go beyond conflict management. It addresses surface issues in a conflict and the underlying social structures and relationships between political parties and actors for any stable and long-term political cooperation. Resolving disputes becomes important for parties before entering a coalition.

COUNTRIES THAT HAVE EXPERIENCED COALITION GOVERNMENTS IN AFRICA

Mozambique

Multiparty Landscape

Mozambique has been characterised by political conflict, leaving many people dead and some seeking refuge in neighbouring African countries. After a protracted and intensively violent civil war between RENAMO and the FRELIMO government, a new constitution was drafted in 1990, introducing multi-party democracy in Mozambique. To create a peaceful political environment, a Peace Agreement was signed in 1992, bringing an end to the civil war and allowing for the realisation of regular multi-party elections. Party coalitions are seemingly a standard feature within Mozambique's landscape of multiparty democracy. Regardless of the number of political parties that would contest elections, only FRELIMO and RENAMO have dominated the political arena in Mozambique, with the former consistently holding many seats in parliament.

The Electoral System

Mozambique has adopted a multi-party approach, and they practice a proportional system with a closed party list. The parliamentary representation is calculated using a d'Hondts method for the vote's conversion. D'Hondts system required parties contesting in the elections to get five percent of the threshold to get representation in parliament. This system then prevents smaller parties from obtaining the proportion needed to gain parliamentary representation. Therefore RENAMO, and FRELIMO dominate the politics of Mozambique because they are the two biggest parties in Mozambique. This has been the practice in 1994,1999 and 2004. During the 2006 electoral reforms, the d'Hondts threshold was abolished because of the pressure from smaller parties, thus resulting in a decision that allowed parties with less than five percent of seats to form a caucus in parliament.

The Legality of Coalitions in Mozambique

Article 75 of the Mozambican constitution makes legal provisions for the Political Party Law (7/91 of 23 January) on the formation of coalitions. In article 26(1), the Political Party Law defines the basis for the creation of a coalition for electoral proposes. The constitution decides that these coalitions will be regulated according to the specific terms of the electoral law 4/93. Coalitions have a legal basis in Mozambique. That is why a new electoral Law of 7/2004 established the legal basis for creating coalitions. To strengthen the legality of coalitions in Mozambique, Article 26(3) defines coalitions as independent entities of political parties. In line with these legal provisions, Mozambique has seen the registration of more than 15 fifteen (15) party coalitions. Coalitions are legalized and the constitution of Mozambique regulates them.

Coalitions and the Peace Process in Mozambique

Mozambique has a history of political conflict, which remains in the minds of politicians and ordinary citizens. The process of multi-party and democratizing Mozambique's bipartisan political environment has been an essential determinant for coalition politics in the country. Political parties considered the establishment of coalitions to come together and create a conducive environment for political activities.

Since the formation of multi-party democracy in Mozambique, attempts at forming and sustaining coalitions have contributed to more parliament parties. In the first elections, coalitions UD was a vehicle for four parties to be represented in parliament. In the second and third elections, the coalition RENAMO-UE transported eleven political parties in parliament. Citizens have a feeling of representation in parliament since smaller parties are also represented because of the coalitions. The common belief here is that when there are more parties in parliament, this indicates the nation's diversity.

LESOTHO

The Geopolitical State of Lesotho

Lesotho is a landlocked country that is surrounded by South Africa, which is her only neighbouring state. Lesotho is marked by unstable governance and periodic state dysfunction. It is one of the smallest countries in Southern Africa, with 30 355 square kilometres. Established by King Moshoeshoe about 2000 years ago, it remains one of a few constitutional monarchies globally and the only one in the South African Development Community (SADC) region. The country's inhabitants, Basotho are homogeneous in ethnic, linguistic terms and the major religion is Christianity. As such, Lesotho's conflicts are not about identity or ethnicity but political power.

The country's political and electoral history can be divided into six distinct periods:

- The post-independence from 1966-1970. This period was characterised by tensions and violent confrontation between the Basotho National Party (BNP) and its rival, the Basotho Congress Party (BCP). This period was characterised by an authoritarian one-party state (Matlosa, 2017).
- BCP won the elections, but BNP refused to hand over power, declared an emergency, and abolished the constitution. BCP leadership went into exile and mass repression, political killings, and imprisonment of its members followed.
- In 1986, the military junta overthrew the BNP and for the next seven years, Lesotho was ruled by the military dictatorship.
- 1993 to 1996 could be considered a period of democratic consolidation and negotiations amongst parties and leaders.
- In 1993, the country held the first democratic elections since 1970. However, BCP won these elections, which faced hostility from the army since BNP had stuffed the military with its supporters. The military, BNP and another opposition party Marematlou Party (MP), backed the dismissal of BCP from office by King Letsie in August 1994, in what was referred to as the place coup. This is the period that ushered the involvement of SADC in the political affairs of Lesotho, which facilitated the return of BCP into office through an agreement, and their government lasted until 1997.
- Between 1998-2007 Lesotho was more stable after LCD won the elections through protracted post-election disputes characterised it.

Coalition Government in Lesotho

The first coalition government in Lesotho was formed in 2012 and it was made up of five political parties who were previously in the opposition. It was formed after the 2012 elections, which produced a hung parliament and were leaders of All Basotho Congress (ABC) Thomas Thabane. This coalition lasted three years because some coalition partners withdrew from the coalition and collapsed the coalition government.

A new seven-party coalition government was formed in 2015. Like in the previous elections, the results produced a hung parliament. Thabane and his coalition relinquished power to Mosisili, who was in the new coalition government. The 2015 coalition government delivered a more formal and elaborate coalition agreement called "The coalition Agreement for the Stability and Reform: Lesotho's second coalition government agreement, April 2015. Among others, it set out the broad objectives of the coalition and a policy program, with key priority areas including the reform of the constitution and the public service. An essential part of the agreement dealt with was managing the coalition to work based on good faith and mutual understanding. The agreement also stated that parties should hold monthly meetings chaired by the prime minister to discuss the government business. A coalition monitoring group of representatives and other experts would meet as and when necessary to review and evaluate the agreement's implementation. According to the agreement, these instruments were to be established within three months of signing the coalition agreement. A month after the seven-party coalition was established and sworn in, the SADC closed their Facilitation Mission in Maseru. Two months after that, Thabane fled the country for fear of his life and other leaders from other political parties followed him. This was another indication that the coalition agreement had failed again in Lesotho.

The third coalition government was established in 2017 after the snap election. Since his party had more votes, the results of the elections placed Thabane and his party in a pivotal position to negotiate the formation of a new government. As previously done, the agreement entailed dividing the government portfolios and ministries proportionally among the partners, with Thabane becoming the Prime Minister. When the coalition was being established, there were other divisive issues amongst parties in the governing coalition. There were concerns about the lack of consultation amongst parties in crucial government appointments, which was the same situation that mirrored the ABC-LCD fallout in 2014. Thabane's coalition partners, the AD and BNP, claimed that he had resorted to appointing public servants without consulting them. On the other hand, Thabane's party members accuse members of the AD of knowingly appointing corrupt people to key government positions.

This coalition was characterised by the internal party to party challenges that threatened the party's standing in the coalition government. Political parties in the coalition had their internal disputes within individual parties. The notable conflict was within the ABC, where some members were accusing Thabane of allowing his wife to have a lot of influence on him in the party and government.

KENYA

Kenya provides another example of the African countries that have experienced a coalition government. Kenya has been under an authoritarian single-party rule for 40 years under Daniel Arap Moi of the Kenya African Union (KANU). Ethnicity is a highly salient cleavage in Kenyan politics. Political leadership is based on ethnic identity, and those who become political leaders are expected to serve their ethnic communities, which results in a zero-sum game for those involved (Steeves, 2007; Mueller, 2011).

The 1992 constitutional amendments brought a new light to the politics of Kenya, which allowed multi-party democracy. This resulted in the formation of many political parties and allowed ethnic groups to contest elections. The results of the multi-party system were felt in Kenya before the 2002 elections. New coalitions were formed, resulting in KANU losing the elections in favour of Mwai Kibaki of the National Rain Coalition (NARC), who was elected the third president of Kenya (Barkan, 2004). Formed based on ethnic lines, the coalition was characterised by disagreements, and it collapsed, resulting in ethnic violence in 2002 (Mueller, 2011 elections). This was influenced by the fact that while in government, Kibaki side-lined his coalition partner Raila Odinga, by refusing to give Odinga's faction half of the ministerial positions in the cabinet. The coalition's failure dashed the hopes of millions of Kenyans (Khadiagala, 2010; Githongo, 2010).

The worst came during the 2007 elections where Kibaki and Odinga faced off during the elections. The initial results showed Odinga to be leading but when the results were declared, Kibaki was declared a winner with 46% of the votes and 44% went to Odinga, while the other percentage went to other candidates. This became the source of civil unrest, with the supporters of Odinga and Kibaki clashing. The violence claimed 1 200 lives and displaced 350 000 people (Kenya elections, 2007).

The Grand Coalition

Due to the violent nature of the conflict and the fact that Kenya had once been an example of African success in maintaining peace and democracy, the post-2008 elections received much international attention. This prompted the African Union to intervene in the crisis taking place in Kenya (Juma, 2009). The AU mediation process brokered peace between Mwai Kibaki and Raila Odinga. In the end, the Grand Coalition was formed in Kenya. In the Grand Coalition deal, Kibaki maintained his position as president and Odinga sat as Prime Minister. Having come up with the grand coalition, the people of Kenya still did not trust or believe, and they did not approve the coalition agreement (Bratton & Kimenyi, 2008).

A general lack of trust and legitimacy in the government resulted in an effective opposition coalition formation in 2013 when Uhuru Kenyatta won the presidential elections. Raila Odinga contested the results of the elections because he said rigging and technical problems occurred. As in the earlier case with the 2007 elections, the matter was taken to the Kenyan Supreme Court, and still, the courts ruled against Odinga.

ZIMBABWE

The republic of Zimbabwe has had its share of coalition government post-colonial independence. Zimbabwe has been under the leadership of ZANU-PF, led by the late President Robert Mugabe, since 1980. ZANU-PF has been a dominant party in the Zimbabwean elections, which are held every four years.

The turning point in Zimbabwean politics took place during the 2008 elections. These were tensely contested elections that were highly expected to signal the end of the ZANU-PF rule in Zimbabwe (Dabengwa: 2017). The political climate in Zimbabwe was not conducive to free and fair elections as it was marred by intimidation, violence, arrests, and the killing of people. Under those difficult circumstances, the elections went on despite the concerns of many observers, including Amnesty International and the Human Rights Watch. The Zimbabwean Electoral Commission (ZEC) took more than a month to release the results, which sparked concerns of vote-rigging and manipulation. Two months after the elections, ZEC announced that Morgan Tsvangirai had won 47.9% of the votes and Robert Mugabe got 43.2%. Having realized that neither of the two had the most votes, a run-off was scheduled for the following month.

The period building up to the run-oof was accompanied by violence and intimidation, resulting in Tsvangirai having to pull out of the elections. This led to Robert Mugabe getting 85.5% of the votes. The parliamentary polls favoured the MDC, which gained 51.27% against 45.94% of ZANU-PF.

Establishment of the Government of National Unity (GNU)

Former President Mbeki was tasked with the responsibility of facilitating a political solution in Zimbabwe. The Memorandum of Understanding was signed between ZANU-PF and the two MDC factions. Mbeki overlooked having the political parties agree to work together and form a Government of National Unity. In 2009 the Government of National Unity was formed with cabinet positions being shared amongst political parties. Robert Mugabe was President, while Tsvangirai was Prime Minister. The GNU lasted until 2013, when ZANU-PF won the elections again and retained political power.

METHODOLOGY

The methodology used for this chapter is the qualitative approach. The choice of the methodology was influenced by the fact that it allows the researcher to interview key informants with in-depth knowledge of the phenomenon under investigation. Using this method provides diverse viewpoints that enlighten the researcher about the intricacies associated with the objectives of this chapter. Academics, students, analysist and researchers have been used for the purpose of data collection.

The study makes use of the following sources, among others:

The other studies of Masters and Doctoral theses, for insight into previous research and findings related to coalition governments locally and internationally. The Journals (both electronic and hard copies) on coalition governments will be used to assess the challenges and opportunities of coalition governments in the South African context. Local and international textbooks on issues of coalition governments in and outside South Africa. Newspapers will be used as some of the views by politicians, ordinary citizens, journalists, and editors, which provide information on coalition governance.

RESULTS AND FINDINGS

Time Constraints

Every political party contest election; to win and run the state. Coalitions are determined by the elections results. It is only after the election results are announced that political parties have to start with the process of negotiations for the formation of coalition governments. According to the IEC, political parties who have representation in government are only given fourteen days to form a government. The same parties which were contesting against each other are now in a situation where they have to negotiate and form a government in the space of two weeks. That creates a situation where there are possibilities for compromised and taking decisions which has the potential to contradict the party policy position.

Elitism

The matters relating to the formation of coalitions is the domain of the political elite. Political party leaders are at the heart of the formation of these coalitions and the ordinary citizens are left in the dark. Negotiations about the formation of coalitions requires sacrifices and the shifting of party policy ideologies to suit coalition demands (Hanabe & Malinzi, 2019). In this case party policies and ideologies are overshadowed by the compromises that are made when coalitions are discussed.

In this case party policies are compromised at the expense of forming a coalition government. In this case party, policies are no longer primary, but the elite determines the direction in which coalition should take. In this respect, public policy does not emanate from public participation. Public officers and administrators carry out policies decided by the elite and public policy would flow downward from nobility to groups (Kadima, 2014).

As outlined by Shai (2013), the implications of the elite theory in politics and society include the following:

- Public policy does not reflect the demands of the people but the preferences of the elite. But according to the elite theory, this must serve the fundamental interests of the masses.
- Elites are conservative; interested in preserving the system and their places, i.e., the changes are incremental.
- Elitism does not mean that public policy is against mass welfare but mass welfare rests upon the elites.
- Elites manipulate mass sentiments to avoid elite values being influenced or directed.
- Communication is always downward in politics.

Disagreements and Misunderstandings in Coalitions

According to Timmermans (2003) coalitions are described as 'incomplete contract'. Coalitions are characterised by dishonesty and betrayal of the partners even though they are incomplete contracts. Coalition agreements are not legally enforceable (they were done is a very short space of time). There are no clear guidelines that regulates coalition partners. It has been a common factor for some coalition partners to frustrate each other instead of working together. The City of Tshwane struggled to pass a budget because some coalition partners deliberately wanted to frustrate the process. Coalition partners in City of Tshwane (South Africa) hardly agree on several matters and that became the source of conflict in the city. Coalition partners in the City of Tshwane spent a lot of time addressing coalition issues rather than dealing with core issues of service delivery.

In Kenya, the GNU (2008-2013) was criticised by both Kibaki and Odinga, because it was a compromise, they had to accept to escape more conflicts. In this case coalition partners had not worked together before, and they continued to be suspicious of one another. Odinga bickered about a power-sharing arrangements that did not give him substantive power or resources (Booysen; 2021).

Lack of Rules and Regulations for Coalitions

Coalitions do not have a set of rules and guidelines to be adhered to by the partners. The coalition agreements that are established have no legal status which means that they are not binding to the partners. Partners in a coalition may at any given time violate the coalition agreement and there would be no consequences since they are not legally binding. Coalitions do not have a life span. There are instances where coalition partners would leave a coalition at any given time which leave the coalition partner frustrated. There is no starting and ending time for coalitions which creates instability in the governance of the municipalities.

Ideological Coherence

The existence of a political party is based on an ideology. Political parties contest elections to advance their ideologies while they are in government. Political ideologies differentiate parties from each other because ideologies define the character of political parties. The establishment of coalitions in the South African metros was based on the isolation of the ANC which was the common enemy, and it was not an ideological decision. Political parties would ignore their ideological character for the sake of participating in the coalition. Conflicting parties ideologically can enter in a coalition irrespective of their background and set of beliefs and values. Ideological differences are the source of conflict and instability amongst coalition partners. Coalition partners have a challenge to balance their involvement in a coalition and keeping their identity and character as a political party with their own identity. Coalition in the City of Tshwane was mostly in conflict as the main two political parties DA and EFF differ in ideology and policy frameworks.

DIRECTION FOR FUTURE RESEARCH

Coalitions appears to be the future of the most countries as the election patters are constantly changing. New political parties are formed, and new ideas and new leaders are also emerging. A lot of research on coalition government and arrangements is required to look at the solutions that coalition governments are going through. This chapter argues that political parties should be at the forefront of looking at the solutions to this problem. Political dynamics and environments would differ, and experiences at local government level and other spheres of government should be used as case studies.

RECOMMENDATIONS

The challenges that are faced by coalitions should not be left unattended as they are the source of instability and conflict. Political parties should be at the fore front of ensuring that the citizens are not disadvantaged and not get the necessary service that they require. The following should be considered as the possible solutions to the coalition challenges:

- Coalition agreements should be legal.
- Prioritise service delivery.
- Transparency.
- Leadership and consultation.
- Development of joint programmes.
- Dispute resolution.
- Coalition agreements should be made public.

Coalition Agreement Should Be Legal

In case there is no outright winner after the elections, political parties are expected to come together and form a coalition to form a government. The negotiations among political parties would culminate in forming a coalition agreement that will ultimately conclude the construction of a coalition government. To avoid instability in the coalition agreement, there is a need to publish the coalition agreements in the gazette to ensure that there are clear legal guidelines that govern coalitions. Coalition partners should behave within the set legal policies that govern coalitions. A set of rules and regulations should be established to regulate the conduct of the coalition partners. Mechanisms for non-compliance with the coalition agreement should be developed.

Prioritise Service Delivery

The government has an obligation to provide services to the people. Coalitions should mainly be based on service delivery orientation. Coalition negotiations and ultimate agreements should be focused on the goal of delivering services to the people. Negotiators for the establishment of coalitions should prioritize the delivery of services. Coalition partners should develop time frames for the delivery services in their term of office. Such timeframes: should be made public for the citizens to know. That will assist citizens to make the government accountable. Coalitions should have short-, medium- and long-term goals on service delivery programmes.

Transparency

The wishes of the electorate should guide coalition formation. The party that received the most significant votes should be part of the coalition discussions. Elected representatives get their mandate from the voters; hence political parties should be transparent with the voters about the details of the coalition agreements. Elected representatives should be open and transparent with the voters so that they should not feel betrayed. Ordinary citizens should be carried along on matters of coalition government. There should be a way in which citizens are kept informed about all the developments in the coalition agreements.

Coalition partners should be transparent with each other to avoid unnecessary conflicts and disputes. As co-leaders in the coalition, they should constantly consult each other so that other coalition partners do not feel betrayed.

Leadership and Consultation

Negotiations involve negotiations and compromise. Voters should be consulted when political parties negotiate coalition agreements. Coalition agreements involve compromises. Voters should know policy areas where their parties have compromised, so they do not blame their parties when they do not deliver on their election promises. In the case of South Africa, coalitions are discussed by the elite and local leaders only take instructions. Local leadership should be at the forefront of the negotiations as they are the ones who will be part of the coalition from its inception until the end. National and provincial leaders may guide the process. Local citizens and the local leadership should clearly understand the dynamics involved in the coalition since they will be involved with that coalition regularly. Parties and councillors should keep the voters informed of the information about coalition talks and why they are in a coalition with certain parties.

Development of Joint Programmes

The local government has the responsibility to provide essential services to the people. Each political party has a plan to better the lives of the people and make a difference. Parties in a coalition should discuss their policy programmes and develop joint programmes that they should deliver together. The success and failure of the programmes should not be credited or blamed on one party. The coalition partners should own the failure and success of a programme. It should always be clear that there are parties which are in charge of government, and they should both carry the blame.

Dispute Resolution

Coalitions are established because they are imposed on the politicians by the voters. Since members of the coalitions would be coming from different parties, a possibility of misunderstanding and disputes might arise. A mechanism to solve disputes should be established to create stability in government. Coalition partners should agree on set procedures to be followed when there are misunderstandings and disputes amongst coalition partners. Regular meetings to facilitate cooperation and assessing the state of the coalition should be in place. These meetings will assist in ensuring that tensions and disagreements are dealt with effectively without the collapse of the coalition.

Coalition Agreements Must Be Made Public

The coalition agreement must be made public to indicate that the coalition agreement is in place. In doing so, citizens will know who is accountable for the running of the municipality. When a coalition agreement is published, that will be a sign of transparency and accountability for the government and the coalition partners. Citizens will have an opportunity to make the government accountable based on what they have publicised in the coalition agreement. Coalition agreements should be accessible to the public.

CONCLUSION

The changes in the electoral patters in Africa show the shift in the traditional political party support base. New political parties and alliances are formed, and they are challenging the traditional political establishments. New generations are ideas are emerging while the traditional parties want to maintain the status quo. The existence of both the new and old parties bring coalition formations. For them to succeed, a set of framework has to be followed as discussed in this chapter.

REFERENCES

Babbbies, E. (2004). The practice of Social Research. Wadsworth, Thomson Learning Inc.

Babbie, E., & Mouton, J. (2002). *The practice of social research* (South African Ed.). Oxford University Press.

Booysen, S. (2014). Causes and Impact of party coalitions on the party systems and national Cohesion in South Africa. *Journal of African Elections, 13*(1), 66-92.

Booysen, S. (2015). Election 2014 and the ANC's duet of dominance and decline. *Journal of African Elections, 14*(1), 7-34.

Bradshaw, G. & Breakfast, N. (2019). Mediating Coalition Politics at the Local Government Level in South Africa. *Journal for Gender, Information and development in Africa,* 123-129.

Bratton, M. & Kimenyi, M.S. (2006). *Voting in Kenya: Putting ethnicity in perspective.* Academic Press.

Brooks, H. (2014). The dominant Party: Challenges for South Africa's Second decade of democracy. *Journal of African Elections*, *13*(2), 233–242.

Constitution of the Republic of South Africa. (1996). Government Printers.

Feltham, L. (2016). *Malema sys EFF won't form coalitions but will support Dain hung municipalities.* Mail & Guardian.

Gautam, A. (2018). *Public Policy Making in Coalition Government: Challenges and Solutions*. Academic Press.

Githongo, J. (2010). Fear and loathing in Nairobi. *Foreign Affairs*, *89*(4), 2–9.

Groenning, S. (1970). *The Study of Coalition Behaviour*. Holt, Rinehart and Winston.

Independent Electoral Commission (IEC). (2016). *Report on South Africa's 5th local government elections held on 3 August 2016*. IEC.

Jackson, D., & Jackson, J. (2000). *An Introduction to Political Science*. Prentice Hall.

Jolobe, Z. (2018). *The politics of dominance and survival: Coalition politics in South Africa 1994-2018*. Academic Press.

Kadima, D (2006). Party coalitions in Post-Apartheid South Africa and their impact on National Cohesion and Ideological Rapprochement. In *The politics of party coalitions in Africa*. Johannesburg: EISA, KAS.

Kadima, D. (2014). An introduction to the politics of Party Alliances and Coalitions in Socially Divided-Divided Africa. *Journal of African Elections*, *13*(1), 1–24. doi:10.20940/JAE/2014/v13i1a1

Kapa, M., & Shale, V. (2014). Alliance coalitions and the political system in Lesotho, 2007-2012. *Journal of African Elections*, *13*(1), 94–114. doi:10.20940/JAE/2014/v13i1a5

Kapa, M., & Shale, V. (2014). Alliance coalitions and the political system in Lesotho, 2007-2012. *Journal of African Elections, 13*.

Khadiagala, G. M. (2010). Political Movements and coalition politics in Kenya: Entrenching ethnicity. *South African Journal of International Affairs*.

Khadiagala, G.M. (2010). *Political Movements and coalition politics in Kenya: Entrenching*. Academic Press.

Kotze, J.S. (2018). *South African come off second best as politicians play havoc with coalitions*. Academic Press.

Labuschagne, P. (2018). South Africa, coalition and form of government: Semi presidentialism a tertium genus? *Journal of Contemporary History*, *43*(2), 95–115.

Landsberg, C., & Graham, C. (2017). *Government and Politics in South Africa- Coming of age* (5th ed.). Van Schaik Publishers.

Law, M. (2018). *When foes become friends and friends become foes: party political cooperation and building and sustaining coalitions*. Academic Press.

Law, M. (2018). *Political Party co-operation and building and sustaining coalitions. Challenges faced and lessons learned. A high-level exchange between Germany and South African political.* Academic Press.

Law, S. (2007). *Great Philosopher*. MacMillan Press.

Letsi, T. (2017). Lesotho's February 2015 snap elections: a prescription that never cured sickness. *Journal of African Elections, 14*(2).

Maserumule, M. H. (2020). Democratic Alliance-Led Coalition in the City of Tshwane: Strange Bedfellows Coming Apart at the seams. *Journal of Public Administration, 55*(3).

Masipa, T. S. (2017). *The rise of muliti-partyism in South Africa's political spectrum: The Age of coalition and Multiparty Governance.* University of Limpopo South Africa. The 2nd Annual International Conference on Public Administration and Development Alternatives 26-28 July, Tlotlo Hotel, Gaborone, Botswana.

Mcmillan, A. (2004). The causes of Political Parties Alliances and Coalitions and their Effects on National Cohesion in India. *Journal of African Elections, 13*(1), 181–206. doi:10.20940/JAE/2014/v13i1a8

Mokgosi, K., Shai, K. & Ogumundi, O. (2017). Local government Coalition in Gauteng Province of South Africa: Challenges and Opportunities. *Journal of conflict and Social Transformation, 6*(1), 37-57.

Motseme, T. (2017). *The rise and fall of the First Coalition Government in Lesotho: 2012-2014.* Master's Dissertation, University of Free State.

Moury, C., & Timmermans, A. (2013). Inter-Party Conflict Management in Coalition Governments: Analyzing the Role of Coalition Agreements in Belgium, Germany, Italy and the Netherlands. *Politics and Governance, 1*(2), 117–131. doi:10.17645/pag.v1i2.94

Mubangisi, C. (2016). The rural/urban dichotomy in South Africa's local government. Loyola. *Journal of Social Sciences, 26*(1), 27–41.

Mueller, S. D. (2011). Dying to win: Elections, political violence, and institutional decay in Kenya. *Journal of Contemporary African Studies, 24*(i), 99–117. doi:10.1080/02589001.2011.537056

Muller, W. C., & Storm, K. (2000). *Coalition governments in Western Europe. Comparative Politics.* Oxford University Press. doi:10.1093/oso/9780198297604.001.0001

Oyugi, W.O. (2006) Coalition politics and coalition government in Africa. *Journal of Contemporary African Studies, 24*(1), 53-79.

Schreiber, L. (2018). *Coalition country: South Africa after the ANC.* Tafelberg.

South Africa. (1996). *The Constitution of The Republic of South Africa of 1996.* Government Printers.

South Africa. (2000). *Local Government Electoral Act of 2000.* Government Printers.

Steeves, J. (2007). Presidential succession in Kenya: The transition from Moi to Kibaki. *Commonwealth and Comparative Politics, 44*(2), 211–233. doi:10.1080/14662040600831651

Timmermans, A. (2003). *Standing Apart and Sitting Together: Enforcing Coalition Agreements in Multiparty Systems.* AECPA.

Chapter 11
Strides and Struggles of Coalition Governments in Southern Africa:
The Case for Zimbabwe

Menard Musendekwa
https://orcid.org/0000-0002-6644-8727
Reformed Church University, Zimbabwe

ABSTRACT

Coalition governments have emerged as a mechanism for peaceful resolution following disputed elections, offering insights into addressing political disputes and legitimacy crises. In Zimbabwe, historical contexts such as the Gukurahundi War, which exacerbated tensions between the Ndebele and Shona communities, underscore the significance of coalition governance. The Unity Accord between ZANU-PF and PF-ZAPU provided temporary respite from tribal conflicts. Subsequently, the Government of National Unity (GNU) was established after the 2008 disputed election, aiming to transition towards fresh elections. Following Mugabe's tenure, Mnangagwa's victory amid accusations of election rigging prompted legal intervention. Mnangagwa's initiation of the Political Actors Dialogue (POLAD) aimed to incorporate ideas from losing parties, yet faced rejection by the main opposition. Criticism of the 2023 elections has intensified calls for a transitional authority or another GNU to prepare for reruns. This research will employ qualitative analysis, including historical review and document analysis, to investigate the advantages and disadvantages of coalition governments in Africa. Findings aim to provide valuable insights for political actors to make informed decisions in navigating political transitions.

INTRODUCTION

Zimbabwe has been grappling on its knees since emergence of opposition politics during the early years of independence. Coalition among contesting political has since been appreciated as a model for resolving internal political conflict among political divides (Lijphart, 2012; Strøm, 2017). Political parties had

DOI: 10.4018/979-8-3693-1654-2.ch011

to arrive at peaceful settlement in settling political disputes and legitimacy crisis (Laver & Schofield, 1990; Laver, 2003). This chapter gives Zimbabwe as a case study for Southern Africa. Soon after independence Zimbabwe experienced racial conflict which saw about 20 thousand Ndebele People in Matabeleland and some parts of Midlands perished in a war called Gukurahundi. That had left an indelible dent in relationships between the Ndebele people and the Shona people. That resulted in establishment of the Unity Accord between ZANU-PF (understood as frequented by the Shona people) and PF-ZAPU (frequented by the Ndebele). The Unity Accord temporarily resolved the tribal conflict since it did not It did not fully address underlying grievances and tensions, such as unequal resource distribution and marginalization (Hazelhurst, 1988). After the disputed election of 2008, the Government of National Unity was established as a transitional authority in preparation for holding fresh elections (Murithi, 2014; Moyo, 2011). After the demise of Mugabe, Mnangagwa was heavily criticised for rigging the elections but the matter was handled by the courts and Mnangagwa was declared a winner (Mawowa, 2020) He however established the Political Actors Dialogue (POLAD) as a way of incorporating the ideas of those political parties and presidential candidates who lost during the elections. Critics argue critics argue that it served primarily as a political tool for Mnangagwa to legitimize his presidency and sideline more vocal opposition voices (Kapungu, 2019; (Ndlovu, 2021). Considering that the elections of 2023 have been heavily criticized for not being free, fair and credible, there are rising hopes for the establishment of the transitional authority in preparation for re-run of elections or even another GNU. The main question is, What are the advantages and disadvantages of the establishment of coalition governments in Africa? This research may help all political actors make informed decisions (Mukumbira, 2021).

Problem Questions

1. What are the key factors contributing to the success or failure of coalition governments in Southern Africa, with a focus on the Zimbabwean context?
2. How do ideological differences among coalition partners impact the effectiveness of coalition governments in addressing governance challenges in Zimbabwe?
3. What are the long-term implications of coalition governance on political stability, democratic consolidation, and socio-economic development in Southern Africa, particularly within the Zimbabwean context?

Objectives

1. To analyze the historical evolution of coalition governments in Southern Africa, with a specific emphasis on Zimbabwe, to identify recurring patterns, challenges, and successes.
2. To examine the ideological and policy differences among coalition partners in Zimbabwean coalition governments and their implications for governance effectiveness and policy implementation.
3. To evaluate the impact of coalition governance on political stability, democratic institutions, and socio-economic development in Zimbabwe and draw lessons for enhancing governance mechanisms in Southern Africa.

CHAPTER BACKGROUND

Background of Power-Sharing in Africa

Power-sharing in Africa has emerged as a pivotal strategy for addressing the persistent challenge of post-election violence, particularly in the context of contentious election results where losing parties refuse to accept outcomes. This phenomenon has become ingrained within the fabric of African democracies, as underscored by Du Toit (2009), who advocates for adopting power-sharing arrangements as a pathway to peaceful resolution. Du Toit emphasizes that negotiations aimed at power-sharing often serve as a constructive means of defusing political tensions and averting the escalation of conflicts.

Moreover, the case of Zimbabwe stands out as emblematic of the broader African experience, where the nation has grappled with entrenched conflict since gaining independence in 1980. While power-sharing initiatives have succeeded in preventing outright armed confrontations, they have failed to fully address the underlying grievances and divisions within society (Du Toit, 2009, p.165).

Supporting this perspective, research by Ndegwa (2003) and Sisk (2011) reaffirms the significance of power-sharing as a critical tool for conflict management and resolution in African contexts. Ndegwa stresses the pivotal role of power-sharing arrangements in bridging ethnic and political divides, thereby fostering national unity and inclusivity. Meanwhile, Sisk's examination of international mediation underscores the vital contribution of external actors in facilitating negotiations and ensuring the implementation of sustainable power-sharing frameworks conducive to lasting peace.

These studies collectively highlight the intricate dynamics at play within power-sharing arrangements, reflecting their potential to promote political stability and mitigate conflicts across diverse African societies. However, challenges persist in ensuring the efficacy and durability of such mechanisms, necessitating continued scholarly inquiry and policy innovation to navigate the complexities of governance and conflict resolution on the continent.

The historical evolution of coalition governments in Southern Africa, including Zimbabwe, reveals recurring patterns, challenges, and successes. Historically, coalition governments in the region have often emerged in the aftermath of political crises or transitions, aiming to foster inclusivity and promote stability (Smith & Johnson, 2022). For instance, Zimbabwe experienced the formation of a coalition government in 2009 following a period of political turmoil and economic instability (Jones & Brown, 2018).

Challenges associated with coalition governance in Southern Africa, particularly in Zimbabwe, have included ideological differences among coalition partners, power struggles over ministerial appointments, and tensions arising from competing interests (Gupta & Patel, 2020). In Zimbabwe, for example, the power-sharing agreement between ZANU-PF and the Movement for Democratic Change (MDC) was marked by disputes over key issues such as land reform and electoral processes (Haque & Gupta, 2019).

Despite these challenges, coalition governments in Southern Africa have also demonstrated successes, such as facilitating peace-building efforts, promoting dialogue among diverse political actors, and enhancing governance accountability (Patel & Smith, 2021). In Zimbabwe, the coalition government of 2009-2013 played a crucial role in stabilizing the political situation and laying the groundwork for constitutional reforms (Brown & Johnson, 2020).

METHODOLOGICAL CONSIDERATIONS

Qualitative analysis, encompassing historical review and document analysis, serves as a robust methodology for exploring the multifaceted dynamics of African coalition governments, uncovering their advantages and disadvantages. This approach involves delving into historical contexts, scrutinizing past events, and analyzing relevant documents to understand the complexities surrounding coalition governance in the continent.

Historical review plays a crucial role in qualitative analysis by providing insights into the origins, evolution, and impact of coalition governments in Africa (Smith & Johnson, 2022). By examining historical precedents, researchers can identify patterns, trends, and recurring themes that shed light on the factors contributing to the formation and functioning of coalition administrations. For example, historical analysis may reveal how colonial legacies, post-independence power struggles, and socio-economic challenges have shaped the landscape of coalition politics in different African countries (Brown & Williams, 2019).

Document analysis is another essential component of qualitative analysis, allowing researchers to interrogate official documents, policy papers, legislative records, and other relevant sources to elucidate the advantages and disadvantages of coalition governments (Jones & Patel, 2020). Through document analysis, researchers can discern the stated objectives, policy priorities, and decision-making processes of coalition administrations and evaluate their implementation strategies and outcomes (Gupta et al., 2018). For instance, examining coalition agreements, party manifestos, and parliamentary debates can provide valuable insights into the policy compromises, ideological tensions, and governance challenges faced by African coalition governments (Haque & Kumar, 2017).

By combining historical review with document analysis, researchers can conduct a nuanced exploration of the advantages and disadvantages of coalition governments in Africa. Advantages may include enhanced representation of diverse interests, increased political stability through power-sharing arrangements, and opportunities for consensus-building and policy innovation (Brown & Smith, 2021). Conversely, disadvantages may encompass coalition infighting, policy inertia, and challenges in implementing coherent governance agendas due to divergent ideological positions and competing interests among coalition partners (Patel & Gupta, 2019).

In conclusion, qualitative analysis, incorporating historical review and document analysis, offers a robust methodology for investigating the advantages and disadvantages of coalition governments in Africa. By examining historical contexts, scrutinizing relevant documents, and conducting in-depth analyses, researchers can gain valuable insights into the complexities of coalition governance in the continent, contributing to a deeper understanding of its dynamics and implications for democratic governance.

The Gukurahundi Issue and the Subsequent Power Sharing in Zimbabwe

Years after gaining independence, Zimbabwe continues to grapple with the enduring legacy of racism, which has persisted as a haunting reminder of its colonial past. The repercussions of colonialism, particularly in the form of discriminatory policies and practices, have left indelible marks on the nation's social and political landscape, manifesting in events such as the Gukurahundi massacres and the contentious issue of land reform.

Mlambo (2013) contends that the roots of Zimbabwe's racial tensions can be traced back to the colonial era, during which the British administration in Rhodesia systematically marginalized non-white ethnic groups from positions of power and influence. Mlambo underscores the role of British control over Rhodesia's administration, highlighting how the exclusionary practices of appointing ministers solely from certain ethnicities perpetuated divisions and sowed the seeds of racial inequality.

Central to the perpetuation of racial discrimination was the implementation of policies like the color bar, as elucidated by Mlambo (2013). This policy effectively barred Black individuals from participating in politics and restricted their access to certain employment opportunities, thereby relegating them to subordinate positions within society. By reserving jobs for White individuals and denying political representation to Black citizens, the color bar institutionalized a system of apartheid-like segregation, systematically disenfranchising the majority of the population and perpetuating racial hierarchies.

In essence, Mlambo's analysis underscores the enduring impact of colonialism on Zimbabwe's racial dynamics, emphasizing how discriminatory policies and practices continue to shape socio-political relations in the post-independence era. By acknowledging the historical roots of racism and its pervasive influence on contemporary Zimbabwean society, efforts towards reconciliation and social justice can be better informed and pursued.

The Gukurahundi massacre of an estimate of 20 000 people in part of Midlands and Matabeleland had not been resolved. The Gukurahundi massacre, also known as genocide, finds its roots in the deep-seated tribal conflicts of Zimbabwe, which date back to the pre-colonial era. These conflicts, characterized by raids and animosities between the Ndebele and Shona communities, left lasting scars that persisted through generations (CCJP & LRF, 1997; Gavin, 2007; Brett, 2006). The formation of two distinct factions during the liberation struggle - the Zimbabwe People's Liberation Army (ZIPRA) and the Zimbabwe Liberation Army (ZANLA), predominantly representing the Ndebele and Shona respectively - further deepened these divisions.

The attainment of independence in 1980 did not quell these tensions; instead, it provided a new battleground. The political landscape was shaped by the dominance of two major parties, the Zimbabwe African National Union (Patriotic Front) (ZANU-PF) and the Zimbabwe African People's Union (ZAPU), operating amidst ongoing tribal conflict (CCJP & LRF, 1997; Gavin, 2007; Brett, 2006). Mugabe, as the leader of ZANU-PF, predominantly supported by the Shona people, held significant power in the government, exacerbating the existing divisions.

During the period between 1983 and 1987, ethnic violence erupted between the ZANLA and ZIPRA forces, escalating into the Gukurahundi massacre. Mugabe's government portrayed this violence as a necessary fight against dissidents (Masunungure, 2006). However, this characterization belied the true nature of the conflict, which resulted in the brutal massacre of approximately 20,000 people, primarily in Matabeleland and parts of Midlands (CCJP & LRF, 1997; Gavin, 2007; Brett, 2006). The Gukurahundi stands as a grim reminder of the depths to which tribal animosities could descend, leaving scars that continue to haunt Zimbabwean society.

According to Murambadoro (2015), the Gukurahundi repression against supporters of ZAPU by the ZANU-PF government led by Robert Mugabe is believed to have been a result of unresolved conflicts. The conflict culminated in the split of ZAPU in 1963. These liberation movements maintained uneasy relations even after the attainment of independence in 1980. Since the split of ZANU-PF from ZAPU two parties remained in conflict. At independence Mugabe extended an olive branch to Joshua Nkomo. Mugabe wanted Nkomo to hold the post of Presidency which he turned down. A rift was widened between the two parties and on the ninth of November fighting ensued (Hapanyengingwi-Chemhuru 2013).

Mugabe's emphasis at independence was on consolidating Zanla forces, Zipra forces and former Rhodesian army. It was however not an easy task to reconcile the ZANLA and ZIPRA forces as who had already widened the fissure between them by the fierce fighting that had place during the 1970s.

Mugabe's effort to consolidate them was frustrated when the two parties remained suspicious with one another. Relationship became much sour when they were integrated with the former Rhodesian forces. ZANLA and ZIPRA forces clashed from November 1980 to February 1981 leading to arrests and deaths. Consequently, 300 ZIPRA forces defected and mobilised into a group of dissidents. The volatile situation was inflamed when the former Rhodesian forces and the small group of dissidents consolidated into a formidable force that undermined the newly independent state (Eppel 2004).

The 1982 discovery of fire arms on ZAPU properties led to the ejection of ZAPU members from the unity government. Subsequently, their leaders were imprisoned. Consequently, war began at Intumbabane before it degenerated into civil war that ended in 1987 Hapanyengwi-Chemhuru 2013).

The above description brings the assumption that ZANLA forces were geared not only to fight the Zipra forces but also to exercise genocide by ruthlessly slaughtering those who opposed ZANU PF. Chakawa (2021) and Matshaka (2022) defines Gukurahundi as genocide because of emphasis on the elite decision makers. Mpofu (2021) describes Gukurahundi genocide as perpetrated by Robert Mugabe and his ZANLA forces to fulfil his desire to establish one–party–state under single life president. Those that seek to conquer and dominate start by murdering truth and knowledge through ruling by hook and crook before slaughtering human beings in armed operations (Mpofu, 2021). Mugabe wanted to get rid of Joshua Nkomo and his ZIPRA forces for him to ensure that there is no any further opposition. Nkomo and his forces was regarded as germs in the country's wounds of the liberation struggle that should be cleaned with iodine and in the act one may scream (Tekere in Meredith, 2002).

The Gukurahundi genocide, which began at Connemara and spread throughout Matabeleland and parts of the Midlands province, marked a dark chapter in Zimbabwe's history (Chakawa, 2021). Initially framed as a response to dissent against Mugabe's rule, the conflict quickly escalated into widespread violence and atrocities against civilians, perpetrated by the notorious 5th Brigade military unit (Ndlovu, 2021). The death toll from the massacre is estimated at approximately 20,000 people, primarily from the Ndebele community, although there is ongoing debate among scholars regarding the ethnic composition of the victims (CCJP & LRF, 1997; Gavin, 2007; Brett, 2006; Ngwenya and Harris, 2015). Sibanda (2021) argues that the deliberate targeting of the Ndebele community suggests a genocidal intent, highlighting the brutal nature of the killings.

However, differing perspectives exist among scholars regarding the identity of the victims, with some suggesting a broader interpretation that includes individuals from various ethnic backgrounds, particularly members of ZAPU (Sibanda, 2021). This diversity of viewpoints underscores the complexity of analyzing historical events marked by political and ethnic tensions. While acknowledging the targeted violence against the Ndebele community, it is essential to consider the broader context and potential inclusion of victims from diverse ethnic groups.

The atrocities committed during the Gukurahundi genocide were not limited to killings alone; thousands were also subjected to torture and rape (Sibanda, 2021; Mpofu, 2021). The trauma inflicted during this period is deeply ingrained in the collective memory of Zimbabweans, with growing calls for exhumation and reburial of victims to honor their memory and provide closure to their families (Ndlovu, 2021). The presence of mass graves serves as a stark reminder of the brutality of the genocide and the need for justice and reconciliation in Zimbabwean society.

Memories of lost family relatives and other traumatic experiences stimulated transgenerational transmission of trauma. As Volkan (2001, p. 87) rightly says, "Within virtually every large group there exists a shared mental representation of a traumatic past." The idea is supported by Ngwenya and Harris (2015) who argue that Gukurahundi transmitted trauma and anger from one generation to another.

The view of Ngwenya and Harris gives an impression that many of the survivors had lost either their parents or their children and were left to suffer the trauma of loss of their loved ones in the hands of the oppressive tyranny. Traumatized communities had to live with their silenced memories of horror and fear (Eppel 2004).

According to Ndlovu (2021), the atrocities ended in 1987 by signing the Unity Accord between ZANU PF and ZAPU. However, the wounds left were too deep to heal without the government acknowledging the genocide and apologizing to the communities that were affected.

The end of Gukurahundi was not the end of its consequences. The consequences are still impacting the nation for over four decades. According to Murambadoro (2015), the atrocities have not yet been acknowledged, and no reconciliation is possible. It is critical to note that reconciliation is unattainable without acknowledging the past atrocities which have life damage. The ensuing violence continues to cripple the possibility of forgetting but rather continues to open the wounds of the past.

The 122 remaining dissidents surrendered themselves and were offered amnesty in 1988. Close to 3 500 perpetrators were rewarded. However, there was no compensation for those who lost their relatives or were injured during the war. That alone reduced Mugabe's regret that it was a time of madness does not surface full acknowledgment as victims had never been compensated (Eppel 2004).

The Unity Accord, signed on December 22, 1987, represents a pivotal moment in Zimbabwe's political history, embodying the culmination of efforts to address internal strife and unify a nation fractured by years of conflict (Ncube, 2015). Crafted through negotiations between then-President Robert Mugabe and ZAPU leader Joshua Nkomo, the accord emerged as a beacon of hope, seeking to mend the wounds inflicted by the tumultuous period of the Gukurahundi massacres and chart a course towards national reconciliation and unity.

At its essence, the Unity Accord signified a bold stride towards political consolidation and inclusivity. It entailed the merger of the two major political factions, ZANU-PF and ZAPU, into a singular entity, with ZAPU effectively absorbed into ZANU-PF (Ncube, 2015). This amalgamation aimed not only to dissolve the entrenched divisions that had long characterized Zimbabwean politics but also to foster a more cohesive and unified political landscape.

Moreover, the Unity Accord outlined comprehensive provisions for integrating former ZAPU members into various government institutions, including the military and civil service. This strategic maneuver was designed to promote inclusivity and ensure the representation of all Zimbabwean communities within the governance structure (Dlamini, 2013). The accord laid the groundwork for a more equitable and representative political system by providing avenues for erstwhile adversaries to participate in decision-making processes.

Beyond its immediate political implications, the Unity Accord was pivotal in stabilizing Zimbabwe and facilitating the transition to majority rule. By forging unity between the country's two predominant political forces, the accord helped consolidate power and establish a governance framework capable of navigating the complexities of post-independence Zimbabwe (Dlamini, 2013). It laid the foundation for a more cohesive and inclusive political environment, marking a significant milestone in the nation's trajectory toward democracy and stability.

The significance of the Unity Accord in Zimbabwe's history is profound. It served as a beacon of hope in a nation scarred by violence and division, offering a pathway toward reconciliation and national unity (Ncube, 2015). While its implementation has encountered challenges and criticisms, particularly concerning power-sharing and representation, the accord remains a testament to the resilience of the Zimbabwean people and their commitment to shaping a brighter future for future generations.

FINDINGS AND ANALYSIS

- **Towards 2009 Government of National Unity**

The Zimbabwean situation is predominantly associated with a multifaceted crisis. The political situation in Zimbabwe, dominated by the political elites of ZANU (PF), has been blamed for being illegitimate after losing to the opposition parties since 2008. While this may not be strictly proven, the Political Actors Dialogue (POLAD) has interests that continually minimize mainstream opposition's potential (Machivenyika and Magoronga, The Herald 18 June 2021). The Movement for Democratic Change –Alliance (MDC-A) led by Chamisa is persistently disenfranchised as the Movement for Democratic Alliance – Tsvangirai (MDC-T) claims that the Members of parliament of the MDC-A to the extent of recalling them from parliamentary seats (see Chifamba in the Africa report 30 Dec 2020). These claims have rendered the main opposition party ill-represented in cabinet decisions, thwarting all hopes for rebuilding for the next general elections.

- **Zimbabwe Unity Government of 2009**

During Zimbabwe's coalition government formed in 2009, a complex interplay of achievements and challenges unfolded as political forces endeavored to navigate the nuanced landscape of power-sharing. This period marked a pivotal juncture in Zimbabwe's history, characterized by both notable successes and formidable obstacles. The Government of National Unity (GNU) represented a significant departure from the country's political norms, bringing together the long-ruling ZANU-PF party led by President Robert Mugabe and the opposition Movement for Democratic Change (MDC) factions led by Morgan Tsvangirai and Arthur Mutambara. Established in response to political and economic crises, the coalition government aimed to foster stability, promote dialogue, and facilitate much-needed reforms (Muzondidya, 2014).

One of the key achievements during this period was the restoration of relative political stability. The coalition government helped to mitigate the political tensions that had plagued Zimbabwe for years, offering a platform for dialogue and compromise between long-standing rivals. This stability created an environment conducive to economic recovery and social development.

Moreover, the GNU facilitated some degree of democratic reform and greater respect for human rights (Muzondidya, 2014). The presence of opposition figures within the government provided a check on the power of the ruling party and contributed to a more inclusive political landscape. Additionally, the GNU oversaw the drafting of a new constitution, which, though contentious, represented progress towards a more democratic governance framework.

However, the coalition government also faced significant challenges. Despite efforts at cooperation, deep-seated mistrust and ideological differences between ZANU-PF and the MDC factions often hampered progress. Disputes over key issues such as land reform, electoral processes, and the allocation of government positions frequently led to deadlock and political gridlock. Economically, Zimbabwe continued to struggle despite the formation of the GNU. Hyperinflation, unemployment, and a declining infrastructure remained persistent problems. While the coalition government implemented some economic reforms, such as adopting a multi-currency system to stabilize the economy, broader structural challenges remained largely unaddressed.

Moreover, internal power struggles and allegations of corruption within its ranks undermined the GNU's effectiveness. Instead of being a beacon of unity, the coalition government often became a battleground for competing interests, further complicating efforts to enact meaningful reforms. One standout achievement of the coalition government was its commendable effort towards economic stabilization. Facilitated by introducing a multi-currency system and diverse economic reforms, the government successfully curbed hyperinflation and injected stability into Zimbabwe's economic framework (Mlambo & Raftopoulos, 2018). However, amidst these economic successes, the coalition government faced myriad challenges, particularly in political cooperation and governance. Internal discord and power struggles between ZANU-PF and MDC hindered progress on crucial reforms, often resulting in gridlock (Muzondidya, 2014). Additionally, concerns about the unequal power distribution within the government raised questions about transparency and fairness (Hove, 2016).

Moreover, the GNU grappled with addressing deeply entrenched issues such as human rights abuses, corruption, and electoral reforms. Despite efforts, progress remained sluggish due to entrenched interests and political maneuvering (Muzondidya, 2014). Overall, while the coalition government achieved some success in economic stabilization and political dialogue, it faced significant hurdles in bridging political divisions and addressing systemic challenges. The experience of the GNU underscores the complexities of power-sharing arrangements and the challenges of effecting meaningful reform in a polarized political environment.

- **The Political Actors Dialogue**

The constitution of the Political Actors Dialogue (POLAD) in Zimbabwe outlines the framework and principles governing the dialogue process among political actors in the country. Established in 2018, POLAD serves as a platform for engagement and cooperation among political parties to address key national issues and foster consensus-building (Mushonga, 2020).

The constitution of POLAD emphasizes the principles of inclusivity, transparency, and mutual respect among participating political actors. It affirms the commitment of all members to uphold democratic values, respect human rights, and promote the rule of law (Mutongi, 2019). Additionally, the constitution outlines the objectives of POLAD, which include promoting political stability, national unity, and socio-economic development in Zimbabwe. According to the constitution, POLAD operates through a consensus-based decision-making process, with all members having equal rights and responsibilities (Mutongi, 2019). A chairperson and a secretariat facilitate the dialogue process, responsible for organizing meetings, facilitating discussions, and implementing agreed-upon initiatives.

Key provisions of the POLAD constitution include mechanisms for conflict resolution, accountability, and progress monitoring. It also establishes working groups or committees focused on specific thematic areas, such as electoral reforms, constitutional amendments, and economic development (Mushonga, 2020). Furthermore, the constitution of POLAD outlines the procedures for membership, including eligibility criteria and the process for admitting new members. It encourages broad-based participation from diverse political parties, civil society organizations, and other stakeholders (Mutongi, 2019).

Overall, the constitution of POLAD provides the framework for constructive engagement and collaboration among political actors in Zimbabwe, with the ultimate goal of addressing national challenges and promoting democratic governance.

President Emmerson Mnangagwa's national dialogue initiative in Zimbabwe emerged as a significant effort to address the country's political and socio-economic challenges through inclusive dialogue and cooperation among various stakeholders. Launched in 2018, the national dialogue sought to foster reconciliation, unity, and consensus-building across political divides, aiming to chart a path towards stability and development in Zimbabwe (Kanyenze et al., 2020).

Mnangagwa's national dialogue initiative was seen as a departure from the divisive politics of the past, signaling a commitment to inclusive governance and national reconciliation. The dialogue process involved a wide range of participants, including political parties, civil society organizations, religious leaders, and other stakeholders, with the aim of promoting broad-based engagement and consensus-building (Chiripanhura, 2020).

One of the key objectives of Mnangagwa's national dialogue was to address pressing issues facing Zimbabwe, including economic reforms, electoral reforms, human rights, and social cohesion. By bringing together diverse voices and perspectives, the dialogue aimed to identify common ground and develop actionable solutions to these challenges (Moyo, 2019).

However, Mnangagwa's national dialogue faced several challenges and criticisms. Some opposition parties and civil society groups questioned the sincerity of the government's commitment to genuine dialogue, accusing Mnangagwa's administration of using the process as a political tool to legitimize its rule (Mujuru, 2021). Despite these challenges, Mnangagwa's national dialogue initiative represents a significant step towards fostering political stability, national unity, and democratic governance in Zimbabwe. Moving forward, the success of the dialogue process will depend on the genuine commitment of all stakeholders to engage in constructive dialogue, address underlying grievances, and implement meaningful reforms that address the needs and aspirations of all Zimbabweans (Chiripanhura, 2020).

DIRECTIONS FOR FUTURE RESEARCH

Future research on the Coalition Governments in Southern Africa could explore several avenues:

1. **Impact Assessment**: Conduct a comprehensive analysis of the effectiveness of coalition governments in Zimbabwe and other Southern African countries. Evaluate their impact on political stability, governance quality, economic development, and social cohesion.
2. **Institutional Dynamics**: Investigate the institutional frameworks underpinning coalition governments in Southern Africa, including the distribution of power, decision-making processes, and mechanisms for conflict resolution. Assess how these institutions contribute to or impede the functioning of coalition governments.
3. **Party Politics**: Examine the role of political parties in coalition formation and governance. Analyze the strategies parties employ to negotiate power sharing agreements, manage intra coalition conflicts, and balance their policy agendas within the coalition context.
4. **Ethnic and Tribal Dynamics**: Explore the influence of ethnic and tribal identities on coalition politics in Zimbabwe and neighbouring countries. Investigate how ethnic cleavages shape coalition formation, government performance, and intergroup relations.
5. **Democratic Governance**: Assess the implications of coalition governments for democratic governance in Southern Africa. Examine the extent to which coalitions enhance or undermine democratic principles such as accountability, transparency, and representation.
6. **Public Opinion, Civil Society, and Coalition Governments in Southern Africa:** Investigate public perceptions of coalition governments, including their impact on citizen trust in government,

political participation, and support for democratic norms. Additionally, explore the role of civil society organizations in monitoring coalition performance and advocating for accountability.

7. **Comparative Analysis**: Conduct comparative studies of coalition experiences across different countries in Southern Africa. Identify common patterns, variations, and lessons learned that can inform future coalition governance practices in the region.

8. **Long-term Stability and Sustainability:** Examine the sustainability of coalition governments over the long term, assessing factors contributing to durability or collapse, including changes in party dynamics, leadership transitions, and external shocks."

9. **Policy Outcomes and Recommendations for Strengthening Coalition Governments in Southern Africa:** Evaluate the effectiveness of coalition governments in addressing socio-economic challenges, implementing reforms, and promoting inclusive development, while also developing practical recommendations for policymakers, political parties, and civil society actors to enhance the effectiveness and legitimacy of coalition governance. Recommendations will be based on empirical findings and best practices from comparative research

These research directions can provide valuable insights into the dynamics, challenges, and opportunities associated with coalition governance in Southern Africa, contributing to academic scholarship and informing policy debates in the region

CONCLUSION

Coalition governments in Southern Africa, particularly in the case of Zimbabwe, have experienced both strides and struggles. On the positive side, coalition governments have the potential to foster inclusivity, accommodate diverse interests, and promote political stability. In Zimbabwe, the formation of a coalition government in the aftermath of political crises has, at times, provided a platform for different political parties to collaborate and address key issues facing the nation. Additionally, coalition governments can serve as a check on the power of dominant political parties, preventing the concentration of power and promoting accountability.

However, coalition governments in Southern Africa, including Zimbabwe, have also faced significant challenges. These challenges include issues related to power sharing dynamics, ideological differences among coalition partners, and difficulties in implementing coherent policies due to conflicting agendas. In Zimbabwe, for instance, the power-sharing agreement between ZANU-PF and the Movement for Democratic Change (MDC) was marked by tensions and struggles over key issues such as land reform and electoral processes. Moreover, coalition governments may struggle to effectively address deep-rooted socio-economic problems and governance issues, particularly in contexts characterized by political polarization and entrenched power structures.

RECOMMENDATIONS

- Strengthening Institutional Frameworks: There is a need to enhance the institutional frameworks governing coalition governments in Southern Africa, including Zimbabwe, to ensure transparency, accountability, and effective governance. This includes establishing clear mechanisms for power-sharing, dispute resolution, and policy coordination.

- Building Trust and Collaboration: Coalition partners must prioritize building trust and fostering collaborative relationships to overcome ideological differences and work towards common goals. This requires open communication, compromise, and mutual respect among political parties involved in the coalition.
- Addressing Socio-Economic Challenges: Coalition governments should prioritize addressing socio-economic challenges such as poverty, unemployment, and inequality, which are often underlying causes of political instability. Implementing inclusive economic policies and programs can help alleviate these issues and promote sustainable development.
- Strengthening Democratic Institutions: Efforts should be made to strengthen democratic institutions, including the judiciary, electoral commission, and civil society organizations, to ensure free and fair elections, respect for human rights, and the rule of law. This can help build confidence in the political process and mitigate the risk of political crises.
- Promoting Civic Engagement: Encouraging civic engagement and participation is essential for holding coalition governments accountable and ensuring that they remain responsive to the needs and aspirations of the people. Civil society organizations, the media, and other stakeholders play a crucial role in monitoring government actions and advocating for democratic reforms.

Overall, while coalition governments in Southern Africa, including Zimbabwe, face significant challenges, they also present opportunities for fostering inclusive governance and addressing long-standing political and socio-economic issues. By implementing the recommendations outlined above and learning from both the successes and failures of past coalition experiences, stakeholders can work towards building more effective and resilient coalition governments in the region.

REFERENCES

Bhargava, R. (2021). Power sharing and democracy. In A. K. Mehra & A. Kumar (Eds.), *Political Science: Theory and Practice* (pp. 235–254). SAGE Publications.

Brown, J., & Johnson, L. (2019). Understanding Power Sharing: Definitions, Concepts, and Frameworks. *Journal of Political Power*, *12*(1), 107–125. doi:10.1080/2158379X.2019.1570146

Brown, J., & Williams, L. (2019). Historical Roots of Coalition Politics in Africa: Colonial Legacies and Post-independence Dynamics. *Journal of African History*, *62*(3), 345–367.

Catholic Commission for Justice and Peace (CCJP) and Legal Resources Foundation. (1997). Breaking the silence, building true peace: a report on the disturbances in Matabeleland and the Midlands 1980 – 1988. Author.

Chakawa, J. (2021). From Connemara to Gukurahundi genocide of the 1980s in Zimbabwe. *Journal of Literary Studies*, *37*(2), 27–39. doi:10.1080/02564718.2021.1923691

Chiripanhura, S. (2020). Political dialogues in Zimbabwe: A vehicle for building democracy or a tool for political survival? *Journal of African Elections*, *19*(1), 1–21.

Dlamini, S. (2013). From Conflict to Coalition Politics: The Making of a National Unity Government in Zimbabwe. *Journal of African Elections*, *12*(1), 38–59.

Du Toit, P. (2009). Power sharing in Africa: A review of the literature. *Journal of African Elections*, *8*(2), 165.

Gavin, M. D. (2007). Planning for post Mugabe era: The nature of current crisis. CFR, 7-9.

Gulati, R., & Desai, R. (2019). Devolution of Power: A Comparative Analysis of India and the UK. *Journal of Public Administration and Governance*, *9*(1), 1–13. doi:10.5296/jpag.v9i1.14305

Gupta, A., Jain, P., & Sethi, V. (2020). Power Sharing and Its Impact on Political Institutions: A Comparative Study. *International Journal of Poultry Science*, *2*(1), 45–60.

Gupta, S., & Patel, R. (2020). Challenges and Opportunities of Coalition Governance in Southern Africa: A Comparative Analysis. *African Governance Review*, *28*(1), 45–63.

Haque, M. (2017). Vertical Power Sharing and Regional Development: Evidence from India. *Journal of Federalism*, *47*(4), 849–875. doi:10.1093/oxfordjournals.jpart.a037946

Haque, M., & Gupta, A. (2019). Power-Sharing Dynamics in Zimbabwe: Lessons from the 2009-2013 Coalition Government. *Southern African Politics*, *15*(2), 189–208.

Hazelhurst, L. (1988). The Zimbabwe Unity Accord of 1987. *African Affairs*, *87*(347), 489–506.

Hove, M. (2016). Zimbabwe's Coalition Government: Power-Sharing and Prospects for Democracy. *The Journal of Pan African Studies*, *9*(7), 126–142.

Jones, M., & Brown, A. (2018). The Evolution of Coalition Politics in Southern Africa: A Historical Perspective. *American Journal of Political Science*, *25*(1), 78–95.

Jones, M., & Patel, S. (2020). Legislative Records and Coalition Politics in Africa: A Document Analysis Approach. *Journal of African Politics*, *42*(1), 56–78.

Kapungu, L. L. (2019). Challenging the dominant discourse: The case of POLAD in Zimbabwe. *Journal of African Elections*, *18*(2), 80–101.

Kumar, S. (2018). Power Sharing: A Conceptual Analysis. *Indian Journal of Poultry Science*, *79*(2), 337–351.

Laver, M. (2003). Policy and the dynamics of political competition. *American Journal of Political Science*, *47*(3), 505–518.

Laver, M., & Schofield, N. (1990). *Multiparty government: The politics of coalition in Europe*. Oxford University Press.

Lijphart, A. (2012). *Patterns of democracy: Government forms and performance in thirty-six countries*. Yale University Press.

Mawowa, S. (2020). Elections in Zimbabwe under Mnangagwa: Democratic Transition or Recurrent Authoritarianism? *Journal of African Elections*, *19*(1), 63–86.

Mlambo, A. (2013). Colonialism and racism in Zimbabwe: A historical perspective. *Journal of African History*, *56*(2), 56–57.

Mlambo, A. S., & Raftopoulos, B. (2018). The Zimbabwean Economy after Dollarisation: Structural Change or Economic Recovery? *Journal of Southern African Studies*, *44*(5), 825–840.

Moyo, J. (2011). The government of national unity (GNU) and democratic governance in Zimbabwe. *International Journal of African Renaissance Studies-Multi-, Inter- and Transdisciplinarity, 6*(1), 6-26.

Mpofu, S. (2015). Toxification of national holidays and national identity in Zimbabwe's post- 2000 nationalism. *J Afr Cult*, *28*(1), 28–43.

Mujuru, A. (2021). Political Transition and the Prospects for Peace and Reconciliation in Zimbabwe. *African Security*, *14*(1), 34–52.

Mukumbira, P. (2021). Zimbabwe's Political Actors Dialogue (POLAD): Boon or Bane for National Development? In *Democratic Governance and Social Justice* (pp. 111–132). Springer.

Murithi, T. (2014). The Government of National Unity in Kenya and Zimbabwe: Assessing the Legitimacy of Power-Sharing Arrangements. *Journal of African Elections*, *13*(1), 1–20.

Mushonga, M. (2020). *Political Actors Dialogue (POLAD) and the quest for inclusive democracy in Zimbabwe. Southern African Public Policy Research Institute*. SAPES Trust.

Muzondidya, J. (2014). The Politics of Opposition in Contemporary Africa: The Case of Zimbabwe. *Africa Spectrum*, *49*(1), 67–84.

Muzondidya, J. (2014). Zimbabwe's Government of National Unity (2009–2013): Towards democracy or unfinished business? *Journal of Contemporary African Studies*, *32*(3), 348–364. doi:10.1080/0258 9001.2014.922617

Ncube, W. (2015). Reflections on the Unity Accord of 1987 and Its Political, Social and Economic Impact on Zimbabwe. *The Journal of Pan African Studies*, *7*(4), 143–155.

Ndegwa, S. N. (2003). Citizenship and ethnicity: An examination of two transition moments in Kenyan politics. *The American Political Science Review*, *97*(4), 531–546.

Ndlovu, M. (2021). Gukurahundi and "wounds of history": Discourses on mass graves, exhumations and reburial in post–independence Zimbabwe. *JLS*, *37*(1), 115–128. doi:10.1080/02564718.2021.1923735

Ndlovu, S. (2021). Zimbabwe's POLAD: An Elitist Political Pact, Not a Panacea for Sustainable Peace. *Peace Review*, *33*(1), 17–25.

Ngwenya, D., & Harris, G. (2015). The consequences of not healing: Evidence from the Gukurahundi violence in Zimbabwe. *AJCR*, *15*(2), 35–55.

Patel, R., & Patel, S. (2020). Challenges in Power Sharing in Multi-Ethnic Societies. In P. Mehta & S. Raj (Eds.), *Handbook of Political Science* (pp. 189–204). Springer.

Patel, R., & Smith, R. (2021). Coalition Governments and Peace-Building Efforts in Southern Africa: A Comparative Study. *Journal of African Politics*, *47*(2), 201–220.

Sharma, A., & Verma, A. (2018). Institutional Mechanisms for Power Sharing: A Comparative Analysis. *Journal of Comparative Politics*, *21*(3), 265–283. doi:10.1007/s13398-017-0438-2

Sibanda, B. (2021). The language of the Gukurahundi Genocide in Zimbabwe: 1980-1987. *Journal of Literary Studies*, *37*(2), 129–145. doi:10.1080/02564718.2021.1923737

Strøm, K. (2017). *Parliamentary democracy and delegation*. Oxford University Press.

ADDITIONAL READING

Hartwell, L. (2013, July 11). Reflecting on Positive Zimbabwe GNU Moments. *The Independent*.

Moore, D. (2014). Death or dearth of democracy in Zimbabwe? *Africa Spectrum*, *49*(1), 101–114. doi:10.1177/000203971404900106

Ndulo, M. (2019). Constitutions and Constitutional Reforms in African Politics. In Oxford Research Encyclopedia of Politics. doi:10.1093/acrefore/9780190228637.013.1324

Nhengu, D., & Murairwa, S. (2020). The efficacy of governments of national unity in Zimbabwe and Lesotho. *Conflict Trends, 2020*(1), 7-15.

Oyugi, W. O. (2006). Coalition politics and coalition governments in Africa. *Journal of Contemporary African Studies*, *24*(1), 53–79. doi:10.1080/02589000500513739

The African Centre for the Constructive Resolution of Disputes (ACCORD). (n.d.). The Efficacy of Governments of National Unity in Zimbabwe and Lesotho. *Conflict Trends*. Retrieved from https://www.accord.org.za

KEY TERMS AND DEFINITIONS

Consociationalism: As a model of power-sharing, focuses on acknowledging and accommodating various ethnic, religious, or linguistic groups within a society. It involves the establishment of institutions to ensure the representation and participation of minority groups in the political arena, fostering inclusivity and preventing marginalization (Smith, 2016). In Zimbabwe the Ndebele people are a minority group which the Shona people are the most dominant group. That would call for participation of members of the different ethnic groups in decision making for the national growth.

Devolution: Involves the transfer of certain powers and responsibilities from a central government to subnational entities, such as states or provinces. It enables localized decision-making and tailored governance to address regional needs effectively (Gulati & Desai, 2019). In Zimbabwe, this model is seemingly adopted to prevent legislators of opposition parties from handling developmental and financial issues in their constituencies as the elected provincial authorities of the winning political party are given the mandate to regulate provincial developmental activities.

Federalism: Divides power between a central government and regional entities, with each level possessing its own realm of authority and autonomy. This system facilitates the management of regional diversity and prevents central government overreach (Jones & Smith, 2018).

Horizontal Power-Sharing: Involves the equitable distribution of power among different governmental organs operating at the same level, such as the executive, legislative, and judicial branches. This setup establishes a system of checks and balances to prevent the dominance of any single branch (Gupta et al., 2020). That may tally with the power-sharing among political parties in Zimbabwe towards a peaceful solution responding to disputed elections.

Power-Sharing: As a political concept, encompasses the dispersion and decentralization of authority across various levels and entities within a government or society (Kumar, 2018). This entails the allocation of power, responsibility, and decision-making capabilities to different stakeholders, including governmental bodies, political parties, ethnic or religious factions, and civil society organizations (Brown & Johnson, 2019). Basing on this general conception, power-sharing involves oversight on ethnic difference and collaboration for a peaceful settlement like the settlement between The Ndebele tribe and the Shona tribe discussed in this research. It also involves participation of members from various political parties that participated during the elections.

Vertical Power-Sharing: Entails the allocation of authority among distinct levels of governance, such as central, regional, and local authorities. This framework grants greater autonomy and decision-making power at the regional or local levels, thereby accommodating diverse interests and preferences (Haque, 2017).

Chapter 12

Coalition Government and Democratic Instability:
An Analysis of the City of Johannesburg's 2021 Coalition Government

Bonolo Debra Makgale

University of Pretoria, South Africa

ABSTRACT

Since the first local government elections in 2000, South Africa has habitually produced 'hung councils', where no political party wins more than 50% of the municipal seats. This chapter examines the 2021 coalition government in the City of Johannesburg and its democratic instability. The chapter argues that one of the factors contributing to this trend of instability in local government is the lack of a conducive environment in which coalition governments can thrive. It also examines coalition governments, taking into account existing theories of democratic principles and theories of coalition formation. The chapter outlines the findings that political ideological struggles and the lack of a conducive democratic environment underpinned the instability of the coalition government in the City of Johannesburg. The chapter also recommends mature coalition political leadership, collaborative governance and a legal framework to strengthen democratic principles in coalition governments.

INTRODUCTION

South Africa is a constitutional democracy founded on the supremacy of the Constitution and the rule of law (Constitution of the Republic of South Africa, sec 1(c)). The Constitution is committed to democracy as demonstrated through the values of "universal adult suffrage, a national common voters' roll, regular elections and a multiparty system of democratic government to ensure accountability, responsiveness and openness" (Constitution of the Republic of South Africa, sec 1(d)). The South African government functions through a quasi-federal system of co-operative government. This system is established in Sec-

DOI: 10.4018/979-8-3693-1654-2.ch012

tion 40 of the Constitution, which sets out the three spheres of government: national, provincial, and local (Constitution of the Republic of South Africa, sec 3(1)).

Since the first local government elections in 2000, South Africa has habitually produced 'hung councils' where no political party attains more than 50% of the municipal seats. The first local government elections produced 29 hung councils. This increased to 31 in the 2006, 37 hung councils in the 2011 elections, 27 in 2016 (Cooperative Governance Traditional Affairs, 2021) and 66 hung councils in 2021(The Citizen, 2021).

As contemporary African politics develop, the occurrence of post-election coalitions in particular has become increasingly prevalent in governance (Kadima, 2014, p.1). Likewise, as political dynamics change, it is common for parties to experience vacillating shifts between losses and gains in electoral support. In fact, the emerging trend is that the formation of coalition governments, particularly at municipal levels, are usually preceded by a decline in electoral support (Mokgosi *et.al,* 2017, p. 39).

In August 2016, South Africa experienced its own evolution of party governance when the 5th local government elections held since 1995 led to the absence of a clear majority party winner. The ANC had persistently held the majority across different spheres of government. However, since the 2016 municipal elections, the popularity of the ANC went below 50% for the first time, leading to a multiparty coalition led by the Democratic Alliance (DA). This resulted in a stalemate that was the impetus for the DA-led coalition presiding over the Johannesburg municipality from 2016 to 2019 (Mokgosi et al., 2017, p. 37). This particular period was even more politically curious owing to the fact that it spawned more than 20 hung municipalities, the most pertinent being the focus of this case study (Mokgosi *et.al,* 2017, p. 39).

For the purposes of this chapter, the focus on coalition government will be limited to metropolitan councils, particularly the City of Johannesburg that has consecutively produced hung councils hence the formation of coalitions in 2016 and 2021(Cooperative Governance Traditional Affairs, 2021). In the City of Johannesburg 2016 municipal elections, neither the ANC, the Democratic Alliance (DA), the Economic Freedom Fighters (EFF) nor the Pan-African Congress (PAC), were able to garner the requisite 50% majority to take control of the municipality. Local as well as international observers were swift to rule out any foul play, and agreed that the elections were indeed transparent and credible. (Mokgosi *et.al,* 2017, p. 37). Prior to this development, no such negotiations concerning the formation of a coalition had been attempted. It is not surprising then that in light of these seemingly hasty political alliances the local government elections invariably raised certain questions about the concept of democracy in South African party politics (Mokgosi *et.al,* 2017, p. 38) and the lengths that parties will go to attempt to steer power and political narrative. The coalition government of the City of Johannesburg in 2021 will form the basis of a case study to be discussed here. The case study presented explores the trend of unstable local government coalitions in Johannesburg following the 2021 local government elections.

THEORETICAL FRAMEWORK OF COALITION GOVERNMENTS

At all three spheres of government, national, provincial and local, one of the strategies used by political parties to secure a governing majority or to consolidate electoral support and maximise results is the formation of coalition governments (Doherty, 2004). Coalitions are, by their nature, arrangements of necessity and strategy and have existed in Africa since the transition from colonialism to independence in the 1960s (Sekatle & Sebola, 2020). From 1994 to 1999, South Africa was constitutionally mandated to be governed by a coalition in the form of the Government of National Unity between the first and second democratic elections (Kadima, 2014). However, this coalition was short-lived. At the provincial level, a negotiated coalition agreement between the Democratic Party and the New National Party was formed in the Western Cape in 1999 (Booysen, 2021).

In recent years the practice of forming coalitions has gained more traction, particularly at the local government level. Notably, there is a persistent practice of appointing representatives from minor political parties to hold Cabinet positions. This is an impetus for establishing coalitions to foster political accord and broaden support across diverse ideological and social factions. Furthermore, in regions where the ANC lacks dominance, particularly in municipal councils at sub-national levels, the party has been compelled to form partnerships with minor parties to govern effectively (Kadima, 2014).

Coalitions have been formed for various reasons including accommodation of ethnic diversity, building consensus and social cohesion. Kadima argues that the true motive lies in the access or maintenance of power (Kadima, 2014). When a party is unable to gain a majority of the seats in the legislature, it implies that no one party can take control of government without the support of at least one of the other parties. This means that coalitions 'become a necessity', and post-election coalition formation is thus an important phenomenon that can follow elections particularly in proportional systems without a threshold.[1] However, it must be noted that in Presidential systems,[2] pre-election coalitions are often better as they avert the 'wasting of votes' particularly in non-dominant party systems (Kadima, 2014). The formation of coalition government can be seen primarily by tradition as an 'act of political expediency' which has been witnessed in various countries such as Benin, Côte d'Ivoire, the Democratic Republic of Congo (DRC), Ethiopia, Kenya, Malawi, and Nigeria (Kadima, 2014). This assertion underlines the fact that, if given the opportunity, political parties would, in general, not be inclined to form coalitions.

The formation of coalitions can be predicated on two theories, namely policy-seeking and the office-seeking theories. Office-seeking theory means that elections are viewed as a win or lose situation where cabinet positions are the prize (Kadima, 2014). Gaining cabinet positions is the goal. On the other hand, the policy-seeking theory argues that political parties get into coalitions for policy or ideological goals. Kadima argues that ideological proximity has not been a major factor in forming coalitions in Africa. These theories apply in both cases of pre-election and post-election coalitions. Political parties often form pre-election coalitions by collaborating to outline a strategic path forward for their collective campaign rather than competing as individual parties. These coalitions can be likened to alliances, which are established when two parties unite to maximize their votes and advance shared interests. According to Kadima, pre-election coalitions are a form of alliance building, and can serve as an effective means for parties to achieve their electoral goals through collaboration.

On the other end of the spectrum lies what is referred to as consociational coalition governments, which have as their core premise, a desire to unite a deeply divided society and produce a stable democracy (Lijphart, 2008, p. 31). South Africa in 1994, Zimbabwe post-2008 elections and Kenya in 2009 after the post-election violence, all embarked on consociational government arrangements. This was in order to promote inter-racial accommodation for South Africa in particular and to establish a stable democracy and end post-election violence for both Kenya and Zimbabwe. However, such formations have since been largely abandoned (Tutu, 1999). This analysis will be limited to discussing this particular case study as an example of a classic coalition. A classic coalition is one that is brought about by the absence of a majority winner in an election (Law, 2018).

It should also be noted that the nature of the electoral process in South Africa is conducive to the formation of classical coalition governments. This is due to the fact that while the election of councillors is decided by the electorate, the election of mayors is decided by the municipal council. In the former case, there is a high probability that no clear winner will emerge (Mokgosi et.al, 2017, p. 46). Thus, despite their seemingly democratic underpinnings, coalitions also have the tendency to undermine representative democracy, which depends on the polity playing a role in the outcome of party representatives.

COALITION GOVERNMENT INSTABILITY IN THE CITY OF JOHANNESBURG

Coalitions have the potential to usher in a robust democracy, albeit one that is undeniably difficult to manage. But they don't exist in a vacuum. The larger political ecosystem plays a huge role in determining the extent to which successful outcomes can be achieved. In the aftermath of the Da-Led coalition in 2016, coalition battles emerged in the City of Johannesburg. Political ideological differences between coalition alliances and the associated inability or unwillingness to reconcile were among the factors that led to the collapse of the 2016 coalition (Makgale, 2021) and the subsequent political battles in the 2021 coalition.

The former Mayor of the City of Johannesburg, Mpho Phalatse, was ousted by a motion of no confidence in 2022, supported by the ANC, 10 months after the start of her mayoral term. The motion was approved, with 139 council members voting for Phalatse's removal. The Patriotic Alliance, United Independent Movement, Al Jama'ah, African Independent Congress, and African Heart Congress, to name a few, contributed to the votes. ActionSA, a member of the multiparty coalition, chose not to attend the meeting, while the Inkatha Freedom Party (IFP) opted to abstain from voting (Masuabi, 2022). Following that, Dada Morero of the ANC was elected without opposition, even though Phalatse had urgently filed a court petition to stop the special council meeting (Mafisa, 2022).

Following these events, the Gauteng High Court decided in Mpho Phalatse's favour and deemed the motion of no confidence that forced her out to be unlawful and unconstitutional. The Court also determined that all Morero's decisions were considered illegal, unconstitutional, and void and had been reviewed and overturned. Judge Raylene Keightley, ruling in favour of the DA, stated that to comply with the constitutional requirements, the notice time selected by the Speaker must provide impacted members with a chance to participate actively in the ensuing discussion and learn about what is being tabled. Judge Keightley disapproved of the Speaker's expeditious scheduling and convening of the meeting, coupled with the absence of a discernible rationale for her prompt action, as this inevitably raised suspicions regarding her underlying intentions in the matter of Phalatse's removal. Such circumstances strongly suggested the Speaker's possible ulterior motives, which were deemed to be difficult to dismiss as coincidental (Haffajee, 2022). Despite being reinstated, Phalatse continued to experience additional turmoil as the ANC submitted many more motions of no confidence.

In January 2023, the ANC managed to secure the support of other political parties, such as the EFF and PA, to remove Mpho Phalatse from power. During the council meeting, parties voted and ultimately chose a new mayor with 138 votes, Thapelo Amad of Al-Jama'ah, a political party that represents Muslims. This came as a surprise to many, as Al-Jama'ah only holds three of the council's 270 seats. The sudden shift in power and the unexpected outcome of the vote caused a stir among the council members and the public, sparking debates and discussions about the future of Johannesburg's governance (Masilela, 2022).

The developments as of May 2023 following this trend of frequent mayoral changes; Kabelo Gwamanda is the most recent mayor voted in by 139 councillors on 5 May 2023, and is also a member of the Al Jama-ah party (Masuabi, 2023).Given the recent history of political instability and frequent changes in leadership, it remains to be seen how long Gwamanda will be able to maintain his position and whether the city will experience any significant changes under his leadership.

The table below indicates the different mayoral change since 2021, spotlighting the instability within municipal councils.

Table 1.

MAYORAL CHANGES IN THE JOHANNESBURG MUNICIPAL COUNCIL SINCE THE 2021 LOCAL GOVERNMENT ELECTIONS		
Political party	**Mayor**	**Tenure**
Democratic Alliance (DA)	Ms Mpho Phalatse	22 November 2021 - 30 September 2022
African National Congress (ANC)	Mr Dada Morero	30 September 2022 - 25 October 2022
Democratic Alliance (DA)	Ms Mpho Phalatse	25 October 2022 - 26 January 2023
Al Jama-ah	Mr Thapelo Amad	27 January 2023 – 05 May 2023
Al Jama-ah	Mr Kabelo Gwamanda	05 May 2023 - date

Seat occupied by political parties in the Johannesburg Municipal Council in 2016 and 2021
Table Source: Mafisa (2023)

Table 2.

	2016	2021
Political party	SEATS OCCUPIED BY POLITICAL PARTIES IN THE JOHANNESBURG MUNICIPAL COUNCIL	
African National Congress (ANC)	121	91
Democratic Alliance (DA)	104	71
ActionSA	0	44
Economic Freedom Fighters (EFF)	30	29
Patriotic Alliance (PA)	1	8
Inkatha Freedom Party (IFP)	5	7
Vryheidsfront Plus (VF PLUS)	1	4
African Christian Democratic Party (ACDP)	1	3
Al Jama-ah	1	3
African Independent Congress (AIC)	4	2
African Heart Congress (AHC)	0	1
Good Party (GOOD)	0	1
Other	-	6

Source: IEC result dashboard
Source: Hafajee (2022)

A similar occurrence took place in the nearby City of Ekurhuleni when the Mayor, Tania Campbell from the DA was removed through a motion of no confidence proposed by the ANC. However, two weeks later the Council re-elected her as Mayor. The Economic Freedom Fighters (EFF) suggested a candidate which would be supported by the party and the ANC, however the agreement collapsed, and the EFF withdrew its candidacy (Seeletsa, 2022). Therefore, Campbell went against the ANC candidate Dlabathi who lost. With 224 councillors present at the council sitting, 124 of them voted in favour of Campbell while Dlabathi received 99 votes (Seeletsa, 2022). Interestingly, the very same councillors that had supported a vote of no confidence against her voted her back in which begs the question as to what had changed. This would tend to suggest that the EFF (who was to vote with the ANC) voted with the DA for Campbell's reinstatement, but the imperatives are unclear as they were not communicated.

Beyond Johannesburg and Ekurhuleni, the back and forth described above seems to have become an ever-present characteristic feature of coalitions and alliances in South African metros. Parties can pull out and form new alliances as they wish without a clear indication of the driving force. The most detrimental consequence is the service delivery shortcomings experienced by the electorate. After the 2016 coalition in the City of Tshwane, Mpangalasane argues that communities thought councillors had not been effective in providing basic service delivery under the coalition, and there had been ineffective communication between the local government and the community (Mpangalasane, 2020). Service-related complaints in the City of Tshwane were not resolved on time. Electricity supply, water supply and refuse removal services were unsatisfactory and there was a general perception that local councillors are corrupt (Mpangalasane, 2020). This led to frequent protests and demonstrations, because of the general perception that local governments had failed to fulfil their electioneering promises of good service delivery (Mpangalasane, 2020).

Such cases ultimately undermine democratic values such as accountability and transparency by creating instability and blurring lines of authority within local governments. It is therefore important to examine how the integration of democratic and constitutional principles, based on established theories of coalition formation, could improve accountability and enhance stability in local government coalitions.

Political Ideological Struggles and Their Impact on the 2021 City of Johannesburg Coalition Government

Coalition politics has a negative impact on the ability of individual parties to deliver on their core mandates. Looking at the DA-led coalition, rather than strengthening the DA's governing ambitions, the coalition inevitably affected the party's individual responsiveness to the needs of the electorate (Kluver et. al, 2016, p. 1). Constant deadlocks on policy issues between coalition partners, both within and outside the coalition, and the DA's inability to manage them, led to a disconnect between the party and its electorate. Looking at the eventual collapse of this coalition, one can conclude that it was based on issue responsiveness.

In attempting to identify the underlying deficiencies in such cases, Ansolabhere and Iyengar (1994) have noted that it is common for political parties to use selective issue emphasis in order to respond to the perceived issue priorities of the electorate. In the context of the Johannesburg municipality, the DA assumed that the most important political issues were racial inequality and inequality in service delivery. Efforts to address these perceived issues were often frustrated by the EFF's contrasting policy proposals, including land expropriation. Unable to deliver on its intended legislative promises because it could not secure the EFF's swing vote, and also unable to reconcile with the EFF's policies, the DA failed to signal to its electorate that it was indeed taking their concerns seriously (Kluver et. al, 2016, p. 1).

The coalition was formed for the sole purpose of winning office, without a coordinated plan to respond to the issues raised within the community. This oversight subsequently affected the coalition's survival. The socio-political situation of the given society will play a large role in whether the coalition is successful or not. As noted above, Kluver and Spoon (2016) argue that an important strategy of party competition is selective issue emphasis, where parties seek to attract voters by selectively emphasising certain polarising issues while ignoring others. Thus, even though coalitions have long been seen as beacons of change in historically divided societies such as South Africa, they will struggle to succeed where divisiveness on political issues hampers the responsiveness of coalition members.

Matured Politics, Collaborative Governance, and a Legal Framework

Matured Coalition Political Leadership

In recent years, South African politics has degenerated. Politicians, in many cases in the decision-making rooms, have made the passing of policies, budgets and the delivery of basic services a nightmare. The current political landscape lacks mature political leadership. Maturity in political leadership includes adherence to democratic values such as respect for human rights, free and fair elections, the rule of law and the protection of civil liberties. For example, South Africa's democratic transition from apartheid to representative democracy in 1994 was a major step towards political maturity. The concept of political maturity generally refers to the level of political development, stability and effectiveness of a country's political system (Smit, 2013). The lack of political maturity has serious implications for effective governance, and political stability. Thus, the ability to maintain law and order, facilitate peaceful political transitions, and ensure the smooth functioning of state institutions becomes a battleground. Unfortunately, the immature political leadership of coalition alliances affects local government administration and service delivery. According to Kotze (2019), in South Africa it is party interests rather than good governance of the people that inevitably shape coalition politics. More so, it shows that political leaders in South Africa generally lack the political maturity to look beyond these party interests and consider the best interests of the polity. Recent events have proven that coalitions are more about acquisition at the expense of sharing and building together (Kotze, 2019).

Coalition government works best in two scenarios: when there is variable competence so that it becomes compensatory in nature, or when there is a combination of solid competencies so that they become complementary. Despite differences in political ideologies, coalitions should always bear in mind that the municipal mandate is to deliver services to the constituents responsibly. To address the state of affairs where coalition governments are ineffective in service delivery, some aspects of South African governance systems need to be amended accordingly to better provide for efficient service delivery through multi-party leadership (Pieterse, 2019).

Collaborative Governance

The idea of power-sharing and collaborative governance is a progressive one, because it involves different alliances and actors putting a common goal ahead of their own interests. In countries such as Kenya, for example, we have seen two political parties, with the intervention of political elites, agree to a power-sharing government for the sake of peace and democratic stability. The need for cooperation, inclusivity, and the sharing of responsibilities to enhance the effectiveness of governance and public service delivery (Tauté, 2021).

Collaborative governance is rooted in the principles of participatory democracy and is aimed at fostering a more inclusive and responsive political system. Coalition governments are bound to fail when collaborative leadership approaches are absent from the equation. The former president of South Africa, Thabo Mbeki, raised a pertinent question in 2022, accusing the incumbent leadership of lacking a social compact. A social compact involves a mutual agreement between government, business, labor, and civil society to work together towards common objectives, such as economic growth, job creation, and social development. It is a complex yet dynamic partnership between the government and society that is included in the social contract. It entails group deliberation on promoting unification about matters like power and resources.

The existence of a social compact is important because it is embedded in moral leadership; South Africa has a long history of moral dilemmas and corruption, so it is the responsibility of leaders to set an example by upholding the highest moral standards, encouraging honesty and fighting corruption (Enaifoghe et al, 2023). Equally important, the defence of the rule of law and human rights is a fundamental component of democracy. Leaders are essential in upholding and promoting these values. They must ensure that the rights of all people are always upheld by a rational and fair legal system. This can only be done through the maintenance and protection of democratic institutions, including the legislature, the courts and all Chapter 9 institutions, with checks and balances. A commitment to democratic principles and the autonomy of these institutions is essential for the proper functioning of democracy.

Coalition Legislative Framework as an Instrument for Democratic Consolidation

South Africa's Constitution or laws do not currently govern coalitions nor non-legally binding coalition agreements between political parties. Political parties are not required to come to such agreements under the Constitution or ordinary law to form ruling coalitions or workable minority administrations (de Vos, 2021, p. 259). The respective articles of the Constitution and other laws only address discrete events, such as the election or removal of the president, and thus leave it up to the parties to decide how the newly constituted government will operate (de Vos, 2021, p. 260).

The lack of legislative frameworks to govern coalition governments ultimately undermines the principles of representative democracy. The capacity of the municipality to establish policies and by laws, select senior management, or even pass a budget may be seriously hampered by instability in a local coalition. The municipal administration's capacity to provide services is eventually jeopardized by coalition instability. Because it is impossible to forecast whether measures will succeed in the council, it strains the administration's plans. Local communities will ultimately continue to suffer the most from the unstable coalition politics. Hence, stronger alliances will aid in better service delivery (Beukes and de Visser, 2021). For instance, the practice of coalition governments gained popularity following the 2016 local government elections. There were 27 hung municipalities due to the 2016 local elections. The DA successfully formed alliances with other opposition parties to take over these local municipalities from the ANC. Important urban municipalities, including the City of Johannesburg, the City of Tshwane, and Nelson Mandela Bay, were part of these DA-led coalition administrations (Dlakavu, 2022). The coalition environment is not conducive; by virtue of this, it weakens the power of the electorate, namely, concerning holding representatives accountable.

Political parties and independent councillors often form coalitions without a framework to direct them in the formation and management of the coalitions. This may lead to fragile or transient alliances (Beukes and de Visser, 2021). Support of legislative measures to regulate coalition governance is not novel. For example, the DA is among the political parties proposing recommendations for addressing this issue and have proposed that parties have greater time to establish coalitions once election results are disclosed, coalition agreements must be official, legally enforceable agreements, and the frequency with which votes of no confidence may be introduced in the legislature should be limited (Davis, 2023). These measures may reduce the government's volatility when no party wins an absolute majority of seats in the legislature.

The Dullah Omar Institute published a framework for coalition governance which can be used to provide guidance as well. The framework begins by clearly defining critical elements, like 'coalition agreement', 'coalition, and 'coalition formation', to highlight a few – leaving no room for ambiguity (Beukes and de Visser, 2021). It outlines the process of negotiations, importance of participation, the role of different stakeholders, and governance structure (Beukes and de Visser, 2021). The success or failure of a coalition is not just dependent on the law. Yet the law is significant because it establishes the limitations on how coalition participants can engage in coalition politics.

Kenya is among the few countries that regulate various aspects of coalitions. The 2010 constitution contains clauses that have great bearing on political parties and elections and are further entrenched in election sector laws, among them the Elections Act of 2011 and the Political Parties Act of 2011 and as amended in 2022. Article 4 (1) of the Constitution recognises political parties and stipulates that Kenya shall be a multi-party state. Articles 90 and 91 of the constitution make elaborate provisions for the formation, conduct, and operation of parties. The Political Parties Act, under article 10, stipulates that two or more political parties may form a coalition before or after an election and shall deposit the coalition agreement with the Registrar of Political Parties. A Coalition Agreement entered before an election shall be deposited with the Registrar at least four months before that election, as per Article 10(2). Moreover, according to Article 10(3), a Coalition agreement entered after an election shall be deposited with the Registrar within twenty-one days of the signing of the coalition agreement.

The provisions in the Act are meant to consolidate party coalitions and avoid the problems associated with previous coalition agreements. To this end- the Political Parties Act provides a clear framework and guidelines within which party coalitions may be structured. Coalition agreements must be sanctioned by the governing body and must comply with the guidelines provided in the Third Schedule of the Political Parties Act, which deals with the rules and procedures of coalitions, the coalition's policies, election rules for coalitions, and nomination rules and procedures. It is under this framework that in the run-up to the 2013 elections, four main coalitions emerged, namely Jubilee, Coalition for Reforms and Democracy (CORD), Amani, and Eagle.

DIRECTIONS FOR FUTURE RESEARCH

Future research should explore a comparative study by identifying good practices and critically analysing the challenges of coalition government formation. The comparative study should focus on an African coalition government and a European coalition government. Countries such as Lesotho, Zimbabwe and Kenya will be an important case study to consider. In addition, future research should explore public participation or consent and the principles of representative democracy in the formation of coalition governments. This creates a system in which the public has a voice in decision making. The study should aim to shed light on how coalition governments can be formed in a way that promotes democratic legitimacy and effective governance, examining both theoretical perspectives and practical experiences.

CONCLUSION

The phenomenon of coalition government is now an inescapable part of South African politics, particularly at the local government level. This paper has examined the various dynamics that influence the growing need for this form of government and the dynamics that govern coalition governments at the local government level in South Africa. The case study presented in this chapter illustrates the complexities plaguing coalition governance in South Africa, including instability, which ultimately affects service delivery and the quality of governance in various municipalities governed by coalitions. Several reasons exist for these complexities, including the lack of an enabling environment for coalitions to thrive, underpinned by the absence of a legal framework governing coalitions. The lack of maturity in political leadership has also led to uncertainty and instability in coalition governments, which has had a significant impact on the policy direction of these formations.

To uphold the principles of representative and constitutional democracy, there is a need to change the way coalition governments are managed at local government level in South Africa. This chapter has argued for the need for a legal framework to govern these coalition governments; there are examples on the continent - notably Kenya - where coalitions, their formation and duration are sanctioned by law. It is also essential for political actors to transform the current political landscape towards political maturity, which will also improve the quality of decision and policy making at the political level and is likely to have a positive impact on the nature of coalitions formed. Integrating democratic principles based on established theories of coalition government formation through the various mechanisms outlined above, as well as learning from the lessons of failed coalitions and their impact on the electorate and democracy, is likely to improve the quality of coalitions formed in South Africa and enhance the stability of the aforementioned.

REFERENCES

Beukes, J., & de Visser, J. (2021). *A framework for coalitions in local government*. Dullah Omar Institute. https://www.cogta.gov.za/cgta_2016/wp-content/uploads/2021/11/A-Framework-for-Coalitions-in-Local-Government_Dullah_Omar_.pdf

Booysen, S. (2021). *Marriages of Inconvenience: The Politics of Coalition South Africa. Mapungubwe Institute for Strategic Reflection*. MISTRA. doi:10.2307/j.ctv2z6qdx6

Cooperative Governance Traditional Affairs. (2021). *A Framework for Coalitions in Local Government – Cooperative Governance and Traditional Affairs*. https://www.cogta.gov.za/index.php/2021/11/22/a-framework-for-coalitions-in-local-government/

Davis, R. (2023). Eight reasons why SA metro coalitions are imploding. *Daily Maverick*. https://www.dailymaverick.co.za/article/2023-01-30-eight-reasons-why-sa-metro-coalitions-are-imploding/

De Vos, P. (2021). The constitutional-legal dimensions of coalition politics and government in South Africa. In S. Booysen (Ed.), *Marriages of Inconvenience The politics of coalitions in South Africa (2021)*. doi:10.2307/j.ctv2z6qdx6.16

Dlakavu, A. (2022). South African electoral trends: Prospects for coalition governance at national and provincial spheres in 2024. *Politikon: South African Journal of Political Studies*, *49*(4), 482. doi:10.10 80/02589346.2022.2151682

Doherty, I. (2004). *Coalition Best Practices*. National Democratic Institute West Bank and Gaza.

Haffajee, F. (2022). ANC's Dada Morero steps down after 25 days in office as DA's Mpho Phalatse reinstated as Joburg mayor. *Daily Maverick*. https://www.dailymaverick.co.za/article/2022-10-25-ancs-dada-morero-steps-down-after-25-days-in-office-as-das-mpho-phalatse-reinstated-as-joburg-mayor/

Kadima, D. (2014). An introduction to the politics of party alliances and coalitions in socially-divided Africa. *Journal of African Elections*, *13*(1), 9. doi:10.20940/JAE/2014/v13i1a1

Kotze, J. S. (2019). *Local Council Turmoil Shows South Africa Isn't Very Good at Coalitions*. Retrieved at https:www.google.co.za/amp/s/theconversation.com/amp/local-council-turmoil-shows-south-africa-isnt-very-good-at-coalitions-128489

Mafisa, I. (2022). *ANC back in power in Johannesburg, Dada Morero elected mayor*. IOL News. https://www.iol.co.za/the-star/news/anc-back-in-power-in-johannesburg-dada-morero-elected-mayor-e358ef61-82e5-426b-b896-319681415679

Makgale, B. (2021). Power, Politics and Ideology: Understanding Councillors' views on the tug of war in the City of Johannesburg. In S. Booysen (Ed.), *Marriage of Incontinence. The politics of coalitions in South African (2021)*. doi:10.2307/j.ctv2z6qdx6.18

Masilela, B. (2023). *Thapelo Amad is the new mayor in town. This is what you need to know about Joburg politics and the election of the new number one citizen*. IOL News. https://www.iol.co.za/news/politics/thapelo-amad-is-the-new-mayor-in-town-this-is-what-you-need-to-know-about-joburg-politics-and-the-election-of-the-new-number-one-citizen-73152cdf-36cd-4165-9f2e-a21739d20f8a

Masuabi, Q. (2022). A dramatic Friday as City of Joburg elects Dada Morero as mayor after Mpho Phalatse gets the chop. *Daily Maverick*. https://www.dailymaverick.co.za/article/2022-09-30-dramatic-friday-joburg-elects-dada-morero-as-mayor-as-phalatse-gets-chop/

Masuabi, Q. (2023). Al Jama-ah's Kabelo Gwamanda voted in as latest mayor of Joburg. *Daily Maverick*. https://www.dailymaverick.co.za/article/2023-05-05-al-jama-ahs-kabelo-gwamanda-voted-in-as-latest-mayor-of-joburg/

Mokgosi, K., Shai, K., & Ogunnubi, O. (2017). Local government coalition in Gauteng province of South Africa: Challenges and Opportunities. *Ubuntu: Journal of Conflict and Social Transformation*, *6*(1), 37–57. doi:10.31920/2050-4950/2017/v6n1a2

Mpangalasane, C. (2020). *The impact of coalition government on service delivery: City of Tshwane metropolitan*. Mini-dissertation, North-West University, http://hdl.handle.net/10394/35622

Pieterse, M. (2019). *What's needed to fix collapsing coalitions in South Africa's cities?* Retrieved at https:www.wits.ac.za/news/latest-news/opinion/2019/2019-12/whats-needed-to-fix-collapsing-coalitions-in-south-africa-cities.html

Republic of Kenya. (2022). Political Parties Act (Amendment) 2022.

Republic of South Africa. (1996). Constitution of the Republic of South Africa.

Seeletsa, M. (2022, November 8). DA's Tania Campbell re-elected as City of Ekurhuleni mayor. *The Citizen.* https://www.citizen.co.za/news/south-africa/elections/local-2021/these-are-the-hung-councils-in-south-africa/

Sekatle, K., & Sebola, M. (2020). The choice of coalition governments for promotion of national unity in Africa: Does the model work for unity and political stability? *The Business and Management Review, 11.*

Smith, M. (n.d.). Compatibility of learner democracy. *De Jure Law Journal, 1*(46) https://www.dejure.up.ac.za/articles-vol-46-1/smit-m

Tutu, D. (1999). *No future without forgiveness.* University of Michigan: Doubleday. doi:10.1111/j.1540-5842.1999.tb00012.x

KEY TERMS AND DEFINITIONS

City of Johannesburg: The City of Johannesburg is the largest city in South Africa and the provincial capital of Gauteng. It is a major economic and financial hub, known for its diversity, cultural richness, and significant role in the country's history.

Coalition Government: A coalition government is formed when multiple political parties cooperate to establish a majority in the legislature, often following an election where no single party achieved a majority of seats.

Collaborative Governance: Collaborative governance is an approach where different sectors of society, including government, private sector, and civil society, work together to make decisions and solve problems.

Democratic Consolidation: This refers to the process through which a new democracy matures, becoming stable and enduring. It involves the deepening of democratic institutions and practices, including the establishment of a strong civil society, independent judiciary, and a culture of political participation and competition.

Democratic Principles: These are fundamental beliefs and norms that underpin the operation of a democratic system. Key democratic principles include the rule of law, protection of human rights, separation of powers, pluralism, free and fair elections, and accountability of government officials.

Hung Council: A hung council occurs when no single political party or coalition of parties has an outright majority of seats in a municipal council, resulting in a situation where the balance of power is held by one or more smaller parties.

Legislative Framework: This term refers to the collection of laws, regulations, and legal principles that establish the legal environment within which individuals, organizations, and governments operate.

Mature Political Leadership: Mature political leadership refers to leaders who demonstrate wisdom, experience, and a deep understanding of the political landscape. They are characterized by their ability to make prudent decisions, manage conflicts, and guide their communities or countries through challenges, often prioritizing long-term stability and prosperity over short-term gains.

Service Delivery: Service delivery in a governmental context refers to the process through which public services, such as healthcare, education, sanitation, and infrastructure, are provided to the population.

ENDNOTES

[1] A proportional system without a threshold means that there's no minimum percentage of votes a party needs to get seats in a legislative body. This can lead to more diverse representation but may also result in many smaller parties.

[2] A presidential system is a type of government where a single person, the president, serves as both the head of state and head of government. The president is elected independently, has significant executive powers, and has a fixed term. A key example is the United States of America.

Chapter 13
The Confluence of Soft Power Diplomacy and Coalition Politics:
A Comparative Analysis of China's Strategies in Africa and the Middle East

Mohamad Zreik
https://orcid.org/0000-0002-6812-6529
Sun Yat-sen University, China

ABSTRACT

China's growing influence through soft power diplomacy is a parallel storyline to Africa's current experience with coalition politics and electoral democracy, especially in the Middle East and East Asia. This chapter examines how China employs coalition politics to enhance its larger diplomatic efforts in Africa with the goal of connecting these two crucial storylines. This chapter uses examples from the Middle East and East Asia to explore the complexities of coalition governments in Africa and how they might help or hurt China's soft power ambitions. This study, which takes an interdisciplinary approach, will shed new light on the complex dynamics at play when coalitions of politicians, democratic governments, and foreign governments interact. The chapter finishes with concrete suggestions for policymakers, stressing the importance of a comprehensive knowledge of these overlapping domains for the development of effective and democratic approaches to government in Africa. Policymakers, academics, and practitioners in the fields of politics, international relations, development studies, and sociology are among the many who will find value in this chapter.

DOI: 10.4018/979-8-3693-1654-2.ch013

1. INTRODUCTION

Over the past few decades, China has established itself as a major actor on the international stage, contributing to the development of international politics, economy, and culture (Falkner, 2016). Modern China has shown a subtle yet assertive stance in foreign affairs, emerging from a past marked by revolutions, reforms, and a period of isolation (Garver, 2015). Its contacts with Africa and the Middle East, two regions of strategic importance in terms of resources, trade, and geopolitics, have been particularly indicative of this policy. China's ascension to global power status, propelled by its economic and diplomatic capabilities, provides an interesting context against which to analyze its strategic moves in these areas.

The countries of Africa and the Middle East are as varied as their rich tapestry, and each faces its own set of difficulties and possibilities. Election democracy and long-term economic growth in Africa have been hampered by coalition politics (Le Van, 2011). These coalitions, whose durability and efficacy can vary widely, provide a testing ground for democratic administration but complicate international diplomacy. Similarly, the Middle East, which is widely regarded as a complex maze of religion, ethnicity, and politics, has emerged as a difficult but indispensable ally in international affairs (Jackson, 2013). The economic, social, and political policies, as well as the use of soft power, that make up China's engagement with these areas go beyond simple trade agreements.

Many of China's soft power projects in Africa have focused on fostering win-win cooperation models, fostering cultural interchange, and investing heavily in infrastructure and human development (Zreik, 2021a). China's financial support for infrastructure projects in Africa's key development areas—including transportation, electricity, and education—has been a game-changer (Rolland, 2017). China has taken a measured, nuanced approach to the Middle East, navigating the region's political intricacies in order to build economic partnerships, with an emphasis on the region's abundant oil resources (Kalantzakos, 2017). These initiatives are typically carried out in tandem with Western involvement, giving these regions new avenues for collaboration and throwing a wrench into the traditional East vs. West storyline.

This means that the complexities of local political environments, such as coalition politics, are essential to comprehending China's influence in Africa and the Middle East. This chapter's goal is to clarify this interface by providing an interdisciplinary understanding of the entangled nature of these linkages. Connecting these two important narratives, and learning how China uses coalition politics to bolster its bigger diplomatic efforts in Africa and the Middle East, will aid policymakers in developing successful and democratic responses to these troubled regions. This research is an important contribution to the fields of international relations, development studies, and political sociology, and should be read by academics, professionals, and policymakers in these areas.

The chapter's discussion of these topics not only adds to our knowledge of China's place in global politics, but also sheds light on the fascinating relationship between soft power diplomacy and coalition building. As China continues to increase its worldwide presence through a carefully calibrated blend of hard and soft power, this perspective allows the reader to grasp the multifaceted interactions and intricate dynamics at play.

China's soft power and Africa's coalition politics are generally discussed separately in academic and policy debates. There has been a noticeable lack of research into the intersection of China's soft power initiatives and the rise of coalition politics as a significant feature in Africa's governance landscape, despite the fact that there is a growing body of literature devoted to understanding the nuances of China's global reach through these initiatives. This split-brain thinking ignores the mutually beneficial or antagonistic nature of these two fields of study, as well as the impact that their interactions may have on domestic administration and foreign relations.

The repercussions of not fully comprehending this connection are extensive. For instance, African officials may lack the knowledge and tools necessary to negotiate accords and collaborations with China that take into account the nuances of African politics, such as the complexities of coalition governments, without an interdisciplinary study (Collins & Bilge, 2020). The efficiency and longevity of China's soft power operations may be jeopardized if its strategists are unable to successfully navigate a maze of political uncertainty informed by a comprehensive understanding of coalition politics.

Moreover, the voids in our knowledge have implications for international relations and academic paradigms more generally than just the local stakeholders. When coalition politics' influence on soft power diplomacy is understudied, it can lead to a lack of the holistic understanding that is essential for constructing efficient, fair, and democratic systems of government.

This chapter seeks to fill this knowledge and experience gap by assessing China's use of coalition politics to boost its soft power activities in Africa and the effects these initiatives have on China. Studying China's position in Africa is important in and of itself, but such research is also vital because it can shed light on how to foster the spread and maintenance of democratic rule across the African continent. Exploring this underexplored junction has the potential to deepen the understanding of both areas and lead to more sophisticated approaches to global cooperation and municipal administration.

This chapter is driven by the question, "How does China utilize coalition politics to enhance its soft power diplomacy in Africa, and what are the reciprocal impacts of this intersection on democratic governance in the region?" The answer to this question can shed light on the complex interplay between China's soft power goals and the politics of coalition governments in Africa. The world is becoming more interconnected but also more politically fractured, and this helps us appreciate the complexity and multidimensionality of international interactions.

There are several goals for this chapter. The primary goal is to provide a thorough analysis of the literature concerning China's soft power initiatives around the world, with an emphasis on Africa and the Middle East. This establishes a scholarly framework for examining our study question.

Second, the chapter intends to analyze the structure of African political coalitions. The complexity, difficulties, and potential rewards of coalitions in various African nations will provide a foundation for investigating their dealings with other powers, primarily China.

Third, the chapter intends to compare and contrast China's soft power initiatives in Africa and the Middle East. This will provide light on whether or not China's approach to these politically varied regions shares any commonalities.

Finally, it is hoped to use this research to propose concrete policy changes. These recommendations will encourage more just and productive collaborations between African and Chinese governments.

To achieve these goals, this chapter will provide new insights into the intersection of soft power diplomacy and coalition politics in the contexts of governance, development, and diplomacy, and so contribute to an interdisciplinary knowledge of international relations.

2. CONCEPTUAL FRAMEWORK

2.1. Definition of Soft Power

The term "soft power," invented by American political scientist Joseph Nye, has become more important in the field of diplomacy and international affairs. Soft power refers to a country's ability to influence the opinions of others without resorting to force or coercion (Nye Jr, 2008). The groundwork for understanding how governments might exercise influence without relying solely on military force or economic inducements was built by Nye's seminal work on the issue. Soft power's subtle application in today's linked global world has the potential to profoundly affect international alliances, partnerships, and long-term ties (Ikenberry, Mastanduno, & Wohlforth, 2009).

Culture, political values, and foreign policies are the three main tenets on which Joseph Nye built his theory of soft power. Let's delve into each one.

Culture

The first pillar of soft power is cultural influence, which is also the most obvious and accessible. Arts, language, food, and popular entertainment are all examples of cultural exports that can arouse curiosity and even affection for a place abroad (Nye, 2012). For instance, China has made excellent use of the widespread interest in its ancient cultural practices like acupuncture and tai chi, as well as the widespread impact of Chinese cuisine and festivals (De Mente, 2011). Mutual appreciation and understanding are cultivated through cultural exchanges, which can pave the way for stronger diplomatic and economic ties (Zreik, 2021b).

Political Ideals

The second pillar, political ideas, consists of a nation's cherished beliefs and preferred methods of government (Aronczyk, 2013). Human rights, the rule of law, and democratic administration are all aspects of a country's political system that might attract the attention of other countries (Diamond & Morlino, 2004). Among countries that perceive China as an alternative to Western methods of administration, the advocacy of a model that combines economic growth and social stability has gained popularity.

Foreign Policies

Diplomatic efforts, international collaboration, and the formulation of global projects are all part of a country's foreign policies, the third pillar. National soft power is often increased through policies that promote international cooperation, economic justice, and peaceful coexistence (DeLisle, 2010). The Belt and Road Initiative, spearheaded by the Chinese government, is emblematic of this type of foreign policy, which seeks to build economic and cultural linkages between countries in different regions of the world (Yu, 2020).

The complexity of soft power can be dissected using this three-pronged framework. Countries like China can use these factors to their advantage by devising varied ways to acquire support abroad, including the attractiveness of their political principles and the deft formulation of their foreign policy. Recognizing the sources, techniques, and implications of soft power is crucial as we negotiate the intricate web of international relations in Africa and the Middle East.

2.2. The Anatomy of Coalition Politics

Coalition politics, especially as it pertains to the political system in Africa, is a fascinating and difficult field of study. A fractured election mandate, in which no single party can claim an outright majority, frequently leads to the creation of coalition governments (Cheibub, 2007). Parties with different platforms and ideologies may establish a coalition in such a situation, with the expectation of mutually beneficial power and decision sharing. Coalition governments in Africa are not a universal occurrence; rather, they vary greatly according on the nation's unique history, culture, and set of issues (Beck & Grande, 2010). But in the end, they all want the same thing: to establish order and authority via cooperation.

Coalition politics is intrinsically linked to democracy and pluralism in many African countries. Africa's diverse population and colonial past make coalition governments a feasible way to secure more equitable representation in government (Cheeseman & Larmer, 2015). They have the ability to foster political inclusiveness and contribute to more equitable development outcomes by giving a voice to underrepresented groups and smaller parties in the policymaking process (Clayton, O'Brien, & Piscopo, 2019).

Coalitions, though, aren't problem-free. Coalition politics are necessary because of societal heterogeneity, but this diversity may also be a political minefield. Policy paralysis, infighting, and corruption are common problems for coalition administrations due to the competition between competing interests (Borzutzky, 2019). Unstable coalitions can disrupt long-term planning and growth by leading to frequent shifts in government and policy focus (Jenkins-Smith et al., 2018). The need to negotiate with coalition partners who may have divergent or even opposing agendas often leads to the compromise or watering down of policy objectives (Dodds, Donoghue, & Roesch, 2016).

Foreign policy goals, such as connections with large global powers like China, mix intriguingly with the imperatives of coalition politics in the African environment (Gilpin, 2016). Coalition governments often have competing objectives, which can make forming foreign alliances difficult. While some in a coalition may be enthusiastic about China's offer of infrastructure development, others may be wary of the country's financial stability and the effect it may have on domestic industries (Bunte, 2019). When large global powers like China seek to expand their soft power influence through diplomatic, cultural, or economic methods, these dynamics take on added significance (Lee, 2011).

Any thorough examination of the governance models and international relations of Africa must begin with an understanding of the anatomy of coalition politics on the continent. Coalitions are crucial to all aspects of politics, from the formation of policies to the negotiation of international relations, and are not solely a function of electoral math. That's why it's important to consider the complex terrain of coalition politics, with all its advantages and disadvantages, when trying to comprehend the part that countries like China play in Africa's growth.

3. CHINA'S SOFT POWER DIPLOMACY: AN OVERVIEW

3.1. Historical Evolution

There has been a noticeable change in China's approach to soft power diplomacy over the years, from one of relative passivity to one of active and strategic involvement with the globe (Lai & Lu, 2012). China spent most of the twentieth century tackling problems on its own territory, such as social upheaval, economic reform, and the introduction of modern technology (Guthrie, 2012). But as it has developed into the world's second largest economy, China has come to recognize the importance of soft power in addition to its economic and military might.

The pivotal moment occurred in the early 2000s, when then-President Hu Jintao publicly recognized the importance of soft power, calling on China to increase its cultural impact as a strategic asset (Pan & Lo, 2017). Since then, China has put considerable resources into a variety of soft power programs, such as the launch of global media networks like CGTN to tell the "China Story" and the establishment of Confucius Institutes around the world to spread the Chinese language and culture (Zreik, 2023).

China's desire to restructure the international order in accordance with its interests and ideals has been a driving force behind its emphasis on soft power. China has increased its use of soft power in international relations since the Belt and Road Initiative was introduced in 2013 (Voon & Xu, 2020). The goal of this huge infrastructure project is to not only promote China's culture, technology, and governance models but also to link Asia, Europe, and Africa together through a system of railways, highways, and ports (Zreik, 2022).

Chinese participation in the United Nations, the World Trade Organization, and the World Health Organization is further evidence of the country's dedication to international cooperation and good governance (Woods, 2008). At the same time, China has worked to deepen its bilateral relationships with specific nations through cultural exchanges, educational alliances, and technology cooperation.

It's interesting to see that China's soft power efforts extend beyond the traditional spheres of politics and economics. The nation has positioned itself as a leader in solving global concerns like climate change while also serving as a center of technology innovation and cultural vitality (Calthorpe, 2015). These aspects of China's soft power not only improve the country's international reputation but also bring in new people, businesses, and collaborations (Yang, 2010).

It is important to remember, though, that China's efforts to increase its soft power have been welcomed with both enthusiasm and mistrust. Others see China's activities as attempts to impose excessive influence or as a mask for more strategic geopolitical objectives, but many countries have welcomed China's initiatives as possibilities for mutual progress.

3.2. Application in Africa

China's soft power operations in Africa cover a wide range of fields, from infrastructure building and economic cooperation to cultural exchanges and educational alliances, and their reach is only growing. China's soft power diplomacy takes many forms, like these, and aims not just at short-term economic gains but at building lasting ties based on mutual respect and common interests.

Infrastructure and Economic Projects

China's strong dedication to infrastructure development in Africa is one of the most obvious examples of its soft power there. Transformative in terms of physical infrastructure and in terms of their potential to drive economic growth and regional integration include projects like Kenya's Mombasa-Nairobi Standard Gauge Railway, Ethiopia's Addis Ababa-Djibouti Railway, and other hydroelectric dams across the continent (Ehizuelen & Abdi, 2018). The Belt and Road Initiative, of which these projects are a part, aims to create conditions favorable to trade and investment by linking Asia, Europe, and Africa through a system of logistical channels (Zreik, 2023).

Cultural Exchanges

Using venues as diverse as Confucius Institutes, art exhibitions, and cultural festivals, China has been actively fostering cultural links with Africa (Brazys & Dukalskis, 2019). The long-term goal of these endeavors is to strengthen diplomatic ties by fostering mutual knowledge and admiration of Chinese culture. The Spring Festival and Chinese film festivals, for example, have become hugely popular in many African nations because they provide a vivid window into China's cultural wealth (Gobe, 2010).

Educational Partnerships

China's soft power strategy in Africa includes an increased focus on academic exchanges. Opportunities for knowledge transfer and capacity building are provided by Chinese government scholarships for African students and by cooperation between Chinese and African universities (Makundi et al., 2017). These programs not only foster the development of future leaders and professionals, but also create interpersonal bonds that can strengthen bilateral ties (Zreik, 2021b).

Medical and Technological Collaboration

China's soft power has grown in recent years thanks to its increased medical help and technology collaborations. The deployment of medical teams, the provision of medical supplies, and the dissemination of knowledge in fields such as telemedicine and public health are all on the rise. China's role in supplying vaccines and medical aid to African countries during pandemics like the COVID-19 outbreak bolstered the country's reputation as a trustworthy partner (Lee, 2021).

Political Consultation and Training Programs

Training programs, policy discussions, and consultative forums are commonplace in China for their African guests, many of whom are African politicians, bureaucrats, and professionals (Brautigam, 2011). These events give African leaders an opportunity to learn about China's political and economic institutions, as well as its governance models, economic policies, and technical developments.

3.3. Application in the Middle East

China's worldwide policy places special emphasis on the Middle East, which presents both opportunities and challenges. China's connection with the Middle East is characterized by a more complex blend of trade agreements, cultural initiatives, and diplomatic maneuvering than its relationship with Africa, where infrastructure and development aid are the major forms of participation. China has shown its sophisticated awareness of the geopolitical complexities of the region and its intention to use soft power as a viable weapon for establishing closer relations through this diverse approach.

Trade Agreements

One of China's most important interactions with the Middle East is commercial. Countries in the region, including Saudi Arabia and Iran, are major exporters of oil to China (Garlick, 2023). In consequence, the Middle East provides a prosperous marketplace for Chinese consumer electronics and building materials (Yeung, 2017). Also, several different FTAs and commercial partnerships are being discussed or already in place with Middle Eastern countries. China's status as a vital economic partner in the area is strengthened by the interdependence that is created by these monetary links (Fulton, 2020).

Cultural Initiatives

China recognizes the importance of culture in the Middle East and has initiated a number of cultural projects to promote peace and understanding. Several countries in the Middle East, such as the United Arab Emirates and Egypt, have opened Confucius Institutes to spread Chinese language and culture (Yellinek, Mann, & Lebel, 2020). In addition, China has taken the initiative to host cultural festivals, art exhibitions, and academic exchanges, all of which serve as a forum for intercultural communication and break down barriers of mistrust (Zreik, 2021b).

Diplomatic Relationships

China's diplomacy in the Middle East is finely tuned to account for the region's nuanced political situation. Despite their differences, Beijing keeps open diplomatic channels with both Iran and Saudi Arabia and strikes a similar diplomatic balance with Israel and Palestine (Zhu, 2016). The governments of the Middle East tend to view China as a less judgmental partner than Western countries because of China's non-interventionist policies and its emphasis on win-win cooperation (Kamel, 2018).

Strategic Partnerships

China's efforts to build strategic relationships extend far beyond the realm of commerce and culture to include fields as diverse as defense and aerospace. Joint ventures, research partnerships, and direct investments are all common types of this type of cooperation. These partnerships not only help China gain a foothold in strategic sectors, but also give Middle Eastern nations access to China's cutting-edge technology for their own economic growth.

Soft Power Through Humanitarian Aid

China's humanitarian aid in the Middle East, especially in war zones and after natural disasters, has been increasing in recent years (Hoh, 2019). China hopes to improve its reputation as a responsible global actor by offering assistance free of overt political conditions (Regilme, Jr & Hodzi, 2021).

4. THE LANDSCAPE OF COALITION POLITICS IN AFRICA

4.1. Case Studies

The need to balance competing ethnic, regional, and political interests inside a single African state has given rise to a broad array of coalition political frameworks. Coalition administrations are on the increase in African countries like Kenya, South Africa, and Zimbabwe, and this has complicated their diplomatic relationships with other countries, particularly China (Shen, 2020). In order to comprehend the interplay between African coalition politics and China's soft power diplomacy, some of the most striking case cases are examined.

Kenya: A Test Case for Infrastructure Diplomacy

Major Chinese infrastructure projects, such as the Mombasa-Nairobi Standard Gauge Railway, were made possible in part by the coalition administration in Kenya, especially during the time of the 'Grand Coalition' between 2008 and 2013 (Basu & Janiec, 2021). China was able to successfully negotiate the intricate coalition politics of Kenya by proposing terms that were acceptable to all parties (Chiyemura, Gambino, & Zajontz, 2023). Despite its share of critics, the project has come to represent the potential gains from China's infrastructure diplomacy in Africa (Basu & Janiec, 2021).

South Africa: The Tripartite Alliance and BRICS

The African National Congress (ANC), the Congress of South African Trade Unions (COSATU), and the South African Communist Party (SACP) in South Africa form a compelling example of a relatively stable Tripartite Alliance (Govo & Muguti, 2023). China's relationship with South Africa is nuanced, primarily because of the country's BRICS membership, which adds an additional layer of geopolitical considerations. The two countries' trade and investment flows have been healthy, and they've managed to keep their connections solid despite political upheaval within the alliance (Blas & Farchy, 2021).

Zimbabwe: Coalition Politics and the 'Look East' Policy

As a result of the 'Look East' policy implemented by the coalition government in power in Zimbabwe from 2009 to 2013, the country's ties to China have grown considerably stronger (Tinarwo & Babu, 2023). As a counterweight to Western dominance, the coalition as a whole agreed to deepen ties with China, despite internal battles and divisions. As a result, China has investments across Zimbabwe's economy, from agriculture to the mining industry (Chipaike & Bischoff, 2019).

Ethiopia: Federalism and Infrastructure

Ethiopia's system of ethnic federalism necessitates a kind of power-sharing that is similar to coalition dynamics, but is not a coalition government in the strict sense. Ethiopia has benefited greatly from China's investment in Africa, particularly in the construction and industrial sectors (Carmody & Murphy, 2022). China's success in navigating Ethiopia's convoluted bureaucracy is shown by the Grand Ethiopian Renaissance Dam, which received funding from Beijing (Barton, 2022).

Senegal: Unity Government and Cultural Diplomacy

The new Senegalese government, which represents a broad coalition of political factions, is eager to improve ties with China (Rukema, 2023). Confucius Institutes and Chinese language programs are growing popularity in this area, demonstrating China's soft power in the sphere of cultural diplomacy (Lee, 2021).

4.2. Democratic Governance and Coalition Politics

Coalition politics' recent ascent in Africa makes for an intriguing case study of the continent's developing democratic system. The alternate approach to governing provided by coalition governments, which are generally partnerships between multiple political parties, can strengthen democratic processes. This is especially important in Africa because of the profound impact that ethnic variety, historical legacies, and economic inequality have on the continent's social and political climate. The following provides an exploration of how coalition politics may help foster democratic leadership in Africa.

Checks and Balances

Coalition politics has a built-in system of checks and balances, which is one of its main advantages (Przybylski, 2018). There is no single party with an outright majority in a coalition government, thus negotiations and compromise are essential. In addition to reducing the possibility of authoritarian leadership, this also fosters the accountability and transparency that are essential to a healthy democracy (Norris, 2012).

Political Inclusivity

Coalitions encourage political openness since they frequently necessitate the participation of parties that represent a wide range of society, including marginalized communities (Grant, 2021). This is especially important in Africa because many African countries are highly multicultural (Fearon, 2003). Coalition politics can result in a more legitimate political system by establishing a more representative form of government.

Policy Moderation

Coalition administrations frequently produce more moderate policies because the coalition partners moderate one other's more extreme positions (Lowndes & Pratchett, 2012). As a result, socioeconomic disparities, which are typically worsened by one-party control, may be mitigated by more equitable development plans that appeal to varied constituencies in the African environment.

Encouragement of Civil Society

Coalition governments, due to the participation of many political parties, typically provide avenues for citizens to have a voice in shaping public policy (Abelson, 2018). This may be especially important in Africa, where a strong civil society can help give a voice to the underrepresented and promote more just and fair government.

Conflict Resolution

Coalition politics can help bring peace to countries plagued by interethnic and intraregional tensions. Coalitions can help reduce tensions and create social cohesion by involving more people from different backgrounds in decision-making (Cornago, 1999).

Strengthening Democratic Institutions

The sheer essence of coalition politics requires the fortification of democratic institutions. Institutions that play a vital role in coalition politics, such as the judiciary (which may need to judge coalition conflicts) and the electoral commission (which must oversee fair coalition-forming processes), are bolstered by the coalition system.

Coalition politics, though, are no silver bullet for fixing Africa's governance problems. They can be riddled with insecurity, policy stagnation, and coalitions formed for opportunistic reasons rather than the common benefit. Therefore, coalition politics must be embedded within a broader institutional structure that promotes transparency, accountability, and public participation in order to actually produce democratic governance.

5. COMPARATIVE ANALYSIS: CHINA'S STRATEGIES IN AFRICA VS. THE MIDDLE EAST

5.1. Cultural Exchange and Influence

China's diplomatic use of soft power is nuanced and flexible, changing course in response to shifting regional dynamics and sensitivity. China has global ambitions in both Africa and the Middle East, but its strategy in these two regions is very different, especially when it comes to cultural interchange and impact.

Confucius Institutes and Cultural Centers

China has been very active in establishing Confucius Institutes across Africa to spread the language and culture of China (Li, 2021). These centers, which are often part of larger colleges, have become crucial channels through which China disseminates its cultural heritage. In contrast, there are less Confucius Institutes in the Middle East, which may be due to the region's long-standing cultural traditions and the prevalence of Islam, which may be seen as at odds with Confucian thought (Yellinek, Mann, & Lebel, 2020).

Cultural Festivals and Exchanges

China has hosted cultural festivals in both locations, showcasing Chinese art, music, and cuisine. However, in Africa, events frequently promote Afro-Chinese partnerships in music and art, and the emphasis is on recognizing shared cultural values (Thornber, 2016). The theological and socioeconomic complexity of the Middle East may contribute to the region's more circumspect approach. Larger in scale and scope, these festivals are planned to avoid offending local sensibilities in their host countries (Salman, Pieper, & Geeraerts, 2015).

Educational Exchanges

Scholarships for study in China and study in Africa are common parts of educational exchange programs in Africa. Science and technology are frequently highlighted, with the goals of strengthening institutional frameworks and meeting Africa's development requirements (Zreik, 2021a). Language study and collaborations in cutting-edge scientific fields like artificial intelligence and sustainable energy are only two examples of the many facets of educational exchange programs in the Middle East (Wang, Xu, & Guo, 2018). This larger focus reflects the more developed educational system in the Middle East compared to many African countries.

Media Outreach

The influence of state-run Chinese media like CCTV and Xinhua has grown in both of these areas (Hu & Ji, 2012). However, the material is adapted to reflect local tastes. China's dedication to development initiatives and mutual growth in Africa is frequently highlighted in media reports (Zhang, 2018). To reach a more politically astute readership, Middle Eastern media outlets tend to present China as a moderating force on the international stage (Scobell & Nader, 2016).

Traditional and Folk Diplomacy

China's use of martial arts and traditional Chinese medicine as tools of traditional and folk diplomacy in Africa is one example (Zhan, 2009). China prefers high-profile, state-led cultural programs that are consistent with regional diplomatic norms, but this is less common in the Middle East.

Public Diplomacy Through Humanitarian Aid

As part of China's broader cultural and diplomatic engagement in Africa, humanitarian aid is frequently promoted with the goal of portraying China as a kind partner (Regilme, Jr & Hodzi, 2021). Humanitarian aid in the Middle East is nuanced, as it seeks to strike a neutral tone in an otherwise highly charged political climate (Kamel, 2018).

5.2. Political Alliances and Coalition Involvement

China's diplomatic interventions in Africa and the Middle East have both been distinguished by a deliberate engagement with coalition governments, albeit with differing goals and techniques adapted to each region's distinct political situation. To better understand China's complicated coalition politics in these widely dispersed but strategically important regions, this section goes into the nuances of these interactions.

Engaging African Coalitions: Pragmatism Over Ideology

Pragmatism has defined China's interactions with African coalition governments like those in Kenya and South Africa. Economic collaboration, infrastructure building, and resource extraction are the main points of emphasis. China hopes to guarantee its projects and investments by working with various political factions within these coalitions, reducing exposure to potential political instability or regime change (Ehizuelen & Abdi, 2018). China's "no strings attached" approach makes it an appealing partner for members of diverse coalitions with differing views, in contrast to the practices of many Western countries (Carbone, 2014).

Navigating the Middle Eastern Quagmire: A Balancing Act

Given the region's convoluted network of alliances, sectarian splits, and geopolitical rivalry, the Middle East poses a considerably more sophisticated problem for China to solve (Zreik, 2022). Countries like Lebanon and Iraq, which have coalition or unity governments, require China to use delicate diplomatic maneuvering. China's strategy here is less concerned with direct financial investment and more concerned with striking a balance of engagement that will allow it to keep working with various groups. This includes not just monetary transactions but also diplomatic initiatives for peace and stability in the region and even mediation between rival coalition members (Hoh, 2019).

Belt and Road Initiative (BRI) as a Common Denominator

China's involvement in both areas has been fundamentally based on the Belt and Road Initiative. In Africa, coalition partners generally agree that the BRI is a good way to stimulate the continent's flagging economy (Oriaifo, Torres de Oliveira, & Ellis, 2020). With its emphasis on regional connectivity and economic opportunity rather than ideological or sectarian differences, the BRI is a project that can win over multiple parties in the Middle East (Scobell & Nader, 2016).

Security Concerns: A Delicate Dance

There is a notable distinction between the two regions with regards to China's security engagements. Some African governments have benefited from China's military assistance and training programs, and their coalition partners have generally welcomed this development (Brautigam, 2011). When it comes to the Middle East, where complex ties and long-running conflicts raise security worries, China treads more carefully. Its security presence is minimal, typically confined to UN-sanctioned anti-piracy or peacekeeping activities (Zreik, 2019).

Soft Power Through Educational and Cultural Initiatives

China's educational and cultural activities as a kind of soft power have met with greater success in Africa, but in the Middle East, with its distinct religious and cultural identity, a different approach has been necessary (Makundi et al., 2017). The Chinese government places greater emphasis on intellectually nuanced soft power in this area by encouraging academic exchanges, think tank partnerships, and scholarly discussions involving politicians from across coalition factions (Kamel, 2018).

6. SYNERGIES AND DISSONANCES BETWEEN SOFT POWER DIPLOMACY AND COALITION POLITICS

China's engagement strategy for coalition governments and its nuanced approach to soft power diplomacy go hand in hand, especially in terms of fostering adaptability and long-term stability in international relations. China is able to target a wide audience with its soft power initiatives because of the diversity of interests and ideologies present in coalition governments. China's focus on economic growth, for instance, has widespread appeal in Africa, connecting with a wide range of coalition members who may otherwise have competing goals (Shen, 2020). The diplomatic landscape is strengthened by the congruence of interests, providing a firmer footing for China's diplomatic initiatives.

Furthermore, China's soft power measures are methods for nurturing long-term partnerships in addition to immediate diplomatic tools. The public's impression of China can be drastically altered by initiatives like cultural exchanges and educational alliances, paving the way for more constructive diplomatic and commercial engagements. When dealing with coalition administrations, whose political environment can be volatile and vulnerable to quick changes, these long-term ties become more crucial. China's influence on these coalition governments will remain stable as long as it continues to invest in social and cultural ties, regardless of political shifts within individual parties (Dreyer, 2018).

Soft power diplomacy and coalition politics make an interesting couple, but they are not without their risks. The complex and frequently delicate balance of interests within coalition governments could be disrupted by poorly timed soft power initiatives (Nye, 2021). If diplomatic or economic efforts are hampered because of a failure to account for cultural sensitivity or cross political red lines, the entire process could be derailed.

7. POLICY RECOMMENDATIONS

7.1. For African Governments

When African governments have a deeper appreciation for China's soft power diplomacy, they are better able to create relationships that benefit both parties. First and foremost, African officials must acknowledge the complexity of China's soft power efforts. This includes everything from large-scale investments in infrastructure and development projects to smaller-scale educational exchanges and cultural activities. African nations can benefit more from their dealings with Beijing if they have a better understanding of China's soft power and its broader context.

Using China's soft power could help African countries build healthier relationships with their neighbors. African countries could propose a mutually beneficial cultural exchange program in exchange for Chinese language courses and art exhibitions. Examples of this could be exchange programs that bring prominent African intellectuals, scholars, and artists to Chinese universities and other venues. These countries can help balance the scales by introducing Chinese society to African cultural and intellectual contributions, so fostering a two-way flow of soft power and reducing the imbalance of power.

Furthermore, African governments may better assess the long-term ramifications of their partnerships with China if they have a solid understanding of soft power dynamics. For instance, China's geopolitical interests on the continent may be served by large-scale infrastructure projects that are widely viewed as good for economic growth. African politicians might use their knowledge of soft power to negotiate terms that align China's soft power aspirations with their own development goals by insisting on the continued involvement and benefit of local communities.

In addition, African governments can strengthen their bargaining positions through the use of soft power strategies of their own design. Africa's cultural wealth and human resources might be used to establish ties with many segments of Chinese society, raising the continent's profile in the eyes of the Chinese people and government.

7.2. For Chinese Policymakers

Chinese policymakers need a nuanced approach beyond economic investments or diplomatic treaties to successfully navigate the complex domain of African politics, particularly the complexities of coalition administrations. Coalition politics, in which different parties or factions come together to create a government, further complicate Africa's political environment. Given this reality, adopting a cookie-cutter approach to ensuring China's long-term interests on the continent is unlikely to be fruitful, and may even backfire.

Coalition administrations are notoriously unstable, so it's important to keep that in mind while forming long-term alliances. Different, even diametrically opposed, interests and ideologies are often brought together in these coalitions. If these differences aren't taken into account, China's diplomatic and economic endeavors could be jeopardized because a policy supported by one group in a coalition administration could be opposed to or even overturned by another. This means that Chinese policymakers must take a more pluralistic approach that recognizes the intricacies of coalition governments in order to effectively work with them.

In this respect, the idea of soft power can be an effective strategy. While economic investments and infrastructural projects have their benefits, they are insufficient to establish the robust relationships that may be achieved through soft power. Exchanges in the fields of culture and education, for instance, can have a significant effect on public opinion and make diplomatic negotiations simpler. Moreover, such projects can find support within a wider range of the coalition government, creating a more solid foundation for long-term collaboration.

Chinese policymakers can benefit from an understanding of the nuances of coalition politics in order to foresee potential difficulties brought on by political upheavals in African nations. Coalition governments have the potential to be unstable due to the frequent realignment or even total reform that may occur inside them. China's diplomatic and economic contacts in Africa will be more stable across the political tides if the country has a deep and nuanced awareness of the coalitions inside the continent.

8. CONCLUSION

The forces that affect and shape today's complex international scene are examined in this chapter, and some light is shown on the intriguing interplay between China's soft power diplomacy and the delicate domain of coalition politics in Africa. The truth is much more nuanced than the simplistic idea that each thread — whether soft power programs or political coalitions — operates independently. There are possibilities and threats for all parties involved because of the ways in which these fields overlap, clash, and sometimes synergize.

China's ascension to global superpower status has prompted the country to take a more sophisticated approach to foreign policy, especially in volatile regions like Africa and the Middle East. By embracing soft power as a diplomatic instrument, countries are acknowledging that there are other factors besides economic and military strength that contribute to their influence. It draws on the social and intellectual foundations of countries to support more material kinds of interaction such as trade deals and building projects. However, there is no assurance that these soft power initiatives would be successful. The political climate in each country plays a significant role, as does the nature of the coalitions that exist inside those governments.

The continent of Africa is at a turning point. The continent is attracting more and more interest not only because of its abundant natural resources, but also because of its rapidly developing human capital and rising geopolitical relevance. The need for coalition governments to govern varied and sometimes fractured societies brings with it both opportunity and danger. They have the potential to serve as hubs for inclusive governance or as dangerous flashpoints. The way these alliances engage with major countries like China can have far-reaching consequences for national progress, regional peace, and international politics.

The policy suggestions in this chapter are meant to help bring about a more equal partnership between African and Chinese parties. The asymmetry that is often evident in contacts with global powers can be mitigated if African countries make use of their knowledge of soft power dynamics. Chinese policymakers, if they want to maintain meaningful and mutually beneficial ties, must learn to understand the intricate interplay of interests among African coalition governments.

There is little space for error and big stakes. In light of China's ongoing global engagement and Africa's efforts to improve its own system of sustainable development and governance, this comparative analysis couldn't be more pertinent. Soft power diplomacy and coalition politics are complex and nuanced, and both sides would do well to take this into account. Such nuance is necessary if they are to establish connections that are transformational rather than merely transactional, serving the interests of all stakeholders both now and in the future.

REFERENCES

Abelson, D. E. (2018). *Do think tanks matter? Assessing the impact of public policy institutes*. McGill-Queen's Press-MQUP. doi:10.1515/9780773553859

Aronczyk, M. (2013). *Branding the nation: The global business of national identity*. Oxford University Press. doi:10.1093/acprof:oso/9780199752164.001.0001

Barton, B. (2022). *The Doraleh Disputes: Infrastructure Politics in the Global South*. Springer Nature.

Basu, P., & Janiec, M. (2021). Kenya's regional ambitions or China's Belt-and-Road? News media representations of the Mombasa-Nairobi Standard Gauge Railway. *Singapore Journal of Tropical Geography*, *42*(1), 45–64. doi:10.1111/sjtg.12350

Beck, U., & Grande, E. (2010). Varieties of second modernity: The cosmopolitan turn in social and political theory and research. *The British Journal of Sociology*, *61*(3), 409–443. doi:10.1111/j.1468-4446.2010.01320.x PMID:20857607

Blas, J., & Farchy, J. (2021). *The world for sale: money, power, and the traders who barter the earth's resources*. Oxford University Press.

Borzutzky, S. (2019). You win some, you lose some: Pension reform in Bachelet's first and second administrations. *Journal of Politics in Latin America*, *11*(2), 204–230. doi:10.1177/1866802X19861491

Brautigam, D. (2011). *The dragon's gift: the real story of China in Africa*. Oxford University Press.

Brazys, S., & Dukalskis, A. (2019). Rising powers and grassroots image management: Confucius Institutes and China in the media. *The Chinese Journal of International Politics*, *12*(4), 557–584. doi:10.1093/cjip/poz012

Bunte, J. B. (2019). *Raise the debt: How developing countries choose their creditors*. Oxford University Press. doi:10.1093/oso/9780190866167.001.0001

Calthorpe, P. (2015). Urbanism in the age of climate change. In *The city reader* (pp. 555–568). Routledge.

Carbone, M. (2014). The European Union and China's rise in Africa: Competing visions, external coherence and trilateral cooperation. In *China's Rise in Africa* (pp. 75–93). Routledge.

Carmody, P. R., & Murphy, J. T. (2022). Chinese neoglobalization in East Africa: Logics, couplings and impacts. *Space and Polity*, *26*(1), 20–43. doi:10.1080/13562576.2022.2104631

Cheeseman, N., & Larmer, M. (2015). Ethnopopulism in Africa: Opposition mobilization in diverse and unequal societies. *Democratization*, *22*(1), 22–50. doi:10.1080/13510347.2013.809065

Cheibub, J. A. (2007). *Presidentialism, parliamentarism, and democracy*. Cambridge University Press.

Chipaike, R., & Bischoff, P. H. (2019). Chinese engagement of Zimbabwe and the limits of elite agency. *Journal of Asian and African Studies*, *54*(7), 947–964. doi:10.1177/0021909619848783

Chiyemura, F., Gambino, E., & Zajontz, T. (2023). Infrastructure and the politics of African state agency: Shaping the Belt and Road Initiative in East Africa. *Chinese Political Science Review*, *8*(1), 105–131. doi:10.1007/s41111-022-00214-8

Clayton, A., O'Brien, D. Z., & Piscopo, J. M. (2019). All male panels? Representation and democratic legitimacy. *American Journal of Political Science*, *63*(1), 113–129. doi:10.1111/ajps.12391

Collins, P. H., & Bilge, S. (2020). *Intersectionality*. John Wiley & Sons.

Cornago, N. (1999). Diplomacy and paradiplomacy in the redefinition of international security: Dimensions of conflict and co-operation. *Regional & Federal Studies*, *9*(1), 40–57. doi:10.1080/13597569908421070

De Mente, B. L. (2011). *Chinese mind: Understanding traditional Chinese beliefs and their influence on contemporary culture*. Tuttle Publishing.

DeLisle, J. (2010). Soft power in a hard place: China, Taiwan, cross-strait relations and US policy. *Orbis*, *54*(4), 493–524. doi:10.1016/j.orbis.2010.07.002

Diamond, L., & Morlino, L. (2004). The quality of democracy: An overview. *Journal of Democracy*, *15*(4), 20–31. doi:10.1353/jod.2004.0060

Dodds, F., Donoghue, A. D., & Roesch, J. L. (2016). *Negotiating the sustainable development goals: a transformational agenda for an insecure world*. Taylor & Francis. doi:10.4324/9781315527093

Dreyer, J. T. (2018). *China's political system: Modernization and tradition*. Routledge. doi:10.4324/9781315144399

Ehizuelen, M. M. O., & Abdi, H. O. (2018). Sustaining China-Africa relations: Slotting Africa into China's one belt, one road initiative makes economic sense. *Asian Journal of Comparative Politics*, *3*(4), 285–310. doi:10.1177/2057891117727901

Falkner, R. (2016). The Paris Agreement and the new logic of international climate politics. *International Affairs*, *92*(5), 1107–1125. doi:10.1111/1468-2346.12708

Fearon, J. D. (2003). Ethnic and cultural diversity by country. *Journal of Economic Growth*, *8*(2), 195–222. doi:10.1023/A:1024419522867

Fulton, J. (2020). Situating Saudi Arabia in China's belt and road initiative. *Asian Politics & Policy*, *12*(3), 362–383. doi:10.1111/aspp.12549

Garlick, J. (2023). China's Hedged Economic Diplomacy in Saudi Arabia and Iran: A Strategy of Risk Mitigation. In *China's Engagement with the Islamic Nations: A Clash or Collaboration of Modern Civilisation?* (pp. 117–136). Springer Nature Switzerland. doi:10.1007/978-3-031-31042-3_7

Garver, J. W. (2015). *China's Quest: The History of the Foreign Relations of the People's Republic of China*. Oxford University Press.

Gilpin, R. G. (2016). *The political economy of international relations*. Princeton University Press.

Gobe, M. (2010). *Emotional branding: The new paradigm for connecting brands to people*. Simon and Schuster.

Govo, N., & Muguti, T. (2023). Constitutionalism and Leadership Renewal in the African National Congress: Lessons for Other African States. In *Military, Politics and Democratization in Southern Africa: The Quest for Political Transition* (pp. 209-231). Cham: Springer Nature Switzerland.

Grant, W. (2021). Pressure groups. In Politics UK (pp. 266-288). Routledge. doi:10.4324/9781003028574-18

Guthrie, D. (2012). *China and globalization: The social, economic, and political transformation of Chinese society*. Routledge. doi:10.4324/9780203121450

Hoh, A. (2019). China's belt and road initiative in Central Asia and the Middle East. *Domes*, *28*(2), 241–276. doi:10.1111/dome.12191

Hu, Z., & Ji, D. (2012). Ambiguities in communicating with the world: The "Going-out" policy of China's media and its multilayered contexts. *Chinese Journal of Communication*, *5*(1), 32–37. doi:10.1080/17544750.2011.647741

Ikenberry, G. J., Mastanduno, M., & Wohlforth, W. C. (2009). Unipolarity, state behavior, and systemic consequences. *World Politics*, *61*(1), 1–27. doi:10.1017/S004388710900001X

Jackson, R. J. (2013). *Global politics in the 21st century*. Cambridge University Press. doi:10.1017/CBO9781139015660

Jenkins-Smith, H. C., Nohrstedt, D., Weible, C. M., & Ingold, K. (2018). The advocacy coalition framework: An overview of the research program. *Theories of the Policy Process, 4*, 135-171.

Kalantzakos, S. (2017). *China and the geopolitics of rare earths*. Oxford University Press. doi:10.1093/oso/9780190670931.001.0001

Kamel, M. S. (2018). China's belt and road initiative: Implications for the Middle East. *Cambridge Review of International Affairs*, *31*(1), 76–95. doi:10.1080/09557571.2018.1480592

Lai, H., & Lu, Y. (Eds.). (2012). *China's soft power and international relations*. Routledge. doi:10.4324/9780203122099

Le Van, A. C. (2011). Power sharing and inclusive politics in Africa's uncertain democracies. *Governance: An International Journal of Policy, Administration and Institutions*, *24*(1), 31–53. doi:10.1111/j.1468-0491.2010.01514.x

Lee, S. T. (2021). Vaccine diplomacy: Nation branding and China's COVID-19 soft power play. *Place Branding and Public Diplomacy*, *19*(1), 64–78. doi:10.1057/s41254-021-00224-4

Lee, S. W. (2011). The theory and reality of soft power: Practical approaches in East Asia. In *Public diplomacy and soft power in East Asia* (pp. 11–32). Palgrave Macmillan US. doi:10.1057/9780230118447_2

Li, S. (2021). China's Confucius Institute in Africa: A different story? *International Journal of Comparative Education and Development*, *23*(4), 353–366. doi:10.1108/IJCED-02-2021-0014

Lowndes, V., & Pratchett, L. (2012). Local governance under the coalition government: Austerity, localism and the 'Big Society'. *Local Government Studies*, *38*(1), 21–40. doi:10.1080/03003930.2011.642949

Makundi, H., Huyse, H., Develtere, P., Mongula, B., & Rutashobya, L. (2017). Training abroad and technological capacity building: Analysing the role of Chinese training and scholarship programmes for Tanzanians. *International Journal of Educational Development*, *57*, 11–20. doi:10.1016/j.ijedudev.2017.08.012

Norris, P. (2012). *Making democratic governance work: How regimes shape prosperity, welfare, and peace*. Cambridge University Press. doi:10.1017/CBO9781139061902

Nye, J. S. Jr. (2008). Public diplomacy and soft power. *The Annals of the American Academy of Political and Social Science*, *616*(1), 94–109. doi:10.1177/0002716207311699

Nye, J. S. (2012). China and soft power. *South African Journal of International Affairs*, *19*(2), 151–155. doi:10.1080/10220461.2012.706889

Nye, J. S. (2021). Soft power: The evolution of a concept. *Journal of Political Power*, *14*(1), 196–208. doi:10.1080/2158379X.2021.1879572

Oriaifo, J., Torres de Oliveira, R., & Ellis, K. M. (2020). Going above and beyond: How intermediaries enhance change in emerging economy institutions to facilitate small to medium enterprise development. *Strategic Entrepreneurship Journal*, *14*(3), 501–531. doi:10.1002/sej.1349

Pan, S. Y., & Lo, J. T. Y. (2017). Re-conceptualizing China's rise as a global power: A neo-tributary perspective. *The Pacific Review*, *30*(1), 1–25. doi:10.1080/09512748.2015.1075578

Przybylski, W. (2018). Explaining eastern Europe: Can Poland's backsliding be stopped? *Journal of Democracy*, *29*(3), 52–64. doi:10.1353/jod.2018.0044

Regilme, S. S. F. Jr, & Hodzi, O. (2021). Comparing US and Chinese foreign aid in the era of rising powers. *The International Spectator*, *56*(2), 114–131. doi:10.1080/03932729.2020.1855904

Rolland, N. (2017). China's "Belt and Road Initiative": Underwhelming or game-changer? *The Washington Quarterly*, *40*(1), 127–142. doi:10.1080/0163660X.2017.1302743

Rukema, J. R. (2023). Last Kicks of a Dying Horse: The Waning Influence of France in Africa. *Journal of African Foreign Affairs*, *10*(2), 7–26. doi:10.31920/2056-5658/2023/v10n2a1

Salman, M., Pieper, M., & Geeraerts, G. (2015). Hedging in the Middle East and China-US Competition. *Asian Politics & Policy*, *7*(4), 575–596. doi:10.1111/aspp.12225

Scobell, A., & Nader, A. (2016). *China in the Middle East: the wary dragon*. RAND Corporation.

Shen, W. (2020). China's role in Africa's energy transition: A critical review of its intensity, institutions, and impacts. *Energy Research & Social Science*, *68*, 101578. doi:10.1016/j.erss.2020.101578

Thornber, K. L. (2016). Breaking Discipline, Integrating Literature: Africa–China Relationships Reconsidered. *Comparative Literature Studies*, *53*(4), 694–721. doi:10.5325/complitstudies.53.4.0694

Tinarwo, J., & Babu, S. C. (2023). Chinese and Indian economic relations and development assistance to Zimbabwe: Rationale, controversies and significance. *Journal of International Development*, *35*(4), 655–667. doi:10.1002/jid.3704

Voon, J. P., & Xu, X. (2020). Impact of the Belt and Road Initiative on China's soft power: Preliminary evidence. *Asia-Pacific Journal of Accounting & Economics*, *27*(1), 120–131. doi:10.1080/16081625.2020.1686841

Wang, X., Xu, W., & Guo, L. (2018). The status quo and ways of STEAM education promoting China's future social sustainable development. *Sustainability (Basel)*, *10*(12), 4417. doi:10.3390/su10124417

Woods, N. (2008). Whose aid? Whose influence? China, emerging donors and the silent revolution in development assistance. *International Affairs*, *84*(6), 1205–1221. doi:10.1111/j.1468-2346.2008.00765.x

Yang, R. (2010). Soft power and higher education: An examination of China's Confucius Institutes. *Globalisation, Societies and Education*, 8(2), 235–245. doi:10.1080/14767721003779746

Yellinek, R., Mann, Y., & Lebel, U. (2020). Chinese Soft-Power in the Arab world–China's Confucius Institutes as a central tool of influence. *Comparative Strategy*, 39(6), 517–534. doi:10.1080/01495933.2020.1826843

Yeung, H. W. C. (2017). Governing the market in a globalizing era: Developmental states, global production networks and inter-firm dynamics in East Asia. In *Global Value Chains and Global Production Networks* (pp. 70–101). Routledge.

Yu, H. (2020). Motivation behind China's 'One Belt, One Road'initiatives and establishment of the Asian infrastructure investment bank. In *China's New Global Strategy* (pp. 3–18). Routledge. doi:10.4324/9780429317002-2

Zhan, M. (2009). *Other-worldly: Making Chinese medicine through transnational frames*. Duke University Press.

Zhang, D. (2018). The concept of 'community of common destiny'in China's diplomacy: Meaning, motives and implications. *Asia & the Pacific Policy Studies*, 5(2), 196–207. doi:10.1002/app5.231

Zhu, Z. (2016). *China's new diplomacy: Rationale, strategies and significance*. Routledge. doi:10.4324/9781315260440

Zreik, M. (2019). China's Involvement in The Syrian Crisis and The Implications of Its Neutral Stance in The War. *RUDN. Journal of Political Science*, 21(1), 56–65.

Zreik, M. (2021a). China and Europe in Africa: Competition or Cooperation? *Malaysian Journal of International Relations, 9*(1), 51-67.

Zreik, M. (2021b). Academic Exchange Programs between China and the Arab Region: A Means of Cultural Harmony or Indirect Chinese Influence?*Arab Studies Quarterly, 43*(2), 172–188. doi:10.13169/arabstudquar.43.2.0172

Zreik, M. (2022). The Chinese presence in the Arab region: Lebanon at the heart of the Belt and Road Initiative. *International Journal of Business and Systems Research*, 16(5-6), 644–662. doi:10.1504/IJBSR.2022.125477

Zreik, M. (2023). Navigating the Dragon: China's Ascent as a Global Power Through Public Diplomacy. In S. Kavoğlu & E. Köksoy (Eds.), *Global Perspectives on the Emerging Trends in Public Diplomacy* (pp. 50–74). IGI Global. doi:10.4018/978-1-6684-9161-4.ch003

KEY TERMS AND DEFINITIONS

Asymmetry in Relations: An imbalance of power, influence, or resources between two parties in a relationship. This term is often used to describe relationships where one party, such as a country, has significantly more power or influence than the other.

Coalition Politics: The process by which multiple political parties or factions collaborate to form a government, often due to the inability of a single party to secure a majority of seats in the legislature. Coalition politics often involve compromise, negotiation, and a blending of different political platforms.

Comparative Analysis: A research methodology that involves the systematic comparison of different variables or cases to identify patterns, similarities, and differences. In this context, it refers to comparing China's strategies in Africa and the Middle East.

Cultural Exchange: The mutual sharing of cultural elements, such as art, language, and traditions, between different countries or societies. Cultural exchange often forms a crucial component of soft power diplomacy.

Democratic Governance: A system of government based on democratic principles, including citizen participation, rule of law, transparency, and accountability. Democratic governance may exist in various forms, such as direct democracy or representative democracy.

Geopolitical Significance: The strategic importance of a geographic area, often due to its location, natural resources, or influence over key international routes. In the context of this chapter, it refers to Africa's emerging role in global geopolitics.

Multipolar System: An international system characterized by multiple centers of power, rather than dominance by a single superpower or a bipolar division. In a multipolar system, influence is more diffuse, and relationships are often more complex.

Sino-African Relations: The diplomatic, economic, and cultural relationships between China and countries in Africa. This term encompasses a broad range of interactions, from trade and investment to diplomatic initiatives and cultural exchanges.

Soft Power Diplomacy: The use of attraction and persuasion rather than coercion or economic incentives to shape the preferences and behaviors of other actors in the international system. This includes cultural exchanges, educational initiatives, and public diplomacy.

Strategic Interests: Long-term goals or objectives that are important for the security, economic prosperity, or influence of a nation. Strategic interests guide policy decisions and diplomatic interactions.

Chapter 14
Navigating Coalition Dynamics in the City of Johannesburg:
A Lefortian Perspective on Political Power

Mpho Tladi

https://orcid.org/0000-0003-0474-7294

University of the Witwatersrand, South Africa

ABSTRACT

This chapter offers a theoretical analysis of coalition politics in South Africa, with a focus on the City of Johannesburg's Metropolitan Municipality. It uses Claude Lefort's political theories to examine the fluctuating dynamics of political power in the nation's coalition governments, particularly at the local government level. The chapter traces the emergence and instability of coalitions, highlighted by the African National Congress' (ANC) loss of majority and the subsequent power shifts in Johannesburg. These changes, including the formation of different coalition arrangements and the 2021 Local Government Elections' outcomes, reflect the unstable nature of coalitions in South Africa. The chapter aims to discuss the impacts of these coalitions on governance quality and service delivery, addressing the broader socio-political and economic challenges of the country. Two case studies, focusing on fiscal management and trust in Johannesburg's coalition government, will provide deeper insights into the practical implications of such political arrangements.

INTRODUCTION

In a nation where political alliances are in constant flux, prominent French political theorist Claude Lefort's theories on the shifting political power dynamics offer an intuitive lens through which to scrutinise South Africa's complex coalition politics. Coalition governments in South Africa have increasingly become a feature of the political landscape, particularly at the local government level. The emergence of such arrangements can be traced back to significant shifts in voter sentiment, which has resulted in the traditionally dominant political party, the African National Congress (ANC) losing its outright majority. For instance, the ANC experienced a loss of power for the very first time since the advent of South

DOI: 10.4018/979-8-3693-1654-2.ch014

Africa's democracy in the City[1] of Johannesburg Metropolitan Municipality in 2016. This event marked a historical moment when an informal coalition between the Democratic Alliance (DA) and the relative newcomer to the political scene, the Economic Freedom Fighters (EFF) took the reins of governance (Mawere et al, 2022).

BACKGROUND

Coalition governments in South Africa have often proved to be unstable. As witnessed in Johannesburg, the initial 2016 arrangement between the liberal democratic DA and socialist EFF fell apart. The 'voting arrangement' between the two opposition parties ended before the end of the political term of five years. This came because of Herman Mashaba's resignation as Mayor who was a DA member at the time. The reason for Mashaba's resignation as Mayor and as a DA member was because he felt that the DA had a problem with his approach and leadership style. Moreover, he felt that the party had disagreed with his implementation of EFF policies such as the insourcing of 7,000 workers (Mvumvu, 2019). Mashaba viewed this as a step towards promoting racial integration and addressing economic inequality in Johannesburg.

These events subsequently led to the ANC's return to power in 2019. This episode resulted in the formation of the Government of Local Unity (GLU), and this signified the first formal coalition structure in the city (Makhubo, 2020). Such experiences underline the fluctuating nature of coalitions, as political parties usually aim to complete their five-year term of office as prescribed by the Constitution of South Africa.

The dynamics of coalition governance were again assessed during the 2021 Local Government Elections (LGEs), which saw another power shift. The DA along with a few other political parties formed a new Multi-Party Government (MPG) which ousted the ANC, only to be subsequently replaced by the GLU (Madia, 2022). Throughout these changes, numerous motions of no confidence have been levelled against various mayors in the city, with the GLU managing to retain power. This ever-changing landscape of coalition governance in the city is seen also in other larger municipalities across South Africa such as the City of Ekurhuleni and the City of Tshwane (Mawere et al, 2022). This raises critical questions about the durability, efficacy, and democratic implications of such arrangements, this prevalence in tandem sets the stage for an in-depth examination in this chapter.

In the main, the chapter constitutes a theoretical analysis of the scholarly and non-scholarly theoretical positions on offer from a deep engagement with the literature in political theory within the broad domain of the South African political scene, with a primary focus on Johannesburg. The importance of such an undertaking cannot be overstated as shifting power dynamics have created a potent level of uncertainty within all spheres of life throughout the country. This is especially significant because in 2024 South Africa goes into its seventh general National and Provincial democratic elections (Khoza, 2023). The year also marks 30 years of democracy following apartheid colonialism and domination through white minority rule.

Let us consider how coalition politics in South Africa reflect the evolving socio-political dynamics inclusive of exacerbating economic challenges and a culture of general mistrust among political actors as well as the ordinary citizenry (Katzenellenbogen, 2023). While coalitions offer the potential for significant electoral gains and a more inclusive governance structure, they also bring about challenges in decision-making, owing to the need for negotiation among potential partners.

To elucidate this complexity, two brief examples will be considered. One is on the 'Financial Management and Governance in Johannesburg's Coalition Government,' and the other is on 'Navigating Trust in the Shadow of Coalition Politics in Johannesburg.' The first example is important because financial management is essential to governing municipalities. The second example is important because public trust is an indicator of good governance. Both examples offer deeper insight into the practical implications of coalition arrangements.

At the local government level, coalitions have had both a positive and negative impact; on the one hand, they reflect the diversifying political landscape and voter sentiments, but on the other, they have at times grossly affected governance quality, as seen in Johannesburg between 2016 and 2019 detailed above. The transformation that coalitions bring to the political landscape signifies a shift towards a more pluralistic political discourse, yet the stability and effectiveness of coalition governments remain critical for addressing South Africa's socio-economic challenges and ensuring a satisfactory quality of governance and service delivery.

METHODOLOGY

Integrating Burawoy's Extended Case Method

Drawing from Michael Burawoy, his extended case method acts as a bridge between theory and empirical research to guide the problematisation of Johannesburg's political system, and to find solutions to the challenges coalitions have brought. Burawoy's approach is useful in its overall assertion, describing theories as maps that help us make sense of the world. In addition, it argues that rather than being distant observers, researchers using the extended case method (through its reflexive model) are engaged and involved in the world they study. Johannesburg's political landscape thus serves as the empirical component of that 'world of study' and research area for this project.

A useful alternative to Burawoy includes Norman Fairclough's (2001) Critical Discourse Theory which focuses on how language is used to construct meaning and power. It could assist in analysing the narratives and rhetoric used by different political parties within coalitions. However, it is limited in the sense that the researcher remains an observer who uses data and information to reach a conclusion. Whereas Burawoy's approach allows the researcher to be an active participant in not only knowledge gathering but also knowledge generation within the field.

This enquiry is anchored in situating Lefort's conceptualisation of power within the intricacies of coalition politics in Johannesburg. However, it is also necessary to mention here that the author is a research practitioner specialising in strategy and planning within the City of Johannesburg, who actively engages with the political complexities of the metro. The author's dual role as a researcher in strategy and planning for the city lends a distinctive vantage point that is both deeply embedded in the 'world of study' and reflexively in line with the theoretical frameworks that guide this analysis. On the one hand, this nexus of theoretical engagement and practical involvement provides a unique lens through which to examine the 'empty place of power' and its manifestation in the governance of Johannesburg. On the other hand, this dual role may lead to potential biases, as professional commitments and preconceived notions could colour the analysis.

The author addresses the issue of bias by adopting a multifaceted approach, particularly suitable given its theoretical focus. This is done by incorporating a variety of materials, including academic literature, media reports, public records, and data from both governmental and non-governmental organisations outside the Johannesburg Municipality framework. These additional sources offer a broader context, revealing insights and issues not apparent in the official narratives.

Additionally, the author makes use of case studies from different contexts to highlight similar challenges or policy initiatives that cut across the discussion on coalitions. This comparative analysis provides valuable insights into the effectiveness of different approaches, enriching the theoretical understanding of the subject.

Burawoy's framework further posits theory as a valuable tool in understanding dynamic social contexts. More importantly, it also makes theory an object of inquiry in its own right. The approach to the questions addressed in this study is anchored in Lefort's notion of the 'empty place of power.' By critically assessing his theory, the intention is to evaluate how well it fits within the context of the politics of Johannesburg.

The City of Johannesburg's political system is underpinned by the fact that every five years South Africa enters its Municipal or Local Government Elections (LGEs). Therefore, the measure of the quality in the social, economic, and political instances within Johannesburg is centered on the level at which the local electorate can appreciate the concept of modern democracy as expressed at the local government level. In other words, the level at which the people of Johannesburg get to publicly decide whom they would like to see temporarily occupying the place of power in the City to ensure better lives for themselves.

The notion of political life focuses not only on the institutions or formal modes of governing but also on the meaningful involvement of Johannesburg's residents through participatory governing. This includes the various institutions within all instances of society under the umbrella of a modern democratic government. Intricately linked to these factors is the important consideration of who it is that speaks in the name of the people who in this instance are the Johannesburg residents i.e., their local electoral representation.

Lefort's Theory of Power and Thought in Johannesburg's Political System

To explain the relationship between local government coalition dynamics characterised by profound uncertainty within a modern democracy, this chapter engages with political theory to gain deeper insights. Particularly, Lefort's seminal work on his theory of the 'empty place of power'- the idea that power is indeterminate and therefore always contestable (Lefort, 1988). This approach gives valuable perspectives that can aid in understanding the omnipotent contestation and struggle for control and political power that has come to define South Africa's political landscape, particularly in post-2016 when the ANC lost majority control over major municipalities including the City of Johannesburg.

For Lefort, the continual process of differentiation is articulated as the empty place of power in that it removes the permanence of power through the 'dissolution of the markers of certitude' which means the undermining or fading away of established signs of certainty or stability and the destruction of the 'body of the king' which represents the dismantling or disruption of traditional symbols of authority and monarchy (Lefort, 1988). Understood also as a process of interrogation, 'the place' is the terrain of contestation of power which is always present (Marchart, 2007). As such 'the locus of power becomes *an empty place*' (Lefort, 1988, p. 17).

Put differently, Lefort (1986) contends that democracy embodies a contradictory nature, wherein the place of power is 'empty', as power perpetually shifts hands through electoral processes. In Lefort's view, this 'place' of power is not held by any individual or group; rather, it persists as a realm of ongoing contestation and negotiation among various political actors.

We trace Lefort's understanding of power from his analysis which posits that traditionally, power was captured in a single individual, often termed 'the prince' (or king), signifying a centralisation of authority within a society, with the prince embodying this authority (Marchart, 2007). This model of centralised or 'closed' power coordinated societal structure around monarchy through the prince, who emerged as the site that conferred the form and order of society.

In contrast, within a democracy, this consolidation of power in a singular entity is subjected to perpetual disruption (Lefort, 1986). Rather than being anchored in a sole authoritative figure, the place of power is vacated to facilitate shared governance through publicly elected representatives. This disruption of a concentrated power centre to a more dispersed public arrangement overturns the conventional model of power being in the body of the prince or monarch. As such this symbolises a shift towards a more democratic, participatory structure of governance.

As with any other theory, the important disclaimer that should be stated is that it should not be assumed the idea of the 'empty place of power' fully resonates with South African politics. This is why when critiquing Lefort the chapter examines aspects of Johannesburg's political landscape that are in alignment with Lefort's theoretical framework, and conversely, those that diverge from it—all the while seeking other technical and theoretical mechanisms in the form of arguments by political theorists that may assist in making Lefort more politically sound for the position this chapter takes.

Core Question

· To what extent does Lefort's theory of the 'empty place of power' offer explanatory value in understanding the dynamics of political competition and governance in Johannesburg?

The questions that follow are presented here as sub-questions which will guide how the chapter responds to the core question above:

Insight from a Lefortian Lens

What aspects of Johannesburg's political competition and governance dynamics give the most insight from Lefort's theory of the 'empty place of power'?

Historical Power Shifts

How do the historical shifts in power, particularly the loss of control by the ANC in 2016, relate to Lefort's conceptual framework of the 'empty place of power'?

Electoral Processes and Power Dynamics

In applying Lefort's theory to the Johannesburg context, what insights emerge regarding the role of electoral processes in shaping the dynamics of political power and governance?

Hypothesis

An appreciation and deeper understanding of Lefort's theory of the 'empty place of power' will provide a nuanced understanding of the dynamics of political competition and governance in Johannesburg, particularly shedding light on the implications of coalition politics and electoral shifts since 2016.

This chapter delves into the intricate dynamics of coalition politics within Johannesburg's local government space through a theoretical lens, specifically using Lefort's conceptual framework of the 'empty place of power.' This chapter brings a nuanced theoretical understanding to the overarching discourse of the book on coalitions. The chapter bridges the theoretical discourse with the practical political shifts and coalition dynamics experienced in the local government landscape i.e., the City of Johannesburg Metropolitan Municipality, enriching the book's broader exploration of coalitions. Furthermore, it gauges whether coalition governments consolidate or undermine electoral democracy using the site of metropolitan local government as the strategic context.

By navigating the murky political landscape of Johannesburg through a Lefortian lens, the chapter extends a well-rounded analysis that articulates both theoretical and empirical dimensions of coalition politics. This approach aligns with the book's objective of providing a comprehensive exploration of coalitions, augmenting the discourse with a blend of theoretical and contextual analysis that extends beyond the conventional narratives. Through investigating the microcosm of Johannesburg's political landscape, the chapter offers valuable insights that resonate with the wider thematic discussions of the book, thereby enhancing the overall understanding of theoretical discourses underpinning coalition politics and coalition governments.

A Snapshot of the Johannesburg Metropolitan Hub

At the time of writing, the City of Johannesburg boasted a population of 4.8 million residents (Stats SA, 2022). With a growth rate of about 0.8% every ten years. Around 871 485 persons aged between 5-24 years in school attendance in the city (ibid). Established in the year 1886, the city marks 137 years of its existence, distinguishing itself as one of the youngest major cities on the global stage. Notably, it is unique in its inception, being the singular major city not situated on a significant waterway such as a bay or a vast river (City of Johannesburg, 2023).

Throughout its relatively short but dynamic history, Johannesburg has undergone a series of transformations, having been reconstructed on four distinct occasions. Initially emerging as a rudimentary tented encampment to serve the gold mining industry, the city has since transitioned through a phase of tin shanties (ibid). It further developed into an area characterized by four-storey buildings of Edwardian architectural design, culminating in the contemporary skyline dominated by modern high-rise structures.

Encompassing an area of approximately 1,645 square kilometres, with the greater metropolitan region extending to about 2,300 square kilometres, Johannesburg's geographical footprint is greater than that of internationally recognized cities such as Sydney, London, and New York, aligning more closely in scale with the expansive reach of Los Angeles. The metropolis is colloquially referred to as *Egoli*, translated from Zulu to mean 'place of gold,' a nickname that reflects its historical and economic roots (ibid). Indeed, the Witwatersrand, the gold-bearing reef on which the city is founded, is the site where an estimated 40% of the world's gold has been extracted (ibid).

Johannesburg's Political and Economic Significance: Understanding Democratic Contestation

The information detailing Johannesburg's profile above depicts the contextual foundation for this chapter, and it covers the elements that make such a city a site for intense and ongoing political contestation. Johannesburg's history as a city founded on wealth (gold) and its rapid development arguably influences its political, social, and economic structures. As such the city occupies a significant position as the centre of economic enterprise not only in South Africa but also in the entire African continent (Smith, 2020). This prominent position has given a considerable amount of attention from various scholars and analysts, who have mainly characterised Johannesburg as a microcosm of South Africa (Harrison, 2018).

While it is crucial to consider this statement with subtlety, Johannesburg's distinct economic characteristics, especially in terms of income disparity, urban restructuring, and availability of fundamental amenities, position it as a key site for grasping the complex interplay of political forces in South Africa. This perspective is reinforced by studies that go on to emphasize the city's role in mirroring wider sociopolitical trends across the nation (Turok 2017; Leach & Mkhize, 2019).

This chapter intends to delve deeper into this narrative, examining how Johannesburg's diverse social composition and its responses within coalition governance structures to shifting economic and political landscapes provide essential insights into democracy. Additionally, at a broader level, it looks at how these factors influence South Africa's current challenges and opportunities. This exploration contributes to a more comprehensive understanding of the country's intricate dynamics zooming in on a metropolitan space.

FINDINGS AND ANALYSIS

Conceptual Framework: Coalition Frameworks and Lefort's Take on Power

To contextualize the discussion, it is important to define the term 'coalition.' As elucidated by Jaygopal Biswas (2019), the term originates from the Medieval Latin *coalitio*, and from the Latin *coalescere*, meaning to come together or unite. A coalition government forms when two or more political parties collaborate to establish a governing body, often necessitated when no single party gains enough majority to govern independently. As Makhubo (2020) and Biswas point out, these coalitions represent a union of diverse groups uniting under a shared program for collective action and are common in places with dynamic political environments like India.

Moshodi (2018) builds on this by referring to various scholarly works. Ka-Daylan (2017) views a coalition as a practical alliance between political parties, formed to establish a majority within the government—a perspective supported by Rose (1974), who highlights the role of coalitions in consolidating governance power. Moshodi also notes that opposition parties often form coalitions to challenge the dominance of incumbent parties, as indicated by Matlosa (2008). This phenomenon is not limited to smaller parties; in countries like Britain, even major parties such as the Conservatives and Labour function as coalitions, representing a spectrum of viewpoints.

Further, Amutabi and Nasong'o (2013) argue that coalitions can empower opposition parties, especially in dominant-party systems, by amalgamating diverse political forces. However, challenges arise in aligning different political interests and policy views.

Turning to the South African metropolitan context, particularly in major cities like Johannesburg, Tshwane, and Ekurhuleni, the usefulness of these definitions comes into question (Knowles 2021, Makgale 2020, Mpangalasane 2020, Ndou 2022). South Africa's multiparty landscape, with its varied interests and ideologies, is a prime setting for coalition politics. The theoretical frameworks provided by Biswas and Moshodi highlight coalitions as entities formed from necessity in the absence of a majority. Yet, in South Africa, coalitions often represent more than just a pragmatic convergence for majority rule. They embody complex negotiations of power, where parties with different agendas and regional priorities must cooperate (MISTRA, 2021). This calls for an in-depth understanding of the intricate balance between shared objectives and the competing political, social, economic, and ideological interests unique to South African metros.

Lefort presents a distinctive viewpoint on the struggle for dominance in these three key areas, particularly: political, social, and economic. His theory of the 'empty place of power' is based on the concept of a comprehensive social structure, which he views as inherently symbolic (Flynn, 2005). To fully grasp Lefort's ideas, it is essential first to understand his interpretation of the symbolic. Only then can we appreciate how he perceives power as occupying an 'empty place.' With this foundation, we can explore how his concepts unify the political, social, and economic realms.

Interpreting Symbolic Frameworks in Society

To examine how democratic principles are exemplified within an urban metropolitan context, insights from theorists Bernard Flynn (2005) and Oliver Marchart (2007) are drawn upon, interpreting Lefort's ideas within the framework of societal evolution—from pre-democratic to democratic, and then to totalitarian regimes. Lefort views power as fundamentally political, forming the cornerstone that binds together all societal forms, irrespective of their chosen structure (Lefort, 2005). This perspective is crucial in understanding the transitions between different societal forms.

Delving deeper into Lefort's theory, Flynn and Marchart bring in the symbolic realm, referring to Ferdinand de Saussure's (1974) seminal work in linguistics. Saussure's concepts of 'signifiers' and 'signifieds,' or the 'signifying dyad,' are instrumental in understanding the arbitrary nature of symbolic relationships. This idea is important to Lefort's analysis of power within a democratic context, focusing on the arbitrary relationship between symbols or ideas (Hudson, 2019).

In Lefort's view, the symbolic realm is self generated or 'sui generis,' which means that it functions autonomously without dependence on external foundations. Its structure is like a linguistic system, which consists of a network of signifiers that are inherently defined, and unrelated though to any transcendental entities or material realities. The essence of this language system is illustrated by the analogy of the identification of colours within the colour spectrum, where the significance of each colour arises from its relationship and differentiation from others (Saussure, 1974). For example, 'brown' only gains meaning when contrasted with other colours, emphasizing the relational nature of meaning.

Lefort applies this relational logic to the societal structure, arguing that society is a symbolic construction where meanings and relations are constantly evolving (Lefort, 1986). He uses this framework to highlight the inherent fluidity in societal organization, evidenced by historical shifts from pre-democratic to democratic and totalitarian forms (Marchart, 2007). This perspective suggests that society is dynamic, always in a state of being deconstructed and reconstructed.

For Lefort, the division of society into subsystems such as the political, social, and economic, and the constant restructuring thereof is not merely an administrative function but one that also carries significant political weight (Lefort, 1988). This viewpoint highlights the political implications of how society is organised, and governed, and how power is distributed and executed (Marchart, 2007).

The Political Philosophy Behind the Empty Place of Power

From a broad perspective, Lefort's view on the concept of 'thought' is seen as a continuous process of inquiry, without any fixed foundations. This perspective is also understood as the 'realm of the uncertain' (Marchart, 2007). He argues that constructing final definitions and concepts from an interrogation process is impossible, as interrogation is always about constant questioning. Lefort understands that the absence of a foundation is the only true foundation. His understanding of the continuous process of inquiry and the absence of fixed foundations challenges traditional notions of knowledge and truth. In his view, knowledge and truth are not fixed entities to be discovered or defined, but instead, they emerge through an ongoing process of questioning and reflection (Lefort, 1986). This perspective has significant implications for a study on democracy and political power.

This approach challenges the idea that there is a definitive, objective truth or knowledge that can be used as a basis for governing a society (Flynn, 2005). Instead, Lefort's perspective suggests that democracy should be understood as a continuous process of inquiry and dialogue, where multiple perspectives and voices are valued. Coming from the political, he defines this process as the 'proper field of interrogation' (Lefort, 1988). This perspective regarding the concepts of knowledge and truth also challenges the notion that political power should be concentrated in the hands of the few who claim to possess the ultimate truth or knowledge.

As such, Lefort's type of thinking is about people always being able to ask political questions, not only those which revolve around material or sustenance but also their physiological existence (Lefort, 1988). In referring to an idea by Marchart's take on Lefort, elsewhere the author writes that:

The political dimension therefore always opens up the boundaries of every particular social domain, and it operates on the logic of inquiry into the origin of the principle of differentiation between social spheres (or social systems) in modernity. (Tladi, 2020).

To explain the significance of reviving political philosophy, which is also partly the reason for his ideas around power, Lefort remarks that:

For the sole motivation behind political philosophy has always been a desire to escape the servitude of collective beliefs and to win the freedom to think about freedom in society; it has always borne in mind the essential difference between the regime of freedom and despotism, or indeed tyranny. (Lefort, 1988, p. 9)

At its core then, the philosophy of the 'empty place of power' is based on recognising what he motions as, the political being the proper field of interrogation, which is about opening the space for debating which forms of society would best suit a particular community. It is observed from the quote above, as well, that Lefort is comparing freedom or democracy with its opposite which is some form of tyranny. The latter gives the impression that despotism is not possible under democratic conditions.

Lefort acknowledges a critical viewpoint within democratic societies: they are often imperfect, tending to crystallize into a singular, unyielding form. This tendency, he notes, runs counter to his philosophy of the 'empty place of power.' This concept recalls Tocqueville's idea of the 'tyranny of the majority,' where the dominant group's interests and values overshadow and suppress those of the minority (Lefort, 1988). However, Lefort counters this by emphasizing the fundamental appreciation of the conditions that foster a democratic society. According to Lefort (1988), understanding and valuing these underlying conditions is key to grasping what he describes as the 'ontological premise' of the social structure. In his view, this premise underpins the very essence and credibility of democratic governance.

Lefort, further interpreting Tocqueville, explores the nuanced relationship between individual subjects and the collective entity of society in a democratic setting. Central to this discussion is the concept of 'escaping servitude' (ibid, p. 1), which, as Lefort describes, involves distancing oneself not from public opinion, but from the confines of political philosophy as conventionally understood. This 'escape' signifies a profound desire to break free from the shackles of collective beliefs, allowing the freedom to think independently about freedom in society. Lefort emphasizes that political philosophy, in its truest form, is driven by the aspiration to discern and appreciate the fundamental difference between a regime of freedom and forms of despotism or tyranny (Lefort, 1986).

In this light, he encourages a perspective shift from viewing society as an abstract concept or as separate from its individuals. Instead, he advocates for recognizing a shared identity of 'the people'—a collective composed of unique individuals. This collective is not a homogenous entity but a diverse consolidation of subjective experiences and viewpoints, each contributing to and shaping the democratic experience (Lefort, 1988). Such an approach contrasts with traditional, more abstract views of society, highlighting the dynamic interplay of individual identities within the democratic process. 'The people,' thus, emerge not just as a theoretical construct but as a living embodiment of democracy, where freedom is continually redefined and enriched through the diverse contributions of its members.

At the heart of this argument is the idea that individuals within a democracy are not lost in the collective identity of 'the people;' they do not become mere parts of a larger machine. Instead, they remain conscious and appreciative of their individuality, understanding that it is their collective actions and decisions that shape societal norms, values, and structures (Lefort, 1986). This collective shaping of society does not strip them of their individual freedoms; rather, it is the mechanism through which they exercise their freedoms. By participating in society as 'the people,' they create and modify the societal landscape, reflecting both their collective will and their individual choices.

In foregrounding his understanding of the 'empty place of power' political theorist Saul Newman gives his account of the concept of power by first referring to, and then critiquing Michel Foucault's configuration of the idea of power. He does this as a way of building up to introduce Lefort's understanding as an alternative. Newman argues that for Foucault power is not something that individuals or groups possess, but rather it is a network of relationships that are encompassing in society (Newman, 2004). According to him, Foucault's perspective shifts from the notion of power being confined to a particular location or controlled by a specific entity. Instead, it implies that power is omnipresent and manifested through social interactions and conventions.

However, Newman is useful here because of his modification of Foucault's relational idea of power to frame it more like the concept of the 'place' of power. He argues that traditional political theory often depicted power as coming from a central and symbolic place. In referencing Thomas Hobbes, for instance, he says Hobbs envisioned power as 'centered in the political body of the sovereign, whose temporal authority was preferred to the 'rapine savagery' of war' (ibid, p. 140).

As with Lefort's destruction of the body of the prince, Foucault's perspective has significantly influenced how we understand power in his articulation of the 'decapitation' of the idea of a central, sovereign figure that wields power—a figure that has been the cornerstone of political theory for centuries. Newman argues that decentralisation presents a significant challenge to conventional radical politics because it undermines the traditional dichotomy of oppressor and oppressed (Newman, 2004).

In summary, according to Lefort, the place of power is perpetually in flux and subject to multiple interpretations. This is because 'the political revolution aimed at seizing or overthrowing power in society is the logical counterpart to the centrality of power in society' (ibid). Power itself does not disappear; it is rather the 'place' that becomes vacant, but at the same time this 'place' continues to function as an operative dimension. According to Marchart (2007), Lefort's understanding is that society lacks a firm foundation, with the 'empty place' of power symbolising this unstable base. In a democracy, power is understood as a site that, although it might not be persistently occupied (its intrinsic essence may fade), is consistently subject to being cleared out (ibid).

Lefort maintains that the philosophy of political thought rests on the continuous process of interrogation. Marchart expands on this, showing that Lefort's ideas on the political and politics do not establish concrete foundations but rather highlight the absence of a constitutive foundation for reasoning and action. In other words, the political as well as politics open what Lefort calls an indeterminate field for interrogation (Marchart, 2007). This indeterminate field, as he explains further later in the chapter, is what constitutes the 'empty place of power.' Finally, according to Lefort, the political instance is the most critical area for investigation as it is necessary to continually question what goes beyond the boundaries of any given social instance. In other words, this ongoing investigation and expansion is what he sees as the essence of the political.

Electoral Processes and the Dynamics of Power in Modern Democracy

Elections represent a unique dynamic in the realm of power and society. They are a fundamental feature of democracy which constitutes the idea of an indeterminate field. Elections present the moment where the 'universal' – a concept encompassing the collective societal will – is temporarily filled by something more specific, like a political party or leader (Hudson, 2015). This 'particular'[2] claims its dominance under the guise of social cohesion, but it is not truly universal. It merely occupies the place meant for the universal, temporarily.

In the context of modernity, elections symbolize the liberation of the individual. Each person is reduced to a mere number – a vote. Collectively, these votes transform the populace into a 'real' entity, shaped and defined through everyday discourse. Marchart suggests that a society can only exist by defining itself against an 'other' – creating a sense of identity through difference (Marchart, 2007).

Electoral processes are a critical intersection in a society's life, acting as a 'vanishing mediator' – which means the moment when power is suspended temporarily, from disincarnation to incarnation (Hudson, 2015). In this period, power hangs in the balance as society transitions from indecision to decision, from a state of potential to one of actualisation. Here, the particular assumes the role of the universal. However, this process is inherently limited. The universal cannot fully and equally represent every particular. Modern power dynamics, especially in democracies, are shaped by this cycle of elections. No single party or leader has the right to permanently hold the position of the universal.

Lefort describes modernity as an experience of the indefinite, a constant grappling with uncertainty and the unknown. This is mirrored in the unpredictable nature of election outcomes, which are central to important societal decisions (Lefort, 1988). Elections embody the indefinite nature of power in modern democracies. They demonstrate the system's legitimacy: the idea that no one permanently controls power. While elections are a set process, their outcomes are never certain. The fluidity and changeability of election results are vital to the social structure of democracy. This constant state of flux and contestation ensures that power remains a circulating force, never settling permanently in one place.

Detailed Recent Political History of Johannesburg

The 2016 LGEs marked a fundamental moment in Johannesburg's multiparty political landscape. The ANC, which had been the predominant force in the city's politics since the end of apartheid, lost its majority in the City Council. This event highlighted the inherent volatility in multiparty systems as described by Booysen, where power dynamics are subject to continuous change (MISTRA, 2021). The DA seized this opportunity to form a minority coalition government, a clear example of the fluid and adaptive nature of coalitions in such systems. This coalition, notably including smaller parties like the EFF, represented a significant shift from the ANC's longstanding dominance. On the one hand this change embodies Booysen's observations on the flexible alliances within multiparty politics (ibid). On the other hand, this flexibility speaks to Lefort's ideas on openness and the embracing of various possibilities within the political dimension.

The ANC's dominance was attributed mainly to the struggle against apartheid, during which it emerged as the primary vehicle for anti-apartheid activism and resistance. However, its dominance in Johannesburg politics began to decrease in the face of mounting dissatisfaction and disillusionment among voters. Issues such as corruption, service delivery failures, and internal factionalism eroded public trust in the ANC-led government, leading to a gradual erosion of its electoral support base (Besseling, 2016).

By the 2021 LGEs, the political configuration of Johannesburg had transformed again, showing Booysen's insight into the evolving nature of coalition dynamics. The DA, strengthened by its coalition partners, managed to further consolidate its influence, effectively replacing the ANC to establish a new MPG (ibid). This change reflected the continuous flux in power balances that characterises multiparty systems. However, the political narrative of Johannesburg continued to evolve, with the MPG soon being ousted and replaced by the GLU, indicating another significant shift in the coalition landscape.

During these shifts, Johannesburg's leadership faced challenges, including several motions of no confidence, highlighting the competitive and unstable nature of multiparty governance as described by Booysen. Despite these challenges, the GLU emerged as the predominant coalition (see Table 1 below)[3], navigating through the intricate and ever-shifting dynamics of Johannesburg's political landscape, a real-world manifestation of Booysen's analysis of coalition politics in multiparty systems.

Table 1. Mayoral succession in the City of Johannesburg, detailing the terms of office, political affiliations, and reasons for changes in mayoral leadership

Name	Term of office		Political party	Reason for Change
Herman Mashaba	**2016**	**2019**	**Democratic Alliance**	**Motion of No Confidence**
Geoff Makhubo	2019	2021	African National Congress	Untimely Passing of Mayor
Jolidee Matongo	2021	2021	African National Congress	Untimely Passing of Mayor
Mpho Moerane	2021	2021	African National Congress	Untimely Passing of Mayor
Mpho Phalatse	2021	2022	Democratic Alliance	Elections
Dada Morero	2022	2022	African National Congress	Motion of No Confidence
Mpho Phalatse	2022	2023	Democratic Alliance	Motion of No Confidence
Thapelo Amad	2023	2023	Al Jama-ah	Resignation
Kabelo Gwamanda	2023	present	Al Jama-ah	

Source: Author's own analysis

Challenges in the city that are related to coalition governing have in many instances been the result of a lack of cooperation, the struggle to secure political power and the instability in key political positions by the different political parties. This has often not been a result of ideological differences as the manifestos of the different parties are similar. However, the coalition agreements break down due to failures to stick to terms agreed upon before assuming office. These agreements often have to do with representation in the constitution of the Mayor and Members of the Mayoral Committee and various other political and administrative positions.

Table 2[4] below shows the political parties that constitute two of the main coalitions in the City of Johannesburg:

Table 2. Coalition formations in the city of Johannesburg

Government of Local Unity		Multi-Party Government	
Political Party	**Acronym**	**Political Party**	**Acronym**
African National Congress	ANC	Democratic Alliance	DA
Economic Freedom Fighters	EFF	Inkatha Freedom Party	IFP
Patriotic Alliance	PA	United Democratic Movement	UDM
Al-Jama-Ah	Al-Jama-Ah	ActionSA	ActionSA
Congress of the People	COPE	African Christian Democratic Party	ACDP
Others	Various	Freedom Front Plus	FF+
		Others	Various

At the time of writing the Johannesburg council was constituted in Table 3 below as follows:

Table 3. Johannesburg council seat allocation and coalition affiliation

Party	Seats	Coalition
African National Congress (ANC)	91	ANC-led Coalition
Democratic Alliance (DA)	71	DA-led Coalition
ActionSA	44	DA-led Coalition
Economic Freedom Fighters (EFF)	29	ANC-led Coalition
Patriotic Alliance (PA)	9	ANC-led Coalition
Inkatha Freedom Party (IFP)	7	DA-led Coalition
Freedom Front Plus (VF PLUS)	4	DA-led Coalition
African Christian Democratic Party (ACDP)	3	DA-led Coalition
Al Jama-ah (ALJAMA)	3	ANC-led Coalition
African Independent Congress (AIC)	2	ANC-led Coalition
African Hope Congress (AHC)	1	Unknown
African People's Convention (APC)	1	Unknown
African Transformation Movement (ATM)	1	Unknown
Congress of the People (COPE)	1	ANC-led Coalition
GOOD	1	Unknown
Pan Africanist Congress (PAC)	1	Unknown
United Democratic Movement (UDM)	1	DA-led Coalition
United Independent Movement (UIM)	1	Unknown

Source: (National Government, 2023)

Lefort's Theory and the Dynamics of Johannesburg's Coalitions

In the context of Johannesburg's political landscape between 2016 and 2023, the functioning of coalitions reveals a dynamic and often volatile interplay of political forces, alliances, and strategies. This period has been marked by a distinct lack of majority wins during elections by any single political party in the city's political landscape. This has led to the formation of various coalition governments as detailed earlier. Importantly, however, this scenario aligns with Lefort's theoretical perspective on democracy, where the place of power is continually subjected to being emptied.

Lefort's concept is particularly relevant in understanding Johannesburg's coalition politics. The city's political arena during this period exemplifies a fluid and unstable exercise of power, where no single entity permanently occupies the position of authority. This is evident from the fact that there have been at least nine different mayors from 2016 to 2023, each representing either the DA-led MPG or the ANC-led GLU coalition arrangements as they have come to be known. This frequent change in leadership underscores the volatility and the transient nature of coalition agreements in Johannesburg.

The coalitions in Johannesburg, hence, can be viewed as practical cases of Lefort's idea of the democratic 'dissolution of the markers of certitude.' In Lefort's view, democracy is characterized by a form of society where power, law, and knowledge are subject to a radical indeterminacy, meaning that they are always open to question and reconfiguration. This is mirrored in the Johannesburg context, where coalitions are continually negotiated, reformed, and sometimes dissolved, reflecting a constant state of political fluidity and contestation (MISTRA, 2021).

Moreover, this period in Johannesburg's political history illustrates the complex relationships and decision-making processes inherent in coalition governance. The coalitions are not merely alliances for convenience or power-sharing but are instead sites of intense political negotiation, strategy, and compromise. They are shaped by a myriad of factors, including ideological alignments, policy priorities, power dynamics within and between parties, and the response to the city's socio-economic challenges.

Johannesburg's recent coalition politics as such serve as a real-world example of Lefort's theoretical insights into the nature of democratic politics. The political landscape in the city highlights the inherently unstable and dynamic nature of coalitions in a context where no single party can claim an absolute majority. This instability, while challenging for consistent governance, also reflects the essential democratic principle of power being an 'empty place,' constantly contested and redefined through political engagement and public discourse.

Example One. Financial Management and Governance in Johannesburg's Coalition Government

Introduction

The City of Johannesburg, since August 2016, has undergone a significant political shift from a single party to a coalition government. This example examines the impacts of this transition on fiscal management and governance. Drawing from the comprehensive analysis provided in 'The State of Financial Management and Governance in Municipalities with Coalition Governance' by the late Executive Mayor of the City of Johannesburg Geoff Makhubo[5]. A document he tabled at the sixth session of the National Council of Provinces local government week in September 2020. This section explores the challenges and opportunities presented by coalition governance in Johannesburg.

Transition to Coalition Governance

According to Makhubo, the emergence of coalition governments in Johannesburg marked a fundamental change in its political landscape. This transition brought forth a blend of various political entities, each with distinct ideologies and governance approaches. The coalition government, while presenting a democratic plurality, faced challenges in maintaining a cohesive approach to governance, particularly in financial management and adherence to legislative mandates (Makhubo, 2020, pp. 3-5).

Financial Management in the Coalition Era

Fiscal management within this new political framework encountered several challenges. Key among these were the varying capacities and expectations of coalition partners, and the ability of technocrats to navigate and execute responsibilities in this complex environment. Effective fiscal management was critical for the stability and success of the coalition government (ibid, pp. 7-11). Makhubo argues that the strategies the GLU government deployed to enhance this included fostering effective communication channels, ensuring transparency, and building a collective understanding of financial priorities.

Governance Challenges and Opportunities

Coalition governance in Johannesburg faced hurdles such as delayed decision-making processes, the inexperience of some coalition partners, and potential governance lapses in municipal entities. Makhubo adds that these challenges were exacerbated by economic constraints and the need for effective public participation. However, this period also presented opportunities for shared policy development and enhanced governance, facilitated by a system of checks and balances inherent in coalition politics (ibid, pp. 14-16).

Lessons Learnt and Recommendations

The experience of Johannesburg's coalition government offers vital lessons in coalition governance. The necessity for clear coalition agreements and shared policy positions emerged as key components to mitigate governance challenges. Additionally, the presentation by Makhubo showed the importance of respecting institutional systems, broad-based consultation, and maintaining transparency and accountability in decision-making (ibid, pp. 24-25).

Conclusion

This example has shown that the City of Johannesburg's experience with coalition government provides a nuanced understanding of the complexities involved in managing financial and governance aspects under coalition politics. It highlights both the challenges faced and the opportunities that arose, offering valuable insights into effective management and governance strategies in politically diverse environments. It further serves as a significant example for understanding the dynamics of coalition governments in urban settings, reflecting Lefort's conceptualization of power in such political constructs.

Example Two. Navigating Trust in the Shadow of Coalition Politics in Johannesburg

Introduction

In the landscape of Johannesburg's governance, coalition politics have emerged as a significant factor shaping public perception and trust in local government. Let us first consider the Quality of Life Survey 6 2021 (QoL). The QoL Survey conducted by the research institute Gauteng City-Region Observatory (GCRO) measures how residents perceive the government's performance using a number of indexes and combining them to reach an average score. Secondly, the Customer Satisfaction Survey 2022 (CSS) conducted by the City of Johannesburg every two years to measure residents' satisfaction with services. Both surveys provide an insightful lens into the dynamics of this trust, revealing a complex interplay between government satisfaction, awareness of political leadership, and public participation.

Findings on Public Trust and Satisfaction

A pervasive sense of dissatisfaction characterises the public's perception of local government in Johannesburg. More than half of the respondents expressed dissatisfaction with their local government, with a notable 53% dissatisfied with provincial government and 58% with local government (GCRO, 2021). Interestingly, the City of Johannesburg recorded the lowest proportion of respondents who explicitly distrust government leaders, suggesting a nuanced landscape of public opinion.

The awareness of local political figures plays a crucial role in shaping this trust. About 31% of respondents were unaware of their local councillor, varying significantly across municipalities (ibid). This lack of awareness correlates with higher levels of dissatisfaction and distrust, underlining the importance of visibility and recognition in fostering public trust.

The Role of Coalition Politics

In the context of coalition politics, these findings gain additional layers of complexity. Coalitions, by their very nature, bring together diverse political entities with varying agendas and leadership styles (MISTRA, 2021). This diversity can both challenge and enhance the public's trust in government, depending on the coalition's ability to present a united front and effectively communicate its policies and achievements to the public.

Strategies for Building Trust

The surveys suggest that improving public perception and participation is crucial for increasing trust in local government. Key strategies include continuous communication of new initiatives, effective use of technology, and robust relationships with the media (City of Johannesburg, 2022). This approach is particularly pertinent in a coalition government setting, where the need for cohesive and transparent communication by the relevant actors is amplified.

Conclusion

In the shadow of coalition politics, the City of Johannesburg faces the critical task of navigating and nurturing public trust. This trust is not static but is continually influenced by the visibility and perceived effectiveness of local government officials and their policies. Understanding and addressing the nuances of public perception, as highlighted in these surveys, is essential for crafting governance strategies that resonate with the residents of Johannesburg.

Public Perceptions in the Shadow of Coalition Politics

The analysis of the QoL 6 and the CSS of 2022 provides a valuable insight into public trust and perception in the context of coalition politics in Johannesburg. These surveys reflect a significant level of dissatisfaction among residents towards local government, influenced by the visibility and effectiveness of political leadership, as well as public participation in governance processes. Considering Lefort's theoretical framework, the essence of democracy is the idea discussed earlier about the dissolution of the markers of certitude, which can be paralleled with the nature of coalition politics where there is no single locus of power but a continuous negotiation among multiple political entities.

As witnessed in Johannesburg this inherent characteristic of coalition governments – their fragmented and negotiated power structure – can lead to an unclear or inconsistent policy direction, impacting public trust negatively. The diverse agendas within a coalition can confuse the public perception of the government's effectiveness and direction, which is critical for fostering trust according to Lefort's conception of any democratic arrangement being legitimate.

Lefortian Democracy and Johannesburg's Politics Since 2016

It is valuable to consider South Africa as a democracy, and more specifically, to view its political parties with coalitions through a Lefortian lens of democracy. Doing so helps us connect Lefort's theory of 'the empty place of power' with the nuances of South African political dialogue. For example, the shifts in Johannesburg's governance between different coalition groupings from 2016 to 2023 are practical examples of Hudson's 'vanishing mediator' moment where power is subjected to being temporarily suspended from one coalition to another. In this instance, however, the 'vanishing mediator' moment is not limited to formal LGEs that happen every five years. In Johannesburg, we see that there are numerous 'vanishing mediator' moments. These are instances where the coalition dynamics in Johannesburg reflect Lefort's notion of power as indeterminate and contestable.

In drawing an analytical link between the concepts discussed earlier by Lefort regarding the people freeing themselves through the symbolic destruction of the king and the contemporary political role of the EFF as 'King Makers' in South Africa (Marrian, 2019), we can focus on the shift in the locus of power and how it resonates in modern politics.

Lefort's analysis of the symbolic destruction of the king in the democratic revolution highlights a crucial shift: power moving from a central, unquestioned authority (the king) to the people. In this shift, the people gain the power to define and choose their leaders, making the essence of power contingent and subject to the will and dynamics of society. In contemporary South African politics and particularly in Johannesburg, the EFF's role as 'King Makers' can be seen as a modern embodiment of this democratic principle. Although they do not hold absolute power themselves, their influence and ability to sway political outcomes place them in a position where they can significantly determine who gets to wield power.

There have been numerous occasions recently where the EFF has been co-opted either by the ANC or the DA to form an alliance. However, focusing on the 2016 election results, these led to a hung council marking a significant shift in South African politics. None of the three biggest parties – the ANC with 44.6%, the DA with 38.4%, and the EFF with 11.1% – could secure a majority to control the municipality. The ANC obtained 121 out of 270 seats, while the DA formed a coalition with several smaller parties, including the IFP, the African Christian Democratic Party (ACDP), and others, culminating in 115 council seats. The EFF, holding 30 seats, chose a strategic, non-committal position, offering conditional support to the DA-led coalition rather than forming an official alliance (MISTRA, 2021, p. 308).

This scenario, especially the role of the EFF, echoes Lefort's concept of the symbolic destruction of the king and the subsequent empowerment of the people in a democratic society. In Lefort's view, the dissolution of a central, unchallenged authority – symbolized by the king – leads to a scenario where power becomes contingent, resting on the shifting sands of societal will and political dynamics. The EFF, by exercising its 'King Maker' role, demonstrated this fluidity and contingency of power. While not the majority, their ability to influence the outcome of the coalition talks underlined the symbolic nature of power in modern democracies. It is not solely about having a majority; it is also about the ability to sway, negotiate, and align strategically.

Moreover, the election results showed a significant decline in ANC support, dropping around twenty percentage points from 2006 to 2016, while the DA experienced an approximate eleven percentage point increase. This shift in voter sentiment further illustrates the dynamic nature of democratic power and agency, resonating with the democratic principles of change and adaptability that Lefort emphasizes. Just as the symbolic destruction of the king represents the empowerment of the people and the openness of societal structures, the changing political landscape in Johannesburg, marked by the EFF's strategic positioning, reflects the ongoing redefinition and reshaping of power in a modern democratic context.

CONCLUSION

Reflections on Lefort's Relevance to Johannesburg Politics

In South Africa, the concept of power is dynamic and not fixed to any specific political group. This understanding is mirrored in the Constitution and various governance institutions, which implicitly or explicitly recognize that no particular group has an inherent right to indefinitely hold power. This idea resonates with Lefort's principle of a society being open-ended or indeterminate, lacking a rigid and absolute structure. Consequently, those who wield power in such a society are also not permanent or absolute. This notion of the 'emptiness of the place of power' is equivalent to the fluidity of social identities, which are not preordained but symbolically constructed (Hudson, 2019).

We see this being the case in the City of Johannesburg, whereby the varied interests and ideologies of different political parties underpin coalitions. As highlighted by Lefort's theory, coalitions are made up of complex negotiations for power. And because no majority wins, parties with different agendas and priorities are forced to cooperate, as argued by Knowles (2021).

In the South African context, the Constitution upholds a liberal democratic framework, mandating regular elections conducted in a manner that upholds freedom and equality. These are fundamental prerequisites for an 'empty place of power.' Additionally, our democracy is reinforced by various institutions, such as Chapter Nine institutions which play an independent oversight role in areas such as Human Rights and Corruption. South Africa also has a parliamentary committee system. These structures collectively reinforce democratic governance. Coalitions and the plurality of views between the political parties which constitute them function as constructs keeping the place of power subject to a permanent openness.

Therefore, the politics of the City of Johannesburg are also subject to these institutions. Hence, political parties are forced to play within the 'rules of the game.' This chapter has shown while political parties are after their own interests, they would much rather negotiate than to flout democracy. This is also another representation of Lefort's theory: that political parties would much rather embrace the domain of contestation, rather than lock themselves into a form of despotism at the municipal level.

Although various motions of no confidence are a sign of upholding the empty place of power, too many motions of no confidence prove to be counterintuitive and obstructive to service delivery. There first needs to be trust and maturity, particularly among the dominant coalitions, whether in the ANC-led GLU or the DA-led MPG coalition. Secondly, and accompanying this, should be political calls for limits to how many motions of no confidence can be allowed in a term of office.

A comprehensive understanding of the empty place of power extends beyond the exclusive access of political parties within competitive politics. It also entails the people, drawing from their diverse life experiences, being empowered to actively participate in society and shape its trajectory. Moreover, they would have several options at their disposal. This is what Lefort refers to as opening up the social fabric i.e. the impossibility of constructing final definitions and concepts from an interrogation process is impossible. Multiple social constructs are all negotiating to expand their possibilities and perhaps even opportunities. What is particularly intriguing is that democracy brings this notion into the open for all to witness and even experience, ensuring that even the smallest political party qualifies to participate in governance, as witnessed in the City of Johannesburg.

REFERENCES

Amutabi, N. M. (2013). *Regime Change and Succession Politics in Africa: Five Decades of Misrule.* Routledge Taylor & Francis. doi:10.4324/9780203080191

Ash, P. (2021). *OBITUARY: Geoff Makhubo — a respected, tainted veteran politician.* Retrieved December 3, 2023, from https://www.timeslive.co.za/politics/2021-07-09-obituary-geoff-makhubo-a-respected-tainted-veteran-politician/

Besseling, R. (2016). *The slow demise of the ANC: Political change, economic decline, and state corruption in South Africa. Africa Policy Brief.* Egmont Institute.

Biswas, J. (2019). Coalition Government and its Challenges of 21st Century in India. *Ensemble, A Peer Revied Academic Journal, 1*(1), 36-40.

Chutel, J. E. (2023). *Johannesburg, Where Mayors Last Just Months, or Even Only Weeks.* Retrieved November 12, 2023, from https://www.nytimes.com/2023/05/17/world/africa/south-africa-johannesburg-mayor.html

City of Johannesburg. (2022). *2021/22 Customer Satisfaction Survey.* City of Johannesburg.

City of Johannesburg. (2023). *Overview of Johanneburg.* City of Johannesburg.

Fairclough, N. (2001). *Critical Discourse Analysis.* Lancaster University.

Flynn, B. (2005). *The Philosophy of Claude Lefort: Interpreting the Political* (1st ed.). Northwestern University Press.

GCRO. (2021). *Quality Of Life Survey 6 (2020/21) Municipal Report: City of Johannesburg.* GCRO.

Harrison, P. (2018). *Johannesburg: A Cultural and Literary History.* Signal Books.

Hudson, P. (2015). *Lecture on the Exceptional State.* University of the Witwatersrand.

Hussain, M. (2023). *TIMELINE | How Johannesburg managed to go through 4 mayors – and counting – in 18 months.* Retrieved November 12, 2023, from https://www.news24.com/news24/opinions/analysis/timeline-how-johannesburg-managed-to-go-through-4-mayors-and-counting-in-18-months-20230503

Ka-Ndyalvan, D. (2017). *Beyond 2019: A coalition government is a threat to South Africa's economic recovery.* Academic Press.

Katzenellenbogen, J. (2023). *Coalitions and Consequences - Polity.* Institute of Race Relations.

Khoza, A. (2023). *Election season kicks off but no date yet.* https://www.businesslive.co.za/bd/national/2023-10-24-election-season-kicks-off-but-no-date-yet/

Knowles, K. (2021). An Analysis Of Emerging Governing Coalitions At The Local Level. In *South Africa With a Specific Focus on Johannesburg and Nelson Mandela Bay*. University of the Free State.

Leach, M., & Mkhize, S. (2019). *Racial Geographies, Housing Segregation and Dispossession in Johannesburg*. Springer.

Lefort, C. (1986). *The Political Forms of Modern Society: Bureaucracy, Democracy, Totalitarianism*. Polity Press.

Lefort, C. (1988). Democracy and Political Theory. London: Polity Press.

Madia, M. (2022). *City of Joburg Elects New Section 79 Committee Chairs Despite Tense Meeting*. Retrieved May 22, 2022, from https://ewn.co.za/2022/01/27/city-of-joburg-elects-new-section-79-committee-chairs-despite-tense-council

Makgale, B. (2020). *Coalition Politics and Urban Governance in Johannesburg's Housing Policy*. Wits Graduate School of Governance.

Makhubo, G. (2020). *The State of Financial Management and Governance in Municipalities with Coalition Government: A Case for Constructive Coalition Governance*. Parliament of South Africa.

Marchart, O. (2007). *Post-Foundational Political Thought: Political Difference in Nancy, Lefort, Badiou and Laclau*. Edinburgh University Press.

Marrian, N. (2019). *The tables could turn on kingmaker EFF*. Retrieved November 30, 2023, from https://mg.co.za/article/2019-04-26-00-the-tables-could-turn-on-kingmaker-eff/

Matlosa, K. (2008). Political Parties and Democratisation in the Southern African Development Community Region: The Weakest link? *EISA Report, 15*.

Mawere, J., Matoane, J., & Khalo, T. (2022). Coalition Governance and Service Delivery in South Africa: A Case Study of Tshwane, Johannesburg and Ekurhuleni Metropolitan Municipalities. *Journal of Public Administration, 57*(2), 272–283.

MISTRA. (2021). Marriages of Inconvenience: The Politics of Coalitions in South Africa. Johannesburg: Mapungubwe Institute for Strategic Reflection.

Moshodi, J. (2018). *Coalition politics a new political landscape in South Africa*. University of the Free State.

Mpangalasane, C. (2020). *The impact of coalition government on service delivery: City of Tshwane metropolitan*. North-West University.

Mvumvu, Z. (2019). *Herman Mashaba resigns as mayor of Johannesburg, says 'I will always choose the country ahead of the party*. Retrieved March 31, 2024, from https://www.timeslive.co.za/politics/2019-10-21-herman-mashaba-resigns-as-mayor-of-johannesburg-says-not-in-my-nature-to-wait-to-be-pushed/

Mwareya, R. (2023). *South Africa: Johannesburg's circus of eight mayors in two years*. Retrieved November 12, 2023, from https://www.theafricareport.com/309452/south-africa-johannesburgs-circus-of-eight-mayors-in-two-years/

National Government. (2023). *City of Johannesburg Metropolitan Municipality (JHB)*. Retrieved December 3, 2023, from https://municipalities.co.za/management/2/city-of-johannesburg-metropolitan-municipality

Ndou, L. L. (2022). *The Impact of Coalition Government on Service Delivery: City of Tshwane Metropolitan*. North West University.

Newman, S. (2004). The Place of Power in Political Discourse. *International Political Science Review / Revue internationale de science politique, 25*(2), 139-157.

Pather, R. (2016, January 14). *EFF strikes a deal with the DA: Here is how Johannesburg will look*. Retrieved from Mail & Gaurdian: https://mg.co.za/article/2016-08-17-the-effs-deal-with-the-da-in-johannesburg-and-how-the-country-will-look/

Rose, R. (1974). *The Problem of Party Government. Professor of Politics*. University of Strathclyde. The MacMillian Press.

Saussure, F. d. (1974). Course in General Linguistics. Academic Press.

Smith, A. (2020). *The Economic Importance of Johannesburg*. WorldAtlas.

Stats, S. A. (2022). *Provinces At a Glance*. Tshwane.

Tladi, M. (2020). *Is the Place of Power Empty? Reading Claude Lefort in South Africa*. University of the Witwatersrand.

Turok, I. (2017). Johannesburg: Warts and All. Urban Forum.

ENDNOTES

[1] City = The Johannesburg Metropolitan Municipality (the institution). city = Johannesburg (the geographic territory).

[2] The 'universal' and 'particular' are terms used to describe concepts within political theory. The 'universal' refers to the collective will or interest of society as a whole, often embodied in the abstract principles of democracy that serve the common good. The 'particular', on the other hand, signifies the specific interests of individual parties or leaders that come to power representing a section of society. While they may claim to serve the universal, they are by definition not all-encompassing and only hold the 'universal' place temporarily until the next electoral cycle. This distinction highlights the tension between the ideals of democracy and the practical realities of political representation. (Marchart, Post-Foundational Political Thought: Political Difference in Nancy, Lefort, Badiou and Laclau., 2007).

[3] Table 1 represents a compilation of mayoral successions in Johannesburg from 2016 to 2023, which I have assembled from various sources, including (Chutel, 2023) (Hussain, 2023) (Mwareya, 2023).

[4] Note: The table provides a general overview of the political parties that constitute two main coalitions in the City of Johannesburg. Please note that the composition of coalitions may change over time due to political dynamics and elections. Information in the table is based on the Author's interpretation.

5   Geoff Makhubo, the former mayor of Johannesburg, passed away on July 9, 2021, due to Covid-19 related complications. Source: (Ash, 2021).

Chapter 15
The Role of Coalition Governments as Sustainable Democracy Enhancing in South Africa

Mukesh Shankar Bharti

https://orcid.org/0000-0002-3693-7247

Jawaharlal Nehru University, India

ABSTRACT

The aim of this study is to discuss the nature of coalition government and its role in strengthening the norms of democracy in South Africa. Over the past two decades, South Africa has continued to focus on the progressive development of the country's political institutions under the ethos of the democratic principle of coalition government. This chapter also discusses the various South African governments' roles in the establishment of democratization in the country. The research method used in this study is the qualitative approach to search for actual research output. The empirical method would also involve discussing research gaps on the nature and characteristics of coalition government for better governance. Moreover, this study will answer the following research questions: How is the coalition government in South Africa paving the way for the healthiest democracy? There is the second question: Why are the people of South Africa electing a coalition government in the country? This study also uses the third wave of democratization theory of Samuel P. Huntington, which contributed to the democratic transition and the establishment of democratic governments in the late 1980s in developing countries, namely in Africa, Latin America, and Central and Eastern Europe. Apart from Samuel P. Huntington's idea on democratization, this study also utilises other modern democratic theories to discuss South Africa's democratization process under the coalition government. Finally, the chapter outlines how political alliances are conceptualized and operationalized for the democratization of South Africa.

DOI: 10.4018/979-8-3693-1654-2.ch015

INTRODUCTION

The most significant event was the end of apartheid and the establishment of a democratic government in 1994. This marked the beginning of a new era characterized by non-racialism, democracy, and equality under the leadership of the African National Congress (ANC) and its leader, Nelson Mandela. South Africa has held several democratic elections since 1994, with the ANC winning the majority of votes in each election. The country's political landscape has seen the emergence of opposition parties such as the Democratic Alliance (DA) and the Economic Freedom Fighters (EFF), contributing to a more pluralistic political environment. Despite the progress made since 1994, South Africa continues to face significant challenges, including poverty, inequality, unemployment, and crime. The government has implemented various social welfare programs and economic policies aimed at addressing these issues, but progress has been uneven. The several past governments of South Africa had made tremendous efforts to address historical injustices and inequalities have included initiatives such as Black Economic Empowerment (BEE) and affirmative action policies aimed at promoting the participation of previously disadvantaged groups in the economy and society.

Land ownership remains a contentious issue in South Africa, with calls for land redistribution to address historical injustices. The government has initiated land reform programs, including land restitution and redistribution, although progress has been slow and uneven. South Africa has played an active role in regional and international affairs, advocating for human rights, democracy, and development. It has also been involved in peacekeeping efforts on the African continent and has sought to strengthen ties with other emerging economies through platforms such as BRICS (Brazil, Russia, India, China, South Africa). Overall, South Africa's post-1994 journey has been characterized by both progress and challenges as the country continues to grapple with the legacy of apartheid while striving to build a more inclusive, equitable, and prosperous society through enhancement of sustainable democratic development in the country. As South Africa transitioned to democracy, traditional authorities saw a decline in their popularity, particularly among younger generations and those advocating for greater democratic accountability and participation. However, it's important to note that traditional leadership still held significance for many rural communities, particularly in matters of culture, identity, and local governance.

This study examines various factors that influence the formation and functioning of coalitions in South Africa. This includes analyzing trends in political party electoral performance, ideological differences among prospective coalition partners, policy preferences, and the personalities and qualities of political leaders. Understanding these factors helps identify areas of potential cooperation, compromise, consensus, and divergence among coalition partners, which are critical for the success and sustainability of coalition governments. The feasibility, efficiency, effectiveness, and sustainability of coalition governments in South Africa depend on several factors, including the degree of ideological alignment among coalition partners, the strength of leadership within the coalition, the ability to forge consensus on key policy issues, and the capacity to manage intra-coalition conflicts and disagreements (Dlakavu, 2022; Mnwana, 2015). By examining these factors, analysts can assess the prospects for successful coalition governance and identify potential challenges and areas for improvement.

The South African Constitution establishes a three-tier governance model consisting of national, provincial, and local government spheres. Each tier has its own set of powers, responsibilities, and functions. This decentralized structure aims to ensure effective governance and service delivery at different levels of government, while also promoting accountability and responsiveness to local needs. The Constitution also mandates the use of a proportional representation (PR) system for elections at all levels of government. Under this system, political parties are allocated seats in legislative bodies based on the proportion of votes they receive in elections. This ensures that minority parties have representation in government, proportional to their level of electoral support (Hanabe & Malinzi, 2019). An embracing a coalition governance model and implementing electoral reforms to strengthen checks and balances, South Africa can enhance accountability mechanisms within its political system. This approach promotes transparency, fosters public trust, and ensures that elected officials are held accountable for their actions, ultimately contributing to a healthier and more democratic political environment.

REVIEW OF LITERATURE

Williams and Papa (2020) discuss under the norms of Commonwealth, South Africa's reintegration in it adopted the market-based economy and promoted the values of liberal democracy in the country. Since the adoption of objectives of the Commonwealth and its open support to South Africa has been implemented in the democratization process in the entire country. Moreover, the other democratic value-based countries had paved the way for successful democracy promotion in the country. The Non-Alignment Movement (NAM) is one of the key international organizations which had supported democratic ethos with liberal multipolar world for its Member States instead of militarization or part of the power block to support a bipolar world. South Africa chaired the NAM from 1998-2003 and the G-77 as well. At the valedictory session of the 1998 NAM summit in Durban, South Africa Nelson Mandela highlighted the construction of the world economic order should be the prime objective of the developing countries, and the restructuring of the UN which is responsible organization to make world politics towards the path of demarcation promotion and establishment of its ideas in the countries (Mandela, 1998).

South Africa is a key country on the African continent which is implementing the norms of democratisation under a coalition government and fulfilling the African Union's (AU) approaches to democratic institutions. South Africa has been improving and advancing democracy in the country and encouraging other African countries to adopt the values of democracy promotion in regional blocks of the continent (Moshoeshoe & Dzinesa, 2024). Fish (2006) describes that in the context of class divisions and race are still considered structural inequalities in the foundation of a democratic institutional building under the coalition government in South Africa. Several structural inequalities in the political and public institutions have created recurring contradictions between gender balances and actual representation in the new democratic environment to the complete transformation in the governance process. Thus, political institutions and other government machinery are unable to fill the gap in gender justice and the absence of gender-based policy to make a complete transition to enhancing democracy in the country. On the other hand, South Africa's coalition form of government system is focusing on filling the gap of race, class and geography in the context of women's representation in the various institutions. The higher level of the government system's governance of South Africa is becoming reliable to institutionalise the local level government in favour of city inhabitants. The local-level coalition governments are working with more reality and enhancing sustainable democratic institutions (Barber, 2013; Benit-Gbaffou et al., 2013; Bosire, 2011; Frug, 1999; Lambright, 2014; Pieterse, 2019; Schragger, 2016).

Karume (2003) the prevalence of coalition governance as a component of politics in several African countries such as Kenya, Nigeria, Zimbabwe, and Uganda, as well as in Central Europe. In these regions, politics are often influenced by factors such as ethnic, cultural, and regional affiliations, leading to fragmented political landscapes where no single party can mobilize enough support to win elections outright. That is an elaboration on how coalition governance becomes integral in such contexts: The African National Congress (ANC) has played a pivotal role in African politics since the era of apartheid in South Africa. Since 1994, the ANC has been the main ruling party in the country and has successfully conducted democratic exercises under the coalition of several governments. In South Africa, the coalition form of government dominated by Nelson Mandela, Mbeki and Zuma presidencies in the country and strengthened democratic practices as well (Naidoo, 2019). Aiyede (2023) explains the democratic government is elected for a certain period to govern the country by the popular vote of the common people. The people's vote is important to form the majority or coalition form of government in democratic countries. South Africa is an example of an African continent that exercises coalition governments. Thus, in democratic countries political parties need support from people to exercise governance even under the coalition format of popular government. The government became legitimate and effectiveness through public support in the electoral process.

Gable (2024) discusses the upcoming 2024 national election in South Africa is poised to be a significant moment in the country's democratic history, marking the seventh election since the end of apartheid. Despite the African National Congress (ANC) holding majority support for the past three decades, the political landscape remains vibrant and diverse, with a multitude of parties competing for representation in parliament. The increasing number of registered parties and the inclusion of independent candidates on the ballot offer voters a wider selection of options than ever before. This proliferation of choices reflects the ongoing contestation and dynamism within South Africa's democracy, demonstrating the pluralism and diversity of political voices in the country. However, the ANC faces mounting challenges as it campaigns for re-election. The party's ability to tout its track record of economic and social progress is diminishing, given the country's sluggish economic growth and stagnant per capita income.

With average economic growth at a mere 0.4 percent over the past five years and per capita income lower than it was in 2010, the ANC must confront growing discontent among voters who have not experienced the promised improvements in their living standards. These economic challenges, coupled with concerns about corruption, service delivery, and inequality, present formidable obstacles for the ANC as it seeks to maintain its dominance in South African politics (Gable, 2024). The upcoming election will test the party's ability to address these pressing issues and regain the trust and confidence of the electorate. Although, opposition parties have an opportunity to capitalize on public dissatisfaction and offer alternative visions for the country's future. Their performance in the election will shape the political landscape and potentially challenge the ANC's hegemony, signaling a potential shift in South Africa's political dynamics. The 2024 election promises to be a pivotal moment in South Africa's democratic journey, offering voters the opportunity to hold their leaders accountable and shape the country's trajectory for years to come.

METHODS AND TECHNIQUES

The empirical research conducted delves deeply into understanding the dynamics of democratic development within the context of coalition governments. This involves examining various aspects of governance, political participation, policy-making, and decision-making processes under coalition arrangements. The research aims to assess how coalition governments contribute to democratic development in South Africa. This includes evaluating the extent to which coalition governments promote political pluralism, consensus-building, inclusivity, and accountability within the political system. The focus on coalition governments recognizes their importance in South Africa's political landscape. By studying coalition dynamics, researchers seek to uncover the opportunities and challenges associated with governing through cooperation and negotiation among multiple political parties. The study relies on empirical evidence, including data analysis, case studies, surveys, and speeches of prominent leaders and academicians, to provide insights into the functioning and outcomes of coalition governments in South Africa. This empirical approach enhances the credibility and validity of the findings of this study.

The research presented here employs a qualitative approach with deductive methods to investigate the in-depth democratic development in South Africa under coalition governments. This research draws on primary and secondary resources to provide comprehensive insights into the dynamics of governance and democratic processes within the context of coalition politics. The qualitative approach allows researchers to explore the complexities of democratic development in South Africa under coalition governments. This involves examining nuanced political relationships, institutional dynamics, and societal factors that shape governance outcomes. Deductive methods involve the formulation of theories and answering questions which are based on existing knowledge and theoretical frameworks. This study applies deductive reasoning to analyze data collected from primary and secondary sources in relation to democratic theories to describe South Africa's political and democratic transformation (Mnwana, 2015). Primary resources may include interviews, surveys, focus groups, and direct observations conducted by the researchers. These methods allow for the collection of firsthand data from key stakeholders, including politicians, policymakers, civil society representatives, and citizens, to gain insights into their perspectives and experiences with coalition governance. Secondary resources encompass existing literature, academic studies, government reports, media sources, and archival materials related to coalition politics and democratic development in South Africa.

The research employs in-depth analysis techniques to unpack the complexities of democratic development under coalition governments. This involves examining patterns, trends, and case studies to identify key factors influencing governance outcomes, such as coalition formation, policy implementation, institutional stability, and citizen engagement. By integrating primary and secondary resources, the research aims to provide comprehensive insights into the challenges and opportunities associated with coalition governance in South Africa. This approach enhances the depth and richness of the findings, allowing for a nuanced understanding of democratic development dynamics in a diverse and evolving political landscape.

THEORETICAL DISCUSSION AND APPROACH

The "waves of democratization" played an important role in promoting the ethos of democratic norms in the African continent. Samuel P. Huntington pioneered the third wave of democratization in the context of Central and Eastern Europe (CEE), Asia, Latin America and Africa. Since the 1970s this democratic wave spread all over the world when phases of decolonization started and the fall of communism across the world (Huntington, 1991, 1993, 1997; Huntington S.P, 1991; Kurzman, 1998). The concept of the third wave of democratic transformation brought major democratic changes in the world in the late twentieth century. Samuel P. Huntington explains this democratic transition is responsible for the establishment of democratic institutions in countries of Africa. South Africa has been a great example of democratic promotion since 1990 and the concept of waves of democratization supports enhancing the democratization process in the country.

Arend Lijphart explained the theory of consociational democracy in pluralistic societies. Lijphart described the democratic transformation and institutional development in the "Democracy in Plural Societies." The democratic stability is possible through an institutional mechanism in the case of South Africa because an ethnically divided country focuses on uniting the mass inhabitants to cooperate with the government to run a democratic set-up. He envisages that consociational democracy is far better than any other theoretical approach to nurture South Africa's democratic transition. Lijphart's model emphasises inclusivity, cooperation, and power-sharing among different segments of society as essential elements for stable governance in deeply divided societies. The consociational democracy model of democracy is designed to accommodate societies deeply divided along ethnic, religious, or cultural lines. It involves power-sharing arrangements among different segments of society to prevent one group from dominating others (Connors, 1996; Lijphart, 1977). Lijphart advocates for power-sharing mechanisms, such as consociational democracy, which accommodate and recognize the diversity of identities within a society. By acknowledging and accommodating primordial loyalties through inclusive governance structures, Lijphart argues that societies can better manage their differences and work towards stability and cooperation.

In a consociational democracy, proportional representation ensures that the composition of the government reflects the diverse makeup of society. This means that political parties or groups receive seats in government in proportion to their level of support among the population. Proportional representation helps prevent the marginalization of minority groups and encourages political pluralism. Lijphart suggests that having multiple cleavages (divisions) within and between segments of society can promote moderation and consensus. When individuals belong to multiple groups with different interests, they may be more inclined to seek compromise and cooperation rather than pursuing extreme positions. Lijphart argues that for consociational democracy to succeed, it's important for the broader population to exhibit political inertness or passivity. This means that the general populace should not be highly politicized or actively engaged in challenging the political status quo. Instead, a degree of political apathy or acceptance of the existing power-sharing arrangements can contribute to stability. The importance of cross-cutting cleavages and political quietism, Lijphart suggests that consociational democracy functions best in societies where there is a balance of power among different segments and where there is not significant popular pressure for radical change. This approach aims to mitigate conflict and promote cooperation by accommodating diverse interests and maintaining a relatively stable political environment. Lijphart, echoing the sentiments of the apartheid government, argues against a majoritarian approach to governance in South Africa. Majoritarianism, which prioritizes the rule of the numerical majority, is seen as potentially detrimental to minority rights in a deeply divided society like South Africa (Lijphart, 1987, 2023).

Lijphart suggests that a consociational solution, based on power-sharing and accommodation of minority interests, is the most viable option for South Africa. Consociational democracy, with its emphasis on inclusive governance and protection of minority rights, is presented as the only approach that the major factions in South Africa are likely to agree upon. By advocating for consociationalism in South Africa, Lijphart emphasizes the importance of recognizing and accommodating the diverse interests and identities within the country to foster stability, reconciliation, and democratic governance. This approach reflects an attempt to address the legacy of apartheid and build a more inclusive and equitable society. Coalition governance is seen as a mechanism to prevent a "winner-takes-all" scenario, where a single dominant party exercises unchecked power. By involving multiple parties in decision-making processes, coalition governments can create a system of checks and balances, ensuring that power is distributed and decisions are subject to scrutiny and consensus-building (Booysen, 2018).

POLITICAL CULTURE OF SOUTH AFRICA

The South African Native National Congress (SANNC), later renamed the African National Congress (ANC), indeed had a leadership primarily composed of members of the African middle class during its formative years. These leaders represented various professions and backgrounds, including lawyers, doctors, journalists, and landowners. At the time of its formation in 1912, South Africa was under British colonial rule, and the political landscape was dominated by racially discriminatory laws and policies. The SANNC was established to advocate for the rights and interests of black South Africans, particularly in the face of discriminatory legislation such as the Natives Land Act of 1913, which severely restricted black land ownership. the leadership of the ANC during its formative years reflects the importance of educated, professional, and politically engaged individuals in the struggle for equality and justice in South Africa. Their efforts laid the foundation for the ANC's role as a leading force in the anti-apartheid movement and its eventual transition to governing party after the end of apartheid in 1994 (de Jager & Sebudubudu, 2017). The ANC demonstrated a willingness to engage in dialogue and negotiation to facilitate a peaceful transition to democracy. The moderation of their positions during this period was essential for reaching a consensus on the future of South Africa and laying the foundation for a more inclusive and democratic society (Molomo, 2000).

The tendency of liberation movements to centralize power and uphold a one-party system is acknowledged. This was partly due to the need for cohesion in the face of oppressive regimes and the desire to maintain control over the liberation narrative. However, the ANC's transition from a liberation movement to a governing party in a democratic South Africa involved a shift towards embracing democratic principles, pluralism, and inclusivity. While it retained its historical identity and ideology, it also recognized the importance of building a multi-party democracy and accommodating diverse interests within South Africa. The National Party (NP) and the ANC had historical legacies that deviated from classic liberal democracy, their moderation and willingness to engage in negotiations during South Africa's transition period were instrumental in facilitating the country's transition to democracy. This transition involved a complex negotiation of competing interests, ideologies, and historical legacies, ultimately leading to the establishment of a democratic South Africa (Giliomee, 1995).

There has been a noticeable increase in popular discontent within South African society. This discontent often stems from frustrations with socioeconomic inequalities, inadequate service delivery, corruption, and perceived failures of governance. These issues have led to disillusionment among segments of the population and a loss of trust in political institutions. The expression of popular discontent has often manifested in threatening and angry discourse. This includes public protests, social media activism, and community mobilization, where grievances are articulated forcefully and sometimes confrontationally. Such discourse reflects the depth of frustration and anger felt by many citizens. The observation about social mobilization of disgruntled citizens relying on violence rather than political structures highlights a significant challenge to democratic governance. When citizens feel marginalized or ignored by formal political channels, they may resort to extra-institutional means, such as protests or violence, to voice their concerns and press for change. The coalition governments of South Africa need to address these challenges and require a multifaceted approach that includes improving governance, enhancing service delivery, tackling corruption, and fostering inclusive political participation. It also necessitates building trust between citizens and political institutions, as well as promoting dialogue and peaceful avenues for expressing grievances. Failure to address these underlying issues risks further polarization and instability within South African society (Reddy, 2010).

COALITION GOVERNMENTS IN SOUTH AFRICA

To effectively analyze and navigate coalition politics in South Africa, it's crucial to have a clear conceptual understanding of what coalitions are and how they function, as well as operational knowledge of the practical aspects of coalition formation, governance, and management. This includes understanding the motivations behind coalition-building, the mechanisms by which coalitions are formed and sustained, and the dynamics of power-sharing and decision-making within coalition governments. The unbanning of political parties in February 1990 marked a critical turning point in South Africa's history. This included the unbanning of key liberation movements such as the African National Congress (ANC), South African Communist Party (SACP), Pan Africanist Congress (PAC), and the Black Consciousness Movement (BCM). The unbanning of these organizations paved the way for the negotiation process towards democratic governance and the end of apartheid. The first democratic election in April 1994 was a landmark event in South Africa's history. It was the first time that all South Africans, regardless of race, were able to participate in a democratic election. The election resulted in the ANC winning a decisive victory, with Nelson Mandela becoming the country's first democratically elected president. This election marked the end of apartheid and the beginning of a new era of democracy in South Africa. The use of a proportional representation (PR) electoral system in the democratic elections helped to solidify the ANC's dominance in Parliament. This electoral system ensured that parties received seats in proportion to their share of the national vote. The ANC's dominance in Parliament peaked in 2004, with the party winning a significant majority of seats (Booysen, 2014).

The formation of the Government of National Unity (GNU) was established as part of the interim Constitution of 1993, which provided for a transitional period leading up to the first democratic elections in 1994. The GNU included the African National Congress (ANC), the National Party (NP), and the Inkatha Freedom Party (IFP). This grand alliance brought together political parties and liberation movements that had been adversaries during the apartheid era. The GNU was formed with the objective of fostering reconciliation, promoting stability, and facilitating the transition to democracy in South Africa. It represented a commitment to inclusivity and shared governance, with representatives from different political backgrounds working together to oversee the transition process. The Government of National Unity in 1993-94 reflected the spirit of cooperation and compromise that characterized South Africa's transition to democracy. While the alliance component was eventually omitted from the final constitution, the GNU played a crucial role in laying the groundwork for democratic governance and reconciliation in post-apartheid South Africa. The 1994 Government of National Unity in South Africa as a power-sharing arrangement. This government was formed as a compromise to manage the transition from apartheid to democracy and included the African National Congress (ANC), the Inkatha Freedom Party (IFP), and the National Party (NP). The arrangement aimed to foster reconciliation, promote stability, and ensure the representation of diverse interests in the post-apartheid political landscape (Arnolds, 2023).

There were indications that political debate within the ruling alliance had become more controlled, with a greater emphasis on conformity and loyalty to the dominant faction within the African National Congress (ANC). This suggests a narrowing of political discourse and a decrease in the openness to diverse opinions and viewpoints within the alliance. The attempts by the ANC to contain a potential split within the Congress of South African Trade Unions (COSATU) were seen as crucial, as such a split could have ramifications for the ANC's electoral dominance. COSATU, as a key ally of the ANC, played a significant role in mobilizing support for the party, and a split within COSATU could weaken the ANC's electoral base. The South African Communist Party (SACP) had become closely aligned with the ANC and wielded significant influence within the government. The SACP's integration into the ANC and its perceived role in shaping government actions indicate a blurring of lines between the two organizations, with the SACP playing a significant role in setting the tone for government policies and decisions (Booysen, 2014; Dlakavu, 2022).

Despite the dominance of the African National Congress (ANC) in South African politics, there has been a noticeable growth of the Democratic Alliance (DA) over the years, particularly from 2004 to 2014. The DA's consistent growth in successive elections indicated the emergence of a viable second party within the political landscape, challenging the ANC's dominance. The DA played a significant role in fostering the development of a two-party system by strategically reaching out to minor opposition parties and consolidating their support. By drawing minor opposition parties into its camp, the DA aimed to strengthen its position as the primary alternative to the ANC and build momentum as the second leg of the two-party system. The emergence of the Economic Freedom Fighters (EFF) in the 2014 elections introduced a new dynamic to South African politics. As a split-off from the ANC, the EFF positioned itself as a left-opposition alternative to the ANC, challenging the traditional dominance of the ANC and potentially disrupting the emerging two-party configuration. The rise of the EFF as a significant new entrant in electoral politics posed a potential challenge to the established order dominated by the ANC. The EFF's focus on issues of economic inequality and social justice appealed to a segment of the electorate disillusioned with the ANC, positioning the party as a potential contender to displace the ANC's dominant position in the political landscape (Booysen, 2014).

FORMATION OF A MULTI-PARTY COALITION

The formation of a seven-party coalition government in the City of Cape Town after the 2006 elections reflects the complexity of local politics in the Western Cape. This coalition included diverse political parties such as the Democratic Alliance (DA), African Christian Democratic Party (ACDP), Freedom Front Plus (FFP), and United Democratic Movement (UDM), among others. The seven-party coalition government in the City of Cape Town after the 2006 elections demonstrates that multi-party coalitions can be effective in local government settings, even with diverse coalition partners. The stability and success of this coalition highlight the potential for cooperation and consensus-building among political parties to govern effectively and address the needs of the community (Arnolds, 2023).

The significant political shift observed in South Africa during the 2016 local government elections, particularly in Gauteng-based metros, where the African National Congress (ANC) lost control, leading to 27 hung municipalities nationally. The loss of control over all three Gauteng-based metros by the ANC marked a significant departure from its historical dominance since the dawn of democracy in 1994. This electoral outcome signaled a potential decline in the ANC's political influence at the local government level. The emergence of 27 hung municipalities nationwide indicated a fragmented political landscape, where no single party held a majority to govern independently. This situation necessitated the formation of coalitions or agreements among multiple parties to govern effectively. Despite South Africa experiencing 97 coalitions before 2016, there is a lack of comprehensive research on the performance of coalitions, particularly at the municipal level. This gap underscores the need for a thorough assessment of coalition governance to understand its effectiveness and impact on service delivery and governance outcomes. The 2016 local government elections and the subsequent rise of coalition governments in several municipalities, evaluating the performance of these coalitions is crucial. Such assessments can provide insights into the strengths and weaknesses of coalition governance, identify best practices, and inform future decision-making and policy development (Pietersen, 2021).

The outcomes of the 2021 local government elections in South Africa, particularly in Tshwane, Johannesburg, and Ekurhuleni, where the African National Congress (ANC) lost electoral power to opposition parties, have resulted in hung municipalities. In these municipalities, no single party received a majority of votes to independently govern, leading to the need for political parties to negotiate and form co-governing coalitions. However, the article contends that the policy agendas and governing principles of the political parties involved are fundamentally incompatible. Therefore, should these parties decide to enter into coalition governments, the divergent policy agendas and principles will hinder the effective delivery of services to residents. The political parties involved in the potential coalitions have distinct policy priorities and approaches to governance (Joshua et al., 2022). These differences may relate to economic policies, social welfare programs, infrastructure development, or other key areas of municipal governance. The study suggests that reconciling these divergent agendas within a coalition framework would be challenging and could lead to policy gridlock or compromises that do not fully address the needs of residents.

DISCUSSION

Coalition governments typically involve parties from diverse ideological, social, and cultural backgrounds. By bringing together representatives from different segments of society, coalition governments can reflect the country's diversity and ensure that various perspectives are represented in decision-making processes. In coalition governments, parties must negotiate and compromise on policy priorities and governance strategies. This process promotes consensus-building and cooperation among parties with different agendas, fostering a culture of dialogue and collaboration that can extend to the broader society. The formation of a coalition government comprising parties with disparate backgrounds sends a powerful symbolic message of unity and inclusivity. It demonstrates a commitment to overcoming divisions and working together towards common goals, irrespective of ideological or cultural differences. South Africa's history of apartheid has left deep-seated cultural and racial divisions in society (Bradshaw & Breakfast, 2019). Coalition governance provides an opportunity to address these divisions by promoting collaboration and mutual understanding among diverse groups. By transcending historical divisions, coalition governments can contribute to healing wounds and promoting reconciliation. Social cohesion among political parties in South Africa can serve as a model for co-existence and non-violent behavior among citizens. By demonstrating respectful dialogue and peaceful conflict resolution, political leaders can set a positive example for the broader society, helping to mitigate the high rates of violence that persist in democratic South Africa.

The political brinkmanship exhibited by the Democratic Alliance (DA) in the aftermath of the 2021 local government elections in South Africa. Despite not having a majority in key metros like Tshwane, Ekurhuleni, and Johannesburg, the DA insisted on unilateral control over the coalition agreement and refused to engage with the Economic Freedom Fighters (EFF) due to ideological differences. The DA's approach to coalition negotiations reflects an unwillingness to compromise and engage constructively with other parties. By prioritizing ideological differences over the practical necessity of coalition-building, the DA risked undermining the formation of stable coalition governments in municipalities where it lacked a majority. the DA's behavior was perceived as immature and counterproductive, given the urgency of forming functional governments to address pressing municipal issues. By engaging in political brinkmanship, the DA may have alienated potential coalition partners and hindered efforts to establish effective governance structures. Effective coalition governance requires parties to set aside ideological differences and prioritize the common good. Instead of engaging in brinkmanship, political parties should demonstrate maturity and flexibility in negotiations, seeking common ground and compromising where necessary to ensure the stability and effectiveness of coalition governments (Electoral Commission of South Africa, 2021).

Ideological and ethnocultural differences among political parties can exacerbate divisions within societies, undermining social cohesion and national unity. Instead of fostering diversity and inclusivity, these differences may accentuate existing fault lines and contribute to polarization along ethnic, racial, or ideological lines. In countries like South Africa, Nigeria, Uganda, and Zimbabwe, political parties often attract support from specific ethnic or cultural groups, reflecting the country's diverse population. This phenomenon can lead to the formation of parties that closely resemble the ethnic or racial makeup of their supporters, further reinforcing identity-based divisions in politics. Political leaders in South Africa, such as Julius Malema of the Economic Freedom Fighters (EFF) and Cornie Mulder from the Freedom Front Plus (FF+), employ populist rhetoric to mobilize support among their respective constituencies. By appealing to racial and ideological identities, these leaders seek to garner electoral support and advance their political agendas. The use of populist rhetoric by leaders like Malema and Mulder highlights the paradoxical nature of identity-based politics. While these leaders may champion the interests of specific ethnic or racial groups, their rhetoric can also deepen divisions and perpetuate societal tensions, rather than fostering genuine dialogue and understanding across diverse communities (Ngwane, 2019; Nyenhuis, 2020).

India has historically maintained close ties with South Africa, particularly due to their shared histories of colonialism and struggles for independence. India has supported South Africa's political and democratic development through diplomatic engagement, technical assistance, and capacity-building initiatives. Additionally, India has provided developmental aid and investments in various sectors, contributing to South Africa's socio-economic progress. China has emerged as a key economic partner for many African countries, including South Africa, through initiatives such as the Belt and Road Initiative (BRI). Under the BRI framework, China has invested heavily in infrastructure projects, trade, and economic cooperation across the African continent. In South Africa, Chinese investments have funded major infrastructure projects, including ports, railways, and telecommunications networks. While both India and China support South Africa's development, their approaches differ significantly. India emphasizes diplomatic relations, cultural exchanges, and capacity-building initiatives, focusing on soft power and people-to-people ties. In contrast, China's involvement is primarily driven by economic interests, with a focus on infrastructure development, trade, and investment, often through state-led initiatives (Bharti, 2022a, 2022b, 2023a, 2023d, 2023b, 2023c). India and China's involvement in South Africa's political and democratic development can have both positive and negative impacts. While economic cooperation with China can stimulate growth and infrastructure development, it also raises concerns about debt sustainability, environmental impacts, and socio-economic inequalities. India's support, on the other hand, may promote democratic values, good governance, and sustainable development, but it may also face challenges in competing with China's economic influence.

CONCLUSION

This paper identified that "waves of democratization" rises in the world as the level of democratic promotion in South Africa as well. Since 1990, South Africa's democratic transformation attracted another neighbourhood country of Africa. The development of democratic institutions has been working beautifully in the country to provide space for common people and decrease the gap of discrimination against coloured people. The coalition governments have been implementing all democratic culture in the country. South African governments have been enhanced democratic norms to the establishment of welfare programs for the inhabitants. The study also highlights the coalition government in South Africa bridging the poverty gap among the people. At the international development indicator also shows that South Africa is an emerging nation in the African continent. South Africa has been successfully organizing international summits in the different cities of the countries and shows enormous temperament towards a democratic base development in the country.

This study finds out the inter-party alliances and coalitions during this period played a crucial role in reshaping South Africa's political landscape. These alliances, particularly between the ANC, NNP, and DA, led to significant changes in party dynamics and electoral outcomes. The formation of alliances helped absorb the support base of the New National Party (NNP), which had experienced a decline in popularity since the 1994 elections. The NNP's support, which stood at 20% in the 1994 elections, was gradually disseminated among various recipient parties. A substantial portion of this support went to the Democratic Party (DP)-DA alliance, positioning the DA as a major challenger to the ANC. By mid-2014, indicators suggested that South Africa was moving towards a two-party system, with the ANC and DA emerging as the two main political contenders. This shift reflected changes in voter preferences and party dynamics influenced by inter-party alliances and coalition-building efforts. Party alliances and coalitions have occasionally aimed to build social cohesion by bringing together diverse political forces and constituencies. The formation of the United Democratic Movement (UDM), which combined split-offs from the ANC and the NNP, represents one such effort to bridge political divides and promote unity.

The coalition form of government in South Africa has played a crucial role in enhancing sustainable democracy, even amid political turmoil following the 2014 parliamentary elections. Despite challenges, coalition governments have contributed to democratic stability and governance effectiveness in several ways:

Inclusivity and Representation: Coalition governments often involve multiple parties representing diverse constituencies. This inclusivity ensures that a broader range of voices and perspectives are represented in decision-making processes, enhancing democratic legitimacy and responsiveness to citizens' needs. The presence of multiple parties within a coalition government provides built-in checks and balances, preventing any single party from monopolizing power. This helps to mitigate the risk of authoritarianism or abuse of power, contributing to the consolidation of democratic norms and principles. In coalition governments, parties often need to find common ground on policy issues, leading to innovative solutions and pragmatic governance approaches. This flexibility and adaptability are essential for addressing complex challenges and advancing sustainable development goals in a dynamic political environment. Despite political turmoil and differences between parties' ideology, coalition governments can provide stability and continuity in governance. By bringing together diverse parties with a shared commitment to democratic principles and constitutional norms, coalition arrangements help prevent political instability and ensure the smooth functioning of government institutions. In a dynamic political environment, coalition governments may be better equipped to adapt to changing circumstances and shifting electoral landscapes. By fostering cooperation and flexibility, coalition arrangements can help navigate uncertain political terrain and maintain stability in times of turmoil.

This study highlights the coalition governance in South Africa has the potential to promote social cohesion by fostering a culture of collaboration, unity, and mutual respect among citizens and political leaders. By transcending ideological and cultural differences, coalition governments can contribute to building a more inclusive and harmonious society, while also addressing the legacy of apartheid and promoting peaceful coexistence. Coalition governments, formed by multiple parties, often face challenges in maintaining transparency and accountability due to the complexity of their agreements and decision-making processes (Morrison, 2023). Moreover, focusing on citizen well-being over political power is essential for the effective functioning of democracy. Governments should prioritize policies and actions that benefit the entire society, rather than serving narrow partisan interests. This requires cooperation and compromise among coalition partners to achieve common goals that promote the welfare of citizens. Encouraging participation from all sectors of society, including citizens, is fundamental for a healthy democracy. When citizens are informed and engaged in the political process, they can contribute valuable insights and perspectives, leading to more inclusive and effective governance. Thus, public coalition agreements and a focus on citizen well-being are crucial elements for fostering accountability and participation in representative democracies. By implementing these principles, governments can better serve the interests of their constituents and strengthen democratic institutions.

REFERENCES

Aiyede, E. R. (2023). Governance and Politics of Public Policy in Africa. In E. R. Aiyede & B. Muganda (Eds.), *Public Policy and Research in Africa* (pp. 87–121). Springer International Publishing. doi:10.1007/978-3-030-99724-3_5

Arnolds, M. (2023). *Department of Cooperative Governance and Traditional Affairs.* Retrieved from https://www.cogta.gov.za/cgta_2016/wp-content/uploads/2023/08/AIC-Coalition-Framework-scheme.pdf

Barber, B. R. (2013). *If Mayors Ruled the World: Dysfunctional Nations, Rising Cities.* Yale University Press.

Benit-Gbaffou, C., Dubresson, A., Fourchard, L., Ginisty, K., Jaglin, S., Olukoju, A., Owuor, S., & Vivet, J. (2013). Exploring the Role of Party Politics in the Governance of African Cities. In S. Bekker & L. Fourchard (Eds.), *Governing Cities in Africa* (pp. 17–42). HSRC Press.

Bharti, M. S. (2022a). The Development of China's Economic Cooperation in the Horn of Africa: Special Reference to the Belt and Road Initiative. *African Journal of Economics. Politics and Social Studies, 1*(1), 17–30. doi:10.15804/ajepss.2022.1.12

Bharti, M. S. (2022b). The Indo-US Strategic Cooperation and How China's Influence Challenges to India-US Alliance in the Indo-Pacific. *Tamkang Journal of International Affairs, 26*(1), 71–127. doi:10.6185/TJIA.V.202209_26(1).0002

Bharti, M. S. (2023a). Global Development and International Order Transition: The Role of China. In M. O. Dinçsoy & H. Can (Eds.), *Optimizing Energy Efficiency During a Global Energy Crisis* (pp. 200–212). IGI Global. doi:10.4018/979-8-3693-0400-6.ch013

Bharti, M. S. (2023b). The Geo-Economics Approach to the European Union Strategic Partnership in the Indo-Pacific Region. In R. A. Castanho (Ed.), *Handbook of Research on Current Advances and Challenges of Borderlands, Migration, and Geopolitics* (pp. 297–311). IGI Global. doi:10.4018/978-1-6684-7020-6.ch015

Bharti, M. S. (2023c). The Strategic Partnership Between India and the United States of America and How China's Influence Challenges the India-Us Alliance in the Indo-Pacific Region. *Regional Formation and Development Studies*, *39*(1), 16–26. doi:10.15181/rfds.v36i1.2507

Bharti, M. S. (2023d). The Sustainable Development and Economic Impact of China's Belt and Road Initiative in Ethiopia. *East Asia (Piscataway, N.J.)*, *40*(2), 175–194. doi:10.1007/s12140-023-09402-y PMID:37065271

Booysen, S. (2014). *Causes And Impact Of Party Alliances And Coalitions On The Party System And National Cohesion In South Africa*. Electoral Institute For Sustainable Democracy In Africa. Retrieved from https://www.eisa.org/wp-content/uploads/2023/05/2014-journal-of-african-elections-v13n1-causes-impact-party-alliances-coalitions-party-system-national-cohesion-south-africa-eisa.pdf

Booysen, S. (2018). Coalitions and alliances demarcate crossroads in ANC trajectories. *New Agenda: South African Journal of Social and Economic Policy*, *68*, 6–10.

Bosire, C. M. (2011). Local Government and Human Rights: Building Institutional Links for the Effective Protection and Realisation of Human Rights in Africa. *African Human Rights Law Journal*, *11*(1), 147–170.

Bradshaw, G., & Breakfast, N. (2019). Mediating coalition politics at the local government level in South Africa, 2016-2019. *Journal of Gender. Information and Development in Africa*, *8*(2), 113–129.

Connors, M. K. (1996). The eclipse of consociationalism in South Africa's Democratic Transition. *Democratization*, *3*(4), 420–434. doi:10.1080/13510349608403488

de Jager, N., & Sebudubudu, D. (2017). Towards understanding Botswana and South Africa's ambivalence to liberal democracy. *Journal of Contemporary African Studies*, *35*(1), 15–33. doi:10.1080/02589001.2016.1246682

Dlakavu, A. (2022). South African electoral trends: Prospects for coalition governance at national and provincial spheres in 2024. *Politikon: South African Journal of Political Studies*, *49*(4), 476–490. doi:10.1080/02589346.2022.2151682

Electoral Commission of South Africa. (2021). *2021 Municipal Elections-Electoral Commission of South Africa*. Retrieved from https://www.elections.org.za/pw/

Fish, J. N. (2006). Engendering Democracy: Domestic Labour and Coalition-Building in South Africa. *Journal of Southern African Studies*, *32*(1), 107–127. doi:10.1080/03057070500493811

Frug, G. E. (1999). *City Making: Building Communities Without Building Walls*. Princeton University Press.

Gable, J. (2024, February 6). *South Africa faces prospect of multi-party coalition*. OMFIF. Retrieved from https://www.omfif.org/2024/02/south-africa-faces-prospect-of-multi-party-coalition/

Giliomee, H. (1995). Democratization in South Africa. *Political Science Quarterly, 110*(1), 83–104. doi:10.2307/2152052

Hanabe, L. D., & Malinzi, U. (2019). Party coalition as a model to govern municipalities in South Africa. *Journal of Public Administration, 54*(1), 41–51.

Huntington, S. P. (1991). How countries democratize. *Political Science Quarterly, 106*(4), 579–616. doi:10.2307/2151795

Huntington, S. P. (1991). *The Third Wave: Democratization in the late Twentieth Century*. University of Oklahoma Press.

Huntington, S. P. (1993). he third wave: Democratization in the late twentieth century (Vol. 4). University of Oklahoma press.

Huntington, S. P. (1997). After twenty years: The future of the third wave. *Journal of Democracy, 8*(4), 3–12. doi:10.1353/jod.1997.0059

Joshua, M., James, M., & Titos, K. (2022). Coalition Governance and Service Delivery in South Africa: A Case Study of Tshwane, Johannesburg and Ekurhuleni Metropolitan Municipalities. *Journal of Public Administration, 57*(2).

Karume, S. (2003). *Conceptual understanding of political coalitions in South Africa: An integration of concepts and practice.* Paper presented at Electoral Institute of Southern Africa (EISA) Roundtable on political party coalitions: Strengthening democracy through party coalition building (Vol. 19). Electoral Institute of Southern Africa round table on Strengthening Democracy through Party Coalition Building.

Kurzman, C. (1998). Waves of democratization. *Studies in Comparative International Development, 33*(1), 42–64. doi:10.1007/BF02788194

Lambright, G. M. S. (2014). Opposition Politics and Urban Service Delivery in Kampala, Uganda. *Development Policy Review, 32*(s1, S1), S39–S60. doi:10.1111/dpr.12068

Lijphart, A. (1977). *Democracy in plural societies: A comparative exploration*. Yale University Press.

Lijphart, A. (1987). Power Sharing in South Africa. Institute of International Studies, University of California.

Lijphart, A. (2023). *The politics of accommodation: Pluralism and democracy in the Netherlands*. University of California Press. doi:10.2307/jj.8501386

Mandela, N. (1998, September 3). *Closing address by President Nelson Mandela at the 12th Summit Meeting of Heads of State and Government of the countries of the Non-Aligned Movement.* Retrieved from http://www.mandela.gov.za/mandela_speeches/1998/980903_nam.htm

Mnwana, S. (2015). Democracy, development and chieftaincy along South Africa's 'Platinum Highway': Some emerging issues. *Journal of Contemporary African Studies, 33*(4), 510–529. doi:10.1080/02589 001.2015.1117730

Molomo, M. G. (2000). Democracy under Siege: The Presidency and Executive Powers in Botswana. *Pula: Botswana Journal of African Studies, 14*(1), 95–108.

Morrison, S. (2023, December 5). *Understanding South Africa's Political Landscape*. Good Governance Africa. Retrieved from https://gga.org/understanding-south-africas-coalition-landscape/

Moshoeshoe, M. L., & Dzinesa, G. A. (2024). More Democracy, More Security? Regionalism and Political [In]Security in East and Southern Africa. *Global Society*, 1–26. doi:10.1080/13600826.2023.2301067

Naidoo, V. (2019). Transitional Politics and Machinery of Government Change in South Africa. *Journal of Southern African Studies*, *45*(3), 575–595. doi:10.1080/03057070.2019.1622309

Ngwane, T. (2019). Insurgent democracy: Post-apartheid South Africa's freedom fighters. *Journal of Southern African Studies*, *45*(1), 229–245. doi:10.1080/03057070.2019.1548136

Nyenhuis, R. (2020). The political struggle for 'the people': Populist discourse in the 2019 South African elections. *Commonwealth and Comparative Politics*, *58*(4), 409–432. doi:10.1080/14662043.2020.1746040

Pieterse, M. (2019). A Year of Living Dangerously? Urban Assertiveness, Cooperative Governance and the First Year of Three Coalition-Led Metropolitan Municipalities in South Africa. *Politikon: South African Journal of Political Studies*, *46*(1), 51–70. doi:10.1080/02589346.2018.1518759

Pietersen, J. M. (2021). Assessment of Coalition Governments (2016-2021) in Metropolitan Cities of Gauteng Province Using the Theory of Democracy. *Journal of Public Administration*, *56*(3), 488–506.

Reddy, T. (2010). ANC Decline, Social Mobilization and Political Society: Understanding South Africa's Evolving Political Culture. *Politikon: South African Journal of Political Studies*, *37*(2–3), 185–206. doi:10.1080/02589346.2010.522329

Schragger, R. (2016). *City Power: Urban Governance in a Global Age*. Oxford University Press.

Williams, C., & Papa, M. (2020). Rethinking "Alliances": The Case of South Africa as a Rising Power. *African Security*, *13*(4), 325–352. doi:10.1080/19392206.2020.1871796

ADDITIONAL READING

Greben, J. (2012). Voter movements between elections – linking the 2011 and preceding election results using cluster trend matrices. In S. Booysen (Ed.), *Local elections in South Africa: Parties, people, politics*. Sun Press with Konrad Adenhauer Stiftung.

Jolobe, Z. (2012). A party for all the people? The DA and the 2011 elections. In S. Booysen (Ed.), *Local elections in South Africa: Parties, people, politics*. Sun Press with Konrad Adenhauer Stiftung.

Kotzé, H. (2001). The potential constituency of the DA: What dowries do the DP and NNP bring to the marriage? In *Opposition in South Africa's new democracy*. KAS.

Lodge, T. (2004). *EISA Election Update – South Africa 2004. Update No 1*. EISA.

Masaka, D. (2022). Political violence in Africa and the search for an ideal democracy model. *African Identities*, 1–19. doi:10.1080/14725843.2022.2108371

Sarakinsky, I. (2007). Political Party Finance in South Africa: Disclosure Versus Secrecy. *Democratization*, *14*(1), 111–128. doi:10.1080/13510340601024330

KEY TERMS AND DEFINITIONS

ANC in South Africa: The African National Congress (ANC) is a prominent political party in South Africa with a rich history deeply intertwined with the country's struggle against apartheid and its transition to democracy. Throughout the apartheid era, the ANC, alongside other liberation movements like the Pan Africanist Congress (PAC) and the South African Communist Party (SACP), fought against racial segregation, discrimination, and the brutal policies of the apartheid government.

Coalition Governments: Coalition governments play a significant role in many democracies worldwide, offering a means to represent diverse interests and promote stability. However, they also require effective communication, compromise, and transparency to address the challenges associated with shared governance and maintain accountability to the electorate.

Future Prospects of South African Democracy: In recent years, the ANC has grappled with internal divisions, allegations of corruption, and declining public trust. Infighting within the party, as well as concerns about mismanagement and state capture, have raised questions about its ability to effectively govern and deliver on its promises. The ANC has pursued a range of economic policies aimed at promoting growth, job creation, and social welfare. These policies include Black Economic Empowerment (BEE) initiatives to redress economic imbalances inherited from apartheid, as well as social welfare programs targeting poverty and inequality. Despite facing challenges, the ANC remains a dominant force in South African politics, with significant support among voters, particularly in rural and historically marginalized communities. Its ability to address internal divisions, combat corruption, and deliver on its promises will be key factors in shaping its future trajectory. By and large, the ANC's legacy is deeply intertwined with South Africa's history and its ongoing journey towards building a more inclusive, democratic, and prosperous society.

Post-Apartheid Governance in South Africa: Since the end of apartheid, the ANC has been the ruling party in South Africa, winning successive elections and holding power at the national level. It has implemented various policies aimed at redressing the legacies of apartheid, promoting social justice, and addressing economic inequality. However, the party has faced criticism for issues such as corruption, service delivery failures, and internal divisions.

Sustainable Democracy: Sustainable democracy seeks to create a resilient and inclusive political system that can effectively address contemporary challenges while safeguarding the rights and interests of future generations. It requires continuous efforts from governments, civil society, and citizens to uphold democratic values and institutions for the well-being of society as a whole.

Transition to Democracy in South Africa: The ANC played a pivotal role in negotiating an end to apartheid and facilitating South Africa's transition to democracy in the early 1990s. Mandela, who became the country's first black president in 1994, led the ANC during this historic period of change.

Chapter 16
Coalitions in South African Local Government and the Implications for Public Service Delivery

Thokozani Ian Nzimakwe

https://orcid.org/0000-0001-5817-9910
University of KwaZulu-Natal, South Africa

Sakhile Zondi
University of KwaZulu-Natal, South Africa

ABSTRACT

The decision to establish coalition governments in South Africa is one that lies firmly on political parties. Ultimately the electorate does not have a say in its formation. It is assumed that representative democracy finds expression in the formation of coalitions. The stability of the government will formally depend on the urges of the elected representatives of political parties in a legislative body. It is more likely to depend on political party leaders who, for various reasons, retain considerable control over the conduct of their elected representatives. Coalitions seem to be the solution when political parties in democracies do not win by outright margins and majority governments have to be constituted. Yet, the way in which political parties and politicians practice coalitions in South Africa means coalitions are, at best, a tense alternative. The South African Constitution of 1996 vests legislative and executive authority in the municipal council. As the highest decision-making body, the council must steer the municipality, determine its strategic direction, and take crucial decisions. In coalitions, this requires close cooperation between coalition partners to ensure that the responsibilities of the council are carried out effectively. This chapter argues that, however, in practice, coalition governments have often been unstable and terminated before the end of the council term. Instability in a local coalition can have a severe impact as it may compromise the municipality's ability to adopt policies and by-laws, make senior management appointments, or even adopt a budget. Ultimately, local communities will continue to bear the brunt of unstable coalition politics. The conclusion is that more stable coalitions will therefore contribute to improved service delivery.

DOI: 10.4018/979-8-3693-1654-2.ch016

INTRODUCTION

In the evolving landscape of South African politics, coalition governments represent a defining feature of a contemporary governance system that characterise many local municipalities. The notion of coalition governance is in line with the practice of representative democracy – a political system in which the politicians are entitled to represent the electorates in all democratic processes (Bouton, 2013). Since 1994, the majority of South African citizens have been accustomed to one political party dominating the others. This has been a defining feature of the post-apartheid politics at the national, provincial and local government levels (Kinsel, 2009) in essence, coalitions are not a new phenomenon, particularly at a municipal level. It is supported by the Constitution of the Republic of South Africa (1996) which encourages the notion of freedom of association. Consequently, the South African citizens are entitled to floor crossing or establish new political parties which are in line with the country's post 1994 political system (Dladla, 2019).

This chapter seeks to analyse coalition governance complexities across the South African municipalities and to examine its service delivery implications. As such the thematic areas that are covered in this chapter include, *inter alia* (i) evolution of coalition governance: from global to local experiences (ii) coalition governance and implication for public service delivery in South Africa (iii) legislative and policy framework for coalition governance; (iv) (iv) Challenges of coalition governance in South Africa, (v) research methodology and presentation of findings; and (vi) conclusion and recommendations.

BACKGROUND

At the onset of the South African democracy, coalition government was experienced when the late former President Mandela, under the leadership of the African National Congress (ANC) co-operated with the opposition parties to form the Government of National Unity (South African History Online (SAHO), 2018). Section 88 of the 1993 Interim Constitution of the Republic of South Africa makes provision for the creation of the Government of National Unity. The GNU played a significant role to transform South Africa and reverse the atrocities of the apartheid regimes and further paved the way for the new set of government policies (SAHO, 2018). It is against this background that various researchers, academics and politicians have noted that coalition governance is not a completely novel practice, rather it has become a popular and growing trend especially after the 2016 and 2021 local government elections in South Africa (Mpangalasane, 2020). The governing ANC has been a dominant political party in the South African political landscape since the attainment of democracy in 1994. The support and political hegemony of the ANC is evident with impressive election outcomes since 1994 at national, provincial and local levels. The party has held a majority of the seats in the National Assembly since 1994, being re-elected with increasing majorities in 1999 and 2004, 2009 and with a slight fall in its support in 2014. During first decade of democracy (1994-2014) the ANC has entrenched strong moral and ethical leadership in the South African society which has also amplified massive social transformation and service delivery outputs (Burgess, Jadwab & Miguel, 2015). However, despite these achievements, the political dominance of the ANC has been gradually eroding (Makgale, 2020). To this end, the outcomes of the local government elections in 2016, and 2021 respectively were indeed a watershed moment for the country's democracy as they introduced a large number of coalition governments in the local government sphere. While the the smaller political parties (Democratic Alliance (DA), Economic Freedom Fighters (EFF) Freedom Front Plus (FF+) and Inkatha Freedom Party (IFP) flourished as more competitive oppositions - changing the country's voting patterns, the ANC recorded a decline in its support base by 14% (Ndou, 2022). The emergence smaller political parties and the decline in support of the ANC have necessitated the formulation of coalition governments in the administration of the South African municipalities (Makole, Ntshangase & Adewumi, 2022). Consequently, the ANC had to move out of leadership positions in many municipalities as the opposition parties negotiated with the smaller parties to constitute the new leadership (municipal councils) (Kariuki, Reddy and Wissink (2022). Since 2000, the number of political parties who partake in the local government elections increased from 98 to 323 in 2021. The growing number of political parties allows the electorates an opportunity for a broader choice, hence there would be no outright winner (Ndou, 2022). To this end, coalitions are now an integral part of the South African politics at the municipal level and can even spread to the national and provincial in the future elections (McCain, 2020, 2018).

In terms of conceptual definition, coalition governance is defined by the South African Local Government Association (SALGA, 2022) as a collaborative initiative between two or more political parties who agree to collaborate in governing together as a ruling coalition government. Collaboration, negotiation, and strategic politics were required to form governments (Tselane, 2023). On a similar vein, Gautam (2022) opines that a coalition government in the local government context is a typology of government that merges multiple political formations who possess different political ideologies co-operating to achieve a common objective of advancing service delivery.

As highlighted in the above section, the coalition governments emerged as a result of the governing party's decline in popularity and support due to a number of reasons which are discussed later in this chapter. According to Makole *et al* (2022:24) coalition governance should be analysed from a context of enhancing and improving multi-party democracy through freedom of choice and association as articulated in the South African Constitution of 1996.

The decision by former President Zuma to denounce the ANC and announce his support for the newly formed Mkhonto Wesizwe (MK) Party is viewed as a major setback for the ANC's ambitions to regain political support of the electorates in the 2024 general elections (Daily Maverick, 2024). In these elections, the ANC is expected to face fierce competition from the opposition parties (MK Party, IFP, DA, EFF, and FF+. The smaller parties and independent candidates could be crucial in case of coalition negotiations (Maserumule, 2020).

LITERATURE REVIEW

Evolution of Coalition Governance from Global to Local Experiences

This section draws best international practices of coalition governance from countries that are renowned for implementing effective and efficient regulatory systems to manage coalitions, such as United Kingdom (UK), India, Kenya and Malaysia) (Tselane, 2023:4).

Coalition has become common governance trend in the western countries due to the growing improbability of a one-party states (Kluver & Back, 2019, cited in Makole and Ntshangase, 2022:24). Therefore, coalitions in the South African context typifies the Western experiences, though there are some differences in the manner in which they are implemented. The modus operand to succeed with coalition governance in the aforementioned countries include consensus-building, emphasis on good governance, abilities to manage conflicting ideologies and responsiveness to urgent needs of the electorates (Tselane, 2023:4). Schreiber (2018) avers that many European countries have successfully adopted coalition-based governance systems in which co-operation, mutual trust and compromise inherent to governing through coalitions have been instrumental to sustain political lives of the coalition parties. The majority of the United Nations Development Programme (UNDP) countries were in coalition governance model except for the Singapore. Schreiber (2018) assert that for the period between 1945 and 2014, 88% of the European governance has flourished significantly under coalition arrangements. Therefore, Europe should be considered as a cornerstone for coalition governance for countries in Africa in particular to draw best practices. In recent years, Germany, Denmark and France have been the cases of coalitions.

Muller and Strom (2000) noted that the success of coalition governance in Europe has been under-pinned by four pillars, including:

- **Coalition politics as a strategic collaboration**: coalition governance is a voluntary choice that is advanced by political organisations that are involved in the pact. These actors are directed/influenced by a set of political ideologies derived from common objectives. This has not been the case in the South African context where different ideologies have been the main challenge that led to the unsustainability of coalition governments.
- **Coalition as an equal partnership between political parties:** coalition requires progressive partnership and strong support base from constituencies. In essence, close relationships between political leaders and constituencies is a key defining feature for the European coalition governments.
- **Coalitions governments are institutionally conditioned:** the institutional internal environments are imperative for the success of coalition partnership. This construct includes the ability of coalition partners to embrace diversity and remain neutral from their political philosophies.
- **Coalitions governance is the pursuit of common political goals and interests:** a coalition group of rival political actors are brought together by perceiving a common threat or harnessing collective energies. They establish a coalition to achieve their goals because they might not achieve such goals when working separately.

It is evident from the above discussion that coalitions exist for many reasons that differ according to the political and legal landscape of a country's socio-economic, cultural, and institutional context and the time at which the coalition is formed However, in more general terms, the traditional rationale for coalition formation is to win elections and hold office (Kadima, 2014).

This chapter draws international best practices of coalition governance from the United Kingdom, India, Malaysia and Kenya.

Coalition Governance in the United Kingdom

Coalitions have been a defining feature of the British politics for centuries. During this period, several agreements, regulatory frameworks and mechanisms were formulated in order to formalise coalition agreements between the British political parties (Labuschagne, 2018). The growing popularity of coalitions was witnessed during the wartime economic depression in Britain in the "Month of May" (Ndou, 2022). In 1918, the Liberal Party formed and led a coalition governance with minority parties which paved the way for the post war economic recovery and reconstruction (Timmermans, 2003). Again, in 1940, In 1940, Winston Churchill established a Coalition National Government, which lasted until May 1945, when the General elections were held (Labuschagne, 2018). British politics have always been dominated by the Conservative Party and the Labour Party. Though these two major parties would exchange each other in running the country, coalitions remained the dominant factor of the British political arrangement. In 2010, the Liberal Democratic Party formed a coalition government with the Conservative Party. Some Liberal Democrats supporters were dismayed by the decision to form a coalition with the Conservative Party due to different political ideologies that existed between these parties (Matthews, 2018).

The case study of coalition governance in the United Kingdom reveals two important lessons that are also instrumental for the South African politics.

- First, coalition governance is formulated for a specific reason to abolish a notion of one-party state and allow opposition parties and smaller political parties to participate in the governance affairs of their communities. The poor management of coalition governments negatively impacts on public service delivery. Therefore, coalition governments require clear guidelines and frameworks to avoid unnecessary conflict in government (Booysen, 2018).
- Second, electorates are an integral part of the coalition because they vote for a party based on its policy direction and commitment to improve political and socio-economic lives. When an agreement is made to form a coalition without proper consultation with the electorates, they feel betrayed and excluded. Therefore, a proper coalition should be characterised with rigorous consultation, participation and compromise as it merges diverse groups of people to form a shared common identity (Ndou, 2022).

Coalition Governance in India

India, a country in Asia with the second biggest population of approximately 1.2 billion people provides an interesting case study of coalition governance. India gained her independence from Great Britain in 1947. Since then, the Indian politics has been largely influenced by the Indian National Congress (INC) as a dominant party which controlled the government and enjoyed overwhelming support (reference). After 1977, the INC became unpopular to its constituencies due to authoritarian rule, bad governance and corruption which triggered a series of violent protests (Schreiber, 2018). Many INC party leaders were found guilty of fraud by the Hight Court. Consequently, the High Court ruled that they should vacate their parliamentary seats and be banned from participating in the governance affairs. These events contributed to the collapse of INC, and was subsequently outvoted in the elections that took place in 1982 (reference). These elections paved the way for the coalition governance in India in which the Junata Alliance, a merger of seven parties took over the Indian government (reference).

The case of India resembles the events that contributed to growing trend of political pluralism in the management of South African municipalities. The ANC to deal with corruption, restore order for municipal governance and deliver community services is singled out as a main reason for its decline and growing popularity of coalition governance at a local government sphere.

Coalition Governances in Kenya

The Republic of Kenya in Africa presents another intriguing case of coalition government which became prevalent after presidential elections that were closely contested in 2007. The dispute of election results after these elections changed the political landscape of the country and paved the way for the creation of coalition governance. According to Donnelley (2015), from 1962 to 1995, a monolithic or one-party dominance system became entrenched in Kenya, and was characterized by authoritarianism and gross violation of human rights (Bigambo, 2017). The repeal of some sections of the country's Constitution led to the introduction of the multi-party system. Although this decision was described as a major political transformation, it lacked legal and effective administrative backup, resulting in a weak legislative framework for elections. As a result of this transformation, numerous political parties and non-partisan individuals were allowed to contest elections (Bigambo, 2017).

In the elections that took place in 2007, President Mwai Kibaki of the Party of National Unity (PNU) was declared the winner of presidential elections. This declaration was challenged by the supporters of the Azimio Laumoja, a country's main opposition party under the leadership of Ralia Odinga. In an attempt to circumvent this violence, the resolution was taken to form the Kenyan Grand Coalition Government in 2008 (Donnelley, 2015) This decision was largely based on the conviction that such government has the potential to promote compromise and conciliation between adversarial factions.

Coalition Governance in Malaysia

Like European, Asian and African countries, the Malaysia has had a rich history of coalition governments which has been part of the country's political landscape for many decades. Since 1957, the country's federal government has never been controlled by a single political party (reference). The first federal government was formed by the amalgamation of a three-party alliance comprising of United Malays National Organisations (UMNO), the Malaysian Chinese Association (MCA), and the Malaysian Indian Congress (MIC) (Luebbert, 2012). In 2018, the Malaysian new coalition government between the Pakatan Harapan (PH) and the Sabah Heritage Party took over the government (Luebbert, 2012).

Coalition Governance and Implication for Public Service Delivery in South Africa

As discussed in the above section, coalition governance has throughout the global community became a growing trend in major constitutional democracies such as the United Kingdom, Malaysia, India, and Kenya. Mnguni (2023:374) assets that the spread of coalition governments at a global and local context has been the dubiousness associated with one-party governments. Consequently, in the post-colonial era, most African states have adopted coalition model. Coalition governments have also been motivated by the zeal of the coalition pacts to stimulate service delivery, thus improving socio-economic conditions for local populace (Dassah, 2012).

Given that local government is a sphere closest to the people, coalitions at a municipal level have a social responsibility of providing basic services to the communities (Ndevu and Muller, 2018). Furthermore, the South African Constitution vests legislative powers on municipalities to entrench democratic values in all local communities, facilitate quality service delivery, enhance socio-economic development, promote clean and safe environment and to encourage community involvement in policy formulation and service delivery planning at a municipal level (RSA Constitution, 1996).

Despite this constitutional mandate, service delivery remains a colossal challenge that has prompted violent protests for many municipalities across South Africa (Kariuki, Reddy & Wissink, 2022). Therefore, there is an expectation that the coalition-led municipality should meet service delivery needs of the South African municipalities. On the similar vein, Ndou (2022) points out that the primary objective of coalition governance in South Africa should be to transform service delivery and improve lives for the local populace. This view is also endorsed by SALGA (2022) that to be effective, the coalition governments will have to become more citizen-centric to meet the expectations of the local citizenry. In the long-term, if coalition led municipalities are responsive to community needs, they will change the way in which current municipalities are managed and ensure their efficiency, effectiveness and sustainability.

The Legislative and Policy Framework for Coalition Governance in South Africa

The global experiences of coalition governance that are discussed in the above sections have alluded to the role and importance of effective legal and administrative environment for the regulation of effective coalition governance. Effective legislative and policy as far as coalition governance is concerned is imperative for the capable and developmental local government which is envisioned by the White Paper on Local Government of 1998. The Developmental mandate of local government requires municipalities to play a more active roles in terms of promoting continuous engagement with local communities towards unlocking their urgent socio-economic needs (Chambers, 2022). Furthermore, this developmental mandate should be prioritised, irrespective of which political party is occupying the leadership positions in a municipal council.

Despite the growing popularity of coalitions governance in South Africa since the local government elections in 2016, there is no specific legislative and policy framework that regulates party coalitions (De Vos, 2021; Dladla, 2019). Likewise, the South African Local Government Association (SALGA, 2022) notes that despite being a dominating feature in the South African local government sphere, coalitions governments are not institutionalised. The South African constitution omits key regulations that promote and safeguard the creation of coalition governments in the 3 spheres of the South African government (National, provincial and local) (Le Roux and Davis, 2019). This implies that there are no guidelines or rules to determine how coalition relationship between parties should be regulated. Currently, the coalitions are created and underpinned by informal binding arrangements and agreements among coalition parties (Kariuki, Reddy and Wissink, 2022). The challenge in this practice emerges when the party with outright majority of votes opts to use its own philosophy to define the values of the coalition partnership (Kariuki, Reddy and Wissink, 2022). As illustrated in the contemporary literature of municipal governance in the South African context, the lack of legislative framework for coalition governance is a colossal challenge that requires urgent intervention. The legislative framework will be instrumental to guide political parties in structuring their coalition politics.

Beukes (2021:13) propose the following responsibilities of the legislative and policy framework for coalition governance in South Africa:

- It should consider public inputs and define the programme of action for the incoming administration;
- Formalise coalition agreements/arrangements between parries involved in the coalition governance.
- It should be customised to meet service delivery needs of the community and political needs of the coalition parties.
- It should be strengthened by coalition partners in practice and made public so that it is deemed as public knowledge.

In this way, the coalition partnerships in local government will commit them to the course to pursue the political aspirations of their constituencies. The notion of violating coalition agreement in favour of more reading proposals elsewhere will be avoided. It should however be noted that in some instances, the coalition will collapse due to policy differences and political ideologies between the coalition partners. This has been the case with ANC-DA and EFF-IFP coalitions.

Challenges of Coalition Governance in the South African Local Government Sphere

The majority of the country's 257 municipalities have been ruled by coalition governments since the 2016 local government elections and are experiencing numerous challenges. Gant, (2021) notes that coalition governments have collapse in various municipalities because dominant parties are not making enough compromises and smaller parties are often made to feel excluded. Various sources of literature outline the following challenges of coalition governments in the South African local government. Such challenges raise uncertainties for the future prospects of coalitions at the national and provincial levels.

- **Strained administrative-political interface:** This aspect points to a challenge in terms of elected leadership and continuity of administration in municipal governance. leadership changes often derail the provision of community changes as it has been the case with Johannesburg, nelson Mandela and Tshwane metropolitan municipalities. It is therefore imperative that service delivery is maintained while the municipality undergoes leadership changes.
- **Lack of continuity and service delivery disruption:** upon coming into power, the parties in a coalition relationship will bring new changes and explore the ways to sustain the functionality of their pact. During this period, service delivery will be disrupted.
- **Smaller parties lack governance capacity:** they can not deliver the mandate which they promised when campaigning for elections. To govern municipalities effectively, they will have to compromise with well established parties and who have bigger voter proportions. Even though small parties typically pursue their own distinct policy goals, they don't always succeed in communicating their policy stances.
- **Diversity of coalition parties:** coalition governments are collaborations of political parties with different scopes and philosophies. In this situation, reaching consensus will be a challenge, derailing the implementation of service delivery priorities.
- **Coalitions are formulated upon weak leaderships:** There is a general observation by academics, practitioners and policymakers alike that poor leadership has been a panacea of coalition governance in the South African municipalities. This observation is informed by the recognition that some coalition pacts are formed by the parties who not have leadership experience (Conrad, 2013).

Improving coalition governments at municipal level will require all parties involved in the pact to co-operate towards decision making, policy formulation and service delivery implementation. Various case studies from the South African context have revealed that coalition governments are only effective when the coalition pact is in a position to reach compromises and work mutually for a common purpose.

RESEARCH METHODOLOGY

The research methodology considered in this chapter is premised on the paradigm of unobtrusive research typology, comprising of conceptual and rigorous analysis of secondary sources of literature. Weiner (2010) explains that unobtrusive research implies data collection methods that excludes research subjects/ participants of the study because the methods are not obtrusive. In the fields of social sciences, unobtrusive research is used in both qualitative and quantitative researches. Sociologist, public administrators, anthropologists and historians who are interested in public affairs are more likely to use unobtrusive research. In the South African context, there has been an increasing volume of literature detailing the nature of coalition governments, hence it was convenient for this chapter to analyse secondary sources of information, including books, policy briefs, research documents, government policies, online sources, and journal articles.

FINDINGS AND ANALYSIS

A rigorous analysis of approximately 35 case studies of coalition government in local government spanning 7 years (2016–2023). The findings extracted from various literature sources under the broad thematic content relating to the current and future prospects for the institutionalisation of coalition governments across the South African municipalities, the findings pointed out that:

- **Public perception on Coalition-led municipalities**: seven in 10 South Africans (70%) are dissatisfied with the way in which local democracy works in their respective municipalities, while only one-quarter (25%) express satisfaction. The dissatisfaction about local democracy stems from the way in which coalition are handled in numerous municipalities. For example, the decision to formulate a coalition government is a decision of political parties and does not include public inputs and the electorates in particular. The pressing challenges relating to municipal service delivery that should be addressed by coalition governments include the water and sanitation, energy crisis/ load shedding, unemployment, crumbling infrastructure, and crime (Afro Barometer, 2023).
- **Citizens and relationships with their political parties**: the majority (63%) of citizens feel that they are excluded by their political parties from meaningful participation in the political affairs and policy formulation. Among the citizens who identify with their political parties, 28% indicated that they feel close to the ANC politics, 17% indicated their close relationships with the DA, 12% for the EFF and 7% for the IFP.
- **Factors Influencing the formation of Coalitions:** the majority of participants revealed that the loss of dominance by the ANC has contributed to forming a coalition government. Since 1994, the ANC has been a major political organisation that consistently won elections at the national, provincial and local levels. However, the decline of support for the ANC since 2016 local government elections have paved the way for coalition governments affording political powers to the opposition parties such as the DA, EFF, IFP, FF+ etc. Similar findings were also generated by the Mail & Guardian (2023) that almost few months to the 2024 presidential elections, the discussions about coalition governments and their implications on political stability are proliferating because the government party is at the risk of losing its majority of voter share.

- **Declining support for one-party state in South Africa:** the study conducted by Labuschagne (2018) indicated that coalition governments are inevitable when the political parties could not get an outright victor (two-third majority) in the election. Usually, coalitions are considered to avoid the rerun of the elections as this may have financial implications. The findings of the study conducted by Jolobe (2022) in relation to coalition government that excludes the ANC in the City of Tshwane, the opposition parties indicated their excitement for the ANC to lose support of the City of Tshwane as they wanted to form the government without ANC at all costs.
- **The implications of coalition governments for municipal service delivery:** coalition governments are generally created to maximise service delivery impact for local communities. This view is also expressed in Kariuki, Reddy and Wissink (2022) that in dealing with current challenges facing the Country's 257 municipalities, it is anticipated that the new coalitions-led municipalities will prioritise service delivery and accelerate socio-economic development aspirations that have been unattended for many years.

It is evident with various literature sources that in light of the political dynamics facing the ANC, the coalition government will be inevitable after the 2024 elections. These negative experiences of the citizens about service delivery and load shedding in particular have also contributed to a growing mistrust of the current political leadership.

CONCLUSION AND RECOMMENDATIONS

The chapter has analysed coalitions across South African local government sphere with specific reference on its implications for public service delivery. The practice of coalition governments in South Africa is has become an institutional norm and is motivated by the political background of the country which promoted proportional representation. That is, political parties are represented in government according to their proportion of the vote received in an election. While there are currently many challenges affecting coalition governance in many municipalities, numerous authors believe that this governance system reflect political maturity of the South African citizens who have undergone a paradigm shift in terms of their voting patterns (Gumede, 2021). For example, they have shifted from emotionally associating with certain political parties and began to apply their minds in affording political powers to the leaders with potential to represent their aspirations (Gumede, 2021). The challenges of coalition pertaining to inconsistencies and party conflicts that have been noted in many municipalities across South Africa have dire consequences for the country's democracy. Municipal service delivery obligations are also affected. Therefore, there is an urgent need for effective legislative and policy framework that will regulate coalition governments. This chapter has indicated that coalition governments at the municipal levels are currently underpinned by informal agreements/arrangements. Streamlining coalition governments will assist coalition parties to find common ground and work progressively in pursuit of public service delivery. The issues of ideological differences between parties in the coalition pact is another challenge that require policy intervention geared towards infrastructure development. The chapter has revealed that political ideological conflicts dominate many coalition governments and their implications on service delivery have devastating effects for local communities.

REFERENCES

Beukes, J. (2021). Coalition governments: guidelines for coalition agreements. *Local Government Bulletin*, *16*(1). https://dullahomarinstitute.org.za/multilevel-govt/local-government

Bigambo, J. (2017). *The Concept of Selective Communication: Shaping the Needs of Conflict and Human Resource Management in Kenya: A Case Study of Action Aid Kenya – Western Region*. Unpublished Human Resource Management report.

Booysen, S. (2018). Coalitions and alliances demarcate crossroads in ANC trajectories. *The New Agenda*, (68), 6–1.

Bouton, L. (2013). A Theory of Strategic Voting in Runoff Elections. *The American Economic Review*, *103*(4), 1248–1288. doi:10.1257/aer.103.4.1248

Burgess, R., Jedwab, R., Miguel, E., Morjaria, A., & Padró-i-Miquel, G. (2015). The Value of Democracy: Evidence from Road Building in Kenya. *The American Economic Review*, *105*(6), 1817–1851. doi:10.1257/aer.20131031

Chambers, D. (2022). Wanted: some adults to make a coalition work. *Sunday Times*. https://www.timeslive.co.za/sunday-times/opinion-and-analysis/opinion/2022-09-18-wanted-some-adultsto-make-a-coalition-work

Conrad, H. (2013). *Handbook of Public Leadership Theories*. Rand - McNally.

Dassah, M. O. (2012). A critical analysis of factors underlying service delivery protests in South Africa. *Journal of African and Asian Local Government Studies*, *1*(2), 1–28.

De Vos, P. (2021). The constitutional-legal dimensions of coalition politics and government in South Africa. Johannesburg: Mapungubwe (Mistra) Publishers. doi:10.2307/j.ctv2z6qdx6.16

Dladla, K. F. (2019). *The impact of the legal framework for local government in building and sustaining coalitions in municipal councils*. Master's dissertation. Cape Town: University of Western Cape. https://etd.uwc. ac.za/handle/11394/6401

Donnelly, J. (2015). *Universal Human Rights in Theory & Practice* (2nd ed.). Cornell University Press.

Gant, D. (2021). A government of national unity: one small step for President Ramaphosa, one giant leap for South Africa. *Daily Maverick*. https://www.dailymaverick.co.za/opinionista/2021-12-02

Gautam, A. K. (2022). Public policy making in coalition government: Challenges and solutions. *Asian Research Journal of Arts and Social Sciences*, *7*(3), 1-8.

Gumede, W. (2021). New laws needed to make political coalition work. *Sunday Times*, *5*(December), 22. https://journals.co.za/doi/full/10.10520/ejc-ajpa_v12_n1_a2

Jolobe, Z. (2018). The politics of dominance and survival: Coalition politics in South Africa 1994-2018. Academic Press.

Kadima, D. (2014). An introduction to the Politics of Party Alliances and Coalitions in Socially-divided Africa. *Journal of African Elections*, *13*(1), 1–24. doi:10.20940/JAE/2014/v13i1a1

Kariuki, P., Reddy, P. S., & Wissink, H. (2022). Implications for municipal leadership and Service Delivery: Coalition Building and Municipal Governance in South Africa. Academic Press.

Kinsel, A. (2009). *Post-apartheid Political Culture in South Africa, 1994-2004*. Unpublished Masters dissertation. University of Central Florida, United States of America. https://stars.library.ucf.edu/cgi/viewcontent.cgi?article=5084&context=etd

Labuschagne, P. (2018). South Africa, coalition and form of government: Semi presidentialism a tertium genus? *Journal of Contemporary History*, *43*(2), 95–115.

Le Roux, M., & Davis, D. (2019). *Lawfare: Judging politics in South Africa*. Jonathan Ball Publishers.

Lefebvre, B., & Robin, C. (2009). *Pre-electoral Coalitions, Party System and Electoral Geography: A Decade of General Elections in India 1999-2009*. Routledge.

Luebbert, G. M., Dodd, L., & Swaan, A. D. (2012, January). 'Coalition Theory and Government Formation in Multiparty Democracies'. *Comparative Politics*, *15*(2), 235. doi:10.2307/421678

Mail & Guardian. (2023). *Understanding South Africa's coalition landscape*, available https://mg.co.za/thought-leader/opinion/2023-12-05-understanding-south-africas-coalition-landscape

Makgale, B. (2020). *Coalition politics and urban governance in Johannesburg's housing policy*. Master's dissertation. Johannesburg: University of the Witwatersrand.

Makole, K. R., Ntshangase, B. A., & Adewumi, S. A. (2022). Coalition Governance: Unchartered Waters in South African Political Landscape. *Business Ethics and Leadership*, *6*(4), 23–37. doi:10.21272/bel.6(4).23-37.2022

Maserumule, M. H. (2020). Democratic Alliance-Led Coalition in the City of Tshwane: Strange Bedfellows Coming Apart at the seams. *Journal of Public Administration*, *55*(3).

Maverick, D. (2024). *What we know about Jacob Zuma's new party*. https://www.dailymaverick.co.za/article/2024-01-09-umkhonto-wesizwe-what-we-know-about-zumas-new-party

McCain, N. (2020). *Mangaung mayor ousted in motion of no confidence*. News24. https://www.news24.com/news24/SouthAfrica/ News/mangaung-mayor-ousted-in-motion-of-no-confidence-20200808

Mnguni, H. (2023). Public Service Delivery in Rural South Africa: The Influence of Coalition Politics at Local Government Level. *International Journal of Social Science Research*, *11*(3), 371–37.

Mpangalasane, C. (2020). *The impact of coalition government on service delivery: City of Tshwane metropolitan*. Unpublished Master's dissertation. Potchefstroom: North-West University.

Muller, W. C., & Storm, K. (2000). *Coalition governments in Western Europe. Comparative Politics*. Oxford University Press. doi:10.1093/oso/9780198297604.001.0001

Ndevu, Z., & Muller, K. (2018). A Conceptual Framework for Improving Service Delivery at Local Government in South Africa. *African Journal of Public Affairs.*, *10*(4), 181–195.

Ndou, L. L. (2022). *An analysis of a coalition government: A new path in administration and governance at local government level in South Africa*. Unpublished PhD Thesis. University of the North West, South Africa.

Republic of South Africa. (1993). *Interim Constitution of the Republic of South Africa 1993*. Government Printer.

Republic of South Africa. (1996). *Constitution of the Republic of South Africa 1996*. Government Printer.

Republic of South Africa. (1998). *White Paper on Local Government of 1998*. Government Printer.

Republic of South Africa. (1998). *Local Government: Municipal Structures Act 117 of 1998*. Government Printer.

Schreiber, L. (2018). *Coalition country: South Africa after the ANC*. Tafelberg.

South African History Online. (2018). *South African Government of National Unity (GNU) – 1994-1999*. https://www.sahistory.org.za/article/south-african-government-national-unity-gnu-1994-1999

South African Local Government Association. (2022). *A Framework for Coalitions in Local Government*. https://dullahomarinstitute.org.za/multilevel-govt/publications/04112021-a-framework-for-coalitions-in-local-government-1.pdf/view

Timmermans, A. (2003). *Standing Apart and Sitting Together: Enforcing Coalition Agreements in Multiparty Systems*. AECPA.

Tselane, N. (2023). *Regulation of coalition governments in South Africa. Concept Document*. Institute of Election Management in Africa.

Weiner, M. (2010). *Power, protest, and the public schools: Jewish and African American struggles in New York City*. Rutgers University Press.

KEY TERMS AND DEFINITIONS

Coalition: A coalition is formed when two or more people or groups temporarily work together to achieve a common goal. The term is most frequently used to denote a formation of power in political or economic spaces.

Constitution: Is a body of fundamental principles or established precedents according to which a state or other organization is acknowledged to be governed.

Democracy: Government by the people, especially rule of the majority. Is a government in which the supreme power is vested in the people and exercised by them directly or indirectly through a system of representation usually involving periodically held free elections.

Governance: the act or process of governing or overseeing the control and direction of something (such as a country or an organization). Is the action or manner of governing a state or organisation.

Local Government: Local government is the public administration of towns, cities, counties and districts. Local government includes both county and municipal government structures.

Municipality: A city or town with its own local government, or this local government itself.

Service Delivery: Service delivery is a business idea and framework, the main goal of which is to provide services from a vendor to a customer. This includes the regular interactions between the two parties throughout the entire process of the business supplying the service and the client purchasing it.

Chapter 17
Examining the Impact of Coalition Governments on Service Delivery:
The Case of ANC–Led All

Mbuyiseni Simon Mathonsi
University of KwaZulu-Natal, South Africa

Ndwakhulu Stephen Tshishonga
University of KwaZulu-Natal, South Africa

ABSTRACT

Formation of coalition governments and politics before and after elections is the manifestation of the absence of overwhelming winner in national, provincial, or local government elections. This chapter aims to contribute to the nascent literature on coalition government and politics within the context of South Africa by examining the historic coalition of the ANC, SACP, COSATU, and SANCO. The chapter is conceptual in approach and it uses a desktop method. The research acknowledges that the tripartite coalition/alliance is without precedent on the African continent and with few parallels throughout the world. Coalition governing is now a phenomenon defining South African body politics, and it is likely to be the future system of government in this country. In terms of the South African system of government, national, provincial, and local governments are critical platforms for service delivery and the overall development of the country that is currently riddled by the triple challenges of unemployment, poverty, and inequality.

DOI: 10.4018/979-8-3693-1654-2.ch017

INTRODUCTION

South Africa will be going to its 7th round of National and Provincial elections in 2024. This happens while the cracks between the ruling coalitions that has governed South Africa since 1994 has become increasingly very difficult to mend and that is likely to impact negatively on coalition's upcoming election hopes (COSATU political report, 2022). There is serious tensions among the different parties of the ANC led- and ruling coalition made up of two political parties, the African National Congress (ANC) and the South African Communist Party (SACP) the largest workers federation known as the Congress of the South African Trade Unions (COSATU). And the Civic Organisation called South African National Civic Organisation (SANCO). This is a rather permanent, historical and left wing ideological alliance existing outside government but with each party represented in the South African government. The alliance is currently loosing its popularity as demonstrated by the 2019 national elections and 2021 local government elections. To the extent that a number of the South African people have abandoned the ruling coalition for the newly formed party called uMkhonto Wesizwe Party (MKP). MKP is the party announced on the 16th of December 2023 by the former ANC and South African State President, Mr Jacob Zuma. Given the popularity of Jacob Zuma amongst ANC members, the MKP is expected to have a sizable impact on the election campaign of the ANC-led Alliance (Omorjee, 2023).

Political parties are organisations representing modern politics whose tasks are to channel societal participation, express social interests, occupy government posts and produce policy (Vercesi, 2016). Resnick (2013) considers political parties as critical institutions to make representative democracy possible either as they govern individually or as part of coalition arrangements. There are but not mutually exclusive definitions of government coalitions. Resnick (2013) defines coalition government as a cabinet of a parliamentary government in which several parties come together using economies of scale to pull together resources (both human and financial) into a more substantial collection and conduct a larger campaign to form a unity government. Coalition is the association of two or more parties who agree to work together to form government based on election outcomes (Mokgosi, Shai, Ogunnubi, 2017). Kadima (2014) argues that coalitions are objectives driven and are processes of organising coalition parties towards a common goal which is explicit agenda to control the executive. This chapter aims to contribute to the nascent literature on coalition government and politics within the context of South Africa, by examining the historic pre-election coalition of the ANC, SACP, COSATU and SANCO currently ruling the country, under the topic "Examining the service delivery impact of Coalition governments and politics: The Classical Case of ANC-led Coalition formed of the ANC, SACP, COSATU and SANCO. Referring to this coalition then formed by ANC, SACP and COSATU, Oliver Reginald Tambo (former ANC president), the longest serving and former President of the ANC, at the 60th Anniversary of the South African Communist Party on 30 July 1986 had this to say:

Ours is not a paper alliance, created at conference tables and finalised through the signing of documents and representing only the agreement of leaders. Our Alliance is a living organism that has grown out of struggle. It was built of our separate and common experiences.

South Africa's governing coalition is, therefore, a product of the history of struggle. The partnership was first started by the ANC and SACP in the late 1940s and were joined by the South African Congress of Trade Unions (SACTU), the pre-cursor to now COSATU in 1955 and SANCO in 1992. This Alliance/coalition may have played a role in inspiring the formation of the Zimbabwean Alliance formed by ZANU (Zimbabwe African National Union) led by Robert Mugabe and ZAPU (Zimbabwe African People's Union) led by Joshwa Nkomo formed as Patriotic Front in 1976.

The ANC alliance can also be likened to China's Revolutionary alliance of 1911 led by Dr Sun Yat – sen (who led the first Chinese revolution) against a Qing Empire, as well as the left wing alliance of Koumintang, communists, students and intellectuals that was set up to complete China's revolution. However because of the emergence of right wing elements within Kuomintang, the Alliance broke up leaving the communists to complete the revolution in 1949. The two alliances (Zimbabwe and China) directly relate to the ANC alliance because they both were conceptualised in the field of struggle to defeat colonialism or monarchy rule to form democratic governments.

The Coalition produced a governing blue-print document referred to as Freedom Chatter, their vision of an equal, non-racial and democratic South Africa. This makes the ANC-led Alliance very unique from alliances or coalitions formed only for purposes of election or formed consequential to hung election results or failure by parties to meet a required election threshold where parties resolve to form post-election coalition. Neither is the ANC-led Coalition similar to pre-election arrangements formed immediately before elections and in anticipation of election threshold challenges. The above coalition arrangements should be considered as being spontaneous, opportunist or forced class of alliances different from the organic, tried and tested ANC-led coalition which was formed out of the struggle anti-democracy system perpetuated by the Apartheid colonialist National Party government of South Africa to bring about an environment where democracy can flourish. This is the coalition that ultimately brought about South African democracy that was first experienced in 1994.

The tensions in the ruling coalition are mainly between the self-proclaimed left axis (SACP and COSATU) and the ANC. ANC, a multi-class formation, is accused of pursuing a "counter-revolutionary" and neoliberal agenda of white monopoly capital (Rametse, 2014). The SACP and COSATU argue that the ANC has abandoned the alliance pact for governance called the National Democratic Revolution (NDR). As a result, it is argued, the country is suffering deepening poverty, unemployment and inequality making the life even more difficult for the working class and the poor. SACP and COSATU Joint Statement (2022) highlighted that:

We remain concerned about the rise of anti-majoritarian forces who are hell-bent on implementing neoliberal policy reforms and following the same path that brought us to this economic crisis. We will not keep quiet and watch the gains of the national Democratic Revolution being reversed.

In support of the above view, McKinley (2001), in his paper "Democracy, Power and Patronage: Debate and Opposition within the ANC and the Tripartite Alliance since 1994", already wrote that:

The ANC's embrace of what is a very minimalist conception of democracy has, since 1994, given rise to serious ideological opposition and class confrontation within its own ranks and those of its alliance partners

Neoliberalism is the political approach that favours free-market capitalism and deregulation, and reduction in government spending (Truter, 2023).

According to Truter (2023) NDR is a program adopted as early as 1920' and formalised in the SACP 1962 program and its main content is the liberation of Africans in particular and Blacks in general from political, social and economic bondage. This is a program that provided a philosophical basis for the establishment of a the ANC led Alliance formed by the united front of black trade union members, the nationalists and the communists from late 20's via 1950's and beyond. This program was further consolidated through the adoption of the SACP 1962 document that provided a theorised Model of the then existential South African State called "Colonialism of a Special Type (CST). The document succinctly characterised the nature and uniqueness of the then exploitative South African colonial state which it referred to as the colony of the "Special Type" and it largely incorporates the objects of the Freedom Chatter. Truter (2023) posits that this revolutionary program serves as a promise directed to those who suffered deprivations and oppression by apartheid colonialist government of South Africa that their quality of life would improve post transition. The Freedom Charter is a document which was written and adopted by the Congress Alliance, a broad coalition which was formed by ANC, the South African Coloured People's Organisation (SACPO), the South African Indian Congress (SAIC), the South African Congress of Democrats (SACD) and other organisations of Civil Society (Rametse, 2014). This document was an embodiment of the aspirational principles that later served as cornerstones for Freedom and democracy.

1. THE HISTORY OF SOUTH AFRICA STRUGGLE FOR DEMOCRACY: THE ROLE OF THE TRIPARTITE ALLIANCE ANC-LED POLITICAL AND GOVERNANCE COALITION

The 2024 round of National and Provincial elections will be the 7th general election within 30 years of democratic breakthrough. This follows a struggle by the indigenous people against colonial rule. South Africa was among the last African countries to be liberated when the ANC led coalition took over government in 2014 and formed the first ever democratic state (Rametse, 2014). The struggle of South Africa is inextricably linked to the liberation struggle by all progressive forces in the African continent. These struggles, Rametse, 2014) contends were general and unique at the same time and they were sparked by the 1884-1885 Berlin Conference which conducted for the purposes of auctioning and demarcate Africa among colonial and foreign political and socio-economic powers with the major beneficiaries being German, Italy, Portugal and Britain (Gumede & Oloruntoba, 2018). The demarcation was done for the purposes of exploiting Africa natural resources for imperial expansion, making Africa the satellite of these powers (Aluko, 2023). It is in this process that African people were not only acculturated but were also transformed into slaves and pariahs in their own countries and abroad and plunged into positions of indignity and subjugation (Honwana, 2013). It is this imperialist and colonial onslaught that had deepened the socio-economic and political underdevelopment in Africa in general and South Africa in Particular (Aluko, 2023) Kornegay Jnr & Mthembu, 2020). Hence the ANC was formed in 1912 and the SACP in 1921 directly for the objectives to fight back against colonial rule and return the land to its rightful owners, the indigenous people and later SACTU (the workers trade Union) joined this coalition when it was formed in 1955 (Kornegay Jnr & Mthembu, 2020). Clearly, unlike many coalitions that are formed on the eve of or post elections, the ANC led coalition was formed as an instrument of struggle to bring about the removal of the apartheid colonial state from power and replace it with the democratic state ushered in through a democratic electoral system, the dream that only came through in 1994 after a long decades of struggle (Mokgosi, Shai and Ogunnubi (2017,)

The depth and seriousness of the tensions within the ANC -led coalition has led to bigger sections of COSATU and SACP agitating for the SACP to consider contesting 2024 national elections independently and thereby break the historic coalition (Cosatu Central Committee Document, 2023). According to Mokgosi, Shai, and Ogunnubi (2017), the ANC –led Coalition became popular and it appealed to a broader constituency consisting of community, civil society, communists and workers. Mokgosi at al. (2017) define coalition building as a "process of organizing parties collectively in pursuit of a common goal" to purposely and explicitly control the executive. Similarly the ANC –led coalition had a longer term goal to bring about a non-racial, non-sexist and democratic society through the National Democratic Revolution program (Truter (2023).

2. SOUTH AFRICA'S PRESENT ELECTORAL SYSTEM AND THE USHERING IN OF FIRST COALITION GOVERNMENT

2.1. RSA Electoral System of Choice

Since 1910 the apartheid colonialist South African Government had been using a British model of electing representatives called the "first-past-post" (FPTP) to elect national legislatures (Truter, 2023). Truter (2023) explains that this apartheid election system was used in its varied and adapted forms to elect provincial legislatures of South West Africa, now Namibia and former homeland legislatures and later adapted for elections of the three-chamber parliament which came as the result of the 1983 constitutional amendments.

South Africa had used the British first-past-the-post (FPTP) system of electing representatives for parliament for more than eighty years. It remained essentially unchanged since its implementation at unification in 1910 until its replacement by a new electoral system with the 1993 Interim Constitution and the subsequent election of April 1994. Variations of the FPTP system were also used for the election of the old provincial councils in South Africa, as well as the provincial legislature of South West Africa, now Namibia and this system was also used for the former system of homelands with its various legislatures, and it was adapted to suit the needs of the three-chamber parliament brought about by the 1983 Constitution (Truter, 2023). The three chamber parliament, also called Trilateral Parliament that operated until 1994 and its aim was to give some limited to political voice to Coloured and Indian races of RSA as part of the apartheid government's strategy of divide-and-rule (Rametse, 2014). This initiative was done as a deliberate move to demonstrate the erstwhile government's revulsion of the black African majority and the enticement of the two included racial groups (Truter, 2023). The black African majority were relegated into black homelands and/or "Bantustans" which largely had no political role rather than being an extension of the brutal Nationalist Party political power and influence. This system of electing representatives finally became out of use as South Africa adopted its interim constitution in 1993.

The South African electoral system choice was preceded by extensive debate between two relatively large groups of negotiators being divided to their choice of what they considered as a suitable electoral system, i.e. the constituency (backed largely by ANC) and the proportional representation (backed largely by NP) systems (Pottie, 2014). Proportional representation is an electoral system that attempts to guarantee that as many subgroups as possible reflect in a proportionate way in the elected bodies while in the constituency –based system the country gets divided into constituencies and each political party nominate a candidate to represent it in that constituency and the candidate getting more vote represents the party in parliament (Pottie, 2014). However, these debates were conducted within the context of creating a stable and inclusive transitional government at the first instance and were concerned more about how best ethnic and racial groups can be accommodated so as to create trust and legitimacy in the electoral process and procedures (Pottie, 2014). This latter system was finally not preferred since it was thought to limit the participation of small parties in the governing of the country and further curtail the overarching vision of building cross-racial and national ties. After the adoption of a proportional representation (PR) list system in 1993 the constitution got amended and the country was ready to put it to test in the 1994 election which it did.

2.2. Composition of South African Parliament

The proportional representation system structured South African Parliament as follows:

STATE ORGAN	NUMBER OF MEMBERS
National Assembly	400
National Council of Provinces	90
Provincial Legislatures	430

The South Africa Yearbook (2021/2022) gives a summary of government operations and the relationship between different layers of government as follows:

The South African Parliament is made up of two Houses (National Assembly {NA} and National Council of Provinces {NCOP}) and its overarching role is to promote and superintend over adherence to the values of human dignity, equality, non-racism, non-sexism and the rest of the rights enshrined in the Bill of rights and implement dictates of the constitution and "see to it that the independence, impartiality, accessibility and effectiveness of the Judiciary and other state institutions is upheld." It performs its role in terms of Chapter 4 of the Constitution of the Republic which inaugurates and sets out its role function as a Parliament elected by the people and that should be governed by the people and epitomise the interests of all provinces in the National Sphere of government. Hence it is the function of Parliament to elect the State President, ensure creation of forum for public consideration of issues, pass legislation, scrutinise and oversee all executive actions

The mandate of Parliament is based on the provisions of Chapter 4 of the Constitution, which establishes Parliament and sets out the functions it performs. Parliament is elected to represent the people, ensure government by the people under the Constitution, and represent the interests of provinces in the national sphere of government.

Parliament (through MPs) elect the President, provide a national forum for the public consideration of issues, pass legislation, and scrutinise and oversee executive action in line with National plans of the country.

2.2.1. The National Assembly (NA)

The system provided for the National Assembly (NA - the first house of Parliament) of 400 members, 200 of whom would be deployed using a national party lists while another 200 would be from provincial lists with the population size of each province determining the its fraction of 200 members. The principal office Bearers of the NA is the Speaker and in his/her absence, the deputy speaker. The Speaker (and Deputy Speaker) are elected directly by the members of the NA, keep order and ensure compliance with House rules, serves as representative and speaker of the NA, and act as Chief Executive officer of Parliament together with the chairperson of Council. In performing his duties the Speaker is assisted by the Deputy Speaker and the three House Chairperson and the whips – the party political functionaries appointed by parties to manage party business and ensure that their parliamentary members are kept abreast of House developments and that the members attend committee meetings.

2.2.2. The National Council of Provinces

The National Council of Provinces (2nd house of Parliament) consist of 90 provincial delegates, 10 of which come from each of the 9 province. The NCOP is constitutionally mandated to ensure that provincial interests are taken very seriously by National parliament. Hence NCOP members are entitled to be part of parliament where issues affecting provinces are discussed. The deployment of the NCOP members is determined by the strength of political parties as reflected in the representation they have at respective provincial legislatures.

2.2.3. Provincial Legislatures

Provincial Legislatures is the legislative branch of government chaired by the Speaker and Deputy Speaker who are nominated by the members of the legislatures and its size is determined by the provincial population size, provided that each legislature has a minimum of 30 and maximum of 80 members. The proportional representation electoral system has allocated seats at provincial legislatures as follows:

Table 1.

Legislature	Seats	
		Total
Eastern Cape Provincial Legislature		63
Free State Legislature		30
Gauteng Provincial Legislature		73
KwaZulu-Natal Legislature		80
Limpopo Legislature		49
Mpumalanga Provincial Legislature		30
North West Provincial Legislature		33
Northern Cape Provincial Legislature		30
Western Cape Provincial Parliament		42
Totals		430

The South Africa Yearbook (2021/2022) further tabulates the mandate of the legislatures as follows:

- Pass legislation as per powers given by the RSA Constitution …. Of … in other areas such power is shared with the national parliament
- It covers such fields and or areas as: health, education (except universities), agriculture, housing, environmental protection, and development planning. However on areas outside its power, it may recommend legislation to the National Assembly.
- It can also endorse a constitution for that province provided it gets the nod of two-thirds of its members.
- It appoints and dismiss the Premier and members of the Executive. Though the task of appointing the executive is the role of Premier, the legislature can pass a motion of no-confidence to compel the Premier to release a member from their posts.
- From its members, it deploys provincial delegates to the NCOP
- It allocates delegates to parties that met the threshold respective to the seats they acquired in the legislature.
- It superintends over the administration of the provincial government, the Premier and the members of the Executive Council who all are mandatory to account to the legislature about their performance based on their delegations.
- It controls the finances of the provincial government based on through use of the appropriation bills, it determines and controls the provincial budget.

Truter (2023) differentiates between the functions of Apartheid Colonial Administration (1910-1994) and that of the democratic dispensation (1994 t0 present)

- While the current legislatures appoint both the head and its executive, during the apartheid administration there was a Provincial Council (legislature) which was only limited to appointing the Executive Council (cabinet) and the appointment of Executive Head was the preserve of the Governor General (prior to 1961) or State President (after 1961).
- The apartheid colonial state also had only four provinces (Natal, Orange Free State, Cape Town and Transvaal) and had curtailed powers and given only responsible for a few topics compared to the post-1994 Legislatures with as many as 9 legislatures which enjoy more powers and more independence.
- It is also worth noting that in 1986 the provincial legislatures were totally abolished and the State president assumed the powers of appointing the Provincial Councils.

2.2.4. Election of members into NA, NCOP, and Provincial Legislatures (PLs)

Pottie, (2014) reports that since the current electoral system is a multi-party system (a ballot consists of the list of competing parties and not individual candidates), so during the voting process, each voter is accorded two ballots to indicate their party of choice for the NA and PLs. Before elections, registered parties ought to submit lists of their candidates to the Independent Electoral Commission (IEC) for scrutiny and ensuring compliance, the submission of lists are subject to guidelines determined by IEC (Pottie, 2014). The number of votes each party achieves during elections determines the number of that party's candidates to be deployed to parliament and legislatures while NCP representation is made up of 10 members per province based on the seats each party received as per allocation by the proportional representation system.

3. 1994-1999: FIRST EXPERIENCE OF SOUTH AFRICAN COALITION GOVERNMENT

To create an environment for free and fair elections, the South African parties negotiating transition agreed to establish critical organs to manage transition. These were the Transitional Executive Council (TEC). This was a multiparty structure to manage the transition to democracy amid a lot of political wars and conflicts between and amongst different parties mainly the ANC and IFP and violence unleashed by apartheid government apparatuses (Pottie, 2014). Another milestone achieved was the adoption of an interim Constitution tailor made to govern the country during the transition. It is this interim constitution that established the IEC as a State organ to manage and administer South African first democratic elections (Rametse, 2014). As part of the negotiations for a transitional government, the agreement was reached amicably by all parties that to ensure a smooth transitional and inaugural administration, a form of government known as the Government of national Unity (GNU) was proposed and implemented for 5 years between 1994 and 1999. The decision to form a coalition government was a common phenomenon in Africa as a means to avoid after election conflict and possibly violence, especially by parties who lose and feel left out of the democratic process (Vercesi, 2015).

The State President then, Mr FW de Klerk announced 27 April 1994 as the election date, yet another milestone, and 19 political parties registered accordingly, with the ANC-led alliance as the only confirmed to contest elections as a coalition. Following under are parties that registered for elections: The National Assembly general election was contested by 19 political parties: African National Congress (ANC) – led coalition, National Party (NP), Inkatha Freedom Party (IFP), Pan Africanist Congress of Azania (PAC), Freedom Front (FF), Democratic Party (DP), African Christian Democratic Party (ACDP), Africa Muslim Party (AMP), African Moderates Congress (AMC), Dikwankwetla Party of South Africa (DPSA), Federal Party (FP), Minority Front (MF), Sport Organisation for Collective Contributions and Equal Rights (SOCCER), African Democratic Movement (ADM), Women's Right Peace Party (WRPP), Ximoko Progressive Party (XPP), Keep It Straight & Simple Party (KISS), Worker's List Party (WLP), and Luso-South Africa Party (LUSO).

Later after 19.5 million people had cast their votes, the ANC-led coalition was announced as the winner of the 1994 elections, followed by the New National Party (NNP) as number 2 and IFP as number 3 and this meant that the Country's Constitution and the Bill of Rights had to take effect and a new and democratic, non-racial and no-sexist South Africa began, abolishing the system of racial apartheid and the homeland system (Vercesi, 2015). The ANC manifesto emphasised the building of non-racialism, non-sexism, democracy, workers' rights, and elimination of poverty, prioritise education, health and housing while The NNP emphasised the supremacy of law and order, free-market Economy and non-racial democracy, protection of minority rights and cultural rights (Pottie, 2014). The IFP, the 3rd largest party campaigned on Free Economy, eradication of corruption, exploitation and intimidation, equal opportunities for all and promotion of worthy customs and culture (Pottie, 2014). On 9 May 1994 the Government of National Unity led by President Nelson Mandela and 1st Deputy President Thabo Mbeki of the ANC-led Coalition which had attained 252 seats, 2nd Deputy President de Frederick Willem de Klerk of the NNP with 82 seats while the of Mr Mangosuthu Buthelezi of the IFP with 43 seats enjoyed Ministerial presence in government. However it is important to indicate that the ANC-led Coalition had won 7 of the 9 provinces (Vercesi, 2015).

This South African GNU is considered by Pottie (2014) as an enforced party coalition where parties who managed to reach the threshold of 10% formed an integral part of the GNU. However in June 1996 the New Nationalist party of Mr FW De Clerk withdrew from GNU largely because the NNP constituency felt not accommodated enough in the decision-making process. This according, to Resnick (2013), is a norm in coalitions because in many instances, political results emanating from these working together agreements are, more often than not, the function of leaders and less a function of voters. Resnick (2013) believe that there is a large invisible hand of party positioning and interparty bargaining at the exclusion of the voters. The coalition governments were also formed between the period 1994-2004 in KwaZulu- Natal between the IFP that had won the provincial elections and the 2nd placed ANC-led coalition (Vercesi, 2015). The same has been the case in the Western Cape Province and coalitions were mainly National Party, the winner of provincial election and. However all these coalitions were from time to time mired with conflicts emanating from distrusts. Resnick (2013) explains that failure of many coalitions is mainly due to the absence of conflict resolution mechanism which should be built into the coalition government system.

4. THE HISTORY OF DEMOCRACY: CONTENT AND CHARACTER OF COALITIONS GOVERNMENT

4.1. Advent of Democracy, Government, and Politics

The advent of state and history of democracy have become ongoing subjects for many research studies. This is because of the multiplicity of views about when and how states and democracy came into being. Some researchers like Isakhan and Stockwell, (2011) believe that the quest to understand the history of democracy should be preceded by the need to respond to the general question on how people have been governed in the first place, both in the ancient and modern times. Archaeologically, predominant forms of societal management/government include, but are not limited to, aristocracy, timocracy, oligarchy, democracy, theocracy and tyranny. Isakhan and Stockwell (2011) claim that these systems of government are not mutually exclusive as one government may have mixed forms of management. Hence they posit that, therefore, the study concerned about any philosophy of governments and democracy should first discover how political office is obtained between the two ways of attaining power: electoral contest or hereditary succession. These researchers believe that since government is the system or group of people governing an organized community (state) it should therefore be of concern to seek to know how this process was undertaken

Resnick (2013) contends that in governance 3 kinds of constitution can be reflected and all of them are both idyllic and corrupt depending on governance is performed. For an example the "rule by one" person is the Monarchy system at its best and a Tyranny at its worst, and that the "rule by the few" is Aristocracy at best and Oligarchy at degenerative form, while the "rule by many is polity at best and its perverted form is Democracy. Democracy, according to Isakhan and Stockwell (2011) is a word derived from Greek word "demokratia" created from the Greek word "demos", which means ("people") and "kratos" which means "rule". This word was developed mid-5th century and it represented a Greek political system which was conducted in many city states, and Athens in particular. Greece, according to Rosenfeld (2018), did not only discover democracy but it also discovered politics, which he defined as the "art of arriving at decisions through open (public) debates or discussion and then submitting to those decisions as an essential condition of cultured and civilised social existence. This "primitive" democracy developed in Greece and Rome replaced the political system of monarchy, despotism, aristocracy and oligarchy which rose within the contradictions of "natural system" of hunting and gathering (Isakhan and Stockwell, 2011). Hunting and gathering was the political system of government where the tribal elders enjoyed popular participation in government affairs and which, however, was replaced by the monarchy and the aristocratic forms of administrations during the period where tribal people began to settle down as community and adopting agriculture as the mode of production. Under such circumstances, the inequality of wealth was created which led to formation of systems of monarchy and aristocracy (Rosenfeld, 2018). Rosenfeld (20180 posits that the distinguishing feature of the democratic approach is the notion of a "constitution" which is defined as an organisation of offices, which all citizens distribute among themselves based on the power held by different classes. This distribution of offices, Isakhan and Stockwell (2011) reasoned, can bring about different forms and shapes of government based on either two –party or multiparty systems of governance. The multi-party (also called proportional representation) systems, by their nature, are the most appropriate in endeavours to accommodate small parties and limit the dominance of larger ones. Hence, when parties fail to win enough legislative support, they resort to forming coalition governments consisting of two or more parties (Rosenfeld, 2018). Rosenfeld (2018) argues further that the eighteenth century also marked the beginning of modern democracy, politics and governments, signifying a radical departure from ancient politics and government. He draws his construct from key intellectual figures of the eighteenth and nineteenth centuries—such as Immanuel Kant, John Dewey, and Thomas Jefferson.

4.2. The Character and Content of Coalition Governments

To give meaning to coalition government phenomenon, Hobolt and Karp (2010) presents data on the frequency of coalition government drawn from 479 government from 17 West European countries. The data showed that coalition governments have, by the year 2010, already became a norm. By the same year at least seventeen out of the thirty OECD member states were already governed by multiparty co-alition governments. Coalition governments are even more common and happening at least 65 percent of the time (Armstrong and Duch, 2010). Sekatle and Sebola, 2020) define coalition government as a group of organisations or political groupings that come together for the purpose of gaining more influence and power than the individual organisations can achieve on their own. Oyugi (2006) clarifies that government coalitions are state administrations formed either before or after elections in presidential or parliamentary or mixed systems and are usually a manifestation of failure of the competing political parties to garner majority of votes required to control parliaments or legislative assemblies. According to Oyigi (2006), the term has now received more popularity and Altman (2000) defined it as;

Temporary combination of groups or individuals formed to pursue specific objectives through joint action. Specifically it is a set of parliamentary political parties that agree pursue common goal, or a common set of goals; pool their resources together in pursuit of this goal; communicate and form building commitments concerning their goal; (and0 agree on distribution of pay-offs to be received on obtaining their goal.

In support to Atman, Dobratz (2015) define coalition government as the cabinet of a parliamentary officials in government where several parties join together to create a unitary government. The notion of coalition governments foregrounds political parties as key actors in representative democracy. It is exactly within this notion of party evolution, organisation and modification that we will examine the topic of study related to ANC-led coalition and historical role of the different parties in it. Western Europe, for example, roughly three-fourths of all governments formed in the post-war era have been composed of multiple political parties (Gallagher, Laver and Mair, 2005). In Africa, in particular, coalition's government had been used as a reactionary tool either to avert instability in the political environment or to arrest one. Hence Sekatle and Sebola (2020) posits that African political leaders have employed this governing strategy mainly as a short term intervention to cultivate the mood of national unity within a country. For an example, in the period 1994 – 1999, South Africa formed the Government of National Unity (GNU) to smoothen transition to a fully-fledged democratic dispensation. The coalition had 3 different political parties: The ANC as the coalition leader, the NNP and the IFP. The same strategy was used in Zimbabwe where the coalition government was preferred between the Zanu-PF led by Robert Mugabe whose organisation had ruled for three-decades and two MDC factions (Sekatle and Sebola (2020). The same approach of governing was also promoted in Lesotho by the coming together of All Basotho Convention (ABDC), of Thomas Thabane, Basotho National Party formed by Leabua Jonathan and Lesotho Congress of Democracy LCD) of Ntsu Mokhehle and Lesotho's first experience in coalition government was in 2012 (Motamai, 2012:1). Such arrangements afford multiparty governments some degree of legitimacy (Henry, 2009) and can be employed in both presidential and parliamentary systems of government.

5. THEORIES INFORMING POLITICAL PARTIES' CHOICE OF COALITION PARTNERS

Using the theories of "rational choice institutionalism" and "bounded rationality", the coalition government scholarship has always sought to answer critical questions surrounding coalitions. These are questions such as how do political parties choose one another, how do they arrive at policy choices, how they divide and distribute offices, what causes intra-coalition conflict and how it is managed? etc. (Miller and Muller, 2010). The theory of "bounded Rationality" postulates that rationality gets limited when individuals are confronted by the task of decision making leading them preferring a decision that is satisfactory rather than best or optimal (Simon, 1957). According to Shepsle (2006). The theory of "rational choice institutionalism" has its origins in economics and organisational theory and it considers institutions as systems of rules and incentives. It believes that rules are contested so that one group of political actors can leverage over another.

Based on "rational choice institutionalism" theory, Hall and Taylor (1996, 944-5) arrived at the conclusion that such institutionalism possesses four main characteristics as follows:

a. Actors in institutions have a fixed set of preferences and aim to their maximization instrumentally;
b. It regards politics as a set of shared action of dilemmas;
c. Actors behave in a strategic manner; and
d. Institutions control the behaviours of individuals and can serve as both constraints and instruments that can deliver benefits from cooperation.

Basically the framework from both these theories assumes that political actors are rational and choose their actions rationally. However, that does not necessarily presuppose that individuals always adhere to such a principle in real life. These theories characteristically place members of a coalition government as veto players and as unrestrained unitary actors determined to exploit well-defined possessions or goods like office, policy or votes. The parties' prospects of participating in winning government coalition are influenced by the external negotiating power of other parties based on their mandatory power and policy position (Miller and Muller, 2010). Miller and Muller (2010) argue further that there is an assumptions that parties prefer coalitions "that (a) embrace themselves as members and (b) are not too far from them on policy positions.

Bäck, Müller and Nyblade (2017) maintain that the study of coalition governments should starts with the understanding of the formation stage of a coalition and develop through all stages until its dissolution. These researchers believe that an understanding of the intricacies of coalition also involves following the coalition behaviour from all its developmental studies. Arguing in support of the above position, Motamai (2012) calls for researchers to pay attentiveness right at the beginning of the life of coalition government when parties unpack such questions as "who gets in and who gets what". It is also important, Motamai (2012) posits, to understand factors fixed at any stage of government formation and those include grasping the initial coalition bargain which may outline matters like coalition size, ideological compatibility and the way of distributing offices. The second responsibility will be about studying of how partners run the-day-to-day functions of government and how they respond to different contextual and institutional/coalition conditions. Motamai (2012) summarises his model of studying government coalitions as follows: Researchers should strive to grasp how coalition actors play their coalition game from the birth to the end of government; how they manage contradictions emanating from differences in cultures, ideology, priorities etc; how they deal with conflict situations; and what informs the need to amend pacts/agreements as well as what motivates the need for compromises and what is the role of the voters in all these processes

5.1. Types of Coalition Governments

Lane and Preker (2018) posit that the political parties, as main actors in government formation are critical in the distribution of executive power, their corresponding seats and its exercise. Political parties are formed with one aim and one aim only, the attainment of highest political office in the country and the exercise of its power. Hence, Weber (2012) retorts that political parties are not the end in themselves but they are instruments by which the masses seek to capture the state power and all it represents. This, therefore, places political parties as only means to an end. Jessop (2012) advances the view that since the "state" power is interconnected with class relations in economics, politics and ideology, hence it becomes an instrument critical to secure the conditions for economic class domination. In support of Jessop, Lane and Preker (2018) argue just like Jessop (2012) that political parties reside in the sphere of power and that n capitalist societies parties are essentially establishments for job patronage that are simply concerned with putting their leader into the top position so that they can turn over state offices to address their narrow and selfish interests (Jessop, 2012). It is further argued that political parties as ideological platforms enter into coalition governments with an intention to accomplish the realisation of substantive political ideals (Lane and Preker, 2018; Jessop, 2012). Coalition governments, like singly majority party governments, are instruments that either alter or reconfigure power relations in line with a particular mode for class domination. Coalitions are not interpersonal phenomenon lacking deeper foundations in the social structure, hence Jessop (2012) advices that any study of government formations should focus more on the causal interconnectedness of the exercise of (state) power and either the reproduction and/or transformation of class domination.

However, it is worth noting that coalition governments themselves are not permanent means. Resnick (2013) posits that coalition governments represent an association of political parties who come together to form a temporary government because the elections produced no outright winner. Some classic theories assume that political parties are office-seeking actors and given that coalition formation is a zero-sum game, parties are inclined to enter into "minimum" winning coalitions with the lowest number of parties (Lane and Preker, 2018) to avoid plurality of views or ideologies. Resnick (2013) singles out two forms of coalitions which he referred to as Pre-Electoral and Post-Electoral coalitions. He defines pre –electoral coalitions as the conjoining of two or more political parties who develop their agenda before elections and conduct elections under one banner to capture presidential or legislative elections. This includes the ANC-led coalition which took power in 1994 and the Zimbabwean ZUPU and ZANU coalition which took power in 1980 and defeated colonial rule. On the other hand Post –electoral coalitions are arrangements where parties compete under their different banners and form negotiated packs post-elections. This is an example of the coalition formed mainly between Economic Freedom Fighters (EFF) and the Democratic Alliance in South Africa to capture Johannesburg and Tswane Metros, largest economic hubs of Gauteng Province following local government elections of November 2021. This coalition which was mainly office-seeking than ideologically compact was aimed at ousting ANC from power.

Since coalition governance is more dominant and is traced to have been formally established in Western Europe, Kadima (2014) employed the same theories to compare the Western Experience with an African experience of coalition governance albeit with different contexts. Theories of coalition emerged from study of coalitions in Western Europe during 1960s and 1970s (Gamson 1961, Riker 1962, Axelrod 1970, De Swan 1973, Dodd 1976; Luebbert 1983) and are based on the effects of coalition size and ideology on coalition formation – by William Gamson (1961) and William Riker (1962). These theories are divided into office-seeking and policy seeking approaches or models. The Office-seeking approach foregrounds access state power or attainment of cabinet posts as a prerequisite irrespective of the nature of ideological foundations of alliance partners (Kadima, 2014). This, Kadima (2014) posits, is indicative of a win-lose scenario where government posts are used as pay-offs – based on minimum winning hypothesis. The agitators of this theory reject any possible existence of minority governments and instead prefer what is termed minimal winning governments with as few political parties as possible just enough to pass legislature decisions or win legislature vote of "confidence". These are minimal winning governments which believe in carrying "no passengers" and believe that such an approach makes it much easier to reach consensus. It is believed that these arrangements are dominant in Africa and are used for the satisfaction and accommodation of different competing interests like different ethnic groups, races and religions the accommodation of which creates stability in the country (Kadima 2014). Contrary to office-seeking, policy –seeking approach prioritises policy seamlessness to cabinet posts distribution. They form coalitions based on ideological adjacency and pursue maximisation of benefits while minimising coalition's bargaining costs caused, mainly, by too much policy compromises (Jessop 2012). Paul Warwick discovered and argued this as early as 1994 that ideologically diverse parties do not survive because parties are forced to make greater policy compromises and also that, however, the end of Cold war has forced a shift by ideologically based pre and post electoral alliances (for an example in South Africa and Mauritius, etc.) to the centre and adopted market economies in attempts to fast-track socio-economic development and as attempts to address social cleavages.

The theory of size and ideology focusses on the potential size of a coalition and ideological convergence among coalition actors (Kadima, 2014). This approach concludes that some parties enter coalitions to maximise both office-seeking and policy-seeking priorities and also that political parties choose to enter into coalitions with parties that will contribute to achieving as minimal a number of political parties as possible and this has benefits of ensuring that gains associated with office incumbency are maximised (Kadima, 2014).

6. CONTRADICTORY VIEWS ON THE EFFICACY OF COALITIONS

There are conflicting views by different scholars and or researchers about the effects of coalition government.

6.1. Anti-Coalition School

Distinguishing between "strong and "weak" governments, Bryce, as early as 1921 already placed coalition governments in the "weak" category. The belief was that school of coalition governments are a liability (weak category) not only to the general management and administration of government but also to fiscal management (Back, Muller and Nyblade, 2017). These scholars believe that traditional single party majority governments are associated with political stability and effective management and administration, while coalitions are normally associated with less economic efficacy expressed through slow growth, higher public debt, huge budget deficit etc. Following under are some of the reasons advanced by Back, Muller and Nyblade (2017) and anti-coalition team why coalition governments should be the option:

Coalition governments are often confronted by more severe "common pool problems". This is caused by the fact that parties in these form of governments, ministers control their spending without considering full tax implications and in coalitions, the Minister of finance has no direct Coalition governments usually create more posts to accommodate more members to satisfy all coalition parties and in the process incur budget deficits

Meyer (2010) claims that multiparty governments also bear delegation challenges and possess inherent structural weaknesses in that ministers tend to adhere more to their individual party interests than to collective goals of the coalition. While in singly party cabinets party interest serves to counterbalance individual incentives. Bawn and Rosenbluth (2006, p. 251) argue that coalitions of fragmented parties is usually associated with reaching less proficiency because a multiplicity of political interests needs representation in cabinets and parliament which also has a bearing on government spending. Meyer (2010) agrees and contends that coalition arrangements retards government performance because of their portfolio allocation model that deploys coalition party ministers or party officials to particular portfolios which are considered the ultimate jurisdiction of those deployed ministers often without any mechanism for oversight. This model, according to Meyer (2010) leave portfolio holders with a privilege to implement as per their discretion, hence this type of coalition governance has been called "ministerial government" or "fiefdom or Ministerial governments". These "ministerial governments" distorts the ways of policy formulation and decision making Martin and Vanberg (2013). Blais et al. (2010); maintains that one amongst other advantages of the single majority parties is that their competition with opposition parties drives the incumbent parties to efficient policies since they are motivated by the need to remain in power, while coalitions more often than not create conflicts and confrontations that do not only retard service delivery but also induce unwarranted government spending. According to (Blais et al. 2010) in coalition government, political outcomes are often less a function of voters' choices than of that of largely invisible processes of party positioning and interparty bargaining.

6.2. Pro-Coalition School of Thought

This group of academics and researchers maintains that coalitions are an important instruments of multi-party democracy, not only because they give a voice to and address the interest of small constituency, but more because they prevent the possibility for the retrogression of democracy into autocracy (Martin and Vanberg, 2013). Misunderstandings that sometimes break coalition governments often results from power asymmetry and hence parties that feel unaccommodated or ill-treated in these government arrangements will obviously resort to revolt (De Haan et al., 2013). The pro-coalition government researchers believe that any system of government will collapse if there are no mechanisms for control and enforcement (Müller and Strøm, 2008). The party that deploys Prime Minister automatically bears both decision and policy making powers than the rest of the parties. To counterbalance this, de Haan et al. (2013) suggests that parties in a coalition must anticipate this and take a decision and ensure that power is in equilibrium de Haan et al. (2013) also suggests that coalitions function well in conditions where the powers of the Prime Minister (PM) are curtailed and certain aspects of it decentralised among representatives of other parties. According to Back, Muller and Nyblade (2017), the study of coalition cabinets formed in 17 Western European countries between 1970 and 1998 supported the claim that coalitions get sustained, coalition agreements matter and performance of multiparty cabinets improved where PM power was low. de Haan et al. (2013) concurs that multi-party settings devoid of power asymmetries in the cabinet perform well and fragmentation is reduced.

Another critical control mechanism that make coalition government work is when the parties in-volved draft and adopt a comprehensive coalition policy agreement or coalition pact/contract that limits policy discretion of individual parties and ministries in their delineated portfolios and jurisdictions (de Haan et al. (2013). This type of argument is also reinforced by "fiscal institutionalists" as they suggest that negotiated spending targets for each ministry should lead to smaller deficits (Martin and Vanberg, 2013). it is therefore concluded that coalition governance mechanisms have enough capability to equi-poise inherent structural weaknesses of the multiparty formation. In the presence of a comprehensive agreement not only institutional fragmentation on public spending is reduced but also public spending emanating from common pool problems is mitigated, especially if at the centre of the coalition pact is the symmetrical distribution of power in the cabinet.

On disproportionate or extreme public spending, the pro-coalition point to the fact that there is a variety of fiscal institutionalism based strategies that can be employed to moderate such. The multiparty formation can use the "delegation approach" to decrease common problem pool through allocating veto rights to other offices, for an example the office of the Finance Minister (Martin and Vanberg, 2013). This minister, according to Martin and Vanberg, 2013) should not be bound by specific interests of spending departments. Delegating veto powers away from known traditional offices gives more weight to the collective interest of government than individual ministers or officers. (de Haan et al., 2013) asserts that the delegation approach should be used as an instrument to help the coalition government negotiate overall spending targets. Rules should also be established at the beginning of the term of office so that all ministers proceed under predetermined limits of spending. Excessive government spending can also be avoided by the development and adoption of fiscal rules that subject all government decisions to specific but agreed upon constraints (Hallerberg et al. 2009). Martin and Vanberg (2013) further posit that fiscal rules are also dependent on how well they are applied in practice and observed in action whether they are embedded in public law or are just peripheral rules of convenience. Political cooperation, proper and sequential programming, financial planning, timeous monitoring and evaluation, promptly undertaken, can mitigate for any loses and instead strengthen service delivery (Lipsmeyer and Pierce, 2011).

In conclusion, Bäck et al. (2011) argues that, however, political parties in multiparty formations should understand that all the above measures to improve coalition performance, heal the drift and refocus all endeavours towards efficiency should viewed as systems that cannot be attained through legal means but must be considered a political function that requires political maturity and tolerance. Hence (Bäck et al. 2011) supports the above construct and further maintains that since political coalitions are products of bargaining strategies, conflict management and conflict resolution measures should be built into the coalition government system (Moury, 2011). The above measures and formulations, according to Moury (2011) should, however, not be considered as a panacea and that even when supported by the conditions above, they remain not permanent but incomplete contracts.

Ashman (2015) posit that since its formation in 1990, the alliance has encountered a number of difficulties, such as the requirement to create a programme that upholds the mass nature of the alliance, the ANC's attempts to ease tensions within COSATU, and the alliance's difficulty in continuing in its current form because of goals for labour that do not seem to be compatible. Nevin, (2005) contends that the coalition won all three seats in parliament and formed a tripartite partnership to rule the nation, with the ANC serving as the senior partner, as the article "We are not the ANC's lapdog--Cosatu: South Africa's government" emphasizes. Twala and Kompi, (2012) note that the ANC-led coalition's service delivery record may be impacted by these issues as they may have an impact on efficient public service delivery and governance.

7. ANC LED COALITION APPROACH TO NATIONAL AND LOCAL GOVERNMENT ELECTIONS AND THE SERVICE DELIVERY RECORD

According to Rapanyane (2022) the African National Congress (ANC) has led South Africa's government since the end of apartheid in 1994. The African National Congress (ANC) has prioritized defending its majority and serving the interests of voters in the run-up to the national and municipal elections. Breytenbach (2019) posit that since apartheid ended, the ANC's track record in providing impoverished South Africans with basic amenities including power, water, and sanitary facilities as well as housing has been uneven. There are still significant backlogs in infrastructure, particularly in rural regions and informal settlements. Southall (2017) highlights that the Congress of South African Trade Unions (CO-SATU) and the South African Communist Party (SACP), two minor associated organizations, form a partnership under the leadership of the ANC, the federal ruling party. The ANC coalition's manifesto for national and municipal elections has always rhetorical of its role in bringing democracy to South Africa and putting an end to apartheid. Lodge (2014) argues that the party bragged about its history of freedom and connections to renowned anti-apartheid figures like Nelson Mandela.

As a result of disenchantment by many of its erstwhile voters, after the 2021 local government elections of November 2021, the ANC found itself occupying opposition benches in at least 3 more big Metropolis Statement in addition Cape Town which it lost long ago (Johannesburg, Tswane, and Nelson Mandela with the first two in Gauteng province and the latter in the Eastern Cape. People of South Africa apportioned blame to the ANC about, among other things, load-shedding (periodic cut in electricity), growing unemployment, increase in poverty and with workers complaining about ANC government undermining of collective bargaining. In its statement of (2021), the ANC indicated that where necessary it would approach coalition building with a stance grounded in principle rather than expediency and informed by the will, mandate, and interests of the electorate. According to Mokgosi, Shai and Ogunnubi (2017), there have been conversations regarding the likelihood of a coalition administration at the national level as a result of the ANC's dwindling vote support. These discussions have included possible coalition partners and the difficulties of building coalitions with parties that have different political philosophies and policy platforms. Mlambo (2019) apportion blame to the shifting internal political environment for the ANC-led alliance's service delivery record. According to Thakur and Nel (2023) this environment includes reports of attempted assassinations, factionalism and corruption. Howver, Morrison (2023) posits that despite the ANC's long-standing dominance in local and national politics, the move to coalition governments has given the party both possibilities and problems in terms of preserving its majority and providing services. Morrison (2023) further notes that in spite of the shift away from official coalition administrations, the ANC has collaborated with other political parties bridging ideological divides, and national-level coalitions have been established in South Africa before.

8. INTRA-PARTY TENSIONS AND ITS IMPACT ON THE SERVICE DELIVERY MANDATE OF THE ANC-LED COALITION

The coalition's mandate to deliver services has been significantly impacted by intra-party conflicts within the ANC alliance. It is argued that this is caused by both ideological and some internal subjective weaknesses. At an ideological front, the COSATU 2022 Congress political report (page 3) read;

It is against this background that officially it has been possible for the dominant right-wing opportunism within the African National Congress to propound reactionary neoliberal economic and social policies first imposed in 1996 in the form of GEAR as part of the pursuit the NDR

Unpacking this report, Mr Ntshalintshali, the then General secretary of COSATU, argued that the alliance lacked ideological cohesion from the beginning when the ANC majority rejected the class content (class struggle) of the NDR and preferred the narrow nationalist route leading to National Democratic Society (NDS) whose content is reactionary. These ideological differences, Ntshalintshali asserted, are reflected in both government policy formation and implementation, and the that lack of qualitative service delivery or reversal of democratic gains are as a result of the neoliberal policy the ANC government has adopted since 1996.

On internal subjective weaknesses, Thakur and Nel (2023) assert that factionalism, purported murder attempts, and the establishment of coalition councils following drops in ANC support in local elections are some of the causes of these conflicts. For Powell, O'Donovan and De Visser (2015), these internal party conflicts have undermined continuity in municipal service delivery by resulting in unstable coalitions, ongoing political infighting, and frequent leadership changes.

Pillay (2018) claims that public protests about inadequate services have put more strain on the ANC alliance. The idea of a coalition administration at the national level has been discussed, along with potential coalition partners and the difficulties of building coalitions with parties that have different political philosophies and policy platforms, as a result of the ANC's declining vote share. Thakur and Nel (2023) posit that these conflicts have impacted the ANC's service delivery record as they can result in political instability, contestation, and factionalism, all of which can impede efficient government and the provision of public services. Morrison (2023) opines that historically, the African National Congress (ANC) has dominated both national and municipal government. However, as more governments transition to coalition governments, the ANC has had both possibilities and problems in terms of sustaining its majority and providing services.

9. CHALLENGES OF TRIPARTITE ALLIANCE OR COALITION

There have been a number of difficulties for the African National Congress (ANC), the Congress of South African Trade Unions (COSATU), and the South African Communist Party (SACP), which form the tripartite alliance in South Africa. According to Ashman (2015) the ANC's attempts to arbitrate conflicts within COSATU, the necessity to create a program that preserves the alliance's mass character, and the alliance's difficulties in maintaining its current shape because of seemingly incompatible labour goals are some of these problems.

The article "A coalition's toughest challenge - the ANC-bloated State" addresses the alliance's major difficulty, which is managing a state that has been under ANC leadership for thirty years. Gumede (2023) posits that the idea of a coalition administration at the national level has been discussed, along with potential coalition partners and the difficulties of building coalitions with parties that have different political philosophies and policy platforms, as a result of the ANC's declining vote share. These issues have an impact on the ANC-led coalition's track record of providing services since they can hinder efficient public service delivery and governance.

Some of the challenges faced by South Africa's tripartite alliance between the ANC, COSATU and SACP according to Buhlungu, (2003) is that the working class and union support for the ANC has decreased as a result of COSATU and SACP disapproval of ANC economic policies like GEAR, which they perceived as being overly neoliberal. This jeopardizes the alliance's cohesion and power. Butler (2017) posit that the ANC has embraced more pro-business and market-oriented economic policies, such as inflation targeting and privatization, which the SACP and COSATU have resisted. Due to ideological disagreements in economic policy, this has caused problems within the alliance. Southall (2013) contends that there is a contention that the ANC has excluded its alliance partners from the decision-making process and has only consulted them following the adoption of policy. Undermining the partnership is the marginalization of SACP and COSATU. McKinley (2015) asserts that tensions and mistrust have been injected into the tripartite alliance as a result of personal disputes between the alliance parties' senior leaders, such as that between Zuma and former COSATU president Zwelinzima Vavi. Seidman (2016) indicates that the solidarity of labour with the ANC was weakened when former COSATU members, such as NUMSA, split away to create alternative labour federations. Coherence of the tripartite coalition is challenged by this fracturing.

10. DIRECTIONS FOR FUTURE RESEARCH

The research study on the tripartite alliance and its impact of service delivery was a desktop research, the investigation of secondary material, further research study that collects data from primary sources may shed more light on this subject. Also the research study was only based on the South African situation and covering only three coalition partners, further research may be required that will examine coalition government at an international level and probably covering more coalition formed by only three partners from a variety of parties.

11. CONCLUSION

The objective of the study was to examine the impact of the ANC-led coalition on service delivery. The paper concludes that the coalition made up of the tripartite alliance is historic and unmatched in Africa since for the purposes of first engage in the struggle to remove an autocratic rule and in its place install the democratic government which it then ran since 1994. The paper reveals that the ideological or policy based conflicts among the coalition partners has had a negative impact on quality service delivery to the people. The study recommends that for coalition government to succeed in their governance work, the parties must first agree on the coalition government service deliver pacts that would regulate the behavior of parties and politicians deployed to ministerial posts. It also advices that the coalition partners must build in conflict resolution mechanisms in their system of government.

REFERENCES

Aluko, O. (2023). Political Unrest and Tyre Burning Theory in Developed Democracies and Developing Democracies. In Insights and Explorations in Democracy, Political Unrest, and Propaganda in Elections (pp. 38-46). IGI Global. doi:10.4018/978-1-6684-8629-0.ch004

ANC Statement. (2021). *Statement of the ANC on Local Government Elections 2021 preliminary results. 3 Nov 2021 – ANC.* Retrieved January 20, 2024, from https://www.anc1912.org.za/statement-of-the-anc-on-local-government-elections-2021-preliminary-results-3-nov-2021/

Ashman, S. (2015). The social crisis of labour and the crisis of labour politics in South Africa. *Revue Tiers Monde*, *224*(4), 47–66. doi:10.3917/rtm.224.0047

Breytenbach, W. (2019). The Presidency, Service Delivery and Protest in Post-Apartheid South Africa. *Journal of Southern African Studies*, *45*(4), 789–807.

Buhlungu, S. (2003). The state of trade unionism in post-apartheid South Africa. *State of the nation: South Africa,* 184-203.

Butler, A. (2017). *Contemporary South Africa.* Bloomsbury Publishing. doi:10.1057/978-1-137-37338-0

Cedras, J. P. (2021). The ANC-led Alliance in Government: A Question of Legitimacy and Trust. *African Journal of Public Affairs*, *12*(1), 63–82.

Gumede, W. (2023). *Policy Brief 46: Improving Coalition Governance.* Retrieved January 18, 2024, from https://www.democracyworks.org.za/policy-brief-improving-coalition-governance/

Jessop, B. (2012). Marxist approaches to power. The Wiley-Blackwell companion to political sociology, 1-14.

Lane, J. E., & Preker, A. M. (2018). Political Parties, Coalitions and Democracy. *Open Journal of Political Science*, 8(4), 447–466. doi:10.4236/ojps.2018.84029

Lodge, T. (2014). Neo-patrimonial politics in the ANC. *African Affairs*, 113(450), 1–23. doi:10.1093/afraf/adt069

Martin, L. W., & Vanberg, G. (2020). Coalition government, legislative institutions, and public policy in parliamentary democracies. *American Journal of Political Science*, 64(2), 325–340. doi:10.1111/ajps.12453

McKinley, D. (2001). Democracy, Power and Patronage: Debate and Opposition within the ANC and the Tripartite Alliance since 1994. In Seminar Report, Konrad Adenauer Stiftung and Rhodes University, Johannesburg (No. 2, pp. 65-79). Academic Press.

McKinley, D. T. (2015). *The ANC and the liberation struggle: A critical political biography*. Jacana Media.

Mlambo, D. N. (2019). Governance and service delivery in the public sector: The case of South Africa under Jacob Zuma (2009–2018). *African Renaissance*, 16(3), 207–224. doi:10.31920/2516-5305/2019/V16n3a11

Mokgosi, K., Shai, K., & Ogunnubi, O. (2017). Local government coalition in Gauteng province of South Africa: Challenges and opportunities. *Ubuntu: Journal of Conflict and Social Transformation*, 6(1), 37–57. doi:10.31920/2050-4950/2017/v6n1a2

Morrison, S. (2023). *Understanding South Africa's coalition landscape | Good Governance Africa*. Retrieved January 20, 2024, from https://gga.org/understanding-south-africas-coalition-landscape/

Nevin, T. (2005). We are not the ANC's lapdog—Cosatu: South Africa's government, writes Tom Nevin, is facing its biggest ever political crisis as one member of the ruling tripartite alliance, the labour movement Cosatu, is threatening to break away. *African Business*, (305). https://link.gale.com/apps/doc/A127937983/EAIM?u=anon~ee4e08ca&sid=sitemap&xid=967b63b8

Oyugi, W. O. (2006). Coalition politics and coalition governments in Africa. *Journal of Contemporary African Studies*, 24(1), 53–79. doi:10.1080/02589000500513739

Pillay, K. (2018). Service delivery protests, populism and the right to the city: Implications for urban governance and management in South Africa. *Journal of Public Affairs*, 18(3), e1819.

Pottie, D. (2014). The electoral system and opposition parties in South Africa. In *Opposition and democracy in South Africa* (pp. 25–52). Routledge.

Powell, D. M., O'Donovan, M., & De Visser, J. (2015). *Civic protests barometer 2007–2014*. Dullah Omar Institute.

Rametse, M. 2014. *The roots of factional tensions over the ANC government's policies in the ruling alliance in South Africa* (Doctoral dissertation, Murdoch University).

Rapanyane, M. B. (2022). Key Challenges Facing the African National Congress-led Government in South Africa: An Afrocentric Perspective. *Insight on Africa*, 14(1), 57–72. doi:10.1177/09750878211049484

Resnick, D. (2013). Do electoral coalitions facilitate democratic consolidation in Africa? *Party Politics*, *19*(5), 735–757. doi:10.1177/1354068811410369

Rosenfeld, S. (2018). *Democracy and truth: A short history*. University of Pennsylvania Press.

Seidman, G. (2016). Is South Africa heading towards a mass strike? Organized labor and the political origins of the 2012 labor unrest. *Labor History*, *57*(5), 618–639.

Sekatle, K. M., & Sebola, M. P. (2020). The choice of coalition governments for promotion of national unity in Africa: Does the model work for unity and political stability? *The Business & Management Review*, *11*(1), 25–32. doi:10.24052/BMR/V11NU01/ART-04

Southall, R. (2013). Liberation movements as governments in Africa. *Representation (McDougall Trust)*, *49*(4), 447–461.

Southall, R. (2017). From liberation movement to party machine? The ANC in South Africa. In *Postcolonial struggles for a democratic Southern Africa* (pp. 61–78). Routledge.

Thakur, S. S., & Nel, A. (2023, December). Alter-nation? Factions, Coalitions and Environmental Governance in the Context of Contested Post-apartheid Local State Democratisation. In *Urban Forum* (pp. 1-20). Springer Netherlands.

Truter, J. (2023). *The National Democratic Revolution: A 'Utopian' Blueprint for South Africa*. Academic Press.

Twala, C., & Kompi, B. (2012). The Congress of South African Trade Unions (COSATU) and the Tripartite Alliance: A marriage of (in) convenience? *Journal of Contemporary History*, *37*(1), 171–190.

Vercesi, M. (2016). Coalition Politics and Inter-Party Conflict Management: A Theoretical Framework. *Politics & Policy*, *44*(2), 168–219. doi:10.1111/polp.12154

ADDITIONAL READING

Bellamy, R. (2012). Democracy, compromise and the representation paradox: Coalition government and political integrity. *Government and Opposition*, *47*(3), 441–465. doi:10.1111/j.1477-7053.2012.01370.x

Dobratz, B. (2015). *Power, politics, and society: an introduction to political sociology*. Routledge. doi:10.4324/9781315663166

Giannetti, D., & Benoit, K. (Eds.). (2008). *Intra-party politics and coalition governments*. Routledge. doi:10.4324/9780203889220

Hobolt, S. B., & Karp, J. A. (2010). Voters and coalition governments. *Electoral Studies*, *29*(3), 299–307. doi:10.1016/j.electstud.2010.03.010

Mthembi, P. (2014). *Repositioning of the South African Communist Party (SACP) in the politics of post-apartheid South Africa: a critical study of SACP from 1990-2010* (Doctoral dissertation, University of Limpopo).

Pedersen, H. H. (2010). How intra-party power relations affect the coalition behaviour of political parties. *Party Politics*, *16*(6), 737–754. doi:10.1177/1354068809345855

KEY TERMS AND DEFINITIONS

African National Congress: The African National Congress (ANC) is a political party in South Africa formed in 1912.

Colonialism of a Special Type: Was a program created by the Tripartite Alliance of the ANC, SACP and COSATU that serves as a promise to liberate South African people who were supressed by apartheid colonialism.

Congress of South African Trade Unions: The Congress of South African Trade Unions (COSATU) is the largest trade union federation in South Africa founded in 1985.

Government of National Unity: The Government of National Unity is the South African Coalition Government formed after 1994 elections and was led by the ANC and joined by NNP and IFP.

Inkatha Freedom Party: The Inkatha Freedom Party (IFP) is a South African political organization, established by Chief Mangosuthu Buthelezi in 1975.

National Assembly: The National Assembly is the first house of South African Parliament consisting of 400 members.

National Council of Provinces: The National Council of Provinces (NCOP) is the upper house of the Parliament of South Africa under the (post-apartheid) constitution which came into full effect in 1997.

National Democratic Revolution: Was the ANC-alliance ideological program to overthrow the colonial state and establish a united, democratic and non-racial South Africa.

Republic of South Africa: South Africa, officially the Republic of South Africa, is the southernmost country in Africa and it got its liberation in 1994.

South African Coloured People's Organisation: The South African Coloured People's Organisation (SACPO) was formed in 1953 at a Coloured People's Convention in Cape Town to unite Coloureds against the efforts to remove them from the common voters rolls.

South African Communist Party: The South African Communist Party is The Communist Party of South Africa which was founded in 1921.

South African Congress of Democrats: The South African Congress of Democrats (SACOD) was a radical left-wing white, anti-apartheid organization founded in South Africa early 1950s.

South African Indian Congress: The South African Indian Congress (SAIC) was an umbrella body founded in 1921 to coordinate political organisations representing Indians in the various provinces of South Africa.

Chapter 18
Investigating the Dynamics of Coalition Governance in South African Local Government

Mohale Ernest Selelo

https://orcid.org/0000-0002-1995-0036

University of Limpopo, South Africa

Khutso Piet Lebotsa

University of Limpopo, South Africa

ABSTRACT

The dynamics of coalitions in South Africa's democratic landscape can be attributed to the ANC government's shortcomings or failure in providing services to communities and its pervasive issues of corruption. The chapter argues that enhancing governance, service delivery, and fostering unity in South Africa requires a political centre, consistent policy agenda, and capable politicians. This is essential to fulfil the service delivery mandate, and it also suggests the need for a legislative framework to regulate coalition governments, considering their inevitability in the current political climate of South Africa. The current South African political climate of coalitions is clouded by political immaturity which is a receipt for poor service delivery. An analysis of several motions of confidence passed in coalition governance in many municipalities across the country shows that coalition governance in the contemporary South African political climate is characterized by instability, political egos, no commonality of interest, and political patronage which are ingredients of poor service delivery, particularly as the next 2024 national and provincial elections draw near. Coalition governments typically include parties with varied ideological orientations and policy preferences. The task of reconciling these differences to establish a unified policy agenda can pose significant conundrums and delays in service delivery. What ordinary people need on the ground is very simple, which is just the provision of basic services not political ideologies. However, different policy agendas from political parties haunt the delivery of basic services to the constituencies. This chapter sees it as imperative to demonstrate contextual and institutional effects that supplement emergent discoveries in the literature of coalition governance. Thus, it adopts a literature-based approach, which is conceptual, to assess the dynamics of coalition governance in South African local government, looking at policy implementation, political stability, and service delivery inter alia.

DOI: 10.4018/979-8-3693-1654-2.ch018

INTRODUCTION AND BACKGROUND

Coalition, "a marriage of inconvenience" as described by Dorey and Garnett, (2016) is currently topping the agenda in government and political parties. Yerankar (2015) proffers that a coalition is a characteristic feature of a multi-party government, wherein several minority parties collaborate to collectively govern when individual party rule is not feasible. The author further lengthens that the formation of a coalition occurs when multiple groups reach a consensus and establish a shared program or agenda to guide their collaborative efforts in governance. One could infer that personal arranged marriages have transitioned to government in the name of coalitions in South African local government. Because in a personal arranged marriage, the bride and the groom make some compromises to a certain extent for the sake of a sustainable marriage. At times the newlyweds would even compromise their happiness for the sake of keeping an arranged marriage alive. Same applies to political parties in coalition. According to Law and Calland (2018), coalitions provide medium to smaller parties with the opportunity to enhance their public visibility and wield disproportionate influence. The Economic Freedom Fighters (EFF) serves as a prime example of a party that strategically positioned itself as a kingmaker in the Johannesburg Municipality. Instead of officially joining the coalition, it opted to exert its significant influence to secure voting power (Makgale, 2020).

The 2016 local government elections which is currently paving a way to the national dialogue on coalitions especially anticipating the 2024 national elections. This arranged marriage on inconvenience, inconveniences good governance, consistent policy and service delivery. Unfortunately, several motions of no confidence passed in the city of Tshwane against Mayors such as Solly Msimanga (Makgale, 2020) for incompetence and lack of service delivery, clearly demonstrate that coalitions have their own setbacks. Coalition governments typically arise when no single party commands an outright majority in the nation's parliament or legislative body following an election. Such alliances serve to diminish the dominance of any single political party, and the pursuit of power stands out as a primary motivation for the formation of coalition governments (Longley, 2023). This is the case in South Africa, following the 2016 local government elections wherein the ANC lost total dominance and power in some local government entities, municipalities and metros.

The outcomes of the 2016 local government elections led to the formation of a coalition between the Democratic Alliance (DA) and the Economic Freedom Fighters (EFF), along with other smaller parties. This coalition aimed to remove the ANC from power in the City of Johannesburg, Tshwane, and Nelson Mandela Bay Metros (Ndou, 2022). The debate on coalition government should be blamed on the ANC for failing to deliver services and for a continuous looting, corruption and lack of accountability amongst others. The question is, would coalitions serve the best interests of the people or advance political interests of different political parties? In an attempt to answer this question, one wonders how these arranged marriages would be sustainable due to policy differences from political parties. Longley (2023) postulates that in the face of having to make policy concessions or compromises, a political party would prefer to retain some degree of power rather than having none whatsoever.

The current political wind in South Africa resembles a circus filled with amusing characters, and the initiation of the national dialogue on coalition governments is capturing the interest of diverse stakeholders. As political parties and various participants convene to deliberate on the complexities of coalition politics and governance, it raises the question of whether these political entities will transcend the immaturity that characterized them in the previous decade (Fakir, 2023). The author further demonstrates that the present-day politics are marred by erratic political parties advancing self-referential policies within unresponsive public institutions detached from societal needs. This disconnection has resulted in a decline in public trust in politics and democratic governance, leading people to disengage from political and public life. This chapter shows the inconsistencies of policy implementation, poor governance, poor service delivery and political instability in local government due to coalitions. Hence, Ndou (2022) argues that coalition governments in South Africa in metropolitan areas exhibit conflict and instability, undermining service delivery and governance through frequent changes in leadership. Additionally, it is noteworthy that coalitions in South Africa lack regulation.

RESEARCH METHODOLOGY

The chapter used literature-based methodology which is at time a desktop study to collect secondary data. Researchers used this approach to collect secondary data through access to different data bases such as google scholar, Sabinet, science direct, ProQuest, internet sources, newspaper publications and other government publications to achieve the aim and purpose of the chapter. This means that the chapter is purely conceptual and has used this methodological approach to validate its hypothesis and results. Mamokhere and Kgobe (2023) proffer that this kind of an approach is qualitative and has long been used by philosophers of the time to provide some philosophical arguments through thorough analysis, explanations and descriptions of different phenomena.

The chapter adopted Thematic Content Analysis (TCA) to analyse quantitative or literature data. TCS by Cengiz (2020) refers to a method of synthesizing quantitative data. It also refers to a method of analysing textual data (Anderson, 2007). Through this analysis, themes were developed in an attempt to achieve the purpose of the chapter. The themes developed in literature were interpreted, provided with meanings, explanations, justification and elucidated to makes sense and gist of selection thereof.

LITERATURE REVIEW

Service Delivery Does Not Have an Ideology: People Need Services Not Ideas

Amidst the controversies associated with coalition government in certain South African municipalities, Peyper (2016) believes that service delivery might be further relegated to the background. The realm of qualitative governance and efficient service delivery has been thoroughly explored in numerous literature reviews, emerging as a prominent theme in administrative studies. In recent years, there has been a rise in the prevalence of coalition governments worldwide (Gautam, 2018). Consequently, these coalitions create disorder in parliamentary democracies by introducing chaos to public policymaking based on party platforms, stemming from ideological gaps and differences in working dimensions among the involved parties (Mpangalasane, 2020). The disorder, chaos, anarchy, inconstancies, political differences also characterise the marriage of inconvenience (coalition) in local government in South Africa. One examples of such chaos in the City of Tshwane that has passed more than 3 motion of no confidence against mayors.

What people need on the ground is just a provision of basic services such as safe water, proper roads, schools and clinics, streetlights and food *inter alia,* not political ideology. Because people cannot eat and satisfy their basic needs through ideologies. These are services that continues to haunt most of the communities in South Africa, and such could be associated with the failure of the ANC government to deliver basic services. Post democratic dispensation and 30 years of democracy has become melancholic for most ordinary people that they still have to live without some of basic services as enshrined in the constitution, bill of rights. The promises of the ANC to deliver basic services causes an upset to the citizens. Because one cannot promise a person without legs that you would provide them with shoes. It is for that reason that the coalitions are the order of the day in metropolitan and local municipalities in South Africa and such is succinctly attributed to the failure of the ANC led government. Meanwhile, the failure of the ANC to delivery basic services is due to unpalatable and unprecedented levels of corruption within government institutions (Manamela, Mulaudzi, Selelo & Hussein, 2020), exacerbated by weak accountability and perhaps internal control measures such as the adherences to ethical principles (Batho Pele Principles).

Makgale (2020) investigated coalition politics and urban governance in Johannesburg's housing policy and shows that there is a delay in the provision of housing due to the dynamics of a coalition government. Mpangalasane (2020: 70) finds that some residents indicated that they are not satisfied with provision of basic services such as water, electricity, and refuse removal in the City of Tshwane. The research conducted by Ndou (2022) identified various obstacles in the formation of coalition governments in South Africa. These difficulties encompassed issues such as the instability within coalitions, their breakdown, subpar service delivery, and the frequent turnover of leadership, all of which could adversely impact the effective governance of municipalities (Ndou, 2022: v).

Political Patronage and Political Instability

Recently, the emergence of the South African coalition local government has been painted with political interference/patronage which are used to run the institutions and thus, in turn, causes political instabilities due to different political and policy interests. Hicken, Aspinall and Weiss (2019) and Anastacio and Morandarte (2023) observe that political patronage is being applied and used in Philippines local politics. However, political patronage and interference tend to circumvent a merit system of personnel and embrace a spoils system. In that the phrase "to the victor belong the spoils" gives the leading party in coalition government more advantage to pursues their policy positions and at times dictate terms. Mungwini (2018) refers to the phrase "*to the victor belong the spoils*" as the triumphant individual claims it all; for instance, not only did he emerge victorious in the tournament, but he also secured numerous profitable endorsements. Indeed, the spoils belong to the victor. In the realm of politics and governance, a spoils system (also referred to as a patronage system) is a custom wherein a political party, upon winning an election, allocates government positions to its supporters, allies (cronyism), and family members (nepotism) as a token of appreciation for contributing to victory and as an encouragement to remain dedicated to the party (Panizza, Peters & Ramos Larraburu, 2019).

This stands in contrast to a merit system, where appointments or promotions are based on a certain level of achievement, irrespective of political involvement (Wijaya, Kartika, Zauhar & Mardiyono, 2019). Hence, the conflicts, anarchy and motions of no confidence passed in both metropolitan and municipalities are as a result of political patronage and political interests. Therefore, all these causes political instabilities in a coalition government in South Africa. While coalition governments offer the advantage of representing a more diverse range of people and facilitating smoother administrative continuity, it present significant risks such as potential instability and the possibility of undemocratic decision-making (Islam, Ahmed & Sakachep, 2023). Assessing these factors is crucial when evaluating the drawbacks of a coalition government. In certain instances, the process of coalition negotiations as a result of political patronage/political interference may extend to a certain period, posing challenges to the formation of a government, while people wait for basic services on the ground. In his study Mpangalasane (2020:75) finds that 73% of the respondents show that there is political interference in the governance and administration of the City of Tshwane that is a coalition government.

Political Party Factions at Council Meetings

Persico, Pueblita & Silverman, (2011) assert that political party factions are an organised groups within a political party which attempts, at a minimum, to command power of decision-making positions of the party. At municipal councils, political parties form interparty factions to connive against the minority parties with the aim to occupy more and strategic positions or defend previously occupied positions and ultimately take decision making powers of municipal councils (Thakur & Nel, 2023). Maneng (2022) cites the 2019 City of Johannesburg Metropolitan scenario, wherein the Democratic Alliance's (DA) internal dynamics led to the resignation of former Mayor Herman Mashaba. The African National Congress (ANC) did not hesitate to capitalise on the opportunity to vote-in Geoff Makhubo as the Mayor-elect of Johannesburg, seized power again through the alliance with smaller parties. This was as a result that the Economic Freedom Fighters (EFF) vowed to abstain from voting with the DA in municipalities wherein they voted for DA candidates after 2016 Local Government Elections (LGE). According to Maneng (2022) this posture was impelled by the EFF and the DA failure to reach an agreement over negotiations for Member of Mayoral Committee (MMC) positions in City of Johannesburg and Tshwane Metropolitans.

The current coalition scenarios in South Africa demonstrate dispersed leadership, factions, mistrust, and ideological conflicts that result in unreliable service delivery and local municipalities placed under administration (Thakur & Nel, 2023). It is clear that the absence of legal frameworks to regulate coalition partners, often coalition governments create a vacuum for political party factions at local government councils. Joshua, James, and Titos (2022) note that interparty factions at council meetings have a bearing on the stability of the coalition, which leads to poor service delivery. The existence of factions in local government councils has demonstrated that power battles over resources and decision-making positions are prevalent in the South African local governments (Thakur & Nel, 2023).

Political Egos, Party Policies, and Ideological Misalignments

According to Maneng (2022), parties need to find a coalition partner whose visions coincide with their own or with whom they may share common ground whenever coalition relationships become necessary following elections. In such instances, each political group represented in a coalition would hope to be given some authority or respect in order to forward its own goals or ideologies (Makgale, 2020). However, due to varying or misaligned political party ideologies, policies, and egos such is never realised since all represented parties deem their political ideology and policies to be relevant to the discourse.

According to Makgale (2020), participants in coalition governments are compelled to negotiate on a shared policy posture, which implies that partners in a coalition arrangement must leave a room for compromise. Sometimes, the concession might be expensive since one party may have to give up a desired course of action that would have produced favourable outcomes in order to appease the expectations of its coalition ally. As a result of the unavoidable compromise, parties find themselves unable to carry out all of the goals and initiatives they had committed to the public and its constituency (Makgale, 2020). One further drawback of coalition governance is the potential for departmental bureaucrats from different coalition partners to apply their nonpartisan discretion when formulating policies, thus undermining the agreement by slanting policy in a party-specific orientation. The stability of a coalition is impacted by the division, disintegration, and ideological variation among political parties (Meydani & Ofek, 2016). From the above scenario of the EFF and DA, their ideological complexity and disintegration led to the instability and collapse of their coalition government in the City of Johannesburg Metropolitan (Maneng, 2022).

The EFF suggests taking land from the nation without providing compensation in exchange for a fair allocation among the populace, in accordance with its principles of economic freedom (Makgale, 2022). According to the EFF's basic manifesto, strengthening government and state capability is necessary in order to do away with tenders (EFF Manifesto, 2013). While the DA wants to employ the profit-motivated private sector to tackle the housing issues, whereas the EFF supports the state's ability to provide amenities, particularly housing (Booysen, 2021). Contrary to the DA's viewpoint, the EFF argues that the government should solve people's problems without consulting the business sector.

The defence, advancement, and expansion of the following ideas form the foundation of the DA's vision: everyone has the right to private property and unrestricted participation in the market economy (Makgale, 2022). The EFF, on the other hand, is of the belief that massive development would be expedited and realised by the uncompensated nationalisation of mining, banks, and other strategically important economic sectors in order to control competition among market participants (BusinessTech, 2019). The EFF also maintains that even with the achievement of political independence, there are still elements of colonial and apartheid economic structures, ownership, and control. The DA envisions a single South African nation with a shared destiny based on equity, liberty, and opportunity for everyone (Makgale, 2022). However, the EFF contends that even twenty years after formal political freedom was achieved, South Africa's black population still faces extreme mass poverty, landlessness, and a dearth of prospects for employment for young people. Additionally, all demographic groups are commonly mistreated and denigrated in the midst of affluence (BusinessTech, 2019).

Maneng (2022) asserts that coalitions can advance politics centred on unanimity and consequently, more accountable administrations. Bradshaw and Ntsikeleko (2019) recommend a panacea to abate differences and disputes that lead to coalition uncertainties. The two authors assert that coalition partners ought to agree on accords that, among other things, provide for the appointment of an arbitrator to arbitrate disputes between parties. They also suggest that party leaders and members be trained in conflict resolution, negotiation, and mediation techniques. It goes without saying that political party egos, policies, and ideological misalignments are the underpinning or causing factors of conflicts and disagreements that lead to coalition instabilities. Nzimakwe (2022) highlights that the issues with coalition governance arise when parties concede that each party will be dominant in the policy domains under the purview of the departments it oversees. This could result in a governance structure where the needs of society are negated in pursuit of political ends (Makgale, 2020).

The Impact of Coalitions on Municipal Administrations

Booysen (2021) believes that the relationship between political parties and bureaucracies constituted intrinsically tense and that political parties' involvement in the appointments to the bureaucracy may have terrible consequences. According to Alford, Hartley, Yates, and Hughes (2017) bureaucrats and politicians have a relationship that is marked by reciprocity of influence, wide contact, different but intersecting functions, and coexistence of political supremacy and administrative submission. The author, continue to assert that there is a blurry boundary between politicians and bureaucrats, a zone of interaction where a variety of actions and behaviours occur. The Municipal Structures Act (1998) provides council the with the authority to designate municipal executives as the municipality's administrative leaders and to supervise the hiring of departmental directors who report to the municipal manager. Thus, it follows that legislators also indirectly have an impact on the responsibilities of a municipal executives, particularly with regard to the issuance of tenders (Mukwedeya, 2015).

The legislative framework for local government in South Africa clearly distinguishes between the executive mayor or executive committee, which is responsible for providing oversight, policy reviews, and recommendations to council, and the municipal manager, who serves as the person in charge of administration and municipal accounting officer (Booysen, 2014). According to Olver (2021) there may be some legal inconsistency in the term "*executive committee or executive mayor*," which could contribute to ongoing issues with the interactions between administrative and so-called executive departments as well as the interactions between the political sphere, council members, and political figures represented in council, and municipal administration officials. Although there have been some surprisingly successful coalitions in local government that have been able to shield the administrative from factionalism in politics and create functioning administrations, coalitions generally serve to highlight issues in the political-administrative landscape (Mpangalasane, 2020).

Pros and Cons of Coalition Governments

Mokgosi, Shai, and Ogunnubi (2017) point out that there are numerous arguments in favour of the idea that coalitions are beneficial. They increase the number of parties in power, which frequently results in a broader spectrum of communities in nations that are separated along racial and ethnic lines getting a taste of democracy. The authors further assert that this can provide opposition parties access to power rather than keeping them out of government under a dominant party structure like South Africa, where the ANC has consistently received a sizable majority of the vote. Mokgosi et al (2017) assert that coalition governments give small opposition parties an opportunity to strengthen their electoral support, advocacy for democratic change, creation of public policy, and come to consensus on government programmes and policies with the ruling party. Coalition governments have the potential to enhance democratic practices and governance, even as they spark social transformation and improve governance through diversity management (Mpangalasane, 2020). On the other hand, coalition governments have the potential to limit a party's ability to uphold its own political distinctiveness whilst trying to honour the obligations of the coalition agreement, construct systems for collaborating with coalition partners, and inform party members and the general public of their goals and accomplishments (Mokgosi *et al.*, 2017). Ashiagbor and Tora (2015) assert that coalitions have a propensity to erode parties' fundamental values while simultaneously offering all parties special chances and difficult hurdles, which may have an impact on their ability to survive and perform well in later elections.

Metros and Local Municipalities in Coalition Post 2016 Local Government Elections

Between August 2016 and October 2019, the City of Johannesburg experienced governance through a coalition led by the Democratic Alliance, which included the Inkatha Freedom Party, African Christian Democratic Party (ACDP), Congress of the People (COPE), United Democratic Movement (UDM),

Freedom Front Plus (VF), and Al Jama-ah. However, Al Jama-ah withdrew from the coalition during this period. They received backing from the EFF, which, although not officially part of the coalition agreement, frequently aligned with the minority government on a case-by-case basis when it came to voting (The city of Joburg, n.d). Since December 4, 2019, the City has been governed by a coalition comprising the African National Congress, Inkatha Freedom Party (IFP), Patriotic Alliance (PA), United Democratic Movement, African Independent Congress (AIC), and Congress of the People (COPE) (The City of Joburg, n.d; Makgale, 2020).

The coalition dynamics in Nelson Mandela Bay highlight a concerning pattern of disintegration among political elites. The then-mayor, Athol Trollip of the DA, was replaced by the UDM's Bobani. These changes were all efforts by political parties to establish a form of representative and unbiased coalition governance, but unfortunately, the outcomes were disappointing, especially in terms of service delivery (Makgale, 2020). The political landscape was further marred by scandals, leading to the removal of Mayor Mongameli Bobani. The unanimous decision by the DA and ANC concluded that his leadership had been detrimental to the city. Hence, the metro faced political discord related to the removal of Deputy Mayor Mongameli Bobani, a UDM member (Makgale, 2020).

The Prince Albert Municipality in the Western Cape Province was under the ANC and Patriotic Alliance (PA) coalition until the DA took over the municipality (Charles, 2022). There were several concerns that were raised including that there were thuggish behaviour and lack of trust amongst council members (Charles, 2022). One other scenario of a coalition is the Rustenburg Local Municipality, wherein the ANC has reached some agreement with the independent candidates and opposition parties including Arona representative and the African Independent Congress (AIC) (Connect Radio News, 2021). One of the agreement is to have ethical governance and advance the delivery of basic services to the people. The Mookgophong Local Municipality in Limpopo was under the DA-Led coalition with the EFF and Freedom Front Plus (VF) after the 2016 local government elections (SABC News, 2021). The municipality was put under administration in 2018 due to bankruptcy because of maladministration and mismanagement (Mailovich, 2018). Clearly, coalition government are characterised by different aspects such as conflicts, policy differences and slow service delivery. Be that as it may be, coalition governments are not all bad because they seek to enforce democracy, wherein small parties and independent candidates at least participate in council meeting. Perhaps, coalitions symbolises a representative democracy.

Policy/Manifesto Implications on Service Delivery: A Case of the ANC, DA, and EFF

Because the right of all people to private ownership and to participate freely in the market economy must be maintained, the EFF holds a different view, as it foresees that immense growth would be accelerated and realized by the nationalization of mines, banks, and other strategic sectors of the economy without compensation in order to regulate competition between market players (Makgale, 2020: 34). While the EFF advocates for the capacitation of the state to deliver services, including houses, the DA intends to utilize the private sector in addressing the housing challenges, which sector is by its nature profit driven (Makgale, 2020: 34). The difference in political manifestos and policies is what creates instabilities in coalition governments. This is proven by constant infighting and conflicts that arises in a coalition government such as the City of Tshwane, the City of Johannesburg and Nelson Mandela Bay Metropolitan Municipality. Because of such policy/manifesto differences, service delivery ends up being compromised and delayed. Below is a brief table that indicates policy differences which must top the agenda in coalition arrangements.

Table 1. Policy/manifesto implications

Policy/Manifesto	ANC	DA	EFF
Wage Gap	The minimum wages for domestic and care work are significantly lower than the national minimum wage	Suggest allowing employees to choose to waive the minimum wage requirement, enabling employers to offer a job under the condition that the employee agrees to be paid below the established minimum.	The plan involves raising minimum wages across the board, but in sectors predominantly occupied by women (such as cleaning/domestic work), the proposed increases are considerably lower than those in male-dominated fields (such as mining, petrol attendants, and private security)
Land	The act of seizing property without compensation is endorsed, with the specific conditions to be outlined at a later date	No expropriation without compensation	Expropriation without compensation immediately – including urban land
Higher education	Continue the provision of higher education at no cost using the existing model	Will provide scholarships/bursaries with a variable scale.	Will provide four years of compulsory, free higher education all

Source: (Dullah Omar Institute, 2019)

Different Coalition Scenarios: What Can South Africa Learn?

In the 2010 general election, David Cameron's Conservative Party secured the most seats in the House of Commons but failed to achieve an overall majority (Seldon, Finn & Thoms, 2015). Consequently, the party forged a coalition agreement with the Liberal Democrats, led by Nick Clegg, deviating from the traditional single-party rule in the United Kingdom. The coalition agreement detailed compromises and shared policy objectives encompassing various issues, such as the economy, social policies, constitutional reforms, and foreign affairs (Williams & Scott, 2016). The primary aim was to bring stability to the government and address the country's challenges, especially in the aftermath of the global financial crisis. However, due to different political interests, it was difficult to achieve all those aspects (social policies, economy, foreign affairs and strengthening the government capacity amongst others) (Williams & Scott, 2016).

Over time, a perception emerged that the Liberal Democrats, as the junior coalition partner, had limited success in influencing government policies (Martin & Vanberg, 2020). Critics contended that decision-making was predominantly dominated by the Conservative Party, and the implemented policies more closely aligned with their priorities than with the compromises outlined in the coalition agreement (Martin & Vanberg, 2020). By the 2015 general election, dissatisfaction with the coalition government became apparent, as the Liberal Democrats suffered significant losses, securing only a fraction of their previous seats (Dorey, Garnett, 2016; Martin, & Vanberg, 2020). This outcome was interpreted as indicative of the party's perceived inability to effectively exert influence and distinguish itself from the Conservatives within the coalition.

In the broader context of political dynamics, coalition governments often entail challenges and compromises for the smaller partner as they navigate the delicate balance between pursuing their own agenda and upholding the coalition's stability (Matthews & Flinders, 2017). The experience of the 2010-2015 coalition government in the United Kingdom stands as a noteworthy case study illustrating the intricacies of coalition politics. Clearly, coalition governments are ineffective due to different policy agendas and political interest which ultimately delay the provision of basic services.

India is no exception when it comes to coalitions. India has experienced coalition governments both at the national level and in various states for the past thirty years (Yerankar, 2015). The prevalence of coalition governments is not a recent development in India. Since 1967, over 60 coalition governments have operated within the Indian political landscape (Yerankar, 2015). More than 10 coalitions have been formed in India. The eleventh coalition was established in May 2014, with Narendra Modi at the helm, operating under the banner of the National Democratic Alliance (NDA) (Yerankar, 2015; Makkalanban, 2015). This simply shows that coalitions are just temporary formations because they always keep on changing.

SCOPE AND LIMITATIONS OF THE CHAPTER

This chapter focused solely on coalition government in South African local municipalities. It delved into metros and rural municipalities to detail the implications of coalition government in terms of policy objectives and service delivery. Although it gave different international scenarios of coalition government, it still focused on its scope and did not divert from the initial argument.

FINDINGS AND DISCUSSION

This chapter finds that indeed, coalition governments have their own conundrums and to a certain extent not all coalitions are bad. Because literature suggests that coalition governments also provide some degree of latitude, freedom and space for smaller parties to also make their input regarding the affairs of governance in coalition. Hence, small parties in South Africa such as IFP, AIC, VF, UDM and perhaps the opposition parties such as DA and EFF have managed to participate in a coalition government and give the ANC headache in terms of influencing policy directions and coming with some policy proposals on how to provide people with services. In part, coalition governments are democratic because they permit for diversity of ideologies from different parties.

This chapter also finds that coalition governments lead to sluggishness of service delivery. The chapter finds and makes reference to Mpangalasane (2020: 70) who finds that the City of Tshwane that is currently under coalition is struggling to provide some basic services such as water, electricity, and housing. This may be linked to the dynamics associated with coalition governments. Clearly, the squabbles from the coalition government lead to bad governance. This chapter also highlighted some policy implications in a coalition government. It shows that different parties have their own policy that they want to execute when they get into coalition. The only difficult situation is when compromises must be made and who is willing to compromise their policy and for what good reasons or what and how would political arrangements benefit them.

DIRECTIONS FOR FUTURE RESEARCH

Regarding the qualms, quandaries and prospects on the dynamics of coalition governance at the local level, a study is needed to examine how coalition government affects public support, strategic planning, leadership, and labour division which play a part in coalition governments' success or failure. Future studies can look into the opportunities and difficulties that coalition government faces when tackling difficult problems like social justice, economic inequality, and climate change. There is currently no existing legislative policy or framework that regulates coalition governance, therefore, a study is needed is needed.

CONCLUSION

From the above debates and analysis, the chapter discussed in length, the nature of coalition government by delving deeply into prospects and challenges of a coalition government. As South Africa is fast approaching the provincial and national elections (2024), there is currently a heated debate held on different platforms such as seminars, webinars, and mainstream media in an attempt define the future of the country by looking into the possibilities of a coalition government. Be that as it may be, one cannot predict how the national election would unfold, rather one could make informed political analysis, even if they are informed analysis, they cannot be guaranteed because politics are elastic. The chapter succinctly shows that coalition governance is all about compromises. Although, compromises are made in coalition government, coalitions are democratic because even the small parties are able to partake at least in provincial and local legislatures. Most significantly, the chapter indicates that coalition government have some unpalatable effects on service delivery. Establishing collaboration and consensus-building among coalition partners to overcome policy differences and promote effective governance. This could involve highlighting examples of successful coalition governments prioritizing cooperation and compromise in decision-making processes, leading to positive governance and service delivery outcomes.

A coalition agreement is a political pact that resembles a contract and "binds" the parties that make up the coalition to any concessions made during the talks (Sithole, 2023). Regarding the terms and conditions that the coalition parties agreed to throughout the discussions, the coalition agreement is meant to act as a point of reference. The coalition agreement covers the procedural regulations for making choices in the coalition, recommends regulations for coalition behaviour, offers for the coalition initiative and demonstrates the structure of the coalition as well as the nature and responsibilities of every party in the coalition in an attempt to try to successfully restrict parties from swaying from the concurred coalition terms (Beukes, 2021). Hence, the drafting and creation of a real, tangible coalition agreement or document is crucial. The real procedures of the arrangement must have been entered, and the document must include the arrangements of the coalition members together with its stipulations.

REFERENCES

Alford, J., Hartley, J., Yates, S., & Hughes, O. (2017). Into the purple zone: Deconstructing the politics/administration distinction. *American Review of Public Administration, 47*(7), 752–763. doi:10.1177/0275074016638481

AnastacioA.MorandarteN. (2023). Political patronage in philippine local politics. *Available at* SSRN 4362736.

Anderson, R. (2007). Thematic content analysis (TCA). *Descriptive Presentation of Qualitative Data, 3,* 1-4.

Ashiagbor, S., & Tora, B. (2015). *Coalitions: a guide for political parties.* The National Democratic Institute and the Oslo Center for Peace and Human Rights.

Beukes, J. (2021). *Dullah Omar Institute.* https://dullahomarinstitute.org.za/multilevel-govt/local-government-bulletin/archives/volume-16-issue-1-march-2021/coalition-governments-guidelines-for-coalition-agreements

Booysen, S. (2014). Causes and impact of party alliances and coalitions on the party system and national cohesion in South Africa. *Journal of African Elections*, *13*(1), 66–92. doi:10.20940/JAE/2014/v13i1a4

Booysen, S. (Ed.). (2021). *Marriages of inconvenience: the politics of coalitions in South Africa.* African Books Collective. doi:10.2307/j.ctv2z6qdx6

Bradshaw, G., & Ntsikeleo, B. (2019). Mediating Coalition Politics at the Local Government Level in South Africa, 2016-2019. *Journal of Information. Gender and Development in Africa*, (Special Issue), 123–139.

BusinessTech. (2019). *ANC vs DA vs EFF: Promises on land reform, jobs and fighting corruption.* https://businesstech.co.za/news/government/302086/anc-vs-da-vs-eff-promises-on-land-reform-jobs-and-fighting-corruption/

Cengiz, E. (2020). A thematic content analysis of the qualitative studies on faith project in Turkey. *Journal of Theoretical Educational Science*, *13*(1), 251–276. doi:10.30831/akukeg.565421

Charles, M. (2022). *DA takes over two key positions in Western Cape municipality.* Academic Press.

Connect Radio News. (2021). *ANC in North West signs coalition agreement with opposition parties, independent candidate.* https://connectradio.co.za/radio/news/anc-in-north-west-signs-coalition-agreements-with-opposition-parties/

Dorey, P., & Garnett, M. (2016). *The British coalition government, 2010-2015: a marriage of inconvenience.* Springer. doi:10.1057/978-1-137-02377-3

Dullah Omar Institute. (2019). *Feminist analysis of ANC, EFF and DA manifestos – in brief.* https://dullahomarinstitute.org.za/women-and-democracy/submissions/feminis-analysis-anc-eff-da-in-brief.pdf

Fakir, E. (2023). *Coalition politics and government – a power and predation roller coaster ride, or means of curbing excess?* https://www.dailymaverick.co.za/opinionista/2023-08-03-coalition-politics-and-government-a-power-and-predation-roller-coaster-ride-or-means-of-curbing-excess/

Gautam, R. (2018). Politics in India: The dynamics of formation of coalition government. *IMPACT: International Journal of Research in Humanities, Arts and Literature, 6,* 167-172.

Hicken, A., Aspinall, E., & Weiss, M. (2019). *Electoral dynamics in the philippines: money politics, patronage and clientelism at the grassroots.* National University of Singapore Press. doi:10.2307/j.ctv136c5vg

Islam, N., Ahmed, M., & Sakachep, M. (2023). Governance in collaboration: Evaluating the advantages and challenges of coalition politics. *The Journal of Research Administration*, 5(2), 2142–2149.

Joshua, M., James, M., & Titos, K. (2022). Coalition Governance and Service Delivery in South Africa: A case study of Tshwane, Johannesburg and Ekurhuleni Metropolitan Municipalities. *Journal of Public Administration*, 57(2), 272–283.

Law, M., & Calland, R. (2018). *Political party co-operation and the building and sustaining of coalitions: Challenges Faced and Lessons Learned.* A High-Level Exchange between South African and German political leaders Symposium, Cape Town, South Africa.

Longley, R. (2023). *What Is a coalition government?* https://www.thoughtco.com/what-is-a-coalition-government-6832794

Mailovich, C. (2018). *Limpopo places coalition-led Modimolle under administration.* https://www.businesslive.co.za/bd/national/2018-06-01-limpopo-places-coalition-led-modimolle-under-administration/

Makgale, B. (2020). *Coalition politics and urban governance in Johannesburg's housing policy* (Doctoral dissertation, Master's dissertation. Johannesburg: University of the Witwatersrand).

Makkalanban, D. S. (2015). Coalition's in Indian political process: A critical analysis. *Indian Journal of Poultry Science*, 76(3), 397–401.

Mamokhere, J., & Kgobe, F. K. L. (2023). One District, one approach, one budget, one plan: Understanding district development model as an initiative for improving service delivery and socio-economic development in South Africa. *International Journal of Social Science Research*, 11(3), 362–370.

Maneng, N. S. (2022). *Power-sharing in South Africa's municipalities: The case of Ekurhuleni and Nelson Mandela Bay Metropolitan municipalities from 2016.* University of the Free State.

ManifestoE. F. F. (2013). Available at https://www.effonline.org/eff-elections-manifesto-2016

Martin, L. W., & Vanberg, G. (2020). Coalition government, legislative institutions, and public policy in parliamentary democracies. *American Journal of Political Science*, 64(2), 325–340. doi:10.1111/ajps.12453

Matthews, F., & Flinders, M. (2017). Patterns of democracy: Coalition governance and majoritarian modification in the United Kingdom, 2010–2015. *British Politics*, 12(2), 157–182. doi:10.1057/s41293-016-0041-5

Meydani, D., & Ofek, D. (2016). A new integrated model of the formation of coalitions: Perspectives on the Twentieth Knesset. *Israel Affairs*, 22(3-4), 612–662.

Mokgosi, K., Shai, K. & Ogunnubi, O. (2017). Local government coalition in Gauteng Province of South Africa: challenges and opportunities. *Ubuntu: Journal of Conflict Transformation*, 37-57.

Mpangalasane, C. (2020). *The impact of coalition government on service delivery: City of Tshwane metropolitan* (Doctoral dissertation, North-West University (South Africa).

Mukwedeya, T. G. (2015). The enemy within: Factionalism in ANC local structures—The case of Buffalo City (East London). *Transformation (Durban)*, *87*(1), 117–134. doi:10.1353/trn.2015.0005

Mukwedeya, T. G. (2016). *Intraparty politics and the local state: Factionalism, patronage, and power in Bufalo City Metropolitan Municipality* (Doctoral dissertation, University of the Witwatersrand, Faculty of Humanities, School of Social Science). https://core.ac.uk/download/pdf/188770832.pdf

Mungwini, P. (2018). To the victor belong the spoils' reflections on ethics and political values in postcolonial Africa. *Proceedings of the XXIII World Congress of Philosophy, 68*, 87-93. 10.5840/wcp232018681517

Ndou, L. L. (2022). *An analysis of a coalition government: a new path in administration and governance at local government level in South Africa* (Doctoral dissertation, North-West University, South Africa).

Nzimakwe, I. (2022). *Status of Coalition Governance in South African municipalities: influence of legislative and policy framework. coalition building and municipal governance in South Africa*. University KwaZulu-Natal.

Olver, C. (2021). The impact of coalitions on South Africa's metropolitan administrations. *Marriages of Inconvenience: The politics of coalitions in South Africa*, 267.

Panizza, F., Peters, B. G., & Ramos Larraburu, C. R. (2019). Roles, trust and skills: A typology of patronage appointments. *Public Administration*, *97*(1), 47–161. doi:10.1111/padm.12560

Persico, N., Pueblita, J. C., & Silverman, D. (2011). Factions and political competition. *Journal of Political Economy*, *119*(2), 242–288. doi:10.1086/660298

Peyper, L. (2016). *Coalition-run metros will hurt service delivery*. https://www.fin24.com/Economy/coalition-run-metros-will-hurt-service-delivery-105analyst-20160707

Republic of South Africa. (1998). *Local Government: Municipal Structures Act, 1998 (Act 117 of 1998)*. Government Printers.

SABC News. (2021). *ANC's Sinah Langa elected Speaker in Modimolle–Mookgophong*. https://elections.sabc.co.za/elections2021/anc/ancs-sinah-langa-elected-speaker-in-modimolle-mookgophong/

Seldon, A., Finn, M., & Thoms, I. (Eds.). (2015). *The coalition effect, 2010–2015*. Cambridge University Press. doi:10.1017/CBO9781139946551

Sithole, D. (2023). Coalitions in South African local municipalities: Is the constitution enabling democracy or not? *Journal for Inclusive Public Policy*, *3*(2), 52–62.

Thakur, S. S., & Nel, A. (2023). Alter-nation? Factions, coalitions and environmental governance in the context of contested post-apartheid local state democratisation. In *Urban Forum* (pp. 1-20). Springer Netherlands.

The City of Joburg. (n.d.). *The state of financial management and governance in municipalities with coalition government: A case for constructive coalition governance.* https://www.parliament.gov.za/storage/app/media/Pages/2020/september/02-092020_National_Council_of_Provinces_Local_Government_Week/docs/session6/The_State_of_Financial_Management_and_Governance_in_Municipalities_with_Coalition_Government.pdf

Weber, M. (1978). *Economy and Society: An outline of interpretive sociology.* University of California Press.

Wijaya, A. F., Kartika, R., Zauhar, S., & Mardiyono, M. (2019). Perspective merit system on placement regulation of high level official civil servants. *HOLISTICA–Journal of Business and Public Administration, 10*(2), 187–206. doi:10.2478/hjbpa-2019-0025

Williams, S. & Scott, P. (2016). The UK coalition government 2010–15: An Overview. *Employment Relations Under Coalition Government,* 3-26.

Yerankar, S. (2015). Coalition politics in India. *Indian Journal of Poultry Science, 76*(3), 402–406.

ADDITIONAL READING

Badran, S. (2020). Grand coalition government: The case of Lebanon. *Arab Law Quarterly, 35*(3), 249–276. doi:10.1163/15730255-14030661

Bergman, T., Back, H., & Hellström, J. (Eds.). (2021). *Coalition governance in western.* doi:10.1093/oso/9780198868484.001.0001

Krauss, S., & Kluever, H. (2023). Cabinet formation and coalition governance: The effect of portfolio allocation on coalition agreements. *Government and Opposition, 58*(4), 862–881. doi:10.1017/gov.2021.68

Sozzi, F. (2024). Controlling Uncertainty in Coalition Governments. *Government and Opposition, 59*(1), 91–108. doi:10.1017/gov.2023.6

KEY TERMS AND DEFINITIONS

Coalition: A coalition is a temporary arrangement between group political parties or organizations that join forces with the aim of achieving greater influence and power than each group could accomplish separately.

Coalition Governance: It refers to compromised policy arrangements by political parties in coalition which are necessary to run government institutions.

Coalition Government: It is a form of government whereby two or more political parties converge to form a government after an election, when no party has secured an absolute majority.

Local Government: Local government is a sphere of government which is close and convenient to the local people who need services.

Political Stability: Political instability refers to the likelihood of a government disintegrating or collapsing due to disputes or intense rivalry and anarchy among different political parties.

Service Delivery: It is the provision of socio-economic goods or services to the people such as water, electricity, houses, schools, clinics, and market stalls by government.

Chapter 19
Critical Reflections on Coalition Governments in the 30th Year of South African Democracy

Daniel N. Mlambo
Tshwane University Technology, South Africa

Thamsanqa Buys
https://orcid.org/0009-0006-1694-5377
Tshwane University of Technology, South Africa

Thabo Francis Saul
Tshwane University of Technology, South Africa

ABSTRACT

This chapter comprehensively explores the detailed evaluations of coalition governments in the 30th year of South African democracy. Despite being a relatively recent concept in our political discussions, implementing coalition arrangements is frequently mishandled, posing a hurdle to efficient administration in local municipalities. The main contention of this chapter is that if coalition agreements in South Africa were motivated by a sincere aspiration for effective governance and the provision of services, they would have had positive outcomes for the general public.

INTRODUCTION

In 1948, the National Party, led by Daniel Francois Malan, won the election on an apartheid platform. Apartheid was a conscious decision to deny black South Africans their rights and liberties. Apartheid was not an entirely new policy. Since the late 19th-century mineral discoveries, Africans have experienced a growing deprivation of their rights, along with the implementation of segregationist policies. The police were granted unrestricted authority. Detention without trial was implemented and became frequent. Individuals were detained without charges for both 90 and 180 days and frequently subjected to torture. South Africa's transition to democracy came about with the 1993 Interim Constitution, cre-

DOI: 10.4018/979-8-3693-1654-2.ch019

ated through discussions between different political parties in the Convention for a Democratic South Africa (CODESA). This led to the country's inaugural non-racial election in 1994 (Waldmeir, 1998).

Booysen (2014) contends that South Africa's first decade of democracy, 1994-2004, delivered a high volume of governing and opposition alliances and coalitions in South Africa. These alliances and coalitions catalyzed the party system and facilitated the consolidation of the African National Congress (ANC) power. Simultaneously, alliances in this decade triggered the main opposition party, the Democratic Alliance (DA), which continued to dominate opposition politics numerically through numerous elections. The second decade of democracy, 2004-2014, was characterized by continued ANC dominance, yet instead of the ANC's unremittingly usurping parties, it became subject to splits. Some of the split-offs emerged to become opposition parties. Others fused into alliances with the ANC or existing opposition parties (Mlambo, 2023). This article takes stock of the development during these two decades and looks ahead to budding new alliances that may thrive in lessened ANC dominance. According to Booysen (2014), in his article, which provides an overview of the developments during these two decades, South Africa experienced many governing and opposition alliances and coalitions during its first decade of democracy from 1994 to 2004. These alliances and coalitions played a crucial role in shaping the party system and strengthening the power of the ANC.

Drawing insights from Golding (2015), coalition government is conceptualized as a unique form of government where two or more political parties work collectively to form a governing body. This type of government arises when no party can secure a majority of the votes (50 percent or more) during an election. While many of the coalition governments at the local level in South Africa have failed and continue to witness many challenges, Ndou (2022) contends that coalition governments have now become part of South Africa's political system. However, these coalitions have resulted in instability, paralysis, and failures in service delivery in certain regions/municipalities of South Africa. This can be attributed to the nature of the political parties involved in these coalitions. For instance, political parties advocate for key positions during coalition arrangements in major metropolitan municipalities such as the City of Johannesburg and Tshwane, considered significant cities and economic hubs in South Africa. If consensus cannot be reached, they vote against each other. As a result, and according to Khumalo and Netswera (2020), mayors are often removed from office within a short period when coalition agreements are breached. In a country with more than 540 parties listed on the ballot paper, coalitions are likely to give rise to ideological differences.

The authors believe that lack of adequate institutional capacity, poor financial management, corruption, coalition governments, lack of accountability, and political instability are the causes of these problems. This chapter aims to unearth the drivers and critical reflections of coalition governments in South Africa's 30-year democratic history. This is prompted by the fact that coalition governments have, over the last few years, given rise to poor governance and adequate service delivery in some parts of South Africa, especially since 2016. This is pivotal given the sense (especially since 2016) that coalition governments have become a new phenomenon in South Africa's political and administrative interface. This is given the fact that (1) the changing dynamics in South Africa's political landscape, (2) voter behavior, (3) the increase in political parties contesting elections, (4) ethical leadership and governance from the ruling ANC and (5) the slight and continuous decline of the ANC (Mlambo and Thusi, 2023). Hence, as South Africa gears for the general elections of the 29th of May 2024, at a time when the ANC seems to be losing its grip on power, one may deduce that we can expect to see an increase in the number of coalition governments being formed from 2024 to 2029.

This chapter contends that achieving fair and impartial service delivery goes beyond mere effectiveness and efficiency; it will require a shift in the mindset among municipal leaders through embracing interconnectedness to safeguard democratic achievements further. Apart from this, the chapter proposes that other studies may in the future look at (1) how realistic coalition governments will be in South Africa, taking into consideration the many challenges they face, especially in the metropolitan municipalities, (2) Do other political parties join a coalition government just for specific positions as promised or for the desire and will of serving communities. Such studies will further assist in molding and shaping our understanding of coalition governments in South Africa. To gather information on critical reflections on coalition governments during the 30 years of South African Democracy and to guide our discussion and reflections in the current study, we employed a methodological approach known as qualitative descriptive research (QDR). Secondary sources such as books, newspapers, journals, magazines, and the internet were used as secondary data sources in the study. A qualitative descriptive approach can be used by researchers to determine what was involved, who was involved, and where things happened (Patton, 2015).

Like other qualitative research methodologies, qualitative descriptive studies are characterized by simultaneous data collection and analysis. Merriam (2002) noted that it is essential to comprehend the fundamentals of what quality in qualitative research entails if study findings are to help build our knowledge base. A basic understanding of the many forms of qualitative research can significantly facilitate a reader's evaluation of the study results due to commonality.

BACKGROUND

The local government elections in South Africa on the 3rd of August 2016 were a significant milestone in the country's political landscape. These elections, the fifth since the establishment of democracy in South Africa, witnessed a notable shift in voting patterns and, consequently, the composition of local government. A noteworthy consequence of these elections, which is the focus of this submission, was the unprecedented decline in power of the ruling ANC in the metropolitan municipalities. As a result, several coalition governments were formed with opposition parties based on a simple majority, marking a new era in South African politics (Masina, 2021). Political actors often find it challenging to enforce their agenda without the support and collaboration of others. This necessity to coordinate political efforts with fellow actors leads to the emergence of coalition politics. Weible et al. (2016) state that coalition politics occurs when individuals or organizations unite and synchronize their actions based on shared beliefs regarding governmental actions on a particular issue. However, according to Harshe (2001), coalition building plays a crucial role in governance within socially diverse societies.

The primary objective of all coalitions is to establish a consensus on a shared minimum agenda to ensure their effectiveness. Harshe also highlights that in recent decades, Western European democracies have demonstrated mature approaches to forming coalitions. These coalitions should not be viewed as exclusive entities, regardless of the circumstances. It is worth noting that coalition politics exhibit common patterns worldwide, as evidenced by observations made in South Africa. According to Ndou (2022), South African municipalities face significant challenges in managing the new phenomenon of coalition government, which was introduced in the fifth local government elections in 2016. It has been observed that political parties prioritize their interests over good governance and service delivery. One of the significant issues is the instability in leadership, with mayors being removed within a short period due to disagreements between coalition partners such as the Democratic Alliance (DA) and Economic

Freedom Fighters (EFF) in the City of Tshwane. For instance, in 2022, the City of Tshwane experienced severe disruptions in service delivery due to protests by municipal workers influenced by coalition partners' disagreements. These disagreements have also significantly impacted labour organizations, leading to prolonged disputes over wage increments, dismissal of staff involved in illegal strikes, vandalism of municipal assets, and an ongoing lack of governance stability in this municipality.

Government of National Unity

The commencement of the CODESA negotiations in December 1991 marked the inception of the Government of National Unity (GNU). This agreement established a framework for a transitional constitution. Through the compromises made during the negotiations, the potential threat of civil war was averted, paving the way for forming an elected constitutional assembly tasked with drafting a permanent constitution. According to Van Zyl Slabbert in Fitzgerald, McLennan, and Munslow (1997), South Africa was characterized by the successful completion of the electoral process and the establishment of a GNU, which initially faced and then overcame a crisis of legitimacy.

The elections were highly successful, and an agreement was reached with all political parties, ensuring that even the Pan Africanist Congress of Azania (PAC) and the Freedom Front remained part of the democratic political system. The Inkatha Freedom Party's (IFP's) threat to boycott South Africa's first democratic election was the closest call, but the party was ultimately brought back into the fold at the last moment. A GNU provides the best opportunity to foster national unity, as it brings significant political legitimacy to the new system and encourages former adversaries to come together.

The transition from apartheid to democracy in South Africa was hailed as "a "miracle" due to its negotiations-based approach instead of warfare (Steinberg, 2014), which was a tedious process that included a myriad of compromises by all parties at the negotiation table. A series of discussions, particularly between the ANC and the then-ruling National Party (NP), were held from the late 1980s until the early 1990s (Mapuva, 2010). According to Hamill (1993), when democracy dawned on a country that had suffered colonialism and apartheid for a combined total of over a hundred years. The rebirth of South Africa as a democratic country, with a strong focus on non-racialism amongst a host of other noble ideals, is argued to have the Convention for a Democratic South Africa (CODESA) talks as its bedrock, with all the injustices that took place finding convergence under these talks, wherein they were put to finality and translated to the constitutional democratic dispensation in place 30 years later. These talks, however, did not just happen. There were what Raligilia (2017) calls bargaining about bargaining, or pre-negotiation talks, which refers to the less formal yet extraordinarily significant discussions between the N.P. and key ANC figures such as Nelson Mandela. These discussions (such as the visit of the apartheid Minister of Justice Kobie Coetsee to Nelson Mandela in 1985 at the Volks Hospital in 1985) paved the way for the broader, formal discussions under CODESA.

CODESA I

With consideration of an NP government that lacked legitimacy and an ANC that was gaining national and international support for the end of apartheid, CODESA I took place in December 1991 (Welsh, 1992) at the World Trade Center in Kempton Park, Johannesburg, with the involvement and attendance of nineteen (19) organizations and political parties (Mbambi, n.d.). The NP and ANC, being the more dominant parties, were joined by racially and ideologically diverse formations such as the South African

Communist Party (SACP), Transvaal and Natal Indian Congress, the NP-allied government delegation, the IFP and the Democratic Party (DP) among others. Some of the critical opening speeches included the NP's Dewie dVilliers' expression of regret and apology over the apartheid policy, with another highlight being the NP leader, FW dKlerk's declaration of intent to have a democratically elected government in place (Pahad, 2014). These two statements, in particular, set the tone. They signaled the future of a democratic South Africa with reconciliation and universal suffrage, critical milestones for which many had laid down their lives. Five working groups were created to ensure the seamless running of these talks (see Figure 1), each with its focus areas to ensure that a democratic result would come out of the negotiations.

Table 1. CODESA 1 talks

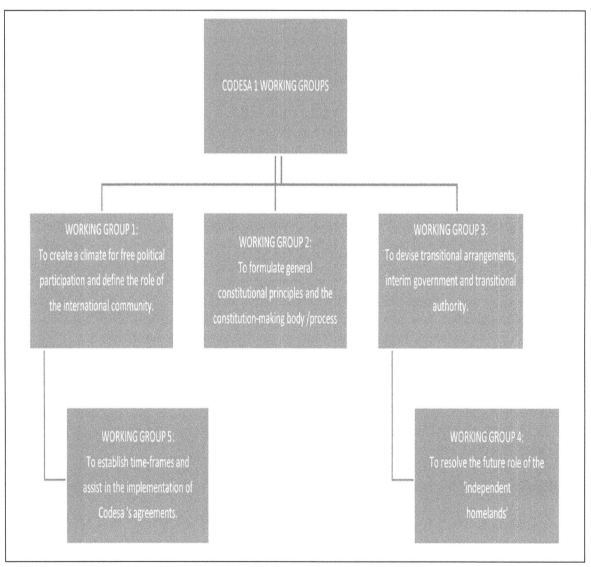

Source: Welsh (1992).

The significance of CODESA I was further highlighted in the Declaration of Intent signed by all parties, including the IFP and the Bophuthatswana Government, stating the following (Pahad, 2014).

- Bringing about an undivided South Africa with one nation sharing a common citizenship
- Working to heal the divisions of the past
- Striving to improve the quality of life of the people and
- To create a climate conducive to peaceful constitutional change by eliminating violence and promoting free political participation, discussion, and debate.

Noble as it was, CODESA I collapsed because of growing mistrust and differing positions between the NP government and the ANC, particularly on issues of the disbanding of the uMkhonto weSizwe and the restructuring of the South African Broadcasting Corporation, coupled with the disagreements on constitutional issues (i.e. the NP wanted a white minority to veto decisions on constitutional amendments while the ANC preferred a two-thirds majority decision-making rule) and the nature and period of existence of the transitional government (Welsh, 1992; Kruger, 1998). This led to a second sitting of negotiations to clarify and agree on outstanding issues through CODESA II.

CODESA II

The plenary of CODESA II started on 15 May 1992 intending to resurrect talks that started under the first plenary (i.e., CODESA I). Despite significant progress in CODESA I talks, some issues remained subject to inflexibility on the part of some parties. These issues led to the stagnation of conclusive progress in the first round of talks. Some of the reports from the previously mentioned working groups (see Table 1) attested to this progress (Kruger, 1998):

Table 2. CODESA working groups

Working Group	Agreement(s)
1	- Despite the priority of releasing political prisoners, the government and ANC should resolve the issue bilaterally and prevent it from hampering progress on other issues. - An interim executive, once it has been established, should be consulted on any state of emergency, and the regulations issued thereunder should be justifiable in a court of law and - Any discriminatory legislation should be repealed.
2	- During the transition period, legislative power would be vested in an interim parliament consisting of two houses, with proportionally elected members and - A final constitution should be drawn up by the national assembly in the interim parliament and accepted by a 70 percent majority.
3	-Multi-party transitional executive council (TEC), in conjunction with existing legislative and executive structures, would facilitate the transition, level the playing field, and create a climate conducive to free political participation and free and fair elections.
4	- The independent homelands would participate in the transitional arrangements. - Independent homelands should be incorporated into South Africa. - Civil servants in the homelands would not be retrenched and would keep their benefits and salaries. - A technical committee would be set up to address all issues about incorporation
5	A drafting committee had to be drawn up to ensure qualified experts were responsible for drawing up legislation arising from agreements reached at CODESA.

Source: Cachalia, (1992); Humphries and Shubane (1992); Raligilia (2017);

CODESA II, however, suffered an ugly fate as the ANC abandoned talks at the back of the brutal Boipatong massacre that claimed 15 lives of ANC supporters at the hands of IFP followers, leading to the ANC blaming this on the NP government for its failure to ensure a quicker end to the discussions. At the same time, Sparks (1996) adds that there was a lack of opportunity to compromise on some issues between the major players (i.e., NP and ANC), and the smaller players lacked the incentive to close the gap. The aftermath of this abandonment was followed by a broader, more inclusive negotiation table in the form of the Multi-party Negotiating Process (MPNP), which included those parties that were not part of or withdrew from CODESA negotiations, such as the IFP and the Afrikaner Freedom Foundation in 1993 (Anglin, 1994).

A year later, this multilateral engagement gave birth to a historic feature of South Africa: a constitutional democracy. The 27th of April 1994 is a day with significant symbolism in the history of South Africa. It was on this day when South Africans took to the polls to ensure the transition from apartheid to a constitutional democratic rule, with universal suffrage seeing an increase from three million voters who were white and the only ones with the right to vote to an estimated eighteen million voters across racial lines (Johnson and Schlemmer, 1996). These elections saw the liberation of the majority black population, Indians, and coloureds from an oppressive system of apartheid that ensured the separate development of whites from the rest of the country's population. It was a difficult election to organize, particularly on the back of loss of lives, decades of oppression, an organizing committee with a lack of insight, and other challenges logistically such as the lack of maps in rural areas and townships, no accurate account of blacks within the country as the last census of this group had taken place in the 1950s (Johnson and Schlemmer, 1996), South Africans managed to cast their all-important votes to put an end to apartheid and give rise to what is today a 30-year-old constitutional democracy. With much jubilation and expectation of a better life for all, South Africans elected the ANC to lead the country to prosperity and equality,

From the Nelson administration's (1994-1998) focus on reconstruction and development, followed by Thabo Mbeki's (1998-2008) efforts to build onto the work of the previous administration and accelerate transformation, to the Jacob Zuma administration (2009-2018) fixated on building service delivery that had been perceived to be neglected in the previous administration (Maserumule, 2021), right to the present Cyril Ramaphosa's leadership, South Africa has always been a country with renewed hope for a better life for all. It has set up a series of laws and institutions to ensure its citizens enjoy the fruits of the hard-fought democracy. It is, however, unfortunate that in the past thirty years, corruption has come to characterize state institutions to the extent that some authors even indicate that the country is losing the battle against this phenomenon, which leads to the bastardization of service delivery ability of the public sector (Krsteski, 2017; Madumo, 2015; Munzhedzi, 2015; Mlambo, Mubecua and Mlambo, 2023).

Coalition Government Within Provinces

A coalition government is formed when multiple political parties or independent representatives join a legislative body or council to establish a governing body and endorse its decisions. This arrangement becomes essential when no single party holds most of the legislative body or council seats. In the context of local government, a governing coalition is focused on electing an executive mayor and other executive members and subsequently backing their initiatives concerning matters such as the budget and municipal policies (Ndou, 2022). Ndletyana (2021) states that the coalitions in local government have been widely discussed in public since the 2016 local elections in South Africa. However, it is essential to note that coalitions are not a new phenomenon. They have been present in the country since the introduction of the new model of local government in 2000. The 2016 local elections marked the fourth occurrence of hung councils, where no party achieved a clear majority.

According to Ndletyana (2021), Mpumalanga Province stands out as the sole province in South Africa that has not witnessed coalition councils. Among the eight provinces that have experienced coalition councils, their frequency and consistency have varied. The Western Cape and Kwa Zulu-Natal have consistently had coalition councils in every local election. Initially, the Western Cape had the highest number of coalition councils, but in 2011, Kwa-Zulu Natal surpassed it. However, in 2016, the Western Cape regained its position, albeit by a narrow margin.

Additionally, Ndletyana (2021) emphasized that the 2011 election also revealed contrasting fluctuations in Kwa-Zulu Natal and the Western Cape compared to the 2006 election. In Kwa-Zulu Natal, the number of hung councils increased by more than half in 2011, while it decreased by a similar margin in the Western Cape. In 2006, the Northern Cape experienced a period of hung councils, but in 2011, it re-emerged with a significantly higher number of hung councils compared to 2000. The Free State, North West, and Limpopo encountered their first hung councils in 2016. This election in 2016 resulted in more provinces, precisely eight out of nine, having hung councils compared to previous elections. Certain municipalities have experienced hung councils on multiple occasions.

The Western Cape stands out with four municipalities, namely Laingsburg, Kannaland, Witzenberg, and Prince Albert, which have had hung councils three times. The Laingsburg municipality even went on to experience a hung council for the fourth. The Northern Cape has also had its fair share of recurrent hung councils in seven and two municipalities, respectively, the remaining six times. Kwa-Zulu Natal and its provinces have only encountered hung councils once. Occasionally, some municipalities have experienced a hung council with only two parties involved rather than the usual involvement of multiple parties.

Theoretical Framework

Without delving into the specifics, this chapter examines the significance of Gawerc and Meyer's (2021) theory on Positive Political Theory (PPT). Positive Political Theory has been utilized to analyze democratic institutions and political bargaining. It allows researchers to evaluate how the outcomes of political bargaining differ depending on the distribution of power among political actors, whether equal or unequal. Furthermore, PPT enables the identification of institutional and contextual mechanisms that grant certain group members more significant influence in determining collective outcomes. By focusing on these mechanisms; researchers can determine whether outcomes arise from asymmetric bargaining or deliberative persuasion. The study employs formal methods such as social choice theory, game theory, and statistical analysis to analyze and comprehend the performance of these coalitions. The process of political parties engaging in democratic institutions and political bargaining is of utmost importance. Municipalities in South Africa are regarded as integral components of our democracy, and political parties negotiate coalition agreements (Monkam, 2014). However, the power distribution among political parties may not be equitable based on their votes. This can result in certain parties wielding more significant influence, potentially leading to the collapse of the coalition. This observation holds particular relevance in South Africa, where the ANC government has maintained power, and coalitions in Tshwane Municipality, Johannesburg Municipality, and Nelson Mandela Bay have experienced varying durations.

On the other hand, in their article, Khumalo and Netswera (2020) aimed to explore the intricacies surrounding political coalitions within municipal leadership. They discuss how political parties with different ideologies often form alliances and make compromises to gain control, referring to these alliances as "marriages of convenience." These coalitions arise when there are no clear winners or when winners do not have a majority stake, and they present numerous challenges to the smooth functioning of municipalities. It is important to note that local government plays a crucial role in driving development, and the state of this sphere of government significantly impacts the effectiveness and efficiency of service delivery.

Re-Emergence of Coalition Governments: 2016 to Present

In August 2016, Mokgosi, Shai, and Ogunnubi (2017) reported that South Africa experienced its fifth round of local government elections since 1995. Despite a few challenges faced by the Independent Electoral Commission of South Africa (IEC) during this election, the results were accepted by all participating political parties. Similar to the previous four cycles, local and international observers deemed the latest edition of the elections as transparent, credible, and democratic. The 2016 local government election marked a significant turning point in the declining electoral support for the ruling party, the African National Congress (ANC). The ANC's loss of significant electoral support benefited opposition parties, particularly the Democratic Alliance (DA), Economic Freedom Fighters (EFF), and smaller parties like the PAC. The closely contested 2016 local government election presented challenges and opportunities for all participating parties. In some regions of Gauteng province, such as the City of Tshwane, Johannesburg, and Ekurhuleni, no party obtained the required majority votes (50% plus 1) to form a municipal government independently. This situation created opportunities for political parties to negotiate and form coalitions to govern certain municipalities.

Masina (2021) highlights the importance of the 2016 local government elections in South Africa, which occurred in August of that year. These elections marked a significant moment in the country's political landscape. The author emphasizes a noticeable change in voting patterns during these fifth local government elections in democratic South Africa, resulting in a transformation in the makeup of local government. As discussed in the submission, one significant outcome of these elections was the unprecedented loss of power by the ruling ANC in the country's metropolitan municipalities. This led to several coalition governments with opposition parties based on a simple majority. Before these elections, the ANC governed seven out of the eight metros in the country, including the City of Tshwane, the City of Johannesburg, the City of Ekurhuleni, Nelson Mandela Metropolitan Municipality, and Buffalo City Metropolitan. The remaining four metros were governed through coalitions, while the City of Cape Town remained firmly under the DA, South Africa's largest opposition party.

Hazell and Yong (2012) assert that coalition governments face unique challenges. One such challenge is instability, which gives rise to various difficulties. In Europe, coalition governments have a shorter lifespan than single-party majority governments. Approximately half of the coalition governments dissolve due to conflicts between the governing parties or within them. Therefore, it is essential to establish effective procedures for managing conflicts, resolving disputes between coalition partners, and promoting communication and coordination.

Coalitions/Roles

Coalitions are undeniably gaining significance within the structures of local and municipal governments. Political parties that previously lacked representation are now discovering a suitable platform to operate and exert their influence within local councils. The main goal of an opposition party when forming a coalition is to overthrow the current governing party. In contrast, the ruling party's primary objective is to secure its position of power (Kadima, 2014). This chapter aligns with Ngubane's (2018) assertion regarding the pivotal role of coalitions in South African municipalities. It suggests that when countries emerging from conflicts establish coalition governments, they aim to promote collective action in addressing broader social, political, and economic transformation, ultimately fostering peace-building.

Consequently, it is imperative to ensure the efficient execution of these vested functions. Municipal councils are widely recognized as the highest decision-making authority, serving as the guiding force behind the municipalities they govern. They are responsible for shaping the strategic direction and making crucial decisions that impact the municipalities and the community's overall well-being. This necessitates close collaboration among coalition partners to fulfill the council's responsibilities in coalitions effectively.

Coalitions in the Post-Apartheid Era

This chapter presents the argument that South Africa, in the post-apartheid era, is confronted with the rise of coalitions to address historical inequalities and the challenges of service delivery failures that hinder effective governance in municipalities. The nation is currently grappling with widespread service delivery protests in all municipalities and several municipalities' breakdown of coalition agreements. Governments face challenges in societies characterized by profound inequality in forming robust alliances to back their development plans. Additionally, populist ideas that offer simplistic yet unattainable solutions for the majority tend to gain traction. This phenomenon is especially evident in democratic nations such as South Africa, where marginalized groups possess political influence while the affluent control crucial economic choices. Consequently, a perpetual power struggle ensues, creating constant contention (Makgetla, 2020).

Reddy (2016) examined the correlation between democracy and service delivery in our municipalities, explicitly focusing on the period since 1994. The author emphasized that the democratic government's objective was to address the historical imbalances within our municipalities. Given that the fight for democracy in South Africa originated at the grassroots level, this must translate into an improved quality of life for local communities. Effective political management is vital in achieving enhanced municipal service delivery and promoting good local governance. Following the establishment of the post-1994 democratic developmental South African state, a robust local government system was implemented and enshrined in Chapter 7 of the Constitution of the Republic of South Africa Act 108 of 1996. The politicization of the local bureaucracy was inevitable as the ruling party aimed to ensure that municipal executive leaders shared the same political ideology and vision, thereby facilitating local development. South Africa is considered a "struggle democracy," and development must occur in historically disadvantaged areas where services have been inadequate or nonexistent. Additionally, it is essential to maintain and upgrade historically advantaged areas as they contribute to the financial sustainability of the municipalities.

According to Booysen (2021), coalitions have been a significant part of South African politics since the country achieved democracy in 1994. Initially, a "grand coalition" was formed at the national level through a Government of National Unity, as mandated by the Constitution. Additionally, coalitions have also been observed in various provinces of the country. Following the transition, multi-party governments were established at national and provincial levels due to election outcomes or other political considerations. At the local government level, coalitions have been common since democratically elected municipalities were introduced in 2000.

In many cases, no single party has secured an absolute majority. The prominence of coalition politics increased in 2016, particularly in metropolitan governments and larger towns (Bradshaw and Breakfast, 2019). These coalitions have taken different forms, including co-governance arrangements and service-and-supply activism, which are crucial in ensuring stability. However, it is essential to note that establishing a culture of stable coalition politics in South Africa will require time and practical experience. Given the nature of party politics, this process cannot be achieved linearly or guaranteed indefinitely.

Findings and Analysis

The management of the government in South African municipalities has posed significant challenges to good governance, service delivery, and leadership stability. These challenges arise from the frequent change of political leadership or mayors due to disagreements among coalition partners. According to Beukes and De Visser (2021), the framework for coalitions in local government highlights that since the first democratic local government elections in 2000 until the 2016 elections, there have consistently been "hung councils." A hung council occurs when no political party secures more than 50% of the seats in the municipal council, necessitating the formation of a coalition or minority government. In the initial local government elections, there were 29 hung councils. This number increased to 31 (including the City of Cape Town) in the 2006 elections and peaked at 37 hung councils in 2011. The 2016 elections saw a decrease to 27 hung councils, but it was the first time four out of the eight metropolitan councils experienced hung councils. These four councils were the City of Johannesburg, Ekurhuleni, Nelson Mandela Bay, and Tshwane.

The ongoing debate on the concepts of good governance and service delivery in South Africa after three decades of democracy stems from the various efforts made during South Africa's transition from apartheid to democracy. Vigorous processes of debate and reflection followed, including the adoption of South Africa's new Constitution in 1996, which addressed past imbalances and affirmed people's rights to express democratic values and principles (Kenosi, 2011). Paying particular attention to governance issues, reviewing policies and legislation that govern public administration, and establishing Chapter 9 institutions (i.e., Public Protector and the Auditor General, among others) was crucial to strengthening the government's oversight role. Under Section 152 of the South African Constitution 1996, the local government is the engine of essential service delivery.

Local government is charged, among other things, with ensuring the provision of services to communities in a sustainable manner, promoting social and economic development, and promoting a safe and healthy environment Constitution, 1996. According to Fitzgerald, McLennan, and Munslow (1995), the Constitution emphasizes the importance of public service being nonpartisan, career-oriented, and guided by fair and equitable values. It should encourage effective public service that represents all communities in South Africa. Public officials should serve unbiased and impartially and faithfully carry out government policies.

Public accountability, which increases legitimacy, is the primary benefit of successful government in democratic cultures, claims Mfene (2013). The Public Finance Management Act (PFMA), the Municipal Finance Management Act (MFMA), and the Protocol on Corporate Governance are just a few of the legislative initiatives introduced by the national, provincial, and local governments to encourage accountability and responsibility in the public sector. South Africa has faced significant challenges that have significant implications for good governance and service delivery. 2024 marks 30 years of South African democracy. Since 1994, South Africa has had its ups and downs. In the early days, South African democracy was considered a success story. More recently, it has been classified as a "deficient democracy." The 30th anniversary offers an opportunity to reflect on the past 30 years and look ahead to the next thirty years. However, progress made in the past three decades of democracy is alarming. Today, one of the biggest obstacles to effective governance is corruption.

Von Holdt (2013) describes the continuation of South Africa's marginal socio-economic structure, characterized on the one hand by deep poverty and extreme inequality and on the other by a symbolic and institutional breakdown due to the transition to democracy. This relationship creates a volatile social order in which inter-elite conflicts and violence increase, characterized by new forms of violence and the renewal of old patterns of violence, a social order that can be characterized as a violent democracy. Good governance and service delivery originated in the post-1960s when some African countries gained independence, and in the 1990s in South Africa, during the transition from apartheid to democratic governance. The administrative and political interaction faced significant challenges throughout South Africa's transition from apartheid to democracy. The volatility within the ruling party hindered the transformation goal and impacted the governance and service delivery throughout most government departments. Some South Africans, dissatisfied with the country's inadequate service delivery, declining economic growth, and rising youth unemployment rates, have labeled democracy as defective due to the corruption-tainted distortion of democratic values (Mongale, 2022).

As Wilson (2003) put it, the function of politics is to "set the task for administration" or to give direction. On the other hand, public administration's function is to offer objective expertise to formulate policy. Politics is at the core of public governance since the government apparatus that carries out policies and programs is the public sector. Thomas (2012) contends that good governance concerns the political and institutional practices and outcomes necessary to achieve development goals. The accurate measure of "good" governance is the extent to which it fulfills the promise of human rights: civil, cultural, economic, political, and social rights. However, because of globalization and new public management, governance is now more often understood as a combination of institutional and political authority to ensure the efficient administration and fair distribution of public resources. It explicitly denotes a change in emphasis from a formal hierarchical administrative and control system to a more dynamic system of relationships between structures and stakeholders that influence people's living and working environments.

According to Overall (2015), leadership is vital to improving people's lives and realizing the objectives of good governance. It is the capacity to influence others to carry out objectives and protect and ensure the highest level of quality of life while also providing critically needed guidance for good government. Strong leadership and excellent governance are essential if development and progress are to be achieved in any nation. Strong leadership and good governance are essential to any nation's survival and development. South Africa's challenge is not a systematic problem but a government system that abuses existing gaps by officials in positions of power. Good governance involves more than just using the government's powers in a transparent and participatory manner.

It also entails the excellent and faithful exercise of power and the accomplishment of the three fundamental duties of government, which are to ensure public safety and security, oversee an efficient and accountable public sector framework, and advance the nation's social and economic goals in line with the popular will (Overall, 2015). While many of the coalition governments at the local level in South Africa have failed and continue to witness challenges, coalition governments have now become part of the political system of South Africa presently and into the future, and one wonders how they will continue to shape Africa's political architecture in the following years to come.

South Africa at 30 Years of Democracy and the Challenges of Coalition and Service Delivery

According to Beukes and De Visser (2021), the stability of a coalition is primarily determined by the political dynamics among its partners. These dynamics often go beyond what can be regulated by law, relying on intangible factors such as personal attitudes, political maturity, mutual respect, and leadership styles. Additionally, there are various reasons why a coalition may fail. It could be due to genuine policy differences between the partners or an unforeseen event with significant political consequences. However, it is essential to note that the number and magnitude of failed local coalitions in South Africa are excessive. Coalitions don't need to be a source of instability.

The primary obstacles that affect service provision in South Africa's municipalities are corruption, financial mismanagement, and leadership instability resulting from unsuccessful coalition agreements, as emphasized by the Auditor General's report for 2021/22. Corruption undermines the priority of delivering services, as those in power prioritize personal gains and favoritism towards their associates. Service delivery, which refers to the process of government providing essential services such as water and sanitation, housing, birth and death certificates, among others, to the communities, points to a social contract that binds the taxpayers and their elected representatives for the betterment of the community (Eigeman, 2007). For service delivery to occur, there has to be efficiency, effectiveness, and responsiveness on the part of the government. This requirement is provided under one of the many legislations under the democratic governance of the public sector vis a-vis service delivery (i.e., Batho Pele Principles). Still, it seems to be getting ignored, considering the blatant corruption that has led to community mistrust and discontent.

It is worth noting that where corruption comes in, service delivery makes its way out. When public resources are not used for their intended purpose, the impact is severe as social services form the nucleus of human development. By failing to deliver on issues such as water, housing, and health care, governments are complicit in violating human rights (Mehrotra, Vandemoortele, and Delamonica, 2000 The dissatisfaction with the lack of services has led to citizens taking to the streets in protest, with some of these protests taking a violent turn, with loss of life, destruction of infrastructure, and looting (Kali, 2023). According to Municipal I.Q. (2023), there were 193 recorded service delivery protests in South Africa in 2022, after a relatively lower number in the previous years (102 in 2020 and 121 in 2021). This rise in service delivery protests indicates a citizenry that is frustrated, discontent, and losing trust in the ability across all three spheres of government to deliver on its constitutional obligations.

On The Notion of Coalition Government in Post-Apartheid South Africa

After elections, an arrangement known as a coalition government is formed when two or more political parties join forces to establish a single governing body (Kadima, 2014). The City of Tshwane, the City of Johannesburg, and the City of Ekurhuleni are the three metropolitan municipalities in Gauteng that saw the formation of coalition governments in 2016. The DA and the EFF formed voting agreements to form a coalition as a result of the ANC losing majority power in the legislatures of the two municipalities (Bradshaw and Breakfast, 2019). One should deduce that local government is a vital framework for South Africans' social, economic, and political welfare since section 152(1) of the South African Constitution mandates municipalities to be accountable for service delivery. Mpangalasane (2020) asserts that municipalities in South Africa are essential in steering the national government's development strategy and guaranteeing that the democratic culture is deeply embedded in communities.

To Masuku and Jili (2019), local government is seen as one of the fundamental branches of government, particularly when guaranteeing service delivery. Local government should try to guarantee that service delivery is feasible as part of its duties. Considering that the majority of South Africans still lack access to basic amenities like housing, power, water and sanitation, and other necessities, previous local government elections in the country have sparked concerns about how well municipalities can provide consistent service delivery (Mokgosi, Shai and Ogunnubi, 2017). The point mentioned above brings up intriguing queries about the effectiveness of political parties, particularly those in coalition, in providing for the demands of the general public. This is put into perspective by the fact that there are a variety of divergent opinions in political science and other cognate disciplines regarding the function and effectiveness of political coalitions in satisfying the demands of the public. In South Africa and globally, there are discussions on whether party allegiance and interests in coalitions may be subsumed by service delivery mandates (Bradshaw and Breakfast, 2019). It might be argued that coalitions must be built through time and effort and should share a shared political ideology on providing services (Hornung, Rüsenberg, Eckert, and Bandelow, 2020). One may contend that the ANC has had a great deal of support in municipal government since 1994; however, the South African political landscape was altered by the local government elections of August 2016, which further brought more political changes to South Africa's political landscape (Mpangalasane, 2020).

Seven of the eight metropolitan municipalities were managed by the ANC before 2016, while the City of Cape Town was (and still is) administered by the DA. Coalitions, with their various interests and intentions, can impair service delivery since the squabbles for positions, power, and control can cripple the operational effectiveness of any municipality (Khumalo and Netswera, 2020). As a result, the conversation around local government research has raised the crucial question of whether political coalitions prioritize party interests over their duties to provide services. Hornung et al. (2020) lists six political party characteristics that are associated with parties seeking to enter into coalitions, and these include:

1. Lost many previously held seats in parliament.
2. A common or relatable ideological basis.
3. A large in size (in terms of membership)
4. Been in government for a considerable time.
5. Decentralized structures and
6. Have built trust with targeted coalition partners over time.

Those above usually demonstrate that parties establish coalition administrations for various reasons. Aref and Neal (2020) concur that trust and a common ideological foundation are critical elements that keep coalitions stable. At the same time, coalitions can be a tactic that is employed by dominant political parties to retain and exert their hegemony (Raleigh and Wigmore-Shepherd, 2020). With the support of willing partners, political parties can continue to advance their program even after losing the majority in an election. However, according to Arriola and Johnson (2014), several coalitions on the African continent have been founded on corruption, with minor party members being promised access to state resources like that of larger parties.

In this instance, Kluver and Spoon (2017) noted that two significant challenges must be settled immediately when a coalition administration is established. The first concerns the makeup of the institutions that will be used to distribute power. The second is how the newly formed alliance would mesh with other governmental domains' current local governance frameworks. In most cases, these two topics frequently present the coalition parties' initial obstacles. The requirement to act independently while maintaining the unity of action is another challenging issue that comes to mind. This stems from the fact that two or more political parties that are by nature political rivals and are competing for votes from the same electorate will need to work together, leading to the questioning of the extent to which each is willing to focus less on self-serving, election-winning agenda in the face of rivalry.

FINDINGS AND DISCUSSION

This chapter emphasizes the importance of a robust local government administration in promoting service delivery and democratic values. It highlights the need for policies and legislative imperatives to be upheld, regardless of whether they originate from a coalition government. Protests resulting from poor service delivery undermine the state's legitimacy and weaken the public service's ability to deliver services effectively. Achieving fair and impartial service delivery goes beyond mere effectiveness and efficiency; it requires a shift in mindset among municipal leaders, embracing the philosophy of interconnectedness. The performance of our state institutions is crucial in safeguarding our democratic achievements. Coalition governments have existed in other states globally, such as Germany, Sweden, New Zealand, and India. The importance of their effectiveness in these states is due to the extensive history and practice of this form of government, a relatively new phenomenon in South Africa. This is also coupled with the democratic and political maturity of the parties involved in a coalition agreement (Oppermann and Brummer, 2014; Gautam, 2018). Thus, from a South African perspective, political parties should foster some of the following principles for adequate coalition arrangements:

1. There is a need for unity, stability, good governance, ethical leadership, and effective governance for any coalition to work collectively and respectfully.
2. Political parties should always be aware that what they do is for the benefit of citizens and communities, and citizen's interests should always come first.
3. Effective communication between those is a coalition agreement, and citizens foster collective trust and respect.
4. Clear rules and responsibilities by all parties are essential in keeping the coalition alive and active, as this will avoid any conflict that might arise.

5. Every coalition must regularly access their review through their signed Memorandum of Understanding (MOU).
6. There should be a need for transparency, accountability, ethics, and good governance.

Adhering to the above practices will ensure that citizens do not suffer through coalition disagreements, considering that those in power are there to serve the people through efficient and transparent service delivery.

CONCLUSION

The citizens had high hopes that crucial services, like service delivery, would be given utmost importance. Unfortunately, ever since South Africa emerged from its isolated state and entered the post-1994 era, there has been a significant increase in inadequate governance, difficulties faced by coalition governments, and protests concerning service delivery. These occurrences do not correspond with the aspirations of countless citizens. As South Africa commemorates its 30th year of democracy in 2024, the government's commitments on paper have not been realized and are not visible on the field, especially in rural regions.

Directions for Future Research

From a methodological perspective, this chapter was driven by a secondary research methodology and relied more on secondary sources to reach the needed conclusion and recommendations. As coalitions started to take shape in 2016 in South Africa, researchers can, in the short and long run, direct their research/studies in a primary direction (especially in a municipality in a coalition government) to get views on people on the ground. This will add more nuance to the functioning of coalition government in South Africa. Drawing from the above, it seems from a South African perspective that coalition governments are here to stay, and much research will be done on their stability and how they direct good governance and service delivery.

ACKNOWLEDGMENT

The corresponding author (Daniel N. Mlambo) would like to thank the National Institute for the Humanities and Social Sciences (NIHSS) for their financial support.

REFERENCES

Anglin, D. G. (1995). International monitoring of the transition to democracy in South Africa, 1992-1994. *African Affairs*, *94*(377), 519–543. doi:10.1093/oxfordjournals.afraf.a098872

Aref, S., & Neal, Z. (2020). Detecting coalitions by optimally partitioning signed networks of political collaboration. *Scientific Reports*, *10*(1), 1506. doi:10.1038/s41598-020-58471-z PMID:32001776

Arriola, L. R., & Johnson, M. C. (2014). Ethnic politics and women's empowerment in Africa: Ministerial appointments to executive cabinets. *American Journal of Political Science*, *58*(2), 495–510. doi:10.1111/ajps.12075

Beukes, J., & De Visser, J. (2021). *A framework for coalitions in local government*. https://www.cogta.gov.za/cgta_2016/wp-content/uploads/2021/11/A-Framework-for-Coalitions-in-Local-Government_Dullah_Omar_.pdf

Booysen, S. (2014). Causes and impact of party alliances and coalitions on the party system and national cohesion in South Africa. *Journal of African Elections*, *13*(1), 66–92. doi:10.20940/JAE/2014/v13i1a4

Booysen, S. (Ed.). (2021). *Marriages of inconvenience: the politics of coalitions in South Africa. African Books Collective*. Mapungubwe Institute for Strategic Reflection. doi:10.2307/j.ctv2z6qdx6

Bradshaw, G., & Breakfast, N. (2019). Mediating Coalition Politics at the Local Government Level in South Africa, 2016-2019. JGIDA, 123-139.

Cachalia, F. (1992). A Report on the Convention for a Democratic South Africa. *S. Afr. J. on Hum. Rts.*, *8*, 249.

Chinyere, P. C., & Rukema, J. R. (2020). The Government of National Unity as a Long-Lasting Political and Economic Solution in Zimbabwe. *The Mankind Quarterly*, *61*(2), 163–189. doi:10.46469/mq.2020.61.2.2

Dlakavu, A. (2022). South African electoral trends: Prospects for coalition governance at national and provincial spheres in 2024. *Politikon: South African Journal of Political Studies*, *49*(4), 476–490. doi:10.1080/02589346.2022.2151682

du Toit, D. (2002). Public Service Delivery. In D. du Toit, A. Knipe, D. van Niekerk, G. van der Walt, & M. Dolve (Eds.), *Service excellence in governance* (1st ed., pp. 55–119). Heinemann.

Eigeman, J. (2007). *Service delivery a challenge for local governments*. VNG International.

Gautam, R. (2018). Politics in India: The dynamics of formation of coalition government. *IMPACT: International Journal of Research in Humanities, Arts and Literature*, *6*, 167-172.

Gawerc, M. I., & Meyer, D. S. (2021). William A. Gamson and His Legacy for Academia and Social Movements. *Contention*, *9*(2), 64–86. doi:10.3167/cont.2021.090205

Golding, J. (2015). What has the Coalition Government done for the development of initial teacher education? *London Review of Education*, *13*(2). Advance online publication. doi:10.18546/LRE.13.2.10

Hamill, J. (1993). South Africa: From Codesa to Leipzig? *The World Today*, *49*(1), 12–16.

Harshe, R. (2001). The South African Experiment in Coalition-Building. *Seton Hall J. Dipl. & Int'l Rel.*, *2*, 87.

Hazell, R., & Yong, B. (2012). *The Politics of Coalition: How the Conservative-Liberal Democrat Government Works*. Bloomsbury Publishing.

Hornung, J., Rüsenberg, R., Eckert, F., & Bandelow, N. C. (2020). New Insights into Coalition Negotiations—The Case of German Government Formation. *Negotiation Journal*, *36*(3), 331–352. doi:10.1111/nejo.12310

Humphries, R., & Shubane, K. (1992). Transkei: Referendum, reincorporation, and a new regionalism. *Journal of Contemporary African Studies*, *11*(2), 109–128. doi:10.1080/02589009208729534

Johnson, R. W., & Schlemmer, L. (Eds.). (1996). Launching Democracy in South Africa: the first open election, April 1994. Yale University Press. doi:10.12987/9780300160994

Kadima, D. (2014). An introduction to the politics of party alliances and coalitions in socially- divided A. *Journal of African Elections*, *13*(1), 1–24. doi:10.20940/JAE/2014/v13i1a1

Kali, M. (2023). A comparative analysis of the causes of the protests in Southern Africa. *SN Social Sciences*, *3*(2), 28. doi:10.1007/s43545-023-00613-x PMID:36691644

Kenosi, L. (2011). Good governance, service delivery, and records: The African tragedy. *Journal of the South African Society of Archivists*, *44*, 19–25.

Keping, Y. (2018). Governance and good governance: A new framework for political analysis. *Fudan Journal of the Humanities and Social Sciences*, *11*(1), 1–8. doi:10.1007/s40647-017-0197-4

Khumalo, P., & Netswera, M. M. (2020). The complex nature of coalitions in the local sphere of government in South Africa. *African Journal of Democracy and Governance*, *7*(3-4), 173–192.

Kikasu, E. T., & Pillay, S. S. (2024). Forecasting an Inevitable Coalition Government at the National Level in South Africa: A New Path to Public Administration and Governance. *Open Journal of Political Science*, *14*(01), 28–51. doi:10.4236/ojps.2024.141003

Krsteski, N.G.H. (2017). Corruption in South Africa: genesis and outlook. *Journal of Process Management – New Technologies,* *5*(4), 49-54.

Lodge, T. (1987). State of exile: The African National Congress of South Africa, 1976–86. *Third World Quarterly*, *9*(1), 1–27. doi:10.1080/01436598708419960

Lupia, A., & McCubbins, M. D. (1998). *The democratic dilemma: Can citizens learn what they need to know?* Cambridge University Press.

Madumo, O. S. (2015). Developmental local government challenges and progress in South Africa. *Administratio Publica*, *23*(2), 153–166.

Makgetla, N. (2020). *Inequality in South Africa–An Overview*. Trade & Industrial Policy Strategies.

Mapuva, J. (2010). Government of National Unity (GNU) as a conflict prevention strategy: Case of Zimbabwe and Kenya. *Journal of Sustainable Development in Africa*, *12*(6), 247–263.

Maserumule, H. (2021). Administering national government. In C. Landsberg & S. Graham (Eds.), *Government and politics in South Africa* (pp. 95–128). Van Schaik Publishers.

Masina, M. (2021). *Future Realities of Coalition Governments in South Africa: Reflections on Coalition Governments in the Metros: 2016-2021.* South African Association of Public Administration and Management.

Masuku, M. M., & Jili, N. N. (2019). Public service delivery in South Africa: The political influence at local government level. *Journal of Public Affairs*, *19*(4), e1935. doi:10.1002/pa.1935

Mehrotra, S., Vandemoortele, J., & Delamonica, E. (2000). *Basic services for all? Public spending and the social dimensions of poverty.* https://www.unicef-irc.org/publications/pdf/basice.pdf

Merriam, S. B. (2002). Introduction to qualitative research. *Qualitative research in practice: Examples for discussion and analysis, 1*(1), 1-17.

Mfene, P. N. (2013). Public accountability. *Administratio Publica*, *21*(1), 6–23.

Mlambo, D. N. (2019). Governance and service delivery in the public sector: The case of South Africa under Jacob Zuma (2009–2018). *African Renaissance*, *16*(3), 207–224. doi:10.31920/2516-5305/2019/V16n3a11

Mlambo, D. N. (2023). The Tragedy of the African National Congress (ANC) and its Cadre Deployment Policy: Ramifications for Municipal Stability, Corruption and Service Deliver. *Pan-African Journal of Governance and Development, 4*(1), 3-17.

Mlambo, D. N., Mubecua, M. A., Mpanza, S. E., & Mlambo, V. H. (2019). Corruption and its implications for development and good governance: A perspective from post-colonial Africa. *Journal of Economics and Behavioral Studies*, *11*(1 (J)), 39–47. doi:10.22610/jebs.v11i1(J).2746

Mlambo, D. N., & Thusi, X. (2023). South Africa's Persistent Social Ills Post-1994 and the Deterioration of the African National Congress: Is the Country Heading towards a Failing State? *Politeia, 42*(1).

Mokgosi, K., Shai, K., & Ogunnubi, O. (2017). Local government coalition in Gauteng province of South Africa: Challenges and opportunities. *Ubuntu: Journal of Conflict and Social Transformation*, *6*(1), 37–57. doi:10.31920/2050-4950/2017/v6n1a2

Mongale, C. (2022). *Social Discontent or Criminality? Navigating the Nexus Between Urban Riots and Criminal Activates in Gauteng and KwaZulu-Natal Provinces, South Africa (2021).* https://www.frontiersin.org/articles/10.3389/frsc.2022.865255/full

Monkam, N. F. (2014). Local municipality productive efficiency and its determinants in South Africa. *Development Southern Africa*, *31*(2), 275–298. doi:10.1080/0376835X.2013.875888

Mpangalasane, C. (2020). *The impact of coalition government on service delivery: City of Tshwane metropolitan* (Doctoral dissertation, North-West University, South Africa).

Municipal, I. Q. (2023). *Protest numbers for 2022 bounce back to pre-COVID numbers.* https://www.municipaliq.co.za/index.php?site_page=press.php

Munzhedzi, P. H. (2015). South African local economic development: issues, challenges and opportunities. *The Xenophobic Attacks in South Africa: Reflections and Possible Strategies to Ward Them Off*, 169.

Ndletyana, M. (2021). Local government coalitions across South Africa, 2000–16. *Marriages of inconvenience: The politics of coalitions in South Africa*, 39.

Ndou, L. L. (2022). *An analysis of a coalition government: a new path in administration and governance at local government level in South Africa* (Doctoral dissertation, North-West University, South Africa).

Ngubane, S. (2018). *Africa Dialogue: Complexities of Coalition Politics in Southern Africa.* https://eratrain.uct.ac.za/converis/portal/detail/Publication/54211339?auxfun=&lang=en_GB

Oppermann, K., & Brummer, K. (2014). Patterns of junior partner influence on the foreign policy of coalition governments. *British Journal of Politics and International Relations*, *16*(4), 555–571. doi:10.1111/1467-856X.12025

Overall, J. (2015). A conceptual framework of innovation and performance: The importance of leadership, relationship quality, and knowledge management. *Academy of Entrepreneurship Journal*, *21*(2), 41.

Pahad, A. (2014). *Insurgent Diplomat-Civil Talks or Civil War?* Penguin Random House South Africa.

Patton, M. Q. (2005). *Qualitative research.* Encyclopedia of statistics in behavioral science.

Raleigh, C. & Wigmore-Shepherd, D. (2020). Elite Coalitions and Power Balance across African Regimes: Introducing the African Cabinet and Political Elite Data Project (ACPED). *Ethnopolitics.* Advance online publication. doi:10.1080/17449057.2020.1771840

Raligilia, K. H. (2017). *The impact of the CODESA talks on the socio-economic rights of the majority of South Africans* (Doctoral thesis, University of Pretoria).

Reddy, P. S. (2016). The politics of service delivery in South Africa: The local government sphere in context. *TD: The Journal for Transdisciplinary Research in Southern Africa*, *12*(1), 1–8. doi:10.4102/td.v12i1.337

South Africa. (1996). *The Constitution of the Republic of South Africa as adopted by the Constitutional Assembly on 8 May 1996 and as amended on 11 October 1996.* Government Printers.

Sparks, A. (1996). *Tomorrow is another country: The inside story of South Africa's road to change.* University of Chicago Press.

Spoon, J. J., & Klüver, H. (2017). Does anybody notice? How policy positions of coalition parties are perceived by voters. *European Journal of Political Research*, *56*(1), 115–132. doi:10.1111/1475-6765.12169

Steinberg, J. (2014). Policing, state power, and the transition from apartheid to democracy: A new perspective. *African Affairs*, *113*(451), 173–191. doi:10.1093/afraf/adu004

Thomas, G. W. (2012). Governance, good governance, and global governance: conceptual and actual challenges. In *Thinking about global governance* (pp. 168–189). Routledge.

Thwala, P. (2022). Do Coalitions Have a Future in South Africa? Presentation to the *Mpumalanga Legislature Management Colloquium.*

Von Holdt, K. (2013). South Africa: The transition to violent democracy. *Review of African Political Economy*, *40*(138), 589–604. doi:10.1080/03056244.2013.854040

Waldmeir, P. (1997). *Anatomy of a miracle: The end of apartheid and the birth of the new South Africa.* WW Norton & Company.

Welsh, D. (1992). Hamlet without the Prince: The Codesa impasse. *Indicator South Africa*, *9*(4), 15–22.

Wilson, W. (2003). The study of public administration. *Communication Researchers and Policy-Making, 61*.

KEY TERMS AND DEFINITIONS

African National Congress (ANC): The ANC is a political organization in South Africa. It emerged as a movement for freedom and equality, actively opposing apartheid. It has been in power since 1994, following the historic post-apartheid election that saw Nelson Mandela elected as the President of South Africa (Lodge, 1987).

Coalition: A coalition is characterized as a collective of organizational actors who (1) mutually commit to achieving a shared objective, (2) collaborate in utilizing their resources to attain this objective, and (3) adopt a unified approach in its pursuit (DeGennaro and Mizrahi, 2005). Different coalitions can be formed when multiple political parties agree to collaborate and establish a ruling coalition government. These coalitions encompass a bare majority coalition government, a grand coalition, a government of national unity at the national level, and a minority government (Beukes and De Visser, 2021:7).

Democracy: Democracy is a system of governance that relies on the decisions made by the populace. In contemporary democracies, individuals are elected or appointed to represent the people and entrust legislative bodies, executives, commissions, judges, and juries. These delegations serve as the fundamental pillars of democracy (Lupia and McCubbins, 1998).

Good Governance: According to Keping (2018), good governance often refers to the process by which decisions are made within an organization. This includes ensuring transparency and accountability in the decision-making process, as well as making decisions that are in the best interest of the organization as a whole.

Government of National Unity: A national unity government, also known as a government of national unity (GNU) or national union government, is a comprehensive coalition government comprising all political parties, or at least the major ones, in the legislative body. At its most fundamental level, a GNU refers to a coalition government that is specifically crafted to incorporate all political participants within the governmental framework (Chinyere and Rukema, 2020).

Service Delivery: The term "service delivery" is frequently employed in South Africa to provide essential resources that citizens rely on, such as water, electricity, sanitation infrastructure, land, and housing. (Mlambo, 2019).

Compilation of References

Abdulhalim, N. (2022). *Investment Opportunities in Post-Conflict Countries How Can Post-Conflict Countries Attract Foreign Direct Investment: The Case of Syria* (Doctoral dissertation, Marmara Universitesi, Turkey).

Abelson, D. E. (2018). *Do think tanks matter? Assessing the impact of public policy institutes.* McGill-Queen's Press-MQUP. doi:10.1515/9780773553859

Adejumobi, S. (2000). Elections in Africa: A fading show of democracy? *International Political Science Review, 21*(1), 59-73.

Aiyede, E. R. (2023). Governance and Politics of Public Policy in Africa. In E. R. Aiyede & B. Muganda (Eds.), *Public Policy and Research in Africa* (pp. 87–121). Springer International Publishing. doi:10.1007/978-3-030-99724-3_5

Akgül-Açıkmeşe, S., Kausch, K., Özel, S., & Lecha, E. S. (2023). *Stalled by Division: EU Internal Contestation over the Israeli-Palestinian Conflict.* Academic Press.

Albala, A., Borges, A., & Couto, L. (2023). Pre-electoral coalitions and cabinet stability in presidential systems. *British Journal of Politics and International Relations, 25*(1), 64–82. doi:10.1177/13691481211056852

Alford, J., Hartley, J., Yates, S., & Hughes, O. (2017). Into the purple zone: Deconstructing the politics/administration distinction. *American Review of Public Administration, 47*(7), 752–763. doi:10.1177/0275074016638481

Aluko, O. (2023). Political Unrest and Tyre Burning Theory in Developed Democracies and Developing Democracies. In Insights and Explorations in Democracy, Political Unrest, and Propaganda in Elections (pp. 38-46). IGI Global. doi:10.4018/978-1-6684-8629-0.ch004

Amiar, J. (2023). *Israeli-Palestinian relations are deeply affected.* Mitvim. Retrieved December 27, 2023, from https://mitvim.org.il/en/publication/israeli-palestinian-relations-are-deeply-affected/

Ammar, S. (2022). *National Reconciliation in Libya: Challenges and Perspectives.* Academic Press.

Amtaika, A. (2017). The Particularistic and Universality of political Cultural Beliefs and Values: Western Liberalism, Islamic Fundamentalism and African Theoretical Perspectives. In A. Amtaika (Ed.), *Culture, Democracy and Development in Africa.* Pan-African University Press.

Amutabi, N. M. (2013). *Regime Change and Succession Politics in Africa: Five Decades of Misrule.* Routledge Taylor & Francis. doi:10.4324/9780203080191

AnastacioA.MorandarteN. (2023). Political patronage in philippine local politics. *Available at* SSRN 4362736.

ANC Statement. (2021). *Statement of the ANC on Local Government Elections 2021 preliminary results. 3 Nov 2021 – ANC.* Retrieved January 20, 2024, from https://www.anc1912.org.za/statement-of-the-anc-on-local-government-elections-2021-preliminary-results-3-nov-2021/

Anderson, R. (2007). Thematic content analysis (TCA). *Descriptive Presentation of Qualitative Data, 3,* 1-4.

Andrushko, V.I. (2021). Політична влада: аналіз інноваційних підходів. *Вісник НЮУ імені Ярослава Мудрого. Серія: Філософія, філософія права, політологія, соціологія, 49*(2), 153-168.

Anglin, D. G. (1995). International monitoring of the transition to democracy in South Africa, 1992-1994. *African Affairs, 94*(377), 519–543. doi:10.1093/oxfordjournals.afraf.a098872

Aref, S., & Neal, Z. (2020). Detecting coalitions by optimally partitioning signed networks of political collaboration. *Scientific Reports, 10*(1), 1506. doi:10.1038/s41598-020-58471-z PMID:32001776

Arjakas. (2019). *On the Reciprocal Relation between Israeli foreign and Domestic policy in regard to the Israeli-Palestinian Conflict, 2009-2019.* Academic Press.

Arnold, G. (2017). *Africa A Modern History: 1945-2015.* Atlantic Books.

Arnold, G. (2017). *Africa: A Modern History: 1945-2015.* Atlantic Books.

Arnolds, M. (2023). *Department of Cooperative Governance and Traditional Affairs.* Retrieved from https://www.cogta.gov.za/cgta_2016/wp-content/uploads/2023/08/AIC-Coalition-Framework-scheme.pdf

Aronczyk, M. (2013). *Branding the nation: The global business of national identity.* Oxford University Press. doi:10.1093/acprof:oso/9780199752164.001.0001

Arriola, L. R. (2013). *Multi-ethnic coalitions in Africa: Business financing of opposition election campaigns.* Cambridge University Press.

Arriola, L. R. (2013). *Multiethnic Coalitions in Africa: Business Financing of Opposition Election Campaigns.* Cambridge University Press.

Arriola, L. R., Devaro, J., & Meng, A. (2021). Democratic subversion: Elite cooptation and opposition fragmentation. *The American Political Science Review, 115*(4), 1358–1372. doi:10.1017/S0003055421000629

Arriola, L. R., & Johnson, M. C. (2014). Ethnic politics and women's empowerment in Africa: Ministerial appointments to executive cabinets. *American Journal of Political Science, 58*(2), 495–510. doi:10.1111/ajps.12075

Asante, M. K. (2003). *Afrocentricity: The Theory of Social Change.* African American Images.

Ash, P. (2021). *OBITUARY: Geoff Makhubo — a respected, tainted veteran politician.* Retrieved December 3, 2023, from https://www.timeslive.co.za/politics/2021-07-09-obituary-geoff-makhubo-a-respected-tainted-veteran-politician/

Ashiagbor, S., & Tora, B. (2015). *Coalitions: a guide for political parties.* The National Democratic Institute and the Oslo Center for Peace and Human Rights.

Ashman, S. (2015). The social crisis of labour and the crisis of labour politics in South Africa. *Revue Tiers Monde, 224*(4), 47–66. doi:10.3917/rtm.224.0047

Averbukh, L., & Lintl, P. (2022). *Israel: Half a year under the Bennett government* (No. 4/2022). SWP Comment.

Axelrod, R. M. (1969). *Conflict of Interest: A Theory of Divergent Goals with Applications to Politics.* Yale University.

Babbbies, E. (2004). The practice of Social Research. Wadsworth, Thomson Learning Inc.

Babbie, E., & Mouton, J. (2002). *The practice of social research* (South African Ed.). Oxford University Press.

Baraka, A. (2021). Intractable Conflicts: How Israeli occupation and manifestation of Apartheid policy contribute to social and economic impacts on Palestinians. *Turan-sam*, *13*(51), 147–157.

Barber, B. R. (2013). *If Mayors Ruled the World: Dysfunctional Nations, Rising Cities*. Yale University Press.

Barton, B. (2022). *The Doraleh Disputes: Infrastructure Politics in the Global South*. Springer Nature.

Basson, A & Hunter, Q. (2023). *Who will rule South Africa? The demise of the ANC and the rise of a new democracy*. Flyleaf Publishing & Distribution.

Basson, A & Hunter, Q. (2023). *Who will rule South Africa? The demise of the ANC and the rise of a new Democracy*. Flyleaf Publishing & Distribution.

Basson, A., & Hunter, Q. (2023). *Who will Rule South Africa? The Demise of the ANC and the Rise of a New Democracy*. Flyleaf Publishing & Distribution.

Basu, P., & Janiec, M. (2021). Kenya's regional ambitions or China's Belt-and-Road? News media representations of the Mombasa-Nairobi Standard Gauge Railway. *Singapore Journal of Tropical Geography*, *42*(1), 45–64. doi:10.1111/sjtg.12350

Bawn, K., Cohen, M., Karol, D., Masket, S., Noel, H., & Zaller, J. (2012). A theory of political parties: Groups, policy demands and nominations in American politics. *Perspectives on Politics*, *10*(3), 571–597. doi:10.1017/S1537592712001624

BBC, (2020). *Israel's Netanyahu and Gantz sign unity government deal*. BBC.

BBC. (2021). *Netanyahu out as new Israeli government approved*. BBC.

Beck, M. (2019). *Israel: A Democratic State?* https://www.e-ir.info/2019/08/25/israel-a-democratic-state/

Beck, U., & Grande, E. (2010). Varieties of second modernity: The cosmopolitan turn in social and political theory and research. *The British Journal of Sociology*, *61*(3), 409–443. doi:10.1111/j.1468-4446.2010.01320.x PMID:20857607

Benit-Gbaffou, C., Dubresson, A., Fourchard, L., Ginisty, K., Jaglin, S., Olukoju, A., Owuor, S., & Vivet, J. (2013). Exploring the Role of Party Politics in the Governance of African Cities. In S. Bekker & L. Fourchard (Eds.), *Governing Cities in Africa* (pp. 17–42). HSRC Press.

Bergman, M., Angelova, M., Bäck, H., & Müller, W. C. (2024). Coalition agreements and governments' policy-making productivity. *West European Politics*, *47*(1), 31–60. doi:10.1080/01402382.2022.2161794

Besseling, R. (2016). *The slow demise of the ANC: Political change, economic decline, and state corruption in South Africa. Africa Policy Brief*. Egmont Institute.

Beukes, J. (2021). Coalition governments: guidelines for coalition agreements. *Local Government Bulletin*, *16*(1). https://dullahomarinstitute.org.za/multilevel-govt/local-government

Beukes, J. (2021). *Dullah Omar Institute*. https://dullahomarinstitute.org.za/multilevel-govt/local-government-bulletin/archives/volume-16-issue-1-march-2021/coalition-governments-guidelines-for-coalition-agreements

Beukes, J., & De Visser, J. (2021). *A framework for coalitions in local government*. Academic Press.

Beukes, J., & de Visser, J. (2021). *A framework for coalitions in local government*. Dullah Omar Institute. https://www.cogta.gov.za/cgta_2016/wp-content/uploads/2021/11/A-Framework-for-Coalitions-in-Local-Government_Dullah_Omar_.pdf

Beukes, J., & De Visser, J. (2021). *A framework for coalitions in local government*. https://www.cogta.gov.za/cgta_2016/wp-content/uploads/2021/11/A-Framework-for-Coalitions-in-Local-Government_Dullah_Omar_.pdf

Beukes, J., & de Visser, J. (2021). *A framework for coalitions in local government. Prepared for the South African Local Government Association*. Dullah Omar Institute, University of the Western Cape.

Bhargava, R. (2021). Power sharing and democracy. In A. K. Mehra & A. Kumar (Eds.), *Political Science: Theory and Practice* (pp. 235–254). SAGE Publications.

Bharti, M. S. (2022d). The Economic Integration of the Central and Eastern European Countries into the European Union: Special Reference to Regional Development. *Copernicus Political and Legal Studies, 1*(2), 11–23. https://doi.org/doi.org/10.15804/CPLS.20222.01

Bharti, M. S. (2022a). Democratisation and Institutional Development in Romania after 1989. *Journal of Scientific Papers. Social Development and Security, 12*(1), 104–117. doi:10.33445/sds.2022.12.1.11

Bharti, M. S. (2022b). Political Institution Building in Post-Communist Romania. *Central European Political Studies, 1*(1), 73–97. doi:10.14746/ssp.2022.1.4

Bharti, M. S. (2022b). The Indo-US Strategic Cooperation and How China's Influence Challenges to India-US Alliance in the Indo-Pacific. *Tamkang Journal of International Affairs, 26*(1), 71–127. doi:10.6185/TJIA.V.202209_26(1).0002

Bharti, M. S. (2022c). The Development of China's Economic Cooperation in the Horn of Africa: Special Reference to the Belt and Road Initiative. *African Journal of Economics. Politics and Social Studies, 1*(1), 17–30. doi:10.15804/ajepss.2022.1.12

Bharti, M. S. (2023). The Sustainable Development and Economic Impact of China's Belt and Road Initiative in Ethiopia. *East Asia (Piscataway, N.J.), 40*(2), 175–194. doi:10.1007/s12140-023-09402-y PMID:37065271

Bharti, M. S. (2023a). Global Development and International Order Transition: The Role of China. In M. O. Dinçsoy & H. Can (Eds.), *Optimizing Energy Efficiency During a Global Energy Crisis* (pp. 200–212). IGI Global. doi:10.4018/979-8-3693-0400-6.ch013

Bharti, M. S. (2023b). The Geo-Economics Approach to the European Union Strategic Partnership in the Indo-Pacific Region. In R. A. Castanho (Ed.), *Handbook of Research on Current Advances and Challenges of Borderlands, Migration, and Geopolitics* (pp. 297–311). IGI Global. doi:10.4018/978-1-6684-7020-6.ch015

Bharti, M. S. (2023c). The Strategic Partnership Between India and the United States of America and How China's Influence Challenges the India-Us Alliance in the Indo-Pacific Region. *Regional Formation and Development Studies, 39*(1), 16–26. doi:10.15181/rfds.v36i1.2507

Bigambo, J. (2017). *The Concept of Selective Communication: Shaping the Needs of Conflict and Human Resource Management in Kenya: A Case Study of Action Aid Kenya – Western Region*. Unpublished Human Resource Management report.

Bishara, M. (2023). Fanatics vs generals: The strange Israeli rift over Gaza. *Al Jazeera*. https://www.aljazeera.com/opinions/2023/10/27/fanatics-vs-generals-the-strange-israeli-rift-over-gaza

Biswas, J. (2019). Coalition Government and its Challenges of 21st Century in India. *Ensemble, A Peer Revied Academic Journal, 1*(1), 36-40.

Biti, T. (2018). Rebuilding Zimbabwe: Lessons from a coalition government. Washington DC: Centre for Global Development.

Blais, A., & Massicotte, L. (2002). Electoral systems. In L. LeDuc, R. G. Niemi, & P. Norris (Eds.), *Comparing democracies* (2nd ed., pp. 40–69). Sage.

Blas, J., & Farchy, J. (2021). *The world for sale: money, power, and the traders who barter the earth's resources*. Oxford University Press.

Blondel J., & Muller, R. (Eds.). (2001). *Cabinets in Eastern Europe*. Palgrave.

Bochel, H., & Powell, M. (2016). *Coalition Government and Social Policy*. Policy Press.

Boddy-Evans, A. (2019). *The Freedom Charter in South Africa*. Retrieved March 1, 2019, https://www.thoughtco.com/text-of-the-freedom-charter-43417

Bogdanor, V. (2007). The Historic Legacy of Tony Blair. *Current History (New York, N.Y.)*, *106*(698), 99–105. doi:10.1525/curh.2007.106.698.99

Booysen, S. (2014). *Causes And Impact Of Party Alliances And Coalitions On The Party System And National Cohesion In South Africa*. Electoral Institute For Sustainable Democracy In Africa. Retrieved from https://www.eisa.org/wp-content/uploads/2023/05/2014-journal-of-african-elections-v13n1-causes-impact-party-alliances-coalitions-party-system-national-cohesion-south-africa-eisa.pdf

Booysen, S. (2014). Causes and Impact of party coalitions on the party systems and national Cohesion in South Africa. *Journal of African Elections, 13*(1), 66-92.

Booysen, S. (2015). Election 2014 and the ANC's duet of dominance and decline. *Journal of African Elections, 14*(1), 7-34.

Booysen, S. (2021). The uneven transition from party dominance to coalitions: South Africa's new politics of instability. In Marriages of Inconvenience: The Politics of Coalitions in South Africa (pp. 13-37). Johannesburg: Mapungubwe Institute for Strategic Reflection (MISTRA).

Booysen, S. (2014). Causes and impact of party alliances and coalitions on the party system and national cohesion in South Africa. *Journal of African Elections*, *13*(1), 66–92. doi:10.20940/JAE/2014/v13i1a4

Booysen, S. (2018). Coalitions and alliances demarcate crossroads in ANC trajectories. *New Agenda: South African Journal of Social and Economic Policy*, *68*, 6–10.

Booysen, S. (2018). Coalitions and alliances demarcate crossroads in ANC trajectories. *The New Agenda*, (68), 6–1.

Booysen, S. (2021). *Marriages of Inconvenience: The Politics of Coalition South Africa. Mapungubwe Institute for Strategic Reflection*. MISTRA. doi:10.2307/j.ctv2z6qdx6

Borzutzky, S. (2019). You win some, you lose some: Pension reform in Bachelet's first and second administrations. *Journal of Politics in Latin America*, *11*(2), 204–230. doi:10.1177/1866802X19861491

Bosire, C. M. (2011). Local Government and Human Rights: Building Institutional Links for the Effective Protection and Realisation of Human Rights in Africa. *African Human Rights Law Journal*, *11*(1), 147–170.

Bouton, L. (2013). A Theory of Strategic Voting in Runoff Elections. *The American Economic Review*, *103*(4), 1248–1288. doi:10.1257/aer.103.4.1248

Bowler, S., Freebourn, J., Klüver, H., & Spoon, J. J. (2020). Teten, P., Donovan, T. and Vowles, J., (2023). Preferences for single-party versus multi-party governments. *Party Politics*, *29*(4), 755–765. doi:10.1177/13540688221081783

Bradshaw, G. & Breakfast, N. (2019). Mediating Coalition Politics at the Local Government Level in South Africa. *Journal for Gender, Information and development in Africa,* 123-129.

Bradshaw, G., & Breakfast, N. (2019). Mediating Coalition Politics at the Local Government Level in South Africa, 2016-2019. JGIDA, 123-139.

Bradshaw, G., & Breakfast, N. (2019). Mediating coalition politics at the local government level in South Africa, 2016-2019. *Journal of Gender. Information and Development in Africa*, *8*(2), 113–129.

Bradshaw, G., & Ntsikeleo, B. (2019). Mediating Coalition Politics at the Local Government Level in South Africa, 2016-2019. *Journal of Information. Gender and Development in Africa*, (Special Issue), 123–139.

Bratton, M. & Kimenyi, M.S. (2006). *Voting in Kenya: Putting ethnicity in perspective.* Academic Press.

Brautigam, D. (2011). *The dragon's gift: the real story of China in Africa.* Oxford University Press.

Brazys, S., & Dukalskis, A. (2019). Rising powers and grassroots image management: Confucius Institutes and China in the media. *The Chinese Journal of International Politics*, *12*(4), 557–584. doi:10.1093/cjip/poz012

Breakfast, N. B. (2020). The Nexus between Conflict Management and Coalition Politics in Three Selected Metropolitan Municipalities in South Africa. *African Journal of Peace and Conflict Studies*, *9*(3), 65–80. doi:10.31920/2634-3665/2020/v9n3a4

Brewer, M. B. (1999). The Psychology of Prejudice: Ingroup Love and Outgroup Hate? *The Journal of Social Issues*, *55*(3), 429–444. doi:10.1111/0022-4537.00126

Breytenbach, W. (2019). The Presidency, Service Delivery and Protest in Post-Apartheid South Africa. *Journal of Southern African Studies*, *45*(4), 789–807.

Britx, A., & Tshuma, J. (2013). Heroes fall, oppressors rise: Democratic decay and authoritarianism in Zimbabwe. In N. De Jager & P. Du Toit (Eds.), *Friends or Foe? Dominant Party Systems in Southern Africa.* United Nations University Press.

Brooks, H. (2014). The dominant Party: Challenges for South Africa's Second decade of democracy. *Journal of African Elections*, *13*(2), 233–242.

Brown, N. J., & Hamzawy, A. (2023). *Arab Peace Initiative II: How Arab Leadership Could Design a Peace Plan in Israel and Palestine.* Academic Press.

Brown, J., & Johnson, L. (2019). Understanding Power Sharing: Definitions, Concepts, and Frameworks. *Journal of Political Power*, *12*(1), 107–125.

Brown, J., & Williams, L. (2019). Historical Roots of Coalition Politics in Africa: Colonial Legacies and Post-independence Dynamics. *Journal of African History*, *62*(3), 345–367.

Budge, I. (1993). 'Issues, Dimensions, and Agenda Change in Postwar Democracies: Long-Term Trends in Party Election Programs and Newspaper Reports in Twenty-Three Democracies. In W. H. Riker (Ed.), *Agenda Formation* (pp. 41–80). University of Michigan Press.

Budge, I., & Farlie, D. (1983). *Explaining and predicting elections: issue effects and party strategies in twenty-three democracies.* Allen & Unwin.

Buhlungu, S. (2003). The state of trade unionism in post-apartheid South Africa. *State of the nation: South Africa,* 184-203.

Bunte, J. B. (2019). *Raise the debt: How developing countries choose their creditors.* Oxford University Press. doi:10.1093/oso/9780190866167.001.0001

Burgess, R., Jedwab, R., Miguel, E., Morjaria, A., & Padró-i-Miquel, G. (2015). The Value of Democracy: Evidence from Road Building in Kenya. *The American Economic Review*, *105*(6), 1817–1851. doi:10.1257/aer.20131031

BusinessTech. (2019). *ANC vs DA vs EFF: Promises on land reform, jobs and fighting corruption.* https://businesstech.co.za/news/government/302086/anc-vs-da-vs-eff-promises-on-land-reform-jobs-and-fighting-corruption/

Butler, A. (2017). *Contemporary South Africa*. Bloomsbury Publishing. doi:10.1057/978-1-137-37338-0

Cachalia, F. (1992). A Report on the Convention for a Democratic South Africa. *S. Afr. J. on Hum. Rts.*, *8*, 249.

Caillaud, B., & Tirole, J. (2002). Parties as political intermediaries. *The Quarterly Journal of Economics*, *117*(4), 1453–1489. doi:10.1162/003355302320935070

Callard, R. (2016). *Make or Break: How the next three years will shape South Africa's next three decades*. Zebra Press.

Calthorpe, P. (2015). Urbanism in the age of climate change. In *The city reader* (pp. 555–568). Routledge.

Cameron, A., & Taflaga, M. (2017). Coalition government: The Australian experience. In A. Cameron & M. Taflaga (Eds.), *Coalition governance in post-conflict countries* (pp. 177–192). Springer.

Campbell, K. L. (2020). Democracy in Western Europe. Democracy in Crisis around the World.

Carbone, M. (2014). The European Union and China's rise in Africa: Competing visions, external coherence and trilateral cooperation. In *China's Rise in Africa* (pp. 75–93). Routledge.

Carmody, P. R., & Murphy, J. T. (2022). Chinese neoglobalization in East Africa: Logics, couplings and impacts. *Space and Polity*, *26*(1), 20–43. doi:10.1080/13562576.2022.2104631

Cassimjee, M. (2023, December 1). South Africa weighs a new election outcome: coalitions. Chatham House. Retrieved from https://www.chathamhouse.org/publications/the-world-today/2023-12/south-africa-weighs-new-election-outcome-coalitions

Catholic Commission for Justice and Peace (CCJP) and Legal Resources Foundation. (1997). Breaking the silence, building true peace: a report on the disturbances in Matabeleland and the Midlands 1980 – 1988. Author.

Cedras, J. P. (2021). The ANC-led Alliance in Government: A Question of Legitimacy and Trust. *African Journal of Public Affairs*, *12*(1), 63–82.

Cengiz, E. (2020). A thematic content analysis of the qualitative studies on faith project in Turkey. *Journal of Theoretical Educational Science*, *13*(1), 251–276. doi:10.30831/akukeg.565421

Chakawa, J. (2021). From Connemara to Gukurahundi genocide of the 1980s in Zimbabwe. *Journal of Literary Studies*, *37*(2), 27–39. doi:10.1080/02564718.2021.1923691

Chambers, D. (2022). Wanted: some adults to make a coalition work. *Sunday Times*. https://www.timeslive.co.za/sunday-times/opinion-and-analysis/opinion/2022-09-18-wanted-some-adultsto-make-a-coalition-work

Charles, M. (2022). *DA takes over two key positions in Western Cape municipality*. Academic Press.

Chavula, H. K. (2022). Malawi's Third Republic: Towards a Democratic Developmental State? *Journal of Asian and African Studies*, *57*(4), 773–793. doi:10.1177/00219096211037040

Cheeseman, N., & Larmer, M. (2015). Ethnopopulism in Africa: Opposition mobilization in diverse and unequal societies. *Democratization*, *22*(1), 22–50. doi:10.1080/13510347.2013.809065

Cheibub, J. A. (2007). *Presidentialism, parliamentarism, and democracy*. Cambridge University Press.

Chessa, M., & Fragnelli, V. (2022). The Italian referendum: What can we get from game theory? *Annals of Operations Research*, *318*(2), 849–869. doi:10.1007/s10479-022-04927-6

Chigora, P., & Guzura, T. (2011). The politics of the government of national unity (GNU) and Power Sharing in Zimbabwe: Challenges and prospects for democracy. *African Journal of History and Culture*, *3*(2), 20–26.

Chilemba, S., (2023). Our Malawi. *RSA Journal, 169*(2), 17-19.

Chinyere, P. C., & Rukema, J. R. (2020). The Government of National Unity as a Long-Lasting Political and Economic Solution in Zimbabwe. *The Mankind Quarterly, 61*(2), 163–189. doi:10.46469/mq.2020.61.2.2

Chipaike, R., & Bischoff, P. H. (2019). Chinese engagement of Zimbabwe and the limits of elite agency. *Journal of Asian and African Studies, 54*(7), 947–964. doi:10.1177/0021909619848783

Chiripanhura, S. (2020). Political dialogues in Zimbabwe: A vehicle for building democracy or a tool for political survival? *Journal of African Elections, 19*(1), 1–21.

Chiyemura, F., Gambino, E., & Zajontz, T. (2023). Infrastructure and the politics of African state agency: Shaping the Belt and Road Initiative in East Africa. *Chinese Political Science Review, 8*(1), 105–131. doi:10.1007/s41111-022-00214-8

Chotiner, I. (2023). *How Israel's Democratic Crisis Affects Palestinians.* Retrieved December 27, 2023, from https://www.newyorker.com/news/q-and-a/how-israels-democratic-crisis-affects-palestinian

Chutel, J. E. (2023). *Johannesburg, Where Mayors Last Just Months, or Even Only Weeks.* Retrieved November 12, 2023, from https://www.nytimes.com/2023/05/17/world/africa/south-africa-johannesburg-mayor.html

City of Johannesburg. (2022). *2021/22 Customer Satisfaction Survey.* City of Johannesburg.

City of Johannesburg. (2023). *Overview of Johanneburg.* City of Johannesburg.

Clark, J. G. (n.d.). *The Legal Framework: The Context for an Electoral Management Body (EMB)'s Role and Powers.* Academic Press.

Clark, N. L., & Worger, W. H. (2011). South Africa: The Rise and Fall of Apartheid. Longman.

Clayton, A., O'Brien, D. Z., & Piscopo, J. M. (2019). All male panels? Representation and democratic legitimacy. *American Journal of Political Science, 63*(1), 113–129. doi:10.1111/ajps.12391

Clayton, G., Dorussen, H., & Böhmelt, T. (2021). United Nations peace initiatives 1946-2015: Introducing a new dataset. *International Interactions, 47*(1), 161–180. doi:10.1080/03050629.2020.1772254

Collins, P. H., & Bilge, S. (2020). *Intersectionality.* John Wiley & Sons.

Collins, R. O., & Burns, J. M. (2014). *A History of Sub-Saharan Africa* (2nd ed.). Cambridge University Press.

Connect Radio News. (2021). *ANC in North West signs coalition agreement with opposition parties, independent candidate.* https://connectradio.co.za/radio/news/anc-in-north-west-signs-coalition-agreements-with-opposition-parties/

Connors, M. K. (1996). The eclipse of consociationalism in South Africa's Democratic Transition. *Democratization, 3*(4), 420–434. doi:10.1080/13510349608403488

Conrad, H. (2013). *Handbook of Public Leadership Theories.* Rand - McNally.

Constitution of the Republic of South Africa. (1996). Government Printers.

Conti, N., & Marangoni, F. (Eds.). (2014). *The challenge of coalition government: the Italian case.* Routledge. doi:10.4324/9781315746937

Conti, N., Pedrazzani, A., & Russo, F. (2022). Policy polarisation in Italy: the short and conflictual life of the 'Government of Change' (2018–2019). In *The Politics of Polarisation* (pp. 64–97). Routledge. doi:10.4324/9781003317012-5

Cooperative Governance Traditional Affairs. (2021). *A Framework for Coalitions in Local Government – Cooperative Governance and Traditional Affairs*. https://www.cogta.gov.za/index.php/2021/11/22/a-framework-for-coalitions-in-local-government/

Cornago, N. (1999). Diplomacy and paradiplomacy in the redefinition of international security: Dimensions of conflict and co-operation. *Regional & Federal Studies*, *9*(1), 40–57. doi:10.1080/13597569908421070

Cortês, E. R. D. O. (2018). *Velhos amigos, novos adversários: as disputas, alianças e reconfigurações empresariais na elite política Moçambicana*. PhD Thesis.

Costantini, I., & O'Driscoll, D. (2023). Twenty years of externally promoted security assistance in Iraq: Changing approaches and their limits. *International Peacekeeping*, *30*(5), 562–584. doi:10.1080/13533312.2022.2149501

Cox, G., & Kernell, S. (2019). *The politics of divided government*. Routledge. doi:10.4324/9780429313844

Creswell, J. W., & Miller, D. L. (2000). Determining Validity in Qualitative Inquiry. *Theory into Practice*, *39*(3), 124–130. doi:10.1207/s15430421tip3903_2

Curtice, J. (2013). Politicians, voters and democracy: The 2011 UK referendum on the Alternative Vote. *Electoral Studies*, *32*(2), 215–223. doi:10.1016/j.electstud.2012.10.010

Da Silva, D. C. (2022). *Electoral Integrity in Mozambique–Institutions, Structures and International Players*. Master thesis.

Daddow, O. (2015). Constructing a 'great'role for Britain in an age of austerity: Interpreting coalition foreign policy, 2010–2015. *International Relations*, *29*(3), 303–318. doi:10.1177/0047117815600931

Dalmases, J. M. (2021). *Guide to forming a coalition government*. Edicions Universitat Barcelona.

Damiani, G. (2022). *Looking for a" genuine science of politics": William H. Riker and the game theoretical turn in political science*. Center for the History of Political Economy at Duke University.

Daphi, P., Anderl, F., & Deitelhoff, N. (2022). Bridges or divides? Conflicts and synergies of coalition building across countries and sectors in the Global Justice Movement. *Social Movement Studies*, *21*(1-2), 8–24. doi:10.1080/1474283 7.2019.1676223

Dassah, M. O. (2012). A critical analysis of factors underlying service delivery protests in South Africa. *Journal of African and Asian Local Government Studies*, *1*(2), 1–28.

Davis, R. (2023). Eight reasons why SA metro coalitions are imploding. *Daily Maverick*. https://www.dailymaverick.co.za/article/2023-01-30-eight-reasons-why-sa-metro-coalitions-are-imploding/

Davis, M. (1977). Inheritance, Magoc and Political Power on South East Papua. *Journal of Pacific Studies*, *3*, 69–88.

de Jager, N., & Sebudubudu, D. (2017). Towards understanding Botswana and South Africa's ambivalence to liberal democracy. *Journal of Contemporary African Studies*, *35*(1), 15–33. doi:10.1080/02589001.2016.1246682

De Mente, B. L. (2011). *Chinese mind: Understanding traditional Chinese beliefs and their influence on contemporary culture*. Tuttle Publishing.

De Vos, P. (2021). The constitutional-legal dimensions of coalition politics and government in South Africa. In S. Booysen (Ed.), *Marriages of Inconvenience The politics of coalitions in South Africa (2021)*. doi:10.2307/j.ctv2z6qdx6.16

Dean, H., & Melrose, M. (1999). *Poverty, Riches and Social Citizenship*. Routledge. doi:10.1057/9780230377950

Dearlove, J., & Saunders, P. (1991). *Introduction to British Politics* (2nd ed.). Polity Press.

Dearlove, J., & Saunders, P. R. (2000). *Introduction to British politics*. No Title.

Debus, M., & Gross, M. (2016). Coalition formation at the local level: Institutional constraints, party policy conflict, and office-seeking political parties. *Party Politics*, *22*(6), 835–846. doi:10.1177/1354068815576292

Deleglise, D. (2018). The rise and fall of Lesotho's coalition governments. In Africa Dialogue: Complexities of Coalition Politics in South Africa (pp. 13-45). Durban: The African Centre for the Constructive Resolution of Disputes (ACCORD).

DeLisle, J. (2010). Soft power in a hard place: China, Taiwan, cross-strait relations and US policy. *Orbis*, *54*(4), 493–524. doi:10.1016/j.orbis.2010.07.002

Des Forges, A. (1999). *Leave no one to tell the story: Genocide in Rwanda*. Human Rights Watch.

Diamond, L. (1995). *Developing Democracy: Toward Consolidation*. Johns Hopkins University Press.

Diamond, L. (1999). *Developing democracy: Toward consolidation*. JHU press. doi:10.56021/9780801860140

Diamond, L., & Morlino, L. (2004). The quality of democracy: An overview. *Journal of Democracy*, *15*(4), 20–31. doi:10.1353/jod.2004.0060

Dieckhoff, A. (2016). What Kind of Democracy Is Israel? De Gruyter Oldenbourg. doi:10.1515/9783110351637-050

Dladla, K. F. (2019). *The impact of the legal framework for local government in building and sustaining coalitions in municipal councils*. Master's dissertation. Cape Town: University of Western Cape. https://etd.uwc.ac.za/handle/11394/6401

Dlakavu, A. (2022). South African electoral trends: Prospects for coalition governance at national and provincial spheres in 2024. *Politikon: South African Journal of Political Studies*, *49*(4), 476–490. doi:10.1080/02589346.2022.2151682

Dlamini, S. (2013). From Conflict to Coalition Politics: The Making of a National Unity Government in Zimbabwe. *Journal of African Elections*, *12*(1), 38–59.

Dodd, L. (2015). *Coalitions in parliamentary government* (Vol. 1247). Princeton University Press. doi:10.1515/9781400868070

Dodds, F., Donoghue, A. D., & Roesch, J. L. (2016). *Negotiating the sustainable development goals: a transformational agenda for an insecure world*. Taylor & Francis. doi:10.4324/9781315527093

Doherty, I. (2004). *Coalition Best Practices*. National Democratic Institute West Bank and Gaza.

Donnelly, J. (2015). *Universal Human Rights in Theory & Practice* (2nd ed.). Cornell University Press.

Doorenspleet, R., & Nijzink, L. (2013). One-Party Dominance in African Democracies: A Framework for Analysis. In R. Doorenspleet & L. Nijzink (Eds.), *One-Party Dominance in African Democracies* (pp. 1–25). Lynne Rienner Publishers. doi:10.1515/9781626372658-002

Dorey, P., & Garnett, M. (2016). *The British coalition government, 2010-2015: a marriage of inconvenience*. Springer. doi:10.1057/978-1-137-02377-3

Downs, A. (1957). *An economic theory of democracy*. Harper.

Downs, W. (2008). Coalition. In W. Darity (Ed.), *International Encyclopedia of the social sciences*. Macmillan Reference.

Doyal, L., & Gough, I. (1991). *A Theory of Human Need*. Macmillan. doi:10.1007/978-1-349-21500-3

Drake, P., & Higgins, M. (2012). Lights, camera, election: Celebrity, performance and the 2010 UK general election leadership debates. *British Journal of Politics and International Relations*, *14*(3), 375–391. doi:10.1111/j.1467-856X.2011.00504.x

Dreyer, J. T. (2018). *China's political system: Modernization and tradition*. Routledge. doi:10.4324/9781315144399

du Toit, D. (2002). Public Service Delivery. In D. du Toit, A. Knipe, D. van Niekerk, G. van der Walt, & M. Dolve (Eds.), *Service excellence in governance* (1st ed., pp. 55–119). Heinemann.

Du Toit, P. (2009). Power sharing in Africa: A review of the literature. *Journal of African Elections*, *8*(2), 165.

Dube, F. (2020). Separation of powers and the institutional supremacy of the Constitutional Court over Parliament and the executive. *South African Journal on Human Rights*, *36*(4), 293–318. doi:10.1080/02587203.2021.1925954

Dullah Omar Institute. (2019). *Feminist analysis of ANC, EFF and DA manifestos – in brief*. https://dullahomarinstitute.org.za/women-and-democracy/submissions/feminis-analysis-anc-eff-da-in-brief.pdf

Dunbabin, J. P. D. (1988). Electoral reforms and their outcome in the United Kingdom, 1865–1900. *Later Victorian Britain, 1867–1900*, 93-125.

Dunleavy, P. (2012). *The British general election of 2010 and the advent of coalition government*. Academic Press.

Dworack, S., Lüttmann, C., von Messling, B., & Vimalarajah, L. (2021). Basics of Mediation: Concepts and Definitions. In *Peace Mediation in Germany's Foreign Policy* (pp. 97–110). Nomos Verlagsgesellschaft MbH & Co. KG. doi:10.5771/9783748926160-97

Earsom, J. (2023). It's not as simple as copy/paste: The EU's Remobilisation of the High Ambition Coalition in international climate governance. *International Environmental Agreement: Politics, Law and Economics*, *23*(1), 27–42. doi:10.1007/s10784-023-09592-z

Ehizuelen, M. M. O., & Abdi, H. O. (2018). Sustaining China-Africa relations: Slotting Africa into China's one belt, one road initiative makes economic sense. *Asian Journal of Comparative Politics*, *3*(4), 285–310. doi:10.1177/2057891117727901

Eigeman, J. (2007). *Service delivery a challenge for local governments*. VNG International.

Electoral Commission of South Africa. (2021). *2021 Municipal Elections-Electoral Commission of South Africa*. Retrieved from https://www.elections.org.za/pw/

Etyang, O. (2022). *The Formation and Instability of Coalition Governments in Kenya*. The African. doi:10.1163/1821889X-bja10001

Evans, M. (2014). *Broadcasting the End of Apartheid: Live Television and the Birth of a New South Africa*. I.B. Tauris. doi:10.5040/9780755619061

Evans, M. (2019). Coalitions through a comparative politics lens. *Coalition Government as a Reflection of a Nation's Politics and Society: A Comparative Study of Parliamentary Parties and Cabinets in 12 Countries*.

Fairclough, N. (2001). *Critical Discourse Analysis*. Lancaster University.

Fakir, E. (2023). *Coalition politics and government – a power and predation roller coaster ride, or means of curbing excess?* https://www.dailymaverick.co.za/opinionista/2023-08-03-coalition-politics-and-government-a-power-and-predation-roller-coaster-ride-or-means-of-curbing-excess/

Falco-Gimeno, A. (2014). 'The use of control mechanisms in Coalition governments: The role of preference tangentiality and repeated interactions'. *Party Politics*, *20*(3), 341–356. doi:10.1177/1354068811436052

Falkner, R. (2016). The Paris Agreement and the new logic of international climate politics. *International Affairs*, *92*(5), 1107–1125. doi:10.1111/1468-2346.12708

Fearon, J. D. (2003). Ethnic and cultural diversity by country. *Journal of Economic Growth*, *8*(2), 195–222. doi:10.1023/A:1024419522867

Feltham, L. (2016). *Malema sys EFF won't form coalitions but will support Dain hung municipalities*. Mail & Guardian.

Ferree, K. E. (2013). *Framing the Race in South Africa: The Political Origins of Race-Census Elections*. Cambridge University Press.

Finley, M. (2012). *Coalition Agreement for Stability and Reform*. Cabinet Office.

Finn, M., Seldom, A., & Finn, M. (2015). *The Coalition Effect, 2010-2015*. Cambridge University Press.

Fisher, S. D., & Hobolt, S. B. (2010). Coalition government and electoral accountability. *Electoral Studies*, *29*(3), 358–369. doi:10.1016/j.electstud.2010.03.003

Fish, J. N. (2006). Engendering Democracy: Domestic Labour and Coalition-Building in South Africa. *Journal of Southern African Studies*, *32*(1), 107–127. doi:10.1080/03057070500493811

Flynn, B. (2005). *The Philosophy of Claude Lefort: Interpreting the Political* (1st ed.). Northwestern University Press.

Foa, R.S., Klassen, A., Slade, M., Rand, A., & Collins, R. (2020). *The global satisfaction with democracy report 2020*. Academic Press.

Fortunato, D., Lin, N. C., Stevenson, R. T., & Tromborg, M. W. (2021). Attributing policy influence under coalition governance. *The American Political Science Review*, *115*(1), 252–268. doi:10.1017/S0003055420000763

Fox, J. A. (2010). *Coalitions and networks*. UC Santa Cruz Papers.

France. (2022). *Israel's Netanyahu back with extreme-right government*. Academic Press.

Freeman, W. (2023). Colombia Tries a Transformative Left Turn. *Current History (New York, N.Y.)*, *122*(841), 69–74. doi:10.1525/curh.2023.122.841.69

Frug, G. E. (1999). *City Making: Building Communities Without Building Walls*. Princeton University Press.

Fulton, J. (2020). Situating Saudi Arabia in China's belt and road initiative. *Asian Politics & Policy*, *12*(3), 362–383. doi:10.1111/aspp.12549

Funada-Classen, S. (2013). *The origins of war in Mozambique: A history of unity and division*. African Minds. doi:10.47622/978-1-920489-97-7

Gable, J. (2024, February 6). *South Africa faces prospect of multi-party coalition*. OMFIF. Retrieved from https://www.omfif.org/2024/02/south-africa-faces-prospect-of-multi-party-coalition/

Gallagher, M., Laver, M., & Mair, P. (1992). *Representative Government in Western Europe*. McGraw-Hill, Inc.

Gamson, W. (1961, June). 'A Theory of Coalition Formation'. *American Sociological Review*, *26*(3), 373. doi:10.2307/2090664

Gant, D. (2021). A government of national unity: one small step for President Ramaphosa, one giant leap for South Africa. *Daily Maverick*. https://www.dailymaverick.co.za/opinionista/2021-12-02

Garlick, J. (2023). China's Hedged Economic Diplomacy in Saudi Arabia and Iran: A Strategy of Risk Mitigation. In *China's Engagement with the Islamic Nations: A Clash or Collaboration of Modern Civilisation?* (pp. 117–136). Springer Nature Switzerland. doi:10.1007/978-3-031-31042-3_7

Garver, J. W. (2015). *China's Quest: The History of the Foreign Relations of the People's Republic of China.* Oxford University Press.

Gautam, A. (2018). *Public Policy Making in Coalition Government: Challenges and Solutions.* Academic Press.

Gautam, A. K. (2022). Public policy making in coalition government: Challenges and solutions. *Asian Research Journal of Arts and Social Sciences, 7*(3), 1-8.

Gautam, R. (2018). Politics in India: The dynamics of formation of coalition government. *IMPACT: International Journal of Research in Humanities, Arts and Literature, 6,* 167-172.

Gavin, M. D. (2007). Planning for post Mugabe era: The nature of current crisis. CFR, 7-9.

Gawerc, M. I., & Meyer, D. S. (2021). William A. Gamson and His Legacy for Academia and Social Movements. *Contention, 9*(2), 64–86. doi:10.3167/cont.2021.090205

Gazibo, M. (2016). Democratization in Africa: Achievements and Agenda. In M. Ndulo & M. Gazibo (Eds.), *Growing Democracy in Africa: Elections, Accountable Governance, and Political Economy* (pp. 28–46). Cambridge Scholars Publishing.

GCRO. (2021). *Quality Of Life Survey 6 (2020/21) Municipal Report: City of Johannesburg.* GCRO.

Geenah, N. (2022, Nov. 6). Netanyahu's pact with extremists 'a threat to justice peace'. Sunday World, p. 3.

Gerner, D. J. (2018). *One land, two peoples: The conflict over Palestine.* Routledge. doi:10.4324/9780429494918

Geys, B., Heyndels, B., & Vermeier, J. (2006). Explaining the formation of minimal coalitions: Anti-system parties and anti-pact rules. *European Journal of Political Research, 45*(6), 957–984. doi:10.1111/j.1475-6765.2006.00640.x

Gherghina, S., Tap, P., & Farcas, R. (2023). Informal Power and Short-Term Consequences: Country Presidents and Political Parties in Romania. *Political Studies Review.* doi:10.1177/14789299231187220

Giannetti, D., & Laver, M. (2008). Party cohesion, party discipline, and party factions in Italy. In *Intra-party politics and coalition governments* (pp. 146–168). Routledge. doi:10.4324/9780203889220

Giliomee, H. (1995). Democratization in South Africa. *Political Science Quarterly, 110*(1), 83–104. doi:10.2307/2152052

Gilpin, R. G. (2016). *The political economy of international relations.* Princeton University Press.

Githongo, J. (2010). Fear and loathing in Nairobi. *Foreign Affairs, 89*(4), 2–9.

Glassman, R. (2017). *The Origins of Democracy in Tribes, City-States, and NationStates.* Springer. doi:10.1007/978-3-319-51695-0

Gloppen, S., Kanyongolo, F., Shen-Bayh, F., & Wang, V. (2022). *Democratic Fits and Starts.* Democratic Backsliding in Africa.

Gobe, M. (2010). *Emotional branding: The new paradigm for connecting brands to people.* Simon and Schuster.

Golding, J. (2015). What has the Coalition Government done for the development of initial teacher education? *London Review of Education, 13*(2). Advance online publication. doi:10.18546/LRE.13.2.10

Goodman, N. D., Ullman, T. D., & Tenenbaum, J. B. (2021). *Learning a Theory of Causality*. Retrieved July 1, 2021, https://web.stanford.edu/~ngoodman/papers/LTBC_psychreview_final.pdf

Governo de Moçambique. (2004). *Constituição da República* [Constitution of the Republic]. Boletim da República.

Govo, N., & Muguti, T. (2023). Constitutionalism and Leadership Renewal in the African National Congress: Lessons for Other African States. In *Military, Politics and Democratization in Southern Africa: The Quest for Political Transition* (pp. 209-231). Cham: Springer Nature Switzerland.

Grant, W. (2021). Pressure groups. In Politics UK (pp. 266-288). Routledge. doi:10.4324/9781003028574-18

Green, C., & Otto, L. (2014). *Resource abundance in Mozambique: Avoiding conflict, ensuring prosperity*. Academic Press.

Green, D. (2020)., *How does change happen? Lessons from Malawi*. From Poverty to Power. Retrieved January 19, 2024, from https://frompoverty.oxfam.org.uk/how-does-change-happen-lessons-from-malawi/

Greene, T. (2019). Foreign policy anarchy in multiparty coalitions: When junior parties take rogue decisions. *European Journal of International Relations*, *25*(3), 800–825. doi:10.1177/1354066119828196

Groenning, S. (1970). *The Study of Coalition Behaviour*. Holt, Rinehart and Winston.

Gross, M., & Krauss, S. (2021). Topic coverage of coalition agreements in multi-level settings: The case of Germany. *German Politics*, *30*(2), 227–248. doi:10.1080/09644008.2019.1658077

Grossman, G., Manekin, D., & Margalit, Y. (2018). How sanctions affect public opinion in target countries: Experimental evidence from Israel. *Comparative Political Studies*, *51*(14), 1823–1857. doi:10.1177/0010414018774370

Gulati, R., & Desai, R. (2019). Devolution of Power: A Comparative Analysis of India and the UK. *Journal of Public Administration and Governance*, *9*(1), 1–13. doi:10.5296/jpag.v9i1.14305

Gumede, W. (2023). *Policy Brief 46: Improving Coalition Governance. Democracy Works Foundation*. Retrieved February 14, 2024, from https://www.democracyworks.org.za/policy-brief-improving-coalition-governance/

Gumede, W. (2023). *Policy Brief 46: Improving Coalition Governance*. Retrieved December 29, 2023, from https://www.democracyworks.org.za/policy-brief-improving-coalition-governance/

Gumede, W. (2023). *Policy Brief 46: Improving Coalition Governance*. Retrieved January 18, 2024, from https://www.democracyworks.org.za/policy-brief-improving-coalition-governance/

Gumede, W. (2021). New laws needed to make political coalition work. *Sunday Times*, *5*(December), 22. https://journals.co.za/doi/full/10.10520/ejc-ajpa_v12_n1_a2

Gumede, W. (2023). Coalitions can work well with strange bedfellows. *Sunday Tmes*, *13*(August), 14.

Gunathilake, L. D. (2018). *Electoral Reform in Former British Colonies: A Comparative Case Study of Sri Lanka and South Africa*. Villanova University.

Gupta, A., Jain, P., & Sethi, V. (2020). Power Sharing and Its Impact on Political Institutions: A Comparative Study. *International Journal of Poultry Science*, *2*(1), 45–60.

Gupta, S., & Patel, R. (2020). Challenges and Opportunities of Coalition Governance in Southern Africa: A Comparative Analysis. *African Governance Review*, *28*(1), 45–63.

Guthrie, D. (2012). *China and globalization: The social, economic, and political transformation of Chinese society*. Routledge. doi:10.4324/9780203121450

Gwekwerere, T., Mutasa, D. E., Mpondi, D., & Mubonderi, B. (2019). Patriotic narratives on national leadership in Zimbabwe: Zimbabwe African National Union-Patriotic Front (ZANU-PF) and Movement for Democratic Change (MDC) song texts, ca 2000–2017. *South African Journal of African Languages*, *39*(1), 56–66. doi:10.1080/02572117.2019.1572323

Haffajee, F. (2022). ANC's Dada Morero steps down after 25 days in office as DA's Mpho Phalatse reinstated as Joburg mayor. *Daily Maverick*. https://www.dailymaverick.co.za/article/2022-10-25-ancs-dada-morero-steps-down-after-25-days-in-office-as-das-mpho-phalatse-reinstated-as-joburg-mayor/

Hahm, H., Hilpert, D., & Konig, T. (2023). Divided We Unite: The Nature of Partyism and the Role of Coalition Partnership in Europe. *The American Political Science Review*, 1–19. doi:10.1017/S0003055423000266

Haklai, O., & Norwich, L. (2016). Bound by tradition: The exclusion of minority ethnonational parties from coalition governments—a comparison of Israel and Canada. *Ethnopolitics*, *15*(3), 265–284. doi:10.1080/17449057.2015.1052612

Haklai, O., & Rass, R. A. (2022). The fourth phase of Palestinian Arab politics in Israel: The centripetal turn. *Israel Studies*, *27*(1), 35–60. doi:10.2979/israelstudies.27.1.02

Hamill, J. (1993). South Africa: From Codesa to Leipzig? *The World Today*, *49*(1), 12–16.

Hanabe, L. D., & Malinzi, U. (2019). Party coalition as a model to govern municipalities in South Africa. *Journal of Public Administration*, *54*(1), 41–51.

Hanlon, J. (2020). Integridade eleitoral em Moçambique: Uma perspectiva política e histórica (Ser. Democracia Multipartidária em Moçambique, pp. 151–169). Maputo: EISA Mozambique.

Hanlon, J. (2010). FRELIMO landslide in tainted election in Mozambique. *Review of African Political Economy*, *37*(123), 92–95. doi:10.1080/03056241003638019

Haque, M. (2017). Vertical Power Sharing and Regional Development: Evidence from India. *Journal of Federalism*, *47*(4), 849–875. doi:10.1093/oxfordjournals.jpart.a037946

Haque, M., & Gupta, A. (2019). Power-Sharing Dynamics in Zimbabwe: Lessons from the 2009-2013 Coalition Government. *Southern African Politics*, *15*(2), 189–208.

Harrison, P. (2018). *Johannesburg: A Cultural and Literary History.* Signal Books.

Harshe, R. (2001). The South African Experiment in Coalition-Building. *Seton Hall J. Dipl. & Int'l Rel.*, *2*, 87.

Hartzell, C., & Hoddie, M. (2003). Institutionalising Peace: Power Sharing and Post-Civil War Conflict Management. *American Journal of Political Science*, *47*(2), 318–332. doi:10.1111/1540-5907.00022

Hassan, Q., Algburi, S., Sameen, A. Z., Salman, H. M., & Jaszczur, M. (2023). Implications of strategic photovoltaic deployment on regional electricity self-sufficiency by 2050: A case study in Iraq. *Renewable Energy Focus*, *46*, 338–355. doi:10.1016/j.ref.2023.07.007

Haybe, A. (2024). Somalia: making the most of EU-Somalia Joint Roadmap. *Watch List*, p. 1.

Hazelhurst, L. (1988). The Zimbabwe Unity Accord of 1987. *African Affairs*, *87*(347), 489–506.

Hazell, R., & Yong, B. (2012). *The Politics of Coalition: How the Conservative-Liberal Democrat Government Works.* Bloomsbury Publishing.

Hermann, T. (2020). Public Opinion in Israel. In *The Oxford Handbook of Israeli Politics and Society* (p. 247). Oxford University Press.

Heywood, A. (2019). Politics (5th ed.). MacMillan International & Red Globe Press.

Heywood, A. (1997). *Politics*. Macmillan Foundations. doi:10.1007/978-1-349-25543-6

Heywood, A. (2015). *Global Politics* (2nd ed.). Palgrave MacMillan.

Hicken, A., Aspinall, E., & Weiss, M. (2019). *Electoral dynamics in the philippines: money politics, patronage and clientelism at the grassroots*. National University of Singapore Press. doi:10.2307/j.ctv136c5vg

Hine, D., & Peele, G. (2016). The expenses crisis: Statutory regulation and its difficulties. In *The regulation of standards in British public life* (pp. 104–124). Manchester University Press. doi:10.7228/manchester/9780719097133.003.0005

Hlahla, K. (2020). *Fault-lines within the movement for democratic change: factionalism and Zimbabwe's opposition, 1999-2015*. University of Johannesburg.

Hoh, A. (2019). China's belt and road initiative in Central Asia and the Middle East. *Domes*, *28*(2), 241–276. doi:10.1111/dome.12191

Holmes, O. 2019). Benjamin Netanyahu tells Israeli president he cannot form government. *The Guardian*. www.theguardian.com

Hornung, J., Rüsenberg, R., Eckert, F., & Bandelow, N. C. (2020). New Insights into Coalition Negotiations—The Case of German Government Formation. *Negotiation Journal*, *36*(3), 331–352. doi:10.1111/nejo.12310

Hove, M. (2016). Zimbabwe's Coalition Government: Power-Sharing and Prospects for Democracy. *The Journal of Pan African Studies*, *9*(7), 126–142.

Hristov, J., & Arias, J. C. (2023). Beyond the politics of love: The challenges of paramilitary violence and the land question for Colombia's President Gustavo Petro. *Studies in Political Economy*, *104*(1), 55–68. doi:10.1080/07078552.2023.2186022

Hübscher, E. (2019). The impact of coalition parties on policy output–evidence from Germany. *Journal of Legislative Studies*, *25*(1), 88–118. doi:10.1080/13572334.2019.1570599

Hudson, P. (2015). *Lecture on the Exceptional State*. University of the Witwatersrand.

Hue, T. H. H., & Tung-Wen Sun, M. (2022). Democratic governance: Examining the Influence of citizen participation on local government performance in Vietnam. *International Journal of Public Administration*, *45*(1), 4–22. doi:10.1080/01900692.2021.1939713

Humphries, R., & Shubane, K. (1992). Transkei: Referendum, reincorporation, and a new regionalism. *Journal of Contemporary African Studies*, *11*(2), 109–128. doi:10.1080/02589009208729534

Huntington, S. P. (1993). he third wave: Democratization in the late twentieth century (Vol. 4). University of Oklahoma press.

Huntington, S. P. (1993). he third wave: Democratization in the late twentieth century (Vol. 4). University of Oklahoma Press.

Huntington, S. P. (1991). How countries democratize. *Political Science Quarterly*, *106*(4), 579–616. doi:10.2307/2151795

Huntington, S. P. (1991). *The Third Wave: Democratization in the late Twentieth Century*. University of Oklahoma Press.

Huntington, S. P. (1997). After twenty years: The future of the third wave. *Journal of Democracy*, *8*(4), 3–12. doi:10.1353/jod.1997.0059

Hussain, M. (2023). *TIMELINE | How Johannesburg managed to go through 4 mayors – and counting – in 18 months.* Retrieved November 12, 2023, from https://www.news24.com/news24/opinions/analysis/timeline-how-johannesburg-managed-to-go-through-4-mayors-and-counting-in-18-months-20230503

Hu, Z., & Ji, D. (2012). Ambiguities in communicating with the world: The "Going-out" policy of China's media and its multilayered contexts. *Chinese Journal of Communication, 5*(1), 32–37. doi:10.1080/17544750.2011.647741

Hyden, G. (2016). The Governance Challenges in Africa. In HWO. African Perspectives on Governance. Eritrea: Africa World Press, Inc.

Ideas, M. (2018). *Understanding power dynamics in Cross-Class coalitions.* Mobilizing Ideas. Retrieved October 18, 2023, from https://mobilizingideas.wordpress.com/2018/03/30/class-and-movement-building-how-does-class-shape-participation-in-movements/

Ikenberry, G. J., Mastanduno, M., & Wohlforth, W. C. (2009). Unipolarity, state behavior, and systemic consequences. *World Politics, 61*(1), 1–27. doi:10.1017/S004388710900001X

Independent Electoral Commission (IEC). (2016). *Report on South Africa's 5th local government elections held on 3 August 2016.* IEC.

Isakhan, B., & Stockwell, S. (Eds.). (2011). *The secret history of democracy.* Palgrave Macmillan. doi:10.1057/9780230299467

Islam, N., Ahmed, M., & Sakachep, M. (2023). Governance in collaboration: Evaluating the advantages and challenges of coalition politics. *The Journal of Research Administration, 5*(2), 2142–2149.

Jackson, D., & Jackson, J. (2000). *An Introduction to Political Science.* Prentice Hall.

Jackson, R. J. (2013). *Global politics in the 21st century.* Cambridge University Press. doi:10.1017/CBO9781139015660

Jacobs, C. (2005). *Improving the quality of regulatory impact assessments in the UK* (No. 1649-2016-135960). Academic Press.

Jafari, S. (2016). *Constraints on Diplomacy: The Rise of Right-Wing Political Cultures in Israel.* University of California.

Jalata, A. (2018). The Contested and Expanding Meaning of Democracy. *JIS, 2*(2).

Jalata, A. (2018). The Contested and Expanding Meaning of Democracy. Journal of Interdisciplinary Studies, 2(2), 1-29.

Jatula, V., & Conshello, S. (2021). Democratic Deficits and Underdevelopment in Mozambique. *Journal of the Humanities and Social Sciences, 13*(2).

Jeeves, A., & Cuthbertson, G. (Eds.). (2008). *Fragile Freedom: South African Democracy 1994-2004.* University of South Africa Press.

Jenkins-Smith, H. C., Nohrstedt, D., Weible, C. M., & Ingold, K. (2018). The advocacy coalition framework: An overview of the research program. *Theories of the Policy Process, 4*, 135-171.

Jerusalema Post. (2022a). Yair Lapid officially becomes Prime Minister of Israel. *The Jerusalem Post.*

Jerusalema Post. (2022b). Israeli government to be sworn in on Sunday, coalition complete. *Jerusalem Post.*

Jessop, B. (2012). Marxist approaches to power. The Wiley-Blackwell companion to political sociology, 1-14.

Jobela, Z. (2018). The politics of dominance and Survival: Coalition Politics in South Africa 1994-2018. In Africa Dialogue: Complexities of Coalition Politics in South Africa (pp. 73-106). Durban: The African Centre for the Constructive Resolution of Disputes (ACCORD).

Jobela, Z. (2018). The politics of dominance and Survival: Coalition Politics in South Africa 1994-2018. In S, Ngubane (Ed.), Africa Dialogue: Complexities of Coalition Politics in South Africa (pp. 73-106). Durban: The African Centre for the Constructive Resolution of Disputes (ACCORD).

Johansson, B., & Vigsø, O. (2021). Sweden: Lone hero or stubborn outlier? In Political Communication and COVID-19 (pp. 155-164). Routledge.

John, T. A., & Aderemi, A. K. (2023). The challenges of promoting centripetal forces in Nigeria's sustainable development. *ACU Journal of Social Sciences, 1*(1).

Johnson, P., Chandler, D., Seldon, A., & Finn, M. (2010). The coalition and the economy. *The coalition effect*, 159-193.

Johnson, R. W., & Schlemmer, L. (Eds.). (1996). Launching Democracy in South Africa: the first open election, April 1994. Yale University Press. doi:10.12987/9780300160994

Johnson, J., & Jacobs, S. (Eds.). (2012). *Encyclopedia of South Africa. Scottville*. University of KwaZulu-Natal.

Jolobe, Z. (2018). *The politics of dominance and survival: Coalition politics in South Africa 1994-2018*. Academic Press.

Jones, T., & Jones, T. (2011). Liberals, Owen and the Social Market Economy: 1983–1988. *The Revival of British Liberalism: From Grimond to Clegg*, 118-142.

Jones, B. D., & Frank, R. B. (2005). *The Politics of Attention: How government prioritises problems*. University of Chicago Press.

Jones, M., & Brown, A. (2018). The Evolution of Coalition Politics in Southern Africa: A Historical Perspective. *American Journal of Political Science, 25*(1), 78–95.

Jones, M., & Patel, S. (2020). Legislative Records and Coalition Politics in Africa: A Document Analysis Approach. *Journal of African Politics, 42*(1), 56–78.

Jönsson, A., (2020). *Populism in Israel: A study of the manifestation of populist rhetoric among Israeli right-wing political actors between 2015 and 2020*. Academic Press.

Jopela, A. (2017). *The Heritagization of the Liberation Struggle in Postcolonial Mozambique*. Academic Press.

Joseph, R. (2011, November 9). *Democracy and Reconfigured Power in Africa*. Brookings. Retrieved from https://www.brookings.edu/articles/democracy-and-reconfigured-power-in-africa/

Joshua, M., James, M., & Titos, K. (2022). Coalition Governance and Service Delivery in South Africa: A case study of Tshwane, Johannesburg and Ekurhuleni Metropolitan Municipalities. *Journal of Public Administration, 57*(2), 272–283.

Kadima, D (2006). Party coalitions in Post-Apartheid South Africa and their impact on National Cohesion and Ideological Rapprochement. In *The politics of party coalitions in Africa*. Johannesburg: EISA, KAS.

Kadima, D. (2023, May). *An Introduction to The Politics of Party Alliances and Coalitions in Socially-Divided Africa*. Electoral Institute for Sustainable Democracy in Africa (EISA). Retrieved from https://www.eisa.org/storage/2023/05/2014-journal-of-african-elections-v13n1-introduction-politics-party-alliances-coalitions-socially-divided-africa-eisa.pdf

Kadima, D. K. (2003). Choosing an electoral system: alternatives for the post-war Democratic Republic of Congo. *Journal of African Elections, 2*(1), 33-48.

Kadima, D. (2006). *Party Coalitions in Post-Apartheid South Africa and their Impact on National Cohesion and Ideological Rapprochement*. EISA.

Kadima, D. (2006). The study of party coalitions in Africa: Importance, scope, theory and research methodology. In *The politics of party coalitions in Africa*. Konrad Adenauer Stiftung and EISA.

Kadima, D. (2014). An introduction to the politics of party alliances and coalitions in socially-divided Africa. *Journal of African Elections*, *13*(1), 1–24. doi:10.20940/JAE/2014/v13i1a1

Kadima, D. (Ed.). (2006). *The politics of party Coalitions in Africa*. EISA.

Kagoro, B. (2004). Constitutional Reform as Social Movement: A critical narrative of the constitution-making debate in Zimbabwe, 1997-2000. In B. Raftopoulos & T. Savage (Eds.), *Zimbabwe: Injustice and Political Reconciliation*. Institute for Reconciliation.

Kalantzakos, S. (2017). *China and the geopolitics of rare earths*. Oxford University Press. doi:10.1093/oso/9780190670931.001.0001

Kali, M. (2023). A comparative analysis of the causes of the protests in Southern Africa. *SN Social Sciences*, *3*(2), 28. doi:10.1007/s43545-023-00613-x PMID:36691644

Kamel, M. S. (2018). China's belt and road initiative: Implications for the Middle East. *Cambridge Review of International Affairs*, *31*(1), 76–95. doi:10.1080/09557571.2018.1480592

Kamrava, M. (2005). Democracy and Democratisation. In J. Haynes (Ed.), *Palgrave Advances in Development Studies* (pp. 67–88). doi:10.1057/9780230502864_4

Ka-Ndyalvan, D. (2017). *Beyond 2019: A coalition government is a threat to South Africa's economic recovery*. Academic Press.

Kapa, M., & Shale, V. (2014). Alliance coalitions and the political system in Lesotho, 2007-2012. *Journal of African Elections, 13*.

Kapa, M. A. (2008). The Politics of Coalition Formation and Democracy in Lesotho. *Politikon: South African Journal of Political Studies*, *35*(3), 339–356. doi:10.1080/02589340903017999

Kapa, M. A., & Shale, V. (2014). Alliances, coalitions and the political system in Lesotho 2007-2012. *Journal of African Elections*, *13*(1), 93–114. doi:10.20940/JAE/2014/v13i1a5

Kappeli, A. (2018). *Italy's Vote for Change: Potential Coalitions and their Implications for Development*. Retrieved March 16, 2018, https://www.cgdev.org/blog/italys-vote-change-potential-coalitions-and-their-implications-development

Kapungu, L. L. (2019). Challenging the dominant discourse: The case of POLAD in Zimbabwe. *Journal of African Elections*, *18*(2), 80–101.

Kariuki, P., Reddy, P. S., & Wissink, H. (2022). Implications for municipal leadership and Service Delivery: Coalition Building and Municipal Governance in South Africa. Academic Press.

Karume, S. (2003). *Conceptual understanding of political coalitions in South Africa: An integration of concepts and practice*. Paper presented at Electoral Institute of Southern Africa (EISA) Roundtable on political party coalitions: Strengthening democracy through party coalition building (Vol. 19). Electoral Institute of Southern Africa round table on Strengthening Democracy through Party Coalition Building.

Karume, S. (2003). Conceptual Understanding of Political Coalitions in South Africa: an Integration of Concepts and Practices. *Political Party Coalitions: Strengthening Democracy through Party Coalition Building*.

Kaswan, M. J. (2015). *Politics as the Dynamics of Power*. In Western Political Science Association Annual Conference. Las Vegas, NV.

Katzenellenbogen, J. (2023). *Coalitions and Consequences - Polity*. Institute of Race Relations.

Kenig, O. (2013). *Israeli Government - Coalition building in Israel: A guide for the perplexed*. The Israel Democracy Institute. Retrieved December 23, 2023, from https://en.idi.org.il/articles/10248

Kenosi, L. (2011). Good governance, service delivery, and records: The African tragedy. *Journal of the South African Society of Archivists, 44*, 19–25.

Keping, Y. (2018). Governance and good governance: A new framework for political analysis. *Fudan Journal of the Humanities and Social Sciences, 11*(1), 1–8. doi:10.1007/s40647-017-0197-4

Khadiagala, G. (2021). Coalition Political in Kemya Superficial assemblages and momentary vehicles to attain power. In Marriages of Inconvenience: The Politics of Coalitions in South Africa (pp.157-180). Johannesburg: Mapungubwe Institute for Strategic Reflection (MISTRA).

Khadiagala, G. (2021). Coalition Political in Kenya Superficial assemblages and momentary vehicles to attain power. In S. Booysen (Ed.), Marriages of Inconvenience: The Politics of Coalitions in South Africa (pp. 157-180). Johannesburg: Mapungubwe Institute for Strategic Reflection (MISTRA).

Khadiagala, G. (2021). Coalition politics in Kenya. Marriages of Inconvenience: The politics of coalitions in South Africa, 157.

Khadiagala, G.M. (2010). *Political Movements and coalition politics in Kenya: Entrenching*. Academic Press.

Khadiagala, G. M. (2010). Political Movements and coalition politics in Kenya: Entrenching ethnicity. *South African Journal of International Affairs*.

Khaketla, B. M. (1971). *Lesotho 1970: An African Coup Under the Microscope*. Morija Printing Works.

Khoza, A. (2023). *Election season kicks off but no date yet*. https://www.businesslive.co.za/bd/national/2023-10-24-election-season-kicks-off-but-no-date-yet/

Khoza, A. (2024, January 14th). Assurance comes as SA prepares for backlash from West. *Sunday Times*, ●●●, 7.

Khumalo, P., & Netswera, M. M. (2020). The complex nature of coalitions in the local sphere of government in South Africa. *African Journal of Democracy and Governance, 7*(3-4), 173–192.

Kikasu, E. T., & Pillay, S. S. (2024). Forecasting an Inevitable Coalition Government at the National Level in South Africa: A New Path to Public Administration and Governance. *Open Journal of Political Science, 14*(01), 28–51. doi:10.4236/ojps.2024.141003

King, A. (1993). Cabinet Coordination or Prime Ministerial Dominance? A Conflict of Three Principles of Cabinet Government. In The developing British Political System: 1990s. Longman.

Kingsley, P. (2022). Israel's Government Collapses, Setting Up 5th Election in 3 Years. *The New York Times*.

Kinsel, A. (2009). *Post-apartheid Political Culture in South Africa, 1994-2004*. Unpublished Masters dissertation. University of Central Florida, United States of America. https://stars.library.ucf.edu/cgi/viewcontent.cgi?article=5084&context=etd

Klã, H., Bäck, H., & Krauss, S. (2023). Coalition Agreements as Control Devices: Coalition Governance in Western and Eastern Europe. Oxford University Press.

Klüver, H., & Sagarzazu, I. (2017). Coalition Governments and Party Competition: Political Communication Strategies of Coalition Parties. *Political Science Research and Methods, 5*(2), 333–349. doi:10.1017/psrm.2015.56

Klüver, H., & Spoon, J. J. (2020). Helping or hurting? How governing as a junior coalition partner influences electoral outcomes. *The Journal of Politics, 82*(4), 1231–1242. doi:10.1086/708239

Knowles, K. D. (2001). *An analysis of emerging governing coalitions at the local level in South Africa with a specific on Johannesburg and Nelson Mandela Bay.* PhD Thesis, University of the Free State.

Knowles, K. (2021). An Analysis Of Emerging Governing Coalitions At The Local Level. In *South Africa With a Specific Focus on Johannesburg and Nelson Mandela Bay.* University of the Free State.

Koalitionen. (2021). https://www.bundestagswahl-2021.de/koalitionen

Koeclin, L. (2016). Introduction: The Conceptual Polysemy of Governance. In L. Koechlin & T. Forster (Eds.), *The Politics of Governance: Actors and Articulations in Africa and Beyond* (pp. 1–22). Routledge.

Kondlo, K. (2020). The Context of South African Government and Politics. In Government and Politics in South Africa: Coming of Age. Cape Town: Van Schaik Publisher.

Kostova, D. (2004a). *Coalition Governments and the Decision Making Process in CEE.* Paper prepared for the ECPR Joint Session of Workshops, University of Uppsala, Sweden.

Kotze, D. (2017). South Africa's communist party strips the ANC of its multi-class ruling party status. *The Conversation.* Retrieved December 7, 2017, https://theconversation.com/south-africas-communist-party-strips-the-anc-of-its-multi-class-ruling-party-status-88647

Kotze, J. S. (2019). *Local Council Turmoil Shows South Africa Isn't Very Good at Coalitions.* Retrieved at https:www.google.co.za/amp/s/theconversation.com/amp/local-council-turmoil-shows-south-africa-isnt-very-good-at-coalitions-128489

Kotze, J.S. (2018). *South African come off second best as politicians play havoc with coalitions.* Academic Press.

Kraitzman, A. P., & Ostrom, C. W. Jr. (2023). The Impact of Governmental Characteristics on Prime Ministers' Popularity Ratings: Evidence from Israel. *Political Behavior, 45*(3), 1143–1168. doi:10.1007/s11109-021-09752-4

Krishnarajan, S. (2023). Rationalizing democracy: The perceptual bias and (un) democratic behavior. *The American Political Science Review, 117*(2), 474–496. doi:10.1017/S0003055422000806

Krsteski, N.G.H. (2017). Corruption in South Africa: genesis and outlook. *Journal of Process Management – New Technologies, 5*(4), 49-54.

Kugler, J. (2018). *Political capacity and economic behavior.* Routledge.

Kumar, K. (Ed.). (1998). Post-conflict elections, democratization, and international assistance. Boulder: Lynne Rienner Publishers.

Kumar, S. (2018). Power Sharing: A Conceptual Analysis. *Indian Journal of Poultry Science, 79*(2), 337–351.

Kura, S. (2008). *African Ruling Political Parties and the Making of 'Authoritarian' Democracies.* ACCORD. Retrieved from https://www.accord.org.za/ajcr-issues/african-ruling-political-parties-and-the-making-of-authoritarian-democracies/

Kurzman, C. (1998). Waves of democratization. *Studies in Comparative International Development, 33*(1), 42–64. doi:10.1007/BF02788194

Kuttner, R. (2021). *Britain's Unlikely Grand Coalition (Don't Mention the War).* https://robertkuttner.com

Labuschagne, P. (2018). South Africa, coalition and form of government: Semi presidentialism a tertium genus? *Journal of Contemporary History, 43*(2), 95–115.

Labuschagne, P. (2018). South Africa, Coalition and Form of Government: Semi-Presidentialism A Tertium Genus? *Journal of Contemporary History, 43*(2), 96–116.

Labuschagne, P. (2018). South Africa, coalition and form of government: Semi-presidentialism a tertium genus? *Journal of Contemporary History, 43*(2), 96–116. doi:10.18820/24150509/JCH43.v2.6

Lai, H., & Lu, Y. (Eds.). (2012). *China's soft power and international relations.* Routledge. doi:10.4324/9780203122099

Lambright, G. M. S. (2014). Opposition Politics and Urban Service Delivery in Kampala, Uganda. *Development Policy Review, 32*(s1, S1), S39–S60. doi:10.1111/dpr.12068

Landsberg, C., & Graham, C. (2017). *Government and Politics in South Africa- Coming of age* (5th ed.). Van Schaik Publishers.

Lane, J. E., & Preker, A. M. (2018). Political Parties, Coalitions and Democracy. *Open Journal of Political Science, 8*(4), 447–466. doi:10.4236/ojps.2018.84029

Larsen, H. O. (2002). Directly elected mayors—democratic renewal or constitutional confusion? In *Local Government at the Millenium* (pp. 111–133). VS Verlag für Sozialwissenschaften. doi:10.1007/978-3-663-10679-1_6

Laver, M. (2003). Policy and the dynamics of political competition. *American Journal of Political Science, 47*(3), 505–518.

Laver, M., & Schofield, N. (1991). *Multiparty government: The politics of coalition in Europe.* Oxford University Press.

Law, M. (2018). *Political Party co-operation and building and sustaining coalitions. Challenges faced and lessons learned. A high-level exchange between Germany and South African political.* Academic Press.

Law, M. (2018). *When foes become friends and friends become foes: party political cooperation and building and sustaining coalitions.* Academic Press.

Law, M., & Calland, R. (2018). *Political party co-operation and the building and sustaining of coalitions: Challenges Faced and Lessons Learned.* A High-Level Exchange between South African and German political leaders Symposium, Cape Town, South Africa.

Law, M., & Calland, R. (2018). *South Africa is learning the ropes of coalition politics – and its inherent instability.* The Conversation. Retrieved December 29, 2023, from https://theconversation.com/south-africa-is-learning-the-ropes-of-coalition-politics-and-its-inherent-instability-96483

Law, S. (2007). *Great Philosopher.* MacMillan Press.

Le Roux, M., & Davis, D. (2019). *Lawfare: Judging politics in South Africa.* Jonathan Ball Publishers.

Le Van, A. C. (2011). Power sharing and inclusive politics in Africa's uncertain democracies. *Governance: An International Journal of Policy, Administration and Institutions, 24*(1), 31–53. doi:10.1111/j.1468-0491.2010.01514.x

Leach, M., & Mkhize, S. (2019). *Racial Geographies, Housing Segregation and Dispossession in Johannesburg.* Springer.

LeBas, A. (2011). *From Protest to Parties: Party Building and Democratisation in Africa.* Oxford University Press. doi:10.1093/acprof:oso/9780199546862.001.0001

Lee, S. T. (2021). Vaccine diplomacy: Nation branding and China's COVID-19 soft power play. *Place Branding and Public Diplomacy, 19*(1), 64–78. doi:10.1057/s41254-021-00224-4

Lee, S. W. (2011). The theory and reality of soft power: Practical approaches in East Asia. In *Public diplomacy and soft power in East Asia* (pp. 11–32). Palgrave Macmillan US. doi:10.1057/9780230118447_2

Lees, C. (2011). How unusual is the United Kingdom Coalition (and what are the chances of it happening again)? *The Political Quarterly*, *82*(2), 279–292. doi:10.1111/j.1467-923X.2011.02192.x

Lefebvre, B., & Robin, C. (2009). *Pre-electoral Coalitions, Party System and Electoral Geography: A Decade of General Elections in India 1999-2009*. Routledge.

Lefort, C. (1986). *The Political Forms of Modern Society: Bureaucracy, Democracy, Totalitarianism*. Polity Press.

Lefort, C. (1988). Democracy and Political Theory. London: Polity Press.

Legodi, L. T. (2019). *An exploration of China's foreign policy towards Sudan from 2006 to 2016: An Afrocentric Perspective*. Unpublished Master of Arts (International Politics) dissertation, University of Limpopo.

Lehrs, L. (2016). Jerusalem on the negotiating table: Analyzing the Israeli-Palestinian peace talks on Jerusalem (1993–2015). *Israel Studies*, *21*(3), 179–205. doi:10.2979/israelstudies.21.3.09

Leiserson, M. (1966). *Coalitions in Politics*. Unpublished doctoral dissertation, Yale University.

Lembani, S. (2014). Alliances, coalitions and the weakening of the party system in Malawi. *Journal of African Elections*, *13*(1), 115–149. doi:10.20940/JAE/2014/v13i1a6

Lenine, E. (2020). Modelling coalitions: From concept formation to tailoring empirical explanations. *Games*, *11*(4), 55. doi:10.3390/g11040055

Letsi, T. (2017). Lesotho's February 2015 snap elections: a prescription that never cured sickness. *Journal of African Elections, 14*(2).

Levitsky, S. R., & Way, L. A. (2012). Beyond patronage: Violent struggle, ruling party cohesion, and authoritarian durability. *Perspectives on Politics*, *10*(4), 869–889. doi:10.1017/S1537592712002861

Levush, R. (2019). *Here We Go Again: Forming a Coalition Government Israeli Style*. https://blogs.loc.gov/law/2019/09/here-we-go-again-forming-a-Coalition-government-israeli-style/

Lewis, M. (2011). An Analysis of the Relationship Between Political Blog Reading, Online Political Activity, and Voting During the 2008 Presidential Campaign. *The International Journal of Interdisciplinary Social Sciences: Annual Review*, *6*(3), 11–28. doi:10.18848/1833-1882/CGP/v06i03/52046

Lijphart, A. (1987). Power Sharing in South Africa. Institute of International Studies, University of California.

Lijphart, A. (1977). *Democracy in plural societies: A comparative exploration*. Yale University Press.

Lijphart, A. (1984). *Democracies: Patterns of Majoritarian and Consensus Government in Twenty-One Countries*. Yale University Press. doi:10.2307/j.ctt1ww3w2t

Lijphart, A. (2012). *Patterns of democracy: Government forms and performance in thirty-six countries*. Yale University Press.

Lijphart, A. (2023). *The politics of accommodation: Pluralism and democracy in the Netherlands*. University of California Press. doi:10.2307/jj.8501386

Likoti, F. (2021). The impact of coalition politics on political parties 'ideologies in Lesotho, 2012-2020. *Coalition politics in Lesotho: a multi-disciplinary study of coalitions and their implications for governance, 1*, 157.

Likoti, F. J. (2009). The 2007 General Elections in Lesotho. The Application and Challenges of the Electoral System. *African Studies Quarterly, 10*(4). africa.ufl.edu/asq/v10/v10i4a3.htm

Lindberg, S. (2007). Institutionalization of Party Systems? Stability and Fluidity among Legislative Parties in Africa's Democracies. *Government and Opposition*, *42*(2), 215–241. doi:10.1111/j.1477-7053.2007.00219.x

Lintl, P. (2018). Israel on Its Way to a Majoritarian System? The Current Government's Fight against Principles of Liberal Democracy, the› Constitutional Revolution‹ and the Supreme Court. *Israeli European Policy Network Papers 2018*.

Lintl, P. (2023). *Israel's anti-liberal coalition: the new government is seeking fundamental changes in the political system and in the Israeli-Palestinian conflict* (SWP Comment, 5/2023). Berlin: Stiftung Wissenschaft und Politik -SWPDeutsches Institut für International.

Li, S. (2021). China's Confucius Institute in Africa: A different story? *International Journal of Comparative Education and Development*, *23*(4), 353–366. doi:10.1108/IJCED-02-2021-0014

Lister, R. (2003). *Citizenship: Feminist Perspectives*. Palgrave. doi:10.1007/978-0-230-80253-7

Lodge, T. (1987). State of exile: The African National Congress of South Africa, 1976–86. *Third World Quarterly*, *9*(1), 1–27. doi:10.1080/01436598708419960

Lodge, T. (2014). Neo-patrimonial politics in the ANC. *African Affairs*, *113*(450), 1–23. doi:10.1093/afraf/adt069

Lodge, T. (2014). Some preliminary conclusions on the causes and consequences of political party alliances and coalitions in Africa. *Journal of African Elections*, *13*(1), 233–242. doi:10.20940/2014/v13i1a10

Longley, R. (2023). *What Is a coalition government?* https://www.thoughtco.com/what-is-a-coalition-government-6832794

Lowndes, V., & Pratchett, L. (2012). Local governance under the coalition government: Austerity, localism and the 'Big Society'. *Local Government Studies*, *38*(1), 21–40. doi:10.1080/03003930.2011.642949

Luebbert, G. M., Dodd, L., & Swaan, A. D. (1983). Coalition theory and government formation in multiparty democracies. *Comparative Politics*, *15*(2), 235–249. doi:10.2307/421678

Lu, J., & Chu, Y. H. (2021). *Understandings of democracy: Origins and consequences beyond western democracies*. Oxford University Press.

Lupia, A., & Kaare, S. (1995). Coalition termination and the strategic timing of legislative elections. *The American Political Science Review*, *89*(3), 648–665. doi:10.2307/2082980

Lupia, A., & McCubbins, M. D. (1998). *The democratic dilemma: Can citizens learn what they need to know?* Cambridge University Press.

Lynch, P., & Fairclough, P. (2010). UK Government and Politics. Hachette.

Maathai, W. (2009). *The Challenge for Africa: A New Vision*. William Heinemann.

Madia, M. (2022). *City of Joburg Elects New Section 79 Committee Chairs Despite Tense Meeting*. Retrieved May 22, 2022, from https://ewn.co.za/2022/01/27/city-of-joburg-elects-new-section-79-committee-chairs-despite-tense-council

Madonsela, T. (2023). *Will Human Rights and social Justice Prevail in Gaza?* City Press.

Madubuegwu, C.E. & Maduekwe, C.A., (2022). Federalism and Power-Sharing in Nigeria: A Theoretical Analysis. *Irish International Journal of Law, Political Sciences and Administration*, *6*(5).

Madumo, O. S. (2015). Developmental local government challenges and progress in South Africa. *Administratio Publica*, *23*(2), 153–166.

Mafisa, I. (2022). *ANC back in power in Johannesburg, Dada Morero elected mayor.* IOL News. https://www.iol.co.za/the-star/news/anc-back-in-power-in-johannesburg-dada-morero-elected-mayor-e358ef61-82e5-426b-b896-319681415679

Mahler, G. (2022). Coalition Politics and Government in Contemporary Israel. In *The Palgrave International Handbook of Israel* (pp. 1–20). Springer Singapore.

Mahler, G. S. (2016). *Politics and government in Israel: the maturation of a modern state.* Rowman & Littlefield.

Mail & Guardian. (2023). *Understanding South Africa's coalition landscape,* available https://mg.co.za/thought-leader/opinion/2023-12-05-understanding-south-africas-coalition-landscape

Mailovich, C. (2018). *Limpopo places coalition-led Modimolle under administration.* https://www.businesslive.co.za/bd/national/2018-06-01-limpopo-places-coalition-led-modimolle-under-administration/

Makgale, B. (2020). *Coalition politics and urban governance in Johannesburg's housing policy* (Doctoral dissertation, Master's dissertation. Johannesburg: University of the Witwatersrand).

Makgale, B. (2020). *Coalition politics and urban governance in Johannesburg's housing policy.* Master's dissertation. Johannesburg: University of the Witwatersrand.

Makgale, B. (2020). *Coalition Politics and Urban Governance in Johannesburg's Housing Policy.* Wits Graduate School of Governance.

Makgale, B. (2021). Power, Politics and Ideology: Understanding Councillors' views on the tug of war in the City of Johannesburg. In S. Booysen (Ed.), *Marriage of Incontinence. The politics of coalitions in South African (2021).* doi:10.2307/j.ctv2z6qdx6.18

Makgetla, N. (2020). *Inequality in South Africa–An Overview.* Trade & Industrial Policy Strategies.

Makhubo, G. (2020). *The State of Financial Management and Governance in Municipalities with Coalition Government: A Case for Constructive Coalition Governance.* Parliament of South Africa.

Makkalanban, D. S. (2015). Coalition's in Indian political process: A critical analysis. *Indian Journal of Poultry Science, 76*(3), 397–401.

Makoa, F. K. (2004). Electoral reform and political stability in Lesotho. *African. The Journal of Conflict Resolution, 4*(2), 79–85.

Makole, K. R., Ntshangase, B. A., & Adewumi, S. A. (2022). Coalition Governance: Unchartered Waters in South African Political Landscape. *Business Ethics and Leadership, 6*(4), 23–37. doi:10.21272/bel.6(4).23-37.2022

Makundi, H., Huyse, H., Develtere, P., Mongula, B., & Rutashobya, L. (2017). Training abroad and technological capacity building: Analysing the role of Chinese training and scholarship programmes for Tanzanians. *International Journal of Educational Development, 57,* 11–20. doi:10.1016/j.ijedudev.2017.08.012

Malamud, A. (2020). Mercosur and the European Union: comparative regionalism and interregionalism. Oxford Research Encyclopedia of Politics. doi:10.1093/acrefore/9780190228637.013.1085

Maleka, M. S., & Shai, K. B. (2016). South Africa's Post-Apartheid Foreign Policy Towards Swaziland. *Journal of Public Administration, 51*(2), 194–204.

Malik, A. A. (2023). Parliamentary Democracy: Mechanisms, Challenges, and the Quest for Effective Governance. *Revista Review Index Journal of Multidisciplinary, 3*(4), 1-9.

Malik, F., Abduladjid, S., Mangku, D. G. S., Yuliartini, N. P. R., Wirawan, I. G. M. A. S., & Mahendra, P. R. A. (2021). Legal Protection for People with Disabilities in the Perspective of Human Rights in Indonesia. *International Journal (Toronto, Ont.)*, *10*, 539.

Mamokhere, J. (2022). Understanding the Complex Interplay of Governance, Systematic, and Structural Factors Affecting Service Delivery in South African Municipalities. *Commonwealth Youth & Development*, *20*(2).

Mamokhere, J., & Kgobe, F. K. L. (2023). One District, one approach, one budget, one plan: Understanding district development model as an initiative for improving service delivery and socio-economic development in South Africa. *International Journal of Social Science Research*, *11*(3), 362–370.

Mandela, N. (1998, September 3). *Closing address by President Nelson Mandela at the 12th Summit Meeting of Heads of State and Government of the countries of the Non-Aligned Movement*. Retrieved from http://www.mandela.gov.za/ mandela_speeches/1998/980903_nam.htm

Mandela, N., & Langa, M. (2017). *Dare Not Linger: The Presidential Years*. Macmillan.

Maneng, N. S. (2022). *Power-sharing in South Africa's municipalities: The case of Ekurhuleni and Nelson Mandela Bay Metropolitan municipalities from 2016*. University of the Free State.

Mangwana, P., Dube, N., & Moyo, L. (2013, September). *Panel presentations to the EISA 8th Annua Symposium*. Academic Press.

ManifestoE. F. F. (2013). Available at https://www.effonline.org/eff-elections-manifesto-2016

Manning, C., & Malbrough, M. (2009). Learning the Right Lessons from Mozambique's Transition to Peace. *Taiwan Journal of Democracy*, *5*(1), 77–91.

Mapuva, J. (2010). Government of National Unit (GNU) AS A Conflict Prevention Strategy: Case of Zimbabwe and Kenya. *Journal of Sustainable Development in Africa*, *12*(6), 247–263.

Mapuva, J. (2010). Government of National Unity (GNU) as a conflict prevention strategy: Case of Zimbabwe and Kenya. *Journal of Sustainable Development in Africa*, *12*(6), 247–263.

Marchart, O. (2007). *Post-Foundational Political Thought: Political Difference in Nancy, Lefort, Badiou and Laclau*. Edinburgh University Press.

Mare, G. (2000). Versions of Resistance History in South Africa: The ANC Strand in Inkatha in the 1970s and 1980s. *Review of African Political Economy*, *83*(83), 63 79. doi:10.1080/03056240008704433

Markowski, R. (2020). Plurality support for democratic decay: The 2019 Polish parliamentary election. *West European Politics*, *43*(7), 1513–1525. doi:10.1080/01402382.2020.1720171

Marradi, A. (1975). Abram de Swaan, Coalition Theories and Cabinet Formations, Amsterdam, Elsevier, 1973. Italian Political Science Review/Rivista Italiana Di Scienza Politica, 5(3), 592–594.

Marrian, N. (2019). *The tables could turn on kingmaker EFF*. Retrieved November 30, 2023, from https://mg.co.za/ article/2019-04-26-00-the-tables-could-turn-on-kingmaker-eff/

Marshall, C., & Rossman, G. B. (2011). *Designing Qualitative Research* (5th ed.). Sage Publications.

Martin, L. W., & Georg, V. (2011). *Parliaments and Coalitions: The Role of Legislative Institutions in Multiparty Governance*. Oxford University Press. doi:10.1093/acprof:oso/9780199607884.001.0001

Martin, L. W., & Vanberg, G. (2020). Coalition government, legislative institutions, and public policy in parliamentary democracies. *American Journal of Political Science*, *64*(2), 325–340. doi:10.1111/ajps.12453

Martin, S. (2002). The modernization of UK local Government: Markets, managers, monitors and mixed fortunes. *Public Management Review*, *4*(3), 291–307. doi:10.1080/14616670210151595

Martin, S., & Whitaker, R. (2019). Beyond committees: Parliamentary oversight of coalition government in Britain. *West European Politics*, *42*(7), 1464–1486. doi:10.1080/01402382.2019.1593595

Maseremule, H. (2020). Administering National Government. In C. Landsberg & S. Graham (Eds.), *Government and Politics in South Africa: Coming of Age* (pp. 95–128). Van Schaik Publisher.

Maserumule, M. H. (2011). *Good Governance in the New Partnership for Africa's Development (NEPAD: A Public Administration Perspective*. Unpublished PhD Thesis. Pretoria: University of South Africa.

Maserumule, H. (2021). Administering national government. In C. Landsberg & S. Graham (Eds.), *Government and politics in South Africa* (pp. 95–128). Van Schaik Publishers.

Maserumule, M. H. (2014). In search of African epistemology- a reflection of an editor. *Journal of Public Administration*, *49*(2), 439–441.

Maserumule, M. H. (2020). Democratic Alliance-Led Coalition in the City of Tshwane: Strange Bedfellows Coming Apart at the Seams. *Journal of Public Administration*, *55*(3), 310–341.

Maserumule, M. H. (2020). Democratic Alliance-Led Coalition in the City of Tshwane: Strange Bedfellows Coming Apart at the seams. *Journal of Public Administration, 55*(3).

Mashatile, P. (2023). *Time to build framework for coalitions*. Mail & Guardian.

Mashele, P., & Qobo, M. (2017). *The fall of the ANC: What Next?* Picador Africa.

Masilela, B. (2023). *Thapelo Amad is the new mayor in town. This is what you need to know about Joburg politics and the election of the new number one citizen*. IOL News. https://www.iol.co.za/news/politics/thapelo-amad-is-the-new-mayor-in-town-this-is-what-you-need-to-know-about-joburg-politics-and-the-election-of-the-new-number-one-citizen-73152cdf-36cd-4165-9f2e-a21739d20f8a

Masina, M. (2021). *Future Realities of Coalition Governments in South Africa*. South African Association of Public Administration and Management (SAAPAM).

Masina, M. (2021). *Future Realities of Coalitions in South Africa: Reflections on Colation Government in the Metros: 2016-2021*. SAAPAM.

Masina, M. (2021). *Future Realities of Coalition Governments in South Africa: Reflections on Coalition Governments in the Metros: 2016-2021*. South African Association of Public Administration and Management.

Masipa, T. S. (2017). *The rise of muliti-partyism in South Africa's political spectrum: The Age of coalition and Multiparty Governance*. University of Limpopo South Africa. The 2nd Annual International Conference on Public Administration and Development Alternatives 26-28 July, Tlotlo Hotel, Gaborone, Botswana.

Masterson, G. (2021). The legacy of multipartyism on political coalitions and rent-seeking in African elections. In Marriages of Inconvenience: The Politics of Coalitions in South Africa (pp.127-155). Johannesburg: Mapungubwe Institute for Strategic Reflection (MISTRA). doi:10.2307/j.ctv2z6qdx6.12

Masuabi, Q. (2022). A dramatic Friday as City of Joburg elects Dada Morero as mayor after Mpho Phalatse gets the chop. *Daily Maverick.* https://www.dailymaverick.co.za/article/2022-09-30-dramatic-friday-joburg-elects-dada-morero-as-mayor-as-phalatse-gets-chop/

Masuabi, Q. (2023). Al Jama-ah's Kabelo Gwamanda voted in as latest mayor of Joburg. *Daily Maverick.* https://www.dailymaverick.co.za/article/2023-05-05-al-jama-ahs-kabelo-gwamanda-voted-in-as-latest-mayor-of-joburg/

Masuku, M. M., & Jili, N. N. (2019). Public service delivery in South Africa: The political influence at local government level. *Journal of Public Affairs*, *19*(4), e1935. doi:10.1002/pa.1935

Mathebula, N. E. (2018). Pondering over the Public Administration discipline: A move towards African epistemology. *Bangladesh e-Journal of Sociology*, *15*(2), 17–25.

Matlosa, K. (2002). Review of electoral systems and democratization in Southern Africa. *International Roundtable on the South African Electoral System, Cape Town.*

Matlosa, K. (2008). Political Parties and Democratisation in the Southern African Development Community Region: The Weakest link? *EISA Report, 15.*

Matlosa, K. (2021). Electoral systems, party systems and coalitions: Lessons from Southern Africa. In S. Booysen (Ed.), Marriages of Inconvenience: The Politics of Coalitions in South Africa (pp.97-124). Johannesburg: Mapungubwe Institute for Strategic Reflection (MISTRA).

Matlosa, K., & Lotshwao, K. (2010). *Political integration and democratisation in Southern Africa: Progress, problems and prospects.* Academic Press.

Matlosa, K., & Sello, C. (2005). *Political parties and democratisation in Lesotho.* Academic Press.

Matlosa, K. (1999). Conflict and Conflict Management: Lesotho's Political Crisis after the 1998 Election. *Lesotho Social Science Review*, *5*(1), 163–196.

Matlosa, K. (2003). Political culture and democratic governance in Southern Africa. *American Journal of Political Science*, *8*(1), 85–112.

Matlosa, K. (2017). Understanding Political Crisis of Lesotho's Post-2015 Elections. In M. Thabane (Ed.), *Towards an Anatomy of Political Instability in Lesotho 1966–2016* (pp. 131–161). National University of Lesotho.

Matsika, T. (2019). *The politics of sustainability: discourse and power in post-2000 Zimbabwean political texts* (Doctoral dissertation, University of the Free State).

Matthews, F., & Flinders, M. (2017). Patterns of democracy: Coalition governance and majoritarian modification in the United Kingdom, 2010–2015. *British Politics*, *12*(2), 157–182. doi:10.1057/s41293-016-0041-5

Matusiak, M. (2023). *Netanyahu for the sixth time: The new Israeli government.* Academic Press.

Maverick, D. (2024). *What we know about Jacob Zuma's new party.* https://www.dailymaverick.co.za/article/2024-01-09-umkhonto-wesizwe-what-we-know-about-zumas-new-party

Mawere, J., Matoane, J., & Khalo, T. (2022). Coalition Governance and Service Delivery in South Africa: A Case Study of Tshwane, Johannesburg and Ekurhuleni Metropolitan Municipalities. *Journal of Public Administration*, *57*(2), 272–283.

Mawowa, S. (2020). Elections in Zimbabwe under Mnangagwa: Democratic Transition or Recurrent Authoritarianism? *Journal of African Elections*, *19*(1), 63–86.

Mayes, B. T., & Allen, R. W. (1977). Toward a definition of organizational politics. *Academy of Management Review*, *2*(4), 672–678. doi:10.2307/257520

Mazula, B. (1995). *Moçambique: eleições, democracia e desenvolvimento*. Inter-Africa Group.

Mbete, S. (2015). The Economic Freedom Fighters-South Africa's turn towards populism? *Journal of African Elections*, *14*(1), 35-59.

McCain, N. (2020). *Mangaung mayor ousted in motion of no confidence*. News24. https://www.news24.com/news24/ SouthAfrica/ News/mangaung-mayor-ousted-in-motion-of-no-confidence-20200808

McCulloch, A. (2013). Does moderation pay? Centripetalism in deeply divided societies. *Ethnopolitics*, *12*(2), 111–132. doi:10.1080/17449057.2012.658002

McGarry, J., & O'Leary, B. (2009). Power shared after the deaths of thousands. In R. Taylor (Ed.), *Consociational theory: McGarry & O'Leary and the Northern Ireland conflict* (pp. 15–84). Routledge.

McInnis, K. J. (2013). Lessons in coalition warfare: Past, present and implications for the future. *International Politics Reviews*, *1*(2), 78–90. doi:10.1057/ipr.2013.8

McKinley, D. (2001). Democracy, Power and Patronage: Debate and Opposition within the ANC and the Tripartite Alliance since 1994. In Seminar Report, Konrad Adenauer Stiftung and Rhodes University, Johannesburg (No. 2, pp. 65-79). Academic Press.

McKinley, D. T. (2015). *The ANC and the liberation struggle: A critical political biography*. Jacana Media.

McLean, I. (2010). Calman and Holtham: the public finance of devolution. In PSA: Territorial Politics Conference, Oxford, UK.

McLean, I. (1999). The Jenkins Commission and the implications of electoral reform for the UK constitution. *Government and Opposition*, *34*(2), 143–160. doi:10.1111/j.1477-7053.1999.tb00475.x

Mcmillan, A. (2004). The causes of Political Parties Alliances and Coalitions and their Effects on National Cohesion in India. *Journal of African Elections*, *13*(1), 181–206. doi:10.20940/JAE/2014/v13i1a8

Mehrotra, S., Vandemoortele, J., & Delamonica, E. (2000). *Basic services for all? Public spending and the social dimensions of poverty*. https://www.unicef-irc.org/publications/pdf/basice.pdf

Merriam, S. B. (2002). Introduction to qualitative research. *Qualitative research in practice: Examples for discussion and analysis*, *1*(1), 1-17.

Meydani, D., & Ofek, D. (2016). A new integrated model of the formation of coalitions: Perspectives on the Twentieth Knesset. *Israel Affairs*, *22*(3-4), 612–662.

Mfene, P. N. (2013). Public accountability. *Administratio Publica*, *21*(1), 6–23.

Miller, A. D. (2021). *Israel's new coalition government is more stable than it looks*. Foreign Policy. Retrieved December 28, 2023, from https://foreignpolicy.com/2021/06/14/israel-bennett-coalition-government-stable/

Mills, G. (2023). *Rich State, Poor State: Why Some Countries Succeed and Others Fail*. Penguin Books.

Mills, G. (2023). *Rich State, Poor State: Why Some Countries Succeed and Others Fail?* Penguin Books.

MISTRA. (2021). Marriages of Inconvenience: The politics of coalitions in South Africa. Johannesburg: Mapungubwe Institute for Strategic Reflection.

MISTRA. (2021). Marriages of Inconvenience: The Politics of Coalitions in South Africa. Johannesburg: Mapungubwe Institute for Strategic Reflection.

Mitchell, J. (2000). New parliament, new politics in Scotland. *Parliamentary Affairs*, *53*(3), 605–621. doi:10.1093/pa/53.3.605

Mithani, M. A., & O'Brien, J. P. (2021). So what exactly is a "coalition" within an organization? A review and organizing framework. *Journal of Management*, *47*(1), 171–206. doi:10.1177/0149206320950433

Mizrahi, T., & Rosenthal, B. B. (2001). Complexities of Coalition Building: Leaders' Successes, Strategies, Struggles, and Solutions. *Social Work*, *46*(1), 63–78. doi:10.1093/sw/46.1.63 PMID:11217495

Mkhize, N. 2013. Municipality in turmoil as ANC-NFP pact collapses. *BusinessDay*. Retrieved July 15, 2013, https://www.businesslive.co.za/bd/politics/2013-07-15-municipality-in-turmoil-as-anc-nfp-pact-collapses/

Mlambo, D. N. (2023). The Tragedy of the African National Congress (ANC) and its Cadre Deployment Policy: Ramifications for Municipal Stability, Corruption and Service Deliver. *Pan-African Journal of Governance and Development*, *4*(1), 3-17.

Mlambo, D. N., & Thusi, X. (2023). South Africa's Persistent Social Ills Post-1994 and the Deterioration of the African National Congress: Is the Country Heading towards a Failing State? *Politeia, 42*(1).

Mlambo, A. (2013). Colonialism and racism in Zimbabwe: A historical perspective. *Journal of African History*, *56*(2), 56–57.

Mlambo, A. S., & Raftopoulos, B. (2018). The Zimbabwean Economy after Dollarisation: Structural Change or Economic Recovery? *Journal of Southern African Studies*, *44*(5), 825–840.

Mlambo, D. N. (2019). Governance and service delivery in the public sector: The case of South Africa under Jacob Zuma (2009–2018). *African Renaissance*, *16*(3), 207–224. doi:10.31920/2516-5305/2019/V16n3a11

Mlambo, D. N., Mubecua, M. A., Mpanza, S. E., & Mlambo, V. H. (2019). Corruption and its implications for development and good governance: A perspective from post-colonial Africa. *Journal of Economics and Behavioral Studies*, *11*(1 (J)), 39–47. doi:10.22610/jebs.v11i1(J).2746

Mnguni, H. (2023). Public Service Delivery in Rural South Africa: The Influence of Coalition Politics at Local Government Level. *International Journal of Social Science Research*, *11*(3), 371–37.

Mnwana, S. (2015). Democracy, development and chieftaincy along South Africa's 'Platinum Highway': Some emerging issues. *Journal of Contemporary African Studies*, *33*(4), 510–529. doi:10.1080/02589001.2015.1117730

Modupe, D. S. (2003). The Afrocentric Philosophical Perspective: Narrative Outline. In A. Mazama (Ed.), *The Afrocentric Paradigm*. Africa World Press.

Mokgosi, K., Shai, K. & Ogumundi, O. (2017). Local government Coalition in Gauteng Province of South Africa: Challenges and Opportunities. *Journal of conflict and Social Transformation, 6*(1), 37-57.

Mokgosi, K., Shai, K. & Ogunnubi, O. (2017). Local government coalition in Gauteng Province of South Africa: challenges and opportunities. *Ubuntu: Journal of Conflict Transformation*, 37-57.

Mokgosi, K., Shai, K., & Ogunnubi, O. (2017). Local Government Coalition in Gauteng Province of South Africa: Challenges and opportunities. *Ubuntu: Journal of Conflict and Social Transformation*, *6*(1), 37–57. doi:10.31920/2050-4950/2017/v6n1a2

Molomo, M. G. (2000). Democracy under Siege: The Presidency and Executive Powers in Botswana. *Pula: Botswana Journal of African Studies*, *14*(1), 95–108.

Mongale, C. (2022). *Social Discontent or Criminality? Navigating the Nexus Between Urban Riots and Criminal Activates in Gauteng and KwaZulu-Natal Provinces, South Africa (2021).* https://www.frontiersin.org/articles/10.3389/frsc.2022.865255/full

Monkam, N. F. (2014). Local municipality productive efficiency and its determinants in South Africa. *Development Southern Africa*, *31*(2), 275–298. doi:10.1080/0376835X.2013.875888

Monyake, M. (2020). A. ssurance dilemmas of the endangered institutional reforms process in Lesotho. *Canadian Journal of African Studies / Revue canadienne des études africaines.* https://www.tandfonline.com/loi/rcas20

Moosa, I. A. (2023). Western Exceptionalism: The Rule of Law, Judicial Independence and Transparency. In *The West Versus the Rest and The Myth of Western Exceptionalism* (pp. 91–130). Springer International Publishing. doi:10.1007/978-3-031-26560-0_4

Morrison, S. (2023). *Understanding South Africa's coalition landscape | Good Governance Africa.* Retrieved January 20, 2024, from https://gga.org/understanding-south-africas-coalition-landscape/

Morrison, S. (2023, December 5). *Understanding South Africa's Political Landscape.* Good Governance Africa. Retrieved from https://gga.org/understanding-south-africas-coalition-landscape/

Mosala, S. (2022). From a Liberation Movement to a Governing Party: An Interrogation of the African National Congress (ANC). *Journal of Nation-Building and Policy Studies*, *6*(3), 67–89. doi:10.31920/2516-3132/2022/v6n3a4

Moseme, T. T. (2017). *The rise and fall of the first coalition government in Lesotho: 2012–2014* (Doctoral dissertation, University of the Free State).

Moshodi, J. (2018). *Coalition politics a new political landscape in South Africa.* University of the Free State.

Moshoeshoe, M. L., & Dzinesa, G. A. (2024). More Democracy, More Security? Regionalism and Political [In]Security in East and Southern Africa. *Global Society*, 1–26. doi:10.1080/13600826.2023.2301067

Mosse, M. (2023). *O Estado da Nação é penoso, patetico, pungente,putrefacto e pária. Não se recomenda! Carta de Moçambique.* Available from https://www.cartamz.com/index.php/blog-do-marcelo-mosse/item/15607-o-estado-da-nacao-e-penoso-patetico-pungente-putrefacto-e-paria-nao-se-recomenda

Motsamai, D. (2015). Elections in time of Instability: Challenges for Lesotho beyond 2015 Poll. *Institute for Security Studies, 3,* 1-16.

Motseme, T. (2017). *The rise and fall of the First Coalition Government in Lesotho: 2012-2014.* Master's Dissertation, University of Free State.

Moury, C., & Timmermans, A. (2013). Inter-Party Conflict Management in Coalition Governments: Analyzing the Role of Coalition Agreements in Belgium, Germany, Italy and the Netherlands. *Politics and Governance*, *1*(2), 117–131. doi:10.17645/pag.v1i2.94

Moyo, J. (2011). The government of national unity (GNU) and democratic governance in Zimbabwe. *International Journal of African Renaissance Studies-Multi-, Inter- and Transdisciplinarity, 6*(1), 6-26.

Mpangalasane, C. (2020). *The impact of coalition government on service delivery: City of Tshwane metropolitan* (Doctoral dissertation, North-West University (South Africa).

Mpangalasane, C. (2020). *The impact of coalition government on service delivery: City of Tshwane metropolitan* (Doctoral dissertation, North-West University, South Africa).

Mpangalasane, C. (2020). *The impact of coalition government on service delivery: City of Tshwane metropolitan.* Mini-dissertation, North-West University, http://hdl.handle.net/10394/35622

Mpangalasane, C. (2020). *The impact of coalition government on service delivery: City of Tshwane metropolitan.* Unpublished Master's dissertation. Potchefstroom: North-West University.

Mpangalasane, C. (2020). *The impact of coalition government on service delivery: City of Tshwane metropolitan.* North-West University.

Mpofu, S. (2015). Toxification of national holidays and national identity in Zimbabwe's post- 2000 nationalism. *J Afr Cult, 28*(1), 28–43.

Mubangisi, C. (2016). The rural/urban dichotomy in South Africa's local government. Loyola. *Journal of Social Sciences, 26*(1), 27–41.

Mueller, S. D. (2011). Dying to win: Elections, political violence, and institutional decay in Kenya. *Journal of Contemporary African Studies, 29*(1), 99–117. doi:10.1080/02589001.2011.537056

Mujuru, A. (2021). Political Transition and the Prospects for Peace and Reconciliation in Zimbabwe. *African Security, 14*(1), 34–52.

Mukherjee, B. (2006). Why political power-sharing agreements lead to enduring peaceful resolution of some civil wars, but not others? *International Studies Quarterly, 50*(2), 479–504. doi:10.1111/j.1468-2478.2006.00410.x

Mukoma, W. N. (2008). A caricature of democracy: Zimbabwe's misguided talks. *The International Herald Tribune.* http://iht.com/articles/2008/07/25/opnion/ednug.php?page=2.

Mukuhlani, T. (2014). Zimbabwe's government of national unity: Successes and challenges in restoring peace and order. *Journal of Power. Politics and Governance, 2*(2), 169–180.

Mukumbira, P. (2021). Zimbabwe's Political Actors Dialogue (POLAD): Boon or Bane for National Development? In *Democratic Governance and Social Justice* (pp. 111–132). Springer.

Mukwedeya, T. G. (2016). *Intraparty politics and the local state: Factionalism, patronage, and power in Bufalo City Metropolitan Municipality* (Doctoral dissertation, University of the Witwatersrand, Faculty of Humanities, School of Social Science). https://core.ac.uk/download/pdf/188770832.pdf

Mukwedeya, T. G. (2015). The enemy within: Factionalism in ANC local structures—The case of Buffalo City (East London). *Transformation (Durban), 87*(1), 117–134. doi:10.1353/trn.2015.0005

Muller & Strom. (2008b). Coalition agreements and cabinet governance. In *Cabinets and Coalition Bargaining.* Oxford University Press.

Müller, W. C., Bergman, T., & Ilonszki, G. (2019). Extending the Coalition Life-cycle Approach to Central Eastern. *Coalition Governance in Central Eastern Europe, 1.*

Müller, W. C., & Meyer, T. M. (2014). Meeting the challenges of representation and accountability in multi-party governments. In *Accountability and European Governance* (pp. 137–164). Routledge.

Muller, W. C., & Storm, K. (2000). *Coalition governments in Western Europe. Comparative Politics.* Oxford University Press. doi:10.1093/oso/9780198297604.001.0001

Muller, W., & Kaare, S. (2008a). *Cabinets and Coalition bargaining: The democratic life cycle in Western Europe.* Oxford University Press.

Muller, W., & Thomas, M. M. (2010). Meeting the Challenges of Representation and Accountability in Multiparty Governments. *West European Politics, 33*(5), 1065–1092. doi:10.1080/01402382.2010.486135

Mungwini, P. (2018). To the victor belong the spoils' reflections on ethics and political values in postcolonial Africa. *Proceedings of the XXIII World Congress of Philosophy, 68*, 87-93. 10.5840/wcp232018681517

Municipal, I. Q. (2023). *Protest numbers for 2022 bounce back to pre-COVID numbers.* https://www.municipaliq.co.za/index.php?site_page=press.php

Munzhedzi, P. H. (2015). South African local economic development: issues, challenges and opportunities. *The Xenophobic Attacks in South Africa: Reflections and Possible Strategies to Ward Them Off*, 169.

Murali, K. (2017). Economic Liberalisation, Electoral Coalitions, and Investments Policies in India. In States in Developing World (pp. 248-279). Cambridge University Press.

Murali, K. (2017). Economic Liberation, electrola Coliations and Invsetment Policies in India. In States in the Developing World (pp. 248-290). Cambridge University Press.

Muriaas, R. L. (2013). Party affiliation in new democracies: Local reactions to the split of the ruling party in Malawi. *African Journal of Political Science and International Relations, 7*(4), 190–199. doi:10.5897/AJPSIR10.096

Murithi, T. (2014). The Government of National Unity in Kenya and Zimbabwe: Assessing the Legitimacy of Power-Sharing Arrangements. *Journal of African Elections, 13*(1), 1–20.

Murphy, P. (2022). Queen Elizabeth II and the Commonwealth: Time to Open the Archives. *The Journal of Imperial and Commonwealth History, 50*(5), 821–828. doi:10.1080/03086534.2022.2136299

Mushonga, M. (2020). *Political Actors Dialogue (POLAD) and the quest for inclusive democracy in Zimbabwe. Southern African Public Policy Research Institute.* SAPES Trust.

Muzafer, S., & Sherif, C. W. (1953). *Groups in Harmony and Tension; An Integration of Studies of Intergroup Relations.* Harper & Brothers.

Muzondidya, J. (2014). The Politics of Opposition in Contemporary Africa: The Case of Zimbabwe. *Africa Spectrum, 49*(1), 67–84.

Muzondidya, J. (2014). Zimbabwe's Government of National Unity (2009–2013): Towards democracy or unfinished business? *Journal of Contemporary African Studies, 32*(3), 348–364. doi:10.1080/02589001.2014.922617

Mvumvu, Z. (2019). *Herman Mashaba resigns as mayor of Johannesburg, says 'I will always choose the country ahead of the party.* Retrieved March 31, 2024, from https://www.timeslive.co.za/politics/2019-10-21-herman-mashaba-resigns-as-mayor-of-johannesburg-says-not-in-my-nature-to-wait-to-be-pushed/

Mwangi, O. G. (2021). Conceptual and theoretical approaches to coalitions in parliamentary democracies. *Coalition Politics in Lesotho: A Multi-Disciplinary Study of Coalitions and Their Implications for Governance*, 13-27. https://doi.org/ doi:10.52779/9781991201690/02

Mwareya, R. (2023). *South Africa: Johannesburg's circus of eight mayors in two years.* Retrieved November 12, 2023, from https://www.theafricareport.com/309452/south-africa-johannesburgs-circus-of-eight-mayors-in-two-years/

Mwonzora, G. (2017). A Critical Analysis of the Role of the Movement for Democratic Change (MDC) in the Democratisation Process in Zimbabwe from 2000 to 2016. *Unpublished PhD thesis. Rhodes University.*

Naamna, M. (2018). Political-electoral transformations in Israel in the contemporary period: Historical and political approach. *Moldoscopie*, *83*(4), 91–99.

Naidoo, V. (2019). Transitional Politics and Machinery of Government Change in South Africa. *Journal of Southern African Studies*, *45*(3), 575–595. doi:10.1080/03057070.2019.1622309

Nampewo, Z., Mike, J. H., & Wolff, J. (2022). Respecting, protecting and fulfilling the human right to health. *International Journal for Equity in Health*, *21*(1), 1–13. doi:10.1186/s12939-022-01634-3 PMID:35292027

National Freedom Party. (n.d.). *Coalition governments in South Africa: Navigating Challenges and Confronting Corruption*. Submission.

National Government. (2023). *City of Johannesburg Metropolitan Municipality (JHB)*. Retrieved December 3, 2023, from https://municipalities.co.za/management/2/city-of-johannesburg-metropolitan-municipality

Ncube, W. (2015). Reflections on the Unity Accord of 1987 and Its Political, Social and Economic Impact on Zimbabwe. *The Journal of Pan African Studies*, *7*(4), 143–155.

Ndegwa, S. N. (2003). Citizenship and ethnicity: An examination of two transition moments in Kenyan politics. *The American Political Science Review*, *97*(4), 531–546.

Ndevu, Z., & Muller, K. (2018). A Conceptual Framework for Improving Service Delivery at Local Government in South Africa. *African Journal of Public Affairs.*, *10*(4), 181–195.

Ndletyana, M. (2018). A Note from the Policy Editor: Coalition Councils: Origin, Composition and Impact on Local Governance. Journal of Public Administration, 53(2), 139-141.

Ndletyana, M. (2020). *Anatomy of the ANC in Power: Insights from Port Elizabeth, 1990-2019*. Human Sciences Research Council (HSRC) Press.

Ndletyana, M. (2021). Local government coalitions across South Africa, 2000–16. *Marriages of inconvenience: The politics of coalitions in South Africa*, 39.

Ndletyana, M. (2018, June). Coalition Councils: Origin, composition, and impact on local germanane. *Journal of Public Administration*, *53*(2), 139–141.

Ndlovu, M. (2021). Gukurahundi and "wounds of history": Discourses on mass graves, exhumations and reburial in post–independence Zimbabwe. *JLS*, *37*(1), 115–128. doi:10.1080/02564718.2021.1923735

Ndlovu, S. (2021). Zimbabwe's POLAD: An Elitist Political Pact, Not a Panacea for Sustainable Peace. *Peace Review*, *33*(1), 17–25.

Ndlovu, S. (2021). Zimbabwe's Poland: A Elitist Political Pact, Not a Panacea for Sustainable Peace. *Peace Review*, *33*(1), 17–25.

Ndou, L. L. (2022). *An analysis of a coalition government: a new path in administration and governance at local government level in South Africa* (Doctoral dissertation, North-West University (South Africa)).

Ndou, L. L. (2022). *An analysis of a coalition government: a new path in administration and governance at local government level in South Africa* (Doctoral dissertation, North-West University, South Africa).

Ndou, L. L. (2022). *An analysis of a coalition government: A new path in administration and governance at local government level in South Africa*. Unpublished PhD Thesis. University of the North West, South Africa.

Ndou, L. L. (2022). *The Impact of Coalition Government on Service Delivery: City of Tshwane Metropolitan.* North West University.

Nester, W. R., & Nester, W. R. (1993). *The Shifting Balance of Political Power: Hearts, Minds and Policies.* American Power, the New World Order and the Japanese Challenge.

Netswera, M. M., & Khumalo, P. (2022). The Coalition-building Process in South Africa: Reflection on the 2021 Local Government Elections. *African Journal of Democracy and Governance, 9*(34), 103–125.

Nevin, T. (2005). We are not the ANC's lapdog—Cosatu: South Africa's government, writes Tom Nevin, is facing its biggest ever political crisis as one member of the ruling tripartite alliance, the labour movement Cosatu, is threatening to break away. *African Business,* (305). https://link.gale.com/apps/doc/A127937983/EAIM?u=anon~ee4e08ca&sid=s itemap&xid=967b63b8

Newman, S. (2004). The Place of Power in Political Discourse. *International Political Science Review / Revue internationale de science politique, 25*(2), 139-157.

Ngqulunga, B. (2017). *The Man Who Founded the ANC: A Biography of Pixley ka Isaka Seme.* Penguin Books.

Ngqulunga, B. (2020). The Changing Face of Zulu Nationalism: The Transformation of Mangosuthu Buthelezi's Politics and Public Image. *Politikon: South African Journal of Political Studies, 47*(3), 287–304. doi:10.1080/02589346.2020 .1795992

Ngubane, S. (2018). *Africa Dialogue: Complexities of Coalition Politics in Southern Africa.* https://eratrain.uct.ac.za/ converis/portal/detail/Publication/54211339?auxfun=&lang=en_GB

Ngwane, T. (2019). Insurgent democracy: Post-apartheid South Africa's freedom fighters. *Journal of Southern African Studies, 45*(1), 229–245. doi:10.1080/03057070.2019.1548136

Ngwenya, D., & Harris, G. (2015). The consequences of not healing: Evidence from the Gukurahundi violence in Zimbabwe. *AJCR, 15*(2), 35–55.

Nhede, N.T., (2012). *The Government of National Unity in Zimbabwe: challenges and obstacles to public administration.* Academic Press.

Nnol, O. I. (1986). *Introduction to Politics.* Longman.

Norris, P., Frank, R. W., & Coma, F. M. (Eds.). (2014). *Advancing electoral integrity.* Oxford University Press.

Norris, P. (2004). *Electoral Engineering: Voting Rules and Political Behaviour.* Cambridge University Press. doi:10.1017/ CBO9780511790980

Norris, P. (2012). *Making democratic governance work: How regimes shape prosperity, welfare, and peace.* Cambridge University Press. doi:10.1017/CBO9781139061902

Norton, P. (2020). Fixed-term Parliaments: Fixed or not so fixed? In Governing Britain (pp. 115-127). Manchester University Press.

Nuvunga, A. (2005). *Multiparty Democracy in Mozambique: Strengths, Weaknesses and Challenges.* EISA Report Number 14.

Nuvunga, A. (2014). *From the two-party to the dominant party system in Mozambique, 1994- 2012. Framing Frelimo party dominance in context.* PhD thesis. Erasmus University of Rotterdam.

Nuvunga, A., & Adalima, J. (2011). *Mozambique Democratic Movement (MDM): an analysis of a new opposition party in Mozambique*. Academic Press.

Nyadera, I. N., & Kisaka, M. O. (2022). The State of Israel. In *The Palgrave Handbook of Comparative Public Administration: Concepts and Cases* (pp. 567–592). Springer Nature Singapore. doi:10.1007/978-981-19-1208-5_20

Nye, J. S. (2012). China and soft power. *South African Journal of International Affairs*, *19*(2), 151–155. doi:10.1080/10220461.2012.706889

Nye, J. S. (2021). Soft power: The evolution of a concept. *Journal of Political Power*, *14*(1), 196–208. doi:10.1080/2158379X.2021.1879572

Nye, J. S. Jr. (2008). Public diplomacy and soft power. *The Annals of the American Academy of Political and Social Science*, *616*(1), 94–109. doi:10.1177/0002716207311699

Nyenhuis, R. (2020). The political struggle for 'the people': Populist discourse in the 2019 South African elections. *Commonwealth and Comparative Politics*, *58*(4), 409–432. doi:10.1080/14662043.2020.1746040

Nzimakwe, I. (2022). *Status of Coalition Governance in South African municipalities: influence of legislative and policy framework. coalition building and municipal governance in South Africa*. University KwaZulu-Natal.

Obiagu, U. C., Abada, I. M., & Mbah, P. O. (2021). Autocratization verity: Insights from democratic setbacks in Africa. *African Review (Dar Es Salaam, Tanzania)*, *48*(2), 301–332. doi:10.1163/1821889X-12340051

Oesterdiekhoff, G. W. (2015). Evolution of democracy. Psychological stages and political developments in world history. *Cultura (Iasi, Romania)*, *12*(2), 81–102. doi:10.5840/cultura201512223

Oluwasuji, O. C., & Okajare, O. E. (2021). Participatory Democracy, Local Government Elections and the Politics of the States' Ruling Parties in Nigeria. *International Journal of Research and Innovation in Social Science*, *1*, 370–378.

Olver, C. (2021). The impact of coalitions on South Africa's metropolitan administrations. *Marriages of Inconvenience: The politics of coalitions in South Africa*, 267.

Oppermann, K., & Brummer, K. (2014). Patterns of junior partner influence on the foreign policy of coalition governments. *British Journal of Politics and International Relations*, *16*(4), 555–571. doi:10.1111/1467-856X.12025

Oppermann, K., Brummer, K., & Van Willigen, N. (2017). Coalition governance and foreign policy decision-making. *European Political Science*, *16*(4), 489–501. doi:10.1057/s41304-016-0082-7

Oprea, V. B. (2014). The specific of the power relationship. *International Letters of Social and Humanistic Sciences*, (23), 45–52.

Oriaifo, J., Torres de Oliveira, R., & Ellis, K. M. (2020). Going above and beyond: How intermediaries enhance change in emerging economy institutions to facilitate small to medium enterprise development. *Strategic Entrepreneurship Journal*, *14*(3), 501–531. doi:10.1002/sej.1349

Overall, J. (2015). A conceptual framework of innovation and performance: The importance of leadership, relationship quality, and knowledge management. *Academy of Entrepreneurship Journal*, *21*(2), 41.

Oyugi, W.O. (2006) Coalition politics and coalition government in Africa. *Journal of Contemporary African Studies*, *24*(1), 53-79.

Oyugi, W. (2006). Coalition Politics and Coalition Governments in Africa: Bureaucracy and Democracy. *Journal of Contemporary African Studies*, *24*(1), 253–279. doi:10.1080/02589000500513739

Pahad, A. (2014). *Insurgent Diplomat-Civil Talks or Civil War?* Penguin Random House South Africa.

Panizza, F., Peters, B. G., & Ramos Larraburu, C. R. (2019). Roles, trust and skills: A typology of patronage appointments. *Public Administration*, *97*(1), 47–161. doi:10.1111/padm.12560

Pan, S. Y., & Lo, J. T. Y. (2017). Re-conceptualizing China's rise as a global power: A neo-tributary perspective. *The Pacific Review*, *30*(1), 1–25. doi:10.1080/09512748.2015.1075578

Papagianni, K. (2008). Participation and State Legitimation. In T. Charles (Ed.), *Building States to Build Peace*. Lynne Rienner. doi:10.1515/9781685856670-005

Patel, L. N. (2021). Political parties, alliance politics and the crisis of governance in Malawi. In S. Booysen (Ed.), *Marriages of Inconvenience: The politics of coalitions in South Africa* (p. 207). doi:10.2307/j.ctv2z6qdx6.15

Patel, R., & Patel, S. (2020). Challenges in Power Sharing in Multi-Ethnic Societies. In P. Mehta & S. Raj (Eds.), *Handbook of Political Science* (pp. 189–204). Springer.

Patel, R., & Smith, R. (2021). Coalition Governments and Peace-Building Efforts in Southern Africa: A Comparative Study. *Journal of African Politics*, *47*(2), 201–220.

Pather, R. (2016, January 14). *EFF strikes a deal with the DA: Here is how Johannesburg will look.* Retrieved from Mail & Gaurdian: https://mg.co.za/article/2016-08-17-the-effs-deal-with-the-da-in-johannesburg-and-how-the-country-will-look/

Patton, M. Q. (2005). *Qualitative research.* Encyclopedia of statistics in behavioral science.

Paudel, B. (2021). *Two-state Solution Between Israel And Palestine: Viable or Obsolete Idea* (Doctoral dissertation, Department Of International Relation & Diplomacy).

Paudel, P., Winterford, K., & Selim, Y. (2023). Exploring the Need for an Integrated Conflict Sensitivity Framework in Development Assistance that Contributes to Peaceful and Sustainable Post-conflict Societies. In *Integrated Approaches to Peace and Sustainability* (pp. 11–31). Springer Nature Singapore. doi:10.1007/978-981-19-7295-9_2

Paxton, F., & Peace, T. (2021). Window dressing? The mainstreaming strategy of the rassemblement national in power in French local government. *Government and Opposition*, *56*(3), 545–562. doi:10.1017/gov.2020.11

Pearce, G., Mawson, J., & Ayres, S. (2008). Regional governance in England: A changing role for the Government's regional offices? *Public Administration*, *86*(2), 443–463. doi:10.1111/j.1467-9299.2007.00699.x

Perry, G. E. (2023). Israel and Palestine. In *Government and Politics of the Contemporary Middle East* (pp. 255–344). Routledge. doi:10.4324/9781003198093-10

Persico, N., Pueblita, J. C., & Silverman, D. (2011). Factions and political competition. *Journal of Political Economy*, *119*(2), 242–288. doi:10.1086/660298

Peter, C. (1991). World Politics Since 1945. Longman.

Peyper, L. (2016). *Coalition-run metros will hurt service delivery.* https://www.fin24.com/Economy/coalition-run-metros-will-hurt-service-delivery-105analyst-20160707

Pieterse, M. (2019). *What's needed to fix collapsing coalitions in South Africa's cities?* Retrieved at https:www.wits.ac.za/news/latest-news/opinion/2019/2019-12/whats-needed-to-fix-collapsing-coalitions-in-south-africa-cities.html

Pieterse, M. (2019). A Year of Living Dangerously? Urban Assertiveness, Cooperative Governance and the First Year of Three Coalition-Led Metropolitan Municipalities in South Africa. *Politikon: South African Journal of Political Studies*, *46*(1), 51–70. doi:10.1080/02589346.2018.1518759

Pietersen, J. M. (2021). Assessment of Coalition Governments (2016-2021) in Metropolitan Cities of Gauteng Province Using the Theory of Democracy. *Journal of Public Administration*, *56*(3), 488–506.

Pillay, K. (2018). Service delivery protests, populism and the right to the city: Implications for urban governance and management in South Africa. *Journal of Public Affairs*, *18*(3), e1819.

Pitcher, M. A. (2020). Mozambique elections 2019: Pernicious polarisation, democratic decline, and rising authoritarianism. *African Affairs*, *119*(476), 468–486. doi:10.1093/afraf/adaa012

Plant, R. (2000). Social Justice. In R. Walker (Ed.), *Ending Child Poverty*. Policy Press.

Polovin, R. (2024). We cannot an will not forget tose who were killed on October 7. *Sunday Times*, *14*(January), 13.

Portugues, V. O. A. (2019). *Moçambique Eleições: Perfil de Ossufo Momade*. https://www.voaportugues.com/a/mo%C3%A7ambique-elei%C3%A7%C3%B5es-perfil-de-ossufo-momade/5120507.html

Pottie, D. (2001). Electoral management and democratic governance in Southern Africa. *Politikon: South African Journal of Political Studies*, *28*(2), 133–155. doi:10.1080/02589340120091628

Pottie, D. (2014). The electoral system and opposition parties in South Africa. In *Opposition and democracy in South Africa* (pp. 25–52). Routledge.

Powell, D. M., O'Donovan, M., & De Visser, J. (2015). *Civic protests barometer 2007–2014*. Dullah Omar Institute.

Przybylski, W. (2018). Explaining eastern Europe: Can Poland's backsliding be stopped? *Journal of Democracy*, *29*(3), 52–64. doi:10.1353/jod.2018.0044

Quinn, T., Bara, J., & Bartle, J. (2013). The UK coalition agreement of 2010: Who won? In *The UK General Election of 2010* (pp. 175–192). Routledge.

Rabkin, F. (2024). The Case that Woke up the World. *Sunday Times.*, *11*(January), 11.

Rahat, G., Hazan, R. Y., & Ben-Nun Bloom, P. (2016). Stable blocs and multiple identities: The 2015 elections in Israel. *Representation (McDougall Trust)*, *52*(1), 99–117. doi:10.1080/00344893.2016.1190592

Raleigh, C. & Wigmore-Shepherd, D. (2020). Elite Coalitions and Power Balance across African Regimes: Introducing the African Cabinet and Political Elite Data Project (ACPED). *Ethnopolitics*. Advance online publication. doi:10.1080/17449057.2020.1771840

Raligilia, K. H. (2017). *The impact of the CODESA talks on the socio-economic rights of the majority of South Africans* (Doctoral thesis, University of Pretoria).

Rametse, M. 2014. *The roots of factional tensions over the ANC government's policies in the ruling alliance in South Africa* (Doctoral dissertation, Murdoch University).

Randall, V. (1993). The media and democratisation in the Third World. *Third World Quarterly*, *14*(3), 625–646. doi:10.1080/01436599308420346

Rapanyane, M. B. (2022). Key Challenges Facing the African National Congress-led Government in South Africa: An Afrocentric Perspective. *Insight on Africa*, *14*(1), 57–72. doi:10.1177/09750878211049484

Raphala, M. G., & Shai, K. B. (2016). *Re-evaluating the EU's external human rights and democritisation policy: a critical analysis on Zimbabwe*. Governance in the 21st Century Organisations, the Proceedings of the 1st International Annual Conference on Public Administration and Development Alternatives (IPADA), The Park (Mokopane), South Africa.

Raynor, J. (2011). *What makes an effective coalition? Evidence-based indicators of success*. The California Endowment.

Read, M. (1993). The Place of Parliament. In The developing British Political System: 1990s. Longman.

Reddy, P. S. (2016). The politics of service delivery in South Africa: The local government sphere in context. *TD: The Journal for Transdisciplinary Research in Southern Africa, 12*(1), 1–8. doi:10.4102/td.v12i1.337

Reddy, T. (2010). ANC Decline, Social Mobilization and Political Society: Understanding South Africa's Evolving Political Culture. *Politikon: South African Journal of Political Studies, 37*(2–3), 185–206. doi:10.1080/02589346.2010.522329

Regilme, S. S. F. Jr, & Hodzi, O. (2021). Comparing US and Chinese foreign aid in the era of rising powers. *The International Spectator, 56*(2), 114–131. doi:10.1080/03932729.2020.1855904

Reilly, B. (2003). *International Electoral Assistance: A review of donor's activities and lessons learned* (Ser. Working Paper 17). The Hague: Clingendael Institute.

Reilly, B. (2015). Electoral systems. Routledge handbook of Southeast Asian democratization, 225-236.

Reiter, Y. & Feher, V. (2023). The Politics of Arab Israelis. *Polarization and Consensus-Building in Israel: The Center Cannot Hold.*

Renwick, A. (2011). *The Politics of Electoral Reform: Changing the Rules of Democracy.* Cambridge University Press.

Republic of Kenya. (2022). Political Parties Act (Amendment) 2022.

Republic of South Africa. (1993). *Interim Constitution of the Republic of South Africa 1993.* Government Printer.

Republic of South Africa. (1996). *Constitution of the Republic of South Africa 1996.* Government Printer.

Republic of South Africa. (1996). Constitution of the Republic of South Africa.

Republic of South Africa. (1996). *The Constitution of the Republic of South Africa.* Government Printers.

Republic of South Africa. (1998). *Local Government: Municipal Structures Act 117 of 1998.* Government Printer.

Republic of South Africa. (1998). *Local Government: Municipal Structures Act, 1998 (Act 117 of 1998).* Government Printers.

Republic of South Africa. (1998). *White Paper on Local Government of 1998.* Government Printer.

Resnick, D. (2013). Do electoral coalitions facilitate democratic consolidation in Africa? *Party Politics, 19*(5), 735–757. doi:10.1177/1354068811410369

Riker, W. H. (1962). *The Theory of Political Coalitions.* Yale University Press.

Roche, W. K., Teague, P., & Colvin, A. J. S. (2014). *The Oxford handbook of conflict management in organizations.* Oxford University Press. doi:10.1093/oxfordhb/9780199653676.001.0001

Rodney, W. (2018). How Europe has underdeveloped Africa. London: Bogle L' Ouverture Publications Ltd.

Roessler, P., & Ohls, D. (2018). Self-enforcing power sharing in weak states. *International Organization, 72*(2), 423–454. doi:10.1017/S0020818318000073

Rogers, D. (2019). *Two Weeks in November: The Astonishing Untold Story of the Operation that Toppled Mugabe.* Jonathan Ball Publishers.

Rolland, N. (2017). China's "Belt and Road Initiative": Underwhelming or game-changer? *The Washington Quarterly, 40*(1), 127–142. doi:10.1080/0163660X.2017.1302743

Rosário, D. (2020). *Órgãos de administração eleitoral em Moçambique: Entre a (im)parcialidade, (in)dependência e a procura de transparência nas eleições competitivas em tempos de regimes híbridos: 1994-2019. Democracia Multipartidária em Moçambique.* EISA Mozambique.

Rose, R. (1974). *The Problem of Party Government. Professor of Politics.* University of Strathclyde. The MacMillian Press.

Rosenau, J. N. (2021). Governance in the Twenty-first Century. In *Understanding Global Cooperation* (pp. 16–47). Brill. doi:10.1163/9789004462601_003

Rosenfeld, S. (2018). *Democracy and truth: A short history.* University of Pennsylvania Press.

Rosner, S. (2022). *Israel's Coalition Didn't Fail. It Set a New Bar.* Retrieved December 27, from 2023, https://www.nytimes.com/2022/07/05/opinion/israel-coalition-government-collapse.html

Roy, J. (2001). *Churchill.* Macmillian.

Rukema, J. R. (2023). Last Kicks of a Dying Horse: The Waning Influence of France in Africa. *Journal of African Foreign Affairs, 10*(2), 7–26. doi:10.31920/2056-5658/2023/v10n2a1

Russell, M. (2011). 'Never Allow a Crisis to Go to Waste': The Wright Committee Reforms to Strengthen the House of Commons. *Parliamentary Affairs, 64*(4), 612–633. doi:10.1093/pa/gsr026

Ryan, M. J. (2014). Power Dynamics in Collective Impact. *Stanford Social Innovation Review, 12*(4), A10–A11. doi:10.48558/N8Y6-E936

SABC News. (2021). *ANC's Sinah Langa elected Speaker in Modimolle–Mookgophong.* https://elections.sabc.co.za/elections2021/anc/ancs-sinah-langa-elected-speaker-in-modimolle-mookgophong/

Sachikonye, L. (2009). *Between authoritarianism and democratization: The challenges of a transition process in Zimbabwe.* Paper presented at the Centre for Political and Historical Studies on Africa and the Middle East, University of Bologna.

Sakwa, R. (2022). Democratisation. In *Routledge Handbook of Russian Politics and Society* (pp. 33–45). Routledge. doi:10.4324/9781003218234-5

Salih, M. M. A. (2003). Introduction: The Evolution of African Political Parties. In M. M. A. Salih (Ed.), *African Political Parties: Evolution.* Institutionalisation and Governance.

Salman, M., Pieper, M., & Geeraerts, G. (2015). Hedging in the Middle East and China-US Competition. *Asian Politics & Policy, 7*(4), 575–596. doi:10.1111/aspp.12225

Sandler, T. (2017). International peacekeeping operations: Burden sharing and effectiveness. *The Journal of Conflict Resolution, 61*(9), 1875–1897. doi:10.1177/0022002717708601 PMID:28989181

Sangeeta, Y. (2020). Coalition Governments in India. *Political Perspective Third Concept,* 21–31.

Saraiva, R. (2023). Adaptive Peacebuilding in Mozambique: Examples of Localized International Non-Governmental Organizations (L-INGOs) in a Complex and Uncertain Environment. In *Adaptive Peacebuilding: A New Approach to Sustaining Peace in the 21st Century* (pp. 121–150). Springer International Publishing. doi:10.1007/978-3-031-18219-8_5

Saunders, C. (2020). Visions of Unity: Southern Africa and Liberation. *Visions of African Unity: New Perspectives on the History of Pan-Africanism and African Unification Projects,* 133-155.

Saussure, F. d. (1974). Course in General Linguistics. Academic Press.

Schakel, A. H., & Jeffery, C. (2013). Are regional elections really 'second-order' elections? *Regional Studies, 47*(3), 323–341. doi:10.1080/00343404.2012.690069

Schiff, G. S. (2018). *Tradition and politics: The religious parties of Israel.* Wayne State University Press.

Schoeman, M., & Graham, S. (2020). The political economy of South Africa in a global context. In Government and Politics in South Africa: Coming of Age (pp. 141-161). Cape Town: Van Schaik Publisher.

Schragger, R. (2016). *City Power: Urban Governance in a Global Age.* Oxford University Press.

Schreiber, L. (2018). *Coalition country: South Africa after the ANC.* Tafelberg.

Schreiber, L. (2018). *Coalition country: South Africa after the ANC.* Tafelberg.

Schreiber, L. (2018). *Coalition Country: South Africa after the ANC.* Tafelberg.

Schreiber, L. (2018). *Coalition Cuntry" South Africa after the ANC.* Tafelberg.

Schrire, R. (2010). The realities of opposition in South Africa: Legitimacy, strategies and consequences. *Democratization*, *8*(1), 135–148. doi:10.1080/714000189

Schwella, E. (2017). *South African GovernanceCape Town.* Oxford University Press Southern Africa.

Scobell, A., & Nader, A. (2016). *China in the Middle East: the wary dragon.* RAND Corporation.

Seawright, D. (2013). 'Yes, the census': The 2011 UK Referendum campaign on the Alternative Vote. *British Politics*, *8*(4), 457–475. doi:10.1057/bp.2013.23

Seeletsa, M. (2022, November 8). DA's Tania Campbell re-elected as City of Ekurhuleni mayor. *The Citizen.* https://www.citizen.co.za/news/south-africa/elections/local-2021/these-are-the-hung-councils-in-south-africa/

Seidman, G. (2016). Is South Africa heading towards a mass strike? Organized labor and the political origins of the 2012 labor unrest. *Labor History*, *57*(5), 618–639.

Sekatle, K., & Sebola, M. (2020). The choice of coalition governments for promotion of national unity in Africa: Does the model work for unity and political stability? *The Business and Management Review, 11.*

Sekatle, K. M., & Sebola, M. P. (2020). The choice of coalition governments for promotion of national unity in Africa: Does the model work for unity and political stability? *The Business & Management Review*, *11*(1), 25–32. doi:10.24052/BMR/V11NU01/ART-04

Seldon, A., Finn, M., & Thoms, I. (Eds.). (2015). *The coalition effect, 2010–2015.* Cambridge University Press. doi:10.1017/CBO9781139946551

Shai, K. B. (2016). *An Afrocentric Critique of the United States of America's foreign policy towards Africa: The case studies of Ghana and Tanzania, 1990-2014.* Unpublished PhD Thesis. University of Limpopo.

Shai, K. B. (2021). From the Guest Editor: About Lies, of Truths in Public Administration Scholarship. Journal of Public Administration, 56(1), 1-2.

Shai, K.B. (2009). *Rethinking United States-South Africa Relations.* Hoedspruit: Royal B. Foundation.

Shai, K. B. (2017). South African State Capture: A Symbiotic Affair between Business and State Going Bad. *Insight on Africa*, *9*(1), 62–75. doi:10.1177/0975087816674584

Shai, K. B., & Nyawasha, T. S. (2016). A critical appraisal of the post-Cold War United States of America's foreign policy towards Kenya: An Afrocentric perspective. *Commonwealth Youth and Development*, *14*(2), 151–169. doi:10.25159/1727-7140/1925

Shai, K. B., Nyawasha, T. S., & Ndaguba, E. A. (2018). [De] constructing South Africa's Jacob Zuma led ANC: An Afrocentric perspective. *Journal of Public Affairs*, *18*(4), e1842. Advance online publication. doi:10.1002/pa.1842

Shai, K. B., & Vunza, M. (2021). Gender Mainstreaming in Peacebuilding and Localised Human Security in the Context of the Darfur Genocide: An Africentric Rhetorical Analysis. *Journal of Literary Studies*, *37*(2), 69–84. doi:10.1080/0 2564718.2021.1923715

Shai, K. B., & Zondi, S. (Eds.). (2020). *Dynamising Liberation Movements in Southern Africa: Quo Vadis?* Ziable Publisher and IPAD.

Shamir, M., & Rahat, G. (Eds.). (2022). *The Elections in Israel, 2019–2021.* Taylor & Francis. doi:10.4324/9781003267911

Sharma, A., & Verma, A. (2018). Institutional Mechanisms for Power Sharing: A Comparative Analysis. *Journal of Comparative Politics*, *21*(3), 265–283. doi:10.1007/s13398-017-0438-2

Shen, W. (2020). China's role in Africa's energy transition: A critical review of its intensity, institutions, and impacts. *Energy Research & Social Science*, *68*, 101578. doi:10.1016/j.erss.2020.101578

Shiner, C. (2004, October 28). *Challenges remain to consolidating democracy in several African countries.* Voanews. Retrieved from https://www.voanews.com/english/archive/2004-10/2004-10-28-voa38.cfm?CFID=117984128&CFT OKEN=79037326

Shivambu, F. (2014). *The Coming Revolution.* Jacana.

Sibanda, B. (2021). The language of the Gukurahundi Genocide in Zimbabwe: 1980-1987. *Journal of Literary Studies*, *37*(2), 129–145. doi:10.1080/02564718.2021.1923737

Sithanen, R. (2003). *Coalition politics under the tropics: office seekers, power makers, nation building A case study of Mauritius.* A paper presented at an Electoral Institute of Southern Africa (EISA) Roundtable: Political party coalitions - Strengthening Democracy through Party Coalition, Building Vineyard Hotel, Claremont, Cape Town, 19 June 2003. Retrieved July 1, 2021, https://aceproject.org/ero-en/topics/parties-and-candidates/mauritius.pdf

Sithole, D. (2023). Coalitions in South African local municipalities: Is the constitution enabling democracy or not? *Journal for Inclusive Public Policy*, *3*(2), 52–62.

Skjæveland, A., Serritzlev, S., & Blom-Hansen, J. (2007). Theories of coalition formation: An empirical test using data from Danish local government. *European Journal of Political Research*, *46*(5), 721–745. doi:10.1111/j.1475-6765.2007.00709.x

Smith, M. (n.d.). Compatibility of learner democracy. *De Jure Law Journal*, *1*(46) https://www.dejure.up.ac.za/articles-vol-46-1/smit-m

Smith, S. (2024). Back SA's Israel Genocide case. Mail & Guardian.

Smith, A. (2020). *The Economic Importance of Johannesburg.* WorldAtlas.

South Africa. (1996). *The Constitution of the Republic of South Africa as adopted by the Constitutional Assembly on 8 May 1996 and as amended on 11 October 1996.* Government Printers.

South Africa. (1996). *The Constitution of The Republic of South Africa of 1996.* Government Printers.

South Africa. (2000). *Local Government Electoral Act of 2000.* Government Printers.

South African History Online. (2018). *South African Government of National Unity (GNU) – 1994-1999.* https://www.sahistory.org.za/article/south-african-government-national-unity-gnu-1994-1999

South African Local Government Association. (2022). *A Framework for Coalitions in Local Government*. https://dulla-homarinstitute.org.za/multilevel-govt/publications/04112021-a-framework-for-coalitions-in-local-government-1.pdf/view

Southall, R. (2013). Liberation movements as governments in Africa. *Representation (McDougall Trust)*, *49*(4), 447–461.

Southall, R. (2014). *Liberation Movements in Power: Part & State in Southern Africa*. University of KwaZulu-Natal.

Southall, R. (2017). From liberation movement to party machine? The ANC in South Africa. In *Post-colonial struggles for a democratic Southern Africa* (pp. 61–78). Routledge.

Southall, R. (2019). Electoral systems and democratization in Africa. In *Voting for Democracy* (pp. 19–36). Routledge. doi:10.4324/9780429428036-2

Sparks, A. (1996). *Tomorrow is another country: The inside story of South Africa's road to change*. University of Chicago Press.

Spoon, J. J., & Klüver, H. (2017). Does anybody notice? How policy positions of coalition parties are perceived by voters. *European Journal of Political Research*, *56*(1), 115–132. doi:10.1111/1475-6765.12169

Sriram, C. L. (2008). Justice as peace? Liberal peacebuilding and strategies of transitional justice. *Global Society*, *21*(4), 579–591. doi:10.1080/13600820701562843

Stapleton, S., Biygautane, T., Bhasin, T., & Hallward, M. C. (2023). Democracy Under Occupation: Coalition Government Formation and Survival in Iraq and Palestine. *Middle East Law and Governance*, *15*(3), 398–422. doi:10.1163/18763375-20231397

Stats, S. A. (2022). *Provinces At a Glance*. Tshwane.

Steeves, J. (2007). Presidential succession in Kenya: The transition from Moi to Kibaki. *Commonwealth and Comparative Politics*, *44*(2), 211–233. doi:10.1080/14662040600831651

Steinberg, J. (2014). Policing, state power, and the transition from apartheid to democracy: A new perspective. *African Affairs*, *113*(451), 173–191. doi:10.1093/afraf/adu004

Stieb, J. (2019). *The Regime Change Consensus: Iraq in American Politics, 1990-2003*. The University of North Carolina at Chapel Hill.

Strøm, K. (2017). *Parliamentary democracy and delegation*. Oxford University Press.

Strøm, K., & Müller, W. C. (1999). Political Parties and Hard Choices. In *Policy, Office, or Votes? How Political Parties in Western Europe Make Hard Decisions*. Cambridge University Press. doi:10.1017/CBO9780511625695.001

Strom, K., & Nyblade, B. (2007). Coalition theory and government formation. In C. Boix & S. Stokes (Eds.), *The Oxford handbook of comparative politics* (pp. 782–802). Oxford University Press.

Sumich, J. (2020). 'Just another African country': Socialism, capitalism and temporality in Mozambique. *Third World Quarterly*, *42*(3), 582–598. doi:10.1080/01436597.2020.1788933

Swana, S. (2024). SA takes Israel to the International Court of Justice for Genocide. Sunday World.

Tannam, E. (2001). Explaining the Good Friday agreement: A learning process. *Government and Opposition*, *36*(4), 493–518. doi:10.1111/1477-7053.00078

Terreblanche, S. (2012). *Lost in Transformation: South Africa's search for a New Future since 1986*. KMM Review Publishing Company.

Thakur, S. S., & Nel, A. (2023). Alter-nation? Factions, coalitions and environmental governance in the context of contested post-apartheid local state democratisation. In *Urban Forum* (pp. 1-20). Springer Netherlands.

Thakur, S. S., & Nel, A. (2023, December). Alter-nation? Factions, Coalitions and Environmental Governance in the Context of Contested Post-apartheid Local State Democratisation. In *Urban Forum* (pp. 1-20). Springer Netherlands.

The City of Joburg. (n.d.). *The state of financial management and governance in municipalities with coalition government: A case for constructive coalition governance.* https://www.parliament.gov.za/storage/app/media/Pages/2020/september/02-092020_National_Council_of_Provinces_Local_Government_Week/docs/session6/The_State_of_Financial_Management_and_Governance_in_Municipalities_with_Coalition_Government.pdf

The Coalition Agreement for Stability and Reform. (2015). *Lesotho's Second Coalition Government Agreement.* Author.

The Coalition. (2010). *Our Programme for Government.* London Her Majestry's Government.

The Constitution of Lesotho. (1993). *The Constitution of Lesotho.* Government Printer.

The National Democratic Institute & The Oslo Centre for Peace and Human Rights. (2015). *Coalitions: A guide for political parties.* NDI & Oslo Centre.

The Post Newspaper. (2015, Apr. 16). *The Collapse of Lesotho First Coalition Government.* Author.

Thies, F. F. (2001). Keeping Tabs on Partners: The Logic of Delegation in Coalition Governments. *American Journal of Political Science*, *45*(3), 580–598. doi:10.2307/2669240

Thomas, G. W. (2012). Governance, good governance, and global governance: conceptual and actual challenges. In *Thinking about global governance* (pp. 168–189). Routledge.

Thornber, K. L. (2016). Breaking Discipline, Integrating Literature: Africa–China Relationships Reconsidered. *Comparative Literature Studies*, *53*(4), 694–721. doi:10.5325/complitstudies.53.4.0694

Thwala, P. (2022). Do Coalitions Have a Future in South Africa? Presentation to the *Mpumalanga Legislature Management Colloquium.*

Timmermans, A. (2003). *Standing Apart and Sitting Together: Enforcing Coalition Agreements in Multiparty Systems.* AECPA.

Tinarwo, J., & Babu, S. C. (2023). Chinese and Indian economic relations and development assistance to Zimbabwe: Rationale, controversies and significance. *Journal of International Development*, *35*(4), 655–667. doi:10.1002/jid.3704

Tladi, M. (2020). *Is the Place of Power Empty? Reading Claude Lefort in South Africa.* University of the Witwatersrand.

Tordoff, W. (1988). Parties in Zambia. In V. Randall (Ed.), *Political Parties in the Third World.* Sage Publications.

Truter, J. (2023). *The National Democratic Revolution: A 'Utopian' Blueprint for South Africa.* Academic Press.

Tsebelis, G. (1995). Decision-making in political systems: Veto players in presidentialism, parliamentarism, multilateralism and multipartyism. *British Journal of Political Science*, *25*(3), 289–325. doi:10.1017/S0007123400007225

Tselane, N. (2023). *Regulation of coalition governments in South Africa. Concept Document.* Institute of Election Management in Africa.

Tselane, N. (2023). *Regulation of coalition governments in South Africa. Concept Document. Institute of Election Management Services in South Africa.* IEMSA.

Tshabangu, I. (2024). The Quest for Democratic Citizenship: Contestations and Geopolitical Contradictions. In N. Tshishonga & I. Tshabangu (Eds.), *Democratization of Africa and Its Impact on the Global Economy* (pp. 1–17). IGI. doi:10.4018/979-8-3693-0477-8.ch001

Tshishonga, N. S. (2024). Continental Integration and Trade in the Southern African Development Community (SADC). In N. Tshishonga & I. Tshabangu (Eds.), *Democratization of Africa and Its Impact on the Global Economy* (pp. 238–260). IGI. doi:10.4018/979-8-3693-0477-8.ch014

Turok, I. (2017). Johannesburg: Warts and All. Urban Forum.

Tutu, D. (1999). *No future without forgiveness.* University of Michigan: Doubleday. doi:10.1111/j.1540-5842.1999.tb00012.x

Twala, C., & Kompi, B. (2012). The Congress of South African Trade Unions (COSATU) and the Tripartite Alliance: A marriage of (in) convenience? *Journal of Contemporary History*, *37*(1), 171–190.

UN Envoy. (2023). *Israeli-Palestinian death toll highest since 2005: UN envoy.* UN.

Unger, C., Mar, K. A., & Gürtler, K. (2020). A club's contribution to global climate governance: The Case of the Climate and Clean Air Coalition. *Palgrave Communications*, *6*(1), 99. doi:10.1057/s41599-020-0474-8

United We Stand. (2021). *Coalition Government in the UK.* https://www.Instituteforgovernment.org.uk/publication/united-we-stand

Varieties of Democracy. (2020). *Clean Elections Index.* Varieties of Democracy V-Dem.

Vercesi, M. (2016). Coalition Politics and Inter-Party Conflict Management: A Theoretical Framework. *Politics & Policy*, *44*(2), 168–219. doi:10.1111/polp.12154

Vermeulen, L. (2019). A domum naturalia for public administration in a university structure. *Journal of Public Administration*, *54*(2).

Vines, A. (2017). Afonso Dhlakama and RENAMO's return to armed conflict since 2013: the politics of reintegration in Mozambique. *A. Themnér, Warlord democrats in Africa Ex-military leaders and electoral politics*, 121-152

Vines, A. (2021). Violence, Peacebuilding, and Elite Bargains in Mozambique Since Independence. In T. McNamee & M. Muyangwa (Eds.), *The State of Peacebuilding in Africa: Lessons Learned for Policymakers and Practitioners* (pp. 321–342). Springer International Publishing. doi:10.1007/978-3-030-46636-7_18

Von Holdt, K. (2013). South Africa: The transition to violent democracy. *Review of African Political Economy*, *40*(138), 589–604. doi:10.1080/03056244.2013.854040

Von Neumann, I., & Morgenstern, O. (1953). *Theory of games and economic behaviour.* Princeton University.

Voon, J. P., & Xu, X. (2020). Impact of the Belt and Road Initiative on China's soft power: Preliminary evidence. *Asia-Pacific Journal of Accounting & Economics*, *27*(1), 120–131. doi:10.1080/16081625.2020.1686841

Waldmeir, P. (1997). *Anatomy of a miracle: The end of apartheid and the birth of the new South Africa.* WW Norton & Company.

Waldron, J. (2020). Separation of powers in thought and practice? *Revista de Direito Administrativo*, *279*(3), 17–53. doi:10.12660/rda.v279.2020.82914

Wall, J. A. Jr, & Callister, R. R. (1995). Conflict and its management. *Journal of Management*, *21*(3), 515–558. doi:10.1177/014920639502100306

Wang, X., Xu, W., & Guo, L. (2018). The status quo and ways of STEAM education promoting China's future social sustainable development. *Sustainability (Basel)*, *10*(12), 4417. doi:10.3390/su10124417

Weber, M. (1978). *Economy and Society: An outline of interpretive sociology.* University of California Press.

Weimer, B., & Carrilho, J. (2017). *Political economy of decentralisation in Mozambique— Dynamics, Outcomes, Challenges.* IESE.

Weiner, M. (2010). *Power, protest, and the public schools: Jewish and African American struggles in New York City.* Rutgers University Press.

Welsh, D. (1992). Hamlet without the Prince: The Codesa impasse. *Indicator South Africa*, *9*(4), 15–22.

Welz, M. (2021). *Africa Since Decolonisation: A History and Politics of a Diverse ContinentCambridge.* Cambridge University Press. doi:10.1017/9781108599566

Wert, J. J. (2010). With a little help from a friend: Habeas Corpus and the Magna Carta after Runnymede. *PS, Political Science & Politics*, *43*(3), 475–478. doi:10.1017/S1049096510000600

Wijaya, A. F., Kartika, R., Zauhar, S., & Mardiyono, M. (2019). Perspective merit system on placement regulation of high level official civil servants. *HOLISTICA–Journal of Business and Public Administration*, *10*(2), 187–206. doi:10.2478/hjbpa-2019-0025

Williams, S. & Scott, P. (2016). The UK coalition government 2010–15: An Overview. *Employment Relations Under Coalition Government*, 3-26.

Williams, C., & Papa, M. (2020). Rethinking "Alliances": The Case of South Africa as a Rising Power. *African Security*, *13*(4), 325–352. doi:10.1080/19392206.2020.1871796

Wilson, W. (2003). The study of public administration. *Communication Researchers and Policy-Making, 61.*

Wofford, J. C. (1982). An Integrative Theory of Leadership. *Journal of Management*, *8*(1), 27–47. doi:10.1177/014920638200800102

Woods, N. (2008). Whose aid? Whose influence? China, emerging donors and the silent revolution in development assistance. *International Affairs*, *84*(6), 1205–1221. doi:10.1111/j.1468-2346.2008.00765.x

Wootliff, R. (2020). Israel calls 4th election in 2 years as Netanyahu-Gantz coalition collapses. *Times of Israel.*

World Bank Group. (2020). *Global Economic Prospect: Slow Growth, Policy Challenges.* Retrieved May 20 2021 from: file:///C:/Users/UTAH/Desktop/ Global%20economic%20prospects%202020.pdf

Yang, R. (2010). Soft power and higher education: An examination of China's Confucius Institutes. *Globalisation, Societies and Education*, *8*(2), 235–245. doi:10.1080/14767721003779746

Yellinek, R., Mann, Y., & Lebel, U. (2020). Chinese Soft-Power in the Arab world–China's Confucius Institutes as a central tool of influence. *Comparative Strategy*, *39*(6), 517–534. doi:10.1080/01495933.2020.1826843

Yerankar, S. (2015). Coalition politics in India. *Indian Journal of Poultry Science*, *76*(3), 402–406.

Yermek, B., Zhanna, K., Dinara, B., Gulzhazira, M., Gulim, K., & Lidiya, B. (2020). Human dignity-the basis of human rights to social protection. *Wisdom*, (3 (16)), 143–155.

Yeung, H. W. C. (2017). Governing the market in a globalizing era: Developmental states, global production networks and inter-firm dynamics in East Asia. In *Global Value Chains and Global Production Networks* (pp. 70–101). Routledge.

Yigit, S. (2022). Cicero and the Art of Rhetoric. In *Media Literacy Forum, Social Sciences in the Age of Digital Transformation Proceedings Book*. Iksad Publications.

Yiğit, S. (2015). 2010 Labour Party Leadership Election. Alternatives. *Turkish Journal of International Relations*, *14*(3), 26–35. doi:10.21599/atjir.20754

Yohannes, O. (2002). The United States and Sub-Saharan Africa After the Cold War: Empty Promises and Retreat. *The Black Scholar*, *32*(1), 23–44. doi:10.1080/00064246.2002.11431168

Yu, H. (2020). Motivation behind China's 'One Belt, One Road' initiatives and establishment of the Asian infrastructure investment bank. In *China's New Global Strategy* (pp. 3–18). Routledge. doi:10.4324/9780429317002-2

Zahariadis, N., & Exadaktylos, T. (2016). Policies that succeed and programs that fail: Ambiguity, conflict, and crisis in Greek higher education. *Policy Studies Journal: the Journal of the Policy Studies Organization*, *44*(1), 59–82. doi:10.1111/psj.12129

Zahorik, J. (2018). Ethiopia and the colonial discourse. In Colonialism on the Margins of Africa. Routledge.

Zahorik, J. (2018). Ethiopia and the colonial discourse. In J. Zahorik & L. Piknerova (Eds.), *Colonialism on the Margins of Africa*. Routledge.

Zahorik, J., & Piknerova, L. (Eds.). (2018). *Colonialism on the Margins of Africa*. Routledge.

Zanotti, J. (2021). Israel: Background and US relations in brief (Vol. 16). Congressional Research Service.

Zhang, D. (2018). The concept of 'community of common destiny' in China's diplomacy: Meaning, motives and implications. *Asia & the Pacific Policy Studies*, *5*(2), 196–207. doi:10.1002/app5.231

Zhan, M. (2009). *Other-worldly: Making Chinese medicine through transnational frames*. Duke University Press.

Zhu, Z. (2016). *China's new diplomacy: Rationale, strategies and significance*. Routledge. doi:10.4324/9781315260440

Zreik, M. (2021a). China and Europe in Africa: Competition or Cooperation? *Malaysian Journal of International Relations, 9*(1), 51-67.

Zreik, M. (2019). China's Involvement in The Syrian Crisis and The Implications of Its Neutral Stance in The War. *RUDN. Journal of Political Science*, *21*(1), 56–65.

Zreik, M. (2021b). Academic Exchange Programs between China and the Arab Region: A Means of Cultural Harmony or Indirect Chinese Influence? *Arab Studies Quarterly*, *43*(2), 172–188. doi:10.13169/arabstudquar.43.2.0172

Zreik, M. (2022). The Chinese presence in the Arab region: Lebanon at the heart of the Belt and Road Initiative. *International Journal of Business and Systems Research*, *16*(5-6), 644–662. doi:10.1504/IJBSR.2022.125477

Zreik, M. (2023). Navigating the Dragon: China's Ascent as a Global Power Through Public Diplomacy. In S. Kavoğlu & E. Köksoy (Eds.), *Global Perspectives on the Emerging Trends in Public Diplomacy* (pp. 50–74). IGI Global. doi:10.4018/978-1-6684-9161-4.ch003

About the Contributors

Ndwakhulu Stephen Tshishonga (PhD) is an Africanist academic and a research fellow within the School of Built Environment & Development Studies at the University of KwaZulu-Natal. He specialises in Community Development, local economic development, local governance and citizenship, and African Politics. Over the past two decades, more than 50 scholarly papers and book chapters were contributed to local and international journals and edited books. His academic citizenship includes presenting at both national and international conferences as well engaging government departments in policy issues relating governance, democracy and professionalising community development in South Africa. He is also a Lead for Global Citizenship and Children's Rights Network (GLOCCRIN) and a Political Analysist on African and international Political Affairs.

* * *

Mukesh Shankar Bharti is a research scholar with a research background in foreign policy analysis and social science research. The author holds a PhD degree in International Relations with a specialization in East and Central Europe. His research area includes democracy, political institutions, European Union and South Asia.

Sushant Shankar Bharti is a research scholar with a research background in the Global South and South Asia. He has published many articles in the peer review journal.

Thamsanqa Buys holds a master's degree in Public Management from the University of Pretoria. As a doctoral candidate in Public Affairs with the Tshwane University of Technology where he is currently employed as a lecturer, he is an emerging scholar having contributed to several articles and book chapters nearing publication. Buys is a member of the South African Association of Public Administration and Management and has presented at national conferences including at the South African Local Government Association's Professionalization Indaba. He shares an interest in public policy, local government, higher education and governance.

José Alberto Daniel Chemane is an Applied Ethnomusicologist, drummer, percussionist and educator, born and raised in Maputo, Mozambique. On early age, he developed passion and interest in indigenous music and dance from Mozambique, later becoming an active performer and advocate. He has performed and conducted workshops extensively in Mozambique and abroad. Since 2011, he has been a part-time lecturer of African Music and Dance at University of KwaZulu-Natal. In 2015 he was a member of Local arrangement committee for the 2015 ICTM-First International African Music Symposium held at UKZN. In 2018, he conducted a workshop presentation and performed with Ikusasa lethu at PASMAE International Conference, Seychelles. In August this year, he presented a paper at the ICTM's 47th World conference, Legon, Ghana. José holds a Master of Art Degree in Applied Ethnomusicology and is currently a PhD student in Music at University of KwaZulu-Natal.

Maximino Costumado, with over ten years of experience, has contributed significantly to academia, research, and community development in countries such as Canada, Mozambique and South Africa. Currently, a Community Development lecturer and researcher at the School of Built Environment and Development Studies (SOBEDS), University of Kwazulu Natal (UKZN), Maximino specializes in diverse research areas, including good governance, community mapping, demographics, sustainable development, and public health. His skills encompass designing research instruments, data analysis, technical report preparation, and youth mentoring. A dedicated professional, Maximino is committed to advancing knowledge in Community Development and governance systems. He is a PhD candidate in Community Development at SOBEDS, UKZN, and he holds a master's in population studies.

Delma Da Silva is a Senior Programme Manager with a proven track record of working in the development industry with national and international non-governmental organizations in the design and implementation of programmes and projects to promote good governance and transparency in Mozambique. Interested and active in the field of evidence-based advocacy throughout her more than 10 years of professional career, Delma has been involved in various programs, forums and platforms on issues related to Good Governance, Civic Engagement, Human Rights, Elections and Political Participation of Women and Youth, Gender, at national and international level having gained extensive experience working with various development partners, including public institutions at national and local level in Mozambique. In recent years she has been involved in consultancy in the area of development, having participated in research and studies on Governance and elections, Social Accountability, Human Rights, Gender, as well as Program Evaluations and Capacity Building oriented towards civil society actors and government institutions. Delma has a degree in Public Administration from Eduardo Mondlane University, a Master's degree in Strategic Management from the School of Higher Studies and Business and holds a Master's degree in Management, specializing in Governance and Public Policy from the Wits School of Governance in Johannesburg. Her dissertation was on electoral integrity in the context of Mozambique.

Thokozani Ian Nzimakwe is a senior lecturer in the School of Management, IT and Governance at the University of KwaZulu-Natal, South Africa. His research interests include governance, electronic governance and ICT applications in public sector settings.

Lebotsa Khutso Piet holds the following academic qualifications: Bachelor's degree of Development Studies, Bachelor of Development Honours in Planning and Management, a Masters degree of Development in Planning and Management all from the from the University of Limpopo. An emerging researcher with interest in the field of Development studies, Public Administration, Governance and South African Politics. Published and co-authored journal articles and participated in research conferences such as University of Limpopo, Faculty of Management and Law 5th and 6th Annual Research Day. Also, In 2022, participated and presented a research paper at the 21st Annual South African Association of Public Administration and Management (SAAPAM) and won an award for best research paper under the theme: University Education. Currently pursuing corporate experience in the field of community development. In 2023, worked at the Independent Electoral Commission (IEC) Limpopo Provincial Office as an outreach and communication intern and presently working at Northam Booysendal Platinum Mine as a stakeholder engagement intern. The zeal to get exposure within the corporate space speaks to the scientific findings identified in his masters dissertation about the flaws of academics to inculcate and impart practical knowledge to students and hurdle of graduates in transcending into the corporate space.

Daniel Nkosinathi Mlambo (Ph.D.) holds a Postgraduate Diploma in Teacher Education from the Haaga-Helia University of Applied Sciences School of Vocational Teacher Education (Finland), a Ph.D. and Master's degree in Public Administration, an honours in International Relations, and a junior degree in Development Studies all from the University of Zululand. His research focuses on African Political Economy, Regional Integration, Governance and Democracy, Migration, and Security Studies. He is currently a Post-Doctoral Research Fellow in the Office of the Executive Dean (Faculty of Humanities) at the Tshwane University of Technology (TUT) under the sponsorship of the National Institute for the Humanities and Social Sciences (NIHSS). His broad research interest under the NIHSS fellowship (2022-2024) will be on State Capacity and Institutional Building in South Africa.

Thabo Saul has the ability to work under pressure and meet deadlines, good understanding of policies and procedures, conflict management skills, negotiation skills, planning skills, time management, leadership skills, change management, project management, people skills, interpersonal skills, total quality management and excellent analytical thinking abilities are just some of his strengths. He is a person of integrity, fairness, team player, service oriented, action oriented, proactive, shows initiative, performance driven, sense of urgency, approachable, honesty, tolerant, respect for individuals, trustworthiness, demonstrates patience and firmness are just some of my good qualities.

Mohale Ernest Selelo holds a position as a Part-Time Lecturer in the Department of Development Planning and Management at the University of Limpopo in South Africa. Mr Selelo is presently pursuing a doctoral degree (Doctor of Administration in Planning and Management) at the University of Limpopo. In 2017, he acted as a mentor at the School of Economics and Management at the University of Limpopo. He is a committed and emerging young researcher in the realm of development and public administration. Therefore, he has authored numerous articles in reputable journals and conference papers approved by DHET. His writings primarily centre on development studies, politics, education, fourth industrial revolution and public administration.

Mpho Tladi is a Specialist in Strategy and Research who uses empirical evidence and research to inform future strategic direction and promote optimal organisational performance. He has developed strong analytical, report writing, and perception management skills that enable the delivery of impactful results and insights. Mr Mpho Tladi is also a PhD Candidate in Political Studies at the University of the Witwatersrand, where he explores the dynamics of power, democracy and coalition governance. He has published my work in peer-reviewed journals and received multiple scholarships and awards for academic excellence. He is passionate about advancing knowledge and innovation in the field of political theory and practice and seeks transformative opportunities to apply his expertise and contribute to positive social change.

Sureyya Yigit is a Professor of Politics and International Relations at the School of Politics and Diplomacy at New Vision University in Tbilisi, Georgia. He received his B.Sc. (Econ) in International Relations from the London School of Economics, his M. Phil in International Relations from Cambridge University, and his Ph.D. from Donetsk National University. He has lectured at several universities in Scandinavia, Turkey, and Central Asia. His current research interests focus on Sustainable Development, Soft Power and foreign policy, African development and post-communist transition. He is a consultant at Aeropodium as well as senior consultant to ZDS Women's Democracy Network in the Kyrgyz Republic. He is also a member of the Editorial Board for the three volume IGI Book Series on Conflict Management as well as an Associate Editor for the International Journal of Green Business. His most recent book is "Africa at Crossroads: Society, Security and Geopolitics" published in 2024.

Mohamad Zreik, a Postdoctoral Fellow at Sun Yat-sen University, is a recognized scholar in International Relations, specializing in China's Arab-region foreign policy. His recent work in soft power diplomacy compares China's methods in the Middle East and East Asia. His extensive knowledge spans Middle Eastern Studies, China-Arab relations, East Asian and Asian Affairs, Eurasian geopolitics, and Political Economy, providing him a unique viewpoint in his field. Dr. Zreik is a proud recipient of a PhD from Central China Normal University (Wuhan). He's written numerous acclaimed papers, many focusing on China's Belt and Road Initiative and its Arab-region impact. His groundbreaking research has established him as a leading expert in his field. Presently, he furthers his research on China's soft power diplomacy tactics at Sun Yat-sen University. His significant contributions make him a crucial figure in understanding contemporary international relations.

Index

A

Africa 1-3, 5-7, 14, 17-18, 20-33, 35-37, 46-48, 74-77, 80-99, 102-110, 112-124, 127, 135, 138-141, 143-155, 157-162, 165-166, 168-175, 179, 181-186, 188-190, 194-195, 197-199, 201-203, 205-222, 224-226, 229-230, 240-244, 246-264, 266-269, 272-275, 277-283, 285, 288, 290, 293-306, 308-313, 316-336

African National Congress (ANC) 26, 81-82, 98-99, 102, 108, 209, 223, 247, 249, 252-255, 262, 264, 278, 285, 293, 295, 299, 304, 317, 324, 334, 336

Alliance 1, 16, 18, 32, 37, 39-41, 49, 56, 65, 67, 77-80, 90, 101, 111, 113, 116-119, 125, 128, 131, 135, 145, 148, 156, 159, 170, 179, 189-191, 209, 224, 229, 240, 247, 253-255, 257-259, 264, 267-268, 277-280, 285, 290, 293-299, 301, 304, 306-307, 309, 317-318, 324, 330

ANC 26, 80-82, 84-85, 87, 90-91, 96, 98-99, 102, 108, 113-114, 116-122, 138, 147-148, 152, 166, 169, 171, 189-193, 195, 198, 209, 223-224, 226-227, 234, 240, 242, 247, 249, 252, 254-255, 257, 259, 261-262, 264-265, 267, 271-273, 275, 277-281, 285, 288, 290, 293-304, 306-307, 309, 311, 313, 317-319, 321-324, 329, 334, 336

ANC in South Africa 262, 298

Asymmetry in Relations 221

B

Britain 7-9, 11-12, 14, 45, 51, 53-57, 69-72, 153, 229, 266-267, 280

C

Cabinet 3-5, 8-12, 14-15, 24, 30, 34, 37, 41, 53, 61, 66, 73, 77-78, 81, 118, 127, 129-130, 132-133, 163-164, 179, 190, 278, 284, 287, 290, 292, 314, 335

Campaign 34, 59, 62, 69, 71-73, 82, 100, 133, 159, 190, 278

Challenges 6, 9, 11, 13-16, 18, 20, 22-28, 31, 37-40, 42, 47-48, 50-51, 53, 69, 74-75, 84-88, 90, 92, 95-97, 100-102, 104-105, 107-108, 110, 122, 144-146, 151, 153-154, 157-158, 163, 165, 167, 170-171, 173-175, 178-185, 196, 198, 200, 208, 223-226, 229, 231, 234-235, 237-238, 242, 247, 249-250, 252, 256-259, 262, 264, 270-273, 277, 279, 291, 295, 297, 304, 307-310, 312, 317-318, 322, 324-328, 330, 333-335

China in Africa 201, 217

City of Johannesburg 113-114, 119-120, 159, 188-189, 191, 193, 195, 198-199, 223, 225-226, 228, 235, 237-239, 241-242, 244, 301, 304-307, 317, 324, 326, 329

Claude Lefort 223, 242, 244

Coalition 1-19, 22-24, 26-27, 29-33, 35-56, 59-61, 63-64, 66-96, 101-105, 107, 110-165, 167-175, 179-186, 188-191, 193-199, 201-203, 205, 209-211, 213-216, 219, 222-226, 228-230, 234-244, 246-266, 269-275, 277-281, 285-303, 305-314, 316-319, 322-326, 328-336

Coalition Governance 10, 22, 30-31, 33-37, 47-48, 71, 74-75, 77, 80, 83, 86-88, 92-94, 104-105, 107, 111, 124, 127-128, 139, 141, 144, 155-156, 165, 172-175, 182, 184, 196-198, 224, 229, 237-238, 243, 247-251, 254-256, 258-260, 264-270, 272, 274, 290-292, 296, 300, 304-305, 307, 310, 312-314, 332

Coalition Government 1-5, 7-16, 19, 23, 26-27, 34-36, 38-42, 44-48, 51, 53-55, 59, 61, 64, 70-71, 73, 77-80, 83, 86-88, 90, 101, 124-126, 128-136, 138-139, 141-142, 144-146, 148, 152, 156, 158-160, 162-165, 167-168, 170-171, 174, 179-180, 182, 184, 188-191, 193-194, 196-199, 209-210, 215, 219, 223, 225, 229, 234, 237-239, 242-244, 246, 248, 254-255, 257, 264-265, 267-268, 271-275, 277-278, 281, 285-289, 291-293, 295-299, 301-305, 307-314, 317-318, 322, 329-336

Coalition Partners 3-5, 8, 10, 12, 37, 53, 66-67, 69, 83, 116, 119, 130, 134, 137, 144-145, 149, 152-153, 156-158, 162-163, 166-169, 173-175, 182-183, 193, 205, 210, 213, 234, 237-238, 247, 254, 256, 258, 263, 266, 269-270, 288, 294-296, 304-306, 310, 318-319, 324-326, 329

Coalition Politics 7, 17, 19, 23-24, 27, 32, 36, 50, 72-73, 88-89, 93-94, 104, 112-116, 119-121, 123, 126-127, 130, 135-137, 140-141, 144, 146-147, 150-154, 161, 169-171, 175, 181, 183-184, 186, 193-196, 198, 201-203, 205, 209-211, 213-216, 222-225, 228, 230, 234, 236-239, 243, 250, 253, 259, 263, 266, 269, 273-274, 277, 297-298, 301, 303, 309, 311-312, 314, 318, 326, 332, 335

Coalitions 1-5, 7-9, 11-15, 17-19, 22-24, 28-32, 34-35, 37-38, 43, 46-49, 53-54, 61, 66-69, 74, 77-83, 85-87, 89-90, 93-95, 97-98, 102-103, 105-108, 112-121, 123-134, 136-141, 144-155, 157-161, 163, 165-171, 181, 189-191, 193-199, 201-203, 205, 210-211, 213, 215-216, 223-226, 228-230, 234-235, 237, 239-244, 247, 253-255, 257, 259-260, 263-275, 278-280, 286-295, 297-298, 300-303, 305-307, 309-313, 317-318, 323-326, 328-333, 335-336

Co-Governance 74-75, 77, 326

Collaborative Governance 188, 194-195, 199

Colonialism of a Special Type 280, 299

Comparative Analysis 54, 88, 93, 146, 182, 184, 186, 201, 211, 216, 222, 226, 333

Compromise 3-4, 7, 10-13, 34, 37, 58, 66, 73, 82, 84-86, 96, 110, 113, 126, 133, 158, 166, 168, 179, 183, 205, 210, 222, 237, 247, 251, 253, 255, 258, 262-263, 266-268, 270, 298, 301, 304, 309-310, 322

Congress of South African Trade Unions 116, 209, 253, 293, 295, 298-299

Conservative Party 8-9, 50, 58, 72, 267, 308

Consociationalism 186, 251, 259

Consolidating Democracy 9, 13, 19, 31, 124

Constitution 15, 34, 36, 38-39, 41-42, 44-45, 51, 60, 62, 65-66, 69, 71, 81, 84-86, 94, 97, 103-104, 106, 119, 122, 127, 160-162, 170-171, 179 180, 188-189, 195-196, 199, 224, 235, 241, 247, 253, 263-265, 268-269, 275, 281-282, 284-287, 299, 303, 313, 316, 319, 325-326, 329, 335

Corruption 36, 46, 49, 79, 81-82, 101, 103-104, 111, 113-114, 154, 180, 195, 205, 234, 241-242, 249, 252, 262, 267, 285, 294, 300-301, 303, 311, 317, 322, 327-328, 330, 333-334

COSATU 116-117, 209, 253, 277-280, 293-295, 297-299

Cultural Exchange 211, 215, 222

D

Democracy 1-4, 8-9, 13, 17, 19, 21-22, 25-35, 38, 43-53, 58-59, 67, 70-71, 74-75, 79-80, 83, 85-90, 93-95, 97-105, 107-111, 117, 119-120, 123-126, 131-135, 137-144, 146-147, 154-155, 160-161, 163-164, 170, 178, 183-186, 188-191, 194-197, 199, 201-202, 205, 210, 217-218, 220, 222, 224, 226-229, 231-234, 236, 239-244, 246-249, 251-254, 257-265, 271-273, 275, 278-280, 285-288, 292-293, 296-298, 303, 306-307, 312-313, 316-319, 322-323, 325-328, 331, 333, 335-336

Democratic Alliance (DA) 113, 148, 189, 224, 247, 254-255, 264, 301, 317-318, 324

Democratic Consolidation 2, 18, 26, 31, 162, 173, 188, 195, 199, 298

Democratic Governance 18, 20, 22, 25-28, 35, 74-75, 77, 80, 84-87, 93, 95-97, 99, 103, 105-106, 108-109, 126, 131, 134, 143, 175, 179-181, 185, 201, 203, 210-211, 219, 222, 232, 241, 251-253, 302, 316, 327-328

Democratic Principles 20, 26, 43, 83, 101-102, 104, 181, 188, 195, 197, 199, 222, 230, 241, 252, 257

Democratic Values 24, 87, 97, 102, 104-105, 111, 180, 193-194, 256, 262, 268, 326-327, 330

Democratization 17-20, 22, 27, 29, 31-32, 88, 90-91, 95-97, 107-110, 217-218, 246, 248, 250, 257, 259-260, 262

Devolution 55-56, 60, 71, 184, 186

Domestic Politics 50

Dominant-Party System 98, 125, 143

E

Economic Freedom Fighters (EFF) 99, 113, 149, 159, 189, 193, 224, 247, 254-256, 264, 290, 301, 304, 324

Election System 92, 130, 281

Elections 2-4, 7-11, 14-15, 17-20, 22-23, 25-30, 32, 34-36, 38-39, 42-43, 45, 48, 50, 55-59, 61-62, 64-70, 72, 74-79, 82-83, 85-90, 93-102, 104-110, 113-114, 116-120, 124-126, 128-129, 131, 139, 141-143, 145, 154, 157-167, 169-173, 179, 183-185, 187-190, 194-196, 198-199, 223-224, 226, 233, 236, 241, 244, 247-248, 253-255, 257, 259, 261-262, 264-275, 277-281, 284-287, 290, 293-294, 296, 299-301, 304, 306-307, 310-311, 313, 317-319, 322-324, 326, 329, 332-333

Electoral Democracy 74, 101, 120, 125, 137, 143, 201, 228

Electoral Framework 92

Electoral Systems 7, 13, 19, 23, 37, 56, 95-96, 103-106, 108-109, 111
European Union 28, 33, 44, 49, 114, 217, 259

F

Federalism 39, 46, 89, 184, 187, 210
Framework 2, 7, 19-22, 28, 36, 41, 51-53, 77-78, 92, 94-95, 106, 126, 131, 138, 141, 144, 149-154, 157, 169, 178-180, 187-189, 194-197, 199, 203-204, 219, 226-230, 237, 239, 241, 255-256, 264, 268-269, 272-276, 288, 298, 300, 306, 310, 313, 319, 323, 326, 328-329, 332-333, 335-336
Future Prospects of South African Democracy 262

G

General Election 26-27, 50, 57, 59, 61, 63, 69-70, 72-73, 78, 114, 148, 152, 280, 285, 308
Geopolitical Significance 26, 222
Good Governance 17, 85, 94, 110, 121, 194, 206, 225, 256, 261, 265, 297, 301, 318, 326-327, 330-331, 333-336
Governance 5, 10, 14-28, 30-31, 33-37, 43, 45-49, 51, 54, 58, 60, 66, 69, 71-72, 74-77, 80-90, 92-112, 116-117, 119-122, 125-128, 131, 134, 136-137, 139, 141-147, 155-159, 161, 165-166, 171-175, 178-189, 191, 194-199, 202-203, 205-207, 210-211, 216, 219, 222-225, 227-229, 232, 234, 237-243, 246-262, 264-270, 272, 274-275, 279-280, 286-287, 290-293, 295-298, 300-307, 309-310, 312-314, 316-319, 325-328, 330-336
Governance Structure 24, 92, 127, 178, 196, 224, 305
Governance Structures 18, 93, 103-104, 111, 229, 251, 256
Government 1-5, 7-19, 21-24, 26-27, 29-30, 34-64, 66-67, 69-91, 94-95, 97-101, 103-114, 117-119, 121-122, 124-126, 128-136, 138-149, 152, 154-160, 162-174, 176-191, 193-201, 203-205, 207, 209-211, 214-215, 219, 222-226, 228-229, 234, 236-239, 242-244, 246, 248-251, 253-255, 257, 259-275, 277-294, 296-315, 317-336
Government of National Unity 74-77, 80-81, 84-86, 88, 90, 114, 143, 147, 164, 172-173, 179, 185, 189, 253, 264, 273, 275, 285, 288, 299, 319, 326, 332-333, 336
Government of National Unity, Democratic Governance, Coalition, Governance, Socio-Economic Development 74
Governments 2-7, 9-15, 17-20, 23, 27, 30, 32-38, 42, 44-47, 49-50, 56, 61, 63, 66, 74, 77, 81-82, 86-

88, 92-93, 95-96, 102-104, 110-112, 114, 121, 125-126, 129-134, 136-139, 144-148, 152-155, 157-160, 165, 167, 171-175, 181-183, 185-186, 188-190, 193-195, 197, 199, 201, 203-205, 208, 210-211, 213-216, 223-225, 228, 236-239, 246-248, 250-258, 261-275, 277-279, 286-292, 294-295, 297-298, 300-304, 306-307, 309-310, 314, 316-318, 324-332, 334-335
Grand Coalition 8-9, 14, 144, 148, 156, 164, 209, 268, 314, 326, 336
Gukurahundi 91, 172-173, 175-178, 183, 185-186

H

Horizontal Power-Sharing 187
Hung Council 188, 199, 240, 323, 326
Hung Parliament 1, 7-8, 13, 16, 50, 69, 78, 82, 85, 119, 162

I

Ideology 1, 3-6, 16, 37, 40, 42, 47, 84, 94, 98, 113, 137, 147, 166-167, 198, 213, 252, 257, 289-290, 302, 304, 325, 329
Inkatha Freedom Party 82, 84, 117, 148, 191, 253, 265, 285, 299, 306-307, 319
Instability 7, 10-11, 13, 15, 27, 34-35, 42, 44, 66, 68, 77, 82, 85-88, 96, 101-104, 114, 116, 119, 128, 137, 140, 153, 157, 159, 166-167, 174, 183, 188, 191-193, 195, 197, 213, 223, 235, 237, 252, 257, 263, 288, 294, 300, 302-303, 305, 315, 317-318, 324, 328
Israel 3, 124, 126-143, 208, 312
Israel-Palestine Relations 124

L

Labour Party 8-9, 56-58, 69, 72, 99, 129, 267
Leadership 6, 8-12, 21, 30, 40, 66, 68-70, 72-73, 77, 83, 85, 98-100, 102, 105-107, 115, 117, 123-124, 126, 131, 133, 138, 144, 146, 148-150, 153-154, 159, 162-164, 167-168, 182, 188, 191, 194-195, 197, 200, 210, 218, 224, 234-236, 238-239, 247, 252, 264-265, 268-270, 272-274, 293-295, 302-304, 307, 310, 317-318, 322, 324, 326-328, 330, 335
Legislative Framework 195, 199, 268-269, 300, 306
Liberal Democrat Party 50
Local Government 2, 57-58, 71-72, 83, 85, 90, 94, 99, 101, 106, 108-109, 112-114, 117, 119, 122, 138, 141, 147-148, 154-155, 167-171, 188-190, 193-195, 197-198, 219, 223-226, 228, 237-239,

247, 254-255, 259, 263-265, 267-275, 277-278, 290, 293, 296-297, 300-304, 306-307, 311-314, 318, 322-326, 329-330, 332-335

M

Mature Political Leadership 194, 200
Mnangagwa 172-173, 180-181, 184
Mozambique 6, 92-110, 153, 157, 160-161
Multipolar System 222
Municipalities 32, 34, 107, 112-113, 115, 117, 119-121, 147-149, 157, 159, 166, 170, 189, 195, 197, 224-226, 237, 239, 243-244, 254-255, 260-261, 263-265, 267-272, 300-304, 306, 309, 312-314, 316-318, 323-326, 328-329
Municipality 102, 112-114, 118-121, 169, 189, 193, 195, 223-224, 226, 228, 240, 244, 263, 268, 270, 275, 301, 306-307, 311, 313, 319, 323-324, 329, 331, 334

N

National Assembly 57, 119, 126, 264, 282, 284-285, 299
National Council of Provinces 237, 282-283, 299
National Crisis 1, 8-9, 16
National Democratic Revolution 279, 281, 298-299
NATO 33, 44, 49
NATO (North Atlantic Treaty Organisation) 49

O

One-Party System 143, 252

P

Parliament 1-2, 4-5, 7-11, 13, 15-17, 34, 37, 43, 50, 55-71, 73, 78-79, 81-82, 85, 96, 100-102, 106, 119, 126, 129-130, 132, 143, 149, 158, 160-162, 179, 243, 249, 253, 281-284, 291, 293, 299, 301, 314, 329
Party Alliance 32
Policy 1, 3-6, 8, 10-12, 20-21, 23, 30-32, 36, 38, 41, 43-44, 48, 50-51, 53-55, 57, 68, 70, 78, 84, 87, 98, 103-105, 108, 110, 113, 117, 119, 121-122, 126, 131-132, 136, 138-141, 143, 145-146, 149-150, 162, 165-168, 170, 173-176, 181-185, 190, 193, 197, 202-205, 207-211, 214-216, 218-222, 226, 229, 237-239, 242-243, 247-248, 250, 255, 257-260, 264, 267-274, 278-279, 288-292, 294-298, 300-310, 312-314, 316, 320, 327-328, 333-335
Political Actors Dialogue 172-173, 179-180, 185

Political Alliance 1, 16
Political Leadership 9, 83, 85, 153-154, 163, 188, 194, 197, 200, 238-239, 272, 326
Political Parties 1-9, 11-13, 15-16, 18, 20-22, 24, 30-32, 34-43, 45, 52-54, 59, 67-68, 70, 73, 75-81, 83-84, 86-87, 89-90, 93-94, 96-99, 104, 111, 113-114, 118-120, 124-127, 130-138, 143-149, 151-152, 155-169, 171-173, 180-183, 187, 189-196, 199, 210-211, 222, 224-225, 229, 235, 240-241, 243-244, 248-251, 253-256, 263-272, 278, 283, 285, 287-291, 293-294, 297, 299-301, 304-305, 307, 311, 314-315, 317-319, 322-325, 329-330, 336
Political Power 23, 25, 47, 55, 85, 87, 93, 126, 131-132, 134, 137, 141, 162, 164, 183, 220, 223, 226-227, 231, 235, 258, 281
Political Stability 23, 26-27, 65, 81, 93, 101, 103-104, 107, 126, 136, 159, 173-175, 179-182, 194, 199, 271, 291, 298, 300, 315
Politicians 24, 37, 56, 60, 70, 85, 102, 113, 130-131, 145-147, 150, 152-153, 157-158, 161, 165, 169-170, 194, 201, 207, 214-215, 250, 263-264, 296, 300, 305-306
Politics 1-4, 6-7, 13-15, 17-20, 23-24, 26-32, 36, 40, 42, 44, 48, 50-51, 54, 70-73, 76, 81, 87-91, 93-94, 96-97, 99-101, 104, 107-109, 112-114, 116, 118-123, 125-127, 130-132, 135-142, 144-147, 150-155, 161, 163-166, 169-172, 175-176, 178, 181, 183-186, 189, 193-198, 201-203, 205-206, 209-211, 213-220, 222-228, 230, 233-234, 236-244, 248-250, 253-254, 256, 258-267, 269, 271, 273-274, 277-278, 286-289, 294, 296-299, 301-303, 305-306, 309-314, 317-318, 326-327, 332-333, 335
Post-Apartheid Governance in South Africa 262
Power-Sharing 2, 18, 24, 27, 34, 43, 45, 53, 76-77, 80, 82, 84, 87-89, 110, 137, 143, 150, 166, 174-175, 178-187, 194, 210, 237, 251, 253, 312
Proportional Representative Electoral System 143

R

Rational Choice 1, 16, 146, 288
Republic of South Africa 119, 122, 170-171, 188-189, 199, 264, 275, 299, 313, 325, 335

S

SACP 116-118, 209, 253-254, 262, 277-280, 293, 295, 298-299, 320
SANCO 116-117, 277-278
Service Delivery 103, 107, 119, 148, 153, 166-168,

193-195, 197-198, 200, 223, 225, 234, 241, 243-244, 247, 249, 252, 254, 260, 262-265, 267-274, 276-278, 291, 293-297, 300-304, 307, 309-310, 312-313, 315-319, 322, 324-336
Sino-African Relations 222
Soft Power Diplomacy 201-203, 206, 209, 214, 216, 222
South Africa 2, 5-7, 18, 20, 23, 26-27, 29-31, 33, 37, 74-77, 80-92, 96-99, 102-104, 106, 108-109, 112-122, 124, 135, 138-141, 144-145, 147-150, 152-155, 157, 159, 161, 165-166, 168-171, 188-190, 194-195, 197-199, 209, 213, 223-226, 229-230, 240-244, 246-264, 268-269, 272-275, 277-283, 285, 288, 290, 293-306, 308-313, 316-336
South African Communist Party 116, 209, 253, 262, 278, 293, 295, 298-299, 319
South African Congress of Democrats 280, 299
South African Indian Congress 117, 280, 299
Southern Africa 3, 87-89, 91-93, 95-98, 104-105, 108-109, 113, 123, 162, 172-174, 181-185, 218, 260-261, 298, 333-335
Stability 2-4, 7, 9-16, 19, 23, 26-27, 32, 36, 39, 56, 64-65, 68, 74, 76-77, 80-81, 83, 85, 93, 97, 101, 103-105, 107, 119, 124, 126, 133, 136, 152, 157-159, 162, 169, 173-175, 178-182, 193-194, 197, 199-200, 204-205, 213-214, 225-226, 237, 250-251, 253-254, 256-258, 262-263, 271, 290-291, 298, 300, 304-305, 308-309, 315, 319, 326, 328, 330-331, 334
Strategic Interests 222
Sudanese Communist Party 33, 41, 43, 49
Sustainable Democracy 30, 35, 246, 257, 259, 262
Sustainable Development Goals 35, 49, 218, 257

T

Transition to Democracy in South Africa 253, 262, 331

Transitional Federal Government 38-39, 46, 49
Transitional Military Council 33, 40-41, 49
Trust 3-4, 7, 9, 11-12, 53, 84, 87, 104, 142, 149, 152, 164, 181, 183, 185, 223, 225, 234, 238-241, 248-249, 252, 262, 266, 281, 296, 298, 302, 307, 313, 328-330

U

UN (United Nations) 49
United Kingdom 7, 9, 50-51, 55, 57, 59-60, 63-65, 68, 70-71, 265-268, 308-309, 312
United Nations 33, 35, 47, 49, 87, 95, 206, 266
Unity Accord 172-173, 178, 184-185

V

Vertical Power-Sharing 187

Z

Zimbabwe 24, 27, 74-76, 78, 80-84, 86-91, 96, 98-99, 106, 112, 114, 118, 120, 122, 149, 157, 164, 172-187, 190, 196, 209, 217, 220, 248, 256, 279, 288, 332-333

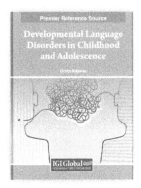

 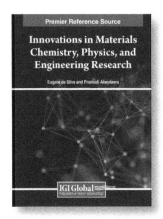 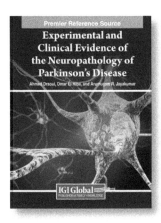 

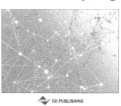

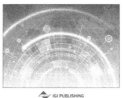

Are You Ready to
Publish Your Research

IGI Global offers book authorship and editorship opportunities across three major subject areas, including Business, STM, and Education.

Benefits of Publishing with IGI Global:

- Free one-on-one editorial and promotional support.

- Expedited publishing timelines that can take your book from start to finish in less than one (1) year.

- Choose from a variety of formats, including Edited and Authored References, Handbooks of Research, Encyclopedias, and Research Insights.

- Utilize IGI Global's eEditorial Discovery® submission system in support of conducting the submission and double-blind peer review process.

- IGI Global maintains a strict adherence to ethical practices due in part to our full membership with the Committee on Publication Ethics (COPE).

- Indexing potential in prestigious indices such as Scopus®, Web of Science™, PsycINFO®, and ERIC – Education Resources Information Center.

- Ability to connect your ORCID iD to your IGI Global publications.

- Earn honorariums and royalties on your full book publications as well as complimentary content and exclusive discounts.

Join Your Colleagues from Prestigious Institutions, Including:

Australian National University

Massachusetts Institute of Technology

JOHNS HOPKINS UNIVERSITY

HARVARD UNIVERSITY

TSINGHUA UNIVERSITY 1911

COLUMBIA UNIVERSITY IN THE CITY OF NEW YORK

Learn More at: www.igi-global.com/publish

or Contact IGI Global's Aquisitions Team at: acquisition@igi-global.com

9 798369 316542